Strategic Management for Hospitality & Travel

TODAY AND TOMORROW

Frederick J. DeMicco, Ph.D. • Marvin Cetron, Ph.D. • Owen Davies

Foreword by Kaye Chon, Ph.D.

Thank you to Tim Flohr of The University of Memphis for his invaluable help with the chapter slides that accompany this text.

Cover image © Shutterstock.com

www.kendallhunt.com
Send all inquiries to:
4050 Westmark Drive
Dubuque, IA 52004-1840

Dedication

This book is dedicated to our mentor and friend Dr. Michael D. Olsen and his lovely and very supportive wife Sandy Olsen of Virginia Polytechnic Institute & State University. The many fortunate Ph.D. students directed by Dr. Olsen (affectionately called the "Olsenites") continue to excel and lead in the world of academia and in the hospitality and tourism profession. We are extremely fortunate and grateful that the Olsens came into our lives.

Brief Contents

Contents

Foreword

By Kaye Chon, Ph.D.
Dean, School of Hotel & Tourism Management, The Hong Kong Polytechnic University

The hospitality and travel manager's goal is to provide guests with the most satisfying experience possible, and thereby to ensure their company's prosperity. As simple as this sounds, doing so effectively requires a remarkable array of skills. The four years required to complete an undergraduate degree in hospitality and travel management are only the beginning of a study that will occupy an entire career.

This text deals with one of the most important skills, and one too often learned by trial and error: developing new competitive methods to attract the guests who give the company both its reason for being and its hope of survival. This is not the only book to touch on this crucial subject. Yet, none I have seen duplicates the concept that makes *Strategic Management for Hospitality and Travel: Today and Tomorrow* uniquely valuable.

This text combines business strategy and forecasting. At first, this may seem an odd pairing. Yet, these topics quickly prove to be the heart of any market-driven enterprise.

Forecasting, as it is meant here, is not the finicky quantitative work of anticipating tourist demand. Instead, the authors try to figure out how the unique circumstances and requirements of each industry segment and company will interact with the broad trends now changing the world. For example, what will it mean for tourism that birth rates are declining throughout the developed countries? How will tomorrow's oil prices affect the bottom line for airlines and cruise operators? How will new technologies change hotel operations?

These are qualitative issues, and getting them right is as much a matter of judgment and experience as of data. Developing them requires, like so many other skills, practice as well as theoretical understanding. In this text, the authors provide both.

They are uniquely qualified to do so. No one in the hospitality industry has as much experience in the use of forecasting to create new competitive methods as the present writers.

Dr. Frederick DeMicco is Professor and ARAMARK International Endowed Chair in the Department of Hotel, Restaurant and Institutional Management at the University of Delaware, among many other appointments. Dr. DeMicco is a knowledgeable educator and hotel consultant on global strategy and innovation to our hospitality industry.

Dr. Marvin Cetron is one of the world's pre-eminent forecasters. He and his colleagues have carried out studies for some 450 of the *Fortune* 500 companies, more than 100 government agencies, and 150 professional and academic associations. In our industry, his clients have included World Travel Market, the National Restaurant Association, the International Association of Exhibition Management, the Hospitality Sales & Marketing Association International, Marriott International, and Carlson Wagonlit.

Owen Davies is a long-time writer and an accomplished forecaster in his own right. Over some three decades, he and Dr. Cetron have collaborated on nine books, including the first edition of this text, and more than 100 studies for business and government. At present, he is Executive Editor at TechCast Global, a forecasting consultancy based in Washington, D.C. He participated in all the studies of hospitality and travel mentioned above.

In these three writers, readers will recognize skills and experience that can help them build productive and rewarding careers.

The Co-Alignment Model of business strategy presented in this volume's early chapters rightly makes forecasting the first step in all strategic planning. It uses the term "environmental scanning," but anticipating future developments is clearly at the core of its process.

In fact, it is not possible, other than by luck, to create a successful new competitive method without forecasting. Business strategies succeed or fail, not in today's environment, but in the one they will meet months or years ahead. If business planners cannot anticipate these future conditions, their competitive methods are likely to fail. So, eventually, will their companies.

This is an essential lesson in an industry such as hospitality and travel, where a single decision can involve hundreds of millions of dollars in investments, years of effort, and thousands of jobs. Teaching it the easy way, rather than by costly experience, is the goal of this text. In this, it succeeds admirably.

As you look back on your professional education some years from now, a few experiences will stand out because they opened your eyes to a uniquely valuable skill. Studying this text is certain to be one of them.

About the Authors

Dr. Fred DeMicco is a Visiting Scholar at Colorado State University and a Visiting Professor at the University of South Florida Sarasota-Manatee and Professor and ARAMARK Endowed Chair Emeritus in the Department of Hotel, Restaurant and Institutional Management at the University of Delaware. He was the Department Chair there for seven years from 2001 to 2007. Formerly, he was Associate Director in the School of Hotel, Restaurant and Recreation Management at Penn State University, where he was Professor-in-Charge of the HRIM undergraduate program (and the Master of Science and PhD graduate program for five years), and he presently is a Conti Distinguished Professor at the Pennsylvania State University's School of Hotel, Restaurant and Recreation Management. Dr. DeMicco is also President of International Academics and Dean of Executive and Professional Programs at the SIAF Campus in Volterra, Tuscany. He has worked in Healthcare at the Massachusetts General Hospital, Boston, and at Walt Disney World in hotel management where he also obtained a Ducktorate Degree from Disney University. Dr. DeMicco is the Founder of the INNternationale, the international student house at the University of Delaware, and has developed and led dozens of Penn State University and University of Delaware student and faculty study abroad programs to six continents, establishing lasting educational and student internship partnerships.

Dr. DeMicco's scholarly interests are: International Strategic Management & Trends related to food and beverage, International Medical Tourism and Wellness, Hospitality Management, Wine & Beverage Management, Managerial Accounting and Innovation. He has worked on projects with ARAMARK International at four Summer Olympic Games (in Atlanta, Australia, Athens and Beijing) and has taught and lead dozens of Study@Sea cruise ship management courses around the world. Since 2007, Dr. DeMicco has been supported and is working with the Foundation of the Bank of Volterra to open a new €25-million campus in the center of Tuscany called the Learning Village in Tuscany for business management students and for all students in the arts & sciences.

He completed his Ph.D. in Hotel, Restaurant and Institutional Management at Virginia Polytechnic Institute and State University under the direction of Dr. Michael D. Olsen. In 1996, he worked in Hotel Management at Walt Disney World, Florida. He has also been employed by Aramark International, Marriott Vacation Club International, and several healthcare operations, including assisted living facilities.

Dr. DeMicco has authored or co-authored nearly 100 refereed articles in the area of tourism and hospitality management, and he has co-authored several books including: Medical Tourism and Wellness, with Apple Academic Press/Taylor Francis; Restaurant Management: A Best Practices Approach, with Kendall-Hunt Publishers (2015) Hospitality 2015: The Future of Hospitality & Travel (2010) with the Educational Institute of the American Hotel and Lodging Association. He is on the Editorial

Advisory Board of the Journal of Hospitality & Tourism Research and several other notable research journals.

Dr. DeMicco was the President, International CHRIE –NENA (North East North American Federation). Recently, he was presented the International CHRIE/Cornell Howard B. Meek Award of Excellence for 2017.

Dr. Marvin Cetron is one of the preeminent forecaster-futurists in the world. For more than 50 years, he has pioneered forecasting for business and government, developing many of the techniques that other forecasters now use daily.

During this long and productive career, Dr. Cetron has consulted for some 450 of the *Fortune* 500 firms, including Marriott International and Capital One; more than 100 government organizations, among them the Central Intelligence Agency, the Transportation Security Administration, and the National Security Agency; and 150 professional and academic associations, including World Travel Market, the National Restaurant Association, the International Association of Exhibition Management, and the Hospitality Sales and Marketing Association International. He served as an advisor to the White House for every administration, Republican and Democratic, from the time of John Kennedy through the Clinton years.

Dr. Cetron's 1994 study, *Terror 2000: The Future Face of Terror*, circulated privately at the Pentagon, predicted virtually the entire course of terrorism in the decade that followed. Specific forecasts included the rise of large-scale terrorist attacks by Muslim extremists, coordinated attacks on widely distant targets, a devastating assault on the World Trade Center, and even the deliberate crash of an airplane into the Pentagon. Overseas hotels and restaurants owned or frequented by Americans led his list of probable targets.

During his 20-year career in R&D planning and forecasting with the U.S. Navy, Dr. Cetron was in charge of the design, development, and implementation of the largest, most comprehensive technological forecast of the United States ever conducted.

Dr. Cetron has a B.S. degree in Industrial Engineering from Pennsylvania State University, a M.S. degree in Production Management from Columbia University, and a Ph.D. in Research and Development Management from American University.

He is a member of the Boards of Advisors of Pennsylvania State University and the University of Delaware.

Owen Davies is a veteran writer and forecaster in the fields of business, technology, and the future. He currently holds the position of Executive Editor at TechCast Global, a forecasting consultancy based in Washington, DC.

Since 1986, he has served as a consultant to Forecasting International, in Fairfax, VA. With FI, he has researched and written approximately 100 studies for commercial clients, professional associations, and government agencies, including Best Western, Capital One, and World Travel Market 2006; the National Restaurant Association, and International Association of Exhibition Management, and the Hospitality Sales and Marketing Association International; and the Department of Defense, Transportation Security Administration, and National Security Agency.

He has written or edited 14 books, uncounted magazine articles, and many business reports and other specialized works, including more than 30 articles for the Hospitality Sales and Marketing Association International *Marketing Review*. He has held staff positions at *Medical World News* (1971–'72), then considered the *Newsweek* of the medical community; *American Druggist* (1976–'77); and *Omni* (1979–'82). He has freelanced for some 45 years.

Davies's books, many of them written with Dr. Marvin J. Cetron, president of Forecasting International, include:

- *Hospitality 2015: The Future of Hospitality and Travel* (American Hotel & Lodging Association), a second forecast of things to come in this fast-changing industry, written as always with Dr. Fred DeMicco and Dr. Cetron

- *Hospitality 2010: The Future of Hospitality and Travel* (Prentice Hall), a look at the future of one of the world's largest and most diverse industries, written with Dr. Fred DeMicco and Dr. Cetron

- *55 Trends Now Shaping the Future of Ground Mass Transportation* (Proteus USA), a forecast of rail and bus transportation over the next 15 years

- *Probable Tomorrows: How Science and Technology Will Transform Our Lives in the Next Twenty Years* (St. Martin's Press), a look at the future of nine critical technologies now reshaping the world

- *Terror 2000: The Future Face of Terrorism*, a study circulated within the Pentagon and distributed to the President and members of Congress, 1994

- *Crystal Globe: The Haves and Have-Nots of the New World Order* (St. Martin's Press), which forecast the reunification of Germany, the Gulf War, and the long-term recession in Japan (and appears to have given President George Bush his favorite description of the post-Soviet world)

- *American Renaissance: Our Life at the Turn of the 21st Century* (St. Martin's Press), a forecast of the future of American society a decade ahead

Preface

"To succeed in war, a general should have full knowledge of his own strengths and weaknesses and full knowledge of the enemy's strengths and weaknesses. Lack of either on might result in defeat."

—Sun Tzu

Reading Sun Tzu's advice above, we cannot help being reminded of the saying, "Business is WAR without bullets." Our purpose here is to give you some of the most effective weapons you will need to win.

The world of hospitality and travel is rapidly changing. Its complexity and dynamism require companies and the people who run them to stay focused on the trends that constantly reshape the competitive environment. In this industry, even more than in most others, sudden developments can have enormous impact literally overnight. Terrorism, corporate selloffs and layoffs, the speed (and hazards) of the cyber age, and the relative ease of introducing new ideas in the flat, interconnected world of the Internet all contribute to this volatility.

Once you finish your studies and begin your hospitality career, you will be called on to be a strategist and a strategic thinker. You will need not only the craft skills that served your older colleagues well at the start of their careers but much more expertise in information and business management. You will be expected to market on the World Wide Web, forge and maintain productive strategic alliances, understand big data, and analyze and synthesize huge volumes of information. You will need to scan and monitor an increasingly complex, demanding, and dynamic competitive environment; understand revenue and pricing strategies; be able to provide information to guests using social media; satisfy their needs for safety and security; and have the leadership acumen and skills to hire and motivate a more diverse group of employees, who also are called upon to be knowledge workers.

The figure below outlines the demanding and complex fund of skill and knowledge that hospitality and travel executives need today to be at the top of their games and reach the highest levels of the industry.

• Economics	• Accounting
• Ecology	• Finance
• Food Science	• Management Information Systems
• Nutrition	• Human Resources
• Organizational Behavior	• Linguistics
• Organization Theory	• Marketing
• Political Science	• Management Science
• Psychology	• Operations
• Technology	• Engineering
• Sociology	• Strategic Management
• Statistics	

(Source: Personal correspondence from Dr. M. Olsen to Dr. F. DeMicco)

Career Opportunities

Your Hospitality and Travel/Tourism Business Management program prepares you for a wide range of roles within the hospitality and travel industry. These may include:

- General Manager
- Assistant General Manager
- Hotel Manager
- Area or Regional Manager/VP
- Director/Manager of Operations
- Chief Financial Officer
- Chief Information Officer
- Chief Marketing or Brand Officer
- Director/Manager of Human Resources
- Director/Manager of Sales and Marketing
- Director/Manager of Revenue Management
- Director/Manager of Brand Management
- Director/Manager of Food and Beverage
- Director/Manager of Banquets and Catering
- Director/Manager of Guest Experience
- Director/Manager of Passenger Experience
- Director/Manager of Brand Standards
- Director/Manager of Communications
- Guest Services Manager
- Restaurant Owner
- Franchise Owner
- Asset Manager
- Development Director
- Feasibility Director
- Product Development
- Hospitality Consultant
- Tourism Marketing Consultant
- Event Manager
- Convention and Meetings Manager
- Special Events Manager
- Entertainment Director
- Chief Entertainment Officer
- GM of a Sports Stadium
- Managing Director of Travel Agency
- Director of Hospitality (for Healthcare/Residential Services)

- Hotel Manager on Cruise Ship
- Cruise Director
- VP of Strategic Management
- Director of Technology and Innovation

(Adapted from a personal communication by Gray Sheehy at the Georgetown University Hospitality Management Program, 2016.)

This book focuses on strategy for companies during a time of both prosperity and uncertainty. It will help you learn to read and interpret the trends in society that bring hospitality firms both opportunity and threats. This book takes an entrepreneurial and an environmental-scanning approach to strategic planning and the management of companies in the hospitality and travel industries. It serves as a primer on these topics while heavily focusing on the scanning and careful observation of the complex, dynamic, and competitive environment the firm operates in. We will refer to this as *environmental scanning*. The book uses environmental scanning as the first (and very important) step in a four-part exercise referred to as the Co-Alignment Model. (See Olson, West, Tse, & DeMicco, 2015.)

The Co-Alignment Model will provide the framework for discussing strategic management for hospitality and travel businesses in this book. The key component of strategic management is being aware of what is going on around the firm, as the environment is fraught with dangers—and also opportunities. In strategic management, executives develop a plan or roadmap to move their company ahead successfully, be good stewards of the environment, and prosper financially—the main primary objective of any business. Our discussion of strategic planning provides the tools we call (not unreasonably, we feel) Strategic Tools, or ST.

The following chapters look at strategic management and the process we call the Co-Alignment Model (Chapter 1). The first step of the Co-Alignment Model is "environmental scanning." By scanning the competitive environment, businesses can identify opportunities and threats that can positively or negatively impact their firm. The next three chapters will look at the remaining steps of this process. They focus on the *strategy* setting, developing the *structure* to serve as a foundation for the strategies we have selected, and *evaluation* of the strategies. Did they make money for the firm (a must), or did they fail?

In Chapter 5, we will discuss *forecasting* in depth. Why is forecasting paramount for strategic managers and planners? Forecasting allows the firm's strategists to identify trends (and fads) in the environment that can positively benefit the business. One example is identifying current trends in new products and services that Millennials may find important when selecting hotels, restaurants, travel destinations, etc. Think how Airbnb and the "Uberization" of travel are changing hospitality and travel today. What will be the next trends, and hence opportunities, for our industry? Strategic forecasting allows us to see these trends and be ready for them.

In essence, our goal as forecasters and strategic planners is to see the future BEFORE it arrives.

Summary

The four-step Co-Alignment Model introduced in the first section of this book—and especially environmental scanning—allows us to forecast trends and gain an advantage over the competition. This is particularly necessary in the complex, fast-changing hospitality and travel space. *Strategic Management 2020* takes a unique approach to strategic planning. It provides the management and forecasting theory and tools that students and practitioners will need for effective strategic planning.

The remaining chapters of the book look at the many segments of the hospitality and tourism industry—cruise ships, hotels, restaurants, airlines, gaming and casinos, sports and entertainment, medical tourism, etc. They will discuss the impact of the most important trends (a complete list is found in Appendix A) for that segment.

At the conclusion of each chapter, a case study that you will find on the Student Ancillary Site (access code included on the inside front cover) will allow you to look at a topic for a specific industry segment and apply the strategic tools learned in Part I.

We believe these end-of-chapter case studies will make it possible to apply the theory we have learned to real-world industry challenges and opportunities, allow for in-depth evaluation, and provide good food for thought and discussion in the classroom or in online forums.

We hope you will enjoy reading this book even as you learn the techniques of strategic forecasting and management and examine the trends that will shape the future of our industry. In the end, you should have the knowledge and skill to recognize the important trends today and anticipate what they will mean for tomorrow; this will give your business and your career an important competitive edge.

Best wishes for success! F.J.D., M.J.C., & O.D.

End of Preface Student Exercise

To help you understand the environment around you and to anticipate the trends that may shape the hospitality and travel industry, *sign up for the following emails.* You will receive these emails just about every day. This should be part of your daily "Scanning of the Environment" (Chapter 1 which follows), to use in this course.

Hospitality, Tourism and Travel Scanning Information

The Skift Daily Travel Newsletter

The Skift Daily Newsletter delivers breaking news, analysis, and insights about the global travel industry directly to your inbox each morning, 6 days a week. If you enjoy what you read here, please consider forwarding. Not getting the daily regularly? Click here to subscribe! https://skift.com/daily/

Hotel and Lodging Scanning

Hotel-Online   Email Contact: newsletter@hotel-online.com

Restaurant and Food Service Scanning

NRA Restaurant SmartBrief   Email contact: restaurant@smartbrief.com
NRN a.m.   Email Contact: news@newsletter.nrn.com

Strategic Management and the Co-Alignment Model: An Overview

This book takes an entrepreneurial and an environmental-scanning approach to strategic planning and management of companies in the hospitality and travel industries. It also serves as a primer on strategy and strategic management, while heavily focusing on the scanning and careful observation of the firm's complex, dynamic, and competitive environment.

This chapter introduces environmental scanning, the first and in some ways most important step of the Co-Alignment Model we use to develop strategies and competitive methods for companies in the hospitality and travel industry. (See Olsen, West, Tse, & DeMicco, 2015.) Chapter 1 also provides a first look at the key trends now changing our world and their use in developing business strategies (Cetron, DeMicco, & Davies, 2016).

Some Background on Strategy Theory

An excellent summary of strategic management theory and application over several decades, *Strategy Safari: A Guide Through the Wilds of Strategic Management*, by Mintzberg, Ahlstrand, and Lampel (1998), provides a guiding light for understanding the many theories, approaches, and applications of strategy for companies. Mintzberg and his colleagues discuss their theories of strategy and apply them to businesses. These include:

1. **The Design School for Strategic Management.** This would include using the SWOT analyses whereby the design school model tries to obtain a "fit" between an organization's internal strengths and the external opportunities in *designing* its strategy. In this model, "structure" should follow strategy. Structure includes company values, social responsibility, and alignment of key resources (e.g., financial, human capital, core competencies) (Mintzberg, et al., 1999).

2. **The Planning School of Strategic Management.** In this strategic management approach, strategies for companies come about from a controlled, conscious process of formal planning, done in progressive steps, described by a checklist, with formal actions and techniques along the process. The CEO has the overall responsibility, with subordinate staff charged with the execution of the strategic plan.

3. **The Positioning School of Strategy.** This school of thought states that only a few key strategies — or "positions" — in the market are necessary in an industry. These positions need to be defended against present and future competitors. Michael Porter's Five Forces theory and the Boston Consulting Group matrix are common theories and tools that are used by the positioning school. These theories are described later in this chapter.

4. **The Entrepreneurial School of Strategy.** Often this school is based on a single leader (or entrepreneur) who creates a vision which is the inspiration for what the firm will do and accomplish. The vision of the leader is an image more than a fully developed strategic plan, but about half of the time with an actual business plan in hand. This leaves the strategic direction flexible, so the leader and firm can deliberate and further develop their strategic plan as the business evolves.

5. **The Cognitive School of Strategy.** This school views strategy formulation as a cognitive process that takes place in the mind of the strategist (Mintzberg, 1999). Thus, strategies emerge as a prospective in the form of concepts, maps that shape how firms deal with the inputs from the surrounding environment (Mintzberg, 1999). Strategies are difficult to attain, and also difficult to change when change is needed. Thus, leaders wish to maintain flexibility in navigating the firm, when organizations and employees can cling to outdated plans due to a cognitive fixation. This can prove to have negative consequences when swift change is needed to correct or chart a new course for the firm amid competition and change.

6. **The Learning School of Strategy.** Organizations learn and thus have evolving strategies. The learning school combines flexibility with effectiveness. This school learns from experience and is not trapped in an out-of-date strategy. A learning organization therefore benefits from its experiments and failures and does not stay bound by the adage, "If it isn't broke, why fix it?" This strategy model "gets it" that managers and employees on the frontline know a great deal and can make strategic contributions for the firm that help it to be competitive, advance, and grow. Learning organizations look outside their own sphere for new knowledge and then propagate what they have learned throughout the company to help achieve success.

7. **The Power School of Strategy.** The power school can use political clout to formulate strategy. This can include joint ventures, technology transfer, strategic alliances, R&D partnerships, and collaborative advertising to name just a few. Mintzberg et al. (1999), states: "Strategy formulation is shaped by power and politics, whether as a process inside the organization or as a behavior of the organization itself and its external environment."

8. **The Cultural School of Strategy.** Strategy formulation for this school is a collective process of social interaction shared by the management and employees of the organization and shaped by their beliefs and culture. This cultural ideology may not actively permit strategic changes, as ideologies tend to perpetuate the existing strategy. Yet, they do promote shifts in position within the firm's overall strategic perspective. It is a strong culture of the firm's beliefs that are passionately shared by members of the organization that uniquely distinguishes one organization from all others. Burger King may be associated with broiling hamburgers, but the ideal of McDonald's is a strong conviction toward "efficiency, service, and cleanliness"(Mintzberg, 1999).

9. **The Environmental School.** The school believes that the environment is the main actor that guides the direction a firm takes. These forces of the competitive environment must be met by readily available responses to threats and opportunities in the marketplace. Leadership must have a plan to adapt flexibly to these environmental forces or else face failure and potential demise.

10. **The Configuration School of Strategy.** In this school, strategy formulation is a process of transformation. A company's strategy must sustain successful stability in the competitive market, but at times during the firm's life cycle it must change course or adapt to a disruptive process without limiting the growth of the firm. The firm can be the disruptor, making quantum advances in new products and/or services to grab a greater piece of the market.

Summary of the Ten Strategy Schools

Figure 1.1 The ten strategy models useful in strategic management offer a "buffet table" of ideas for hospitality and travel executives.

Figure 1.2 Strategy planning uses the ten strategy theories to create and cook up a new "strategy recipe."

We like Mintzberg's ideas about the ten schools, which share some similar processes for strategy, yet have unique attributes for strategic planning. The question arises, should strategists select and choose from among all of these ten ideas, "like customers from a buffet," or should they try to mix and match the strategic theories "as a master chef might try to combine them into a new award-winning recipe in the kitchen?" (Mintzberg, 1999). The answers are "yes" and "yes." Both approaches can and do apply to strategic planning.

The book you're about to read follows these recipes, using existing strategy theory and providing an approach that may look and "taste" somewhat different, yet will be familiar to the strategic management palate.

The strategic model we will present in the following chapters will borrow heavily from many of the theories outlined above. We call our four-step strategic planning process the Co-Alignment Model (Olsen, West, & Tse), and each step of the Co-Alignment Model borrows from the theories and schools above to present a streamlined strategic planning model for the hospitality and travel industry.

The Co-Alignment Model Explained

The four steps of the Co-Alignment Model that we will follow throughout the book are 1. Environmental scanning; 2. Setting the strategy (or competitive methods); 3. Providing structure (resources and core competencies, e.g., human capital) to the firm's strategy; and finally 4. Evaluation (e.g., firm profitability, guest satisfaction, stock price, etc.) of the firm's strategy/competitive methods. Buttressing the Co-Alignment Model and firm strategy are the key trends that impact, or will impact, the firm in the years ahead. (See Appendix A.) We devote our first four chapters to these steps.

For example, step one of the Co-Alignment Model, environmental scanning, determines that terrorism is affecting travel to a part of the world, such as Paris. The spread of terrorism and its effects on travel safety and security are one of the trends in our inventory. In the chapters that follow, strategies and tactics to address this trend will be explained. Another reality in the hospitality and travel environment is technology.

(Appendix A contains several trends dealing with technology.) How are social media influencing how consumers search for hotels and/or restaurants? The chapter on restaurant strategy, among others, will discuss the ubiquitous presence of technology in some detail.

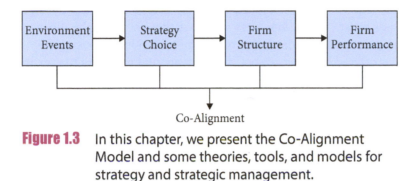

Figure 1.3 In this chapter, we present the Co-Alignment Model and some theories, tools, and models for strategy and strategic management.

Source: Personal correspondence Dr. M. Olsen to Dr. F. DeMicco, 2005.

With this foundation established, Chapter 5 will introduce forecasting and the tools used for it. This process ties into the first step of the Co-Alignment Model, environmental scanning, allowing us to identify trends that could affect the firm's direction and its subsequent strategies. We think of this as (almost) seeing the future before it arrives. Chapter 5 demonstrates how forecasting and environmental scanning help in strategic planning and management for the hospitality and travel firms.

As we have seen, researchers offer a variety of definitions for the concept of strategy and strategy development. Yet, they all recognize that business strategy is an application of environmental analysis used to determine a firm's position in the marketplace and how its resources should be used to reach its major goals. According to Tse and Olsen (1998), the differences among the schools of strategy are found in three primary areas: the breadth of the concept of business strategy, the components of strategy, and the inclusiveness of the strategy-formulation process. The Hofer and Schendel Model identified a fourth component in which the emphasis is on the resource-based view, which stresses the firm's capabilities as the determinant of competitive advantage, and the synergy between all the components. Hofer and Schendel organized the concept of strategy into four components:

1. Scope (product/market and geographic territories);
2. Resource deployments and distinctive competencies;
3. Competitive advantage;
4. Synergy.

Strategic management therefore includes the analysis of the internal and the external environment, the formulation of strategies, and the implementation of strategies and measurement of the company's performance. Olsen et al. (1999) defined strategic management as a continuous process of analyzing the company's internal and external environments, investing in effective competitive methods, and maximizing the utilization of resources.

The authors and their colleagues have conducted extensive research on firms in the hospitality industry and their attempts to gain sustainable competitive advantage. As a result of these studies, we defined strategic management as the ability of the management to align the firm with the forces driving change in the environment in which it competes. This alignment requires that management invest in competitive methods that yield the greatest overall financial value to the company. To accomplish this, managers must create a business structure that consistently allocates resources to those competitive methods that provide the best value over time. By identifying opportunities offered by the forces of change, selecting methods that enable the firm to gain competitive advantage, and allocating sufficient financial resources to those methods, management fulfills its responsibility to the company's owners and investors. This relationship is referred to as the Co-Alignment Model.

The Path to Firm Profitability

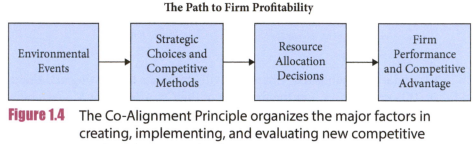

Figure 1.4   The Co-Alignment Principle organizes the major factors in creating, implementing, and evaluating new competitive methods to ensure business success.

Source: Connolly, Daniel J. (2012, December) Embracing the Big Data Phenomenon to Become an Intelligent Organization. PhoCusWright's Spotlight. Sherman, CT: PhoCusWright, Inc.

Strategic management begins with the company's business environment. This is defined as the domain in which the customers, competitors, suppliers, and regulators exist in the context of rapid change and increasing complexity in the broad global environment. In this context, opportunities and threats appear that are both immediate and long-term. In the co-alignment principle, strategic choice refers to the competitive methods that firms invest in to achieve their objectives. According to Olsen, et al., The concept of strategy choice suggests that management is constantly engaged in making choices about how to compete.

In the third stage of the Co-Alignment Model, the firm structure refers to the company's ability to implement that strategy effectively. It represents the ways in which the company's tasks and responsibilities are allocated in the strategy implementation process. Implementation stands for the process of allocating resources, bringing all the firm's resources into alignment to achieve the objectives. Based on the Tse and Olsen work (1999), the alignment between the company's core competencies (its unique resources) and its competitive methods are the most important internal match-up that can be achieved.

If management can identify the correct opportunities in its competitive environment, invest in the best value-adding competitive methods, and create a structure that supports effective implementation and execution of these methods, they will achieve the financial performance expected by investors. The measure of financial performance most commonly utilized today is cash flow per share of owner's/investor's equity. This must be reorganized to become a future-oriented measure of cash flow. Management's task is to maximize its future value. To do this they must estimate the cash flow that can be generated by each possible competitive method over its expected useful life. This future-based orientation is the basis of the Co-Alignment Model.

Strategic Tools Applicable in the Co-Alignment Model

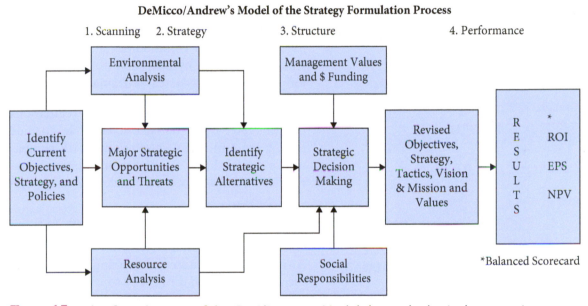

DeMicco/Andrew's Model of the Strategy Formulation Process

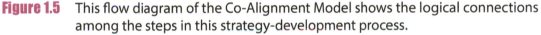

Figure 1.5   This flow diagram of the Co-Alignment Model shows the logical connections among the steps in this strategy-development process.

Source: Dr. F. DeMicco

The task environment includes categories that have more direct impact, usually with more immediate consequences to a firm, than the remote environment. These include market and consumer behavior, industry structure, competitors, government agencies, and suppliers.

Porter's five forces include three from "horizontal" competition—the threat of substitute products or services, the threat of established rivals, and the threat of new entrants—and two forces from "vertical" competition—the bargaining power of suppliers and the bargaining power of customers.

The firm's environment is especially important to hospitality enterprises. For hospitality firms, competition comes from international and national as well as local companies. Hospitality enterprises often compete at all levels, feeling the pressure from international, national, and regional chains and the strength of their marketing and advertising programs, but also feeling competition from local firms.

Figure 1.6 We see here how Porter's Five Forces Model is applied to Step 1, Environmental Scanning.

Source: Dr. F. DeMicco

Under this circumstance, managers can use Porter's Five Forces Model to monitor competition and to understand what forces are driving changes at what levels. New businesses can move into your turf and compete head-on. These often are the same type of enterprise, such as a new business hotel or a Mexican-themed restaurant that opens near established competitors.

There are other risks as well. Customers may gain leverage over the business by researching the price of hotel rooms on the Internet or by reading reviews on Yelp or TripAdvisor, for example. Suppliers have bargaining power when they can increase prices on commodities at will, such as when dairy prices skyrocket and the cost of cheese for pizza restaurant increases dramatically.

Some strategists might place laws and regulations into this category as well. Recent examples include raising the minimum wage, requiring all companies to provide health care for their employees, and restricting the size of a carbonated beverage that can be sold.

Hospitality businesses also face the threat of substitute products. These can include the rise of Airbnb as a substitute for booking hotel rooms, the sale of prepared dinners by supermarkets, and

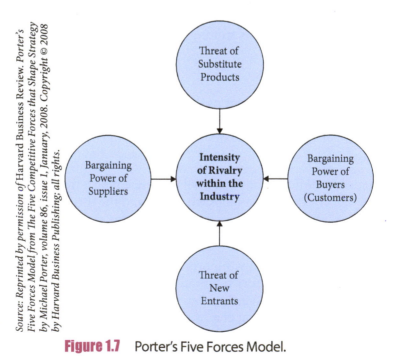

Source: Reprinted by permission of Harvard Business Review. Porter's Five Forces Model from The Five Competitive Forces that Shape Strategy by Michael Porter, volume 86, issue 1, January, 2008. Copyright © 2008 by Harvard Business Publishing; all rights.

Figure 1.7 Porter's Five Forces Model.

the replacement of video stores by online video streaming services. Can you think of other products and services that might threaten companies in the hospitality and travel industry?

Ansoff's Matrix Applied to Domain Definition

The concept of strategic management begins with the firm's business environment. This is defined as the domain in which customers, competitors, suppliers, and regulators impact the company. Today, it exists in a context of rapid change and increasing complexity in the broad global environment.

Management can adopt Ansoff's Matrix to identify the forces that will drive change, to seek opportunities that will add value to the firm in both the short and long terms, to determine the best opportunities for the future, and to invest in competitive methods that will match those opportunities. See http://www.edrawsoft.com/ansoff-matrix.php.

Ansoff's Matrix is a useful tool in crafting product and market-growth strategies. It can offer insights into how to take your product strategy, product marketing, and product management to the next level of performance. Examples of developing new products and new markets include Carnival developing a new cruise line that sails to Cuba from Miami each week or Chipotle developing an Asian or pizza concept (Shop-House and Pizzeria Locale, respectively).

BCG Matrix Applied to Competitive Method Choice

The concept of strategy choice focuses on the competitive methods that firms invest in to achieve their objectives. Competitive methods are defined as the portfolio of products and services that the firm chooses to compete within its environment.

It is the management's responsibility to choose products and services and combine them into a portfolio. The BCG Matrix is a framework created by Boston Consulting Group to evaluate the strategic position of the business's brand portfolio and potential. It helps us to identify competitive methods that require substantial resources to drive revenue, create value, and meet the expectations of customers, employees, and donors. Businesses can use it to see where they stand in the market: how competitive they are (market share), whether there are market-growth opportunities, and whether they need to use Ansoff's Matrix, above, and look at developing new products in existing or new markets.

The BCG Matrix classifies the business portfolio into four categories, based on industry attractiveness (growth rate of that industry) and competitive position (relative market share). These two dimensions reveal the possible profitability of the business portfolio according to the cash needed to support that unit and the cash generated by it. By using the matrix, management can identify competitive methods and adopt strategies for each product and service to optimize the portfolio.

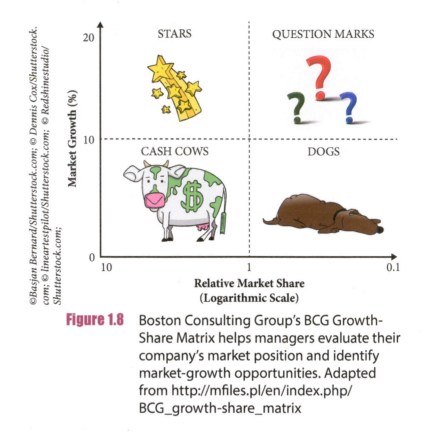

Figure 1.8 Boston Consulting Group's BCG Growth-Share Matrix helps managers evaluate their company's market position and identify market-growth opportunities. Adapted from http://mfiles.pl/en/index.php/BCG_growth-share_matrix

SWOT Analysis Applied to Strengths and Weaknesses Analysis

The Strengths, Weaknesses, Opportunities, and Threats (SWOT Model) is an important and very popular tool that firms can use to identify their strengths and figure out how to use them to seize opportunities in the competitive environment. In addition, the firm can discover weaknesses and vulnerabilities that can be exposed by the competition to limit profitability and success.

Once this has been accomplished, the firm must conduct a thorough review of the strengths and weaknesses of the alignment relationships. To the extent that they constitute strengths, management must determine why, decide how to allocate their resources to preserve them, and strengthen those that offer the greatest cash flow per share. SWOT analysis is an effective analytic tool fit for this purpose. Its framework allows managers to synthesize insights into the firm's strengths and weaknesses with those regarding external opportunities and threats. See http://www.managementguru.net/swot-analysis/

SWOT analysis helps management concentrate on allocating resources and uncovering opportunities to create a sustainable niche in the market. It involves specifying business objectives and identifying the internal and external factors that are favorable and unfavorable for the organization to achieve those objectives.

Some Resources for Environmental Scanning

Event or Trend	Top Three Sources	Timing	Estimate of Validity & Reliability	Influence on Strategic Thinking
Asset and Capital	Wall Street Journal	Daily	Excellent in short term	Very strong
	Business Week	Weekly	Excellent in short term	Strong
	Economist	Weekly	Excellent in both short and long term	Very strong

Figure 1.9 The publications above are some of the most useful resources for scanning the environment.

Source: Personal correspondence Dr. M. Olsen to Dr. F. DeMicco, 2005.

The Life Cycle of a Service Firm

Like so many other things, the economy and companies are subject to recognizable life cycles. The economy cycles between highs—periods of business expansion, and lows—when recessions hit.

When the economy is hitting on all cylinders, employment is high and incomes and confidence are up. People travel more, dine out more, and are more likely to make major purchases. When the economy is down, people generally travel less and dine out less frequently. They even postpone major purchases such as homes and cars. We see this most clearly, of course, in a recession.

Your hospitality or travel business will go through these cycles. In fact, because travel, restaurant meals, and other industry services are commonly elective, hospitality and travel often prove more sensitive than most to economic fluctuations. Therefore, anticipating these cycles is a major part of the Co-Alignment Model, and environmental scanning is the right tool to see the changes coming that can impact your firm. Knowing that change is coming prepares you to face economic down times and perhaps correct your strategic course. For example, it may prove necessary to spend more on marketing, sales, and promotions; update pricing; adjust hiring and/ or employee scheduling; etc.

Past economic cycles suggest that good economic times last about 60 months or so, and down economic times will last from about 18 to 24 months (give or take.) These economic cycles have occurred for more than 100 years. So although we may feel that good times for our hospitality and travel industry will go on forever, a down economic cycle is waiting in the wings. Just understanding the reality of economic cycles will take you a long way towards successful strategic management and the ultimate success of your business (Note: During these economic downturns, more businesses fail and go into bankruptcy because they failed to anticipate change and have a strategy to cope with it successfully.) The figure below shows the vicissitudes of the hotel and lodging industry over many years. The boom times are always followed by economic-cycle declines for the hotel industry.

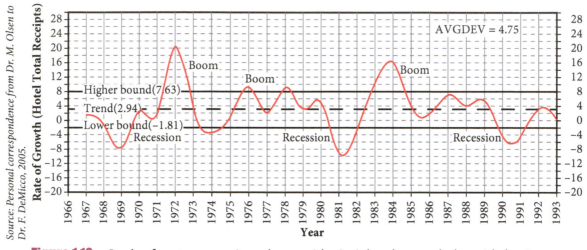

Source: Personal correspondence from Dr. M. Olsen to Dr. F. DeMicco, 2005.

Figure 1.10 Study of past economic cycles provides insights that can help guide business planning.

Businesses, including hotels and restaurants, also go through a characteristic life cycle. They are born with an entrepreneurial stage in which founder and owners have a dream and the vision to start a business. If it is successful, the business may expand by opening similar outlets in other geographical areas. We refer to this as *multi-site expansion*. If the concept is generating sufficient return on investment and the owners are satisfied that the firm is profitable, these multiple business units will continue to expand and multiply and the business enters the *growth stage* of its life cycle. Unfortunately, this stage never seems to last. Eventually, the business will slow down and stop growing. It may even begin to lose earnings. This is the *maturity stage* of the life cycle. (See Sasser, HBS, for more work in this area.)

The concepts of strategic management come into play in these last two stages. They can help your business rise above the completion, continue its growth, and delay its maturity and potential decline. Your skill in strategic planning will guide your strategic choices and tactics in the competitive environment. A restaurant company may come up with new products, new pricing incentives and promotions, and new technologies, for example. It may invest more in research and development (R&D) to anticipate change and continue its growth while other competitors mature, stagnate, and decline.

We have seen this often throughout business history. Even established companies like McDonald's and Chipotle have faced this slow-down. It is the understanding and anticipation of the economic and service-firm life cycle that leads them change strategic direction or introduce new tactics to continue their growth. McDonald's recently hit a slow patch and developed new systems, new technologies, new products (McCafe and the all-day breakfast, for example) to reaccelerate growth. McDonald's also continues to invest in R&D, which can be the secret of success in hospitality and travel. See Marriott for another success story.

As the authors found in a comprehensive study, firms that continue to invest in R&D even during recessionary times perform better than competitors who devote funds only to shorter-term goals such as bringing more money to the bottom line. We contend that even before a firm is "born" into the entrepreneurial stage, it invests in planning and developing its products and services. At this point in their development, many firms have a strong R&D mindset. However, as they grow and expand, they often spend more money on administrative costs and on the "process" of growth and less on the R&D that could generate new products and services and delay the stage of maturity and slow-down. Companies that sustain their success do so because they anticipate change, often because of increased market competition, economic downturn, or growing sameness/staleness of their prod-

ucts and services (or menu diversity and mix). New players with exciting products can take away from your existing business, which was growing but now faces, for example, maturity and falling sales.

Understanding economic cycles enables us to remain successful in a dynamic, competitive, and complex hospitality and travel market environment. Figure 1.11 demonstrates the life cycles of a firm with revenue ($) on the Y-axis and time on the X-axis.

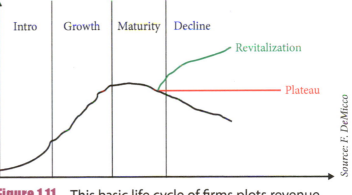

Source: F. DeMicco

Figure 1.11 This basic life cycle of firms plots revenue, on the Y-axis, against time, on the X-axis.

Conclusion

Chapter 1 discussed the strategic planning process and its importance in our hypercompetitive hospitality and travel environment. The Co-Alignment Model is introduced. We have focused on the important first step in strategic management, environmental scanning. Several key strategy concepts are discussed along with some of the strategic tools we use to develop a strategy for the company. One of the most important concepts in strategic management theory, the life cycle of the service firm, is also introduced. It captures the way in which change affects the company over time and points out how the environment can shape the success of the business. Over all, change and competition are consistent and pervasive. And even though most companies follow a low to moderate incremental pattern and eventually slower decline at the end of their life cycle, with proper strategic management and planning the firm can continue to grow and profit in a complex and changing environment. Staying abreast of this change through environmental scanning is required for the survival and sustainability of a hospitality and travel business.

Web Assignment

Log into the student website and complete the end of chapter assignment. Try to utilize some of the works you read about from this chapter and apply the key concepts, terms, and theory in your responses.

The Co-Alignment Model: Step 2 – Strategy Setting

In examining a hospitality and travel firm, Figure 2.1 shows their different strategic elements. At the top of the pyramid below is the overall corporate strategy, indicating what businesses the company is in. Then the business strategy identifies the competitive methods (CMs—or the unique products and services the firm will deploy against their competition or "competitive set"). Finally, the functional strategy or the internal departments or functional business area elements such as marketing, finance, administration, human resources, research and development (R&D), technology, etc. that will be employed to carry out the firm's strategy and competitive methods (CMs).

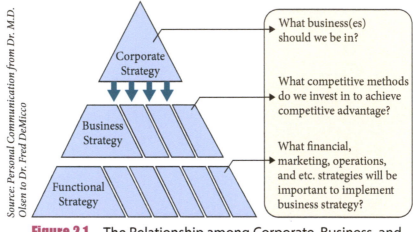

Source: Personal Communication from Dr. M.D. Olsen to Dr. Fred DeMicco

Figure 2.1   The Relationship among Corporate, Business, and Functional Strategies.

After completing step 1 of the Co-Alignment Model and having scanned the environment to determine your firm's strengths and opportunities in a marketplace to begin your new business, or progress the firm into the future, it is time to set (or redirect) the strategic course for the firm. Basically step 2 is defining your strategic "competitive methods" (CMs) that will position your hospitality or travel firm for success in a competitive marketplace. These CMs are your unique tactics that align with your chosen business strategy.

Most competing firms have to have what we refer to as critical success factors (CSF's). These factors are similar to all firms. For example, quick-service restaurants have to have drive-through windows and home delivery to compete. Hotels have to have a reservation system, Wi-Fi, etc. These are a given. What makes a competing firm unique are their competitive methods, which are the selected products (P) and services (S) that are the key strategic elements that will be deployed to win the battle for the customer's wallet. See Figure 2.2 and Figure 2.3 representing the lodging industry, where we see the critical success factors (CSF's) and competitive methods (CMs) working together strategically to increase a firm's net present value (NPV).

Investments in CSFs	NPV $	Investment required $	Investments in CM	NPV $	Investment required S
CSF1	10,000	50,000	CM1	5,000	25,000
CSF2	100,000	40,000	CM2	20,000	150,000
CSF3	1,500,000	800,000	CM3	6,000,000	3,400,000
Total	$1,610,000	$890,000	Total	$6,025,000	$3,575,000

Figure 2.2   A comparison of NPV and investment requirements of CSFs and CMs.

Another way to look at this is in Figure 2.3 showing the strategy portion of the Co-Alignment Model work.

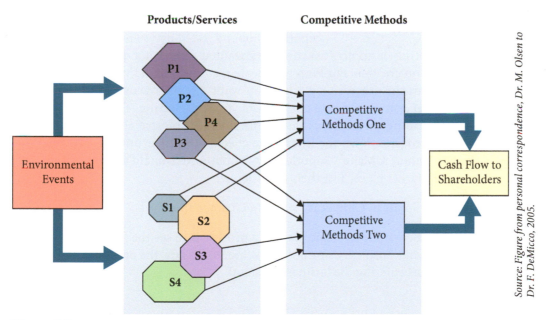

Source: Figure from personal correspondence, Dr. M. Olsen to Dr. F. DeMicco, 2005.

Figure 2.3   Competitive Methods as Combinations of Goods and Services.

Think about companies you know well. McDonald's, Chipotle, or Marriott, for example.

What are Chipotle's unique competitive methods (CMs) compared to Panera?

For example, what are the strengths of Chipotle that attract customers? Can you list these here?

You may have listed its sourcing of products from local farmers, its commitment to freshness, and its focus on sustainability. However, the chain's primary CM is its offering of customized products (P) made in front of you: menu items that are fast and are of fair value for your money. Chipotle is part of the fast-casual restaurant segment. Its other competitive method is its layout and design, referred to as the firm's "technological core." Think about how we begin the dining process at a Chipotle. We queue up in line. We are greeted by the first person who asks if we want a burrito or bowl (or taco). This starts the service process as we select our fresh ingredients added by a succession of servers down the line until we check out. We have part of this visual process right in front of us—every step of the way. This unique technological core is a CM for Chipotle. In fact, their Asian concept and pizza concept use a similar technological core and process. For example, for ShopHouse, the Asian concept the company tested between 2011 and 2017, the

Figure 2.4 Chipotle technological core and competitive method of design and process.

first server greeting customers asked if they wanted rice or noodles to serve as the base of their menu creation. For Pizzeria Locale, a spinoff chain that debuted in 2013, the first server in the process may ask if you want a regular crust, whole wheat (or even gluten-free) crust as the base of the pizza you are selecting. Then this continues down the line adding cheese, toppings and finally into an extremely hot oven as you and the pizza progress down the line to the checkout in their unique "process." So, these are the unique CMs of Chipotle. How about a McDonald's? How is Marriott unique in the market place? List their CMs below:

(Also see the Chipotle in China case study in Chapter 15.)

A good way to look at the strategic planning process is to see the flow of people (and materials) into your business using a systems model to show the processes of employees serving guests entering the business (system).

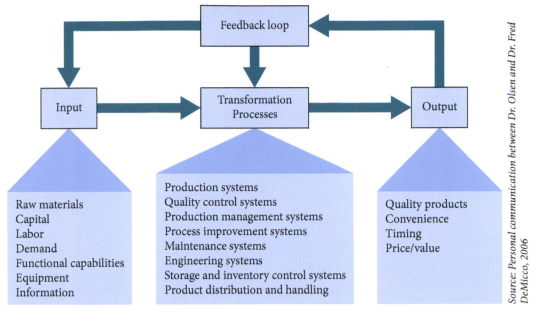

Source: Personal communication between Dr. Olsen and Dr. Fred DeMicco, 2006

Figure 2.5 The System Model of Product.

This helps management view the flow of guests into the restaurant or hotel, for example. Below is a model for a healthcare system to illustrate the service processes of a business (Figure 2.6).

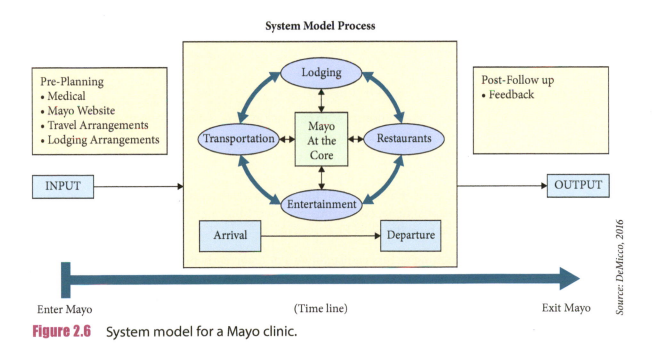

Source: DeMicco, 2016

Figure 2.6 System model for a Mayo clinic.

Scanning the Environment

Drivers from the remote environment have an impact on the firm. Therefore, a scan of the remote environment can influence the decision of whether or not to move into a particular area of activity (or geography) by looking at the broader, more general influences: ecological, environmental, political, socio-cultural, and technological. This often referred to as the PESTEL Model and is another useful tool firm strategists can use.

PESTEL is shown in Figure 2.7 below.

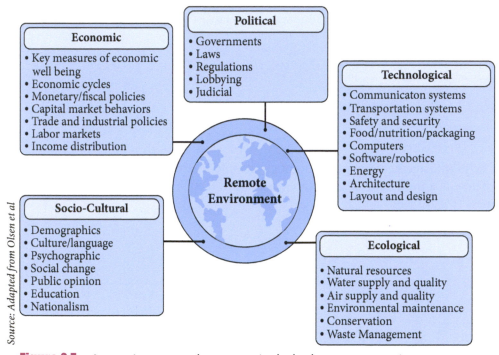

Figure 2.7   An environmental scan can include the remote environment, including these key variables.

Add the legal environment and all the legal mandates (such as minimum wage) and other new laws that impact doing business in the hospitality and travel industry to the above, and you have the PESTEL acronym.

These over-arching factors can facilitate a decision early in the scanning process. The decision to implement new strategies is a difficult one, with many factors coming into play, but if the preliminary scan shows significant problems in a particular place, it may be best to reconsider.

(Note: large insurance companies such as AIG provide good environmental scanning information. They collect big data to glean information on weather patterns, crime in an area, etc., and hospitality and travel firms can use this data in looking at a particular geographical area to open a new unit).

Strategizing in a Complex and Uncertain World

As readers will have recognized by now, strategic planning is a very complex process. It is also relatively obvious that success in such an endeavor is uncertain. In discussing the SWOT analyses above, we considered threats in the form of competition. Another term we can use to describe this red ocean of competition is "complexity." The more complex the business environment is, the more volatile and unstable for our business because the competition is fierce when a hospitality or tourism firm finds itself in a crowded (complex) environment. The firm has to scan the environment constantly, determine what the customers are demanding, and then adjust strategy and tactics accordingly during these unstable and volatile environments.

A certain, or stable, situation has a few, similar aspects, whereas an uncertain, or volatile, situation contains many, disparate facets.

Travel Industry Strategy Application Example: Airlines

As Figure 2.8 shows, the airline industry uses the Co-Alignment Model to choose appropriate strategies by utilizing various strategic tools listed in the diagram to gain a competitive edge in the market. Forecasting is very important at the beginning of any research to give a general idea of the opinions of experts within specific fields. This gives companies a broad view of the most optimistic and the most pessimistic consequences of their choices. First of all, airlines must scan all facets of the environment, including remote, task, functional, and firm environments. Elements to be considered in this process include models showing the forces that could impact a company, the market's certainty and complexity, growth, shares, and SWOT analyses, as well as many other factors. The Strategic Management Modelshows the order of steps from the forecasting stage through strategy development, to the final stages, where the strategy is evaluated. The choice of the strategic competitive methods (CMs) or the unique products and services (P + S) to deploy in the competitive business environment is critical. The life cycles and investments of these competitive methods to the firm can be even more important. See Figure 2.8 and Figure 2.9.

Airlines executives must implement competitive methods they are sure will bring profits to the company. They must scan the environment to see most importantly what is important to their customers. Since time is the most precious commodity, airlines could charge extra for direct, point-to-point flights. Being connected is also extremely important to those in the air. Making Wi-Fi available to travelers is extremely important and is a huge competitive method. People who are traveling in flights without Wi-Fi "are losing time" as they are not able to do things they otherwise would if they

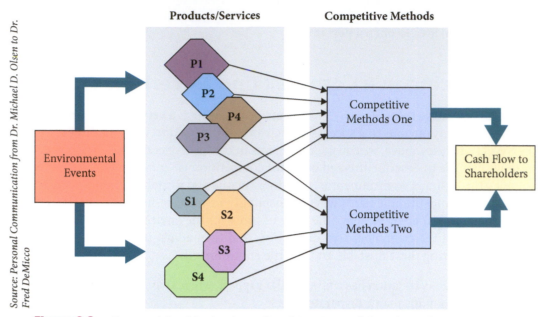

Source: Personal Communication from Dr. Michael D. Olsen to Dr. Fred DeMicco

Figure 2.8   Competitive Methods as Combinations of Goods and Services.

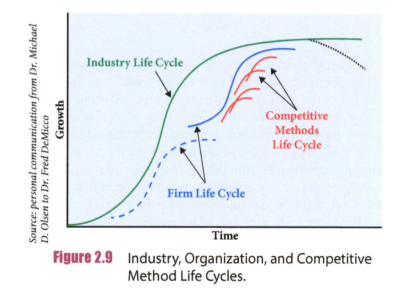

Source: personal communication from Dr. Michael D. Olsen to Dr. Fred DeMicco

Figure 2.9   Industry, Organization, and Competitive Method Life Cycles.

had Wi-Fi, like connecting with people or doing work on their electronic devices. Many customers also feel comfort is one of the main reasons to travel on specific flights. Many people would prefer larger seats and more legroom, and if an airline's managers believe they can make a profit on a newer plane with larger seating then they should do so to improve customer satisfaction.

Strategically chosen competitive methods are what makes a business stand out and are the key to the business's future successes or failure. Making customers happy is the number one goal in every industry, and methods to do so must be chosen that will

Co-Alignment Model

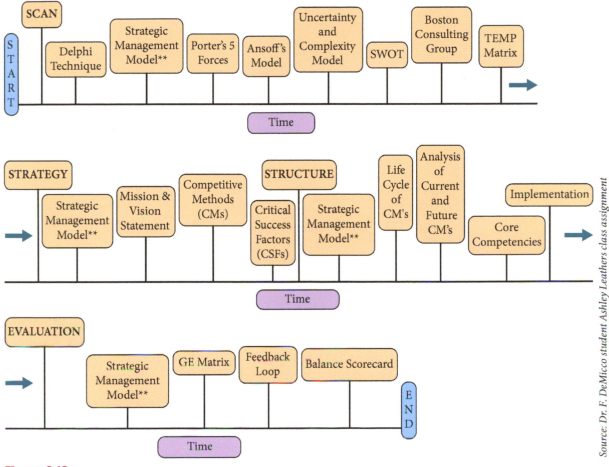

Source: Dr. F. DeMicco student Ashley Leathers class assignment

Figure 2.10

bring profits. Scanning the environment is extremely important: without this first step, strategic decisions will not be made correctly. Choosing effective competitive methods is vital to a business's success, and each competitive method affects every aspect of a business. When a firm is choosing a competitive method, it must be sure that the life cycle of that CM will be long and they that it will add value and be profitable to the firm. The life cycle of a competitive method must be looked at constantly and evaluated to see if the industry is becoming mature and if more investments must be made to maintain the effectiveness of this competitive method. Analyses of competitive methods must also be completed daily to identify and make any necessary adjustments. This is done by constantly scanning the environment (task and remote) and constantly looking at forces driving change, value drivers, critical success factors, and life cycles. After scanning is completed, the company must look at the changes in cash flow over time and the net present value of the chosen competitive method. After all of these factors are taken into account, the assessment of the CM's future performance is made, and decisions about this CM can be made strategically.

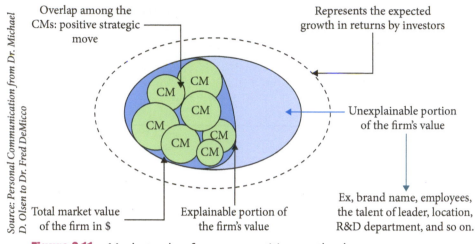

Source: Personal Communication from Dr. Michael D. Olsen to Dr. Fred DeMicco

Figure 2.11   Market value from competitive methods.

The figure above shows that you must maintain a significant inventory of CMs. The more CMs a firm has, the more market value that firm will obtain. The value of the firm can be measured by CMs and the growth that these methods bring to the firm. The firm can also grow by things that cannot be measured in terms of profits, things that are intangible, such as brand name, location, employees, experience, etc. Both tangible and intangible products/services are beneficial to the firm, but only the methods used can be measured to see the value they add.

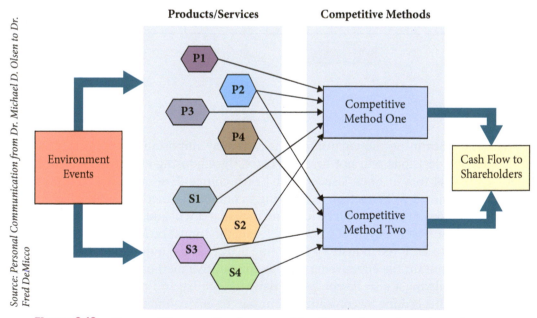

Source: Personal Communication from Dr. Michael D. Olsen to Dr. Fred DeMicco

Figure 2.12   Competition methods as combinations of goods and services.

The airline industry is a market that sells combinations of products and services. An example of this is when customers buy a first-class seat; they will enjoy corresponding services. A bundle of products/services can be viewed as a unique competition method (CM). These CMs must reflect the reality that gains in a competitive edge within the environment can increase profits for investors. Each competitive method in an enterprise should be unique because it will help each individual company to generate revenues specific to that competitive method. Southwest Airlines, for example, was famous for its budget flights. However, more and more competitors have entered this market. Therefore, Southwest must use forces driving change as a strategic tool to regain its competitive edge. In one strategy, Southwest and other budget airlines have designed bundle options to attract and retain more customers. Even though Southwest has provided customers with more options in general, they treat customers who purchase bundle packages with even greater priority than usual. Extra perks for these customers include additional frequent-flier points and an alcoholic drink. They also give up to $28 per flight Business Select upgrades off their unrestricted anytime fares. Additionally, they have begun to sell a new package that allows specific customers to jump to the front of boarding lines. By doing this, Southwest Airlines attracts customers to spend more money for their flights, which in turn brings Southwest more profits.

Strategic Planning: Some New Ideas

A new technique for company strategic planning is called Creative Strategy, and firms can use this as a guide for innovation—innovation being the new products and services that provide a competitive advantage to a firm over another in the competitive marketplace.

Kim and Mauborgne describe Blue Ocean Strategy and propose a way to avoid "red oceans," where competitors bloody each other in wars over similar products and services.They suggest moving into "Blue Oceans" where no firms yet compete. A Blue-Ocean strategy seeks new products and services for new customers. By getting there first and serving new customers a unique competitive method, companies can gain a first-mover advantage (before future competition arrives in the market). Examples of companies benefitting from these Blue Oceans include Cirque de Soleil and Yellow Tail Wines.

But how do you come up with new and attractive competitive methods (i.e., your products and services)?

Duggan (2007) shows how innovation happens in businesses and integrates modern neuroscience into a theory about how we shape our creative strategic ideas. This theory states that current strategic thinking explains how to do research, scan, interpret models, use theories such as SWOT, Porter's Five Forces, etc. But these do not guide firms to the next step: developing creative ideas to give your firm a competitive advantage. Brainstorming does not work particularly well for setting a new strategic plan; it is merely tossing out ideas. Creative strategy follows a natural three-step method based on the science of the human brain: breaking down a problem/challenge into parts, searching for past examples, and creating a new combination to solve the problem (and create new products and services). This is how creative strategy setting for a new strategic innovation for a firm could take place. This technique, called Creative Strategy, has been used by Netflix and even by Henry Ford, when he borrowed ideas from the animal processing industry to build cars (on an assembly line).

Summary

In summary, this chapter focused on step 2 of the Co-Alignment Model: Strategy. Strategic management and planning and setting the strategy with competitive methods (CMs) shape each and every firm and either bring them successes or bring them failures, and, in terms of airlines, competitive methods can be more helpful than anything else in this always-changing industry. It is hoped that as time goes on airlines will find methods that provide them room to grow and prosper, no matter the current global status.

Web Assignment

Log into the student website and complete the end of chapter assignment. Try to utilize some of the works you read about from this chapter and apply the key concepts, terms, and theory in your responses.

CHAPTER 3

Structure: The Third Step of the Strategic Management Co-Alignment Model

We call our strategic management process the Co-Alignment Model because it focuses on the necessary alignment of the factors required for strategic success: the choice of strategy and competitive methods, and the structure that supports them. If these elements are not properly aligned, or if the company fails to provide adequate resources to implement its plan, the strategy will fail. These issues help to explain the life-cycle theory we discussed in Chapter 1 and the eventual maturity and decline of hospitality and travel firms.

In the last chapter, we looked at strategy and competitive methods. The next step is to make sure the company's structure is properly aligned with those CM elements. In this chapter, we will examine this factor and see how it contributes to strategic success.

Organizational Structure

In organizational theory, structure begins with the design of the company hierarchy. An appropriate hierarchy enables the company to carry out its strategic objectives by having the right people in the right place at the right time, and with the authority they need to advance the company's goals. The traditional organizational structure is presented in Figure 3.1.

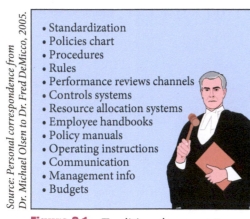

Source: Personal correspondence from Dr. Michael Olsen to Dr. Fred DeMicco, 2005.

- Standardization
- Policies chart
- Procedures
- Rules
- Performance reviews channels
- Controls systems
- Resource allocation systems
- Employee handbooks
- Policy manuals
- Operating instructions
- Communication
- Management info
- Budgets

Figure 3.1 Traditional corporate structure is hierarchical, with precisely defined duties, procedures, and chain of command.

Structure also relates to a firm's flexibility, centralization or decentralization of authority, formalization of the chain of command, and empowerment of employees. In the most effective companies, employees work within a well-defined hierarchy and follow clear rules for reporting to superiors. Yet, they are allowed an elastic span of control to make empowered decisions about what is best for the guest, thereby helping keep guests loyal to their hosts. Other aspects of the hospitality and travel firm's structure relate to locus of control, power, authority, and accountability of managers and employees. These all are part of the firm's values and philosophy, and how these variables are structured either promotes or limits the organization's ability to carry out its tactics and meet goals and objectives of its strategic plan in a competitive environment.

The Co-Alignment Model's Organizational Structure

In the Co-Alignment Model, organizational structure is critical to the company's success because it underpins and supports the firm's strategy, allowing it to be executed effectively. Figure 3.2 illustrates the decision-making process in strategic management. It shows the integration of core competencies with the firm's selected

Integration of the firm's <u>Core Competencies</u> (CC) with its selected <u>Competitive Methods</u> (CM)

I.   <u>Environmental Scanning Process</u>
II.   <u>Determine Opportunities; Determine Competencies and Available Resources</u>
III. <u>Align Opportunities with Competencies</u>
IV. <u>Determine Investment Hurdles and Financial Feasibility</u>
V.   <u>Make Investments Aligning Structure with Strategy</u> (CMs and CCs)
VI. <u>Implement the Strategy and Evaluate Results</u> (See Chapter 4.)

Source: Dr. Fred DeMicco.

Figure 3.2   Many factors influence the choice and implementation of Competitive Methods. These are key.

competitive methods–the structure for defining, organizing, and carrying out the firm's strategy.

Having the right employees and managers properly aligned for all service encounters and delivery is critical for success. It is this element that adds structure to the firm's competitive methods (strategy). The degree of skills, knowledge, and abilities required by employees and managers determines the investment needed in structure. For example, a full-service or luxury hotel or an upscale or fine-dining restaurant requires a large investment in human capital to deliver the services guests expect. Figure 3.3 shows the relationship between the perceived quality of the product and the level of service required in various types of hospitality and travel business.

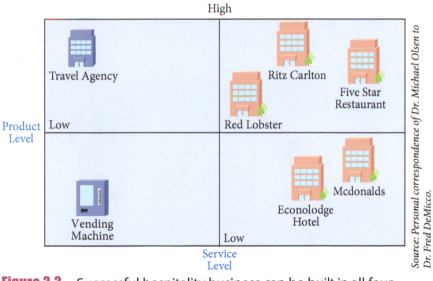
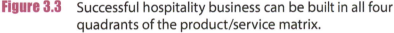

Source: Personal correspondence of Dr. Michael Olsen to Dr. Fred DeMicco.

Figure 3.3   Successful hospitality business can be built in all four quadrants of the product/service matrix.

Ritz-Carlton, in Figure 3.3, is a great example of how having employees engaged with the guests improves the firm's profitability. Their personnel, management, and hotel luxury design—their structure—is aligned with their completive-methods strategy to deliver a high level of product (P) and a high level of service (S).

We refer to encounters between employees and guests as the service "moment of truth." Properly selected, educated and trained, and engaged employees will engage guests at a higher level. This ensures better service, improves guest and employee satisfaction, lowers employee turnover, and increases profitability and guest loyalty. Figures 3.4 and 3.5 illustrate this relationship between employees and guests at the "moment of truth." The end-of-chapter case study takes a close look at how these factors operate at Ritz-Carlton, a Marriott International company, and the importance and impact of this engagement between employees and guests.

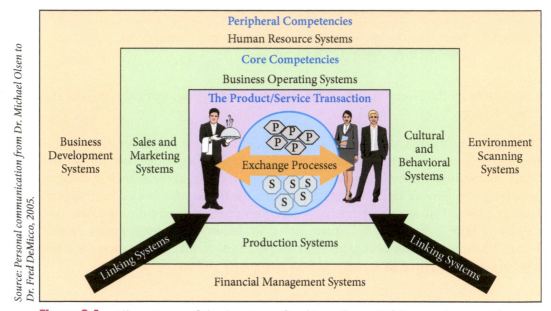

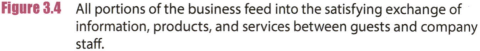

Source: Personal communication from Dr. Michael Olsen to Dr. Fred DeMicco, 2005.

Figure 3.4 All portions of the business feed into the satisfying exchange of information, products, and services between guests and company staff.

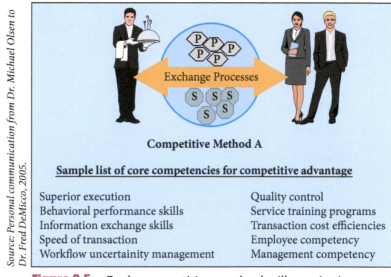

Source: Personal communication from Dr. Michael Olsen to Dr. Fred DeMicco, 2005.

Figure 3.5 Each competitive method will require its own set of skills and resources to support its necessary interactions between staff and guests.

Another useful structure-setting strategy tool, the FRAP Matrix (FRequency And Personalization Matrix), is used to determine the level of guest personalization that is possible, or necessary, based on the competitive method the firm has chosen and the amount of money the company managers have budgeted to achieve it. The FRAP Matrix compares the frequency of repurchase with the personalization of the exchange. Structure decisions are based on collected data, which yields information about the guests and how frequently they return to the facility. If guests visit infrequently, then the lower right-quadrant analytics and "big data" can be used to encourage more frequent stops. Examples of this are often seen among cruise lines, such as Carnival, and destination wellness spas, such as Canyon Ranch. This technique is particularly effective when guests have rated their cruise or spa visit very favorably. It can also be helpful in prospecting for new customers.

As the FRAP Matrix implies, information technology is one more component of organizational structure. The collection of big data, to glean customer expectations, perception of the product and service-delivery levels, and guest-expectation information as seen in Figure 3.6, can give the firm an edge in the competitive hospitality and travel business environment, making it possible to beat the competition and become more successful. Again, this is an example of aligning a component of structure with the company's strategic objectives.

Figure 3.7 illustrates how a firm will align and structure its competitive methods with its core competencies, principally the talent of the organization's managers and employees, to deliver the hospitality and/or travel products and services.

Structure helps to translate competitive methods into corporate benefits such as free cash flow, return on investment, and guest perception. Competitive methods such as marketing campaigns, quality and consistency of products and services, and cultivation of a reputation for corporate social responsibility through social awareness, environmental protection, and other efforts are supported by the

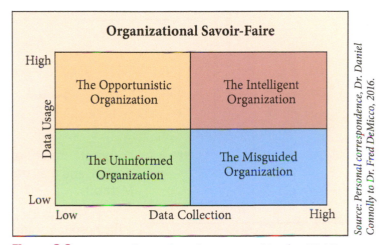

Organizational Savoir-Faire

Data Usage: High / Low

Data Collection: Low / High

- The Opportunistic Organization
- The Intelligent Organization
- The Uninformed Organization
- The Misguided Organization

Source: Personal correspondence, Dr. Daniel Connolly to Dr. Fred DeMicco, 2016.

Figure 3.6   Data collected and organized in the FRAP Matrix goes a long way to determine the company's operational style and success.

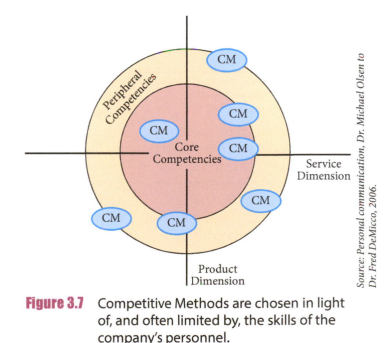

Peripheral Competencies

Core Competencies

Service Dimension

Product Dimension

CM

Source: Personal communication, Dr. Michael Olsen to Dr. Fred DeMicco, 2006.

Figure 3.7   Competitive Methods are chosen in light of, and often limited by, the skills of the company's personnel.

Structure: The Third Step of the Strategic Management Co-Alignment Model   31 firm's structure. Resource allocation, core competencies, and contextual and process variables must be aligned to make the competitive methods effective.

Figure 3.8 presents another way to look at structure and its role in aligning the firm's competitive methods with the appropriate resources.

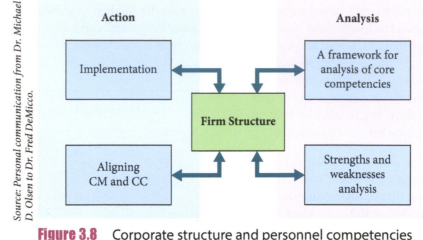

Source: Personal communication from Dr. Michael D. Olsen to Dr. Fred DeMicco.

Figure 3.8 Corporate structure and personnel competencies govern, and may be altered in light of, Competitive Methods.

The hospitality and travel industry offers many examples in which structure and competitive methods must be aligned. In a typical case, management wishes to establish a hotel as the top-rated event center in its city. To do so, the facility will need the best audio-visual (A/V) technology, sound systems, and lighting compared with their competitors. (Their competitive method is to have the top A/V system in the city.) To make it work, executives need to budget for the equipment and personnel to service the technology their goal requires.

Fortunately, there is a strategy tool that can help to determine the technology needs, necessary investments, and appropriate structure in a competitive environment. This is the Strategic Impact Grid or Matrix. It compares technology investment needs and the cost of IT reliability with the need for newness—the firm's need to have the latest and greatest IT hardware and software. For example, two firms that require state-of-the-art IT and would rate high on both axes are Google and Southwest Airlines. They cannot afford to have their systems go down, so reliability is a high priority for them; their business models require the latest and best hardware and software. Google exists to provide unfailing service on the Internet, while the Southwest business model relies on customers booking their own flights on the company website. See Figure 3.9.

Figure 3.9 In information systems, reliability and the need for state-of-the-art technology often are competing priorities. The Strategic Impact Grid helps in deciding their relative importance to the company. Adapted Piccoli, Gabriele. 2008. Information Systems for Managers. Hoboken, NJ: John Wiley & Sons.

Our industry provides many such examples. Airlines that wish to be known as having the best inflight entertainment would need to make a similar investment. A restaurateur who wants his establishment to rate three Michelin stars or five Diamonds would have to spend the money to hire a top chef and assistants and also to invest in the right equipment, furniture, and fixtures. Think about hospitality and travel entities such as a top-level spa, golf course, or cruise ship, and consider the competitive methods and the structure required to support them. Figure 3.10 looks at using technology as a firm's strategy and competitive method and aligning the technology structure to outperform the competition.

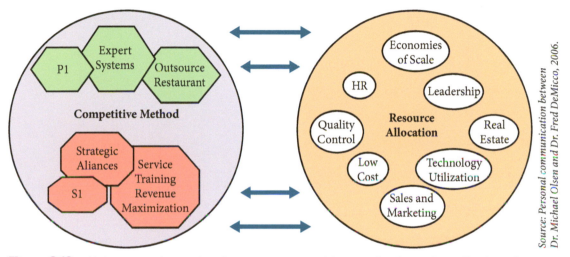

Source: Personal communication between Dr. Michael Olsen and Dr. Fred DeMicco, 2006.

Figure 3.10 Using superior technology as a competitive method requires aligning the company's tech structure to fit.

Can you list some other possible strategies for a hotel or restaurant you know or perhaps work at? Name the unique competitive methods that distinguish them from the competition, and then analyze the aligning structure that allows the firm to realize its unique competitive methods.

In the chapter covering restaurants further, you'll see how proper hiring and training of the service staff provides for a very positive guest encounter. Thus, investing resources in training of the staff can allow a restaurant to execute a top-level guest service experience in a competitive environment. The same principles apply to every segment of the hospitality and travel industry.

Web Assignment

Log into the student website and complete the end of chapter assignment. Try to utilize some of the works you read about from this chapter and apply the key concepts, terms, and theory in your responses.

CHAPTER 4

Did Our Competitive Methods Make Money? Strategy Financials

Businesses can have many goals. They exist to serve their customers, of course. They may take pride in providing steady jobs for their employees or in being good citizens of their communities, which is a competitive method (CM) as well as a purpose. In Google's early days, the company famously stated its top priority as, "Don't be evil." Yet, under the law a company can have only one purpose: to make money, and as much of it as possible. That is management's fiduciary duty to its owners, investors, and stockholders. This brings us to step 4 of the Co-Alignment Model, figuring out whether the company's investment in a CM has advanced the firm and earned it money. Have the chosen CMs made a profit? Both literally and figuratively, that is the bottom line for any business.

There are many ways to gauge a firm's performance. For a publicly traded company, investors might look at the stock's Earnings per Share, dividends paid, and rise or fall of the stock price. However, for management the primary measure of a CM's results is the Return on Investment (ROI). Any investment should make money and/or reduce costs. Ideally, it will do both. ROI can even be estimated beforehand to determine whether the investment in a CM is financially feasible.

Return on Investment (ROI)

A basic formula for ROI is the following:

(Money Made from the Investment in the CM + Money Saved by It)/Cost of the Investment

It can be used in two ways: with estimated figures for income and savings (chances are that the cost will be known) to decide whether the investment is worth making and, after the CM has been implemented, with actual data to evaluate the results. If the resulting ROI is larger than 1.0, then this probably is or was a good investment, as it makes money and/or saves on costs.

Here is an example of ROI calculation:

A new automated espresso machine connected to your point-of-sale terminal (POS) generates an additional $5,500 per year in sales and saves $2,500 on labor. It costs you $4,000. What is the ROI for the year? (Show your work here.)

Using the ROI formula above, you have:

$5,550 (additional revenue) + $2,500 (cost savings) / $4,000 = 2.0

Since 2.0 is greater than 1.0, the ROI is positive and the firm should make the investment in the espresso machine.

Figure 4.1 looks at the evaluation of a firm's strategy, or CMs invested in, to see whether they delivered a financial return on their investment and had a positive effect on the business. This example measures cash flow per share, but targets such as earnings per share, Net Present Value, or ROI would be calculated similarly and would be just as useful.

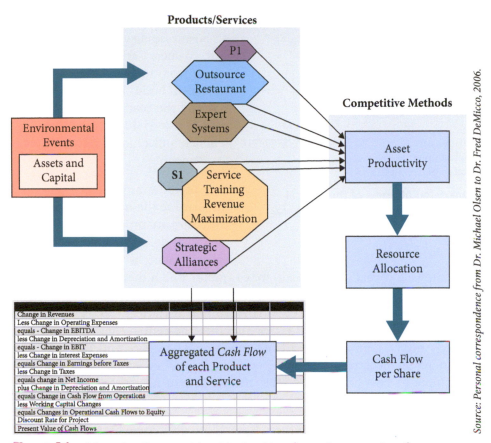

Products/Services

Competitive Methods

Source: Personal correspondence from Dr. Michael Olsen to Dr. Fred DeMicco, 2006.

Figure 4.1 After the Competitive Method has been in operation for a reasonable period, its results must be evaluated by a process similar to the one depicted above.

Cost of Capital

Cost of capital is an important term in finance and a major factor in determining whether the strategic investment in competitive methods—the firm's allocation and deployment of resources (i.e., the structure)—pays off. In many cases, cost of capital equates to the interest rate that must be paid to borrow the funds. However, it also can refer to the opportunity cost of diverting money from its current use to pay for the new competitive method. In this case, it equals the present rate of return on the firm's capital.

The return rate is very important in determining the outcome of the firm's strategic objectives and also investment in its structure. Recall that investment of capital in the strategy or CMs is not a theoretical construct; it costs the business actual money. Add to that the investment of structure by the firm to align with the strategy, including human capital investment, equipment, technology, etc., which are real investment costs to a business. All these affect the bottom line. Figure 4.2 looks at the elements that comprise the *cost of capital*.

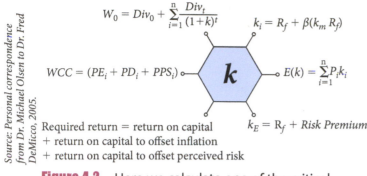

Source: Personal correspondence from Dr. Michael Olsen to Dr. Fred DeMicco, 2005.

$$W_0 = Div_0 + \sum_{i=1}^{n} \frac{Div_t}{(1+k)^t}$$

$$k_i = R_f + \beta(k_m R_f)$$

$$WCC = (PE_i + PD_i + PPS_i)$$

$$E(k) = \sum_{i=1}^{n} P_i k_i$$

Required return = return on capital
+ return on capital to offset inflation
+ return on capital to offset perceived risk

$$k_E = R_f + Risk\ Premium$$

Figure 4.2   Here we calculate one of the critical factors in selecting a new Competitive Method.

In making a financial commitment, all businesses have a required return that owners and/or shareholders *expect* from their investment. Investors also build in the variable of *risk* and the cost of inflation. If perceived risk is high, then investors will demand a higher return on their investment.

Risk includes any factor that could undermine the investment and cost the company money. Typical examples include an unstable economic environment, a hazardous geopolitical climate (the threat of terrorism, for example), and a disruptive technology that will compete with a firm's investment. Similarly, if inflation is projected to be high in a given economic cycle (usually annual inflation risk is taken into account), then investors again will factor this into the return they expect. If the risks are too high, the business will not invest in a strategy and the structure required to achieve the return. The formula in Figure 4.2 explains how a firm might calculate its cost of capital or the interest rate of return needed to justify investing in a strategic CM.

One good example of incorporating these factors into deciding whether to go ahead with a project strategy comes from the ski industry. Managers of a company like publicly traded Vail Resorts must consider many variables in deciding whether to make a strategic investment in a new ski resort. One of the most significant is snow. An uncommonly mild winter could send skiers elsewhere for a season, eating into the resort's profit. More than one such winter could be devastating. This is important even for a major corporation because a new resort can cost a billion dollars or more. However, Vail Resorts and its stockholders face less risk than they might because Vail has ski resorts all over the world and in different climate-impacted areas. If there is no snow in New England, there still might be record snowfalls in the U.S. Rockies or in Canada or at Vail operations elsewhere. Thus, the element of weather risk is mitigated, and it becomes easier to invest in a new resort or to buy the company's stock. Exposure to risks like this is a typical element in deciding whether to invest in a project or company (or not).

This analysis involves four key considerations that govern any possible investment in strategic CMs. These are: estimating the cash flows from the CM; determining the cost of capital, or the borrowing interest rate, for the CM investment; the degree of risk in investing capital in the CM; and finally the investment itself—whether it is financially prudent to invest in the strategic CM at all. See Figure 4.3 for a graphical representation of these factors.

To determine whether the investment is likely to bring the return that investors demand, managers often calculate *Net Present Value (NPV.)* If the cash flows (over the years of the investment) of the strategic CMs are positive (adjusted to present-day dollars) and exceed the financial *investment* (denoted as "I" in Figure 4.4), then it generally makes sense to invest in the strategic CM. It has a positive cash flow and is likely to make money for the company rather than lose it.

Making money is obviously the key measure of success in any business. Yet not all decisions lend themselves to this kind of analysis. For example, a small hotel or resort might consider providing a shuttle for its guests to and from the local airport, even though public transportation is available. Costs are well defined—the price of the vehicle and the cost of its maintenance, interest on any capital borrowed for its purchase, insurance, and salary and benefits for a driver. However, it is nearly impossible to assign a cash flow to the service when making the decision or to identify whatever profit it brings after it enters operation.

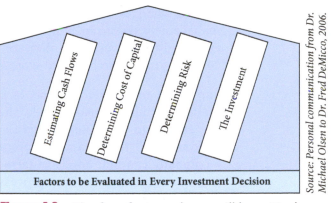

Factors to be Evaluated in Every Investment Decision

Source: Personal communication from Dr. Michael Olsen to Dr. Fred DeMicco, 2006.

Figure 4.3 The four factors above will be critical throughout the manager's career.

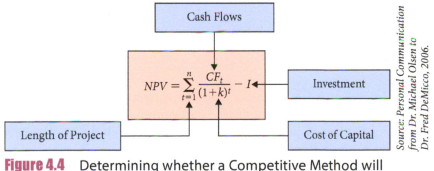

Source: Personal Communication from Dr. Michael Olsen to Dr. Fred DeMicco, 2006.

$$NPV = \sum_{t=1}^{n} \frac{CF_t}{(1+k)^t} - I$$

Figure 4.4 Determining whether a Competitive Method will be a profitable use of investment funds.

This is one of those cases we noted above, where outcomes and expectations other than direct profit may be important for a business. Is the company well regarded and respected by consumers? Is it a good steward of the environment? Are the employees satisfied with their jobs? Are guests satisfied with their experience? Does the hospitality and travel firm invest in education and training for its employees and managers? Weighing these factors is another part of step 4 in the Co-Alignment Model. One tool often used for this purpose is the "Balanced Scorecard."

The Balanced Scorecard Applied to Short-term Objectives and Evaluation

Evaluation is essential to be sure that the strategic investment receives proper execution and follow-through. Management and employees are charged with the responsibility of assessing whether or not the firm is following the correct course to meet its planned strategic objectives. This decision is based on a thorough analysis of the environment and the changes occurring in it. The Balanced Scorecard therefore functions as a management system enabling the firm to set, track, and achieve its key business strategies and objectives. For a diagram of this process go to http://www.erptraining9. com/blog/using-the-balanced-scorecard-to-measure-performance-under-sap-erp/

Supported by the set elements of strategy, the firm's strategic structure, design methods, and automation tools, the *Balanced Scorecard* helps managers to track the execution of strategic activities and to monitor the consequences of their actions. With the Balanced Scorecard at the center of its management systems, a company can monitor short-term results from additional perspectives—1. Customers, 2. Internal business processes, 3. Learning and growth, and 4. Financial performance—and evaluate strategy in the light of recent performance. The Balanced Scorecard thus enables companies to modify strategies to reflect real-time learning. For example, to measure a strategy's effect on customers, firms will collect feedback called guest satisfaction scores, or GSS. (If that shuttle service provides a quantifiable benefit, it is likely to appear here.) Managers will also be evaluated and scored by employees. The Balanced Scorecard also will ask employees to evaluate how well the firm is investing in their knowledge, skills, and abilities. Finally, as we discuss in depth below, they will take account of financial performance and ROI to decide whether the strategic plan and competitive methods have paid dividends for the firm.

BizCafé *

The BizCafé Interpretive Simulation, created by Interpretive Software (www.interpretive.com), replicates the real-life business of running a coffee shop. In BizCafé, students assume the role of coffee shop manager and make all the decisions required to open the business and prosper in the face of competition. In the process, they learn how to sort out priorities and objectives in the context of a limited budget and a changing environment. They develop skill in management, operations, marketing, and accounting.

Above all, they learn about the process of making sound decisions with the help of hard numbers. Many of these decisions are based on the principles introduced in this chapter. They provide sound practical experience in evaluating the promise and results of competitive methods, as hospitality and travel students will be required to do throughout their careers.

Below, we will walk through a typical simulation. Work begins with selecting a name for the business and deciding what furniture and equipment will best meet the company's objectives. After that, there are weekly decisions about how to staff the café, price and promote the product, set shop hours, and purchase supplies to operate the business. In addition, "incidents" (mini-cases) require a response.

As we walk through this case study, think about the decisions participants make in operating their coffee shop. Analyze the data, and figure out which options are most

---

*Adapted from John David McCracken and F.J. DeMicco, 2016

likely to bolster the company's bottom line. Do the math. This experience will not duplicate that of participating in a simulation, but it will be good practice.

In this scenario, Amelia's Coffee Shop secures a loan of $25,000 to set up in business. The company's mission statement tells us much of what we need to know about the business and its goals:

Mission Statement

To achieve the highest Net Income and most importantly Cumulative Revenue in the competitive set, Amelia's will position itself with a high price point (as opposed to a low price point/high volume strategy), monitor and analyze our competitive ranking, test the market demand and maximize revenue by charging premium prices, sell the most coffee, and offer a superior combination of the highest quality coffee product and hospitable service. The costs of goods sold will be controlled to achieve the highest gross margin, and expenses will be maintained at their lowest levels to maximize net income. We will strive for the highest employee and customer satisfaction rankings.

To guide business decisions, the shop receives financial statements each week. The simulation allows only limited information about nine competitors, which received similar loans and set up shop at the same time. Managers can see their current and accumulated revenue, coffee prices, cups sold, number of employees, branding, and customer satisfaction. They also can monitor the pricing, wages, and net income of their competitors, which began with the same budget and set up shop when Amelia's did. These are the factors to be analyzed.

Let's watch Amelia's performance and see whether we would make the same decisions Amelia's manager does.

The beginning Balance Sheet (Figure 4.5) shows an initial capital investment of $25,000, $10,000 of which has been spent on equipment. We can compare this with our ending balance sheet (Appendix V).

Assets		Liabilities	
Cash	$12,500.00	Taxes Payable	$0.00
Deposits	$2,500.00	Loans	$25,000.00
Equipment	$10,000.00	**Total Liabilities**	$25,000.00
Accumulated	$0.00	**Equity**	
Depreciation		Retained Eamings	$0.00
Inventory	$0.00	**Total Equity**	$0.00
Total Assets	$25,000.00	**Total Liab. & Eq.**	$25,000.00

Figure 4.5   Amelia's starting balance sheet.

One of our most important management tools is the Income Statement:

Revenue – Cost Of Goods Sold = Gross Margin
Gross Margin – Total Expenses = Net Income

Each week, we will check Amelia's Income Statement and compare our revenue and net income with those of the competition. Why? Because each week a manager must modify pricing and wages based on what has happened in the past.

Consider: What happens when we raise or lower prices? What happens when we pay our employees above or below average pay rates? Figuring out cause-and-effect relationships will help to improve our predictions in the future.

In the end, we will look at Amelia's Final Cumulative Net Income. What percentage of total revenue is represented by net income?

The Play

Startup Period

Our Startup for BizCafé seeks to generate the highest revenue possible and keep Cost of Goods Sold and Operating Expenses as low as possible in the startup period. An early lead in revenue is a key to success. Success requires a number of decisions.

Background Information

At least two decisions are involved here, but let us take them as given. Assume that each pound of coffee will produce approximately thirty-two to forty cups. Coffee purchases are always made conservatively. Small incremental orders cost only a few more cents per pound than buying in bulk. Better to pay extra than over-purchase and waste product. Amelia's coffee orders grow only as the business does. Conservative purchasing is a good practice providing an indicator, showing increased demand, and control, revealing possible excess usage, theft, or waste. Coffee cups were purchased in bulk throughout the period.

Setting Up Shop

Opening a business requires many tactical decisions. The goal is to keep initial costs as low as possible without compromising the quality and service required by the company's mission statement. Let us look at some of the most important. As we do, please try to figure out what choices you would make to implement the strategy Amelia's management has chosen.

Decision 1: Coffee Price: It costs Amelia's $0.28 to make a cup of coffee. The default price in the area is $3.75. When all products are the same, it may be best to offer low competitive pricing. However, Amelia's offers a high-quality product and service. Does this justify charging more than the competition?

How much should Amelia's charge for a cup of coffee?

A.) More than the competition
B.) The same price as the competition
C.) Less than the competition

Decision 2: Operating Hours: The maximum operating hours are 7:00 a.m. to 11:00 p.m. History tells us that in 1946 the Tote'm convenience stores expanded their hours and renamed the company 7-Eleven. In 1969, they began 24-hour operations. Additional marginal revenue exceeded the costs. With that in mind:

Which of the following schedules would you select? Why?

A.) 7:30 a.m. – 2:00 p.m.
B.) 7:00 a.m. – 8:30 p.m.
C.) 7:00 a.m. – 11:00 p.m.

Decision 3: Staffing: In order to dominate in the marketplace, beginning costs must be kept as low as possible consistent with good service. How many employees should Amelia's hire? The competitors have anywhere from 2 to 25.

For the Startup Period, Amelia's should hire:

A.) More employees than the competition.
B.) The same number as the competition.
C.) Fewer employees than the competition.

Decision 4: Employee Pay: Amelia's will expect a higher level of performance than the competition. In later periods, the shop will rely on superior service to be able to raise coffee prices, challenging the staff to maintain the same level of demand.

How much should Amelia's pay its employees?

A.) Pay below the average.
B.) Pay the average.
C.) Pay above industry averages.

Decision 5: Coffee Machine

Amelia's can buy either a two-cup or a four-cup coffee machine. A four-cup high-capacity coffee machine costs $6,000. The two-cup machine costs less, but Amelia's needs to maximize output, so management calculates the break-even point for covering the cost of the high-capacity machine. To do so, it needs the result from Decision 1: Given its goal of providing a high-quality product, Amelia's charges $3.95 per cup of coffee with a unit cost of $0.28. Knowing this, we can calculate how many cups Amelia's must sell to break even. Amelia's needs to maximize its capacity of output, and the additional cost of the high-capacity machine must be recouped by volume sales.

Is a $6000 coffee machine worth the investment?

Coffee Machine Cost: $6,000, Selling Price is $3.95; Unit Cost per Cup is $0.28.

Break-Even Volume = Fixed Cost ÷ (Unit Selling Price − Unit Cost)
$$= \$6,000 \div (\$3.95 - \$0.28)$$
$$= 6000 \div 3.67$$
$$= 1,634 \text{ Cups}$$

Should we purchase the High-Capacity Coffee Machine?

A.) Yes.   B.) No

Decision 6: Should Amelia's purchase used furniture for $500 or trendy "green" furniture for $4000?

A.) Used furniture for $500.   B.) Trendy "green" furniture for $4000.

Decision 7: How much should Amelia's spend on advertising to develop branding and name recognition?

A.) Spend as much on advertising as you can afford, and support special sales with additional campaigns.

B.) Spend as conservatively as possible, but enough to develop a consistent presence.

Hint: A consistent message on a regular schedule provides the best return for advertising dollar spent. Radio messages in drive times and small newspaper ads work well in combination to develop name recognition and branding for our coffee shop. The size of an ad does not matter as much for a startup business, as long as we are "in the game." Given its satisfactory brand awareness, Amelia's decides to continue this advertising strategy.

Decision 8: Insurance: Equipment insurance is now available. The cost is $600 per month. Many repairs can cost much more than that. Let us assume that within one year two of our critical machines fail, a $3247 dishwasher and a $4000 coffee machine.

Should we purchase insurance to cover repairs for $600?

A.) Yes, purchase insurance.   B.) No, pay for repairs as they arise.

Amelia's Decisions

Amelia's strategy is to establish positioning at a **high price point** in a market that is expected to grow. With this in mind:

As we have just seen, coffee price is set at $3.95 per cup. This is higher than the local average in order to gain an early lead in overall revenue, but—the management hopes—not high enough to discourage potential customers.

The company relies on high standards to attract clients willing to pay slightly more than they would at competing shops, so it needs enough managers and staff to ensure attentive service. Amelia's began with a conservative payroll of thirteen employees. There are two managers, and the company plans to add a third in the second session of the simulation. Pay is set at $650 per week for managers and $9.25 an hour for servers. This is significantly above the local average.

The shop will stay open as from 7:00 a.m. to 11:00 p.m.—as long as it can! Additional revenue from each cup of coffee sold will exceed the extra cost of hourly employees. Shops that limit their evening and weekend hours consistently put themselves at a disadvantage.

Because Amelia's upscale philosophy requires the best aesthetic presentation, management did buy the trendy "green" furnishings. With $3.67 profit per cup, the break-even point is $4000 ÷ $3.67 = 1089 cups.

Amelia's bought the four-cup coffee machine.

It also insured its equipment against breakdowns. The estimated $7247 cost of repairs or replacement, plus lost revenue during down time, would exceed the $7200 annual cost for insurance.

For a startup, the best advertising policy is to provide basic exposure consistently over time to develop branding and name recognition. Amelia's chose to go with three radio ads per day (in drive times) and a small ad in the local newspaper, which are sufficient to develop exposure. Its advertising budget therefore is conservative and likely to prove well spent.

First Period Results

We see how these decisions turned out in Figure 4.6. Numbers that were less than the competition's best for that period appear in red.

Coffee Shop Comparative Analysis Period 1					
Week 1	Revenue ($)	Cups Sold	Net Income ($)	Cum. Inc. ($)	Satisfaction
Perk Up	4764	1356	−899	−899	43.3
Amelia's	6395	1619	−1333	−1333	41.3
M. Business	4187	1674	−1899	−1899	43.3

Figure 4.6 First-period results for the top three coffee shops.

In Figure 4.6, we see that Amelia's trails behind Perk Up in Cups Sold, Net Income, and Cumulative Revenue in this first period. Customer Satisfaction comes in a disappointing third. However, brand awareness (which does not appear in the figure) is second among the ten competitors.

These results present obvious questions. Should Amelia's raise prices in hope of improving its bottom line? Is its extra spending on furnishings and salaries paying off? Please give these issues some thought before continuing.

Cups sold are within 60 of the leader, 1619 to 1674. This suggests the need to increase capacity. Options include hiring more staff, expanding the infrastructure, or reducing prices to stimulate demand. Amelia's management decides to keep prices stable because it is not yet evident what factors affect demand. For infrastructure, self-ordering electronic kiosks and/or tablets to place orders are considerations for Amelia's. In addition, investing in an app for ordering on the smartphone and payment can speed up service (and also help reduce labor). It is too early to reach a verdict on the company's extra spending on upscale furniture and salaries. Management still believes that keeping standards high will enable Amelia's to attract the upscale clientele it needs to support the strategy of pricing coffee higher than the competition.

The conservative spending strategy was effective in that the business never had to borrow, and the checkbook balances showed revenue of $10,819.42 for Week 1, which grew to $14,016.89 within a few weeks. This strategy was also limiting in that other shops with more employees were selling more cups of coffee.

Coffee Shop Comparative Analysis Period 2					
Week 2	Revenue ($)	Cups Sold	Net Income ($)	Cum. Inc. ($)	Satisfaction
Amelia's	8287	2098	2452	1120	52.8
Perk Up	5345	1527	1778	879	51.8
Louvre	6310	1639	573	573	42.6

Figure 4.7 Second-period results for the top three coffee shops.

Management is excited to see that Amelia's figures are now the highest! This indicates that the market is in a period of growth, so Amelia's raises its price from $3.95 per cup to $4.10.

In making this decision, managers analyze the revenue and cups sold of Amelia's closest competitor. Louvre is charging $3.75 per cup, $.20 less than Amelia's. Despite this, Amelia's revenue and cups sold were higher. We see also that Customer Satisfaction and Brand Awareness rankings are now higher for Amelia's than for the competition. The process of deduction tells us that our high-end coffee, furniture, and high-paid team are enabling us to realize higher revenue.

Amelia's hired one more manager and three more servers to increase capacity. We hire conservatively, not overestimating demand. The $650 weekly manager pay and the $9.25 hourly wage rate are maintained.

Coffee Shop Comparative Analysis Period 3					
Week 3	Revenue ($)	Cups Sold	Net Income ($)	Cum. Inc. ($)	Satisfaction
Amelia's	10738	2619	3632	4752	58.5
Perk Up	7441	2126	2543	3422	57.1
Zoe's	8245	2386	1779	−273	60.0

Figure 4.8 Third-period results for the top three coffee shops.

Managers do not want to overestimate demand, resulting in excessive costs. However, it appears that some changes are justified. Continuing to test the demand, Amelia's will increase the price to $4.20 for Week 4. The company hired one more manager and three more servers to increase capacity. The $650 weekly manager pay is increased to $680 per week and the $9.25 hourly wage rate is maintained.

Operations: Coffee cups are bought in bulk at low prices, and Amelia's conservatively ordered coffee in the previous period, and had to purchase another 9 lbs. of coffee during the period. The price difference was nominal, so it still pays to buy conservatively.

The Break-Even Volume in Cups = Fixed Cost ÷ (Unit Selling Price − Unit Cost).

Fixed Costs are $5780, the Selling Price is $3.95, and the Unit Cost per Cup is $0.28.

Break-Even Volume = Fixed Cost ÷ (Unit Selling Price − Unit Cost)
= $5,780 ÷ ($3.95 − $0.28)
= 5780 ÷ 3.67
= 1575 Cups need to be sold to "cover" fixed costs.

Baked Goods: Amelia's has the opportunity to purchase an oven. Should the company bake its own pastries? Experience suggests that 30 percent of coffee buyers will buy pastries at an average price of $2.00 per item. There are two options.

Option 1: After the cost of materials and staff to do the baking, the $4000 oven will allow a $1.50 return per pastry, 75 percent of the average selling price for pastries.

Break-Even Point = Initial Investment ÷ Profit per Pastry
= $4000 ÷ $1.50
= 2666 pastries must be sold to break even.

Option 2: Continue to buy pastries from a bakery. A return of $1.00 requires no initial investment. The return on investment will be $1.00 for each $2.00 pastry, a 50% cost of goods sold, right away and continuously.

Amelia's chose Option 2. Was this a good decision? How long would it have taken to break even on the investment in an oven? One-third of coffee buyers also buy pastries, and in period 3, Amelia's sold 2619 cups of coffee. This means the shop sold approximately 873 pastries. At that rate, it would take exactly 3 months to reach the break-even point.

Given these figures, should Amelia's have purchased the oven?

Coffee Shop Comparative Analysis Period 4

Week 4	Revenue ($)	Cups Sold	Net Income ($)	Cum. Inc. ($)	Satisfaction
Amelia's	12210	2552	4488	9240	56.7
Cure Café	14354	3263	3949	−475	78.2
Zoe's	11061	2545	3445	3172	60.8

Figure 4.9 Fourth-period results for the top three coffee shops.

Amelia's regrets not purchasing the oven! We see the shop sold fewer cups than the competition and brought in less revenue. In response, prices are held consistent at $4.20 per cup, but not lowered. Amelia's also raises the manager's pay from $680 to $700 per week in the hope that this will improve service and profits.

Coffee Shop Comparative Analysis Period 5

Week 5	Revenue ($)	Cups Sold	Net Income ($)	Cum. Inc. ($)	Satisfaction
Cure Café	16454	3761	3444	2969	79.6
Amelia's	13222	2762	2928	12168	57.2
Zoe's	12336	2841	2290	5462	67.9

Figure 4.10 Fifth-period results for the top three coffee shops.

Although Amelia's revenue and cups sold are not the highest, cumulative income is more than double that of the shop's closest competitor.

The company again holds prices at $4.20 per cup, and raises managers' pay from $700 to $720 per week. Hourly rates are increased from $9.25 to $9.30. Industry averages are $693.64 and $8.73, respectively. Amelia's will pay more for higher quality service.

Week 6	Revenue ($)	Cups Sold	Net Income ($)	Cum. Inc. ($)	Satisfaction
Coffee Shop Comparative Analysis Period 6					
Cure Café	17036	3890	6045	9014	81.5
Amelia's	13819	2885	4763	16931	56.9
Zoe's	12670	2763	3299	8761	65.2

Figure 4.11 Sixth-period results for the top three coffee shops.

Revenue and net income again are below the competitions' in week 6. Tracking the competitors' staffing levels shows that coffee shops in our competitive set employ from two to twenty-eight servers. The shop with the largest staff had higher customer satisfaction ratings as well. Amelia's responds by adding four more servers to increase serving capacity.

Operations: Coffee is still purchased conservatively, and cups are purchased in bulk.

Small, Medium, and Large! Amelia's now offers coffee in three sizes! The default prices are $3.40, $4.20 and $4.65 per cup. Amelia's chose these prices to cover a broad spectrum and encourage sales of the relatively low-priced large coffee. An opportunity to upgrade to more costly "green" ingredients is passed by.

Week 7	Revenue ($)	Cups Sold	Net Income ($)	Cum. Inc. ($)	Satisfaction
Coffee Shop Comparative Analysis Period 7					
Cure Café	18839	4431	9135	18149	76.6
Zoe's	16820	3316	6739	15500	60.0
Amelia's	16820	3740	5875	22806	52.1

Figure 4.12 Seventh-period results for the top three coffee shops.

Coffee prices are raised again, as the demand seems endless. Raising coffee prices is not discouraging sales. Three more servers are added to increase capacity. Amelia's pays management and servers substantially more than the competition, based on the belief that higher pay will attract a more hospitality-minded team.

Week 8	Revenue ($)	Cups Sold	Net Income ($)	Cum. Inc. ($)	Satisfaction
Coffee Shop Comparative Analysis Period 8					
Amelia's	19457	4147	9859	32664	52.7
Cure Café	19482	4595	9763	27912	68.3
Zoe's	14719	3672	6479	21979	63.0

Figure 4.13 Eighth-period results for the top three coffee shops.

In response to its continued testing of demand, Amelia's sets its new prices at $3.75, $4.25, and $4.65. We see that the closest competitor's coffee prices are $3.25, $3.75, and $4.25, considerable lower than Amelia's. With 23 employees, Amelia's still lags behind one competitor in the number of cups sold, so management hires seven more staff for a total of thirty.

Amelia's continues to pay managers $720 per week and staff $9.30 per hour, above the industry averages of $702, and $8.86, respectively.

Coffee Shop Comparative Analysis Period 9					
Week 9	Revenue ($)	Cups Sold	Net Income ($)	Cum. Inc. ($)	Satisfaction
Amelia's	22024	4671	9327	41991	55.9
Cure Café	19834	4694	8713	36625	74.8
Zoe's	16655	3826	3605	41991	58.6

Figure 4.14 Ninth-period results for the top three coffee shops.

Amelia's revenue is the highest in our competitive set. We keep prices constant so as not to reduce demand and maintain market share in a growing environment. Management weekly pay is being raised by $20 to $740. The industry average pay is $704 per week, and we want to pay more than our competitors. Our strategy will be to challenge our staff with well-defined goals, and reward accomplishment with pay increases. This strategy ties employees closely to the success of the business, and prevents turnover.

Decision 9: Coffee Roaster: Should Amelia's purchase a $2400 coffee roaster? The roaster will create a savory environment with its aroma. The return on investment calculation involves considering the intangible value created by an aroma that attracts new patrons.

The intangible value of the aroma can be quantified with a conservative value. We will assume that walk-in business increases 10% because the aroma attracts passersby. Approximately 467 additional cups will be sold based on our assumption.

We calculate our current average coffee price of $4.25 x 42% return on each cup, which equals $1.78 profit per cup because net income ($9,327.) represents 42% of revenue ($22,024). Therefore, The coffee roaster investment of $2400 is divided by $1.78 per cup, resulting in a break-even point of 1348 cups. We see for this period that we currently sell 4671 cups; we will pay for our coffee roaster within 1 period, assuming we see the assumed 10% increase in business volume.

Should Amelia's purchase the Coffee Roaster for $2400?
A.) Yes.   B.) No.

Coffee Shop Comparative Analysis Period 10					
Week 10	Revenue ($)	Cups Sold	Net Income ($)	Cum. Inc. ($)	Satisfaction
Amelia's	22129	4695	11181	58173	67.2
Cure Café	19113	4518	10029	46654	83.7
M. Business	11328	3030	4107	17982	66.7

Figure 4.15 Tenth-period results for the top three coffee shops.

This period saw very little growth in revenue and cups sold, so Amelia's management decides to test the market yet again. They keep the small and medium prices at $3.75 and $4.25, and raise the price of a large coffee to $4.65. Manager pay is increased from $750 to $900, and staff pay is raised from $9.39 per hour to $10.75. The expectation is that a highly paid staff will accomplish the company's aggressive goal of charging more for the large size coffee.

Coffee Shop Comparative Analysis Period 11

Week 11	Revenue ($)	Cups Sold	Net Income ($)	Cum. Inc. ($)	Satisfaction
Amelia's	22234	4925	11106	64279	70.7
Cure Café	19338	4570	10539	57193	68.3
Zoe's	17373	4662	7004	38507	70.2

Figure 4.16 Eleventh-period results for the top three coffee shops.

Decision 10: Employee Pay: Amelia's still has the best statistics in the local market, although the competitors' "number of cups sold" are within 10 percent. Managers receive $900 per week, against the average pay of $714. Staff pay is $10.75 per hour, compared to the average of $8.78. Management believes that higher salaries have paid off because employees are able to command the higher prices Amelia's charges.

With revenue figures so close to the competition, should Amelia's increase pay rates yet again?

A.) Yes, award conservative raises.   B.) No pay raises.

Decision 11: Should Amelia's continue to raise prices?

A.) Yes. Increase the large cup price.   B.) No, keep prices the same.

Coffee Shop Comparative Analysis Period 12

Week 12	Revenue ($)	Cups Sold	Net Income ($)	Cum. Inc. ($)	Satisfaction
Amelia's	24044	5097	11197	76256	67.9
Cure Café	19278	4564	10567	67761	83.8
Zoe's	18440	4928	9054	47560	67.0

Figure 4.17 Twelfth-period results for the top three coffee shops.

Amelia's did raise pay modestly, but enough that employees would still see an increase. The raises are tied to financial gains. The substantial increases in week 11 reflected a record-breaking number of cups sold in the previous period. Amelia's did raise the price of the large coffee to $4.65.

Decision 12: We are offered an opportunity to rent more space for $1000. Would this be a wise decision? Should Amelia's expand?

A) Yes   B) No.

It was a hard choice, but in the end Amelia's took the chance. It rented the extra space in the hope that the opportunity to serve more customers would justify the expense.

Coffee Shop Comparative Analysis Period 13

Week 13	Revenue ($)	Cups Sold	Net Income ($)	Cum. Inc. ($)	Satisfaction
Amelia's	29013	6161	12134	88390	69.8
Zoe's	22382	5855	8385	55945	71.1
Cure Café	19300	4564	8164	75925	83.8

Figure 4.18 Thirteenth-period results for the top three coffee shops.

Amelia's thirteenth and final week shows us that the company's strategies have worked! Amelia's charged more for coffee and paid employees more than competitors. Focusing on the single goal of raising the large coffee price has been successful. As shown in the Coffee Shop Comparative Financial Results Table below, Amelia's has achieved the highest Cumulative Income, $88,390, and also the highest number of cups sold!

Afterthoughts

Amelia's mission of setting high standards to attract customers who would pay more worked out well. So did most of the tactical decisions made to implement this strategy. The final income statement gives us the proof. Gross revenue in the 13 simulated weeks comes to $221,394.25, and $88,390.01 filters down to the bottom line as net profit. It is worth looking at Figure 4.20 in the appendix for more details of Amelia's performance, especially compared with the competition.

First, though, let us consider the individual decisions:

Buying a $6000 coffee machine enabled faster service and made it possible to sell more cups per day. With more than 1600 cups sold, Amelia's came within 15 cups of covering its investment in the first week of operation.

The purchase of a roaster in week 9 was even more successful. Sales paid for it in a week with some profit left over.

The company's price for a cup of coffee was higher than most, but customers accepted it in return for the high quality of the shop's product, pleasant surroundings, and helpful staff. This justified both the cost of the coffee and the extra investment in staff and furnishings.

Keeping the shop open as long as possible maximized both revenue and net income.

Beginning with a relatively small staff held costs down when Amelia's was just starting. Hiring managers and servers as the business grew made it possible to maintain high-end service and to serve more customers.

The conservative advertising budget proved enough to develop the Amelia's brand and build name recognition. Spending more probably would not have helped enough to justify the extra cost.

Insuring the shop's equipment saved money in the end.

And renting more space seems to have paid off. Both sales and net income rose in the following period.

There was one disappointing result among all these successes: Amelia's customer satisfaction numbers lagged behind the competition throughout the simulation. We lack the data to explain this, and the shop's best-in-market revenues and net income go a long way to compensate for this single weakness. However, improving customer satisfaction might well make Amelia's even more successful. The management probably needs to carry out some research to learn why this one figure is so low and how it can be improved.

It is worth noting that this is just one simulation and one way to approach a business. There are other ways to make a success in the retail coffee business or any other segment of the hospitality industry. Dunkin' Donuts manages to be highly successful without aiming for a high-end ambience or customer experience.

One last thought: It is possible to do almost everything right and still fail in the end. We knew one local coffee shop that almost duplicated Amelia's strategy, brewing the best coffee the owners could find and offering it at a premium price in a pleasant environment. Unfortunately, a few weeks after the shop opened the town set out to widen the busy street in front of it. Construction took more than a year, sending potential customers to alternative routes. By the time traffic returned, the owners were too short of capital to recover, and a small core of devoted regulars could not support them. The shop closed after two years. A major chain could have weathered the lean period, but small business is always a risk.

The Life-Cycle of a Service Firm Revisited Through a Financial Lens

In a previous chapter of this book we discussed the founding, opening, and "birth of the firm"–or the entrepreneurship stage/phase. As the Figure 4.19 below illustrates, before the firm even opens, there is a lot of required done to design the new concept, do the projections, design the hotel or restaurant, menu concepts, market research, etc. This takes place years before the actual opening of the concept (starting in year T –2 years). We can say that there is an enormous amount of time, expert innovative insight, and energy going into research and development (R&D) for the new concept. Often, once the new firm opens and begins to grow (growth stage), fewer of its resources go into R&D, and more go into the "process," such as structuring the human resources department and advertising. Generally, more attention and resources also focus on running and building the business, potentially expanding it to multiple locations. Our research indicates that this can lead to the maturity phase of the life cycle—as firms are no longer innovating and competing against newcomers to the market, and also against the existing competition. Therefore, for a firm to keep growing (i.e., increasing revenue), it is imperative to keep innovating to continue its upward curve in the more competitive marketplace.

A third dimension to the life cycle has to do with a firm taking risks. The *larger* firms become through growth or expansion, the less *"risk"* they are willing to take. This is also seen in the figure below. We call this the POLaR Matrix (DeMicco, F. © 2016), or the Point Of Low Returns (POLaR). *Polar* may be the appropriate phrase, as revenue *growth* of the firm is slowing down (to a "glacial" pace), almost *frozen* in revenue growth. Therefore, the firm has reached a *point of low returns* or POLaR. The financial performance of the firm likewise is *frozen* to a degree, and the firm must continue to innovate (through R&D strategies). The POLaR Matrix drives home the point that firms need to continue to innovate throughout their life cycle, to continue to grow and prosper (and not mature or suffer a worse fate–declining or going out of business) by continuing to emphasize a culture of research and development (R&D) of new products and services (i.e., their competitive methods to deliver the financial gains that investors and stockholders expect.

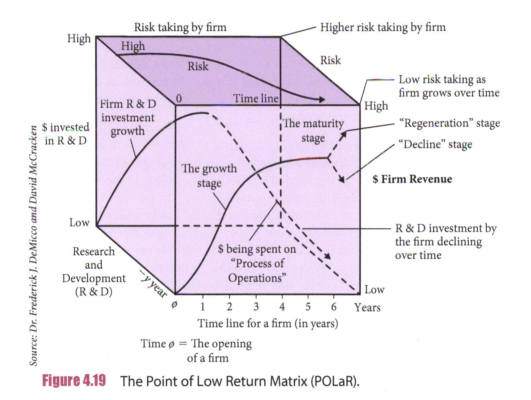

Figure 4.19 The Point of Low Return Matrix (POLaR).

Another Type of Life Cycle Model: Market Category Strategy

Competing today is not always about beating the competition directly. It is also about inventing a new market *category.* Recent research is demonstrating that you cannot build a dominant company without first establishing and building a legendary *category.* In a book called *Play Bigger* by A. Ramadan, D. Peterson, C. Lochhead, and

K. Maney, the authors demonstrate that having the best product or service in the hospitality and travel industry is not enough to compete; you have to have a dominant category.

Category kings include Amazon, Uber, Airbnb, IKEA, and even 5-hour ENERGY. These category leaders are top of mind. These firms are creative and enduring brands and create value to owners and control over seventy percent of their category. Think of Amazon and their grasp on online book and electronic sales and all the other products they sell online. Google is not only a *category*-leading company but also a verb— "Google it."

Category kings are symbolic of an entire category such as Facebook, Uber, and Netflix. When Jeff Bezos, the founder of Amazon, went looking for a new concept and a business category that would dominate the industry, his environmental scan determined that no brick-and-mortar, free-standing book store could carry more than 100,000 titles. But when Amazon.com went live in 1995 it was able to offer a million or more titles in its online catalog.

Amazon became the largest bookstore in the world and a category leader. Today, the overarching and transformational force in the marketplace is the category – thereby creating a new market for a new product or service that often comes (but not always) from a new firm. Today it is paramount that hospitality and travel firms innovate, create, and develop a new and outstanding market category in tandem with building a great company, products, and services.

P.A. Geroski (2009, *The Evolution of New Markets*, Oxford Press) describes new category leadership and development by a firm. In the early stages of the marketplace, the number of companies in the market space explodes. This is the stage when the category is defined and entrants into the market are competing to deliver a new product or service. In the middle stage, the number of companies declines/dives as the category king emerges and the competitors decline and disappear. In the last stage, the number of companies declines further as the market king dominates and controls the market category. We can now add this to our three-dimensional model and show the longer growth curve that demonstrates the sustained growth of the *market category leader*. Look at Figure 4.19 again. Can you think of hospitality and travel market category leaders that have shown sustained growth and leadership like an Amazon?

Would McDonald's be included as a sustained market *category* leader? Why or why not? Can you make a case for Starbucks as a coffee and beverage market *category* leader? Why or why not?

What about a Marriott International? Can you list others?

Appendix: BizCafé Final Results

Weekly Financial and Cups Sold Measures compared with the closest competitor. The figures listed in red represent periods where Amelia's figures were lower than those of the best competitor for that period.

	Amelia's Weekly Metrics				
Week	Revenue	Cups Sold	Net Income	Cum. Inc.	Competitor
1	$6395	1619	$−1333	$−899	
2	8287	2098	2452	1120	879
3	10738	2619	3632	4752	3422
4	12210	2552	4488	9240	6278
5	13222	2762	2928	12168	5462
6	13819	2885	4763	16931	9014
7	16820	3740	5875	22806	18149
8	19457	4147	9859	32664	27912
9	22024	4671	9327	41991	36625
10	22129	4695	11181	58173	46654
11	22234	4925	11106	64279	57193
12	24044	5097	11197	76256	67761
13	29013	6161	12134	88390	75925

Figure 4.20   Summary of Amelia's performance over time.

Web Assignment

Log into the student website and complete the end of chapter assignment. Try to utilize some of the works you read about from this chapter and apply the key concepts, terms, and theory in your responses.

Practical Prophecy for Business Strategy

There are two kinds of environmental scanning. One is the sort any good executive does automatically: Looking for innovations in the industry, new competitive methods created by the competition that may be worth emulating or adapting, that might someday become standard practice. This chapter is about the other kind.

Chapter 1 told us that environmental scanning is the foundation of the Co-Alignment Model. Another term for this is forecasting, in which two of the authors have specialized for many years. By looking at the broad forces shaping the business environment—forecasters tend to think of them as trends—we can often foresee both opportunities and potential threats that could promote or hinder the success of any business in the travel and hospitality industry. Figure 5.1 offers a conceptual model of the relationship between environmental developments and business success.

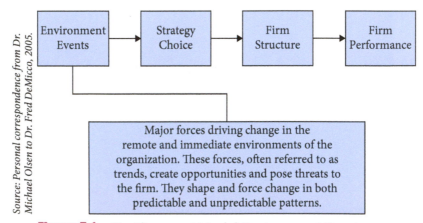

Figure 5.1   Co-Alignment Model-Environment Events

Because—let's call it forecasting from here on—plays such a fundamental role in the Co-Alignment Model, we will devote this chapter to this vital skill. Executives in any firm will need it in making any major business decision, and even in figuring out what decisions are worth making. Forecasting also is a major factor in the second section of this book, so this discussion should help with the chapters ahead.

Consider a few questions you could face during a career in hospitality and travel. What can you expect from the economy over the next one, five, or ten years? How will demographic changes alter the food preferences of diners at mid-priced restaurants? How will technology continue to reshape hotel management? If you do not encounter these exact issues, you will be expected to cope with many like them. The techniques we are about to examine make it possible.

Scanning the environment allows us to see patterns emerging that may require a change in the firm's business strategies. These patterns may be fleeting, as in a fad, or they may turn out to be lasting trends that will certainly have an impact on the hospitality and travel market. Technology, economics, demographics, social values, and many other factors all are subject to change, and therefore to trends. Appendix A at the end of the book offers a good look at the range of trends that can affect the hospitality and travel industry.

It can be difficult to foresee exactly what effects a specific development will have; for example, no one who witnessed the rise of automobiles early in the 20th century foresaw that the privacy of back seats would trigger a teen sexual revolution. Yet, we can usually recognize when a trend will impact hospitality and travel firms. Theoretically, this is the role of deductive thinking, as seen in Figure 5.2. Inductive thinking can then help us to anticipate the effects it will have and identify future signposts that will help to confirm that the change is proceeding as expected.

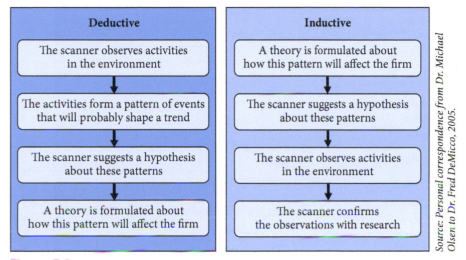

Source: Personal correspondence from Dr. Michael Olsen to Dr. Fred DeMicco, 2005.

Figure 5.2   Comparison of Inductive and Deductive Approaches to Environmental Scanning

Another way to view environmental scanning and forecasting is as part of a broader process called visioning. This includes nearly all aspects of forecasting and business strategy: the search for emerging patterns, identification of the key forces driving change, analysis of the impacts on stakeholders, and the choice of new competitive methods. Each step in the process can involve a variety of techniques, and each provides material for the next. As we see in Figure 5.3, visioning is a continuing process in which strategy choices—creating or selecting new competitive methods—lead to another round of research and analysis.

Visioning in turn feeds into the overall process of managing change. We see a conceptual diagram of this relationship in Figure 5.4.

At the end of this chapter, we will examine a study that applied this kind of business analysis to a major restaurant corporation. First, however, let's consider three of the most important forecasting techniques. Then we will see how they are used to evaluate a common issue in international business.

Consulting the Oracle

One common forecasting technique is the Delphi survey or poll. In a Delphi poll, a panel of experts fills out a questionnaire about the issues under study. The answers from this first survey are then circulated among the participants, and the poll is

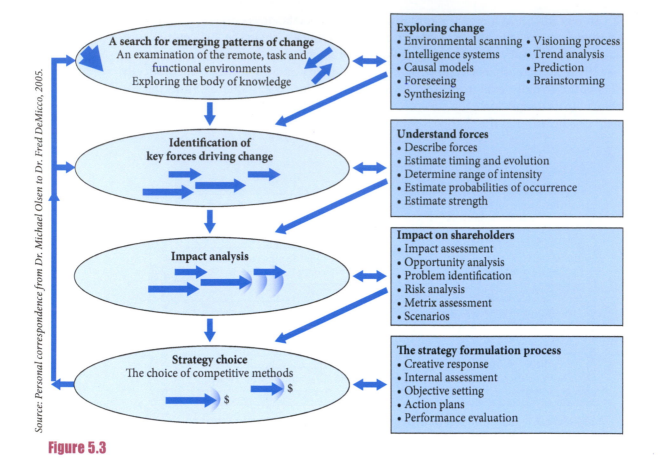

Source: Personal correspondence from Dr. Michael Olsen to Dr. Fred DeMicco, 2005.

Figure 5.3

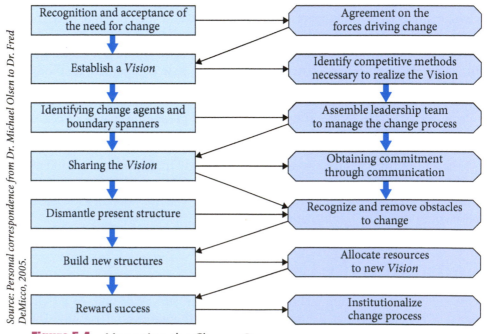

Source: Personal correspondence from Dr. Michael Olsen to Dr. Fred DeMicco, 2005.

Figure 5.4 Managing the Change Process

repeated. In the second round of questioning, participants reconsider their original views in light of the opinions of their peers. This usually results in a narrower range of replies and a more "solid" consensus, as the extreme views are mitigated by further thought and perhaps a bit of peer pressure.

For example, economists are renowned for their widely varied, often conflicting predictions about what will happen in the years ahead. Ask a few dozen of them about the future course of, say, the United States, and you are likely to get answers ranging from record growth to financial collapse. After the second round of questioning, there will still be outliers—economists are at least as reluctant to give up their opinions as the rest of us—but on average, the responses will have converged significantly. And if this Delphi study is like most others, the consensus will accurately predict the future of the American economy. For anyone running a business, this is information worth knowing.

The Delphi technique has been used in several thousand studies and is generally held to produce the most reliable analyses and forecasts available. Forecasting International (FI), the company founded by one of the authors and long employing another, has used Delphi studies with gratifying success in a wide variety of fields.

However, we often modify the basic method by including a number of participants who are professional forecasters, rather than subject specialists. This change frequently produces useful results that a more narrowly focused study might overlook. The forecasters tend to consider data from other fields that the specialists would not, and their insights trigger new ideas from the specialists in the second round of questioning.

For example, in 1994—seven years before the September 11 attacks—we carried out a study of future terrorism for the U.S. Department of Defense. Our Delphi panel included a number of leading forecasters as well as people who had spent entire careers studying terrorism in the United States, Europe, Latin America, Israel, and even the former Soviet Union.

The results were more dire than most of us expected, and much more accurate. The study anticipated virtually the entire course of terrorism as it developed over the next fifteen years. Specific predictions included the rise of international terrorism based in the Muslim extremist movement; a second, much more successful attack on the World Trade Center; a terrorist incident in the Midwest carried out by an American-born extremist connected to the militia movement; and even the deliberate crash of an airplane into the Pentagon. (We omitted that last finding at the request of the State Department, where experts feared giving would-be terrorists an idea they might not have on their own.) In reviewing this study, we concluded that it would not have been nearly so wide-ranging and accurate if it had been limited to the specialists, who then believed that terrorism was a waning problem.

In all, we believe that the Delphi technique thoroughly proved its value in a field marked by limited information and widely varying opinions. We strongly recommend using it to clarify any difficult business issue.

Fictional Futures

Another useful tool is the scenario. Webster's first definition of the word *scenario* is "an outline or synopsis of a play." As descriptions borrowed from other fields go, this one is not bad. Scenarios are portraits of alternative futures that might conceivably develop from today's world. They are not forecasting in that we do not expect tomorrow's reality to resemble them, save in limited and unpredictable ways. A good scenario can make us see the evolution of a future we would scarcely recognize if we were magically transported into the middle of it.

This is very much their purpose. Scenarios are often used in developing forecasts to help identify issues that need further research. They also can broaden our imaginations, allowing us to envision a wider range of possible futures. Sometimes we also use them to broaden the imaginations of our clients, enabling them to consider forecasts that they otherwise might find too "far out" to be taken seriously.

Scenarios begin with drivers, a defined set of forces that we choose to examine. Will new technologies dominate future society? Will the capitalist economic model continue to spread throughout the world? Will a sudden change of heart sweep across the globe, so that environmentalism guides our decisions? Scenarios can spin out any combination of postulates, each one leading to a different, yet convincing, future. The only limitation is that scenarios must be internally consistent. A scenario of economic decline, for example, is unlikely to include full employment or a wealthy middle-class; joblessness and privation are the order of that future day.

One of the most commonly used scenarios, and one that has had a powerful influence on the work of many futurists, including Forecasting International, is the 2050 Global Normative Scenario, created by the United Nations Millennium Project. It represents a consensus vision of the future compiled from the ideas of over 1000 participants in a continuing attempt to anticipate what is to come. In the Millennium Project's scenario, the world of 2050 has changed in many ways. Predictably, it is driven and dominated by science and technology. The Internet, biotechnology, nano machines, and space technology all have contributed to this prosperous New World. In all, technology, global communications, human development, and enlightened economic policies have worked together to make the world a better place than seemed possible in the early years of the 21st century.

Another tool uses three scenarios: one optimistic, one pessimistic, and one that deliberately parts company with most of the trends we see around us today. This variation grew from the work of the Global Scenario Group of the Stockholm Environmental Institute. Over the last few years, the Brookings Institution, the Santa Fe Institute, and FI all have employed them in a wide variety of contexts. They are commonly known as "Market World," "Fortress World," and "Transformed World."

"Market World" projects a glowing capitalist vision of economic reform and technological innovation. In this scenario, developing regions are quickly integrated into the global economy. Countries privatize government-run industries, cut through tangled regulations, trim public spending, and let the market have its way. In the real world, this formula has turned many backward lands into industrial powers. The common liabilities of unrestrained industry, such as rampant pollution and economic inequality, are ignored in this deliberately optimistic scenario.

"Fortress World" represents the dark side of capitalism. Economies grow rapidly, but the boom leaves whole regions of the world untouched. The poor become poorer. The environment suffers. Terrorism grows. By 2050, all we can see ahead is growing desperation and violence, as what little remains of the social contract continues to disintegrate.

"Transformed World" steps outside the either/or of capitalist paradise or nightmare. In this scenario, a pragmatic idealism replaces consumer society's will to get and spend with an altruistic desire to provide for basic human needs and the shared vision of a better life for all. Environmentalism prospers. Urban crime, drug use, and poverty decline as education, employment, and the city environment improve. By 2050, democracy has become almost universal. With many shared values and general tolerance for what differences remain, the world has all but achieved a single global civilization. It is a stable and happy place at last.

These three scenarios are largely generic, and that is much of their value. In the process of adapting them for each study, we often learn things that would not turn up in a more straightforward examination of the future.

One famous scenario-based study gave Royal Dutch Shell a leg up on its competition. In the early 1970s, oil was still cheap, and no one expected that to change. Yet Shell executives considered a scenario in which the Organization of Petroleum Exporting Countries (OPEC) dramatically cut the supply of oil. The effects were so dire that the company made detailed plans to deal with such a crisis. A few years later, Arab members of OPEC imposed an embargo against the United States, and the price of oil, in 2016 dollars, doubled from $20 per barrel to $40 almost overnight. As the global economy reeled and many of its competitors struggled to survive, Shell smoothly implemented its emergency plan. A report by Shell on its scenario program credits this preparation with helping to ensure the company's future success.

Hundreds of forecasts have been performed for the hospitality industry over the years. So far as we know, none of them anticipated the sudden collapse of air travel that followed the September 11 terrorist attacks or the restriction of international passenger traffic that accompanied the SARS (severe acute respiratory syndrome) epidemic of 2003. Doing so would have required insights that could have been derived only by asking "What if?" That is the realm of the scenario.

If This Goes On...

One of the most valuable forecasting techniques is trend analysis. It comes in two forms: trend extrapolation and trend correlation. The basic idea of trend extrapolation is that the changes we see happening around us are likely to continue, and the future will grow out of them. Any reasonable forecast must assume that technology will continue to deliver new miracles, that countries where birthrates are out of control are likely to have much larger populations in the years ahead, and so on. We need good cause to deviate from these straight-line projections, and any reasons to do so can be among the most useful insights derived from the study.

Trend correlation is even simpler in principle. Some trends follow others. Thus, when you know where one is headed, you can be reasonably sure about the other. For example, a rise in the number of construction permits issued in a community reliably foretells an increase in the number of buildings built. A rise in birth rates presages a long-term increase in the demand for housing, schools, and eventually restaurants, and other segments of the hospitality industry.

Some 30 years ago, we developed a unique tool to help with trend analysis. After our first three decades in forecasting, we reviewed what we knew about the future and condensed our knowledge into a list of trends we could see changing the world. We have updated that list frequently over the years. The number of entries varies from time to time as trends mature and die and new forces arise to shift the course of events. At the moment, FI is tracking 50 major trends in world politics, technology, national and international economics, and other important aspects of global society. These are the broad forces that will help to shape the future, and they give us a necessary context in which to consider any specific subject. The latest revision of our list appears as Appendix A.

Since developing our list of trends, we have used them to predict the future of companies, industries, and entire countries. In each study, we look at the specific circumstances of the subject—say, the hospitality industry—and try to figure out how they will interact with the broader trends. How will the economy affect them? What about demographics, technology, and changing societal values?

Trend extrapolation does have its limitations. Unlike scenarios, this is not a technique for "thinking the unthinkable," as the pioneering forecaster Herman Kahn titled a book about nuclear war. Over time, surprises occur that cumulatively change the course of events. Barring a shock on the scale of September 11, forecasts are likely to be very accurate over the next year or two, correct in many ways but mistaken in some ten years ahead, and significantly wrong twenty years out. However, extrapolating trends can be useful even for long-range forecasts, because the process itself helps us to identify the areas in which surprises are most likely to occur and will have the greatest impact. In this way, it provides a basic framework for understanding the future. And when events deviate from their expected course, we can more easily recognize that something new is happening and probably requires study.

Trend analysis is the most valuable tool we have for charting the most likely path of future events. The chapters in the next section all grew out of this process.

Trends for Hospitality and Travel

Dr. Michael Olsen (2013) at Virginia Tech identified a series of trends specific to the hospitality and travel industry. They are likely to be important throughout the careers of today's students. They originated with the "Visioning the Future" workshops, in which researchers across the globe asked industry leaders about the major changes in our field. This research involved over 4,000 industry practitioners who helped identify the forces driving change in this industry and their likely impact on hospitality managers and organizations.

These trends will have significant long-term impact on this industry. They will change the way hospitality organizations are managed and the strategies they will select to compete in the future. In many cases, change is already reshaping industry practices. Here are the eight trends Dr. Olsen identified:

1. The Internet is changing marketing, distribution, and capacity management.

Internet travel-marketing sites such as Expedia and Kayak are giving customers more control over the selection and booking of travel experiences. As a result, the hospitality industry is losing control over the sale of hotel rooms, airline seats, car rentals, tickets to attractions, and seats in restaurants. Most travelers now believe that shopping through the Internet provides them with a convenient and cost-efficient method of booking accommodations, restaurant reservations, and other hospitality services. Shopping through third-party aggregators also tends to reduce prices, making travel more affordable but endangering industry profits.

Because of this trend, we can expect industry marketing to change in the years ahead. This process has already begun. As technology helps destinations to consolidate portfolios of hotels, restaurants, and attractions into a single distribution center (i.e., convention and visitor's bureau websites and, especially, online discount aggregators), brand is becoming secondary. To a great extent, brand marketing is being replaced by destination marketing: Consumers first decide where they want to travel; then they decide how to get there and where to stay. Social media and online booking thus will continue to play a large role in consumers' evaluation and selection of services to spend their money on. Ratings on TripAdvisor and Yelp, for example, will be major drivers and influencers determining where the consumer spends.

2. Safety and security are growing concerns.

In the post-9/11 world, travelers are increasingly confronted with potential risks to personal safety and health. Major issues include potential terrorist attacks and epidemics of diseases such as bird flu, Zika virus, and food poisoning by *E. coli* and other bacteria. These risks have now become the number-one concern of many wealthy and well-informed travelers. Because governments struggle to obtain sufficient funds to protect their own citizens and travelers, individual hospitality enterprises are increasingly required to meet the challenges of security, disease, and other risks on their own. Given the rise of terrorism in Europe and the frequent appearance of new insurgent movements to replace defeated predecessors, this priority can only grow for at least several decades.

3. The global shift to market economies has brought tremendous competition for capital to invest in productive assets.

China and India especially have almost endless appetites for investment capital. This competition directs funds to those investments that provide the greatest return. This puts pressure on all firms to focus on value-adding strategies that will be sustainable over time. It does not bode well for the hospitality industry in mature markets, where many investors find the returns on their capital insufficient. In the future, it is likely to be increasingly difficult for hospitality to fund continuing growth, putting greater pressure on effective strategic management practices. Managers have always needed to focus on competitive methods that generate the best future cash flows for the organization. This requirement is becoming more urgent by the year.

4. Technology is transforming the hospitality industry.

In the hospitality industry, as in all others, the convergence of telecommunications, the computer, and improved data collection is making it possible for firms to compete in new ways. Whether it is in marketing the industry, managing resources, or investigating the future, one thing is clear: Technology will provide some of the most important competitive methods that hospitality firms employ in the future. As long as advances in information technology continue at a rapid pace, IT will continue to drive change in the hospitality industry. Mastering this transformation will be one of the most important new requirements for industry executives.

5. Change is placing ever greater demands on hospitality managers.

The Visioning the Future study made one thing very clear. No matter where in the world the researchers asked, they found that the old way of learning the business is out. Managers are expected to be masters of the business world more than masters of the craft of hospitality. The skills to provide the customer with the most satisfying products and services will always be needed. Yet, tomorrow's manager must be a strategist. Success now demands knowledge of how to use technology, the ability to analyze and synthesize large amounts of information from a variety of sources, and the ability to function effectively in an uncertain environment.

These and other challenges will require the manager to think in an interdisciplinary manner and with an eye to the future. In addition, leadership will be based on performance, not seniority. This change in the leadership paradigm will be driven by the increasingly complex relationships among the customer, employee, and manager. Customer expectation of value and quality and the employees' need for enlightened leadership will continue to drive change in hospitality management.

6. Sustainability is increasingly important.

As the world economy becomes ever more integrated and populations continue to expand, the requirement that growth be sustainable is becoming a mandate for all business leaders. Governments are developing policies that favor sustainable economic development—tax incentives for green projects are a common example—and customers are increasingly likely to weigh their travel plans against this standard. Hospitality leaders therefore must consider the full range of issues that determine whether corporate activities are environmentally sound and require the highest standards in operations and development.

7. **Social issues are gaining new significance in business.**

In many countries, the gap between economic "haves" and "have nots" is a growing concern. One major factor in this issue, of course, is the availability of stable, well-paid jobs. Because hospitality and travel creates more jobs than many other sectors, industry leaders can expect to be called on to help reduce economic inequality wherever their companies operate. This will require that managers effectively develop and utilize the local labor force as well as the physical environment in which their employees live.

This is just one of many such issues. The private sector will be expected to bear an increasingly large share of the social costs related to their role in the community. Social media will ensure that these concerns play a growing part in consumer travel decisions.

8. **Consumers are increasingly concerned with health and wellness.**

In the future, we expect spas, meals that are healthful as well as tasty, and other such amenities to assume greater importance for industry managers. This will be seen most clearly in the growth of medical tourism, where hospitality integrates with hospitals and clinics. (We call this Hospitality Bridging Healthcare or H2H©.) However, this trend will be felt throughout hospitality and travel, helping to shape factors that range from hotel design to staff training.

Although these industry-specific trends are important in their own right, some of the most useful insights are likely to emerge when we examine their interaction with the more general trends in society and with a company's unique circumstances. The ability to analyze such interactions is one of the more useful forecasting skills an aspiring leader can master.

National Stability

Before moving on to our end-of-chapter case study, let us work through a sample analysis. In an age of terrorism, and for an industry that is exposed to risks all over the world, one of the most important issues is the stability of foreign lands. Do we dare to put a new hotel, resort, or conference center in a given country? Can airlines and cruise ships safely visit its ports? Should we consider moving out of existing operations there? Executives at international hospitality companies are likely to face this kind of problem more than once in their careers.

Beginning with this crucial issue has another benefit as well. National stability is such a complex topic that looking into it will turn up much of what we need to know about the country's economy, its demographic future, and many other factors that will affect a hospitality business. It is often a good place to begin a study.

For any work of this sort, we supplement our trends with a wide range of economic, demographic, technological, and military data specific to the nation, industry, or organization of interest. In projecting the future of a company, much of the information we need will be proprietary and supplied by the employer or client. Yet, for national security virtually all critical indicators are readily available. In half a century of working with classified information under government contracts, Forecasting International has found that almost everything you need to know comes from public sources.

The indicators in Appendix B: Vital Signs for National Security have proved especially useful. Not all of them are important for every nation; there is little point in trying to assess the military potential of Costa Rica, which has no army. Each must be weighted according to conditions in the country at hand, and thus far that is largely a task for human judgment and experience. For most, the raw data is readily available from online resources like the CIA World Factbook and the websites of the World Bank and the International Monetary Fund.

Note that data found at many websites are single points. They give us a snapshot of each country, when a video would tell us much more. For a serious study, we would look not only at GDP or military spending, but at trends in those data. The whole point of forecasting is not to find out where the subject stands, but where it is going.

We also must bear in mind that not all data is accurate even when it is found in otherwise reliable collections. For example, a study at the University of Chicago reported in the May 15, 2018 edition of the *Washington Post* used satellite data to find that China, Russia, and other authoritarian countries exaggerate their GDP by anything from 15 to 30 percent. Those official figures, wrong as they are, will be faithfully copied into virtually all of the databases we otherwise would consider to be reliable.

For a better idea of how this works, let us take a country and see what we can learn about it. We will look at Great Britain, which is globally significant and for which reliable data is readily available.

For a start, in 2017, the United Kingdom had a GDP of $2.88 trillion by purchasing power parity (PPP), a measure of local buying power. According to the World Economic Forum, this makes it the fifth largest economy in the world. The CIA World FactBook shows that this translates to a comfortable $43,600 per capita.

You will run into PPP often when looking at economies, so you should be aware of its limitations. Even competent economists often apply PPP in situations where it doesn't make sense.

The CIA's use above is where PPP belongs. A GDP per capita of $43,600 PPP tells us that residents should have enough local buying power to live comfortably. On average, they are likely to possess the disposable income to eat at restaurants, go on vacation, and enjoy other hospitality services.

In the world at large, which is where comparing national economies can be interesting, PPP is approximately meaningless. No one in Riyadh will sell you oil at prices based on your country's PPP. For this purpose, we want raw numbers.

Nonetheless, even the CIA sometimes uses PPP to compare national economies where GDP figures are not reliable. For our money, the proper estimate in such instances is, "We don't know."

Back to the UK's national stability.

Britain is a major exporting country, tenth largest in the world by value of its export products, $436.5 billion in 2017. This is a remarkably good performance. Britain exports over 27 percent as much goods, in dollar terms, as the United States with only 20 percent of the population.

It also ranks eighth in the World Economic Forum's Index of Business Competitiveness for 2017-'18. This is a respectable showing, which should contribute to future prosperity.

In resources, the United Kingdom does not have enough oil or fresh water to rank among the top ten. Neither is it among the largest exporters of farm products. However, Eurostat reports that Britain is the third-largest primary energy producer in Europe. For some purposes, it would help to know where that energy comes from—its oil fields in the North Sea are nearly depleted—but we will ignore that issue for now.

The United Kingdom has a solid base in technology. Its scientists won 96 Nobel prizes through 2017, compared with 268 for the United States and 88 for Germany. It ranks ninth in the number of Internet users, despite a relative shortage of personal computers. However, British residents in in the five years ending 2016 applied for just over one-third as many patents per million population as their American peers. This seems odd, and it might have something to do with patent law rather than inventiveness. Depending on the purpose of our study, this could require more research

Britain also may have the kind of social base that contributes to a stable society. With about two rooms per person, its housing supply is tied for seventh place among the 34 member countries of the Organization for Economic Cooperation and Development. However, the UN Human Development Index does not rate its quality of life among the top ten—it ranks sixteenth—and it lags in 26th place in the number of university students per 100,000 population. This data category also may justify more study.

A few minutes with the Internet reveals that the number of immigrants in the UK doubled between 1993 and 2014, with more than 13 percent of British residents now foreign-born. The three greatest donor nations are India, Poland, and Pakistan. Again, for some purposes this aspect of British society also would rate more study.

Militarily, the United Kingdom is the world's seventh-largest spender. Yet the budget for its armed forces is less than one-tenth that of the United States, consuming only 1.8 percent of GDP. Its active-duty armed forces comprise only 152,350 men and women; as a percentage of the national population, this is the 101st largest military in the world. However, with 215 warheads, Britain owns a significant nuclear deterrent. Unlike Ukraine and many other countries in Eastern Europe, it cannot be casually attacked by a greater power.

Diplomatically, Britain is a permanent member of the United Nations Security Council, which gives it more power than mere population would suggest. It also ranks second among the world's donors of foreign aid, which confers status of its own.

Britain's Corruption Perception Index is 82, signifying that its business and political operations have earned a high degree of public trust. This suggests basic stability, as the governments of unstable countries are seldom known for their rectitude.

A little more time with the Net finds that in 2015 there were about 6.325 million males in the violence-prone ages between 15 and 29, or about 9.8 percent of the population. Unemployment in the 16-to-24 age group, another critical factor, has declined from a recession peak 19 percent to about 12 percent. Both numbers are low compared to countries like Afghanistan and Yemen, where unrest is an obvious danger. For a serious report, we would want to know how youth unemployment is distributed among natives and immigrant groups and whether nativist xenophobia might breed unrest among or toward young migrants in response.

Culturally, Britain appears to consume Hollywood fantasies more than it exports its own. It ranks third, behind China and Japan, in the value of movie tickets sold each year outside North America and is the world's fourth largest producer of feature films, with 298 completed in 2015, compared with 791 in the U.S. (Cultural data tend to lag frustratingly behind the times.) Both countries are behind India, which produced some 2,000 feature films that year, and Nigeria, which completed 997 in 2011, the most recent year for which numbers are available.

Without going into depth, all this paints a picture of the United Kingdom as a significant economic, military, and diplomatic power in the world. It also suggests that we can expect Britain to remain economically comfortable, stable, and influential for some time to come.

However, even this brief study raises some interesting questions:

How dependent is the United Kingdom on energy imports? And how quickly is it converting to renewable sources? In the long run, this will be critical to the country's economy, and we have more work to do in this area.

How long can the United Kingdom remain a global economic leader? The world increasingly depends on technology, and Britain does not seem to be producing all that many college graduates. Can it maintain a strong technological base without them? Does it have some way of training engineers and technicians that does not show up in college data? Perhaps a system of technical schools supplemented by on-the-job training? Or does it rely on technologically sophisticated immigrants? For a serious study of Britain's long-term national security, we would wish to know.

And what does that population of young males indicate? The well-educated industrialized lands almost all have low birth rates and relatively few young people. Does Britain have an unusually large, fertile immigrant population? News reports have said that militant religious leaders in Britain have inspired young Muslims to *jihad* against the West, and there have been several incidents of home-grown terrorism. How many of Britain's young men are potential converts to extremism? How many have fought in Afghanistan or Iraq and returned home with military training and experience. How effective are the country's security departments in keeping an eye on them? Flag this area for more research. It could be critical to the future safety of hospitality businesses and their guests.

We see in many of these questions the power of trend data. Some of them would be answered if we were examining changes over time, rather than looking at single data points.

We see also the value of even a cursory look ahead. In a few minutes of thinking about the most basic data, we have identified several important issues that must be examined further before we can feel confident that our image of Britain will not change abruptly in a few years. Forecasters often carry out such preliminary studies to learn whether a subject merits greater effort. Many do.

Finally, we see the vulnerability of forecasts to unexpected events. In 2016, then-Prime Minister David Cameron somewhat mystifyingly "solved" a short-term political problem by offering British subjects a chance to pull out of the European Union. More than two years later, and less than six months short of the separation date, it still is not clear whether Britain will actually leave the EU or under what conditions it would do so. There even is talk of a second referendum, which almost certainly would support continued membership. As this is written, we cannot be sure what to expect when, or if, Brexit is finalized. If it goes ahead, we can expect a significant reduction in British GDP, a decline in outgoing tourism, and a boost to in-country travel. The wealthy will travel abroad as always, but continued weakness in the UK pound will make it more costly for them. Cancelling Brexit would of course negate all those predictions, but in mid-2018 we view that as the less likely possibility.

There is another lesson here as well. As the Brexit vote drew near, a solid majority of forecasters predicted its defeat despite many polls suggesting its passage. In retrospect, they seem to have put their wishes ahead of their data. The lesson? Always go where your data lead, no matter how unpalatable the result.

This is not an easy rule to follow, as we are seldom truly aware of our biases. Mastering the art of forecasting thus becomes a matter of personal development as well as study and practice.

Most of us learn best by doing something, not by reading about it, so for a more valuable introduction to forecasting why not try this on your own? Pick a country, gather the necessary data, and see what the indicators and trends imply for it. Then figure out how things are likely to evolve over the next ten or twenty years, and weigh the merits of siting a new hotel or resort there. This exercise will give you a far better sense of how much can be accomplished using publicly available data and relatively simple methods of analysis.

Web Assignment

Log into the student website and complete the end of chapter assignment. Try to utilize some of the works you read about from this chapter and apply the key concepts, terms, and theory in your responses.

CHAPTER 6

Today's Environment… And Tomorrow's

In Chapter 5, we introduced the process of forecasting and its application to environmental scanning. We also looked briefly at some specific trends that Dr. Michael Olsen, of Virginia Tech, identified as being important for hospitality and travel. This chapter expands on that introduction. Here, we will examine some of the broader trends in the world and try to figure out how this more general environment will shape the industry in the years ahead. This view of the future will serve as background material for our analyses of specific industry segments in the chapters ahead.

The discussion below demonstrates one of forecasting's limitations: Critical elements of the future cannot be predicted because they depend on decisions that have yet to be made. In these cases, we will look at the most likely possibilities and try to identify some turning points that will reveal which path the world has taken. Anticipating these signposts is one more benefit of making our forecasts explicit rather than allowing them to exist only as hidden assumptions.

We face a second limitation as well. Our discussion of trends and their effects is inevitably general. Yet, what people and companies experience in the years ahead will be thoroughly specific. It does little good to be told that the economy is growing rapidly if most of the profit goes to financiers in New York but you live in Detroit, where the manufacturing jobs that once supported the local economy have all but disappeared. What we say below will be, on average, correct. Yet, in practice it will have to be adapted to local conditions and the specific circumstances of each company. Working out what these variations imply is one of the forecaster's essential skills and most frequent assignments.

We urge readers to examine these and the other trends found in Appendix A on their own. This is more than a matter of practice, although practice is necessary in preparing for any career. This is being written in mid-2018. Your own forecasts will have the benefit of local knowledge and a year or more in which new economic data and events clarify many uncertainties. You also may interpret your data in ways that we would not and come to a different view of the future. Your conclusions need not be more accurate than ours to provide extra value. It is enough to identify a few more indicators that will show whether the forecast is working out or needs revision.

Here, then, are the most important trends for travel and hospitality, their status as this is written, and what they mean for this industry.

The global Economy continues to grow, but not as fast as it used to.

As recently as 2011, the global economy grew by about 4.1 percent per year. By 2015, it had slowed significantly. For 2018 and 2019, the Organization for Economic Cooperation and Development expects it to come in around 3.9 percent, up from 3.1 percent in 2017.

There is a wide gap between economic performance in the most industrialized economies and that of the developing countries. It did not favor the wealthy, who supply most of the demand for travel and hospitality.

The "Group of Twenty," or G20, economies, nineteen countries plus the European Union, provide roughly 85 percent of the world's GDP. They grew by 3.8 percent in

2016. Only three grew faster than that: China, India, and Indonesia. The United States, much of Europe, and Japan all trailed well behind.

In contrast, the world's developing economies grew at an average rate of 4.8 percent. This is a trend we have long seen: Developing economies outpace the developed. This is likely to continue long into the future. The International Monetary Fund estimates that between 2010 and 2030 economies will grow by 5.7 percent annually in Asia, 4.8 percent in Africa, and 4.3 percent in the Middle East, but only 2.6 percent in Europe and the Americas. The World Bank believes that more than half of global economic growth will come from just six countries by 2025—Brazil, China, India, Indonesia, South Korea, and Russia. Of these, all but Korea are still ranked as developing economies.

How long the current prosperity will last is open to question. The International Monetary Fund reports that global debt is now worse than it was before the 2008 financial crisis. By 2016, the most recent figure now available, debt was up to 225 percent of global GDP. That is 12 points higher than the previous record, set in 2009. In the IMF's view, developed economies, emerging markets, and low-income countries all are now at risk of another severe downturn.

Our own view is that there will be another worldwide recession. We simply don't know when. Economies, whether national or global, can remain buoyant or soggy longer than seems reasonable. They also can blow up without obvious warning. Our best guess, and it can be no more, is that it will happen in the middle of the next decade.

Three economies are large enough to change global prospects—the United States, Europe, and China—and we should look at them individually. We will touch on India as well because of its growing importance to hospitality and travel.

United States

In the world's largest economy, GDP has been rising by about 2.4 percent annually since the recession of 2008/'09. In 2017, it grew 2.3 percent. The Congressional Budget Office estimates that real economic growth will average about 1.9 percent through 2028, providing jobs for almost all who want one.

This is not nearly as good as it appears. We learn more about people's well-being if we divide GDP growth by the population. When per-capita GDP grew at more than 2 percent, personal income doubled in 35 years—fast enough for people to feel good about it. It is expected to come in at 2.1 percent in 2018, so for the moment all is well. However, by 2023 it will slow to 0.6 percent, according to IMF estimates. At that rate, doubling personal income will take just under 116 years.

Already, many people feel they are running as fast as they can just to say where they are.

Many of them are correct. Although median income has risen handily since 2016, only city-dwellers have benefited. Those in rural areas have not.

Two more groups also have been losing out. Although average income rose sharply at the end of 2012 and the beginning of 2013, real middle-class incomes have risen only slowly since 1980. Adjusted for price inflation, middle-class buying power is only $1.50 per hour more than it was in 1964. And between 1971 and 2015, the share of the country's income received by the middle class fell from 61 percent to 50.

At the same time, the poor have lost real income, while the well-off and extremely wealthy have received much more. The top 10 percent of U.S. households earn about 28 percent of the country's total income. They also hold 76 percent of the country's wealth. The top 0.1 percent, about 160,000 extremely well-off households—own 22 percent of America's wealth, up from around 7 percent at the low point in the early 1970s. Since the late 1980s, when the lower and middle classes were at their peak, the fraction they own has fallen from about 34 percent to 22 percent. This trend will continue until fundamental policy changes restore middle-class income. In today's political climate, no such changes are imminent.

Looking at the other side of the equation, the three items the middle class has always valued most have grown more expensive much faster than overall inflation. These are homes, education, and healthcare. Between 2000 and 2017, the median home price went up nearly 88 percent, according to the Case-Shiller U.S. National Home Price Index. Private college tuition has been growing at roughly twice the cost of inflation. And between 2000 and 2012, the cost of healthcare rose by 21 percent. Real median household income fell by 8 percent over the same period.

As workers grow increasingly strapped, demand for goods and services has risen largely through borrowing. The recession of 2008 began as a result of the excessive debt incurred by many who could not afford to pay it down. It curtailed their demand, and consumers were slow to resume their free-spending ways. This was a primary reason the U.S. economy grew so slowly for so long after the recession ended. More recently, consumer debt has been growing at much higher annual rates—over 7 percent in 2014 and '15. However, in the first three months of 2018, the growth of consumer debt has slowed to annual rates of 4.7, 4.3, and 3.6 percent. Many economists will welcome this easier pace.

On balance, we usually would accept that the American economy will continue to grow at roughly 2 percent per year well into the 2020s, with any recession shallow and brief. The surprise election of Donald Trump to lead the U.S. changed that. Maybe. Twenty erratic months into his presidency, we still are not sure what he will do or how it will affect the economy.

In the middle of 2018, threats to leave the North American Free Trade Agreement and saddle Chinese imports with prohibitive tariffs appeared to have been abandoned. It would have been tempting to sigh with relief and move on to other matters. Yet, no sooner had this paragraph been drafted than Pres. Trump imposed 25-percent tariffs on imported steel and 10-percent tariffs on aluminum. Three of the country's allies and the largest buyers of American exports—the EU, Canada, and Mexico—were hit, and the EU and Mexico vowed to retaliate with tariffs of their own. All three economies buy more than twice as much in American exports as China does.

Further complicating matters, President Trump suggested as recently as April 2018 that the United States might join the Trans Pacific Partnership after all; before the day was over, his tweets qualified the idea into meaninglessness. In May, he announced sanctions that would have destroyed Chinese telecom giant ZTE and rescinded them only two weeks later. At some point—we have rather lost track, and in this environment it hardly seems to matter—tariffs on EU products were put on hold, while the range of Chinese products subject to them expanded. Anything said of an economy facing such uncertainties is largely speculation.

By the time this text reaches print, the future should be easier to read. Until it is, the future of the hospitality and travel industry remains in flux.

Europe

The economy here struggled for years after the recession of 2008, but it now seems the bad times have passed. Beginning in 2015, GDP growth in Europe has come in at annual rates near or above 2 percent in every quarter, accelerating to 2.5 percent in 2018. Unemployment has fallen as well, to 7.1 percent in May 2018 for the Union as a whole and 8.5 percent in the Euro zone. These were the lowest jobless rates the Continent had seen since December 2008.

In a region that includes 28 countries, such aggregate numbers inevitably hide significant details:

Ireland ended 2017 with an annual growth rate of 8.4 percent for the quarter. It was the best economic performance in the EU.

Next door, the UK came in at 1.2 percent, the slowest in the Union.

Greece and Switzerland were tied at 1.9 percent. This was a particularly good showing for Greece after declines of up to 9.1 percent annually in the recent past. It may do a little better in 2018, but by the early 2020s the Greek economy can be expected to slow to the range of 1 percent.

Unemployment at the beginning of 2018 was stuck at 11.1 percent in Italy, 16.3 percent in Spain, and 20.9 percent in Greece. Youth unemployment—16.1 percent in the EU as a whole, remains at 31.5 percent in Italy, 36 percent in Spain, and 43.7 percent in Greece.

Despite such local weaknesses, our overall expectation for the EU is for continued growth in the range of 1.2 to 1.5 percent through the early 2020s and a few tenths slower for the rest of the decade. This should be good news for hospitality and travel. It will be strong enough to support international travel both within the Continent and outbound, yet not so strong that it raises the Euro's exchange rate enough to discourage inbound vacationers.

One unknown for Europe's economy is Britain's decision to leave the EU. Brexit is "the scariest thing that's happening right now in the markets" according to a mid-2016 headline in the *Washington Post*. We are not entirely convinced. The economic impact of Brexit will remain unclear until the sides agree on the terms of their divorce, assuming they can reach an agreement at all. This is scheduled for later in 2018, with the decision not taking effect until January 1, 2021. Nonetheless, concern about Brexit clearly is strong and widespread. When Britain's GDP growth came in at only 0.1 percent in the first quarter of 2018, the well-respected *Financial Times* cited Brexit worries as part of the explanation.

Most economic forecasts show relatively little impact outside the UK itself. Among ten prominent studies in the year following the Brexit vote, nine forecast shrinkage in the British GDP, with losses ranging up to nearly 8 percent. *EU Exit Analysis – Cross Whitehall Briefing*, a secret government study that became public in January 2018, predicted that the British economy fifteen years after the exit could be anything up to 8 percent smaller than it would have been without Brexit. This could shrink to 2 percent if Britain accepts continued Norway-style membership in the European Economic Area, but Prime Minister Theresa May has ruled out such an arrangement.

Our best estimate currently is that the loss will be close to 5 percent. This would likely weaken the Pound Sterling on foreign exchange markets, reducing leisure travel from the UK to the Continent, but encouraging tourism from abroad and within the country.

China

Asia's leading power has been the great economic success story of the last half-century, the only large country in the world—its population is approaching 1.4 billion—that ever scores double-digit GDP growth, and it did so for years.

This new prosperity has been unevenly distributed. Just 1 percent of the country's households own one-third of its wealth. Yet, since 2000 the middle class has grown from just 4 percent of the population to 68 percent in 2012 and an expected 75 percent in 2022. By 2020, more than 130 million of the country's 250 million households are expected to fit into this category, with half of them classified as affluent.

"Middle class" in China does not mean quite what it does in the West. The Chinese government considers anyone with a household income of $7,250 to $62,500 to be in the middle class. McKinsey defines the Chinese middle-class as those with an income of $11,500 to $43,000 per year. In the United States, incomes at the lower end of these ranges would qualify as poverty. Yet, in China they are enough to pay for food, clothing, and shelter with some disposable income left over. This explains why China has the world's fastest growing fleet of automobiles and is the single largest market for luxury goods.

This rapid growth has been critical to the global economy. For most of thirty years, China has been the engine that drives the world. Many economists believe China's continuing demand for imports powered the world out of its worst downturn in decades.

That is unlikely to happen next time around. China's growth is slowing. Officially, it came in at 6.7 percent in both 2015 and 2016 and 6.9 percent in 2017. Other estimates, arguably more objective, put it as low as 1 percent, at least in the first two years.

This is only the beginning. OECD believes growth will come in at 4 percent in 2025 and 3.5 percent in 2030. By 2050, it will decline to only 1.8 percent, in line with other advanced countries.

At least two factors will block China's return to headier rates of growth:

China once had a big, young workforce with relatively few seniors to support. This single factor accounted for one-fourth of China's economic growth. By 2050, thanks to the infamous one-child policy, almost 40 percent of the population will be retirement-age or older. With few young people to replace them, China's workforce will shrink by nearly 200 million, almost 25 percent. The country's demographic advantage is going away, never to return.

Ironically, the second problem is China's prosperity. In 1978, when the country entered its boom years, the average manufacturing worker earned 597 yuan *per year*—about $35 at a time when median income in the United States was $19,647. By 2015, factory workers averaged 55,300 yuan annually, $7,940 at current exchange rates.

This is good, because it is driving the rise of China's middle class from only 4 percent of the population in 2000 to 68 percent in 2012 and a predicted 75 percent in 2022.

The downside is that companies have begun moving their production to Mexico, where manufacturing workers earn only $4,900 a year. Even Chinese firms are now importing their goods. The export industries that powered China's growth will not drive its future.

The country faces three more important problems.

Officially, China's unemployment rate is 3.95 percent, the lowest it has been in years. However, that hides crucial details. Some 270 million rural peasants migrated to the cities in search of jobs that many now have lost. They are still counted as farm workers and are considered to be employed by definition. Official tallies also miss part-time employment among workers at so called "zombie companies," which survive only because local governments borrow heavily on their behalf. In all, outside observers believe true unemployment has tripled in recent years, to 12 or 13 percent.

Then there is debt. China has more of it than official statistics show. When recession threatened in 2008, Beijing poured $600 billion into the economy. This kept the economy going but left it addicted to easy credit. Government debt was reported to be 47.6 percent of GDP in 2017. Unfortunately, most borrowing in China is from private lenders known as "shadow banks," and their transactions are not officially recorded. Taking them into account, Chinese debt is believed to be nearly 250 percent of GDP.

This is a problem because Chinese banks have poor lending standards, and the shadow banks are believed to be even less cautious. Thus, banks are sitting on an estimated $1 trillion in loans that can never be repaid. No one knows how much more is privately held. This has investors worried, making it harder for banks to get enough capital to remain stable.

There may be another issue as well. We have seen one vaguely plausible suggestion that Chinese debt really totals more than 800 percent of GDP. We don't believe it, and there seems little point in going into the details here. But if it turned out to be correct, we would have no idea what could happen to the country's economy. It is worth being alert for surprises in this area.

That said, here is our current conclusion:

Beijing has a track record of maneuvering its economy through dangerous times, and it is hard to imagine them failing in the immediate future. At its every-five-years Party Congress in 2017, President Xi Jinping declared that bringing down China's debt load was a top priority. He even implied that regulators had gotten a handle on the so-called "shadow banks," which are not bound by the usual banking strictures. Less than a month later, the government announced comprehensive new rules for the asset-management industry, a crackdown on micro loans, and other measures designed to inhibit borrowing. This strengthens our doubt that China will stumble and set off another global recession.

Yet, the issues above make it clear that a financial crash in China is the second-greatest risk to the global economy. A 2016 report from the Bank of England warned that high debt and fast credit expansion made China more vulnerable to a financial crisis than any of the world's other major economies. If there is a global recession in the years ahead, it will not end in China, as the last one did. It might start there.

India

The Indian economy is not nearly as rich as that of the United States, nor as large as China's. Yet, growth of 7.6 percent in 2016 and an estimated 6.7 percent in 2017—7.1 percent, according to Indian government statements—made it the fastest expanding large economy in the world. If the government is correct, 2017 was the fourth consecutive year of GDP growth above 7 percent and only the second time since 1990 that the Indian economy grew faster than China's; the first was 2016. India is expected to remain one of the world's fastest growing economies, averaging 6.4 percent annually between 2015 and 2030.

Yet, this growing wealth is shared among more than 1.26 billion people. Per-capita GDP thus comes in at $1,800, compared with $51,500 for the United States and $38,340 in the Euro zone. This is not as bad as it sounds. Measured by purchasing power parity (PPP), a statistic that attempts to compare the standard of living in different countries, India's per-capita GDP works out to about $6,400 a year. In India, it is enough to get by.

However, income is distributed very unevenly. The World Bank estimates that more than one in five Indians lives in extreme poverty. Borrowing from the Indian government, it defines this as $2 per day based on PPP. In real-number terms, it works out to little more than fifty cents. Either way, it is a starvation-level income.

Most Indians are better off, but estimates of how many and how much better vary widely, depending largely on how analysts define the middle class. At Mumbai University, economists include anyone spending from $2 to $10 per day, based on purchasing power parity (PPP.) By this definition, more than 600 billion people already rank in the middle class, upward of twice as many as in 2004. This seems too inclusive; as we noted above, $2 a day is a starvation-level income, even in India.

A more common definition considers the middle class to be those who can spend between $10.01 and $50 per day, again as PPP. Call it $3,650 to $18,250. This standard pares the middle class to around 50 million people. By 2020, this version of India's middle class will grow to 200 million people, according to Ernst & Young, and 475 million by 2030. Yet another source predicts that the middle class will number 575 million soon after 2025. No wonder outbound travel from India is growing by 25 percent each year.

Bottom Line

After all that, our conclusions are few, unsurprising, and provisional. We expect that the world's economy will continue to grow by roughly 3 percent per year well into the 2020s. The United States and Europe, but probably not China or India, will sink into recession from time to time, with 2021 or '22 being the most likely period for the next significant contraction in the U.S. These episodes will be relatively brief and, although the impact of Brexit is likely to make them a fraction deeper than they otherwise would be, they will have nothing like the global impact of 2008.

Our confidence in this forecast stems largely from our belief that most national leaders are too cautious to steer their countries into economic danger. The EU's ill-considered austerity policy after 2008, shrinking demand just when governments should have been promoting it, is a counter-example that slowed the region's recovery. Yet even that was not enough to cause Europe or the world lasting harm. We believe policies will be no worse in the near future.

The ways in which this forecast might go wrong provide many opportunities to check, and if necessary adjust, our expectations. Obvious signposts include decisions by the United States to leave NAFTA or to sustain tariffs on its trading partners. (For the moment, we assume that they are intended to pressure their targets into trade concessions and will soon be rescinded.) These are by far the most serious risks to the economies of the U.S. and the world. An unrestrained attempt to stimulate the U.S. economy is both more probable and almost certain to guarantee a recession in the United States in the early 2020s. Yet, it seems likely to be much less destructive than 2008, both immediately and in the long run.

In Europe, we can monitor Brexit negotiations. Severe penalties for Britain's secession would impair prospects in the UK, and late in 2017 it has begun to appear that it will suffer more and longer than the optimists once believed. The EU, in contrast, seems poised for continued economic growth. Loss of another member country from the Union could slow the Continental economy and might even contribute to the EU's gradual dissolution. The growth of populism in Italy and France represents the worst such threat. However, the terms of Britain's divorce from the Union seem likely to discourage any such possibilities. In any case, so much of the world's economic growth now depends on Asia and other developing regions that even loss of the EU should have only mild and transient effects on the global economy.

China offers relatively few such markers, largely because its financial and employment data are much less reliable. The most obvious risk is a credit crunch triggered by the country's enormous burden of uncollectible debt. Other possibilities, such as a real-estate collapse, seem less likely to propagate through the economy. China also seems well able to withstand any trade sanctions the Trump administration is likely to put in place without undue stress.

Impact on Travel and Hospitality

In all, we believe the global economic environment will support steady growth in this industry. Much of the travel market in the 2020s will be familiar. Yet, the scale will have changed. Global overnight visitor flow in 2016 was about 5.4 billion. By 2020, this can be expected to reach 6.2 billion, an increase of nearly 15 percent in just four years.

This of course means fast growth in the hotel market. Domestic stays are expected to climb from some 4.8 billion to about 5.2 billion over the period. International stays, which have been outpacing domestic since 2009, will grow from about 5.6 billion in 2016 to about 6.7 billion in 2020.

However, in the long run the industry's product mix may have to change. With the middle class in decline, particularly in the United States but also in Britain and some other countries, products tailored for them—too expensive for the poor and not lavish enough for the rich—are gradually losing their market. As the trend toward inequality continues, travel and hospitality will have to focus on the ends of the spectrum, creating more products for the necessarily frugal and still more of them for the voluntarily free-spending.

Europe will remain the favorite destination for international tourists, bringing in nearly half a billion visitors and about 41 percent of global spending in 2020. North America will still be in third place, receiving about 13 percent.

Elsewhere, tourism to and from the Middle East and Africa will grow significantly. However, the most important trend by far will be the continuing growth of tourism to, from, and within Asia. Outbound travel from the region is expected to grow to more than 177 million trips in 2020. Inbound travel is expected to reach 70.4 million that year.

Not very long ago, we made the daring forecast that by 2020 no fewer than 100 million Chinese tourists would fan out across the world. The number reached 120 million in 2015. It is now expected to pass 220 million by 2025. They will spend $450 billion that year, more than double the amount in 2015. Some 70 million will visit Hong Kong and Macau, which do not require a passport. Sixteen million will tour Japan, more than triple the number only ten years earlier. Dramatic as this growth is, it will leave room for further expansion. Only 12 percent of Chinese are expected to own a passport by 2025.

The Indian market also is expanding rapidly thanks to the rising incomes of the upper middle class and the wealthy. Travel within the country is expected to grow by nearly 10 percent per year through 2020, to 2.24 billion trips. For the same period, international arrivals are expected to grow by 50 percent, to 12 million. Many of them will be from other Asian lands.

Forecasts of Indian outbound tourism and overseas spending vary widely. The one we find most likely says the number of Indians traveling to other countries will expand from 19.9 million to nearly 25 million, with Indian travelers spending some $28 billion in their host countries. The most optimistic estimates put the number of outbound travelers as high as 40 million.

Indian culture ensures that this is only the beginning. In recent years, Indians have come to see travel as a means of exploration, self-realization, and experimenting with lifestyles. In this context, leisure travel is no longer a luxury, but a necessary part of personal development. This is particularly true among young Indians, who will make up tomorrow's travel market.

One inbound segment worth watching is medical tourism. India is currently the fastest growing destination for medical tourists, their numbers climbing by more than 20 percent per year. Spending by this segment is expected to grow from $3 billion in 2015 to roughly $8 billion by 2020.

One more fact is worth noting. Travel has always tended to go from countries with strong currencies to those where weaker currencies make local accommodations and attractions relatively cheap. We see this in the upsurge of travel from Continental

Europe to Britain in 2016, when the pound collapsed on foreign-exchange markets after the Brexit vote. Nothing we can foresee will change this. Travel and hospitality companies will always be seeking ways to take advantage of, or shield their business from, currency fluctuations. Anticipating them is one of the many cases where forecasting may be able to help.

It is worth reminding ourselves that all these predictions are contingent on the continuing health of the global economy. That is, on the European Union's survival after Brexit, China's ability to avoid a financial crisis, and the stability of American trade policy. These all are the most likely outcomes of current developments, but in 2018 that last especially is far from guaranteed. We will need to keep a close watch on the signposts identified earlier in this chapter.

The world's population is growing rapidly, though not as fast as it once did. It is growing older as well.

There were 7.3 billion people in the world in mid-2015. By 2050, there will be 9.6 billion, according to the United Nations, and even that estimate may be too low. The UN been adjusting its forecast upward for several years, and the Center for Strategic and International Studies warns that most official projections underestimate both fertility and future gains in longevity. They probably are correct.

At the same time, the global population age 60 and older is growing rapidly, from about 901 million in 2015 to 2.1 billion in 2050. The number of "oldest old," those age 80 and over, will more than triple, from 125 million in 2015 to 434 million. In all, people over 65 made up only 15 percent of the world's population in 2000. Their numbers will reach 27 percent by 2050.

Both these trends will be distributed unevenly.

It turns out that the slowest growing countries are the ones the United Nations classifies as "most developed." In Europe, Japan, South Korea, and other wealthy lands, populations are shrinking. This is true also in China and Russia, which rank as developing countries but are special cases.

And the fastest growing countries? They are the world's least developed: Angola, Chad, the Democratic Republic of Congo, Mali, and many of their neighbors. These are the countries least able to support their existing populations.

Just nine countries will account for half of global population growth through 2050, 1.2 billion people in all: India, Nigeria, Pakistan, Congo, Ethiopia, Tanzania, Indonesia, Uganda, and the United States, the only industrialized land to make the list.

Of these countries, only the U.S., Indonesia, and conceivably India can hope to feed all their people at mid-century.

The number of elders, too, will vary from one place to another. Aging is most advanced in the high-income countries. In 2015, one-third of Japanese already were age 60 or over. In Germany, it was 28 percent, in Italy 28 percent, and in Finland 27 percent. By 2030, seniors will make up more than one-fourth of the population in Europe and North America, only 6 percent in Africa. The aging of their populations moves faster each year.

To see the issues most clearly, look at the countries destined to drive some of the greatest changes in travel and tourism in the coming decades, China and India.

China's population is approaching its expected peak of just over 1.4 billion. Between 2025 and 2050, it will decline to 1.3 billion. Thanks to the country's one-child policy, the country's working-age population will shrink even faster, from 938 million in 2015 to 908 million in 2025 and only 726 million in 2050.

At the same time, better medical care is creating a much larger population of non-working elders who need support. From about 134 million in 2015, the group age 65 and older will grow to nearly 300 million in 2050.

This combination will make it difficult for China to continue building its economy at anything like its accustomed rate. Much of the country's effort will go to expanding its infrastructure of nursing homes and hospitals. So will a great deal of money. As things stand, the Chinese pension system is expected to build up a deficit of $11 trillion over twenty years. In the long run, real income and quality of life are likely to decline for all. This is one reason China is pushing to automate its economy, to keep its per-capita GDP growing when human workers no longer can.

India faces the opposite challenge. Its retirement-age population is growing, but its workforce is expanding much faster. In 2016, India is home to 1.3 billion people. By 2025, 1.46 billion will make it the most populous country in the world, surpassing even China. By 2050, it will reach 1.7 billion.

The 65-and-over population will grow as well, from 76.7 million to 109 million and then to 234 million. This will be a challenge because the traditional system of senior care, elders living with their children when they grew too old to work, has broken down as younger generations have moved to the cities in search of work and are no longer available to care for elderly parents. So far, India has not developed a modern social-security system to replace it. However, even starting from scratch it faces a smaller problem than its neighbor to the north. As a fraction of the total, its senior population will be roughly 12 percent, only half as large as China's.

At the same time, the working-age population will expand from 874 million in 2016 to 985 million in 2025 and over 1 billion at mid-century. For India, the challenge will be to find useful employment for its vast working-age population. If it succeeds, providing for the country's elders will be a much smaller problem than in China.

Impact on Travel and Hospitality

Growing populations mean growing demand for travel and hospitality, at least in the more prosperous of the developing nations. The industry has already begun adapting to this trend, establishing new facilities wherever local conditions permit. Yet, more will be required of it as population trends progress.

There also will be more demand to get away from overcrowded cities, especially at higher and lower price points. Because of this, it will be increasingly difficult to find

84   **Strategic Management for Hospitality & Travel: Today and Tomorrow**

uncrowded destinations within easy reach of population centers. Companies that succeed in doing so will outperform those that do not. The alternative, creating a sense of space while ensuring privacy, will be an increasingly important competitive method from the 2020s on.

More products in all price ranges will be designed for seniors, who are both the fastest-growing segment of society (outside India) and, on average, the wealthiest. Many future customers will value the senior-oriented conveniences already permeating the industry. Faucet handles that can be operated conveniently by arthritic hands, larger signs with easier-to-read type, and TTY-equipped support lines for the hearing-impaired are obvious examples. Some may require innovations such as systems that slowly raise the light in guest rooms to wake those who may not hear the usual wake-up call.

Manpower needs may grow, as older patrons require a bit more help checking in, coping with luggage, arranging for local transportation, and carrying out other activities that younger customers would comfortably handle on their own. Industry outposts such as destination hotels and resorts and cruise lines may need to expand their medical staff and facilities to cope with guests who are, on average, not as healthy as other generations.

Hospitality staff are well equipped by temperament and training to meet these needs. They will have to be increasingly sensitive to the varying needs and abilities of older patrons, who display a much wider range of capacities than is commonly found among the young.

Off-season tourism by seniors will help to smooth out the annual cycle in cash flow for hotels, motels, resorts, and other travel businesses.

To serve older customers better, hotels, resorts, and cruise lines should arrange for more senior discounts for their patrons at local restaurants and attractions.

Special tours and other activities should be ranked for the amount of walking, energy, or agility they require, so that older customers can easily choose pastimes within their abilities.

The obvious exception to many of these requirements will be China, where tomorrow's elderly may be much poorer than their peers in other countries. Companies doing extensive business there will need to focus more on seniors as the younger generations shrink, but may have to aim for lower-cost attractions.

Technology continues to transform both the economy and society.

New technologies are pushing the state of the art in all fields. They will do so far into the future.

Biotechnology offers to cure disease; improve crop yields and feed a hungry world; provide cheaper, cleaner energy; develop cleaner, more efficient manufacturing processes; and perhaps even to extend the human lifespan well beyond our traditional three score and ten years.

New materials are enabling stronger, lighter structures, some of which can monitor their own wear and even heal damage.

From nanotechnology, we can expect wonders that range from higher-powered, longer-lived batteries to miniature robots that roam the bloodstream to destroy cancers and clean out blocked arteries.

All of these new technologies, and many others, will quickly change our lives in the years ahead, mostly for the better. Someone magically transplanted from the early twentieth century would recognize much of the world around him. Cars, though remarkably improved, are still cars; they will still obviously be cars even when they drive themselves. Airplanes, even more radically transformed, are still airplanes. But computers, televisions, even radio; antibiotics and medical scanners; the Internet, of course; and endless other artifacts would be almost incomprehensible. The ways in which they have changed our lives would be even harder for our time traveler to grasp. The transformation brought by new technologies in the years ahead are likely to be similarly overwhelming.

New technology is spectacularly on display in places like Eatsa, a chain of fully automated restaurants in the United States; Spyce, in Boston, which is helmed by celebrity chef Daniel Boulud; Muten Kurazushi Sushi Restaurant in Japan; and the largely robot-staffed Henn-na hotel in Nagasaki, Japan. At least until the novelty wears off, these installations are proving highly successful. Eatsa has grown to five locations since 2015, and Muten Kurazushi Sushi Restaurant has no fewer than 260. Even Henn-na is opening a second location, near Disney World in Tokyo.

China's Baidu and KFC China have teamed up to build a restaurant in Beijing that uses image recognition software to guess the patron's age and sex and make food suggestions such a customer would be likely to enjoy. Similar installations should soon recognize guests at hotels and resorts and on cruise ships and make it easier to anticipate their needs. Baidu and KFC China also are experimenting with a voice recognition program that allows customers to place their orders by speaking to an automated customer-service agent. We do not expect that to catch on in hospitality outside the fast-food segment, but an Alexa-style bot might offer directions to local destinations or order a cab when the human staff is occupied with other guests.

Much more innovation is going on behind the scenes. We expect to see artificial-intelligence programs that help corporate-level executives manage the company's finances, identify the best location for a new hotel, and simulate the likely success or failure of new competitive methods. Similar programs will optimize deployment of cruise ships for maximum profit. Automatic ordering systems that anticipate the need to stock up on supplies will become much more sophisticated and successful, "talking" directly to vendors' computers. More predictable, repetitive work will be automated every year, improving efficiency and reducing personnel costs in the process.

By far the greatest market for new technologies will be the airlines. Without getting too far into the details, more sophisticated aerodynamics, better engines, and new materials will not make most airliners in the 2020s any faster than they are today. Instead, tomorrow's aircraft will be over 20 percent more fuel-efficient, produce less air pollution, and incur lower maintenance costs. These all are improvements that airlines will welcome. New aircraft designs that incorporate these innovations will not arrive until well into the next decade, but many improvements can be retrofitted to existing airplanes. Airline executives will spend much of their time calculating which technologies will best improve company profits while remaining affordable.

In one of the most significant developments, Boeing, Airbus, and others are working on radical new power trains for aircraft up to the size of a regional airliner. Instead of driving the craft directly, their turbine engines will spin electric generators. They in turn will drive electric motors that provide thrust. A variation will use the generators to recharge batteries that power the motors. By always running their turbines at the optimum speed, these hybrid-electric airplanes are expected to use 30 percent less fuel than today's most efficient models and to release 60 to 75 percent less carbon dioxide. A Swiss startup called Dufour Aerospace says its two-place model will travel up to 500 miles at speeds of 200 mph with the same cost-per-mile as a car. And Seattle-based Zunum Aero, backed by Boeing and JetBlue, is aiming for speeds around 340 mph at 25,000 feet.

It is not clear yet how soon hybrid-electric airliners will begin to displace conventional models. Zunum Aero says it should have a twelve-passenger craft on the market by 2022, with a 50-passenger regional airliner ready for service by the end of the decade. And a consortium of Airbus, Rolls-Royce, and Siemens plans to fly a test aircraft in 2020, with a 50- to 100-passenger airliner due to enter service between 2030 and 2035.

We agree with their target dates. Given the leap in efficiency these aircraft will provide, they are likely to enter service in the very early 2030s, and conceivably in the last couple of years of the previous century, when today's aviation-minded hospitality graduates will begin contributing to major business decisions.

One surprising development may be the return of supersonic passenger aircraft. NASA has developed a one-third-scale demonstrator for a small supersonic airliner. The XB-1 is designed to reduce the loud boom made by supersonic aircraft passing overhead to levels acceptable over land. Flight testing is scheduled to begin in 2018. A full-scale airliner incorporating its technology would be 170 feet long and accommodate up to 55 passengers.

Other groups are working on designs for supersonic airliners. These include Lockheed Martin and Richard Branson's Virgin Group. Virgin is working with Boom Technology, a Denver startup working on a 40-seat airliner. The craft is intended to cruise at nearly 1,700 miles per hour for the price of standard business class. Boom estimates the market for a supersonic airliner at $260 billion. No word yet on when such an airliner will take to the air. However, an operator of time-shared business aircraft called FlexJet has announced that it plans to begin transoceanic flights at speeds over 1,000 mph in 2023.

Yet, the greatest change so far is not in the aircraft themselves but in the air traffic control (ATC) system that guides them from place to place while ensuring that airplanes never try to occupy the same location at the same time. Until recently, commercial aircraft have been required to travel along fixed routes, from one waypoint to another, even though it means taking more time and burning more fuel than would be required if they could go directly from one airport to another. This was not the only way to keep track of aircraft in a crowded sky, but it was the simplest and most effective.

The advent of GPS navigation is changing this. The "NextGen" ATC system now being installed at airports in the United States is designed to handle course decisions and keep aircraft a safe distance from each other. As a result, airliners will be able to fly directly from one point to another instead of using the less efficient airlanes. A similar, compatible system is being installed in Europe.

NextGen offers a number of other features intended to improve aircraft communications, prevent runway accidents, reduce fuel use during landing, and give flight controllers more information about aircraft locations and movement.

To date, airlines have been slow to install the equipment needed to use the NextGen system. In early 2018, the Federal Aviation Administration (FAA) estimated that up to 150,000 aircraft have yet to carry NextGen hardware, which is mandated for 2020. As long ago as 2010, FAA estimated that it would cost the airlines up to $4.5 billion to comply. The projected return through 2035 is only $200 million, and more hardware will be required later as planned features are added to the system.

Despite the official deadline, it is not certain how soon airlines will be required to equip their aircraft for NextGen. The system was supposed to be complete by 2025 and was expected to cost $40 billion. By 2016, stripped of some of its original features, its due date had been pushed off by up to a decade, at a cost two or three times higher than the original estimate.

Farther into the future, another radical aviation development is coming. The U.S. Army and Navy both are developing aircraft flown solely by artificial intelligence (AI). Many airliners already incorporate autoland systems that can safely guide the aircraft to the ground without human intervention. Private companies are at work on similar projects. The Innovative Future Air Transport System now under development in Europe would completely replace human pilots with computers. In case of emergency, a backup pilot on the ground could take over and fly the aircraft much like a drone. The IFATS consortium estimates that a 220-passenger airliner would cost only $1.8 million more if automated. Yet it could hold 10 more passengers, cruise 5 percent faster, and use less fuel, all due to the absence of a cockpit. Annual maintenance cost would be 20 percent lower. As a result, pretax profits would go up 42 percent, from $15.7 million to $22.4 million.

We expect a practical, fully automated prototype airliner to be demonstrated about 2027. However, because aircraft replacement schedules are so long, certification requirements so stringent, and insurance issues likely to be difficult, we do not believe the first commercial flight of an automated airliner will take place until the 2030s—well within the careers of today's travel majors.

At least one more technology could revolutionize travel. In Europe, high-speed rail has long competed successfully against regional airlines. Unlike the Continent, the United States lacks a well-developed network of trains from one major city to another. Entrepreneur Elon Musk's Hyperloop could change that. Traveling at 760 mph through an evacuated tube, it could be faster, cheaper, and safer than even supersonic aircraft for distances up to at least 900 miles.

Musk first proposed the Hyperloop for the run between Los Angeles and San Francisco, which would take only 90 minutes. However, it appears that the first operational Hyperloop system may go into operation in Abu Dhabi. Feasibility studies also have begun in China, Finland, Russia, and the United Kingdom. Musk has even claimed to have a "verbal agreement" to install a Hyperloop line between New York City and Washington, D.C. China's largest maker of railway equipment, CRRC Corp., is reportedly considering a Hyperloop for the 6,213-mile trip from China to Moscow, which it would make in a single day. If any technology seems likely to transform long-distance travel, the Hyperloop is it.

Yet, another technology could be even more revolutionary. This is artificial intelligence. It could upend almost everything we believe about the economy, society, and our own place in the world.

We will not bother to explain AI here. Anyone not living in a cave or a coma already knows that it attempts to duplicate the results of human thought and understanding, if not in exactly the same way that we achieve them. Bots, robots, autonomous vehicles, and automation in all forms could take over many of the activities that now make up our jobs, leaving many of us with nothing to do and–more important–no way of making a living.

Exactly how many jobs could be displaced is a matter of considerable debate. Reports from authorities ranging from the Oxford Martin School, MIT economists, McKinsey, and the Obama White House have forecast job losses ranging almost up to 50 percent of today's employment. The World Bank put it at 57 percent! These include 80 percent of retail jobs and 83 percent of all jobs paying less than $20 per hour. Just for a start, say goodbye to truck drivers, accountants, office managers, HR people, and many doctors in routine specialties such as radiology.

There are two arguments to counter fears of AI-induced job loss. One is that today's routine jobs will be replaced by a wave of new occupations that depend on uniquely human capacities like social skill and creativity. The other is that jobs will not be lost altogether, but will change to emphasize the abilities in which people remain superior to machines. In these improved occupations, AI will augment human workers, not replace them. The otherwise reliable McKinsey & Company says that AI will merely automate 30 percent of the activities in many jobs, leaving human workers to focus on those less-tedious activities only they can do.

There are two flaws in these arguments.

One is in the implied suggestion that automating only 30 percent of the activities in many jobs will mean that human workers have nothing to worry about. We believe this is equivalent to stating that those employment categories will need about 30 percent fewer people. If this proves correct, as now appears inevitable, many of us could soon have plenty of time for travel but no way to pay for it.

The second issue is that new, better, human-centered occupations will appear slowly, while artificial intelligence is likely to displace jobs quickly. A recent study by economists at MIT and Boston University concluded that the decline of human labor has already been underway for at least a decade.

Optimists discussing AI are fond of pointing to the Industrial Revolution, which displaced virtually all of the craft workers who had dominated economies before the mid-1700s but created factory jobs that sustained economies and enriched ever-growing populations until after World War II. They gloss over a key fact: It took factories two generations to deliver jobs for all who needed them. Few of those craftsmen displaced by the Industrial Revolution ever found a home in the brave new mechanized economy. Most lived in poverty for the rest of their lives.

Even if jobs evolve so that automation becomes an aide to human workers instead of their replacement, we are likely to find that many who built careers in the old economy are unable to make the transition. Some will be too old for retraining to make economic sense for them or, especially, for the business managers charged with building a skilled workforce. Others will lack talents the new jobs demand. Very few of the factory workers displaced by the first wave of automation in recent decades found, or could prepare for, jobs working with the machines that replaced them.

A recent study at Oxford Martin School estimated that only one in five workers held jobs likely to be less in demand. Another predicts that AI will begin to transform 60 percent of businesses as soon as 2022, threatening many jobs in the process. It also identified some key skills for the new era: facility with the English language, knowledge of history and philosophy, management, and personal capacities such as social perceptiveness, judgment, originality, and oral expression. At best, some of these will require mid-life retraining of the sort many companies already have been reluctant to support.

We are not as pessimistic about employment as the discussion above sounds. We are inclined to believe that society will "muddle through" this transition. For a while, at least, AI will be limited in the number of human activities it can supplant. And many business processes will require extensive re-engineering to take advantage of the new technology. This will take time during which many of the workers who can do so will retrain themselves in the skills their altered positions will need.

For those who require more time, or who cannot adapt successfully, we suspect most countries will (reluctantly) adopt some form of income guarantee to ensure that no one falls into abject poverty. In the United States, the increasingly dire need to repair and replace worn-out infrastructure may provide jobs of last resort, much as the Works Progress Administration did in the 1930s. In the U.S. and U.K. especially, enacting such programs will require overcoming powerful opposition to the idea that governments should tax their citizens to pay for necessary services. By the end of the 2020s, there is likely to be no alternative.

Taking all such factors into account, unemployment figures seem likely to end up about 5 percent higher than they would have been if AI had not come along. This is enough to be felt, but not a societal disaster.

Impact on Travel and Hospitality

Technological innovations can be expected to make certain operations more efficient and less costly, much as keycards did when they replaced actual keys. In limited ways, they will reduce the need to depend on fallible human workers for essential activities. Yet, it will be quite some time before a robot can tidy a hotel room.

Because this trend is reshaping other industries, the need for skilled technical staff will outgrow the supply, at least until artificial intelligence replaces humans for systems planning, tech support, and other key technology functions. Hospitality and travel will find it increasingly necessary to compete with other industries for the technical staff required to keep their many systems operating reliably, and especially to fix them when something goes wrong. Salaries for these employees and pay for tech-oriented consultants will be a growing line item on corporate balance sheets.

The new technology most likely to bring wholesale change is of course artificial intelligence, so we will begin there.

One forecast of AI dealt specifically with our industry. It said AI would send four out of five hospitality workers to the unemployment lines.

We disagree, of course. Company accountants and other back-office personnel will be at risk. Some hotel cleaners could be displaced by automated vacuums, and porters at mid-priced hotels may face competition from robotic carts that carry the guests' bags and guide them to their rooms. Yet, no one whose job involves significant interpersonal skills is likely to be displaced. Neither will those in high-end establishments, where personal service is one of the most valued amenities.

Nonetheless, hospitality and travel businesses could face a difficult future thanks to AI. If jobs in other industries disappear en masse, the number of potential guests who can afford international travel, stays at even moderately priced hotels and destinations, and other pleasures will decline precipitously. Competition for the remaining jobs will be intense, so wages are likely to fall, leaving still fewer to support the hospitality and travel industry. The wealthy will still visit the most exclusive resorts and restaurants. Business travelers will still travel. However, most of those in the bottom half of today's income range will be limited to "staycations" and facilities that provide a suggestion of luxury at the lowest possible cost. Hospitality businesses meeting the needs of these customers probably have not been designed yet.

One last concern deals with the developing world. In these economies, a much higher proportion of jobs involves the routine activities AI is most able to take over. Governments also could have much smaller tax bases to help them cope with the effects of widespread unemployment. This combination could create large populations of hopeless unemployed, especially among the young men who are most prone to violence. India, where this population is growing fast, is particularly at risk.

There are two implications here.

One is that many countries will become much less hospitable for tourists from wealthier lands. The resulting security problems could dwarf any the world has yet seen. Most would-be tourists will consider such countries unavailable for elective travel. More traditional destinations in Europe, the United States, and a very few other highly secure lands will receive their business instead. The cruise industry, which can provide security onboard ship and opt to visit only their own resorts and the safest ports, also could find its business growing even more rapidly thanks to this concern.

The second issue is that countries such as India may be in a much poorer position to send travelers abroad. After the expected burst of prosperity in the 2020s, their economic growth could slow, and the profits will be even more concentrated among wealthy business owners. The middle classes, no longer expanding as fast as they are today, would be available for international travel.

We do have a counter-argument, which we find almost convincing. Governments like that of India, recognizing a potential disaster ahead, may ban the most job-destroying uses of AI, even though doing so will make their countries' products less competitive in international trade; India already has banned the introduction of driverless cars. And businesses in developing lands may find that investing in new technologies does not pay off, owing to a local shortage of technical skills and the low financial density of many Third-World industries. It could make sense for them to continue employing human workers for many job categories. Security issues then would be much less troubling. However, the routine white-collar jobs that support much of the growing middle class still could be in danger, possibly limiting the outbound tourism now expected to grow quickly in the years ahead.

We will return to the subject of artificial intelligence at the end of this section to consider an alternative scenario.

For aviation, new technologies will be especially critical. Over the next few decades, airlines are likely to spend vast sums equipping their aircraft first to operate within the NextGen system, to buy hybrid-electric aircraft for regional flights, and then to replace human pilots with AI. The first step in automation, which NASA, Boeing, and Airbus all are working on, will be to reduce aircraft from two pilots in the cockpit to just one. This is likely to occur first on cargo airplanes in the early 2020s and on passenger aircraft once a good safety record has been compiled. Completely pilotless aircraft will come later.

The result, if the enthusiasts can be believed, will be faster, cheaper, and even safer air travel. This does seem likely to us, as pilot error is implicated in more than 80 percent of airline accidents and is solely responsible for many of them.

Yet, if the Hyperloop catches on, the regional airlines may find that much of their investment has been in vain. As the network is built out, first in the Middle East, then in Asia and Europe, Hyperloop systems would replace airlines in ranges under 500 miles and eventually for longer distances. In the United States, with its long tradition of resistance to public transportation, this will be a consideration only in the very long term. Elsewhere, we could see a burst of construction in the late 2020s and, especially, in the '30s.

The Hyperloop could have one more effect. By bringing distant cities closer, it will make them more attractive to both business and families and encourage more casual travel among them. In the long run, the Hyperloop could build a much larger market for hotels, restaurants, and other hospitality businesses in some communities that currently do not justify the investment.

From hospitality's point of view, the most remarkable thing about modern technology may not be its growing sophistication so much as how little of it seems likely to affect the patron's view of travel and tourism. Hospitality is, and we believe always will be, an activity where personal attention is the essence of good business. Guests at a low-end motel might accept a robot clerk if doing so meant lower room rates. Those at a luxury hotel or resort will not.

It will matter much less to air travelers that the human in the cockpit has been replaced by a computer. By 2030, they will know from experience that autonomous cars avoid nearly all the accidents that human drivers could not. They are likely to reason that autonomous airliners should be even safer. At 35,000 feet, there are few pedestrians to step out into traffic.

Finally, let us return to those warnings of mass unemployment to come from AI. There is a way in which they could come true. And if they still would not replace many workers in travel and hospitality, where personal contact is essential, their other effects could be felt much more than we expect.

In this scenario, theoretical and engineering breakthroughs will make AI, robotics, and other forms of automation more capable than forecasters now anticipate. There is no way to predict such developments accurately, but we would expect to see the change of trend by about 2025.

Five to ten years later, in this variant future, unemployment will be clearly rising. By 2030, AI will push jobless rates 10 percent or so higher than they otherwise would have been. Travel and hospitality will find bookings starting to slip in mid-range and low-end markets.

By the 2040s, unemployment will be an urgent problem throughout the developed world. It will be clear that the new, more creative jobs optimists once counted on are not helping nearly as much as they imagined. Few displaced workers have or can quickly learn the necessary skills, and AI is taking over jobs that once seemed to require human imagination and insight almost as fast as they appear. However reluctantly, governments recognize that work will never again provide a living wage for anything like the number of people who need it.

In the worst-case scenario, the death-before-taxes philosophy would make it impossible for the United States, Britain, and even parts of the EU to provide an alternative income for those who need it. In that future, poverty of a kind not seen since the 1930s would be more widespread than in the Great Depression. Travel and hospitality would shrink rapidly, leaving viable markets only at the top and very bottom ends of the cost/service spectrum.

One segment of hospitality could benefit, however: quickservice restaurants. For many, other restaurants would be out of reach, and near-total automation of fast-food service will allow investors an acceptable profit even while reducing prices to the minimum.

This is very much an alternative scenario, not what we expect will come to pass. Yet, the possibility is significant enough to require monitoring the key factors: R&D in artificial intelligence, the rate at which companies adapt their processes to take advantage of AI, any uptick in unemployment, and the ability of government to care for the unemployed. These last two especially will be important in both the prosperous countries international tourists call home and in potential destinations in the developing world.

What we know for sure even now is that today's hospitality students will face challenging times in the middle and later parts of their careers.

Energy will gradually become less expensive.

The cost of energy today is effectively the cost of oil. In 2015, 36 percent of the world's energy was derived from petroleum. Natural gas, much of which comes from oil fields, accounted for another 26 percent. Coal supplied 18 percent of energy, nuclear power 9.8 percent. "Other" sources amounted to only 2.1 percent of global energy production. That includes solar energy, wind, geothermal, and all the other renewables, save biofuel. Factors such as environmental concerns and government subsidies complicate this picture. Yet, the price of oil effectively controls demand for the rest. Other energy sources are used if they cost less than oil. If they cost more, they are not.

Analysts at the World Bank believe that 2016's average price of crude oil, just over $40 per barrel (in constant 2010 dollars), is as low as oil will go. They estimate that prices will average $65 per barrel in 2018 and 2019, and $66.3 in 2025. They will, in the World Bank's view, continue to climb through 2050.

At Forecasting International, we have long believed that the "natural" price of oil is no more than $65 per barrel. To move prices even that high, the Organization of the Petroleum Exporting Countries (OPEC) and unaffiliated producers have had to remain uncharacteristically united in limiting their output. We doubt that this discipline can survive forever. When it fails, oil prices will head down again.

Before continuing, it is worth looking at some basic details of the petroleum market. This is a complicated subject, but for now we can simplify it to just four factors:

Total energy demand: The world needs more energy every year. The U.S. Energy Information Administration predicts that global energy consumption will grow by nearly 50 percent between 2012 and 2040. China, India, and other Asian nations will account for more than half of this increase.

Oil demand: Much of this new energy will be derived from oil. Petroleum consumption has grown for decades. In 2018, it is expected to reach 99.3 million barrels per day. The United States takes about 21 percent of that, China 11.5 percent. China alone is responsible for most of the growth in oil consumption the world has seen since 1980. Shell Oil predicts that demand for oil will not begin to decline until the 2040s. We believe China's pollution problems and commitment to renewable energy could slow the growth of oil consumption below current estimates.

Oil supply: Contrary to popular belief, the world is not about to run out of petroleum. In 2013, the U.S. Department of Energy (DoE) put the world's proved oil reserves at 1,646 trillion barrels—more than twice the amount available in 1980 and 65 percent more than in 1990. The United States, one of the smaller producers, has more proved reserves than it did in 1965. In fact, in November 2017 Fatih Berol, executive director of the International Energy Agency (IEA), predicted that new shale-oil production will make the United States "the undisputed leader of global oil and gas markets for decades to come."

Berol may be right. American producers have dramatically reduced their costs in the last few years, and their output is climbing rapidly—by 846,000 barrels per day just in the three months ending in November 2017. The IEA predicted in mid-2018 that the U.S. would be able to export 5 million barrels per day by 2023. Production also is growing quickly in Canada, Brazil, and Norway.

None of this speaks of declining supply. The U.S. Department of Energy forecasts that global oil production will dip slightly through 2019, peak in 2029 at a level 12 percent higher than in 2015, and then decline very gradually through 2050. This will have little or nothing to do with the available supply. It will depend on shrinking demand, due mostly to the replacement of internal-combustion vehicles by cheaper, more efficient electric models.

Competing energy sources: Oil will remain the dominant energy source well into the future. Shell predicts that much of the growing demand for energy will be met by expanding coal production, particularly in the developing countries. The supply of renewable energy is expected to grow by 2.6 percent annually, more than doubling between 2015 and 2040.

Yet the cost of renewables is falling rapidly. The World Economic Forum reports that solar and wind energy are at least as cheap as fossil fuels in more than 30 nations. The cost of solar especially is expected to continue declining until it is cheaper than oil or coal. As a result, investments in renewable energy already have passed those in fossil fuels. This transition is moving fastest in Asia, where coal has long dominated the energy market and environmental problems are among the worst in the world. China, the world's largest emitter of greenhouse gases, has announced plans to spend more than $360 billion on renewable energy by 2020.

All this leads us to a conclusion many energy-industry experts do not share. McKinsey, for example, predicts that the price of oil will rise gradually to $75, or even $80, per barrel by 2020. Other sources see it growing steadily, returning to $100 per barrel around 2040.

We are not convinced. For us, the two critical factors are the steeply declining cost of renewable energy and China's increasingly desperate need to clean up its environment. We suspect that the energy industry consistently underestimates these factors. If we are correct, the price of oil will fluctuate, occasionally spiking over its fair value. Yet, on average, its price will rise little faster than the rate of inflation.

Beginning in the 2020s, the market for oil, like that for coal, is likely to grow slower than global energy demand. Eventually, competition from renewables will begin to put pressure on oil prices. In some markets, it already has. In May 2018, California cut production of solar and wind energy because renewables were driving the cost of electricity so low that grid operators could not earn a profit. California policy requires the state to derive half its energy from non-carbon sources by 2030. The current growth of renewables would let it hit that target a decade early, much faster than the industry can adapt to the change.

Oil may never get much cheaper than it is today because producing countries will throttle back production whenever their profit margin slips below acceptable levels. Yet, if oil moves much above current prices, it will speed the growth of wind and solar energy production, driving it lower again.

However, two factors could upset this forecast. One could drive the cost of energy much lower much sooner than we expect. The other could push it up.

The downward force is the arrival of the electric car. According to researchers at the University of Leeds, all-electric cars already are the cheapest to own. In an average year, the total cost of owning an electric was about 10 percent lower than for a diesel or gas-engine model. In part, electrics owed their advantage over internal-combustion cars to government tax subsidies. However, the study predicts that by 2025 they will be cheaper even without subsidies. Renault puts the date several years earlier.

Most studies assume that electric cars will slowly displace those powered by gas and oil, so that even by 2040 they will account for only 37 percent of all cars in the United States. However, some recent work suggests that about half the cars on American roads could be electric by 2030 and over 90 percent a decade later. Yet another study, which factored in a quick transition from privately owned cars to much cheaper ride-hailing services, concluded that by 2030 electrics could account for 95 percent of all passenger miles.

Transportation uses over 70 percent of the world's energy. In the U.S., more than 65 percent of oil consumed is burned by personal cars and trucks. If that last study proves correct, we can expect a sudden crash in the price of oil, not two decades ahead but well before 2030.

There is another possibility, however. At the end of 2017, a report from researchers at the Massachusetts Institute of Technology revised estimates of future oil production in the United States radically downward. Estimates from the government's Energy Information Agency (EIA), on which most estimates of future oil prices depend, assume that nearly all the recent gains in U.S. oil output stem from the spread of fracking and other technologies that enhance oil recovery. The new forecast suggests that's wrong. Instead, the MIT study attributes the boost in American oil production to low energy prices. In this view, they led drillers to focus on locations where oil and gas are easiest to extract. Once those fields are exhausted, the cost of energy could rise quickly.

If so, we should know soon. Production at places like North Dakota's Bakken Shale deposit will be about 10 percent higher than EIA projections through 2020. After that, output in the MIT scenario will get worse each year as these high-yield deposits are depleted. The U.S. will never become energy-independent after all. This would ensure that crude prices remain at $65 or more well into the future.

The International Energy Agency also warns of a possible spike in oil prices in the coming decade. Global investment in new production has been coming down since 2015, the agency points out, while demand for oil is still growing. In the 2020s, this could reduce the growth of oil output faster than consumption declines. The IEA speculates that this could drive the global price of oil to $80.

At this point, we have no way to determine which of these forecasts will prove true. We will be closely monitoring oil production and consumption and the popularity of ride-hailing services over the next few years and the growing market for electric cars through the 2020s. We recommend that hospitality students and executives do so as well. A key factor will be the relationship between American oil production and Chinese oil consumption. If American supply outgrows Chinese demand, the cost of energy should remain well under control. If the reverse, oil could be selling for $100 per barrel by 2020. We believe this would be a temporary problem, but it would be painful in the medium term. On balance, we expect the cost of oil to remain under control.

By 2025, and perhaps as early as 2020, it should be clear whether the American oil output remains high and the internal-combustion car begins to disappear. If so, energy costs could plummet much faster than our current analysis indicates.

Impact on Travel and Hospitality

In general, travel and hospitality are like most other industries. When the cost of energy is low, demand for their services tends to be high, and profit margins are comfortable. When it is high, markets begin to dry up, and profit margins shrink. However, in this industry a few special concerns deserve attention.

Like technology, any change in the cost of energy is felt most painfully by the airlines. In 2016, with the average price of crude oil at about $44.60 per barrel, fuel represented 19 percent of airline operating costs, according to the International Air Transport Association. In 2012, when crude averaged $111.80 per barrel, fuel made up more than 33 percent of operating costs.

Cruise lines probably come second. A 2015 analysis found that fuel represented about 11 percent of a cruise ship's operating cost. Among onboard expenses, only payroll was more expensive, and that by less than one-quarter percent. A second estimate put the cost of fuel at nearly 13 percent of total expenses, a full percentage point ahead of payroll and related costs.

Clearly, when the cost of oil remains under control, these segments prosper. When it rises significantly faster than the general rate of inflation, profits suffer. The same is true of course of other segments, but the direct impact is not quite so severe.

The indirect impact for hotels, restaurants, and resorts may be greater. When oil prices are high, consumers feel it not only in the cost of gasoline and home heating, but in all their expenses. Their disposable income declines, and with it their spending on luxuries like cruises and resort stays. "Staycations" become more appealing, so local attractions may benefit where more distant ones do not.

If our expectations for energy costs prove correct, the decades ahead should average out as a time of relatively free consumer spending, steady growth of the travel and hospitality markets, and acceptable profits for the industry. If not, we are likely to see frequent periods of highly competitive pricing, discounts, and constrained profits.

Growing stress increasingly erodes our quality of life.

We once thought of this as an issue of "time poverty": People are working longer hours, feeling increasingly harried, and finding less time for themselves. This trend is responsible for many developments in hospitality, from take-out menus and delivery services at mid-range restaurants to mini-vacation packages of two or three days at a four-star hotel.

In fact, some of our stress does result from extended working hours. Technically, American men now work for pay 12 hours a week less than they did 40 years ago. However, email and smartphones have turned off-duty hours into unpaid working time. A study from Harvard Business School reported that 94 percent of professionals averaged at least 50 hours of work per week. Nearly half worked 65 hours. A Gallup survey found that 21 percent of all workers, professional or not, put in 50 to 59 hours each week, while 18 percent report over 60 hours.

It could be worse. On average, Americans work 1,789 hours per year. At least 16 countries work longer hours. In Israel, the average is 1,853 hours. It is 1,985 hours in Russia and 2,228 in Mexico. Workers in Hong Kong, the city with the world's highest average, spend 2,505 hours a year on the job.

Nonetheless, over the years it has become clear that there is more to this trend than long hours. Our lives in general are becoming steadily more demanding and less secure. The loss of personal time we first noticed is only one of the results. Others include growing frustration, poorer health, and a deteriorating quality of life.

Consider working conditions. More than 14 percent of workers interviewed for a study of stress by the European Agency for Safety and Health at Work reported being threatened with physical violence at work. More than 8 percent working in public administration, education, and health reported incidents of actual violence. Many reported harassment.

Still more issues arise at home. Sociologist Arlie Hochschild, who carried out a ground-breaking study of the subject, cited among major causes of stress sullen children, resentful spouses, endless chores, and generalized chaos. Other studies have found that women are on average much less happy at home, where they juggle parenting, housekeeping, shopping, providing emotional support for family members, and many other roles, than at work, where they perform only one.

Yet, the most important cause of stress is almost certainly money. A study certified by the American Psychological Association found that 64 percent of Americans cited it as a "somewhat "or "very significant" source of stress. Nearly three out of four said that money issues had caused them extreme stress in the previous month. Almost one-third of adults with partners reported that money was a major source of conflict in their relationship. Predictably, those with relatively little money suffered more stress than those who were better off.

There are many of them. As we saw above, workers in the United States, at least, live with wages that after inflation have been stagnant for years. In fact, the upper income brackets have been doing quite well. Those in the lower brackets have been losing income once we take inflation into account. For many, the amount left for discretionary spending has fallen to zero. Several studies have reported that about two-thirds of Americans have no savings to cover an unexpected car repair or medical bill. One found that being unable to pay for health insurance contributed to 49,000 deaths in one year.

In addition, in the age of technology, many jobs feel increasingly in danger of disappearing. As we already have seen, authorities from Bank of America Merrill Lynch to the White House have warned that robots and artificial-intelligence software could replace nearly half of human jobs by 2025. The World Economic Forum estimates that one-third of skillsets workers will need in 2020 did not yet exist at the beginning of 2017. Another study estimated that AI will encroach on 83 percent of jobs paying $20 or less per hour, compared with only 4 percent of jobs paying $40 or more. These and other threats to employment appear in the news almost daily, adding to the worries of workers who already have too many.

Stress is more than a subjective issue. In mid-life, it has been linked to a higher risk of heart disease, high blood pressure, alcoholism, mental illness, and dementia. The annual Labour Force Survey in Britain reports that stress-related issues cost the country 11.7 million days of work per year, about 24 per worker. It caused 37 percent of all work-related illnesses and 45 percent of all working days lost to health problems. In the United States, where statistics on such things are harder to come by, one study estimated that workplace stress adds up to $190 billion a year to healthcare costs. Other research found that job-related stress contributes to more than 180,000 deaths per year.

Impact on Travel and Hospitality

Stress is especially high in the hospitality industry. A study of managers and hourly workers at 65 hotels in the United States found that interpersonal tensions and unexpected issues like a malfunctioning computer system were among the most common causes of stress. Problems were most common among management, but all workers were afflicted. Another study, in Europe, found that 9.3 percent of workers in hotels and restaurants had been threatened with violence, and 8.6 percent reported problems with harassment. One in seven hotel and restaurant workers burns out due to chronic stress in the workplace, and the cruise industry can be even more demanding. One shipboard restaurant employee reported working twelve to fifteen hours a day, seven days a week for ten straight months.

All this guarantees that tomorrow's hospitality and travel executives will spend much of their time coping with stress-related problems. Casual workers, who make up a large portion of hotel staff, and those whose working hours vary unpredictably are at the greatest risk.

One small exception to the growth of work-related stress has emerged in France, which mandates a 35-hour work week. Since the beginning of 2017, a "right to disconnect" law has guaranteed workers at companies with 50 or more employees the right to ignore digital communications outside normal business hours. Although this will change management practices in France, for travel and hospitality businesses as much as for others, it seems unlikely to catch on elsewhere.

For the hospitality industry, stress offers positive benefits: It provides opportunities to develop competitive strategies aimed at those for whom stress does have more to do with time and responsibilities than with money. To date, hotels and cruise lines have developed two- and three-day packages and "cruises to nowhere" for these guests. We expect competition for this market to be one of the most innovative areas in the years ahead.

Migration Is Redistributing the World's Population

Historically, population flows have carried people in large numbers from the southern hemisphere to the northern and from the east to the west. Although the specific countries involved have changed somewhat over the years—for example, movement from the former Soviet Union to Western Europe has slowed since the 1990s and early aughts—the basic pattern remains constant.

Some 247 million people have moved out of their native lands. Ninety percent of them have moved voluntarily, usually in search of economic opportunity. About half of all migrants globally have moved from developing to developed countries. In major destination countries, immigrants accounted for 40 to 80 percent of growth in the labor force. One convincing study found that immigrants to Germany who became entrepreneurs and small-business owners created 1.3 million jobs in 2014 alone. This is more than double the annual growth of the German workforce.

Most migration takes place inside geographic regions. For example, in 2015 nearly 23 million people moved from one country in Eastern Europe and Central Asia to another country in that area. Only 10 million moved from Eastern Europe and Central Asia to Western Europe. Some 15 million people moved from one country in sub-Saharan Africa to another. And 10.1 million changed countries within the Middle East and North Africa.

Migration is not only for the poor and imperiled. In 2016, 60 percent of China's wealthiest said they planned to invest abroad and emigrate within three years.

Migrants contribute nearly 10 percent of global GDP. In 2015, that amounted to roughly $6.7 trillion, nearly twice as much as they would have produced in their countries of origin. The developed countries received more than 90 percent of this benefit.

However, 65.6 million people were displaced by conflict and persecution in 2017, the most since the office of the UN High Commissioner for Refugees began keeping records. Nearly 41 million of them are displaced inside their native countries.

Half the world's refugees came from just three countries: Syria, Afghanistan, and Somalia. Nearly all the 1 million-plus refugees who arrived in Europe in 2016 came from these lands.

About 3 million refugees have been resettled in the United States since Congress created the Federal Refugee Resettlement Program in 1980. However, in 2017 President Trump cut the refugee admission quota from 110,000 to only 45,000. The pace of resettlement has slowed sharply since he took office.

In the later 21st century, climate change is likely to be one of the largest causes of migration. In Bangladesh alone, a rise of 1 meter in sea level will flood 20 percent of the country and displace more than 30 million people.

A 2016 survey of people in twenty-seven countries found that two out of three respondents around the world believed national governments should do more to help refugees. More than 75 percent in 20 of the countries would accept refugees into their country. Only 17 percent would refuse.

Impact on Travel and Hospitality

As a large employer of relatively low-wage workers, this industry depends heavily on recent immigrants for its labor force. Continuing migration will ensure a steady supply of workers at prices hospitality and travel businesses can afford to pay.

The large numbers of people who believe in helping refugees and accepting them into their own countries ensures that populist bans on immigration will not survive. However, because the xenophobic minority is much louder, it will be well into the 2020s before the developed countries begin to deal effectively with refugees and integrate them into their populations, rather than banishing them to isolated camps. In the interim, it is possible that businesses in some countries will find the supply of low-wage workers temporarily shrinking and their labor costs rising.

Immigrant populations also are a major cause of growth in the restaurant industry. Wherever large numbers of migrants settle, restaurants will spring up to provide their native cuisines. Like Italian, Mexican, and Chinese restaurants, they will find a ready market among novelty-seeking natives and eventually become fixtures in the industry. In turn, they will provide employment for later waves of immigrants.

New generations are beginning to change society's priorities.

Let us begin with definitions:

Between 1981 and 1997, some 66 million people were born in the United States. These are the Millennials. Thanks to immigration, they are now 75.4 million strong, and their number is expected to peak at 81.1 million in 2036. In 2017, Millennials already made up one-fourth of the world's workforce. By 2020, they will be half.

For our purposes, anyone born after 1997 is a Centennial. Others set different beginnings, and in some cases endpoints, for this generation. Yet one thing everyone agrees on: There are a lot of them. In 2016, the most common estimate held that there were nearly 84 million Centennials in the U.S., some 26 percent of the population. That makes them already the largest generation in history, and their numbers are still growing. By 2020, 40 percent of Americans are expected to be Centennials. Worldwide, there are about 1.3 billion Centennials, with as many as 2 billion expected by 2020.

Note that most generations are somewhat artificial. The Census Bureau recognizes only the Baby Boomers, the 76 million born from 1946 through 1964. The rest are largely marketing constructs defined to help the world's fashion buyers and consultants make a neat, coherent "pitch" to bosses and prospective clients.

Yet, age cohorts do tend to have some common characteristics. Those who grew up during the Depression learned frugality and caution as their grandchildren never did. The teens and young adults of the Second World War were shaped by their experiences as well. So were those who lived through the assassination of President John Kennedy and the time of hippies and "flower power." In the broadest possible terms and with endless individual variations, each age group learned similar lessons and developed at least some of the same values. If these categories are highly simplified, they nonetheless allow us to develop expectations and policies that more or less work.

The Baby Boomers remain in many ways the dominant generation in society. In the United States, they continue to hold much of the power in Washington and in Corporate America. According to the Census Bureau, they also control over 80 percent of personal financial assets and more than half of discretionary spending power. For any consumer-oriented industry, they are a key market. Yet, the focus of business planners and marketers has already begun to move on.

The Millennials are currently of interest not only because there are millions of them, ranging in age from 21 to 37 in 2018, but because they now make up the prime-age workforce and market throughout the world. As the Boomers once were and Centennials will be, the Millennials today are the primary concern for executives hiring and managing mid-level corporate staffs. They also are a group for whom companies will design many of their competitive methods for the next two decades.

Although there is enormous diversity among the world's populations, Generation X (the 55 million born in the U.S. from 1965 through 1980, plus about 11 million immigrants), and especially the Millennials and Centennials, share many characteristics with others in their age groups around the world.

As we look at these traits, please bear in mind that anything said about a group inevitably leaves out essential details and individual variation. There will be Centennials who, though only four years old at the time, remember being frightened when their mothers wept at the 9/11 terrorist attacks and Millennials then in their twenties who somehow slept through them. We speak here in generalities.

Remember, too, that the authors' view their subject across a gap of more decades than we care to think about. If students find that we get some, or even many, things wrong about their generation, please use your insights as a starting point for your own analysis of Millennial and Centennial values, abilities, and attitudes and their implications for hospitality and travel. Understanding our limitations can only help as you begin your careers and must cope with your seniors.

What has shaped these generations?

For a start, of course, their parents.

The Millennials for the most part were children of Boomers. Looking back at their own mistakes and rocky relationships with elders, Baby Boom parents sought above all to keep their children safe, to foster self-expression, and to encourage teamwork.

Parents of Centennials have been less concerned with self-esteem than with self-reliance and confidence based on demonstrated ability. This begins to explain the heavily scheduled lives for which today's young are known. The knowledge that college recruiters these days want to see diverse extracurricular activities on a student's application probably accounts for the rest.

Neither generation's parents have been eager to give them the independence that self-expression and self-reliance would seem to imply. In college and well into their twenties, about one-third of Millennials and Centennials say their mothers still treat them like babies.

Other factors also have helped make these generations "different."

Few Millennials and none of the Centennials have known a time when the United States was at peace. Two Gulf Wars in the 1990s, large-scale combat in Afghanistan, incessant drone strikes in Asia and Africa, and the permanent expectation of terrorism is life as they know it. Whatever else this does, it cannot encourage taking the future for granted, as many Baby Boomers once appeared to do.

Both age groups learned by watching their elders not to count on financial security, either. The recession of 2008 reinforced this lesson. So have frequent warnings from politicians that Social Security might not be there to support them in old age.

So does their own experience. For the young, good jobs are hard to find. As of April 2018, youth unemployment in the U.S. had at last fallen to 8.4 percent, about double the general rate. In parts of Europe, the gap is much higher, and even those young people who find work often find themselves stuck in an endless succession of temp jobs.

Fair warning: We have seen reports of young, experienced hospitality workers in Europe who were in exactly this position.

In the U.S., where such statistics are easy to find, 7 percent of workers receiving the federal minimum wage or less hold a bachelor's degree. Another 34 percent have at least some college or an associate degree. According to the Federal Reserve Bank, about 44 percent of young people with a bachelor's degree are stuck in jobs that college or high-school students once would have held. Over all, those in their twenties now earn about 20 percent less in real buying power than Gen X did at the same age.

For graduates, college brings one more financial challenge. Seventy percent are saddled with student loans they are ill-equipped to repay. Estimates of their average debt in 2016 range from about $28,500 to more than $37,000. Six out of ten have no idea when they will pay it off.

This probably explains why some 40 percent of American adults ages 18 to 34 live with their parents—more of them for the first time on record than are married or cohabiting. In Europe, living with parents is taken for granted; nearly half of those from 18 to 29 do. In the U.S., many elders take it as yet more evidence that something is wrong with young people today.

Add one last factor to the generational equation: technology.

The older Millennials were not all born into the world of laptops, smartphones, and social media, but they came close. Even the eldest were barely into double-digit ages when the public began to figure out what the Internet could do for them. The youngest never knew a world without the Net.

The Centennials are digital natives, not quite born with laptops and smartphones in their hands but often using their parents' computers in preschool and receiving their own hardware much earlier than Millennials did. One survey found that the average pre-teen aged eight to twelve spends six hours a day using electronic media. For those aged thirteen to eighteen, the figure was nearly nine hours. More than half of American teens report feeling addicted to their smartphones. Seventy-two percent say they feel an almost constant need to check for messages and reply as soon as they come in.

Among both generations, modern communications technology has smoothed regional and national differences. Over some 40 years in the twentieth century, television largely homogenized regional dialects and accents; in a limited way, it also spread common values wherever American programs could be seen. Since the mid-1990s, the Internet has been spreading similar values and attitudes throughout the world. As a result, Millennials and Centennials tend are likely to have more in common with their peers on other continents than with their own elders.

All these influences have helped shape today's young people in ways that matter in the workplace. We will look at Millennials first and move on to the Centennials in a few minutes.

Baby Boom parents forged, on average, a generation of "good kids." Studies find that Millennials are likely to be cooperative and to work naturally in groups much better than their individuality-obsessed parents did at the same age. They generally function well in the ad hoc task-oriented teams modern management often relies on to get things done.

Offsetting these virtues, at least in the eyes of their managers, the concern for self-esteem typical of Boomer parents made the Millennials characteristically sure of themselves—perhaps too sure. They are willing to take on whatever challenges their employers throw at them, but much less so to accommodate standard procedures and the working habits of their elders. Yet at the same time many need the constant feedback and rewards their parents gave them. This can be an uncomfortable combination for executives charged with getting the best from them.

The other characteristic Millennials share—we will see it again when we look at the Centennials below—is a comfort and proficiency with technology that their elders can only envy. Ninety-five percent own a smartphone, and most are on it constantly, often while also using other devices, looking up information, checking for text messages from friends and colleagues, and generally convincing older managers that they are paying attention to anything but work.

This also helps explain why 65 percent of Millennials in a 2011 survey said they felt held back by dated and rigid work styles. They often believe technology offers a better way to get things done than corporate procedures allow. They often are right. Yet, it can be difficult to fit Millennial impatience into a corporate culture built by and for the Baby Boom generation.

There is one more generational characteristic that managers often find disquieting. Growing up in an age of insecurity has given the Millennials a general sense of transience and made them skittish about anything or anyone beyond their immediate friends. In a recent study, Pew Research found that only one in five believed most people could be trusted—significantly fewer than among Gen X and barely half as many as in their parents' generation.

Similarly, they are, on average, much less willing to invest in institutions as previous generations have done. Half say they are political independents. Nearly one-third have no religious affiliation. Some 75 percent remain unmarried at ages 18 to 32, compared with just under half of Boomers. All these are the highest numbers for any generation yet recorded.

Executives who complain about Millennials are half right. This characteristic lack of commitment applies to employers as much as it does to any other organization or group. Watching their parents forced to give up on lifetime employment taught them that all jobs are temporary. Growing up in uncertain times has made them focus more on the bottom line than their predecessors did. However, it is their own bottom line, not the company's. Any job is temporary almost by definition—a step on the way to a more responsible, better paid opportunity. This explains why Millennials report that the chance to learn new skills was the top factor that led them to accept their present job. If a position offers too little chance for training and advancement, the search for a better one begins immediately.

Despite this, or perhaps because of it, Millennials tend to be nearly as optimistic about their personal futures as they are pessimistic about so many other things. Only four in ten consider themselves "middle-class," nearly half describing themselves as lower or lower-middle-class. Fewer than half believe that Social Security will be there for them when it is their turn to retire. Yet, one-third say they have enough money to lead the lives they want, and more than half expect to in the future. Even among the unemployed, six out of ten expect eventually to have enough. Two-thirds expect to be better off than their parents' generation.

All these characteristics matter when approaching Millennials as potential customers. Perhaps one in a hundred can be influenced by traditional advertising. A hard sell turns the rest off immediately, and subjecting them to it is a mistake that is difficult to recover from. Cynical about marketing claims, they are much more likely to be convinced by user reviews and personal testimony, though not celebrity endorsements. The fashion industry especially has capitalized on this by employing "online influencers"—bloggers with large and devoted followings—to represent their merchandise.

This is one aspect of "authenticity," a general sense of trustworthiness that Millennials respond to above almost all else. This can mean anything from establishing a consistent corporate identity in frequent messages that do not attempt to sell a specific product to sharing profits with worthy causes. One prominent marketer has built a good business by donating a pair of shoes to the poor in developing countries for each pair sold. This continues to work despite the widely reported tendency of its footwear to self-destruct after a few days or weeks of use.

As this company makes clear, social media are an essential marketing tool. Two-thirds of Millennials say they are much more likely to become loyal customers of brands that engage with them on social networks. They check with trusted blogs before they buy something, and one-third rely mostly on what the blogs tell them. A solid majority report using their smartphones to check prices and user reviews while shopping in a brick-and-mortar store, and even when talking to salespeople.

An effective marketing strategy will approach Millennials through a variety of platforms, at all hours, with messages that look good no matter the hardware. Four out of five messages, and sometimes more, will focus on corporate identity and social responsibility, rather than sales. And it will continue, not for a few weeks or the next quarter, but essentially forever.

Contrary to popular belief, Millennials are as loyal to brands as any other generation. Sixty percent say they usually or always buy the products they currently purchase. Yet, this loyalty must be maintained by constant reminders through a medium and in a style they trust.

In all, the Millennials are not what their elders expected. When approached skillfully they can be effective on the job and rewarding as customers. Yet, they can be hard for older colleagues to work with and for marketers of any age to sell to. Among both, the best strategies and tactics have been debated for so long that the Millennials themselves are growing into management positions and facing generational challenges of their own.

Those challenges involve the Centennials. If they largely missed shocks like 9/11 and, among the younger, the Great Recession, they have spent their lives surrounded by the results. War and terrorism are ever-present in the news. Racial and ethnic tensions have flared—in the U.S. because dominant Caucasians are becoming just another minority, in Europe because waves of immigrants and refugees are replacing casual Christianity with more devout Islam. Gender norms are changing. Economic challenges are a given. Security is not. More than any previous generation, Centennials take such things for granted.

All this has had characteristic effects.

Centennials seldom notice racial and ethnic diversity except when advertising neglects it. Fifty percent more identify themselves as multiracial than Millennials did in 2000.

They accept gender diversity just as readily. In early 2016, a survey by J. Walter Thompson found that only 48 percent identified themselves as "exclusively heterosexual," while 38 percent reported some degree of bisexuality. Some 70 percent supported gender-neutral public restrooms. More than half said they knew someone who had rejected gender-specific language and adopted "they," "them," and other gender-neutral pronouns. Three out of four agreed that "Gender doesn't define a person as much as it used to."

This trend is visible in some other lands as well. A 2015 poll YouGov UK found that half of young adults identified themselves as "something other than 100 percent heterosexual."

Yet, although large majorities of Centennials support issues like same-sex marriage and marijuana legalization, they can be surprisingly conservative in other ways. They are 92 percent more likely than the previous generation to wear seat belts, 43 percent less likely to smoke, 34 percent less likely to be binge drinkers, and 19 percent less likely to have tried alcohol. They even incur 52 percent fewer teen pregnancies.

Where the Millennials were optimists, Centennials are realists. They typically aim for goals they can attain, rather than dreams they probably will not.

Where the Millennials have tended to live in the present, Centennials are always planning for the future. Two-thirds prefer to save money instead of making impulse purchases.

Where many of the Millennials identify themselves as environmentalists, Centennials much less often do so. Yet, three out of four say they do worry about human impact on the planet.

They also want to make the world around them a better place. From age 16 to 19, one in four volunteer in social programs or other public-spirited activities. Sixty percent want their jobs to make a difference.

Like the Millennials, today's youngest are good at teamwork. For proof, visit almost any Starbucks or bookstore café after school, and count the groups working on class assignments. One-third work with classmates online, where a third—not necessarily the same one—watch lessons. Yet, this is less a matter of parental training than it was for Millennials. Today's young simply recognize that some activities work out best when pursued cooperatively.

This feeds into their ambitions. In some studies, 70 percent or more of high-school students want to start a business. Three out of four wish their hobbies would turn into full-time jobs.

Millennials legendarily suffer from the embarrassing information shared years ago in social media. Few Centennials will make the same mistake; they are much more private. One in four left Facebook in 2014 alone. Instead, they prefer social media like Snapchat, Whisper, and Secret, where participants are anonymous and, in some cases, messages automatically disappear when read or after a fixed interval.

Social media are only one aspect of technology, of course, and probably not the most important. Centennials are the first generation who never knew a world without the Internet. Many have never lived without a mobile device. As of 2015, 77 percent of those from age 12 to 17 had a cell phone. They used streaming media before downloading, text messaging before email, which they view as old-fashioned. More than 40 percent spend three hours or more per day on media activities not related to school.

Ubiquitous technology has not turned Centennials into skilled techies, any more than it did the Millennials. Instead, they are skilled users of technology, applying their brains primarily to the things computers cannot handle as well.

Centennials know that information can almost always be found in a few minutes with Google. They don't have to remember it as their elders did, unless they need to pass a test. This can make them appear uninformed to those who learn the hard way.

Although multitasking degrades everyone's performance on mental activities, Centennials tend to do it more successfully than their elders. For preference, the average Millennial multitasks with only two screens. Centennials tend to prefer five: a desktop computer, a laptop, a tablet, a smartphone, and a television to soak up whatever attention the other media do not.

Living with a constant flood of information, Centennials tend to be a lot quicker to integrate new data into their knowledge base. One glance, and it falls into place—for so long as it is remembered.

This may explain another Centennial characteristic. By most measures, they have the attention span of mayflies, all of eight seconds. Advertisers report that Centennials will sit through a ten-second video, but seldom anything longer. This is not quite the shocking decline that pre-Internet generations might imagine; in 2000, the average attention span among Americans of all age groups was only twelve seconds, and older generations also show declines since then. However, the studies we have seen captured only how quickly attention was redirected. That occurs frequently in multitasking, and we wonder whether more detailed research would find that each of the tasks in hand consistently received as much attention as it needed, adding up to much more substantial numbers.

Unexpectedly, Centennials are not as addicted to social media as many of their seniors imagine. Two-thirds still use Facebook, and half check in with it several times a day. However, six out of ten prefer talking with others in person rather than through any online platform. This is not true at work, however, where 41 percent would rather communicate electronically. Predictably, three out of four believe technology makes them more effective on the job.

It also separates them from their less tech-savvy superiors. Many doubt that their bosses really understand how they use computers and the Internet to work more efficiently. This is one more factor making them impatient with established procedures, another trait their superiors often find frustrating. Conspicuous multitasking also can leave managers wondering what youthful employees are up to.

Probably work, as it turns out. Centennials are only half as likely as Millennials to believe talking, texting, or surfing the Web are acceptable during working hours. However, they are nearly twice as likely to think it appropriate to talk on the phone during a job interview. For managers and HR personnel, this will take some adjustment.

In fact, most aspects of dealing with Centennials probably will require adaptation. In many superficial ways, they appear almost to be super-Millennials, even better with technology and multitasking and even less patient with procedures they find getting in their way. Yet to managers and advertisers alike, the differences will matter.

The Centennials also will be the first generation to use virtual reality (VR) and augmented reality (AR) devices. The youngest of them will grow up with VR and AR. It will be interesting to see how this changes their relationship with the world around them. VR, this most immersive of digital technologies, might even capture their attention for longer than eight seconds. With today's state of the art, they will not find it easy to multitask while wearing a VR headset.

Impact on Travel and Hospitality

The Millennials and Centennials have learned from experience that many tasks are better handled as group efforts. On average, this has made them cooperative when it is clear that a chore requires it. This social skill should translate well to an industry as dependent on personal interactions as hospitality is.

Employers and marketers who have not successfully adjusted their policies and practices to suit Millennial workers have almost lost their chance. It is the Centennials' turn now. Both generations thrive on challenge, but in return they expect—and need—recognition, opportunity, and the chance to learn new skills. So far, Centennials appear to depend less on constant reinforcement, but they are at least as concerned with opportunities for learning and advancement.

Job training thus will be even more essential in the years ahead, both to ensure polished, efficient service and to retain good workers. Yet, it may repay the investment less well. Once the opportunity for advancement runs out or some other factor makes the job less satisfying, those new skills will move to another company as fast as possible.

Millennials and Centennials clearly adapt to new technologies more easily than previous generations. They also expect them to be available. Technology budgets may need to expand as a result.

They are less likely than older computer users to be patient with glitches. They expect high-tech gadgetry to work, to help them meet challenges rather than creating new ones.

This applies to marketing as well. Whether on their smartphones or in person, customer experiences need to be streamlined, efficient, uninterrupted, and—for best results—playful. This puts a premium on collecting guest data, making it possible to deliver exactly the information each individual wants in the most painless way possible.

A reputation for "corporate social responsibility"– contributing to the community and serving as good stewards of the environment–will give companies a substantial advantage in both hiring and marketing over less conscientious competitors. Although Centennials are less apt to talk about values than the previous generation, about 60 percent say they probably would leave a job if the company no longer reflected theirs.

And, as we saw in discussing the economy above, a near-universal shortage of disposable income among these generations will place a premium on developing products and services that seem luxurious, yet can be delivered at relatively low cost.

Entrepreneurship is spreading throughout the world, yet shrinking in the United States.

Some 63 percent of 20-something Americans either own their own business or want to start one, according to surveys now a few years old. More recently, a survey of Millennials found that only 22 percent said entrepreneurship was the best plan.

They are expressing this loss of enthusiasm in practical ways. In the U.S., the share of new entrepreneurs aged 20 to 34 has declined from almost 35 percent in 1996 to 25 percent in 2014. Blame student loan payments that make building personal capital difficult to impossible. It does not help that low-credit beginners find it increasingly difficult to attract angel investors or borrow to start or expand a business.

Forecasts say that 40 percent of the American labor force will be "contingent workers" by 2020 and more than 50 percent by 2030. Never permanently employed and always economically insecure, many of them are likely to start businesses because they have few other options.

If they do, it will be an important change. Entrepreneurship in the U.S. has been declining for decades. In 1977, 16 percent of companies were less than one year old, and they employed nearly 6 percent of workers. Both numbers have sunk almost continuously, so that by 2014 only 8 percent of companies were new, and they employed only 2.1 percent of workers. Early data suggests that even high-tech companies are following this trend.

There are two counter-intuitive explanations: Deregulation has made it easier for big, established companies to dominate their markets. And the decline of welfare has deprived the poor of the economic security that would allow them to take risks.

Outside the United States, in contrast, entrepreneurship is spreading rapidly.

China now allows some students to defer coursework while trying out business ideas, and the "Internet Plus" strategy aims to promote net-powered startups. McKinsey estimates that new Internet applications could account for 22 percent of China's GDP growth through 2025.

In Hong Kong, the number of startups grew by 25 percent in 2016, from 1,558 new companies to 1,926. Most reportedly are being founded by young entrepreneurs.

Europe's startup culture also is booming. The High Tech Campus in Eindhoven, Netherlands, is home to more than 130 new companies and some 10,000 entrepreneurs and researchers. Lisbon saw nearly 100 startups created every day in 2014. And early-stage tech companies there raised $13.4 billion in 2015 Credit Silicon Valley for showing the world how much a strong entrepreneurial culture can accomplish.

Nonetheless, early-stage funding has declined sharply in recent years, and the phenomenon is world-wide. Globally, venture capitalists financed some 19,000 tech companies in 2014, only 10,000 in 2017. Funding peaked at $101.3 billion in 2016. A year later, it came to only $83 billion. Early and seed-stage funding has been hit hardest, collapsing from 13, 292 deals worldwide in 2014 to only an estimated 5,900 in 2017. Most of this change reflects the passing of old fads—the funding of businesses consisting solely of an app, slowing of new developments in software-as-a-service, and even a reduction in financial technology startups. Yet, it is clear that new businesses are, at least for now, becoming harder to fund.

Impact on Travel and Hospitality

The decline of entrepreneurship is partly responsible for the slowing of economic growth in the U.S. This is shrinking the middle class and increasing demand for inexpensive travel options that still feel luxurious. It also has helped drive the rise of "staycations." These trends can only continue into the 2020s, and possibly beyond. This will help the bottom lines of local attractions like amusement parks and restaurants a modest step above the casual-dining segment. It will erode profits at destinations designed to serve middle-income guests and unable to shift their offerings toward higher or lower parts of the spectrum.

As an industry with a record of continuous growth for decades, travel and hospitality is an attractive field for startup businesses. In Europe, Asia, and parts of Africa, the growth of entrepreneurship is likely to bring a steady flow of new resorts, restaurants, hotels, and other destinations and travel services. In the most heavily served regions, this could begin to reduce profits by splitting guests among too many providers. Yet, the most new businesses are likely to appear in less heavily trafficked areas, giving travelers appealing new options to choose from. Overall, the growth of entrepreneurship outside the U.S. will help to drive the hospitality and travel industry's continued expansion.

Militant extremism continues to spread and gain power.

Although it sometimes seems, here in the United States, where attention has turned inward, that political violence is on the wane, terrorism remains a force throughout the world. The Global Attack Index compiled by Jane's Terrorism and Insurgency Centre lists 22,487 terrorist events in 2017, resulting in 18,475 deaths. Islamic State, of which we hear less of late, killed 6,500 people in 4,500 incidents. This was the fourth consecutive year in which it ranked as the world's most active terrorist organization.

Nonetheless, there have been fewer terrorist attacks, 22,487 in 2017 compared with 24,202 the previous year, when 77 countries suffered at least one death from terrorism. Fewer victims are dying as well. Among non-militants, fatalities peaked at 48,786 in 2014 and declined to 18,475 only three years later. One reason is that large-scale, centrally planned assaults have been largely replaced by smaller events staged by local groups and "lone-wolf" attackers. This kind of home-grown extremism will be a growing concern in the years ahead.

We see this pattern clearly in the United States, where the attacks of September 11, 2001, remains the only major terrorist incident emanating from a foreign source. As of mid-2018, according to one tally, 36 terrorist events since 9/11 have killed 173 people. (This count omits attacks that caused only injuries or failed entirely and assaults not clearly resulting from religious or political animosities. However, including the failed and non-fatal terrorist incidents would not greatly change the picture.) Nine of the attacks were carried out by American-born terrorists against abortion providers, liberal politicians, or other targets of the far right. Three involved a restaurant or nightclub.

Limiting our attention to the period from 2008 through 2017, the Anti-Defamation League's Center on Extremism counts 372 people killed by political extremists in the United States. Only planned attacks are included in its count, not spontaneous outbursts of violence. Of these, only 26 percent were carried out by Islamist extremists. Three percent were from the political left. The rest, 71 percent, were carried out in roughly equal numbers by white supremacists and anti-government activists. Half emanated from organized cells. Half were carried out by loners.

Terrorism is more active in Europe, where it is aided by proximity to the Middle East and northern Africa, open borders, and plentiful soft targets. In 2016, there were 152 terrorist attacks on the Continent, 76 in the United Kingdom alone. In France, there were 23, in Italy 17. The bloodiest attack was in Manchester, UK, with 22 dead. Barcelona came second with 13.

There may be worse to come. Anti-terrorism specialists in Britain warn that the risk of attack there is growing. Paris suffered coordinated attacks that killed 130 in November 2015. The head of Europol, the EU-wide law enforcement agency, estimates that up to 5,000 European Muslims have already visited the Middle East and returned home radicalized and trained for jihad. In November 2016, Turkey reported that it had 7,670 people from the EU on its no-entry list of foreign terrorist fighters.

Nonetheless, it is important to view terrorism in light of other dangers. The 22,487 terrorism-related deaths throughout the world in 2017 is relatively small compared to the roughly 40,100 Americans killed in traffic accidents that year. People in the United States and Europe have a greater risk of being killed by lightning than by terrorism. This also is true in Israel, arguably the developed world's bull's eye for Muslim extremists. There were 25 terrorist attacks there in 2017 and only 34 deaths. India, where terrorists killed 206 civilians and 81 security personnel in 2017, loses between 2,100 and 2,500 people each year to lightning. A single death from terrorism is a tragedy. Yet it is one that business executives need to keep in proportion.

Impact on Travel and Hospitality

Google "hotel bomb*," and the Internet search returned 38.1 million items early in 2018. Then search for "bomb* restaurant." After filtering out a surprising number of establishments with "bomb" in their name, we are left with 34.9 million entries. The oldest attack in the first few pages of results is the bombing of the King David Hotel in Jerusalem by Zionist militants in 1946. Others may well predate it. Assaults on the travel and hospitality industry are an ancient problem. What better target to inflict the most pain on one's chosen enemies than where they gather, relaxed, happy, and almost always completely undefended? Wherever terrorism strikes, it hits travel and hospitality.

Fortunately, none of the top countries for terrorism is likely to be on anyone's list of tourist destinations. According to the London Institute for Economic and Peace, Iraq comes first, followed by Afghanistan, Nigeria, Syria, and Pakistan. However, a number of popular destinations are among the dozen highest-risk lands. India is in eighth place, Turkey in ninth, Egypt and the Philippines eleventh and twelfth, respectively. Thailand falls in 16th place.

Ukraine shows particularly well both the impact of terrorism and the hospitality industry's exposure to it. In 17th place on the London Institute list, it attracted 14.2 million international tourists in 2017; as recently as 2012, there were 23 million. According to official statistics, there were 124 acts of terror in Ukraine every month in 2017, down from 155 a year earlier. Radisson, Holiday Inn, InterContinental, and Hyatt all operate hotels in Kiev.

Terrorism's greatest impact on hospitality and travel followed the attacks of September 11, 2001. Overseas arrivals in the United States plummeted from about 6.4 million immediately before the event to about 3.75 million in the following quarter. By 2007, they still had not returned to their level of the third quarter of 2001. However, the 9/11 attacks precipitated a widespread recession in the following year; it is not clear how much of the continuing downturn in the travel and hospitality sector was due to fear of a repeat attack and how much resulted from lost prosperity.

The Bali bombings of 2002 and 2005 provide a clearer case. The 2002 attack killed 202 people and generated publicity throughout the world. Immediately after the bombing, tourism was off sharply. For many, though not all, countries of origin, it remained depressed for some time. Australia lost 88 tourists in the attack, and the number of Australian visitors to Indonesia fell from 384,667 in 2002 to 310,742 in 2003. From France, there were 113,434 tourists in 2002, only 81,314 the following year. Tourism from the United States declined from 175,474 arrivals to 141,635.

Tourism from a few countries within the region was almost unaffected. Singapore, Malaysia, India, and China all sent more tourists to Indonesia in 2003 than the year before. However, these were the exceptions. It took two years for visitor counts from Australia and South Korea to reach their former level and three for travel from the United Kingdom to recover. The numbers from Japan, the United States, Taiwan, France, Germany, and the Netherlands did not reach their former levels until the recovery after the recession of 2008.

The 2005 suicide bombings were responsible for at least some of the continued decline. Visitor arrivals in the months after the attack dropped by 31 percent throughout Indonesia and by nearly half in Bali itself.

These incidents give fair warning. Small, little publicized terrorist events will have little effect on tourism. Larger, more widely known attacks can cause lasting damage. Before the attack on Bali in 2002, tourism supplied between 60 percent and 70 percent of the island's economy and directly or indirectly employed some 40 percent of the workforce. Those numbers plummeted after the attacks. This will be a continuing concern for the travel and hospitality industry for many years to come. Hospitality facilities can effectively defend themselves against terrorist attack. It is doubtful that many will wish to do so at the cost of reminding guests that there is reason to worry.

A good security model is Jerusalem's King David Hotel, site of that 1946 bombing. The hotel's upper-story windows can survive a rocket-propelled grenade. The air conditioning can filter out poison gas. Robots tour the sewers searching for bombs. According to one report, the King David even scans its surroundings with infrared cameras carried by balloons. At many hotels in Israel and other places where security is a priority, guests enter through metal detectors. Some hotels scan guests' bags, much as airports do—this is common in India, where "sniffers" also may scan for explosives— and block cars at a safe distance from the hotel itself.

None of these measures seem likely to catch on in the United States or most of Europe. Many will seem too expensive to pay for at locations that do not specifically expect to become targets, and guests are likely to find them unacceptably intrusive. Few restaurants will be able to afford them under any circumstances. Casinos could, but guests often arrive with so many bags that most casino operators have felt scanning them all would be prohibitively difficult.

For casinos, at least, priorities have changed since the October 2017 shooting from a window at the Mandalay Bay in Las Vegas killed 58 people and wounded some 500 others at a music festival across the street. Since then, Mandalay Bay and other properties owned by MGM Resorts have improved their security, and the Wynn Resort has begun scanning guests with metal detectors and putting bags through X-ray machines.

This is likely to be only the beginning. We can expect to see more security cameras nearly everywhere, however, and facial recognition systems—intrusive, but inconspicuous—are likely to become common as their cost declines. This is one more place where AI will make itself felt.

For most future hospitality executives, high-level security will remain in the back of the mind, a concern when events show the potential cost of doing without, but never quite a high enough priority to act on. For those in cities like Jerusalem, Mumbai, Jakarta, and Las Vegas, they will be a daily issue.

Web Assignment

Log into the student website and complete the end of chapter assignment. Try to utilize some of the works you read about from this chapter and apply the key concepts, terms, and theory in your responses.

CHAPTER 7

Medical Tourism and Wellness Trends and Strategy

For most of us, getting sick is a good way to ruin a vacation. However, for growing numbers of people, needing to see the doctor is the whole point of going abroad. When they require surgery or dental work, they combine it with a trip to the Taj Mahal, a photo safari on the African veldt, or a stay at a luxury hotel—or at a hospital that feels like one—all at bargain-basement prices. Simply walking across the bridge from San Ysidro, CA, to Tijuana can cut the cost of dental work in half or less, sometimes much less.

This is medical tourism, and it is one of the hottest niche markets in the hospitality industry. At least, we believe it is. Or will be.

As you may have figured out already, reliable data about medical tourism is remarkably hard to come by. Observers disagree about the size and growth rate of this travel segment. Sometimes, they even disagree with themselves.

Market Projection

One specialist in medical tourism suggests that about 7 million people each year qualify as medical tourists.

On the other hand, the Organization for Economic Cooperation and Development (OECD)—which we trust in most of the fields it studies—estimates that nearly 50 million patients travel abroad for medical services each year.

A third report says the United States alone sent 11 million medical tourists abroad in 2016. That is a little hard to believe; only 35.1 million people left the U.S. for any reason that year, according to the National Travel & Tourism Office, and only 1.2 percent of them—about 421,000—cited health treatment as a primary reason for travel.

In part, this variation results from disagreement about exactly what qualifies as medical tourism. Some authorities count not only visits to hospitals, clinics, and individual providers, but travel to spas and wellness services, and we tend to follow their lead throughout this chapter. However, other analysts do not. This difference alone could reduce the count of medical tourists by 90 percent. In addition, in some regions where undocumented migrants are common, it becomes difficult to count the number of people making the trip. This is particularly an issue in the market for medical services among travelers from the United States to Mexico.

Revenue estimates are just as variable. In 2016, one analyst placed the market for medical tourism at only $5 billion a year. We believe this is considerably too low.

At the other end of the scale, in 2016 VISA and Oxford Economics carried out a major study of medical tourism. The first version of their report put annual revenues at $349 billion worldwide. (One garbled account from no less than the American Medical Association transposed the digits and made it $439 billion!) A hasty revision brought the figure down to around $50 billion per year. In mid-2017, the latest version available online suggests that medical tourism brings in global revenues of $100 billion annually. Call that the highest credible number.

This report also projects revenue growth of 25 percent per year, another number we believe marks the high end of credibility. Starting at $100 billion and expanding at that pace, the medical-tourism market could be worth about $600 billion in 2025. This seems very optimistic, but perhaps not totally impossible.

Unfortunately, the study also predicts that 3 to 4 percent of the world's population will go abroad for medical services in 2025. That is between 230 million and 310 million people. We find even the lower number harder to believe.

Tentatively, then, we will cast our vote with Patients Beyond Borders (PBB), an online clearinghouse of information about medical tourism. They estimate that 14 to 16 million people travel internationally for care each year. They believed about 1.4 million Americans would go travel outside the country for medical care in 2017. Only one in ten go for medical treatment, and 70 percent of them want cosmetic surgery or other elective procedures. The remainder seek a variety of "wellness" services like spa visits, supervised exercise, and dieting. Medical tourists, the company estimated, would spend an average of $3,800 to $6,000 per visit that year, including direct costs for medical services, accommodations, and local and international transportation. This puts revenues anywhere from $45.5 billion to $72 billion per year, PBB estimates. The firm's best guess is that the market is now growing by 15 to 25 percent annually.

For a quick analysis, let's accept that there were about 14 million medical tourists in 2017 and put the revenue and growth numbers in the middle of their ranges, at $50 billion and 20 percent. This multiplies out to about 60 million medical tourists in 2025, producing revenues of $260 billion, or about $4,333 per person. We find these numbers much easier to accept. Until better data becomes available, we will make this our official forecast: Through 2025, expect medical tourism to grow by 20 percent per year, reaching 60 million people and a market value in the neighborhood of $260 billion.

Note that the exact numbers matter a lot. Raising revenues to an average of $5,000 per person adds $40 billion to the bottom line. Accepting the high-end estimate of $60 billion a year in 2016 revenues brings the 2025 forecast to nearly $310 billion. Thank you, compound interest!

Why Get Healthcare Elsewhere?

The United States has the best medical care in the world, or so we are told despite many statistics that say otherwise. Most countries in Europe offer universal health care, either paid for entirely through taxes or heavily subsidized and with relatively modest charges. In fact, 75 of the world's 192 countries have passed legislation mandating universal access to healthcare services independent of income, and in 58, from South Korea to Botswana, at least 90 percent of the population have effective access to necessary medical services. Why go elsewhere for them?

It turns out that medical tourists have several good reasons to seek care away from home, and sometimes far away, even when their countries provide generally adequate care at reasonable cost—as too many do not.

One motivation, particularly in the United States, probably is general dissatisfaction. A study by the Commonwealth Fund rated healthcare systems in eleven prosperous

countries according to satisfaction ratings by both patients and primary-care physicians. Britain, with its much-maligned National Health Service, was rated best in nine of the eleven measures and first over all. In four categories and overall rank, the United States came in dead last. With a fifth-place rating for timeliness of care, the U.S. even landed below the UK, which came in third.

Another benefit of medical tourism is comfort. A private room in a clinic or hospital with the amenities of a four-star hotel is a lot easier to stay in than the bare two- and four-bed cells typical of American hospitals.

Ordinary sight-seeing also is a factor. Why spend time in a hospital at home when you can combine your procedure with a good vacation at lower cost? Almost 90 percent of patients or their companions take advantage of the standard attractions while in the country for care.

Yet, there are more compelling reasons to go abroad, especially for critical care.

In some regions, state-of-the-art medical facilities are hard to come by, if they exist at all. For this reason, patients throughout the Middle East regularly travel to Jordan or Dubai, Asia, and even the U.S. for complicated surgery; close to 1 million Indonesians make a yearly trip to Malaysia or Singapore for routine matters as well as more challenging treatments; and 100,000 Russians annually find care in Israel, Turkey, and the United States.

In other countries, the public health system is overburdened, and needed care can be delayed, particularly for difficult, uncommon, or expensive procedures. In Britain, regulations require the National Health Service to provide surgery no more than 18 weeks after diagnosis. In 2016, more than 193,000 patients waited longer every month. (At that, this is a substantial improvement over the experience reported in the first edition of this text, published in 2006.) In Canada, the waiting list for neurosurgery in 2016 averaged 47 weeks after referral by a general practitioner. Esoteric procedures can take even longer. Waiting times of three months or more are common for stem-cell transplants needed for more than 80 diseases, including several blood cancers. In one well-publicized case from 2016, an 18-year-old girl with acute myeloid leukemia died while waiting for a transplant eight months after learning that several matching donors were available. Until May 2017, cancer patients who had relapsed after chemotherapy were barred from stem-cell transplants that might have saved their lives.

Stem cells bring up another reason to leave home for care. Some procedures not yet approved or banned for nonmedical reasons may be available in others for patients who want and can afford them. Canadians with multiple sclerosis, for example, must leave the country for treatment of abnormal blood drainage from the brain and spinal cord, which a few specialists believe is a factor in the disease. And in the U.S., stem cell transplants are accepted only for patients with certain cancers and a few other disorders. Despite this, nearly 600 clinics across the country offer them for purposes ranging from repair of spinal cord injuries to breast augmentation. However, insurance rarely covers these procedures, and costs of $25,000 or more can make it worth searching for less expensive providers in other countries.

China is another such case. New treatments there are not blocked by ethical or religious sensitivities, but bureaucratic inertia has the same effect. Beijing estimates that half a million of its citizens traveled abroad for medical care in 2016, many of them for cancer and heart disease that required treatment not yet approved at home.

The delay between early research and clinical use of new therapies provides many such examples. In probably the most dramatic, scientists in the last few years have found that giving the elderly blood plasma from the young reverses many effects of aging. To date, these benefits have been clearly demonstrated only in experimental animals. Yet, at least one clinic in the United States already provides these treatments for human patients in the guise of research—at a cost of $8,000 per two-liter dose. Predicting that similar infusions will soon be available much less expensively in any number of developing countries is probably the easiest forecast we will ever make.

This of course brings us to the real attraction of medical tourism for patients from countries where modern healthcare is readily available: price. In polls, nearly 80 percent of medical tourists say they left home to save money on care. They have good reason to do so. Patients Beyond Borders offers some ranges for expected savings on care in ten popular destinations. Compared with costs in the U.S., the savings add up:

- Brazil: 20 to 30 percent;
- Costa Rica: 45 to 65 percent;
- India: 65 to 90 percent;
- Malaysia: 65 to 80 percent;
- Mexico: 40 to 65 percent;
- Singapore: 25 to 40 percent;
- South Korea: 30 to 45 percent;
- Taiwan: 40 to 55 percent;
- Thailand: 50 to 75 percent;
- Turkey: 50 to 65 percent;

For some procedures, the savings can be even greater:

A heart-valve replacement that would cost $200,000 or more in the U.S. goes for as little as $5,000 in India. Call it $10,000 including round-trip air fare and a brief vacation.

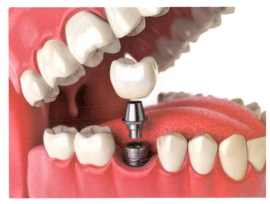

© Maxx-Studio/Shutterstock.com

A coronary artery bypass can cost anywhere from $70,000 to $200,000 in the United States and sometimes more. In India, the price is $7,000 to $9,000.

Dental implants are worth $4,500 or more per tooth in the States. They go for around $770 in Thailand, $600 in Mexico, and as little as $500 in Hungary.

A knee replacement that averages close to $60,000 in the United States—not counting physical therapy—costs as little as $5,000 in Thailand and $3,300 in India.

LASIK eye surgery averages about $2,500 per eye in the U.S. It can be had elsewhere for between $300 and $465.

And a hair transplant that would cost up to $25,000 in the U.S. or Europe costs only $600 to $2,000 in Istanbul.

Quality Concerns

Inferior medical care would not be worth having at any price, and there are still a few skeptics who warn that Third-World surgery cannot be as good as that available in the United States. Many of them speak on behalf of organizations representing American physicians, including the American Medical Association. In fact, there were cases of botched plastic surgery, particularly at some Mexican clinics, in the days before anyone figured out what a gold mine cheap, high-quality care could be for practitioners in developing countries.

Yet, hospitals and clinics that cater to the tourist market often are among the best in the world. Many are staffed by physicians trained at major medical centers in the United States and Europe. Bangkok's Bumrungrad International Hospital has some 900 physicians, including about 220 surgeons who are board-certified in the U.S. One of Singapore's major hospitals is a branch of the prestigious Johns Hopkins University, which collaborates with 18 hospitals around the world. More than 450 hospitals around the world are accredited by the nonprofit Joint Commission International (JCI), a branch of the organization that evaluates and certifies the quality of care provided by medical institutions in the United States. The entire healthcare system in Singapore does a better job than the U.S. in measures such as life expectancy, infant mortality, and maternal deaths in childbirth.

Another indicator that suggests quality care is the number of procedures a facility performs. In a field where experience is as important as technology, Fortis Escorts Heart Institute, in New Delhi, carried out some 70,000 heart operations in 2016. Its death rate among patients during some heart operations is about that of most major hospitals in the United States—a little higher in some years, a little lower in some. In other heart procedures, the hospital's death rate is consistently less than at comparable American institutions.

It can help, too, that clinics specializing in medical tourism in some countries are backed by sophisticated research infrastructures. India is one of the world's leading centers for biotechnology research, while both India and South Korea are pushing ahead with stem cell research at a level of sophistication at least equal to that anywhere else in the world.

Skilled doctors and state-of-the-art equipment are only two of many benefits these medical centers offer foreign patients. In many, the doctors are supported by more registered nurses per patient than any Western facility could afford. Some facilities provide a nurse for each patient 24 hours a day. Many assign patients a personal assistant for the post-hospital recovery period. Some Asian national airlines offer frequent-flyer miles to ease the cost of returning for follow-up care. Some offer special discounts for medical tourists visiting affiliated clinics.

Under the circumstances, it is no surprise that the medical tourism market is growing rapidly. Ten years ago, it was hardly large enough to be noticed. Today, something over 370,000 patients per year visit Singapore alone; nearly half arrive from the Middle East. Thailand attracts perhaps 3 million. Around half a million annually travel to India for medical care; the tourism ministry issued over 170,000 visas specifically for medical tourists in 2016, up 45 percent in a year. Argentina, Costa Rica, Cuba, Jamaica, South Africa, Jordan, Malaysia, Hungary, Latvia, and Estonia all have broken into this lucrative market or are trying to do so, and it seems that a few more countries join the list every year.

Top Destinations

A number of countries entered the market for medical tourism early on or worked hard to develop their offerings quickly, and they have benefited from low wages and other costs. As a result, they have become the most popular destinations in the market today. Here are some details about ten at the top.

Costa Rica has ecological wonders found in few other lands, from some of the largest, best protected rain forests in Central America to the fire show of the Arenal volcano. For those with more urban tastes, the casinos of San Jose, Puntarenas, and Guanacaste provide all the action even a jaded Las Vegas regular could want.

But for North American patients, what Costa Rica really offers is inexpensive, high-quality medical care in their back yard. Two major hospitals are accredited by the Joint Commission International, while many others have specific accreditations for ambulatory health care or ambulatory surgery. In all, the World Health Organization rates Costa Rica's healthcare system as one of the three best in Latin America. Costa Rica received about 2.6 million foreign visitors in 2015; about 130,000 went for medical care or wellness services.

Cosmetic surgery and dental work are the traditional specialties here, but just about any medical service that can be found in the United States can be had in San Jose. Many will be delivered by English-speaking specialists board-certified in the U.S. In the last few years, eye surgery and weight loss procedures have become common among medical tourists there. Wellness clinics and prevention services abound. There even are so-called "recovery retreats," hotels with all the amenities but with nurses and interns on hand to provide medical services for post-surgery patients.

For most procedures, costs can be half those in the United States—not the prices they would find in India or Thailand, but a lot closer to home for medical vacationers with limited travel time or budgets. Get a facelift, and chill on the beach until the bruises go away, and the folks at home will never quite be sure why you suddenly look so good.

Hungary may be the Continent's oldest destination for medical tourism. The wealthy of Europe have been visiting the country's spas for centuries. They still are, and patients are beginning to join them from North America, western Russia, and the Middle East.

Hungary's healthcare system was modeled on the British National Health service, so almost any form of care is readily available. Although cosmetic surgery is a growing market, this country is best known for its dentistry. No wonder. In Manhattan, there is one dentist for every 630 residents. In Prague, Czech Republic, the number is one in 1,200. Hungarian towns near the Austrian border, where dental tourism is at its busiest, average about one for every 200 residents.

This competition, combined Hungary's generally low prices, has the expected benefit for patients. A dental implant that would cost from $3000 to $6000 in the United States goes for as little as $450 in Hungary; the most costly we have heard of was only $1,200. Removing a tooth averages only $50. A root canal that would be up to $900 for a front tooth and $1,400 for a molar averages just $99, with front teeth costing as little as $50. For anyone in Europe, it does not take much work to justify the cost of visiting Budapest.

Add to this spa towns fed by more than 1,000 hot springs, historic castles and palaces, the Danube, and four-star hotels that can cost as little as $85 per night in downtown Budapest, and Hungary becomes one of the more inviting destinations for the medical tourist.

India has a two-tier medical system. In the vast rural areas, doctors are thin on the ground, and an estimated 700,000 who practice as physicians are unlicensed, and many are untrained. In the cities, the wealthy, at least, have access to state-of-the-art hospitals and clinics, and doctors are as skilled as any in the world. It is this second group that medical tourists get to meet.

India is not the oldest "brand" in medical tourism, but it has grown into one of the most inviting and successful. An estimated 500,000 medical tourists visit India each year, and the flow is believed to be growing by 20 percent annually.

Several factors contribute to this success. It helps a lot that English is among the many native languages in India, one spoken by all educated Indians. Unlike some competing nations, India offers a high degree of transparency; visitors need not worry about unexpected problems with their funds or legal status. Some hospitals begin evaluating patients over the Internet, so they are ready to begin treatment as soon as the patient arrives. Some will even take care of travel arrangements from visa applications to making hotel reservations for the patient's family. And, of course, India is the only country in the world where medical tourists can visit the Taj Mahal while convalescing from a kidney transplant.

Yet, India's most obvious attraction is its cost of care, which can be as little as 15 percent of the price in the U.S. and for many procedures is the lowest in the world. Even trips for follow-up care are cheaper than for ordinary vacationers, because Air India subsidizes them with frequent flyer miles.

Another attraction is the range of high-level services available in such a large, technologically advanced country. There are top-notch centers for open heart surgery, pediatric heart surgery, hip and knee replacement, cosmetic surgery, dentistry, bone marrow transplants, cancer therapy, and just about any other specialty a patient could need.

Many of those centers are among the best in the world. Virtually all are equipped with the latest electronic and medical diagnostic equipment—and India, unlike some of its competitors in this market, has the technological sophistication and infrastructure to maintain it. Additionally, Indian pharmaceuticals meet the stringent requirements of the U.S. Food and Drug Administration. It helps, too, that most facilities specializing in medical tourism provide accommodations that could be mistaken for five-star hotels.

Some Indian medical centers even provide services that are uncommon elsewhere. For example, instead of having the entire hip joint replaced, patients can undergo "hip resurfacing," in which damaged bone is scraped away and replaced with chrome alloy. The result is a smoothly functioning joint with less trauma and recovery time than total replacement, and at lower cost. The operation is now widely available in the United States, but Indian tourist clinics offered the procedure long before it received FDA approval; this long practice has given Indian orthopedic clinics success rates better than those of most other institutions in the world. Other advanced services available in Indian clinics include radiotherapy and radiosurgery to destroy cancerous tumors from outside the body, robot-assisted surgery, and bone marrow transplants for genetic disorders yet to receive FDA approval in the United States.

Of course, before surgery or after, India has a broad array of unique and exotic destinations for Western tourists. From attending one of the Dalai Lama's public talks at Dharamsala—you will need to plan well ahead—to a half-day safari in the White Tiger-Bandhavgarh National Park, shopping for handicrafts in the tribal villages of Orissa and Madhya Pradesh, or skin-diving in the Indian Ocean, this 4,000 year-old civilization has something to offer anyone who visits.

Israel these days probably is best known for its long-running conflict with its neighbors and a relatively high risk of terrorist attack. (Of course, "relatively" conceals important detail. Even in Israel, people are statistically more likely to be struck by lightning than by terrorist violence.) Yet, among medical tourists, this country is known for exemplary care, a high doctor-patient ratio, a high-tech manufacturing industry that supplies state-of-the-art equipment, and some of the best hospitals in the world.

These and other advantages bring Israel about 50,000 medical tourists per year, many of them from Russia and other parts of the former Soviet Union. English is spoken almost universally, so travel from the United States also is growing quickly.

If Israel has a medical specialty, it is probably in-vitro fertilization, which is readily available for about one-quarter of American prices and provides success rates higher than those of comparable clinics in the States. Several hospitals and clinics specialize in this field. Others are known for their skill with organ transplants, cancer care, and orthopedic surgery.

The country's other marketable asset for medical tourism is the Dead Sea, where the saline waters–nearly ten times as salty as the ocean–are said to have healing properties. Health and wellness travel to the Sea, on the borders of Jordan and Palestine, is growing quickly, and if the water will not cure psoriasis, as many believe, at least the heated mud baths temporarily ease the pain of arthritis. A side trip to the region's spas and clinics makes a pleasant follow-on to a trip for more serious care.

Malaysia, for many in the West, can seem a lot like staying at home. Although its fundamentally Asian core is always easy to see, the country was a British colony until 1957. It retains a thick veneer of English tradition, particularly in major cities such as Kuala Lumpur and Georgetown.

However, for medical tourism its important asset is not culture but location. Four out of five medical tourists to Malaysia–call it 940,000 in 2016—arrive from Indonesia, just three miles across the Strait of Malacca. Substantial numbers also come from nearby Australia, and many travel from the Middle East; a moderate Islamic culture makes this country a comfortable destination for patients from other Muslim lands. It also helps that Malaysia is only a half-hour flight from Singapore, where prices for equivalent care are up to 50 percent higher. Compared with health costs in the United States, prices are two-thirds or more lower.

Like most destinations these days, Malaysia offers a full range of care, with specific hospitals and clinics known for surgery, pain management, eye care, cancer treatment, dentistry, and weight control. More than one-third of medical tourists come for dental care, with cosmetic surgery and orthopedic treatments close behind. Malaysia also is well known for health screening, which has made it a favorite place for pre-employment physicals for companies throughout the region. For around $500, hospitals and clinics provide an astonishing array of tests, many of which Western patients will never have heard of, much less undergone.

A few years ago, medical tourism to Malaysia was growing by 35 percent per year. It continues to increase quickly, if not quite that fast, thanks substantially to the efforts of the Malaysia Healthcare Travel Council, part of the Ministry of Health. Medical tourism is expected to expand by 30 percent per year, with revenues reaching $3.5 billion by 2024.

Mexico is the obvious destination for American medical tourists, and they travel there en masse. Although statistics are sketchy at best, an estimated eight out of ten Americans who seek health care abroad go one country to the south. Most travel relatively short distances to destinations just across the border from Arizona, California, Nevada, and Texas. Mexico, in turn, receives nearly all its medical tourists from the United States or Canada. One reasonable estimate puts the number of tourists visiting Mexican hospitals and clinics at around 1 million a year. However, many are native Mexicans, and an unknown number of them are undocumented migrants. All this makes the cross-border trade in medical services very difficult to quantify.

Like most destinations, Mexico sees the greatest demand for dentistry and cosmetic surgery. Tijuana alone has twenty dental clinics within three miles of the border, nine in the first mile, and twenty cosmetic-surgery clinics in the same neighborhood. Nuevo Laredo, just over the river from Laredo, TX, is home to nineteen dental practices and ten clinics specializing in cosmetic surgery. Juarez, next door to El Paso, offers twenty dental clinics and fifteen cosmetic surgeons, seven of them sharing office space with dentists. In Nogales, the numbers are nineteen and twelve. In Mexicali we stopped counting at forty and twenty-two. Simply looking at a map tells us why American medical tourists head south.

Singapore is tiny, just 277 square miles. (For comparison, New York City is 309 square miles, London 607.) Yet, this wealthy city-state has one of the world's best medical systems. Fourteen of its twenty hospitals are JCI-accredited. In most measures, Singapore ranks better than healthcare in the United States, Canada, and much of Europe. Its rates of maternal and infant mortality are lower, its life expectancy higher. The medical school at National University of Singapore, a joint venture with Duke University, is prestigious enough that would-be physicians come to study there from Oxford, Cambridge, and the American Ivy League universities.

This is far more medical care than a city of 5.5 million needs, so the government has put a good deal of work into attracting medical tourists to keep its doctors occupied. It has had considerable success. Nearly 600,000 people each year travel to Singapore for care. Most are from neighboring countries, but the number arriving from Europe and the U.S. is growing.

With healthcare so plentiful and skilled, there is little point in thinking about specialties for which medical travelers should consider Singapore. If doctors anywhere in the world can treat, heal, or cure it, their colleagues in Singapore can do it, too, and very possibly better.

However, most patients will find that care is no cheaper than it would be at home. In a private hospital, a heart bypass will cost most patients between $35,000 and $52,000, while replacing a hip will run from $14,000 to $25,000. These prices will seem cheap to patients from the United States, where a bypass average about $75,000 and hip replacement is around $40,000, but travel expenses will eat up much of the saving. For patients elsewhere, Singapore is an option mostly when the highest-quality care is worth the extra cost.

South Korea is not the cheapest destination for American medical tourists. Neither is it the closest. Savings typically range from 30 percent to 45 percent compared with prices in the U.S., and getting to South Korea from North America means spending 11 to 14 hours in the air. As a result, most American medical tourists to the country are expatriates or military personnel assigned to bases in the region. For the rest, at least Korean Air offers nonstop flights from many cities in the United States and Canada.

For certain procedures and for tourists within Asia, South Korea can be much more attractive. Patients needing a heart bypass, valve replacement, or artificial hip or knee can save over 80 percent of the price at American hospitals. For uninsured patients from Japan, care costs much less than it would at home, and travel expenses are nominal. China's National Tourism Administration rates South Korea the most popular destination for its country's outbound medical tourists.

About 600,000 foreign patients visit the country each year. Like the government of Malaysia, Seoul is working hard to attract more medical tourists. Roughly 1 million are expected by 2020. Two years later, medical tourism is forecast to bring the country $2 billion a year in revenues.

What tourists receive for their money is access to one of the most sophisticated, high-tech healthcare systems in the world. All the usual medical services are available, but South Korea is particularly well known for spinal surgery and care, robot-assisted surgery, and organ transplants. One transplant center achieves 96-percent survival rates one year after liver replacement, compared with 88 percent in the U.S.

By some accounts, Seoul is the plastic surgery capital of the world. However, this South Korean specialty has become controversial in the last few years. In 2014, the national health ministry reports, one in four Chinese patients came for cosmetic surgery. So did 28 percent of Russians and 23 percent of Americans. However, this is one specialty that medical authorities do not police, and unregulated clinics are reported to have caused problems. In China particularly, stories of patients who were overcharged or received poor treatment are common. The number of patients seeking cosmetic surgery in South Korea has declined, though estimates of how much vary widely.

Other attractions in South Korea include some spectacular seaside resorts, national parks rated among the world's most beautiful, the serenity of countless Buddhist temples, and a market for medicinal herbs that has been in operation since 1658. The country's mountainous geography, particularly in the north, also means that visitors will not face the heat and humidity found in Southeast Asia.

Thailand got its start in medical tourism in 1997, when the economic crash that hammered much of Asia sent canny healthcare providers looking for new markets. Today, it is one of the world's largest and best-established destinations for foreign patients, particularly from the Japan and the United States. Fifty-three JCI-accredited hospitals are distributed among four major cities: Bangkok, Pataya, Phuket, and Chiang Mai. Nearly 3 million people reportedly visited Thailand for medical care in 2017, another 13 million for wellness treatments. In all, they accounted for more than half of tourist arrivals that year and contributed about $4.7 billion to the economy.

By 2018, Thailand expected to receive some 1 million tourists for medical care and more than 25 million for wellness treatments.

The largest centers for medical tourism are Bangkok and Phuket. No fewer than six medical facilities in Bangkok have hospital accreditation from the United States. Bumrungrad Hospital alone sees 850,000 patients per year, 40 percent of them from abroad. As in most tourist-oriented medical communities, the major attractions are cosmetic surgery and dental treatments. However, eye surgery, kidney dialysis, and organ transplantation are among the most common specialties sought by medical travelers in Thailand. When not pinned down by medical treatments or recovery, patients usually spend their time shopping or sight-seeing.

For vacation possibilities Phuket is clearly your destination, with some of the most spectacular beaches and shorefront scenery on the planet. For a few patients, Phuket has another attraction as well: In all the world, Bangkok Phuket Hospital probably is *the* place to go for sex-change surgery, one of the top ten procedures for which patients visit Thailand.

Turkey may not be the first place Americans think of when considering care overseas. For patients in the Middle East, Russia, North Africa, and parts of Europe, it comes to mind much more readily. One reason is the country's enormous supply of public and private hospitals, over 1,200, including 51 accredited by the Joint Commission International—more than in any other country in the world. Another is the Turkish government's hard work in putting the word out that medical tourists are welcome and will find what they need in Istanbul, Ankara, Izmir, and probably many smaller cities. It helps that Turkish Airlines offers a 50-percent rebate on fares for medical tourists.

These efforts have been remarkably successful. According to the Turkey Health Tourism Development Council, about 750,000 international patients arrived in 2016. Another estimate suggests that 32 percent of patients seen in Turkey are medical tourists. Add perhaps half a million visitors to the country's hot springs, spas, and wellness centers, as some industry analysts do, and the number would be in the neighborhood of 1.25 million medical tourists a year. The Council hopes to attract 2 million actual patients a year by 2023.

For some reason, Turkish hospitals have become especially popular for eye operations, at least among medical tourists. LASIK surgery averages about $2,500 per eye in the United States and perhaps $2,000 in Britain, but around $1,250 in Turkey. Cataract removal is about $3,600 in the U.S. and $4,500 in the U.K. In Turkey, it is only $1,500. There are good reasons to make the journey, especially if a side trip to the Topkapi Palace, the Aya Sofya Museum, or the ruins at Ephesus sounds like a good way to test your eyesight.

The country's second specialty is hair transplants, which go for only a few percent of U.S. and Europen prices. Some 60,000 patients a year visit Turkey for the procedure, most of them from the Middle East. This is one area in which patients need to pick their facilities carefully. Though the law requires that physicians carry out all hair transplants, nurses and technicians do the job at many specialty clinics. One result is an uncommonly high proportion of botched operations. We believe this problem will resolve itself eventually, much as plastic-surgery clinics in Mexico pulled themselves together when word of botched facelifts discouraged American patients. However, we cannot guess how long it will take.

If a medical specialty or service exists, tourists will find it in Turkey, with a generally high standard of care and prices well below those at home. A coronary angioplasty that would cost an average of $30,000 in the United States or about half that in Britain is $5,000 or so in Turkey. A knee replacement that averages about $50,000 in the U.S. and around $17,000 in the U.K. is only $7,500 in Turkey. For patients in Europe, where travel costs to Turkey are low—a flight from London can be had for as little as £85, or about $110—these are obvious bargains.

United States—Americans may find it ironic, dissatisfied as many are with their country's high-cost care, poor insurance coverage, and statistically mediocre results compared with other healthcare systems, but the United States is one of the world's most popular destinations for medical tourists. A look at some of the institutions that actively compete for overseas patients makes the reason obvious. They include the Mayo Clinic, Johns Hopkins, Memorial Sloan Kettering, the Cleveland Clinic, and MD Anderson Cancer Center. These are some of the most prestigious medical institutions in the world, and their quality of care lives up to their reputations. For those who can afford their cost, they are the obvious places to go for treatment, especially when life is at stake.

© BravoKiloVideo/Shutterstock.com

As a result, some 800,000 patients from all over the world seek treatment from American medical centers each year. If the case is complicated or doctors at home have failed, a trip to the United States is often the last resort. For those wealthy enough that cost does not matter, it is often the first.

Top Trends for Medical Tourism

Medical tourism sounds like a specialty where health workers are the only essential personnel, and they do account for many of the jobs in the field. However, opportunities are expanding almost as quickly as the market. Hospitals and clinics catering to medical tourists need planners, coordinators, and marketers to bring in patients, help arrange accommodations and travel for the patient's traveling partners, and often the patient before and after treatment, and to promote the institution's abilities to health travelers in other countries. Several companies serve as intermediaries between medical providers and employers needing low-cost care for their workers. A number of firms have arisen to coordinate medical tourism for patients, making travel reservations much like traditional agents, but also helping to select the right institution for individual needs, arrange for care, setting up accommodations for people accompanying the patient, and planning pre- and post-care vacations. Many more such opportunities are likely to appear in the decade ahead.

Like all these market-segment chapters, this one has given only a snapshot of its topic. Anyone working as a manager in this field, or interested in doing so, will need to assemble a movie of its evolution to help them anticipate changes and develop effective strategies for dealing with them. This, of course, is where the trends come in. Here are five of the most important for this fast-growing market.

Travel (especially international) and tourism are growing fast, as they have done for many years.

This trend, of course, is critical to all segments of the industry. Two statistics are significant for medical tourism.

The UN World Tourism Organization believes that the number of international tourist arrivals will grow by 3.3 percent per year, on average, for the two decades ending in 2030. At that rate, there will be 1.8 billion at the end of the period. Note that travel to developing lands is expected to grow by 4.4 percent annually, compared with only 2.2 percent in the industrialized countries.

The World Travel and Tourism Council predicts that industry's direct contribution to global GDP will grow by 3.8 percent in 2017 and 4.0 percent per year, on average, from 2018 through 2027.

These numbers provide an effective floor for this segment. The number of medical tourists has been growing faster than the travel and hospitality industry as a whole. So has the value of the market.

Let us use the 4.4-percent growth estimate for the developing countries, as that group includes most destinations for medical tourism. If we accept the narrowest definition, there will be about 8.3 million medical tourists in 2020 and 10.3 million in 2025. If we use the broader definition favored by the Organization for Economic Cooperation and Development, the numbers come to about 59.4 million in 2020 and 73.7 million in 2025.

Market value in the years ahead is even less certain. Assume, as we did at the beginning of this chapter, that the current value is in the middle of the range calculated by Patients Beyond Borders, some $50 billion in 2016. Accepting the WTTC estimates, medical tourism would generate $58.4 billion in 2020 and $71 billion in 2025.

Although this segment is likely to grow faster than the international travel market in general, we prefer to be a bit more conservative in our expectations. We will stick with the values we calculated at the beginning of this chapter: Expect to see some 60 million medical tourists in 2025 and worldwide revenues of $300 billion. Yet, there are enough variables to shift these targets by plus or minus 20 percent in the years ahead. Consider these a reasonable baseline for your future calculations.

Economic Growth Is Slowing in Many Countries

Not in all, however, and it turns out that both slowing and accelerating economies can be good for medical tourism. It depends on the countries involved, both as tourist sources and as destinations.

China and India will be critical to the future of medical tourism, and they will take most of our attention here. This is a function of their economic growth at least as much as their billion-plus populations. Both economies are expanding faster than in any other large nation in the world. Even as China's slows to around 4 percent per year in the 2020s, it will remain one of the two growth leaders among countries with populations upward of 50 million. India, of course, will be the other.

As we saw in Chapter 6, the rapid growth of China's economy has raised hundreds of millions of people out of abject poverty and into the middle class. By 2020, some 400 million people may well be able to afford medical care in another country. China is destined to become one of the world's largest markets for medical tourism before the 2020s are over.

The Indian economy is growing even faster, by upward of 7 percent in recent years. It will continue to expand rapidly when China's high-growth period is clearly behind it, averaging 6.4 percent per year through the 2020s. Again, this suggests that the Indian market for medical tourism will grow at least that fast.

In both China and India, healthcare is readily available. At least, that is the theory. In practice, there are large gaps.

About 95 percent of the Chinese population has at least minimal health insurance. On average, it covers about 70 percent of medical expenses, but less for severe or chronic ills. Cancer or heart disease can still leave Chinese families destitute.

Beijing hopes to provide basic healthcare at affordable prices for all its citizens by 2020. That might be expected to minimize the number of people who leave China for care. However, hospitals in China vary widely, with services in major cities generally more modern and effective than those in rural areas. And even in major cities, the best hospitals tend to be profit-making ventures run, or at least partially owned, by foreign healthcare companies. Bills at these hospitals can run ten times those in rural facilities. Throughout the country, medications are expensive and, for some, unaffordable.

The situation is worse in India. Perhaps one in four families are covered by insurance, and even they pay 70 percent of medical expenses out of pocket. The government runs an extensive network of medical facilities. Yet, India has so many people that a community health center with four doctors and thirty beds must cover a population of 80,000 to 120,000. Care at public facilities is free, but shortages of staff and supplies mean that needed services often are unavailable. In a 2016 study by The Lancet, a prestigious medical journal, India's healthcare system rated 154th out of 195 countries. China came in 82nd. Bangladesh, with a per-capita GDP around $4,000 compared with India's $6,700, was 52nd.

All this means that in China, and especially in India, the poor are stuck, unable to afford the price of sophisticated medical care or continuing treatment. In India, they also are likely to find that timely care is unavailable.

The Indian upper middle class and wealthy can buy care at the same high-quality hospitals medical tourists do, and for much less than the same services would cost in the West or in many other tourist destinations. However, Indian culture values travel, and as we have seen destinations like Hungary and Turkey have developed reputations for excellence in particular specialties like cosmetic surgery and eye care. These factors both suggest that many well-off Indians are likely to go elsewhere for care even if strictly economic concerns do not justify it. Medical tourism, like most kinds of travel, will be seen as a luxury and proof of affluence. Even for those in the next tier down, medical tourism may be an attractive option, especially for those who are going abroad for other purposes.

Their peers in China have another reason to travel for healthcare. It may be more expensive in other countries, but at least it is available. It will help a lot, also, that insurance has begun to cover travel expenses for those who cannot find care close to home.

The UN World Tourism Organization expects some 50 million Indians to go abroad in 2020. Around 150 million Chinese will join them. If even one percent of them seek medical care, they will add some 2 million patients to the medical-tourism market. We consider this very possible.

In fact, for Chinese travelers this is a simple projection of the established record. They took an estimated 500,000 outbound medical trips in 2016. The greatest number went to Thailand. Bumrungrad Hospital alone saw 7,500 Chinese patients in 2015—compared with 9,000 for all the hospitals in Singapore—and has added a ward with a Chinese-speaking staff. We expect Indian medical tourists, too, to think of Thailand first when seeking any but the most specialized care elsewhere.

Now consider Europe and, to a lesser extent, the United States and Canada. They are well supplied with skilled doctors and high-quality hospitals, and patients in Europe and Canada are covered by government-supported medical systems. In the United States, we believe the long-term trend leads to establishment of a single-payer health-care system, but only after further delay by politically powerful lobbies. Until then, care will remain expensive and insurance coverage spotty. In the UK and Canada especially, even urgently needed treatment can be delayed by shortages of capacity and other factors.

Economic growth in the developed lands has slowed from the heady pace seen in the late 20th century and the first decade of this one. Through the 2020s, we therefore expect middle-class patients throughout Europe and North America to feel increasingly short of disposable income. They will be eager to save money on healthcare, especially for elective procedures like plastic surgery. It is at least possible, also, that some European countries will choose to cut back on the coverage provided by social programs. (See below.) The UK and Germany, where politicians facing economic problems automatically think first of austerity, seem particularly likely to follow this course.

All these developments will be especially welcome for Hungary and the Czech Republic, which draw most of their foreign patients from other parts of Europe, and for Turkey, where the number of patients from Europe and North America has begun to grow. They will be less significant for Thailand and India, which already receive the largest shares of Western medical tourism and will be proportionally less affected.

Demographic Changes

For medical tourism, it makes sense to consider three trends simultaneously: the growth of the world's population to 9.6 billion in 2050, the global extension of life expectancy, and the dramatic growth of the elderly population in rich and poor countries alike. These trends all foretell rapid expansion of the travel-for-treatment market. Together, they are the largest single reason to expect growth in the medical-tourism market to be even faster than many observers do.

The effect of simple population growth is obvious. If the planet is home to roughly 7 billion people and the number of medical tourists is about 14 million, then when the world's population reaches 9.6 billion, the number of medical tourists should be about 19.2 billion. The real number will, of course, be much higher.

The reason is the stretching of our life expectancy and the growing elderly cohort. As we saw in Chapter 6, better nutrition, new pharmaceuticals and medical technologies, and government health programs raise life expectancy with every generation. In 1950, life expectancy at birth in the United States was 68.2, and an 80-year-old American could look forward to another 6.5 years. Today, life expectancy at birth is up by more than ten years, to 78.9, and the average 80-year old will reach 89.6. In many other places, the average is even greater. In 25 countries, life expectancy at birth is upward of 80 years. In Monaco, it is 89-plus. A life expectancy just under 79 puts the United States in 53rd place. By 2050, most of the world's countries are expected to have more people age 65 and above than younger than 15. In Japan, South Korea, and Germany, more than half of the population in 2050 will be over 50.

As a result, the world's senior population will more than double from 901 million in 2015 to 2.1 billion in 2050. The over-80 population will more than triple, reaching 434 million. Those in their traditional retirement years made up only 15 percent of the global population in 2000. Fifty years later, they will be 27 percent.

© zimmytws/Shutterstock.com

This trend alone guarantees that the cost of medical care will rise quickly in the years ahead. In the United States, health care for the average child costs about $3,550 per year. For working-age adults, it is around $6,600. However, among the elderly, it is nearly $19,000 per year, and much of that goes to the oldest old. Patients in their late 60s make up 26 percent of the Medicare population but account for only 15 percent of the program's cost. Those age 80 and above make up 24 percent of the population but account for one-third of Medicare spending. All these numbers change over time and vary from one country to another. However, the general trend is clear: The older the population, the higher their medical expenses.

This is mostly good news for individuals; in general, we all want to live longer. However, it is much less so for national economies, which will have to spend more and more on healthcare over the next few decades. And that, in turn, is great news for medical tourism.

Exactly how these trends will play out depends on the region. The critical issue is the dependency ratio. This is the number of children and retirees compared with the population in their prime employment years, ages 15 to 64. The smaller a country's dependency ratio, the easier it will be for workers to support those who do not contribute to the economy.

High dependency ratios change the way economies perform. Savings translate to investments that promote growth and, because more money is available to those wishing to borrow, help keep interest rates low. Retirees, on average, begin spending what they have saved, so interest rates go up and economic growth declines. Housing prices also go down; one study of ten countries found that they had sunk, in real terms, by 0.2 percent per year as the ratio of seniors to working-age adults rose. One more likely effect is a shift in consumption from goods to healthcare services. This is particularly true when the elderly population is comparatively large, producing a high "old-age dependency ratio."

In most of the less developed countries and some of the developing, high birth rates and reduced childhood mortality in recent decades are enlarging the workforce, and dependency ratios are falling. In India, for example, the number of children and elders equaled 54 percent of the working-age population in 2010 and is expected to be 48 in 2050. In Nigeria, it is slipping from 88 to 69. These trends should lead to faster economic growth and improved standards of living.

In the developed lands, dependency ratios are climbing rapidly thanks to a combination of low birth rates and longer life expectancies. In the United States, it was 49 in 2010 and will be 66 in 2050. In Germany, it is rising from 52 to 83. In Spain, the dependency ratio began the period at 47 and will end at 94. In Japan, it was 52 and is expected to reach 96!

In all these countries, the change is due primarily to the growing population age 65 and over. In the U.S., there were 19 per 100 people of working age in 2010. By 2050, there will be 36. In Germany, there were 32, and the number is expected to reach 60. In Spain, the increase is from 25 to 67. In Japan, the ratio will double, from 36 to 72. South Korea's age-dependency ratio will reach only 66, but that is more than four times its ratio of only 15 in 2010.

China is a special case, thanks to the one-child policy introduced in 1979 to stem out-of-control population growth and not replaced by a two-child rule until 2016. Population growth has slowed as intended, but as a result more people are now reaching retirement than are entering the workforce. The working-age population is declining, from a peak of 925 million in 2011 to only 700 million expected in 2050. The old-age dependency ratio is more than tripling from 11 in 2010 to 39 in 2050.

China is not the only country with a declining workforce, nor even the one with the greatest percentage loss in the years ahead. Germany's workforce will shrink by about 17 percent over the same period by 2060. Japan's is due to shrink by 12.4 percent, but its high life expectancy means that by 2060 some 40 percent of the population will be age 65 or older.

However, Germany and most other countries of the European Union provide ample programs for retirement pensions and old-age medical care. Japan's are not as generous, but the government is working to expand them before need too badly outstrips availability. China is much less ready for the future. If its social programs are not in crisis already, they are approaching it much faster than they can be improved.

Beijing has attempted to prepare for this future by establishing a variety of new programs and improving others. In 2016, some 890 million people had government-funded pension accounts, 750 million were covered by medical insurance, 220 million by workplace injury insurance.

Unfortunately, these numbers sound more impressive than the reality they represent. Expenses at the five largest government-funded insurance programs are growing about one-third faster than the money available to pay them. Many former military officers already report that they have not received pensions, jobs, or insurance since retiring; some have been waiting twenty years. By 2020, the number of elderly collecting pensions will exceed the working-age population. And when they elderly need geriatric services, few are available. China has about half as many beds per thousand seniors as the developed countries. In the West, between 4 and 8 percent of seniors live in residential care facilities. In China, the number is 1 to 2 percent.

Consider one more factor, the growing shortage of medical personnel in much of the world. In the early 2020s, the United States is expected to have some 90,000 too few doctors and more than 1 million fewer nurses than it needs. Japan will have 200,000 too few nurses by 2020 and 380,000 too few by 2025. China had 500,000 fewer doctors than it needed as early as 2015.

All these factors point in the same direction. In China, Japan, and South Korea; in Western Europe; in Canada and, to a lesser extent, the United States, demand for medical care will grow at least as fast as the supply, and in most cases faster. At the same time, people in many parts of the world will be watching their disposable income shrink even as their expenses grow. People will need much more care in the years ahead, and many of them will be unable to find it at home. Those who can afford the cost of travel will seek it in other countries. Demographic trends guarantee a prosperous future for companies that serve the world's medical tourists.

Important medical advances will continue to appear almost daily.

We do not need to make an exhaustive list here. You can find more details in Appendix A, Trend 34, and every website that publishes medical news. In general, our medical knowledge doubles every four to five years, and faster in some specialties. Clinical knowledge, the kind doctors use in caring for patients, doubles every 18 months. Half of what medical students learn in their freshman year about the cutting edge of medical science and technology is obsolete, revised, or taken for granted before their junior year is over.

Many of the most important discoveries over the next decades will emerge from genetics. Some 10,000 human diseases arise from defects in a single gene. In 2018, researchers already were conducting small human trials of gene editing for the treatment of lung, bladder, prostate, and kidney cancer. Other disorders likely to be treated by genetic therapy, and perhaps even eliminated from our species, include heart disease, HIV/AIDS, and Alzheimer's disease.

Other advances will come from new developments in immunotherapy. Experimental results against some forms of cancer are particularly promising.

Work in regeneration medicine is not yet quite so advanced, but it seems likely that in the 2030s it will be possible to heal paralysis by restoring damaged spinal nerves, and someday even to regrow lost limbs.

By 2025, work on nanotechnology is likely to produce the first cell-sized machines that can travel through the bloodstream, scouring out whatever plaques of artery-clogging cholesterol other therapies have not eliminated and killing cancer cells before they have a chance to form a tumor.

As wonderful as all these developments promise to be, their impact on medical costs may be less welcome. New medical treatments and technologies, however they operate and whatever they cure, have one thing in common: They tend to be expensive, often horrifyingly so. On balance and over time, this latest generation of medical advances seems likely to improve our health in old age enough to bring down the overall cost of care. However, during the transition period—say, the next twenty years—medical expenses are likely to rise sharply.

This is, of course, one more trend that will help grow the market for medical tourism throughout the careers of today's hospitality students. In the healthy, fast-growing market for hospitality and tourism services, this should be one of the most vibrant segments for at least the next twenty years.

CHAPTER 8

Away on Business: The Meetings, Incentives, Conventions, Expositions (MICE) Market

Aparna Sharma & Bill Naylor

© r.classen/Shutterstock.com

Welcome to one of the more challenging and fast-changing segments of hospitality and travel. Become an event planner, coordinator, or manager, and you can look forward to busy days, few of them routine; adequate, if unspectacular pay (median income is about half what a talented software engineer might earn in his first job); more travel than you may want; constant multitasking; and, according to CareerCast, more stress than any occupation but military professionals, fire fighters, airline pilots, and police officers. In one survey, 74 percent of event planners cited time pressure as an important characteristic of their work. You probably won't have enough leisure to be bored.

You probably won't be unemployed, either. There were around 100,000 meeting, convention, and event planners in 2014, according to the U.S. Bureau of Labor Statistics. By 2024, there will be about 10 percent more, making this one of the faster-growing occupations BLS tracks.

Given the size of the American market, 100,000 MICE professionals is remarkably few. There are something over 2 million meetings, conventions, trade shows, incentive meetings, and other MICE activities annually in the United States alone. Call it twenty a year per industry specialist.

We use an industry-standard definition here: Meetings in this sense have ten or more participants and last at least four hours. They take place in a contracted venue, not a company office. And they are strictly business; activities like consumer shows, formal education, recreation or entertainment, and political rallies don't count, even though some of them will require a professional planner, organizer, or manager. About 1.3 million of the U.S. total are corporate or business meetings.

As one might expect, smaller gatherings are the most common. However, at the other end of the scale, there are some 32,000 exhibitions and trade shows each year throughout the world. Europe puts on the most, about 14,000 annually, with 1.4 million exhibitors, but in the United States they average larger. Roughly 11,000 exhibitions and trade shows there attract about 2 million exhibiting companies and an estimated 87 million attendees each year.

According to a report from 2015, the MICE industry adds an estimated $770 billion dollars to the U.S. economy. About $280 billion in of this represents direct spending, with the rest coming from associated industries. This includes some $130 billion in travel and tourism and $107 billion for meeting planners and managers. Including the supporting industries, the MICE market helps provide jobs for an estimated 205 million people. This makes the meeting industry bigger than air and rail transport, spectator sports, or information and data processing services.

Requirements for Success

As a strictly B2B segment, the MICE market is so different from other sectors of travel and hospitality that we will delay our discussion of competitive methods and strategic analysis for a minute and will spend less time in applying the lessons of the first six chapters to this specialty. Instead, let us begin by looking at what it takes to build a career in this field.

Graduates seeking to enter MICE will face an unparalleled breadth of activities and skill requirements. At the relatively straightforward end of the market, managing corporate incentive programs can look a lot like being a conventional travel agent, making travel arrangements and hotel or resort reservations for high-performing company employees. The harder part is finding destinations and activities that incentive recipients will enjoy and remember. This requires both a clear understanding of their values and priorities and a broad knowledge of travel options. Our look at generational changes in Chapter 6 should be a useful beginning, but corporate culture and individual variation will strongly influence these decisions.

For a large meeting or convention, things become more complicated. A database of occupational descriptions and requirements for job seekers can be found at O*Net OnLine. The entry for meeting, convention, and event planners is intimidating at best. It lists no fewer than seventeen extremely varied functions MICE workers are expected to carry out, often simultaneously. A few are relatively simple, like reading trade publications, attending seminars, and consulting with other meeting professionals to keep up with trends and standards in the field. Among the not-so-simple duties, we find developing event topics and choosing featured speakers; promoting the conference, convention, or trade show; and coordinating services for events. These services include accommodation and transportation for participants, facilities, catering, signage, displays, printing, special needs requirements, and event security. For some of us, duties such as planning budgets, reviewing bills and approving payment, and maintaining financial records may be even more difficult. And these functions are just the beginning. The list of "work activities" contains more items.

Necessary skills include being a good reader and listener, speaking well to convey information clearly, writing effectively, and managing time and financial resources. Some requirements may be hard to learn, including complex problem solving, negotiating effectively, making sound judgments and decisions, and persuading others to change their minds or behavior. Social perceptiveness and a service orientation—actively looking for ways to help people—may be more natural talent than learned ability.

Other requirements include facility with English, of course, at least in the U.S.; that includes skill in spelling, composition, and grammar. Add knowledge of business administration and management, public security, media production, relevant aspects of law and government; and computers and electronics. That last may not apply to everyone in the field. You will need a wide variety of software skills, but it seems unlikely that all meeting planners are comfortable tinkering with circuitry.

This brings us to software. Job listings in this field often specify facility with any or all of a dozen categories of software. We can take familiarity with Microsoft Outlook, PowerPoint, and Excel as given, and probably basic knowledge of HTML. Other categories and specific programs most often required include:

Customer relationship management software—Blackbaud's Raiser's Edge NXT nonprofit fundraising program;

Database user interface and query software—FileMaker Pro and Microsoft Access;

Desktop publishing software—Adobe InDesign and Microsoft Publisher;

Financial analysis software—Delphi Technology;

Graphics or photo image editing software—Adobe Photoshop;

Map creation software—ESRI ArcGIS;

Project management software—Microsoft Project and Oracle Primavera Enterprise Project Portfolio Management.

This is probably the longest, most daunting list of job requirements we have ever seen. Not all will apply to every position, particularly at the entry level. However, a broad selection of them will be needed to qualify for promotions and any second or third positions that might come your way. So add one more skill: being an effective life-long learner, even while coping with a high-pressure job that often demands more than the traditional eight hours.

At least you aren't likely to be replaced by a robot.

MICE Basics

Many of us think of trade shows and expositions as the place where companies introduce new products and services. Rather, we used to. This once-prominent part of the market has been in decline. In high-tech especially, manufacturers with a product ready for market in January can no longer afford to delay its introduction for a major trade show that may not take place until June; if it isn't obsolete by then, faster competitors will have captured the market. Because of this, many companies now introduce products at their own smaller, task-specific meetings for reporters, often with Internet feeds to shareholders. Think Apple and the newest iPhone. Online marketing and product announcements are beginning to serve this function for smaller firms.

Yet, companies still rely on large meetings to accomplish a variety of important goals: At Forecasting International, where we have occasionally run meetings of up to several hundred participants, we concentrate on four rewards that make it worth the executive's while to attend a business gathering. Call them the "four Cs:" contacts, contracts, certification, and clarification.

Contacts, of course, are the people attendees meet. Individuals attend these events to establish trust and credibility with new contacts and to meet in person with colleagues whom they ordinarily know only through the impersonal media of text messaging, e-mail, and—difficult as it may be for some in the younger generations to imagine—the telephone. For most attendees, and especially for exhibitors, this is the real return on their investment in the meeting.

For the most successful attendees, who do impress potential new customers or whose potential suppliers impress them, those contacts can result in contracts. Thus, large industry trade shows can have a measurable impact on the bottom line. Some 77 percent of B2B companies identify exhibitions as their primary sales channel.

Certification comes from those workshops held at many association meetings. They provide a base of common knowledge that improves the efficiency of any industry. This is particularly important in highly technical fields such information technology and health care, where any deficiency in professional skills may cost lives.

Clarification can take many forms. It may be just a matter of asking the right question of an expert you would not have met outside the meeting. Clarification also can be more tangible: it's one thing to see a video of new equipment, but quite another to touch the hardware and see and hear it working in person. Some companies thus are using MICE events to train customers in operating their new products. Companies use meetings to promote the exchange of ideas with co-workers and competitors and to train their own people to deal with new products and procedures.

For individual attendees, meetings have one more benefit: They provide an escape from daily routine in a way that still counts as doing business. This makes activities outside the exhibition space nearly as important as what happens inside. In a 2017 interview with more than seven hundred meeting planners, the trade magazine *Meetings Today* found that nearly 40 percent made sure course space was available for attending golfers, while 22 percent arranged for tickets at local sporting events. Nearly 20 percent incorporated trips to local casinos and other gaming venues. One in four often incorporated local attractions and theme parks into their meetings. Thirty percent fit in spas and spa activities, and 27 percent included some sort of wellness component. One-fourth provided activities for the spouses of attendees. Yet, the most common addition to the meeting itself was team-building activities for corporate groups; nearly 45 percent reported often incorporating them. Among all the apparent distractions, providing business value for companies and individual attendees remained the top priority.

All these functions have significant implications for the structure and management of meetings, exhibitions, and trade shows.

Major Trends for MICE

Global and Local Economies

The most general concern for the MICE market also is the most important. This is the economy, both worldwide and in the organizer's home country. Meetings in general are an essential part of the business world. Yet, most specific meetings are elective. Thus, when times get tough they are among the first things companies think to cut. This was a serious problem for the industry during and immediately after the recession of 2008/'09. Had the downturn continued, it would have been a grim time for MICE. Even as it was, when companies realized how bad 2009 had been, they cut back on MICE activities. The U.S. trade show market shrank, for example, in 2010 by about $0.4 billion. It was only a small loss—the market had been worth $11 billion the previous year—but it was the first contraction in years.

For a time, two issues troubled MICE executives. Many feared that management might decide their companies had survived comfortably enough without meetings and conventions during the recession and would not add them back into the budget once the crisis had passed. This has proved not to be the case, as the end of 2016 marked the twenty-fourth consecutive quarter in which the industry's overall performance improved. With recessions as severe as that of 2008 unlikely in the years ahead, we expect it to continue doing so through at least 2025.

The second concern, early in the recovery, was whether the MICE market could grow faster than the economy, a necessity if the market were to expand again at its accustomed pace. Today, of course, we know. The U.S. economy grew by roughly 2 percent annually for years after the recovery began. Yet, the MICE industry in the United States has achieved a CAGR of around 3 percent, and the trade show segment is growing by 4 percent per year.

With the renewed growth of the United States economy and that of the rest of the world, the markets for MICE planning and management and for exposition space are likely to grow rapidly. We can expect this market to continue outpacing the overall economy at least through 2020. Forecasts for the global MICE industry anticipate a market worth $1.245 trillion by 2023.

Yet, this is one field that requires constant attention. As we noted in Chapter 6, several important economies suffer from obvious weaknesses that could send them back into recession and perhaps take the global economy with them. These include China's vast burden of debt, the possible (though unlikely) collapse of the European Union owing to nationalist movements like the one currently, as this is written, dragging Great Britain into economic and social exile, and the potential for trade wars and another banking crisis in the United States. Although we believe all these countries can manage their economic flaws, and probably will, the potential consequences of being wrong about any of them are too great to ignore.

New Generations Dominate

The Boomers and Generation X are still with us, but today the younger generations are reshaping travel and hospitality. The MICE market is no exception.

In the United States, Millennials make up about one-fourth of the workforce and the majority of business travelers. In India, they are half the population. By 2020, this one generation will supply half of the world's labor pool.

At the same time, Centennials are beginning to enter the workforce, bringing attitudes and concerns of their own. There are even more of them than of Millennials, and in the long run they are likely to be more influential. Although Centennial values and attitudes often appear similar to those of Millennials, there are enough variations to keep managers and HR departments slightly ill at ease.

The Millennials did not all grow up with computers, tablets, and smartphones; the Internet and social media. Yet, they came close. Even the eldest among them were barely into double-digit ages when the Internet began to reshape society. The younger never knew a time when the nearest laptop or smartphone could not unite them with all the world's information and everyone they knew.

We should rename Millennials "Generation E," for entrepreneurship, education, English, and email, assets that members of this generation share throughout the world—though that last is now nearly as dated as landline telephones. Thanks to mass media, the Internet, and the shared experiences they deliver, these generations often have more in common with their peers across the globe than with their own parents. Other common characteristics include independence, eagerness for responsibility and recognition, the determination to be successful, doubt about the "American Dream" of upward mobility, and absolute intolerance for traditional marketing.

Throughout the world—with the exception of the United States—Millennials are starting new businesses at an unprecedented rate. They are proving to be even more business-oriented than Gen X, caring for little but the bottom line. We suspect Centennials will be still more hard-nosed when they take their turn as founders.

This characteristic promises new demand for meetings and expositions. Each new company founded by a Millennial or Centennial will translate into rooms occupied during industry gatherings, and the most successful will add to the market for gatherings of corporate executives, product roll-outs, and other single-firm meetings.

One more new-generation characteristic is likely to have a major effect on meetings: For all their hard-nosed attention to the bottom line, the Millennials have a different approach to careers than their Baby-Boom elders. To younger workers, a job is just a part of the bigger picture of life. This approach to work may appear lackadaisical to their elders, but many have grand plans for their futures, of which career is only one facet. Millennials and Centennials are not likely to be as interested as their predecessors in attending meetings unless they can bring their families and put in some quality time in leisure activities.

Another aspect of the latest generations, especially the Centennials, is the increased acceptance of openly gay, lesbian and trans consumers. Events for and by the LGBTQ community are on the rise, with the potential for increased MICE business. A good example is the LGBT Confex. The 4th International LGBT Business Expo was held in Puerto Vallarta, Mexico, where it was first held, in 2014. The number of exhibitors grew from 20 (in 2011) to 60 in 2016, with around 900 business meetings as well. The exhibitors included Human Rights Campaign, American Express, Marriott International, and Out and Equal, among other notables. Puerto Vallarta is home to several LGBTQ-friendly venues, including beaches, bars, clubs, restaurants, tours, and activities. Mexico's Ministry of Tourism, SECTUR, and the Mexico Tourism Board are actively cultivating the LGBTQ market. (Odyssey Media Group, 2013) We can expect to see many more such meetings, and even gay-themed leisure tracks at general-interest meetings, as the Centennials come to dominate employment markets and eventually rise to managerial positions.

Growing Older

At the other end of the age spectrum, we see a second crucial trend. Throughout the developed world, the retirement-age population is growing at an astonishing rate. For example, the over-65 cohort is rising from 12.4 percent of the American population in 2000 to more than 16 percent in 2020. The same trend is seen in Europe, Japan, and even in some developing countries. India's over-60 population is expanding from 56 million in 1991 to 137 million in 2021 and 340 million in 2051.

For destinations that host meetings and expositions, this demographic trend offers one of the most vibrant markets of the next 20 years. A wide range of new goods and services will cater to the needs of the elderly, and particularly those of healthy, active seniors throughout the developed world. At the same time, the health-care industry will continue to grow rapidly to meet the medical needs of less fortunate seniors. Companies delivering these products and services will provide a fast-expanding market for event space, planning, and management.

Aging has a second aspect that could be important. Workers in the traditional retirement years represent the fastest growing employment pool in many developed countries. This resource has yet to be fully or efficiently tapped. Retirement-age workers—generally well-spoken, courteous, and available for part-time work—are especially well suited to the hospitality industry.

Post-retirement workers also are likely to form a growing percentage of meeting attendees, and this will influence the meetings themselves. Venues will need to be "elder-friendly," with brighter-than-average lighting suited to dimming vision, a bit more volume on the sound system, large-type signage, and door levers, rather than knobs, so that arthritic hands can operate them more easily. A wider variety of food and beverages will be required to meet the needs of those on restricted diets. Younger personnel may need some training to speak with the extra formality that many elders expect. This trend also will bring even greater need for precise service and quality control. Older workers, particularly those whose positions are as senior as they are, tend to have less patience with disappointment or delay than others.

Technology Unites the World

The tech industry drives some of the world's largest trade shows. According to one count in 2017, seventeen out of the hundred biggest shows in the U.S. and seven of the top fifty-six in Europe served high-tech industries. Several more dealt with medicine and healthcare, a field in which technology may not be the purpose but for which it provides essential tools.

Yet technology itself has seemed a mixed blessing. For one thing, it has helped to shrink lead times dramatically. A few years ago, event organizers tended to plan meetings three to six months out and often much longer for large groups. For the largest, lead times still run six to ten months. For the rest… worldwide, lead times now average about seven weeks. In Asia, they stretch to two months. In Central and South America, they average six weeks. Only North America has resisted this trend. In the United States and Canada, lead time still averaged eighteen weeks in 2016. Yet, it seems unlikely that American planners can hold out against this trend for much longer. Shorter lead times place new pressure on event planners and managers, and this was not an easy-going profession to begin with.

Technology has brought another concern that in the long run could be even more troubling. Text messaging, Skype, social media, online videoconferencing services, and the like make it easier for executives to maintain contact with customers and colleagues without ever seeing them in person. At some point, it seems almost inevitable that these competing technologies will take attendance from meetings and trade shows. This is particularly an issue with Millennials, who have been honing their skills with high-tech communications at least since their early teens. It can only grow more important as Centennials approach mid-career.

This seems a reasonable concern. The business argument for replacing travel with tele-communications is compelling. On average, putting four people on airplanes to meet with a fifth runs nearly $5,200. In 2008, a simple audio conference cost an average of $689. A videoconference ran $1,700. Today, video conferencing on Skype or Facetime is essentially free.

Yet, so far Millennials have proved as eager to attend industry events as their prede-cessors were. One reason clearly is the opportunity to find new customers and sup-pliers. Another may be that constant exposure to sterile high-tech media leaves even the most devoted users feeling deprived of human contact and needing a business-oriented excuse to meet in person. A third also seems likely: Compared with previous generations, many Millennials often have less disposable income than the previous generation was at the same age. Understandably, most are inclined to avoid spending whenever they can. A trip out of town, entertainment offered as part of the meeting package, and the chance to buy good food and drink on the company credit card are too good to pass up. Millennials have proved to be, if anything, even more willing to enjoy themselves on their employer's tab than their Baby Boom parents were.

Despite this, some MICE industry leaders continue to worry that telecommunications eventually could erode the market for meetngs. The reason, of course, is the rise of the Centennials. After a lifetime of instant messaging and social media, they may be feel less need for direct human contact than Millennials appear to. Or not. Our best guess is that the need to meet in person is a basic part of human psychology that Centenni-als will need as much as their predecessors—and there is still that company-funded entertainment. Yet, MICE executives will continue to monitor this possibility until enough Centennial workers have demonstrated what matters to them.

For MICE providers, the possible risks of technology are offset by clear and immedi-ate benefits. Telecommunications has all but eliminated geographic barriers. A mes-sage can be emailed to hundreds or thousands of potential exhibitors or attendees all over the world at little more cost than sending a note to a colleague down the hall. In the next few years, when both the Internet and telephone systems are equipped to translate conversations accurately among the most common languages in real time, the mechanics of doing business internationally will be easier still.

This has obvious benefit applications for all segments of the MICE market. The Inter-net makes it possible for businesses throughout the world to compete on an even footing with industry leaders. Thus, smaller destinations in developing countries will find it easier to target meeting planners seeking novel sites for high-end gatherings. It also becomes increasingly possible for planners to find and market directly to small companies with private meetings on their schedules—potential clients who probably would have been overlooked before the Internet transformed business processes. And as the Net spreads through neglected parts of Asia and Africa, some of those locations too will become suitable sites for international meetings.

In a recent blog post, students of hospitality technology at the University of Delaware offered a long list of possible competitive methods and other ideas for the future of technology in the MICE market. We offer them as a spur to your own imagination:

- Use Google Glass and similar technologies to translate the meeting into differ-ent languages and use facial recognition technology to connect people on social media by looking at their faces. (QinBian, Yiwen Xu, Yufei, Wang, Yunmei Bai, Nan Jiang, Teng Wang)

- "Avatar Conferencing," a completely virtual conference so that you could hold it anywhere, such as on a safari in a jungle, on top of the Empire State Building, or a New York City street. Each attendee would create their own avatar. Avatars can interact with one another and attend lectures and discussions, and explore the virtual world. (Katelyn Morse, Mary Palma, Allison Hanik, Caroline Sohodski)

- Mobile/Virtual kiosk ordering system that allows you to view the menu and order food from anywhere. Upon ordering, a message provides the location and time to pick up your food. (Jessica Wincott, Schuyler Lehman, Jennifer Turowski)

- GPS tracker with RFID—CRM: Attendees wear a GPS tracker that record exhibits they have already attended and whether they "liked it" or not and suggests other exhibits likely to interest them. (Rachel Borkoski, Samantha Dominguez, Stephanie Hepner, Lindsay Canell)

- "MICE Trap:" Instant LinkedIn. Write a brief profile, and meet other people in conferences. You can chat with them and even meet up with them in the real world. A networking opportunity while technology advances. (Junyi Chung, Michael Diminick, Mattew Heck)

- Pre-arrival: 3-D virtual tour of convention set-up and facility with information on each group sent to iPad, smartphones, and email adresses. (Nina Clark, Robert Serpico, Lindsay Rogers)

- Audio Device and Virtual Food menu cart that plays information from the vineyard on a particular wine being served. (Alexandra Rufo, Megan Smutz, Amy Cohn, Kimberly Lindell)

- Add microphones to MICE conference name badges. (Leigh Redefer, Sara Kazmierski, Jessica Rosenberg)

- Virtual holograms of keynote speakers available in the privacy of your home. You could also follow along with text and slides on a tablet. (Brian Prickrill, Alexander Vellios, Seth Bergman, Anne Truono)

- Phone technology that allows interactive contact sharing without the use of business cards. Contact information is stored directly into your phone/tablet along with links to the person's bio/resume, business position, and company information, automatically add them to "MICE Trap", Facebook, Twitter, Linked-in, and all other social media connection sites. (Callie D'Ambrisi, Alexandra Giannini, Adam Cowperthwait, Stephanie Johnson)

- An all-encompassing smartphone app that can be interfaced with a phone, tablet or computer. Capabilities include:
  - ✓ Provides information on all aspects of the conference: maps, schedules, list of vendors, etc.
  - ✓ Social networking: attendees can share thoughts with one another, network, and post ideas.
  - ✓ Pre-registration and check-in.
  - ✓ Real time responses to questions during speeches.

- All purchasing completed during conference, monitored by the app: Track trends, and order room service. (Jean Thomae, Morgan West, Maria Trasolini, Kaitlyn Wendler)
- Space Conferences: take your meeting to the moon! (Brandon Groux, Alexander Vellions, Lauren Mitchell, Dingchao He, Julie Garafalo)
- Speak at a lower cost. (Anam Ahmed, Justin Tansey, John Guzman)
- Telecommunicator for event guests that can translate foreign languages directly into their ear bud (iPhone) or Google Glass ear piece. (Erin Marshall, Yuchen Song, Fengming Yu, Pinyi Zhao, Nguyen Tran, Jing Zhang; Dr. Frederick DeMicco, 2013)
- Another technological avenue that might bear exploration is the use of interactive gaming, like Wii Fit or XBox One for "Fitness Breaks" during MICE events. From another recent post:

Given the different sports that can be played on the Wii, football, baseball, or basketball could be incorporated into a theme of the sporting event of the day. In ski resort-area hotels, for example, the Wii Fit offers skiing competitions for lounge patrons.

For fitness addicts, an in-room Wii Fit attached to the TV allows guests to do yoga and Pilates in their own rooms. This may appeal to female business travelers not wanting to work out in the hotel's public exercise room. Tying a spa menu to the Wii Fit in-room could up-sell to the fitness segment.

For convention center hotels, the Wii Fit could be incorporated into the mid-morning or mid-afternoon break. Call it a fitness break, where conferees can really stretch and get a little exercise using the Wii after sitting in sessions. We have found this actually stimulates conversation and networking. The Wii break could also be sponsored by a company as a new and innovative type of sponsorship offering: "The Wii Fitness Break sponsored by…" Nutritious foods can be offered during the breaks as well. (Dr. Frederick DeMicco, NINTENDO WII: SAY OUI TO INCREASED F&B SALES, 2009)

Meetings Go Green

For Baby Boomers and Generation X, environmentalism was a defining value. It is less so for Millennials and much less for Centennials, according to many surveys. They agree that the environment is important, but they are much less likely than the previous generations to put that belief into practice.

We suspect this is largely a matter of age and—no pun intended—the environment we examined in Chapter 6. The two newest generations have been bombarded their entire lives by the risk of terrorism, news of multiple wars, and global and national economies that make it hard to build financial security. On top of that, the Centennials are busy getting their lives established. All this does not leave much time or energy for environmental movements.

However, when we dig into the details, it turns out that Millennials and Centennials have incorporated many "green" values into their personal lives. Witness the continuing growth of organic farming and the rise of the "locavore" movement, sourcing food from nearby farms. Even the Centennials often participated in environmental organizations while in high school. The difference is that as adults many say they believe they can best contribute to the cause through company programs and by influencing corporate policy.

These quietly "green" attitudes have only just begun to influence the MICE market. In 2015, a poll of corporate meeting planners found that only one company in four had a policy about green meetings. Only 6 percent reported that they often paid more to implement environmentally friendly measures. Twenty-nine percent sometimes did, 31 percent rarely, and 34 percent never. Nonetheless, 59 percent of companies reported that their meetings were at least somewhat greener than they had been two years earlier.

For hotels and convention centers, being environmentally friendly can make a big difference. Asked whether green certifications influenced their selection of venues, 11 percent of respondents said "Yes, to a great extent." Another 26 percent said that they were "somewhat" significant.

However, when planners were asked how important green policies and procedures were when selecting specific meeting venues, the numbers were higher. Twenty-five percent said they were very important and another 33 percent somewhat important when selecting a hotel. For convention centers or other meeting facilities, the numbers were 28 percent and 32 percent, respectively. For restaurants, the respondents were more lenient. Eighteen percent considered environmental friendliness very important in selecting a place to eat, while 27 percent rated it somewhat important. For all three categories, fewer than one in four considered it "not at all important."

So far, only a few meeting venues have chosen being conspicuously green as an important competitive method. In Monterey, CA, the 379-room Portola Hotel & Spa has a Silver LEED (Leadership in Energy and Environmental Design) certification from the US Green Building Council. Its policies and practices are typical of green facilities. Paper cups are out, reusable china, glassware, and silverware in. Menu items are organic and sustainable. And meetings there produce no waste at all; everything is composted. Go to the hotel's webpage for event planners, and the headline reads "Green Monterey Meeting Space: Sustainable and Efficient."

It turns out that green practices not only draw environment-minded customers, they improve the facility's bottom line. In 2014 , Cornell University researchers found that green hotels reduced their operating costs and gained a few percent in revenue. One Chicago Hyatt reports that green practices have cut their waste hauling by 80 percent. In early 2017, the Green Hotels Association has more than 150 member facilities in the United States and twenty-two more around the world.

It is easy to predict that the trend toward green meeting places is only beginning.

Society Goes Global

Our beliefs and values are shaped by what we see and hear. Throughout the United States, people have long watched the same movies and TV programs. These media have achieved worldwide reach. In the process, they are creating a truly integrated global society. Migration, intermarriage, and the rapid growth of travel for business and pleasure all are hastening this process. In the U.K., some 21 percent of young adults answering a poll viewed themselves as primarily European, rather than British. Some 31 percent of French Gen Xers, 36 percent of Germans, and 42 percent of Italians also said they thought of themselves as European.

Over the next half-century, growing cultural exchanges at the personal level will help to reduce some of the conflict that plagued the twentieth century. However, this has already produced a reactionary backlash in societies where xenophobia is common. Some of the most fervent "culturist" movements spring from religious fundamentalism. Yet, in countries like the United States, the "alt-right" movement presents its views in populist terms, arguing however improbably that immigrants take jobs that otherwise would go to natives. Would-be dictators and strong-men will use these movements to promote their own interests, ensuring that ethnic, sectarian, and regional violence will remain common.

Thus, political risks are likely to grow in areas where there are strong religious or ethnic movements, especially when they may target Western or American interests. Anti-foreign movements are increasingly common in Europe, but anti-American sentiments are widespread throughout the developing world. Terrorism especially will be a continuing problem for meeting destinations in the developing world, and particularly where there are large, conservative Muslim communities. In one poll of meeting attendees long after 9/11, more than 90 percent said that safety was one of the most important factors they considered in choosing whether to attend an event.

However, the trend toward a more homogeneous world culture is generally making life simpler for meeting planners and destination managers. In the most heavily traveled lands, it is quickly becoming easier to host international meetings and expositions, with less risk of unfortunate incidents owing to cultural conflicts. The continuing spread of the English language; the development of a task-focused, profit-oriented global business culture; and the slow, steady replacement of ethnic and sectarian interests by concerns for personal security and material well-being all will help to make international meetings more secure and manageable in the years ahead.

International Exposure

The growing unification of the world into a single market will bring further opportunities for international events. Hotels and resorts with good connections to managers of international meetings and expositions will be especially well positioned to benefit from this trend. Destinations in some developing countries also will benefit from government efforts to build international trade and from the "trendiness" of exotic locales.

In Asia, many national travel authorities are eager to build their country's reputation as a good destination for the international event business. For example, Phuket News stated in 2014, "The island's growing MICE market is a key segment which can help Phuket attract quality visitors." Several organizations met that year to plan for sustainable growth of the Phuket MICE market. Macau, Hong Kong, and many neighboring countries also actively solicit international business events.

Mainland China is an odd exception. Despite its stated eagerness for travel revenue, Beijing makes it relatively difficult for tourists and business travelers to enter the country. It is not clear when, or whether, its restrictive policies will change or how China can build a vibrant MICE sector until they do.

Asian outbound travelers also are becoming a significant force in the international MICE market. First to benefit is Australia. A long day's flight from the U.S., Sydney and Melbourne are only a few hours from East Asia, making them very accessible to those on a more limited budget. With China on deck to be the world's foremost international tourist destination by 2020 and the U.S. being the top long-distance destination for Chinese tourists, the Asian MICE market can be expected to grow quickly at least through the mid 2020s.

South Korea also is focusing on MICE, with considerable success. The Union of International Associations (UIA) counted 10,786 international meetings in 2017. Of these, 1,297, just over 12 percent, took place in South Korea. According to the Korea Tourism Bureau, this made the country the top destination for international meetings by UIA's criteria for the second consecutive year. It also ranked 13th place in rankings by the International Congress and Convention Association, with 279 qualified meetings hosted in South Korea that year. The Korea MICE Bureau is working to raise these numbers still further.

Japan touted Yokohama as "Japan's First Port of Call" in a video released in March 2014. The video was intended to demonstrate Yokohama's history as Japan's gateway to the world. "Yokohama has been the host to several high-profile events" Travel Daily Media pointed out. These included the "Asia Pacific Economic Cooperation forums, the 10th Annual Meeting of the International Society for Stem Cell Research, the Human Proteome Organization 12th Annual World Congress, and the Intergovernmental Panel on Climate Change in 2014. Yokohama's location, as a port city, points up its position as a gateway to tourism, making it ideal for entry from the air and sea as well."

Travel promoters are even marketing the United States as an exotic destination for Asian visitors. For example, in 2014 the Visit USA Committee, India chapter, released its first-ever whitepaper, "Why USA for MICE," presenting the US as a cost-effective destination for Indian event planners. This effort has been remarkably successful. For example, International Indian Film Academy (IIFA) that year held its annual awards event in Tampa Bay, Florida. It brought some 10,000 to 12,000 room-nights of business to the city. An estimated 30,000 local

© MTS_Photo/Shutterstock.com

Yokohama skyline

visitors and $11 million in revenue also came to the Tampa Bay area—and that is likely to be only the beginning of the event's benefits for the region. An estimated 800 million Indian viewers watching the IIFA awards—compared with about 111 million for the Super Bowl—saw their favorite stars touting the wonders of Tampa Bay. Such efforts can only bring more tourists to Tampa Bay in the future.

There are still some issues that could slow the growth of Asia's MICE sector. Overseas markets seeking MICE functions from the West will have to reassure meeting managers about factors such as the availability of manpower and equipment and the financial risks of doing business under an unfamiliar legal system. Of course, the threat of international terrorism also will be a concern for international meetings for many years to come. This will require hotels, resorts, and meeting planners in many areas to take extra care in arranging security for gatherings. The Arab lands, the Middle East, the Philippines, and the Muslim regions of Asia are obvious high-risk areas, but Europe too has significant numbers of radicalized Muslims sympathetic to the terrorist cause. These include some converts who can pass for native Europeans—because that is exactly what they are. It will not be enough to find a venue with suitable barriers to prevent the approach of a truck bomb. For genuine security, the venue's staff must have undergone a rigorous background check. Similarly, any local personnel or services hired to help set up an exhibition also require clearance. In any meeting place, the greatest risk is always from the facility's own staff and suppliers.

Further Trends for Meetings and Expositions

In addition to these industry-specific developments some general trends also seem particularly likely to shape the future of the MICE market. In Chapter 7, we analyzed the most relevant trends for the medical-tourism segment, and we will return to this practice in later discussions. Here, however, we are moved to try something different. Please carry out your own analysis of these trends and their probable influence on the MICE market. We suggest looking at each and taking some time to figure out how they will affect demand for business-oriented events and the planners and managers who run them. Once you have worked out your own analysis of each trend, compare it with the implications found in the appendix. Then consider any differences between them. Given the benefit of another year or two worth of information to build upon, your estimates may well improve on our own. If so, it should be useful reassurance of your increasing skill in strategic forecasting. If not, we hope the experience will help guide your future studies.

Time is becoming the world's most precious commodity.

In the United States, workers spend about 10 percent more time on the job than they did a decade ago. European executives and non-unionized workers face the same trend. In Britain, an Ipsos MORI study found that 32 percent of people who had not visited a museum in the previous year reported having too little time to do so; in 1999, only 6 percent cited that reason. China's rapid economic development means its workers also are experiencing faster-paced and time-pressured lives. In a recent survey by the Chinese news portal Sina, 56 percent of respondents said they felt short of time. Technical workers and executives in India are beginning to report the same job-related stresses, particularly when they work on U.S. and European schedules.

Tourism, vacationing, and travel (especially international) continue to grow with each passing year.

International tourism grew by more than 6 percent in the first half of 2007 thanks in part to global prosperity. This trend slowed briefly during the global recession of 2008 and '09 and recovered quickly. By 2020, international tourist arrivals are expected to reach 1.6 billion annually, up from 842 million in 2006. By 2020, according to the World Trade Organization, 100 million Chinese will fan out across the globe, replacing Americans, Japanese, and Germans as the world's most numerous travelers. Some 50 million Indian tourists will join them.

Education and training are expanding throughout society.

Rapid changes in the job market and work-related technologies will require increased training for almost every worker, just as knowledge turnover in the professions requires continuous retraining and lifelong learning. Thus, a substantial portion of the labor force will be in job retraining programs at any given moment. Such opportunities are an important factor in attracting and retaining Millennial workers. We suspect they will be equally significant for the Centennials reading this text. Although American companies are inclined to view employee training as an expense to be avoided, rather than as an opportunity to build a more capable, productive workforce, they are likely to be responsible for many of these efforts. Others will be the worker's own responsibility.

Women's salaries are approaching equality with men's—but very slowly.

In the 1980s and '90s, women's overall income in the United States was catching up with that of their male co-workers. More recently, it has stagnated. In 1995, university educated women earned 75.7 cents for every dollar earned by men, on average. In 2005, it had fallen to 74.7 cents. During the same period, lower-income women continued to gain on their male peers, though very slowly. One reason may be that women are less interested than men in working 70 hours or more per week during their prime reproductive years, and growing numbers have chosen to stay home and rear their children. Women also appear to be less likely to choose and pursue a career on the basis of income. Studies that attempt to compensate for differences in factors such as education, occupation, experience, and union membership find much smaller income differences than others. One reported that women receive about 91 percent as much as men. Another held that incomes are virtually equal when measured with appropriate rigor. Some studies also suggest that the pay gap has largely disappeared for women in the newest cohort of workers. This would make sense, given the nearly complete gender blindness of the Millennials.

The same trend is visible in most other industrialized countries. According to the European Commission, women on the Continent earn 15 percent less than men, on average, down from 17 percent in 1995. In Britain, the gap was 20 percent, down from 26 percent. Japan is an exception to this trend. The gender gap there remains near 35 percent.

Transportation technology and practice are improving rapidly.

The newest generation of aircraft, such as the Boeing 787 and future Airbus A350 XWB, are using lightweight materials and more efficient engines to cut fuel costs, stretch ranges, and increase cargo capacity. At the same time, rail travel is getting faster. The TGV Est line, which runs 300 km (180 miles) from Paris to Frankfurt, operates at 320 kph (198.8 mph) inside France, compared with 300 kph on other parts of the TGV system. China has been installing a network of high-speed trains to compensate for its shortage of regional air transportation.

Technology is creating a knowledge-dependent global society.

More and more businesses, and entire industries, are based on the production and exchange of information and ideas rather than exclusively on manufactured goods or other tangible products. At the same time, manufacturers and sellers of physical products are able to capture and analyze much more information about buyers' needs and preferences, making the selling process more efficient and effective. The number of Internet users in the United States more than doubled between 2000 and 2007, to nearly 231 million, or 69 percent of the population. Yet the percent of the population online has remained almost unchanged since 2004. And while the percentage of Internet users in China is smaller than in the U.S., the absolute number of users there passed that of the U.S. early in 2008.

People around the world are becoming increasingly sensitive to environmental issues as the consequences of neglect, indifference, and ignorance become ever more apparent.

The World Health Organization (WHO) estimates that 3,000,000 people die each year from the effects of air pollution, about 5 percent of the total deaths. In the United States, an estimated 64,000 people a year die of cardiopulmonary disease caused by breathing particulates. In Sub-Saharan Africa, the toll is between 300,000 and 500,000 deaths per year. Pollution-related respiratory diseases kill about 1.4 million people yearly in China and Southeast Asia, and contaminated water is implicated in 80 percent of the world's health problems, according to WHO. An estimated 40,000 people around the world die each day of diseases directly caused by contaminated water, more than 14,000,000 per year. Growing awareness of such issues is a motivating force in the worldwide "green" movement. Although the environment to date is largely a First-World concern, its influence can be expected to spread as developing countries grow prosperous enough that workers can afford to devote part of their attention to matters beyond immediate survival.

Organizations are simplifying their structures and squeezing out personnel.

Computers and information-management systems have stretched the manager's effective span of control from six to twenty-one subordinates. Information now flows from frontline workers to higher management for analysis. Thus, fewer mid-level managers are needed, flattening the corporate pyramid.

The span of control could stretch again if computer science finally delivers on its long-delayed promise of artificial intelligence. Opportunities for advancement are shrinking, because they come within the worker's narrow specialty, rather than at the broader corporate level. By 2001, only one person in fifty was promoted, compared with one in twenty in 1987. As this trend continues, we may see corporate "right-sizing" cutting into the number of attendees at meetings in the most heavily affected industries.

We hope this exercise in practical trend analysis has been obviously worth your effort. We recommend making similar efforts in the chapters ahead. Read the trends at the end of each. Then try to put our analysis out of your mind and make your own. This is essential practice for any career that requires developing and evaluating competitive methods in the international business environment. This is especially true for managers in the world of hospitality and travel.

Web Assignment

Log into the student website and complete the end of chapter assignment. Try to utilize some of the works you read about from this chapter and apply the key concepts, terms, and theory in your responses.

CHAPTER 9

Clipped Wings: Troubled Times for the Airlines

Ye Guo & Ashley Leathers —contributed to this chapter.

© Matej Kastelic/Shutterstock.com

McGill University law professor Paul Stephen Dempsey once summarized the airline business for the Institute of Air & Space Law, of which he is director. His description, which was headlined "The Curse and Blessing of Commercial Aviation," stands as an invitation and a warning to anyone thinking of a career in the industry. Some years later, it remains the best description of this demanding field we have seen. He wrote:

> "The airline business is a **tough business**. Profit margins are thin, fixed costs are high, capital expenditures are large, government regulation has been unstable, and taxation can be unmerciful. Demand can be chilled by an outbreak of disease, recession, war or terrorism."

> "The airline business also is a **glamorous business**. Its technology is breathtaking. The defiance of gravity, the allure of exotic destinations or primordial geographic domination has drawn investment and managerial talent into the industry at a level surpassing what dispassionate financial analysis seemingly would warrant."

It is a huge business as well. The International Air Transport Association (IATA) reports that there were over 5,000 airlines in the world as of mid-2017. In 2018, they expected to carry more than 4.35 billion passengers and 63.6 million tons of cargo on more than 50,000 routes among over 20,000 unique city pairs. In the process, they should make something like $33.8 billion on $834 billion in revenues, 71 percent of it from passengers and the remainder from cargo operations. This translates to a return on capital of 8.5 percent. It was more than double the $14 billion industry profits in 2014 and one of the largest profits the airlines have earned in this century. The industry's follow-on impact makes that profit appear tiny. According to one estimate, air transport contributes some 4.5 percent of the global GDP. At official exchange rates, that amounted to about $3.9 trillion in 2018. The industry also employs 9.9 million people worldwide and supports a total of 62.7 million jobs.

IATA noted that 2015's net of $36 billion, or 9.7 percent on invested capital, was "the first time in history airlines made a normal level of profitability." They probably are right. Famed investor Warren Buffett estimates that since the first scheduled airline (the St. Petersburg to Tampa Airboat Line) took flight in 1914—1910 if we count the Zeppelins of Deutsche Luftshiffahrts-Aktiengesellshchaft—the industry has run at a loss. This is something students may wish to consider when thinking about a career in this uniquely challenging field.

Yet Another Perfect Storm

These days, it seems that anyone who has suffered business reverses blames them on a "perfect storm," a disastrous combination of forces and events that could not have been foreseen or defended against. If any industry has had the right to use this excuse for its troubles, it is the airlines. Burdened by enormous investments in equipment and maintenance, high fuel and personnel costs, heavy regulation, union conflicts, safety concerns, and endless other issues, it is even more sensitive to the business environment than other segments of the travel industry. Since 2000, that environment has often been dreadful.

When we wrote the first edition of this book, the airline industry had just begun to emerge from one of the most difficult trials in its history. The next was only a year into the future. It would be worse. Much worse.

Before looking at them, we need to step back a few decades. Problems had been building for the major airlines since the 1980s.

Most retail industries are divided into many distinct markets. Clothing, for example, offers segments ranging from the cheap goods found at Walmart and Target to custom tailoring and designer originals. Outlets include department stores, mall chains, local and regional chains, and small boutiques, each competing primarily with others of its kind in its area. Specialty stores offer clothing for men and/or women, for children, for teens, and even for infants. Although their customers overlap, retailers have many ways to differentiate themselves from the competition without endangering their bottom line.

Not so the airline industry. Given basic assumptions of safety and convenient scheduling, few customers care very much who moves them from one place to another. The profitable business and first class passengers often show some degree of brand loyalty, but they are a relatively small fraction of the market and it does not take much of a price hike to send even these customers looking for a cheaper option. Thus, regional carriers and national airlines, full-service carriers and discounters, all compete for the same passengers, and they compete almost exclusively on price.

Worse, they probably do so while carrying enormous debt. Even a well-used Boeing 747 can cost more than $25 million, and an airplane with fewer flight hours can run four times that. A new one is priced in the neighborhood of $379 million. Now add the cost of setting up a maintenance shop; hiring and training pilots, mechanics, and other personnel; and all the associated expenses. JetBlue was careful with its capital and still burned through $45 million before its first airplane left the ground.

It is seldom the largest participants that compete most successfully. Discount carriers generally run tighter operations, pay their employees less, pay out nothing for retirees and much less for benefits, often buy used planes in good condition rather than investing in new equipment, turn them around faster between flights, and pack their passengers tighter. In some markets, including North America, they even are more likely to take off on time. These efficiencies give the discounters lower costs per passenger-mile and better profits than full-service airlines despite charging less than their larger competitors. Surveys show that on average they even achieve higher customer satisfaction ratings.

As a result, discount operators have flourished even as full-fare carriers fought to survive. Low-fare lines held just 4 percent of the North American market in 1991. In early 2004, they accounted for 25 percent. By 2015, Southwest Airlines—a low-fare carrier since its first flight in 1971—owned 18 percent of the U.S. domestic market.

Discount airlines also have achieved steady growth in Europe. Low-fare carriers now handle over half of passenger traffic within Britain and between Britain and the Continent. Within mainland Europe, low-fare and no-frills operations such as Ryanair and easyJet have taken about a third of the airline market.

By the turn of this century, this intense competition was forcing even the industry giants to cut their fares. As a result, airlines entered a long period of consolidation, which is continuing still. And while bankruptcies have always been common among small regional and feeder airlines, now the big operators were in danger. Braniff International went under in 1982. Continental Airlines filed for bankruptcy protection in 1983. Pan American World Airways succumbed in 1991. National Airlines died in 2000, and Trans World Airlines sold out to American in 2001.

That is where the airlines stood at the beginning of this century. Profits were small, debts large, and even the biggest operators were fragile. The last thing any of the airlines needed was a sharp decline in air travel. They faced two of them in less than a decade.

The first trial, of course, was the use of hijacked airliners in the terrorist attacks of September 11, 2001. In the weeks that followed, passenger traffic fell some 35 percent. For the year, it was down 5.9 percent from 2000. It fell another 1.4 percent in 2002. Airlines responded by cutting capacity by nearly 3 percent that year and another 4 percent the next. Revenues worldwide declined to $307 billion in 2001, a loss of $27 billion from the previous year. Bottom-line profits took an even bigger hit. Airlines lost $13 billion in 2001, another $11.3 billion in 2002. Swissair and Sabena went bankrupt within months. In North America, no fewer than six airlines eventually filed for bankruptcy protection.

In 2003, air carriers received yet another blow: The outbreak of severe acute respiratory syndrome in and around China cost the world an estimated $33 billion. That was only 0.1 percent of the global GDP, but the airlines carried much of the burden. Asia Pacific Airlines lost 8 percent of its year's expected traffic. North American Airlines lost about 3.7 percent of its traffic and $1 billion. As catastrophes go, these were relatively small. Yet, coming so soon after 9/11 they had an outsized impact.

It took the industry five years to recover, but by 2006 things were looking up. After losing multiple billions of dollars for six straight years—about $42 billion in all, most of it in the U.S. market—the airlines *almost* broke even. Losses that year amounted to only 0.1 percent of revenues, $500 million. They did even better in 2007, making $5.6 billion on revenues of some $490 billion. Granted, their profit margin was less than 2 percent, and they were $190 billion in debt. By airline standards, 2007 was a good year.

It would be some time before they saw another. In December, the Great Recession arrived. Activity in the world's largest economies almost immediately shrank by 15 to 30 percent. Travel on economy tickets in 2008 fell 5 percent from the previous year. Premium travel, which offers much better profits, was off 13 percent; by early 2009, it was 20 percent below 2007 levels. And as global manufacturing output collapsed, airfreight—a secondary market for passenger carriers but an important source of revenue—was off 22 percent by the end of 2008.

At the same time, fuel prices soared. Between 1990 and 2002, the average cost of crude oil was only $20 per barrel. In 2001, it still held at $24.70 per barrel, and jet fuel averaged $30.50 per barrel for the year. In 2007, average prices were $73.00 and $90.00, respectively. In 2008, they climbed to $99.00 and $126.70. At their peak, crude oil cost over $147 per barrel, jet fuel $199. Per gallon, jet fuel cost about $0.49 in November 2001. By July 2008, it had risen to $3.89. In 2007, fuel accounted for 28 percent of the average airline's operating costs. By mid-2008, it was 40 percent, and even 50 percent for some airlines.

All these figures bury some details. For example, revenue passenger kilometers in international markets actually grew about 5 percent in the first half of 2008. It took some months for the recession's magnitude to sink in. And some airlines were able to cut their capacity quickly and slow the flow of red ink. Yet, this was also the period when deliveries of jet and turboprop airliners, ordered in better times, reached their peak. Airlines took possession of 1,177 new aircraft in 2008, just when they least needed them.

The result was easily predicted. In 2007, the world's airlines brought in $510 billion in revenue and pocketed $14.7 billion in net profit, or 2.9 percent. In 2008, they had $570 in revenues and lost $26.1 billion. Delta alone lost nearly $9 billion that year. By 2009, as the effects of the recession worked their way through the global economy, revenues had fallen to $476 billion, down 16.5 percent from the previous year. Airlines losses during the period totaled about four times as much as after 9/11.

Yet, even in 2009 things were beginning to look up. Thanks to the grounding of unneeded aircraft and technological advances like e-ticketing—it saved $3 billion in costs all on its own—the airlines held their year's losses to $4.6 billion. By 2010, a much leaner industry was profitable again, keeping a net of $17.3 billion on sales of $564 billion.

However, the bad years had taken their toll. From 2008 through 2010 more than sixty European airlines ceased operations or were absorbed by larger, better-funded competitors. Nearly all were small regional carriers. The same cannot be said of North America, where thirty-odd small airlines went under and mergers necessitated financial problems eventually involved Delta, Northwest, Continental, United, American, and US Airways.

Current Status

As we saw at the beginning of this chapter, the world's airlines have come a long way since the financial crisis of 2009 and '10. In 2015, for the first time in history, they made the kind of profit that many other industries would take for granted—this despite a 6-percent decline in revenue.

It helped that demand was up, with about 7.4 percent more passengers in 2015 than the year before. Yet, the single greatest reason for the airlines' prosperity that year and the next had nothing to do with passengers or with the air carriers themselves. Instead, the key factor was the price of oil. From its peak of $147 per barrel in 2008, crude fell briefly to less than $27.82 per barrel in July 2016. In the U.S., the price of jet fuel touched $0.81 per gallon in January 2016, recovering to the mid $50s per barrel by that December. Because oil prices are quoted in U.S. dollars and the dollar was strong on foreign-exchange markets, how much benefit each airline received depended on the value of its own country's currency. In Russia, which had by far the weakest currency of any major economy, jet fuel was about 20 percent cheaper than it had been a year earlier. In other countries, the price fell as much as 60 percent.

The combination of high demand and lower fuel cost has meant good times for the world's airlines. In 2015, the four largest air carriers in the U.S. saved $11 billion on fuel, 36 percent of the previous year's bill. United reported net income of $7.3 billion in 2015, up from $1.1 billion a year earlier. Southwest doubled its net income to $2.2 billion. Over all, U.S. airlines booked $22 billion in operating profits in the first nine months of the year, a 75-percent improvement over 2014.

In Europe, pricing pressure drove Lufthansa's traffic revenues down 4.2 percent. Yet a saving of €798 million on fuel helped raise the company's after-tax profits by nearly 6 percent. In November 2016, Lufthansa reported that its profits were up another 7 percent, thanks in part to a fuel bill 8 percent lower than the year before.

For once, airlines that had signed long-term fuel contracts to hedge their fuel costs against future increases did worse than less cautious operators. As early as March, Delta and United announced that they had abandoned the practice for the foreseeable future, while JetBlue, Spirit Airlines, and some European carriers radically cut back. In 2016, United, Delta, and Southwest expected their combined fuel bill to come in $6.4 billion less than 2015's unusually reasonable expense.

Cheap fuel has also helped the no-frills discount airlines, improving their profits and allowing them to compete more effectively for price-conscious passengers. As a result, ticket prices have been dropping rapidly throughout the industry. At the depths of the recession, the average nonpremium domestic ticket in the United States cost $360. As the economy improved, it grew steadily through the middle of 2014, when the average price neared $500. Over the next eighteen months, under pressure from the low-fare carriers, it declined to $388. By the fourth quarter of 2017, it was only $347.

The combination of lower expenses and higher demand has allowed full-service airlines to change their competitive methods, becoming more like the low-cost carriers. Instead of trying to provide the most luxurious service while keeping ticket prices under control, they are packing more passengers into their aircraft and turning amenities that used to be standard into extra-cost options. At the end of 2016, ticket prices had come down a bit, but profits per passenger had gone up nearly 10 percent.

One profitable tactic was to shrink passenger seats. Seat space is measured in "pitch," the distance from one point on an aircraft seat to the same point on the seat behind. In economy sections, the average seat pitch ranges from 30 to 34 inches. As demand grew, it shrank, with some airlines reducing the distance between seats to 28 inches. "Slim line" seats helped ease the crowding. Thinner padding squeezed the seats down to 1 inch in thickness, allowing airlines to pack in more passengers while keeping pitch at a reasonable 30 to 32 inches.

At the same time, many of the services that passengers once could take for granted now carry a price tag. Passengers willing to do without checked bags, food, or seat upgrades can pay less even as the airlines reap bigger profits.

Baggage fees have become standard throughout the industry. Most airlines still allow passengers one free carry-on bag, but not all. In mid-2018, Spirit Airlines charges from

$20 to $100 for a bag in the overhead bin. A few carriers still allow passengers to check one bag, or even two, without charge, but most charge from $15 to $45 for the first, and prices go up sharply for additional bags. Bags that are oversize or overweight carry hefty fees.

On a few airlines, so do overweight passengers.

Pets have become luggage. Some airlines classify a dog or cat as an extra bag. Others charge specific fees of $100 and up. However, on most airlines seeing-eye dogs and other service animals still travel free.

One typical discount package from a full-service airline is United's "basic economy" class, introduced in 2017. Price-conscious travelers get to pay less, but the new ticket option involves some trade-offs. There are charges for carry-on bags. Passengers are not allowed to upgrade to better classes. Neither are they allowed to change flights. Refunds are only a memory.

In 2015, the Global Business Travel Association reported that average airfares within the U.S. had declined from $392 the previous year to $379. However, the proliferation of ancillary fees negated whatever savings business travelers might have received. In 2017, baggage fees and reservation cancellation/change fees brought airlines some $7 billion in extra revenue, providing half of all industry profits. In 2018, a strong global economy was expected to raise air fares by an average of 3.5 percent.

Frequent flyer programs are changing too. Early in 2016, Delta announced that in 2017 it would begin to calculate award miles according to ticket price rather than miles flown. United, JetBlue, Southwest, and Virgin America all have similar programs. In fact, according to one survey, in mid-2018, only Alaska Airlines still bases its frequent flier program on miles rather than money. This makes both elite status and award tickets harder to come by, but it makes for bigger numbers on the carrier's bottom line.

Another tactic is been the formation of cooperative alliances designed to benefit the partners. The simplest alliances are codeshare agreements in which each airline markets the flight under its own number but only one of the companies handles the flight operation. This allows all partners to profit from the sale of tickets without going to the expense of flying a route that would be unlikely to support multiple airlines. For companies, this reduces the cost of sales offices, operational and maintenance facilities, and personnel. Travelers often benefit from lower prices, more destinations within easy reach, and more departure times. However, alliances can also bring higher prices by reduced competition and flights among cities that multiple partners used to serve.

In 2016, there are three major alliances and several lesser ones. Star Alliance, with twenty-seven members, carries more than 642 million passengers per year. Sky Team, with twenty, moves 665 million. Oneworld, with thirteen airlines, serve 557 million annually. All three have global reach. Three smaller groups, Vanilla Alliance, U-FLY Alliance, and Value Alliance serve Australasia and the Far East. Membership in the three large groupings has changed over the years as companies merge, go out of business, or transfer to another alliance. We can expect to see many more such changes as each company's business strategies evolve.

Combined with a favorable economy, adopting new competitive methods has made a big difference in the balance sheets of some airlines. It even changed the mind of Warren Buffet, who had shunned the industry since buying a piece of US Airways in 1989 and losing most of his $358-million investment. In mid-November 2016, Berkshire Hathaway bought $1.3 billion worth of airline stock. Some $800 million went for shares in American Airlines, a company long burdened by high debt and financial problems. Other companies receiving Buffett money included American, United Continental Holdings, and Southwest. Factors prompting the investment were not announced, but obvious probabilities included rising passenger demand, improved competitive strategies, and the low price of airline shares compared to those of other industries.

Some tinkering with their appearance in the stock market helped as well. In 2016, American, United Continental, Delta, and Southwest all bought back some of their outstanding stock. This meant there was more profit per remaining share, improving their stock's appeal for investors. Stock prices went up, making it easier for the companies to attract needed funding.

While regaining their profitability after the Great Recession, the airlines also faced bad news. Yet, their problems were the kind that air carriers, and most of their passengers, have learned are simply part of the industry.

One is labor unrest. Strikes are a constant for airlines and associated services. In 2016 alone: Lufthansa was forced to cancel more than eight hundred flights when one-thousand-eight-hundred pilots walked off the job. Company pilots also held a one-day strike in June. At Air France, air traffic controllers walked out for a day, check-in staff and flight attendants went on strike, and a strike by pilots was canceled at the last minute. Spanish air traffic controllers briefly went on strike. In mid-December, strikes threatened for later in the month included pilots at Hawaiian Airlines and airport workers at Chicago O'Hare and at eighteen airports in Britain. It was a typical year in commercial aviation.

Airline strikes are not like those in other industries. Because business interruptions are so costly, most are limited to a day or two—long enough to make the workers' point without threatening corporate survival. Strikes can be nerve-wracking, but they are something those in the industry are forced to live with.

The second concern is security. Although there have been no attacks on the scale of 9/11, terrorists have attempted airplane bombings several times since 2001. Two such efforts were successful. In Russia, suicide bombers brought down two domestic flights in 2004, with a combined loss of ninety lives. And a bomb planted by ISIL sympathizers at the Cairo airport took down Metrojet Flight 9268 on October 31, 2015, killing 224 passengers and crew. At least five similar plots have failed.

Several recent incidents have involved computer hacking. An attack on computers operated by LOT, the Polish airline, temporarily stranded 1,400 passengers at Warsaw Chopin Airport. Hackers also attempted to disable the electrical equipment of airplanes at Cairo airport. So far, none of these efforts has been particularly destructive.

There really is not much to be said about the risk of terrorism. In the United States, airlines pay an estimated $7 billion per year for pre-flight security checks by the Transportation Safety Administration. Yet tests find that screeners miss weapons and explosives up to 95 percent of the time, and the most effective gate security could not have prevented the Cairo attack; airport personnel planted that bomb. This problem will remain with us at least for the next two decades. We will not be surprised if it continues long after today's hospitality students have retired.

Nonetheless, it is worth remembering that the airline industry can be its own worst enemy. Early in 2018, Berkshire Hathaway's $1.8 billion investment had grown to some $11 billion. Then airline stocks plummeted on fears that there soon would be a fare war among carriers. In a single day, Berkshire Hathaway's profits shrank by $727 million. In early January 2019, another one-day drop in airline stocks cost the investor about $559 million in Delta, Southwest, United, and American. Berkshire Hathaway was Delta's largest investor and was the second-largest in the other three.

Looking Ahead

In Chapter 6, we offered a broad overview of the future based on the trends in Appendix A. It will be a period of economic growth and demographic evolution that will move the world's financial and political center of gravity notably toward the East. It also will be a time when technology accelerates, bringing change even faster than it has done to date. Commercial aviation will be particularly sensitive to many of these developments, none of which is under its control. In the material ahead, we will examine what some of the most significant trends will mean for airlines and the executives who manage them. However, this will be no more than the beginning of a process that will be a part of daily life for anyone pursuing a career in this challenging industry. We urge readers to examine the trends in Appendix A closely and work out for themselves what they mean for the airlines. It will be good practice.

As this is written, the United States seems to remain in a transitional period. It has been two years, as this is written, since one president widely respected at home and abroad ended his second term in office and another much less well-known and less predictable moved into the White House. Yet, much remains unclear. President Donald Trump espouses policies in many ways very different from those of his predecessor. He advocates much tighter budgets than the country has seen in decades, looser regulation, less involvement in overseas conflicts, and a much harder line with some potential adversaries. As of mid-2018, some of these policies have been applied in unexpected and sometimes incompatible ways. As their effects become clear, some of the forecasts below are very likely to change. Readers will need to adjust them accordingly, making their own analyses as events proceed.

Here are some of the critical issues to consider:

Global economy: Airlines may be even more sensitive to their economic environment than other sectors of the travel and hospitality industry. In good economic times, travel is favorite recreation and a sound investment in new business and effective management. In lean times, would-be tourists with empty pockets stay at home, and businesses often view travel budgets as fat ripe for the trimming.

As we observed in Chapter 6, even moderate prosperity should keep the travel and hospitality industry growing and profitable. Air travel will be no exception—assuming the price of oil remains under control, as we believe it generally will.

Our baseline forecast calls for the continued growth of the global economy at an average rate of about 3 percent annually. At that rate, it will double in size by 2037 and nearly triple by 2050. This is enough to support the growth of the airline industry well beyond 2020.

We expect growth to slow in most of today's industrialized economies, with comparatively rapid expansion among the developing lands.

Lands outside the United States and Europe will account for a much greater part of global economic growth. China will be the single greatest factor in this. Its growth rate can be expected to remain around 6 percent annually in the near future, declining to about 3.5 percent in the next decade and 2.5 percent in the more distant future. The Chinese economy is already larger than that of the U.S. when measured by purchasing power parity. Despite the continued slowing of its growth, by 2025 it will be well on its way to surpassing the United States even in the absolute terms on which international trade operates.

Many other economies will be burgeoning during this period. The Indian economy will not expand as quickly China's used to for many more years, but its share of global prosperity should grow steadily—if New Delhi can restrain the anti-capitalist impulse to throttle its own success. By 2030, we expect it to become as prosperous, when measured by purchasing power parity, as the United States was in 2014.

Other developing economies also are likely to grow rapidly over the long term. Mexico, Indonesia, and Turkey in particular have relatively diversified economies that should serve them well. Within the careers of today's college students, they are likely to become as prosperous as the major European economies are today.

For Russia, Nigeria, and other countries heavily dependent on natural resources for their income, that kind of prosperity will be much harder to achieve. They will need to develop more diversified industries and much better governance. It is not yet clear that they can do so.

Population growth will be a secondary factor in the airline markets. This will be most significant in India and in Africa, which has the world's highest birth rates. In most African countries, resource-based economies will slow development, substantially offsetting the potential benefits of larger working-age populations.

All this tells us where the airline industry can be expected to grow fastest—in China, India, Mexico, Indonesia, and Turkey. It could grow rapidly as well in countries like Malaysia, Nigeria, and Vietnam if their government policies act to promote general prosperity rather than to enrich, or to maintain the dominance of, those in power. In Nigeria and other parts of Africa, this may be too much to expect.

All this points to rapid growth for airline travel both to and within regions that are not yet major airline markets. We see this already in China, where fast economic growth and the gradual loosening of military control over the airspace has resulted in an aviation boom. The decade ahead will see slower, but steady, growth of the airline industry in many other developing-world markets.

The primary risk to this expansion is another worldwide recession. We do not expect to see one unless a great economic power makes a serious and avoidable mistake. Unfortunately, that possibility is great enough and its consequences severe enough that we cannot ignore it. Two obvious hazards are a collapse of the Chinese banking system owing to its enormous burden of uncollectible debt and a prolonged, destructive trade war between the United States and China, and conceivably between the United States and its traditional allies in Europe and Canada. Either would set back the airlines' growth for as long as they continue, and both will need careful monitoring in the near future.

Here in 2018, we have given up trying to predict how the Trump administration will handle trade policy in the years ahead. We have assumed that the president's combative rhetoric on trade was largely a negotiating position, and this remains our default guess about his most inflammatory rhetoric. However, we are a lot less certain of it than we once were. However, we remain confident that even the worst case will represent only a temporary setback for global trade, and therefor the airlines. By 2025, whatever trouble materializes should have passed, and the global economy will return to solid growth. The market for air travel will return with it.

Technology: This is the second factor tomorrow's aviation professionals will have to deal with. If it is not the airline exec's biggest day-to-day worry, in the longer run it will do more to transform the airline industry than any other. For many years, technology will continue to offer better navigation, more efficient aircraft, cleaner burning engines, greater safety—and the continuing need for investment to keep up with both regulatory requirements and the competition.

Into the mid-2020s, the most significant development is a new air traffic control (ATC) system. In the U.S., it is called the Next Generation Transportation System, or NextGen. A similar and compatible system in Europe is known as SESAR, for Single European Sky ATM Research. Parts of NextGen already are in place, while others are scheduled for completion in the coming decade or so. (The schedule has slipped frequently, and we will not be surprised if it does so again.) SESAR is scheduled for deployment between 2024 and 2035.

For roughly half a century, airliners have flown from one airport to another guided by radio beacons along a series of well-defined paths in the sky. Radar watches over the airspace, and ATC personnel monitor their displays and instruct pilots to ensure that aircraft remain safely separated. This system does not fail often, but over the years about two dozen accidents have been caused by human error. This system also wastes fuel and travel time by requiring aircraft to remain within their defined paths rather than flying straight to their destinations.

NextGen was designed to solve these problems by guiding the aircraft with GPS and having the airplanes themselves report their location to nearby aircraft to ensure adequate separation. Budget concerns and problems with project management have stripped away some of the features NextGen was designed to offer. Much more of the responsibility for air safety will remain with human controllers on the ground. However, it still should be a big improvement on the old way of doing things.

For airlines, this will mean improved safety, shorter travel times, and more efficient use of fuel. By reducing the separation distances requiried for safety, NextGen and SESAR also will allow many more aircraft to fly simultaneously as the demand for air travel continues to grow.

For airline executives, it will mean an estimated equipment cost of $15 billion between 2013 and 2030, when the NextGen system is supposed to be complete. Funding and managing this transition will be a significant requirement until the new global ATC system is in place.

Many other technologies also will require funding and management over the next decade. Ground operations already are changing as companies develop robotic baggage handling systems, automated loaders to pack baggage and cargo efficiently into the aircraft, and even unmanned tugs to move airliners to and from boarding gates.

In the air, pilots are slowly being "assisted" more and more by automated systems. Airliners equipped with autoland systems can handle nearly all parts of the landing process without human input. On Airbus aircraft, the control system even overrules pilot input to keep the airplane from maneuvering in ways the engineers did not intend.

In Europe, a proposed technology called the Innovative Future Air Transport System would replace onboard pilots with automated controls and a backup pilot on the ground to oversee the operation and take control of the airplane in an emergency, much like today's military drone pilots. For an estimated $2 million per aircraft, a 220-passenger airliner could carry 230 passengers and crew 5 percent faster, use 5 percent less fuel, cost 20 percent less for maintenance, and spend significantly more time in the air. We do not expect to see such a system begin operation until the mid or late 2030s, but today's students will face the challenges of fitting them into airline budgets and operations while brokering peace with the personnel all this new technology will replace.

Competition: Given a prosperous economy, we can expect to see the rise, and no doubt fall, of many small regional carriers throughout the world. However, new air services may not be the primary rivals that appear in the next few decades. In many parts of the world, that role probably will go to rail systems.

In Europe, trains routinely travel at speeds of 125 mph; a few in Italy top out at nearly twice that. Tracks link all major urban areas and many lesser cities. No surprise then that rail has captured a substantial share of the continent's short-distance travel market. Eurostar, which runs between London and Paris and among several French cities, accounts for 75 percent of the combined rail/air market along its routes. In all, trains carry about 45 percent of the passengers who travel within the EU.

Things are different in the United States. Although the U.S. has the biggest network of rail lines in the world, nearly all that travels along it is cargo. In one recent year, railways in the EU carried nearly 250 billion passenger-miles of traffic. In the U.S., the number was less than 11 billion. Most of that was along the Northeast Corridor from Boston through New York and Philadelphia to Washington, DC.

Amtrak train in Washington, DC

Yet, competition between the airlines and Amtrak, the federally funded passenger rail service, has grown increasingly intense on those routes where passenger trains are available. With high fares, slow security inspection at airports, and frequent delays, the airlines have been losing business in the valuable Northeast Corridor to what in the United States passes for high-speed rail. Although Amtrak's Acela trains can reach 150 mph, the over-all speed from Boston to New York is only 79 mph, and 63 mph from New York to Washington. Despite this, some 75 percent of travelers between Washington and New York go by train. Between New York and Boston, it is more than 50 percent. By 2020, we expect Amtrak to carry twice as many passengers along the Northeast Corridor as it did in 2010.

Another factor is the possible spread of true high-speed rail. In addition to upgrades in the Northeast Corridor to allow speeds up to 150 miles per hour, many new rail routes have been proposed for private development. It appears that a few eventually will carry passengers. These include:

The California High-Speed Rail network from from Anaheim and Los Angeles to San Francisco, with a branch line to Sacramento. Construction of the first segment, from Madera to Fresno, began in 2015. Plans call for the system to be complete by 2029, but heavy political opposition may yet abort the project.

In Florida, the Brightline system is intended eventually to carry passengers from Miami to West Palm Beach with stops in Fort Lauderdale. Construction began in 2014, with service between Fort Lauderdale and West Palm Beach inaugurated in January 2018 and to Miami that May. Service to Orlando is scheduled to begin in 2019.

Other proposed high-speed rail routes would link Portland, OR, with Vancouver; Chicago with St. Louis, MO; Cleveland and Cincinnati in Ohio; Washington, DC, with Raleigh and Charlotte, VA. None of these projects yet has a firm schedule for completion, but they have received federal funding in amounts ranging from $485 million to $2.9 billion. It seems likely that they will eventually begin to siphon off passenger traffic from airlines in their regions.

China has built an enormous network of air service over the last 30 years. At least fifteen airlines provide both domestic and international service, while at least thirty fly exclusively within the country. Their number is growing rapidly. Five domestic airlines began operation between 2014 and 2016 alone.

Domestic air operations in China also face increasing competition from high-speed rail. As recently as 2008, the Chinese rail system provided less than 1.5 billion trips. By 2015, China operated more than 75,000 miles of railways, including nearly 12,000 of high-speed rail. Inter-city trains that year carried more than 2.3 billion passenger trips totaling nearly 700 billion passenger-miles.

China continues to expand its rail system as fast as it can. In 2015, the country began work on some 7,500 miles of high-speed rail corridors forming a grid across much of the country. The system was to be completed in 2020, but the schedule has been moved up and many lines are expected to be in operation before then.

Unlike many other countries, China uses its trains primarily for long-distance travel. Average trip distance there is more than 300 miles. We expect trip distances to continue stretching as high-speed rail lines are completed. As the system grows, rail will provide ever-greater competition for domestic air service. In the next decade, this is likely to trigger a period of consolidation in the Chinese airline industry.

One other potential competitor for inter-city customers is likely to begin operation sometime in the decade after 2020. This is the Hyperloop system proposed by inventor Elon Musk. Traveling through tubes in near-vacuum at speeds up to 760 mph,

Hyperloop could carry passengers from San Francisco to Los Angeles in 30 minutes or from China to Germany in a day. In the U.S., two companies are working to develop the system: Hyperloop One and and Hyperloop Transportation Technologies. Hyperloop One claims it will demonstrate a full-scale Hyperloop by 2020. HTT, meanwhile, has announced plans to build a 10-km test track in Tongren, China. Half of the $300-million cost will be funded by the state-owned Tongren Transportation & Tourism Investment Group.

However promising the Hyperloop system, there are serious obstacles to its construction. Mr. Musk says it would cost about $6 billion to build the line from San Francisco to Los Angeles. Others put the figure much higher. The problem of obtaining right-of-way along such an extensive corridor could be even harder to overcome. Legal and regulatory hurdles may stop the Hyperloop even if technology does not.

For this reason, the first Hyperloop system to be operational is likely to be carrying passengers in another country. Hyperloop One has several deals in the works with potential customers overseas. The company reportedly has been negotiating a possible investment from China's largest maker of railway equipment. It also has signed a Memorandum of Understanding with Summa Group to explore the idea of connecting Moscow's transportation grid to a Hyperloop system. Russia seems a particularly likely market for Hyperloop One. It takes a train sixteen days to travel across the 8,077-mile northern rail route across the country. A Hyperloop train could make the distance in under eleven hours. However, the first system to move passengers probably will appear in the Middle East. In November 2016, Hyperloop One announced that it had agreed with Dubai's Roads and Transport Authority to study potential Hyperloop routes for passengers and cargo in the United Arab Emirates.

Wherever Hyperloop systems are built, air travel clearly will face serious competition. With reasonable ticket prices, Hyperloop might easily dominate its markets.

The Bottom Line

The post-2008 downturn in air travel has had a lasting impact on the industry, just as the contraction after 9/11 did. Boeing estimated that 5 percent fewer passenger-miles would be flown in 2020 than would have been the case if the 9/11 terrorist spectacular had not taken place. That put the market roughly four years behind the growth curve that analysts once expected. The recession of 2008 and '09 further slowed the growth of air travel. Airlines do not expect to see a billion passengers per year in the U.S. until at least 2020.

Yet the real lesson to be drawn is the importance and durability of commercial aviation. The contraction in travel after 9/11 and during the Great Recession could not have been much more painful for airlines and their executives. Yet, the great majority of airlines survived the hard times to prosper when business recovered. And it recovered faster than some other industry sectors. For any future travel executives who welcome challenge in a time of rapid change, the airlines offer careers to consider.

Incorporating Olsen into Airlines

As we have seen, the world's airlines have faced many hardships in recent years—global recession, terrorism, and epidemics among the worst—and while many have been able to survive these challenges others have failed. Success in hard times requires the skilled application of all the techniques we examined in the early chapters of this text.

Because airline companies can be affected both positively and negatively by factors all over the world, airline executives must scan the global environment constantly to identify risks and opportunities that could improve or threaten their performance. The ability to recognize approaching trouble while there is still time to prepare for it can make the difference between success and failure. This is, of course, true in all industries. Yet, because airlines are at the mercy of a uniquely wide range of conflicting forces they may require broader, more continuous environmental scanning and forecasting than other segments of the travel industry.

As we saw in this text's early chapters, environmental scanning is only the beginning. It will do little good unless the airline has its critical success factors (CSF) in place. Some examples in the airline industry are loyalty programs, frequent flier miles programs, and traveler status programs—things that once were unique competitive methods but quickly became taken for granted. Without incentives such as these, even more travelers would choose whatever airline offered the lowest fare, accelerating a race to the bottom in both prices and service. With these CSF in place, customers develop at least some loyalty to their airlines of choice and continue to provide revenue in return for the extra rewards or amenities the carrier offers.

Just as importantly, airlines must choose competitive methods that give them a strategic advantage in the market. Some examples are free checked bags, larger seating (bigger seats, more leg room), complementary pillows or blankets, e-check in, onboard entertainment, Wi-Fi, and food and beverage choices. In the future, airlines can be expected to develop many more ways to make flight more satisfying if not necessarily more comfortable. These competitive methods offer great ways to help guests personalize their flight.

This is one area in which the high operating costs of the legacy airlines make themselves felt. Customers often are willing to pay a premium when airlines offer an extra level of service, and when they pay more for a flight, they feel they deserve something in return from the airline—free snacks, a free checked bag, etc. It is easy to assume that the full-fare airlines are likely to provide more such amenities than cut-price carriers.

This is not always so. Discount airlines, unburdened by enormous debt and retirement payments, often can afford to provide more extras than the legacy airlines. Southwest offers complementary bag check, snacks and non-alcoholic beverages, and thirteen live television channels with seventy-five different television shows. Older competitors may offer their guests more amenities, but extra services are not always complementary and may be available only on select international flights. As airlines compete to offer more rewards, still more customers may decide to save

Co-Alignment Model

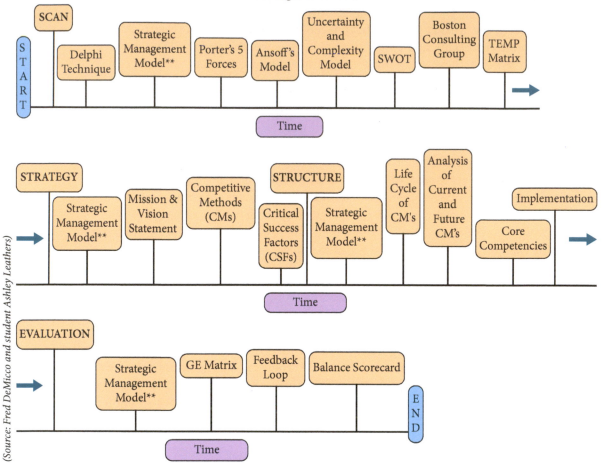

(Source: Fred DeMicco and student Ashley Leathers)

Figure 9.1. The complete process of analyzing competitive methods and critical success factors.

money by flying with the least expensive carrier even if doing so sacrifices a few comforts.

In fact, what the passenger is willing to sacrifice often is the most important issue in selecting competitive methods. For example, customers may be willing to sacrifice extra legroom if they will receive a free checked bag and a free snack. In developing their competitive methods, airline executives must figure out customers want and are willing to pay for. This analysis can be more difficult than in better differentiated markets and more influenced by the competition's choices.

As Figure 9.1 shows, the airline industry uses the Co-Alignment Model to choose appropriate strategies and to gain a competitive edge in the market. Environmental scanning and forecasting are very important at the beginning of this process, both to learn how experts view the opportunities and to anticipate change. Forecasting also can give executives a broad view of the most optimistic and pessimistic consequences of their choices.

The airline's environmental scans and forecasting must take account of a wider variety of factors than many other industries would need to—remote, task, functional, and firm environments all may be uniquely complex, accounting for forces that could impact the company, the market's certainty and complexity, growth, shares, and SWOT analyses, as well as many other factors. In many cases, valid and reliable data may be hard to find.

Once this is accomplished, airline executives must use this information to design strategic methods that will benefit their firm and make it profitable. The Strategic Management Model shown in Figure 9.1 shows the order of steps from the forecasting stage through the final phase, when it is later evaluated.

The choice of competitive methods is important, but their lifecycles and required investments can be even more so. For example, frequent-flier programs began as competitive methods and have long since evolved into critical success factors. Yet, as we saw earlier, in 2016 domestic airlines in the U.S. fundamentally changed their programs. Until then, frequent-flier rewards were always been based on miles flown. Today, they are calculated according to the amount of money spent with the carrier. This provides an extra benefit for first class passengers but penalizes those who are more price-sensitive. Delta Airlines was first to make this change, but many competitors quickly followed its lead. Frequent-flier programs in their original form have come to the end of their lifecycle. As a result, some customers may switch to discount carriers. Forecasting allows us to anticipate such changes. The Strategic Management Model helps us to evaluate them and decide whether the change, on balance, will serve the company well.

Choice of routes provides another competitive method. Since time is everyone's most precious commodity, airlines could charge extra for direct, point-to-point flights. We are likely to see many variations of this method as the NextGen and SESAR air traffic control systems make it possible to shave minutes off flight times.

Communication is increasingly important to those in the air. Making Wi-Fi available to travelers thus is a hugely important competitive method. People on flights without Wi-Fi are "losing time" because they cannot remain connected with their colleagues and clients or use their laptops and tablets to find information online.

Many customers also feel comfort is one of the main reasons to fly with a specific airline. Many would prefer larger seats and more leg room. If the airline believes it can make a profit on a newer plane with larger seating, then it should make the necessary investment to improve customer satisfaction.

In choosing a competitive method, executives must be sure that it will add value for customers and be profitable for the firm over the longest possible lifecycle. As we see with frequent-flier programs, these decisions must be revisited constantly to recognize when changes in the industry require either investing more in the method or replacing it with another.

Reviewing competitive methods thus becomes a daily necessity for airline executives even more than for their peers in other industries. So do scanning the environment (task and remote) and looking at forces driving change, value drivers, critical success factors, and lifecycles. In addition, they must constantly monitor changes in cash flow over time and the net present value of each competitive method. After all these factors are taken into account, the competitive method's future performance can be projected, and decisions about it can be made strategically.

The more CMs the firm has, the more market value it will obtain. The value of the firm can be measured by CMs and shows the growth that these methods bring to the firm. The company also can grow through factors that are not easily measured in terms of profit. Many of these are intangible: brand name, location, employees, experience, etc. Both tangible and intangible products and services are beneficial to the firm, but only the competitive methods used can be measured to determine the value they add.

The airline industry is a market in which companies sell combinations of products and services. For example, when customers buy a first-class seat, they will enjoy services far more elaborate and personal than those granted to passengers farther back in the aircraft. A bundle of products and services like this can be viewed as a single, unique competitive method.

Southwest Airlines, for example, was famous for its budget flights, but more and more competitors have entered into this market. Therefore, Southwest and its competitors are using the forces that drive change as strategic tools to regain their competitive edge. The price of budget-flight tickets usually excludes various fees. Southwest and other airlines have designed bundle options to attract and retain more customers. Even though Southwest has provided all its customers with more options, they treat those who have purchased bundle packages with even greater priority than usual. Extra treats for these customers include more frequent flier points and a free alcoholic drink. Southwest also gives up to $28 per flight Business Select upgrades off their unrestricted anytime fares. Additionally, after strategic analysis, it began to sell a new package that allows specific customers to jump to the front of boarding lines. In this way, Southwest Airlines encourages customers to spend more money for their flights and provide the company with greater profits.

Competitive methods shape each company and bring it success or failure. For airlines, the frequent introduction of new, well-chosen competitive methods has become a critical success factor in this always-changing industry. As time goes on, airlines must constantly develop new and more effective methods that provide them room to grow and prosper, no matter the current global conditions.

References

"2030: The "Perfect Storm" Scenario." Population Institute. <https://www.populationinstitute.org/external/files/reports/The_Perfect_Storm_Scenario_for_2030.pdf>.

"Airline Industry Market Dynamics." Alglas, 2014. Web. 3 May 2014. <http://www.alglas.com/airline_industry_market_dynamics.htm>.

"Annual Crude Oil and Jet Fuel Prices." Airlines for America, 2014. Web. 22 Apr. 2014. <http://www.airlines.org/Pages/Annual-Crude-Oil-and-Jet-Fuel-Prices.aspx>.

"Building the New American. Together." U.S. Airways, 1 Jan. 2014. Web. 26 Apr. 2014. <http://www.usairways.com/en-US/aboutus/pressroom/arriving.html?c=glmus_21225&re=1>.

"Crude Oil Price History." FedPrimeRate.com, 1 Jan. 2014. Web. 1 May 2014. <http://www.fedprimerate.com/crude-oil-price-history.htm>.

"Fact Sheet: Climate Change." IATA, Dec. 2013. Web. 1 May 2014. <https://www.iata.org/pressroom/facts_figures/fact_sheets/pages/environment.aspx>.

"Operational Fuel Efficiency." IATA, 2014. Web. 1 May 2014. <http://www.iata.org/whatwedo/ops-infra/Pages/fuel-efficiency.aspx>.

"United Kingdom (UK) GDP - Gross Domestic Product." countryeconomy.com, 2014. Web. 20 Apr. 2014. <http://countryeconomy.com/gdp/uk>.

"What is the U.S. economic outlook for 2014. Not good." U$ Economic Outlook,2014. Web. 16 Apr. 2014. <http://www.useconomicoutlook2014.com/author/admin#.U3qpMl5H2FI>.

<http://online.wsj.com/news/articles/SB10001424127887323926104578273933631888950>

Carey, Susan. "Why Small Airports Are in Such Big Trouble." **Wall Street Journal** [New York] 8 Apr. 2014, sec. Marketplace: B1, B4. Print.

Dugger, Celia W. "Half the World Soon to be in Citites." The New York Times, 27 June 2007. Web. 20 Apr. 2014. <http://www.nytimes.com/2007/06/27/world/27cnd-population.html?hp>.

Erumban, Abdul A. "Global Economic Outlook 2014, February 2014 Update." The Conference Board, 2014. Web. 20 Apr. 2014. <https://www.conference-board.org/data/globaloutlook.cfm>.

Feigenbaum, Baruch. "Southwest Struggles As Legacy Airlines Establish Solid Business Models. Reason Foundation, 6 Dec. 2013. Web. 1 Apr. 2014. <http://reason.org/blog/show/southwest-struggles-as-legacy-airli>.

Kendall, Brent and Susan Carey. "U.S. Defends Settlement in Air Deal." **Wall Street Journal** [New York] 11 Mar. 2014, sec. Corporate News: B3. Print.

Kirby, Mark. "Andrew Muirhead, Director of Innovation, Lufthansa Technik - on the future of passenger experiences." Red Associates, 2014. Web. 26 Apr. 2014. <http://www.redassociates.com/conversations/enabling-innovation/andrew-muirhead-director-of-innovation-lufthansa-technik-on-the-future-of-passenger-experiences/>.

Mayerowitz, Scott. "The Future of Aviation: Airlines' Leaders Predictions." USA Today, 1 Jan. 2014. Web. 1 Apr. 2014. <http://www.usatoday.com/story/travel/flights/2014/01/01/future-of-aviation-airline-ceos-predictions/4267643/>.

McCartney, Scott . "A Prius With Wings vs. a Guzzler in the Clouds." The Wall Street Journal, 12 Aug. 2010. Web. 28 Apr. 2014. <http://online.wsj.com/news/articles/SB10001424052748704901104575423261677748380>.

McCartney, Scott. "Hey, Let's Just Heat the Runways." The Wall Street Journal, 20 Feb. 2014. Web. 28 Apr. 2014. <http://online.wsj.com/news/articles/SB20001424052702304914204579392883809689994>.

Nicas, Jack. "At the Airport, Bots vs Terrorists." **Wall Street Journal** [New York] 31 Dec. 2013, sec. Marketplace: B1, B2. Print.

Nixon, Ron. "Frustrations of Air Travel Push Passengers to Amtrak." . The New York Times, 15 Aug. 2012. Web. 26 Apr. 2014. <http://www.nytimes.com/2012/08/16/business/hassles-of-air-travel-push-passengers-to-amtrak.html?pagewanted=all>.

Norris, Floyd. "A Dire Economic Forecast Based on New Assumptions." The New York Times, 27 Feb. 2014. Web. 20 Apr. 2014. <http://www.nytimes.com/2014/02/28/business/economy/questioning-a-dire-economic-forecast.html?_r=>.

Plumer, Brad. "How the big U.S. airlines try to avoid competing with each other." The Washington Post, 14 Apr. 2013. Web. 22 Apr. 2014. <http://www.washingtonpost.com/blogs/wonkblog/wp/2013/08/14/heres-how-the-big-u-s-airlines-try-to-avoid-competing-with-each-other/>.

Rapoza, Kenneth. "Global Growth Forecast 2020." Forbes, 26 Mar. 2012. Web. 20 Apr. 2014. <http://www.forbes.com/sites/kenrapoza/2012/03/26/global-growth-forecast-2020/>.

Scott Mccartney. "A New Bundle Jungle for Travelers." Wall Street Journal, 30 Jan. 2013, online.

Wang, Brian. "Cities and Megacities of 2030, 2050 and 2100." nextbigfuture.com, 23 Sept. 2011. Web. 20 Apr. 2014. <http://nextbigfuture.com/2011/09/cities-and-megacities-of-2030-2050-and.html>.

Weisbrot, Mark. "Why has Europe's economy done worse than the US?" theguardian, 16 Jan. 2014. Web. 22 Apr. 2014. <http://www.theguardian.com/commentisfree/2014/jan/16/why-the-european-economy-is-worse>.

Web Assignment

Log into the student website and complete the end of chapter assignment. Try to utilize some of the works you read about from this chapter and apply the key concepts, terms, and theory in your responses.

The Cruise Industry – Trends and Strategy

Cruising is hot, hot, hot, and not just when the weather turns sultry. Demand for cruises has grown by 62 percent in ten years, according to the Cruise Lines International Association (CLIA.) It's only the beginning. Passenger loads in 2001 were a scant 10 million. In 2017, bookings reached 26.7 million, with 27.2 million anticipated in 2018. And by 2027, the world's cruise lines are expected to carry upward of 40 million passengers. At the beginning of 2018, 449 cruise ships plied the world's seas, with room for 537,000 passengers. In 2016, the latest number currently available, they carried some 24.7 million passengers.

Between 2018 and 2026, at least 89 new ships are scheduled to set sail, including 27 in 2018 and 24 more by the end of 2019. They will add 42,488 berths to the world total, well above the record 34,000 seen in 2018. One industry source speculates that as many as 500 cruise ships could be operating by 2027.

Cruise-industry executives clearly are not expecting any sharp contraction in the near future. History is on their side. The cruise industry's trend of steady growth, currently by an average of 7.4 percent per year, is one of the strongest in travel. Even the recession of 2008–'09 could barely interrupt it.

Present Status

CLIA tracks its members closely, so performance numbers for the organization's 54 lines and marketing affiliates are easy to find. They are not entirely comprehensive. The closest we have found to a comprehensive industry census includes 145 separate brands many of them small, independent lines operating in niche markets. In all, however, CLIA members account for 95 percent of global cruise passenger capacity. Data for them is effectively a look at the whole industry.

Their worldwide revenue in 2018 was expected to reach $45.6 billion, up 4.6 percent from 2017. Non-member lines can be expected to add about $8 billion to the total. By 2027, CLIA member revenue is expected to reach some $57 billion. Bookings have been growing by over 6 percent annually for more than two decades and about 7.4 percent per year since the end of the Great Recession.

All this gives cruising outsized impact on the global economy. CLIA's member cruise lines provided the equivalent of full-time employment for over 1 million people in 2016. They paid some $41.1 billion in wages and salaries. In all, the industry added an estimated $126 billion to the world's economic output that year.

The cruise industry is highly centralized, so much of the industry's profit goes to a small handful of companies. Many of the largest cruise lines, including many CLIA members, are owned and managed by larger holding companies—for example, Carnival Corporation owns not only Carnival Cruise Line, but Cunard, Princess Cruises, Holland America, and six others. The three largest cruise line companies have captured no less than 85 percent of the market. They are expected to pick up another percent or so by 2020.

Carnival's nine lines alone account for over 47 percent of cruise passengers and some 39 percent of industry revenue. The company operates 106 cruise ships (including ten on order), with more than 160,000 berths and $17.5 billion in revenue in 2017. The Carnival brand alone carries 22 percent of the world's passengers, with Costa Cruises and Princess each accounting for 6 percent.

© Ruth Peterkin/Shutterstock.com

In second place, Royal Caribbean International owns another quarter of the market and brought in about $8.8 billion in 2017. In mid-2018, the company operates 27 ships among three separate brands, with Royal Caribbean accounting for some 23 percent of the passengers carried and over 20 percent of revenue.

Norwegian Cruise Line comes in third with 9.5 percent of the industry's passengers and over 12 percent of revenue. This is divided among three brands: Norwegian, by far the largest with some 9.5 percent of global bookings; Oceania Cruises; and Regent Seven Seas, each with less than 1 percent.

Outside these three, only MSC Cruises, Disney, Pullmantur, and TUI Cruises carry much over 1 percent of the world's passengers, about 7 percent, 2.3 percent, 1.4 percent, and 2 percent, respectively. TUI is a joint venture between Royal Caribbean and TUI AG, in Germany.

As demand and revenues have grown, cruise lines have been expanding. Counting only CLIA members, cruise ships now visit 2,000 destinations around the world, and guests can choose from among over 30,000 different cruises each year. At least 28 lines specializing in river cruises, only a minority of them belonging to CLIA, add still more capacity for vacations afloat.

The steady growth of the world's cruise fleet will affect both these specialties. Of the 97 new cruise ships scheduled for delivery between 2017 and 2026, eighty of them are ocean-going, and seventeen are designed for river cruises. The marine vessels include four giants of 200,000 tons or more. MSC Cruises will add two of its new World Class designs—one for delivery in 2022, one in 2024—with record-setting capacities of 6,850 passengers. The company has options for two more in 2025 and 2026. Yet the largest physically will be Royal Caribbean's biggest Oasis-class vessels, 1,185 feet long and some 227,000 gross tons. In all, these new vessels will add berths for 230,788 passengers to the world's cruise fleet.

These new ships will not add as many net berths to the world's fleet as one might expect, only a few percent, as aging vessels are being retired. However, the ships coming online over the next decade should be significantly more efficient and profitable than any now afloat. And new ships always attract high demand from passengers with a taste for the latest, greatest, and most glamorous.

Before we consider the various cruise markets and the strategies that companies use to compete in them, Cruise Market Watch, a well-known data source for this industry, offers a breakdown of the average passenger's costs on a cruise and the way the money is divided among the line's expense categories. This kind of information is basic to understanding the industry's priorities and performance. In 2018:

The average cruiser paid $1,293 for the ticket and racked up $498 in onboard spending. Casinos and bars accounted for $274 of shipboard receipts. The cruise line received another $100 for shore excursions and $50 in the spa. All other onboard spending came to $75. This adds up to a total of $1,779 in cruise line revenue for the typical cruiser's voyage.

Operating costs came to $1,564 per passenger. Because their products are relatively complicated and market specialties are so diverse, cruise lines still rely heavily on travel agents for bookings. Thus, the line's single largest cost for the typical passenger's voyage is the agent's commission, $233 on average, or 15 percent of gross revenue.

Fuel costs in 2018 were $193 per passenger, or 12.3 percent of the cruiser's spending. Note that this expense category has varied widely over the years as the cost of oil fluctuates. The peak in 2008 reached an unprecedented $103.67 per barrel, adjusted for inflation to 2017 prices. It has stayed relatively under control since then. By 2015, it had come down to just $43.22. Through 2018 prices reached over $72 per barrel for West Texas Intermediate Crude, one of the industry-standard grades, before declining to $43 in late December. Average price per barrel for the industry in 2018 was 65 for West Texas Intermediate and $72 for the cleaner, easier-to-refine Brent crude oil. As we will see when we look at the most important trends for the industry later in this chapter, we expect fuel costs to remain under control for at least the next decade, and probably longer.

Other expenses eat up much of the cruise line's revenue, as they do in any industry. Corporate operating costs in 2018 totaled $208 per passenger, or 13 percent. Another $197, or 12.6 percent went to payroll; $172, or 11 percent, to depreciation and amortization; $107, or 7 percent to food; and $136, or 8.7 percent, to transportation and miscellaneous shipboard costs. "Other operating costs" were the single biggest expense category, accounting for $260, or 16.6 percent, of per-passenger revenue. That left $212.80 per passenger, 6.6 percent, in gross profit.

As modest as it sounds, this is a pre-tax profit that many industries would envy. In late 2017, hotel profits averaged about 5 percent. Auto and car-component makers brought in only 4.2 percent. Retailers settled for an average of 4 percent. At grocery stores, gross profits from the main aisles came in at a paltry 1 percent.

Competitive Methods

New ships are a powerful attraction for many cruisers, but that appeal does come at a price. Cunard's Queen Mary 2, which made its maiden voyage in 2004, may be the most successful example of what a new ship can do for its owners. At 148,528 gross tons, with 2,620 passengers (2,690 after a refit in 2016), QM2 remains the largest ocean liner ever built. With a cost of some $800 million—$300,000 per passenger berth—she is the most expensive as well. In return for its investment, Cunard has one of the most sought-after ocean liners now in service and probably the first one considered by prosperous vacationers contemplating a round-the-world cruise. Staterooms on Queen Mary 2 are regularly booked up months in advance, and sometimes years.

Predictably, cruise lines have devised many more routine competitive methods to carve out their pieces of the market. Many have been carried over from other travel segments but are adapted to fit the unique needs of hospitality afloat.

One of the most obvious is simply being in the right place when potential customers are selecting a cruise. Some two-thirds of cruise passengers say the port of departure is a significant factor in choosing their voyage. They are far more likely to book a cruise if they can easily drive to the starting point of their journey than if getting there requires an airline flight. Therefore, cruise lines with enough ships to do so usually operate out of multiple ports on both coasts of the United States, various ports of Europe, and in the last few years several ports in China.

As in most industries, market segmentation is key to competition. Cruises and cruise lines are divided along several axes.

Price is the most basic of them. There was a time when an ocean cruise almost defined luxury. If you weren't rich, you weren't going. Today, cruise vacations are available for almost every budget and interest. The distinction between luxury cruises and the rest is still important, but even this is starting to blur.

Divide and Conquer

Industry observers tend to break the cost/luxury spectrum into three categories: affordable, family, and luxury. Although this is convenient, we should remember that such divisions are purely artificial. Participants can be found all along any spectrum, and all but the smallest companies participate in more than one market segment.

Differentiation begins with the cabins. Even the smallest cruise vessels offer a variety of accommodations, and prices, one for each specific combination of square footage, location on the ship, port holes or larger windows, access to a balcony, and various amenities. Quarters may range from small inboard cabins without so much as a porthole to giant suites at the front of the ship, some on two levels. Cabin prices can depend on distance from noisy show lounges, bars, or pools; stability (queasy voyagers will prefer lower, more central accommodations where they feel less roll and sway); niceties like an in-cabin bar, or spa-like fittings such as a fancy showerhead or a yoga mat. Many ships have twenty separate classes of accommodation, and some have upward of thirty.

At the least costly end of the range, affordable cruises are exactly that—low-priced, but not because they shortchange guests on comfort, entertainment, or other amenities. There isn't a seagoing equivalent of Jet Blue or Ryanair, where customers are interested in little more than getting from point A to point B at the lowest cost possible. Instead, economy-class cruises often travel on older ships operated by lines such as Carnival, Royal Caribbean, and Norwegian Cruise Line. Vessels launched in the 1990s or early 2000s are comfortable but without quite the diversity of amusements and Vegas-worthy bling typical of the latest cruise ships. On these vessels, there won't be quite as many restaurants and bars as on those more recently launched. There are likely to be fewer pools as well. Cruisers might even have to endure the absence of a surf simulator or climbing wall. Yet there will be plenty of food, shows, and other activities to relax with between ports.

Affordable cruises generally have a few other common characteristics. They tend to be brief. Three- and four-night cruises are common, and some last a single night—though not in the United States, where since 2016 government regulations require ships to visit at least one foreign port before returning to the U.S. Carnival Cruise Line reports that half its ships are dedicated to voyages of three to five days. The least expensive trips are likely to occur in the off-season—the Caribbean, Mexico, or the Bahamas in autumn; winter in the Mediterranean; and Alaska in May or September. Longer trips often are one-way, sailing when ships are being moved from one market to another for the season—from the eastern U.S. to Europe, or from Alaska to southern California in late autumn. Even better prices can be had by waiting until the last moment and looking for ships with unsold berths.

All these economies can add up to substantial savings. In November 2017, Norwegian Cruise Line offered seven-night cruises of the western Caribbean for as little as $48 per night, with a $1,000 onboard credit for those departing Miami in the next week. A four-night round-trip Carnival cruise to Mexico, leaving from Long Beach, CA, could be had for $42 per night for a single passenger, $49 for two, with up to $500 onboard credit for voyages departing within two weeks. For comparison, one seven-night Mexican cruise out of San Diego with Holland America ran $303 per night. Nothing comparable to the low-cost vacations would have been available to budget travelers a few decades ago.

As recently as the 1990s, many people still thought of cruises as an activity for older, well-to-do consumers. Today, family cruises are the industry's single biggest market segment. According to CLIA, 42 percent of cruise parties include children under the age of 18. For almost any cruise line, save the smaller luxury specialists, this is a critical market. This also is where competition is at its most intense. New competitive methods are likely to debut here, and many remain focused on family vacations.

The older ships seen in the affordable market often host family cruises as well, but this is where many of the newer and larger vessels stand out. Think of them as floating resorts. They carry perhaps 2,500 passengers on average, but also come in plus sizes ranging up to 5,500 double occupancy and 1,000 more at full capacity. Cruisers will find upward of a dozen restaurants; a bar or seven (one ship we know offers fourteen); one or two movie theaters; a gymnasium; a full-service spa; at least one, but frequently two or three fresh-water swimming pools; often a casino; and a host of entertainment options. Royal Caribbean's Quantum of the Seas, launched in 2014, even offers simulated sky diving and a sightseeing capsule on a stalk that can raise passengers 300 feet into the air.

Even in this segment, ticket prices may be relatively low, and it is possible to enjoy a cruise without spending any more. Yet drinks, upscale meals, guided shore excursions, and other amenities often are billed separately. This can add a lot to the net cost of the guest's vacation. It certainly improves the company's bottom line. As we saw above, for a typical passenger, onboard spending supplies the company's entire profit with $200 left over to help cover expenses.

Family cruises are multigenerational by definition, so the range of entertainment available on these voyages is much broader than in the over-18 market. For adults, it can range from Zumba classes or bingo to singers, bands, dance classes, and over-the-top night-time shows, occasionally with X-rated comics. Classes for the studious are a given. Some ships offer tastings of regional wines or single-malt scotch. When three generations travel together, most of these amenities will serve for the grandparents as well.

However, the key to a family cruise is having enough youth-friendly activities so age-conscious children and teens can avoid those who are a few unbridgeable years younger. Almost any ship will offer them in abundance. Climbing walls and surf simulators have become almost routine, though not restricted to the under-eighteen crowd. Ditto extra-cost video arcades. Disney movies are a staple on that company's famously kid-focused cruises. (In one list of the ten best cruise ships for families, Disney supplied four, including the top three.) Teens-only dances can be taken for granted.

Some specialty lines cater to adults, but even in this category the larger generally offer at least some family-friendly cruises.

The luxury, and costly, end of the spectrum, is clearly different. Cabins are more spacious, interior design more stylish. Gourmet meals are promised, and often delivered; restaurants planned and overseen by Michelin-starred chefs won't surprise passengers with experience aboard luxury lines. Fares tend to be all-inclusive—expect free drinks at a minimum—and lines hoping to attract well-to-do parents frequently offer discounts for the younger crowd; in some, those under seventeen travel free. Regent Seven Seas offers all-suite ships, and on most of them all suites have a balcony. Seabourn's mid-size ships carry a huge spa complex and a water-sports marina that retracts into the ship when under way. Silversea provides relatively few scheduled onboard activities, but every cabin comes with butler service. The staff-to-guest ratio is a lot higher as well, with the minimum approaching one crewman for every two passengers.

In this market, we find many smaller players. Silversea Cruises, large for a luxury line, has nine ships. Regent Seven Seas has four; Seabourn, which bills itself as an "ultra-luxury" cruise line, operates five ships, including one new in 2018. Crystal Cruises operates nine ships, including two ocean-going vessels, five river cruisers, and one yacht; an expedition ship is due in 2020, with three more ocean cruisers and another yacht to follow.

Other noteworthy participants in the luxury market include SeaDream Yacht Club, with two 110-passenger yachts; Hapag-Lloyd with four ships, all but one essentially dedicated to the German market; Paul Gauguin Cruises, with a single vessel in French Polynesia and the South Pacific; and Ponant, with eleven, recently expanded from five and scheduled to add two more in 2019.

Luxury ships themselves tend to be smaller as well. Regent's *Seven Seas Navigator* carries 490 passengers in all-suite accommodations. *Star Legend*, owned by Windstar Cruises, carries 212, while *Wind Star* and *Wind Spirit*—both partially powered by sail—are limited to 148 guests. Ponant's *Le Ponant* is a 64-passenger bark. Even the outsized exceptions are small compared with those marketed to less-wealthy voyagers. The largest are operated by Crystal Cruises: *Crystal Symphony*, with space for 922 passengers, and *Crystal Serenity*, which accommodates 1,070.

Of course, luxury costs. It is not hard to find discounts, but expect base prices starting around $300 per night for a stateroom with a balcony. In July 2018, seven nights in the Caribbean on Regent's *Seven Seas Voyager* will set you back $730 per night, a 65 percent discount from the brochure price of $14,898. One tiny, delightful ship we know charges $4,900 for a four-night cruise in its smaller suites. Fortunately for the budget-minded, one of its slightly larger sisters makes the same trip for only $3,200 per suite and an economical $2,000 for a single cabin. Within its specialized market, cruising the upper Amazon, the line has been described as "one of the region's more affordable options."

Blurring the Line

The idea of giving the richest passengers special privileges is not new. Analysts trace it all the way back to 1973, when Cunard refurbished the *Queen Elizabeth 2*. In the process, the company added twenty penthouses to the ship and converted a nearby bar to the Queen's Grill, an exclusive restaurant for high-status guests. Cunard added the status-symbol eatery to *Queen Mary 2* during a 1998 refit and since has built them into the *Queen Elizabeth* and *Queen Victoria*.

More recently, other cruise lines have been trying to split the difference between family and luxury cruising by separating the biggest spenders from the masses. The Haven is a gated community of luxury cabins around a courtyard found on Norwegian Cruise Line's vessels. Royal Caribbean International and Celebrity Cruises offer Suite Class. Holland America has the exclusive-access Neptune Lounge. Carnival's latest ships have abandoned the company's egalitarian tradition, providing the Havana Cabana for use of the poverty-averse. MSC offers the MSC Yacht Club. Even Disney provides Concierge Level service and amenities for those with accommodating travel budgets.

Celebrity Cruises' Luminae is typical of restaurants for the more profitable guests lodging in the ships' suites. They are open for breakfast, lunch (on sea days), and dinner. A new menu each day offers a changing selection of foods not available at other onboard restaurants. Access is included with the suite. Royal Caribbean, Norwegian, and MSC all offer similar facilities.

Many cruise lines also provide exclusive lounges for well-off passengers, like Holland America's Neptune Lounge and Norwegian's Haven. Expect free snacks, specialty coffees, off-schedule meals, and other conveniences.

On most lines, these privileged cruisers receive a host of other niceties, beginning with no-waiting check-in. On some, private lounges in port relieve the tedium of boarding. Butler service is common in the largest suites, though some make do with exclusive concierge service. Disney reserves a number of cabanas on Castaway Cay for Concierge Level guests; others are likely to find that cabanas have already sold out. Lesser amenities include a selection of free items, including things like drinks, Internet time, in-suite movies, bottled water, and even laundry service.

It all adds up to an air of exclusivity that commands premium prices and attracts guests who might otherwise voyage with one of the luxury lines or settle for less costly comforts. Finding new ways of catering to these passengers will be a continuing challenge for tomorrow's cruise executives.

Specialty Cruises

Despite the many similarities of ships at a given price level, cruise lines have found many ways to distinguish their voyages from those of the competition. Theme cruises are a staple. There is at least one ship sailing for almost any interest, and many lines offer partial-ship cruises for specialty groups.

Food and wine probably are the most popular cruise theme. Through 2017, at least, Celebrity Cruises offered *Top Chef* cruises, with kitchen stars from Bravo's popular series providing a meal, cooking classes, and even a TV-style chefs' battle among passengers. Holland America has run a similar cruise based on the competing TV show *MasterChef*. Norwegian Cruise Line's "Meet the Winemaker" cruises feature Q&A sessions and extra-cost wine tastings and five-course wine-paired dinners. Crystal, Seabourn, and Silversea all have specialty food-and-wine cruises.

Holland America builds some specialty vacations around another TV series, *Dancing with the Stars*. Windstar each year offers a unique cruise to the Grand Prix de Monaco. And Norwegian begins some of its cruises in the famed port city of Las Vegas, where guests can transition into vacation mode before sailing from New Orleans or Seattle.

Name a cruise line, and it probably offers at least one voyage for gay and lesbian travelers, who make up one of the industry's most sought-after markets. Many are organized by charter companies that specialize in serving these communities. Cruises often take place on smaller ships, but two of Royal Caribbean's 5,400-passenger vessels also have been chartered for all-gay cruises.

Music-themed cruises abound. The year 2019 will see hip-hop, reggae, and jazz cruises from Carnival; a "Monsters of Rock" cruise with Royal Caribbean; a cruise with house, techno, and trance music from Celebrity; and an "On The Blue Cruise" with oldies groups such as the Zombies, booked on Royal Caribbean.

Specialty cruises cater to fans of NFL football and major-league baseball; fine arts, often with on-board auctions; ballroom dancing; Weight Watchers; wellness; photography; and bird-watching. Also catered to: runners (unlikely as running at sea might sound), golfers (with stops at famous courses), and quilters. Cunard's *Queen Mary 2* even offers a fashion-themed cruise timed to arrive at the start of New York City's Fashion Week, in September. If someone has an interest, a few moments with Google is likely to find at least one cruise that caters to it.

Niche Markets

Many entire lines specialize in markets the larger companies would be hard pressed to serve as efficiently or well. For example, several luxury operators carry their passengers back to the age of sail. Like *Le Ponant*, three of Windstar's vessels are motor-sailers, each with four tall masts carrying half an acre of white sail. Star Clippers offers three sailing ships, two with room for 170 passengers and one a 439-foot, five-masted square-rigger with space for 227 guests. Island Windjammers operates three sailing vessels in the Caribbean—one is a motor-sailer—with accommodations for twelve to 24.

"Voluntourism" is a relatively new and popular specialty. Fathom, the latest brand from Carnival Corp., operated a single 710-passenger ship for cruisers willing to spend a few days teaching English or helping gather crops in the Dominican Republic. Although the Fathom brand has been discontinued, its "social impact" philosophy has been transferred to the company's other brands, which are beginning to offer voluntourism options on some of their cruises. Some passages on Crystal Cruises offer free shore excursions where volunteers may find themselves helping underprivileged children, tending animals, or restoring a state park in Oregon. For less energetic guests, P&O, Holland America, and other lines settle for on-board fund-raising for a wide variety of charities. Although no one closely tracks voluntourism activities industry-wide, this method of competing for some of the socially conscious cruiser's leisure budget is clearly on the rise.

Lindblad Expeditions offers fourteen ships, including three river cruisers and a square-rigger. Nine operate under the National Geographic brand. This probably makes Lindblad's the largest cruise fleet in the luxury market in 2019.

However, as its name suggests, the company does not compete directly with other luxury cruise lines. Lindblad is one of several specialists in expedition cruising, where nature-minded travelers give up some of the comforts and all the crowding of family cruises in return for access to environments and wildlife others will never see outside their televisions.

Lindblad's *National Geographic Quest*, launched in 2017 and carrying 100 passengers, shows the trade-off. It offers a spa and fitness room, a single restaurant and lounge, and a few other amenities. However, cruisers also can enjoy fleet of 24 sea kayaks, a hydrophone for listening to whale song, a video microscope, and lectures by skilled naturalists. The ship also carries full cold-water diving gear for guest experts. It began its cruises in Alaska and the Pacific Northwest, relocated to Costa Rica and Panama at the end of 2017, and will move on to explore Belize and Guatemala—not scenes typically visited by the multi-thousand passenger ships.

Lindblad is not alone in the expedition market:

Norway's Hurtigruten, with thirteen ships and four on order, offers trips along that country's fjord-notched coasts, to Greenland and Iceland, and to the Arctic. The company's 276-passenger *Fram* is a polar expedition ship hardened to survive heavy ice. Ten hardy passengers per trip can sign up for a night ashore in two-person tents. (This experience costs extra; keeping warm aboard does not.)

Quark Expeditions, with seven ships, and Poseidon Expeditions, with three, specialize in journeys to the poles. Both companies market arctic cruises on *50 Years of Victory*, a nuclear-powered icebreaker, formerly a Russian research vessel, that sails from Murmansk to the North Pole each summer.

Scenic nature cruises provide a softer sort of nature expedition. Ships tend to be a bit larger and better supplied with the usual cruise amenities. Activities average less demanding, with sea kayaking and dogsledding competing for the passenger's attention with bird-, whale-, and glacier-watching, swimming and snorkeling, and guided nature hikes. Popular destinations include Alaska, the Arctic and Antarctic, and of course the Galapagos Islands.

Expedition cruises especially are a fast-growing segment of the industry. No fewer than 22 new expedition cruise vessels were on order for delivery in mid-2018 through 2019—out of 33 cruise ships scheduled for the period.

Inland Cruising

Rivers offer still another opportunity for water travel. Cruises along inland waterways often are thought of as a European specialty, but they can be found on every inhabited continent. Their stock in trade is relaxation, the chance just to sit and watch the world drift by. Yet, there is novelty as well. Each day on many cruises offers a chance to explore a town or city, or in some cases more exotic regions.

Aboard ship, river cruises are much like others, but often on a smaller scale. Staterooms are comfortable, but rarely expansive. So are restaurants and lounges. Entertainment tends to be low-key, most of it provided by the scenery passing by. Yet, amenities such as stocked minibars, balconies, and butler service often are available.

River itineraries are remarkably diverse, arguably even more so than those of ocean-going lines, which for most of a journey feature unbroken 360-degree views of water. The largest operator is Viking River Cruises, with upward of seventy ships wandering the waterways of Germany, Russia, Egypt, China, and other locations. American Cruise Lines offers 35 itineraries in the United States, including trips along the Mississippi on paddlewheel riverboats in which Mark Twain would have felt at home—once he figured out the Wi-Fi. Aqua Expeditions operates just two vessels, one on the Amazon and one on the Mekong River in Vietnam, a waterway it shares with at least six other cruise lines. Abercrombie & Kent offers cruises along the rivers of France, Germany, and the Netherlands in Europe; the Mekong and Yangtze in Asia; the Nile in Africa; plus a variety of expedition and barge cruises on chartered vessels. In sub-Saharan Africa, cruise operators like AmaWaterways and tour packagers such as Adventure Life often combine river cruises with a stay in Cape Town or side trips to Victoria Falls, the Serengeti in Tanzania, or the Canary Islands. Apart from the poles, few corners of the world are inaccessible by river.

The Amazon is a kind of crossover destination, with visits by a wide range of cruise lines. Lindblad's luxurious 32-passenger *Delfin II* shares the Amazon with the 929-passenger Braemar, operated by Fred. Olsen Cruise Lines; larger ships from Crystal, Holland America, Oceania, Silversea, and Viking; and several expedition lines, including Aqua Expeditions and International Expeditions.

Barge cruising offers even smaller vessels, often with staterooms in the single digits. *Nymphea*, operated in France by European Waterways, has room for only six guests. Routes are miniaturized, too, traveling along small rivers or canals only forty feet wide. The billboard attraction here is the chance to visit chateaus, castles, small wineries, and villages inaccessible to larger vessels.

However, barge cruise lines frequently offer a kind of luxury that ocean-going lines could find hard to equal. Think of a tiny, many-starred hotel floating through the countryside of France. One travel writer tells of a fellow passenger who requested morels for dinner. They appeared the following night, having been bought fresh at a local market that morning.

River and barge cruises are rarely cheap. A seven-night river cruise in France or Germany starts at about $1,600 in the off season and double that in peak periods. Seven days on a typical barge cruise go for $4,000 and up. Yet no one who enjoys their slow pace, luxurious accommodations, and remarkable service seems to find them too costly.

As a result, river cruises have become one of the industry's fastest growing markets. Over the five years ending in 2017, cruise operators launched more than 120 new river ships. Over two-dozen more were on order for 2018 and '19. It seems likely that river cruising will remain one of the industry's hot markets well into the next decade, and probably beyond.

Proprietary Destinations

In the last few years, cruise lines have found a way to provide unique destinations. In and around the Caribbean, a number of lines have developed private resorts and islands where their passengers can enjoy comforts and amenities not available to others. Typical examples:

Amber Cove, outside Puerto Plata in the Dominican Republic, is a thirty-acre resort shared by Carnival, Costa, Cunard, and Holland America. There isn't a beach, so visitors make do with an enormous swimming pool, bars and lounges, ecotours, and other diversions for the adventurous and pampered layabouts alike. If that is not enough, there are speedboats to Paradise Island, site of the country's top snorkeling reef, a lush national park, and an enjoyable beachfront restaurant.

At Half Moon Cay, near Eleuthera in the Bahamas, passengers with Carnival and its sister line Holland America can enjoy 2,400-acres of sun, sand, and tropical waters. Also available: a large water park, horseback riding, bicycle nature tours, and private butlers bringing hot and cold snacks and drinks to enjoy them with.

The thousand-acre Castaway Key is a Disney exclusive. Most of the facility is designed for family activities, but an adults-only beach gives parents a chance to escape for a couple of hours, while abundant resources cater to children and younger teens (supervised by the staff). Sports like snorkeling, fishing, parasailing, and watercraft skiing are available for the energetic. Glass-bottom boats and other diversions cater to those who are less so.

Norwegian's Harvest Caye is only 78 acres about a mile from the mainland in Belize. Yet it packs an enormous quantity of entertainment into that small area. Seven acres consist of beach, but other attractions include kayaking, bars and restaurants, a nature center, and snorkeling on the world's second largest barrier reef. A fifteen-minute boat ride to the mainland adds diversions such as visits to Mayan ruins, rafting or tubing on a rainforest river, and an ecotour of the local savannah by boat.

Norwegian also operates Great Stirrup Cay, in the Bahamas, which it will share with Regent Seven Seas, Oceania, and MSC Cruises. Already offering most of the standard resort facilities, the island is still under development.

In addition to the lines noted above, Royal Caribbean and Azamara share Labadee, a private resort in Haiti; Princess has Princess Cays, in the Bahamas; Royal Caribbean and its subsidiaries, Celebrity and Azamara, share CocoCay, also in the Bajamas and currently undergoing a $200-million overhaul; Costa Cruises has a private beach, catamaran tours, and rainforest tours on Catalina Island, in the Dominican Republic; Catalina otherwise is protected by UNESCO as a World Heritage Site. Half the world away, Paul Gauguin Cruises offers time at Motu Mahana, a tiny private island in French Polynesia, and a private beach on Bora Bora.

Proprietary destinations like these once qualified as a novel competitive method. They are evolving rapidly into business as usual. Before the 2020s are too far along, cruise executives dealing with proprietary destinations are likely to spend less of their time developing new ones and more of their time trying to make sure the islands and resorts the company already owns appear uniquely attractive among all the competing options at other lines.

Opening the World

Before we look at the trends that will shape the cruise industry over the next decade or so, there are a few special items to consider. These are issues in which long-term trends already are changing the cruise market. They will continue to do so for years to come.

The first is the growth of the global economy, and particularly the benefits it has brought some regions where potential cruise markets were vast but too poor to support even the least costly vacations. Two of these are obvious and growing. A third might become significant in the next decade.

The obvious candidates are in Asia, so it is worth spending a moment to look at the market overall.

In 2013, companies belonging to the Cruise Lines International Association based 43 ships there. By 2017, there were 66. That still is not many, but it represents a combined annual growth rate of 11 percent.

The number of cruises and voyages had grown from 861 in 2013 to 2,086 scheduled for 2017, a growth rate of 25 percent per year.

Passenger capacity had grown even faster, from 1.51 million in 2013 to 4.24 million in 2017, or 29 percent annually. This was nearly 11 percent of the world's total.

The number of passengers was growing fastest of all. Asia provided only 774,536 passengers in 2012. By 2016, there were 3,098,202. It comes out to a CAGR of 41 percent.

China, of course, is the largest and best developed of these markets. In recent years, it has grown from a port of call for long-distance cruises to a major source of new business for the industry. The first international cruise line to base a ship there was Costa Cruises, Carnival Corporation's Italian brand. It began with a single ship that sailed from Shanghai in 2006. Royal Caribbean followed a year later, with routes originating in Shanghai and Hong Kong. These proved to be wise decisions. By 2012, 216,702 cruise passengers embarked from Chinese ports. By 2014, the number had grown to 697,000, an increase of 79 percent in just two years. Three years later, Costa had deployed eight ships to China and hosted its 2 millionth passenger there, with two 4,200-passenger ships designed specifically for the Chinese market to join them in 2019 and 2020.

By 2016, China was providing more than two-thirds of passengers sailing from Asia, according to a study by the CLIA. A year later, more than 2 million passengers were expected to embark from Chinese ports. Estimates suggest that the market will double again by 2020, to some 4.5 million passengers. And by 2030, China is expected to be the world's second-largest cruise market, according to the Chinese Ministry of Transport. In all, the Hong Kong Tourist Board estimates that the Chinese cruise market could ultimately grow to 83 million passengers per year. Yes, that is more than eleven times the size of the American market.

As demand has expanded, the nation's cruise infrastructure is growing rapidly. Although Shanghai remains China's largest cruise port, some fifteen ports on the Yellow Sea, South China Sea, and the Pacific host cruise lines. At least two Chinese shipbuilders have entered the cruise market. In 2016, Chinese travel agents even formed their own specialty organization, the China Cruise Tourism Service Alliance.

The number of cruise lines operating in China is beginning to rise as well. Costa and Royal Caribbean are still there, of course. Carnival has ordered two new ships for the China market, with options for four more; they will be the first cruise ships ever built by a China-based construction firm. Oceania, Regent Seven Seas, MSC Cruises, and Dream Cruises are there. AIDA Cruises added its first China-based ship in 2017. Windstar Cruises offered a few sailings from Hong Kong and Beijing. Norwegian took delivery of its first ship built exclusively for the Chinese market in 2017, the 3,883-passenger *Norwegian Joy*. Princess Cruises has taken delivery of its first built-for-China vessel, *Majestic Princess*, with accommodations for 3,560 passengers. The ship was scheduled to join *Majestic Princess*, already based in Shanghai.

Native Chinese cruise companies also are beginning to appear. Sanya International Cruise Development Co. was operating a cruise ship called *Dream of the South China Sea* as early as 2017. It was expected to add two new ships in 2017 and planned to operate as many as eight ships, all in the South China Sea, by 2022. Hainan Strait Shipping Co. has offered cruises in the sea since April 2013.

The market for inland cruises also is well served. Viking River Cruises is there, offering trips up the Yangtze as well as European sailings exclusively for Chinese cruisers. Viking shares the Yangtze with a number of other lines, including President Cruises, Century Cruises, and Chiangjiang Cruises. All three are native Chinese lines.

Cruise lines have found that serving the Chinese market requires some adaptation.

Although four out of ten Asian cruise passengers are under 40, multigenerational groups are common in China. Those who pay for a cruise are likely to be middle-aged, but they often travel with their adult children, grandchildren, and sometimes elderly parents. *Norwegian Joy* will accommodate this demand by offering staterooms designed for extended families and many connecting staterooms for large family groups traveling together.

Passengers elsewhere are unlikely to want rice and congee for breakfast. In the China market, authentic local cuisine is mandatory. It also is highly profitable. Tuniu, a leading Chinese travel website, reports that Chinese tourists spend an average of $200 on a trip, with a large portion of that going to food. Bars and spas are out, restaurants very much in.

The Broadway-style shows that go over so well in the Caribbean have all but disappeared from China-based cruises. In this market, local celebrities and entertainers are the rule. Passengers can expect karaoke rooms and mahjong as well.

Gambling, a traditional Asian pastime, has proved almost mandatory. Royal Caribbean's *Ovation of the Seas*, with room for 4,905 passengers and designed specifically for the Chinese market, carries a larger-than-average casino featuring state-of-the-art poker machines, baccarat, and a native game called sic bo, which is popular with the older generation. The casino offers one other feature not often found in cruise ships elsewhere: on some Chinese departures, smoking is allowed throughout the casino floor.

© steve estvanik/
Shutterstock.com

In recent years, a number of local operators, reportedly backed by organized crime, have launched casino "cruises to nowhere." They appear to be doing remarkably well. According to a government study, gamblers on casino ships spent an average of HK$45,259 per person, about US$5,800 at late-2017 exchange rates. That was up some twenty-fold since 2012. In nearby Macau, which used to be Asia's richer equivalent of Las Vegas, the average was only HK$7,938, or just over US$1,000.

A second activity critical to the China market is shopping, and particularly for luxury goods. The Royal Esplanade on *Ovation of the Seas* features brands such as Cartier, Kate Spade, Michael Kors, and Swarovski. Port calls, especially outside China, tend to be longer than in other markets so Chinese passengers have plenty of opportunity to stock up on luxury goods. Fukuoka, Japan, is especially popular among shoppers, and getting there on cruise ship costs less than the airlines.

One other mandatory characteristic is flexibility in the face of changing government policy. Early in 2017, Beijing promoted nationalist resentment toward South Korea when that country decided to install American anti-missile systems. At first, cruise operators maintained occupancy levels by offering steep discounts on voyages from China to the neighboring land. This helped minimize the number of empty staterooms, but on one visit to Jeju, a South Korean resort island and the second-most-visited port in Asia, about 3,300 Chinese passengers refused to get off *Costa Serena*.

That April, the Chinese government banned travel to South Korea. Cruise lines responded by switching to alternative ports in Japan or adding sea days to voyages that would have stopped in South Korea. About 40 percent of all cruises from China were affected. At the start of 2018, the boycott was partially rescinded. Nonetheless, of a dozen cruise ships from China scheduled to stop at Incheon in the first half of the year, eight canceled their visits.

This could be a continuing problem for cruise operators in China. Beijing has previously imposed travel bans on the Philippines and Japan over political differences. There also have been unofficial or government-mandated boycotts of products or companies from the Philippines, Japan, France, Norway, and the United States.

Other government policies can be just as disruptive. In 2014 and '15, economic growth in China began to slow when Beijing reduced its stimulus efforts. More recently, a crackdown on corruption has inhibited conspicuous spending, and especially gambling. Lines for the first time had to fill staterooms by discounting ticket prices by as much as 60 percent. An unofficial report says that casino revenues on *Costa Atlantica* fell from nearly $1 million during the February 2014 New Year period to less than $100,000 in the same period of 2015. Such unpredictable headwinds are likely to buffet the Chinese cruise market for many years.

In the last few years, they have added to a problem that cruise lines know all too well. Passenger capacity has expanded faster than the number of vacationers to fill the berths. Beijing's regulations require cruise lines to market through travel agencies, not directly to consumers. As a result, though most state rooms have remained full, passenger yields have been eroding.

Several industry observers have pointed to another problem as well. Cruise lines have adapted to the China market so well that their offerings have become indistinguishable. Essentially all ships offer the same mix of good and plentiful Chinese food, regional entertainment, gambling, shopping, and other attractions. To entice customers more effectively, the lines will have to develop new competitive methods suited to the Chinese market. The battle to fill staterooms is likely to be a permanent feature of this maturing cruise market.

Add one more issue that will be hard to solve. Well-to-do Chinese travelers are generally short of time. They look for three- or four-day excursions so they can get back to work quickly after their break. That means sticking to nearby ports, and there are not many of them. With South Korea and Taiwan effectively off limits, Chinese cruises can visit only Hong Kong and a few ports on Japan's west coast. Mainland tourists looking for novelty—and how many of them aren't?—have little reason to take a cruise. It is hard to see how the industry can overcome this handicap unless they can develop proprietary resorts near the Chinese coast, as cruise lines have done in the Caribbean. This will not be easy. There are about 250 islands in the South China Sea, but ownership of virtually all is contested by China and at least one other country, sometimes more.

For now, many lines have been redeploying ships away from China. Royal Caribbean's *Ovation of the Seas*, formally dedicated to the mainland market, spent part of 2018 in Australia. So did Princess Cruises' *Majestic Princess*, built specifically for China. *Costa Victoria* returned to Europe, while Royal Caribbean's *Mariner of the Seas* headed back to Miami. In all, cruise capacity in the Chinese market in 2018 was expected to be down about 18 percent from the previous year.

This reduction is not likely to last long. MSC Cruises repositioned the 1,984-passenger *MSC Lirica* to Europe, but the ship was scheduled to be replaced by *MSC Splendida*, with room for 4,363. Royal Caribbean still planned to send *Spectrum of the Seas*, the first of its new Quantum Ultra class ships, to China in the spring of 2019. Costa Cruises is scheduled to add two new ships to its China fleet, one each in 2019 and '20. A few years later, Carnival is committed to launch at least two more.

There is every reason to believe Chinese vacationers will be ready to sail on them. Estimates vary widely beyond ten years out, but the consensus is that between 7 million and 10 million will book voyages from local ports in 2030. Given how quickly the market has grown to date, the number seems likely to come in at the higher end of this range, and maybe a little above—if the problems noted above can be overcome. Many of today's hospitality students entering the cruise industry will spend their working days devising new competitive methods suited to this lucrative region.

Two more cruise markets are worth mentioning. Neither is nearly as well developed as China's. Yet one could grow quickly in the years ahead, while the other may be an increasingly frequent destination; it could provide a few outbound bookings as well.

India could offer even greater promise than its northern neighbor in the long run. Royal Caribbean has been marketing cruises there since 1993, Genting's Star Cruises brand since '94. Star Cruises even based the *SuperStar Libra* in Mumbai for the October 2006 to March '07 season. Nearly 40,000 passengers sailed on the ship in that first season, some 81,000 the next. Yet, Star Cruises withdrew the ship after the 2007-'08 season; observers believe unfavorable government policies were to blame.

Clearly, the industry is still getting started in this vast country. With a population of more than 1.3 billion in 2016, India supplied slightly less than 4 percent of Asian cruisers. For comparison, Taiwan, with a population of 23.5 million, yielded 7.6 percent, while Singapore, population barely 5.6 million, provided 6.4 percent.

The vast Indian market is worth pursuing. The second most populous land in the world, India soon will overtake China to become the planet's largest national market. Its economy is growing rapidly—in recent years, India has outpaced even China—so the number of Indians who can afford what for most still counts as a luxury vacation is expanding as well. At a cost of $150 to $200 per night, a cruise is little if any more expensive than a landlocked holiday.

The Indian cruise industry is growing rapidly, though probably not as quickly as it could. In the 2015 to '16 cruise season, around 125,000 Indians took a cruise trip, up from approximately 104,000 a season earlier. Thomas Cook's Indian division reported that cruise bookings were growing by about 22 percent per year. Other sources put the figure as high as 40 percent. In mid-2018, the new India Cruise Lines Association set itself a target of carrying 5 million passengers from India by 2020.

In fact, current statistics understate the subcontinent's cruise market. In 2016, about 100,000 Indians traveled to Singapore before leaving land. This so-called fly-cruise tourism is especially popular in India because the regional-hub port is in much easier reach of many popular destinations. Malaysia, Thailand, and Vietnam all are much closer when cruising from Singapore than from India itself.

Popular destinations for Indian travelers predictably include Hong Kong, Singapore, and Dubai, but the Mediterranean and far-off Caribbean round out the top five.

There still are some obstacles to be overcome before the Indian cruise market lives up to its potential. One is a shortage of infrastructure. Only twelve ports in the country are large enough to host the average cruise ship, and only four—Cochin, Mumbai, Goa, and New Mangalore—had actual cruise terminals in mid-2018. A fifth was under development at Chennai.

Bureaucratic obstacles also have been a problem. Until 2017, the limited immigration facilities provided by the country's Ministry of Shipping made it a hassle for cruisers to deal with their paperwork on departure and arrival. Recently, the government has made it easier to obtain a visa and opened new immigration counters at five of the largest ports. The New Delhi government is expected to extend these improvements to the remaining cruise-capable ports.

However, even that may not be enough to trigger the kind of growth India has long promised the cruise industry. After Star Cruises pulled the *SuperStar Libra* out of the country, it was another eight years before the next cruise ship made India its home. This was Costa Cruises' 1,400-passenger *Costa Neo Classica*, which in December 2016 began sailing from Mumbai to the Maldives with stopovers at new Mangalore, Goa, and Cochin. The route is generally believed to have been economically successful. Yet, the ship made its final voyage in March 2018, when the ship was sold to another line. Scathing reviews of voyages by Indian cruise passengers suggest that Costa, uncharacteristically, may have undermined its own success in an unfamiliar market far from its corporate managers.

It seems that to date the world's cruise operators have not quite figured out the Indian market. Royal Caribbean, Holland America, Norwegian Cruise Line, Genting, MSC, Regent, and of course Costa Cruises all are represented in the country. Most reported bookings growth in the range of 25 percent in 2017. Yet, none has seen enough promise to give this market the kind of push China has long received.

Our current analysis is that India continues to suffer the excessive bureaucracy, distrust of foreign companies, and—we are sorry to say—widespread corruption that have always made it difficult for non-native investors to do business in an otherwise promising market. In recent years, the world's technology companies have managed to succeed in India despite such obstacles. In late 2017, for example, IBM had more employees in India than in the United States. Microsoft had six business units in the country employing about 6500 people. And Google's Indian sales crossed the $1 billion mark in FY 2017, 22 percent above the 2016 tally. We expect the cruise industry to succeed as well before the 2020s are too far along.

For today's hospitality students who find the cruise industry appealing, the Indian market could provide challenges enough to occupy a productive career. Over the coming decades, the rewards should more than justify the effort that developing this vexing market will require.

Cuba is the latest cruise market to begin opening up, and by far the most difficult to predict. Tourism there experienced the beginnings of a boom after President Obama lifted travel restrictions to the country in 2014. Only 6,770 Americans visited Cuba in 2012. By 2016, Americans accounted for 281,000 of the estimated 4 million tourists who visited the island.

Many of them arrived on cruise lines. In mid-2018, 29 major ships were scheduled to visit the island's four ports. Essentially all the big lines offer cruises in Cuba. So do smaller operators such as Azamara Club and Le Ponant.

They should find a ready market. Kayak reports that it found a 173 percent increase in Cuba searches over the year ending in April 2017. The travel website named Cuba its top trending destination at the end of 2016.

Yet, searches are not bookings, and tourism from the U.S. to Cuba still has not begun to approach the 1 million per year that some industry commentators predicted for the near future. The U.S. Department of Transportation has limited air service to only 20 flights per day. Smaller airlines especially have been cutting back their service to Cuba, and some—notably Spirit Airlines, Silver Airways, Frontier, and Alaska Airlines—have dropped it altogether. All this probably works to the cruise lines' advantage.

Americans tend to be high-maintenance travelers. After decades of rule under the Castro brothers and near-total isolation from non-Communist countries, especially the United States, Cuba lacks the modern infrastructure that many travelers from the U.S. demand. Cell phones are not likely to work there. Neither are credit cards. And access to the Internet is limited at best. These are hardships that few relatively pampered Americans are willing to face. A study by insurance company Allianz Global Assistance found that only 24 percent of Americans were at all likely to visit Cuba in 2017, down from 30 percent the previous year. More than one in eight cited the lack of travel infrastructure as a major cause of their reluctance to spend vacation time in Cuba. At the bottom line, only 2 percent of those responding to the poll intended to visit Cuba by the end of 2017.

Yet, for that minority, cruising should be an attractive option. On a cruise, passengers get to take their technology with them. Internet access may not be cheap, but it is always available. Credit cards are guaranteed to work. And if cell phones do not, the ship can provide opportunities to call home.

The greatest question affecting Cuban travel is how many more obstacles the Trump administration will put in its way. In 2017, the State Department twice warned against traveling to Cuba, first because of a series of attacks on tourists in Havana, and again after mysterious illnesses afflicted personnel at the American Embassy there. That second particularly seems more like an excuse to disrupt Cuba tourism, rather than a legitimate concern. Nonetheless, the actual restrictions on travel there announced in November 2017 did little to inhibit travel there. Instead of directly restricting travel to Cuba, U.S. authorities blacklisted hotels, shops, and other businesses linked to Cuban military, intelligence, or security services and required tourists to go as part of an organized group managed by a U.S.-owned company. Cruise lines were quick to point out that their voyages were clearly permitted. In the end, some 619,000 Americans visited Cuba in 2017, up 18 percent from the year before.

Despite American politics, the Cuban cruise market is clearly growing. The cruise-ship port in Havana handled 328,000 passengers in 2017. It was expected to see 700,000 in 2018 and likely many more as its two cruise terminals grow to six by 2024. Royal Caribbean has announced new sailings to Cuba for 2018 and '19. Norwegian Cruise Line announced that it will bring the *Norwegian Sun* four-night cruises to Key West and Havana in 2018. Victory Cruise Lines announced plans to begin two-week journeys around the island in 2018. Carnival added twenty more sailings from Tampa to Cuba to its schedule for 2018, this on top of eleven that had already been scheduled from Tampa and seventeen from Miami. And for 2019, SeaDream Yacht Club has begun to offer seven-day trips that will stop at several Cuban islands in 2019.

Unlike small airlines, the majors also are expanding their service to Cuba. Southwest, JetBlue, American, and Delta all have applied to add new Cuban flights to their schedules. It seems a strong vote of confidence for American tourism to the once-forbidden island.

Cuba is unlikely to become a major tourist destination for the next few years. Yet, travel there will continue to grow. It will accelerate when some future American president rescinds current restrictions. By the mid or late 2020s, Havana will seem less like an exotic, somewhat forbidding destination and more like a standard port of call for cruise lines departing from Florida. As this evolution proceeds, cruise executives will find themselves having to compete harder for tourist dollars in the maturing Cuban market.

They will face one special issue as well. This, of course, is Caribbean weather. In 2017, Hurricane Irma brought winds of 160 mph to Cuba, devastating a broad path along the island's northern coast. Several popular tourist destinations were either destroyed or heavily damaged. The following year, Hurricanes Alberto, Beryl, Isaac, and Michael added to the damage. As climate change makes Caribbean storms more frequent and more powerful, cruise ships throughout the region will have either to hurry back to the mainland or to ride out the winds and waves in a nearer port. Although ship captains will have primary responsibility for their vessel's safety, landlocked executives will have to help plan emergency procedures and make sure the necessary resources are in place to cope with disasters that are not completely predictable.

In all, the Cuban market is likely to be a challenging one for new travel executives assigned to it. Managed well, it should also be a rewarding one for both cruise lines and the hospitality graduates who build a career with them.

Major Trends for the Cruise Industry

In Chapter 7, we discussed the trends that will do most to influence travel and hospitality in the next decade and beyond. Here we will apply the most important of these and other trends shaping the cruise industry today and through the 2020s. They appear in slightly modified form to emphasize those aspects most directly significant to our current topic.

Economic growth continues throughout the world, quickly in the developing lands but much less so in the industrialized nations.

A vacation afloat is even more expensive and less necessary than a Starbucks latte, so the cruise market should be sensitive to the economies of the United States, Europe, and the world. It is, but perhaps less so than one might expect. For a lesson in how challenging the industry can be, and yet how durable, look back to the Great Recession. It was not as bad for cruise lines as it could have been.

Because vacations tend to be planned well ahead, it was 2009 before the recession filtered through to the industry. By then, many who might have taken a cruise had temporarily given up on expensive vacations. They were barely making ends meet and terrified that the next round of pink slips could put them out on the street.

To salvage their year, cruise executives offered sharp discounts on bookings. Carnival cut prices by up to 25 percent for tickets reserved in advance. Holland America reduced fares and offered 50-percent discounts on deposits and cruise tours. Seabourn gave discounts of $1,000 per suite on top of early-booking savings of up to 50 percent. That money-saving staycation did not look so attractive when a cruise hardly cost more.

Sacrificing some of their profit allowed cruise lines to keep the rest. When 2009 was over, cruise ships had carried more than 1.4 million passengers, up from 1.2 million the previous year. Revenue was only $24.9 billion, off $2.4 billion from the previous year. Yet Carnival delivered a return on equity of 8.7 percent for the year. Norwegian, after two disastrous years, brought in 4.13 percent. Royal Caribbean came in at 2.27 percent. If profits were not all they could have been, they were enough to keep the ships sailing and prepare for the better years to come.

As we saw in Chapter 7, today's hospitality students should have long, successful careers without ever facing challenges like those of 2009. It would take a combination of unlikely factors to trigger such a downturn in today's global economy. The most dangerous would be a trade war between the United States and China combined with a debt crisis in Beijing. At the beginning of 2019, that war has been under way for a full year, and we still cannot guess how these developments will play out. Readers, of course, will know what happened.

Even if the world avoids the chaos a serious trade war would bring, other economic pressures could force the cruise industry to reconsider its market priorities. Because economic expansion is slowing, on average, throughout the developed world, the United States and Europe will not be the critical growth areas they once were.

Fortunately, two of the world's fastest-growing economies are in China and India, the only countries with billion-plus populations. Sluggish economies in the United States and Europe will be less important when growth is so fast in countries that each have three times as many people as either of the established markets. Worldwide, the number of potential cruisers will continue to grow through the 2020s and well beyond.

One last factor worth considering here is economic inequality. In a time when government policies steer the benefits of growth almost exclusively to the wealthy, the rich get richer, while those in the bottom half of the economy tread water at best. We see this most clearly in the United States, where inequality is growing fastest, but similar trends are visible in many industrialized nations.

In the U.S., the top 1 percent of adults earned on average twenty-seven times as much as the bottom 50 percent did in 1980. By 2014, they were earning eighty-one times as much. Over the same period, average middle-class income rose about 40 percent. For the top 0.001 percent of richest Americans, income shot up 636 percent! A 2017 analysis by Philip Alston, UN special repporteur on extreme poverty and human rights, found that policies championed by President Trump and the Republican-led Congress would make the United States "the world champion of extreme inequality."

At the same time, the cost of the big-ticket purchases most important to the middle class—a home, healthcare, and a college education for their children—have been growing much faster. Average tuition at private four-year colleges, for example, was $9,500 in 1980. By the 2017–'18 school year, it had nearly quadrupled to $34,740. In 1980, healthcare costs in the U.S. averaged $1,108 per person. By 2017, they skyrocketed to $10,224, nearly double the $5,280 average of other developed countries.

Squeezed by stagnant incomes and soaring expenses, the American middle class is finding it increasingly difficult to afford the luxuries that once seemed a normal part of life. To date, cruise lines have managed to offset this problem by routinely offering discounts and other incentives to maintain booking numbers. We expect them to continue doing so successfully in the years ahead. However, the United States and Europe will never again be the industry's growth markets.

That position will fall to the giants of Asia. With economic growth currently around 6.5 percent per year and a middle-class population estimated at 400 million, China will be the cruise industry's fastest expanding market through the 2020s and beyond. India, with even faster economic growth and a middle-class population of 267 million in 2016 and expected to reach 547 million as soon as 2025, will come in a close second once the country develops the port infrastructure cruise ships require. These two countries will more than compensate for any slowing of growth in the industry's top markets today. By broadening the industry's economic base, they should help cushion the effects of future recessions in the U.S. and Europe.

Populations in the developed world are growing older and more diverse as younger generations gain economic, political, and social power.

Many business executives are as aware of the passage of time and generations as any Woodstock veteran gritting his teeth at yet another article about "the aging Baby Boom generation." In the cruise industry, they have reason to be. Despite the broad range of individual variation, members of each generation have enough in common to make them well-defined markets. They have characteristic needs and preferences and are more receptive to some forms of marketing than others. As each generation moves through its life cycle, industries need to change with them. This has proved especially the case for cruise lines.

Even a few years ago, Baby Boomers were clearly the dominant generation. This was nowhere more true than in the United States and Europe, the cruise industry's most important markets. The Boomers were the largest generation in history and, if they were not yet as well-off as their elders, it was clear they soon would be. Between 1989 and 2013, as younger adults grew poorer, the inflation-adjusted wealth of families age 62 and up rose by 40 percent. This was wealth the Boomers had already begun to inherit when the period began. To marketers hoping for a prosperous future, Boomers seemed the only game in town.

Generation X, largely an afterthought, fortunately displayed much the same product preferences as the Boomers. And there were not nearly as many of them. They could be, and were, largely ignored.

Today, attention is shifting rapidly to the Millennials, who by our definition range in 2019 from age 37 all the way down to 22. There are more of them than there ever were in the baby boom, about 92 million, including a majority of the world's potential wage-earners.

Unfortunately, Millennials can be tight with their money, out of necessity. On average, they have less of it to spend than Boomers did at the same age. Their unemployment rate was about three times the national average, nearly 13 percent in mid-2017. And many are carrying much more debt than they can afford, most of it in college loans. In a 2017 poll, half of Millennials said they would give up their right to vote in the next two presidential elections in it let them escape loan payments for the rest of their lives. The Deloitte 2018 Millennial Study discovered that over half believe their financial situation will be worse than their parents' was. Nearly two-thirds plan to work a "side hustle" to make more money to help them cope with costs of food, transportation, healthcare, and housing prices all rising faster than their incomes.

Despite this, Millennials travel more than any other generation. A survey by the American Society of Travel Agents (ASTA) found that 80 percent took at least one leisure trip in 2016. In fact, they averaged nearly 2.4 vacations that year, 44 percent more than Baby Boomers did. A survey in 2018 found that a third were willing to spend $5,000 or more for their summer vacations. More than half said they expected to to travel more in the following twelve months, compared to only 22 percent of Boomers.

Predictably, cruise lines have found Millennials a receptive market for products that meet their needs and interests—especially when they put out their message on the Internet, where about three Millennials out of four do much of their comparison shopping. Some 27 percent in the ASTA survey reported taking at least one cruise in an average year. Only 14 percent of Baby Boomers could say the same. Fully 90 percent of Millennials who had taken a cruise said they liked cruising, and 61 percent said they "strongly like it."

One reason is that cruise lines have made a serious effort to design products that fit Millennial priorities and tastes. More than seven out of ten Millennials say they would rather spend money on experiences than on products. That obviously includes onboard entertainment. Millennial-era bands like New Kids On The Block and the Backstreet Boys remain a powerful draw for cruisers who grew up listening to them.

For other experiences, "authenticity" is an important value. This is a nebulous word that can mean anything from enjoying local food and wine in an elegant ship's restaurant to meeting the natives. They know it when they see it—and more importantly they know when it seems to be missing.

Authenticity may help explain the recent boom in river cruising. River lines had 16 percent more reservations in 2016 than the year before. Eleven percent of Millennials have taken a river cruise, and upward of 40 percent say they are likely to consider one. Shore excursions are a lot closer to hand on a river than in mid-ocean, with the chance to experience local culture available almost daily.

Similarly, a survey of travel advisors found that the top vacation choice for Millennials is "adventure travel." Show them penguins in Antarctica, give them a chance to climb a mountain or run a marathon in some far-off land, and the cruise line will have made their vacation.

Of course, reliable Internet connections are a must, and preferably built into the ticket price, where they appear to be free.

This ties into a broader Millennial preference: Cruises are most appealing when entertainment, food, sightseeing, and other features are built into one reasonable ticket price. Extra-cost items are much less attractive.

Other priorities unearthed by the ASTA study include the opportunity to relax (64 percent), to "spend quality time with family" (59 percent), and to "see natural sights" (38 percent.) In other surveys, many said that one of the best parts of a cruise is the chance to meet new people from a variety of places.

With all this in mind, cruise lines are catering to Millennial tastes in a variety of new ways.

Carnival's Fathom brand, new in 2015, was designed with 20- and 30-somethings in mind. It pioneered a combination of shipboard self-improvement seminars with "social impact" activities in Cuba and the Dominican Republic. Fathom itself was discontinued after barely a year as a cruise line, but the brand lives on in trips being offered by the company's other brands. A tour of four islands in the Caribbean scheduled by Princess in January 2018 was expected to include optional shore excursions to help local partners repair some of the damage left by 2017's hurricanes.

The idea of Millennial-only cruise ships is a good deal more radical. U by Uniworld will be offering river cruises in France, Germany, and Hungary on two all-black vessels imaginatively named "The A" and "The B." The new line is ticking all the Millennial check-boxes. Both ships are small, only 120 passengers each, so meeting everyone on board will be easy. In early 2019, the U site described the line's attractions as "accommodations on a sexy ship, delicious locally-inspired food and lots of fun activities to choose from." Overnight stops in cities like Paris and Budapest, including guided

tours at night, will "allow passengers to really connect with a city and the people who live there," according to an account by the respected *Cruise Critic*. The company is even describing its new effort as "a line where Instagram moments are made." At all-inclusive prices of $200 to $250 per day, it seems an offering that many Millennials should find irresistible.

So early in the next big demographic transition, these developments barely hint at what must be to come. For the next twenty years, executives at the cruise lines will be devoting more and more of their time to competing for their share of the Millennial travel budget.

Of course, by then the Centennials now taking hospitality courses will have become their own next important market.

Energy will gradually become less expensive as alternative sources displace fossil fuels.

After struggling since late 2014, it seemed three years later that the Organization of Petroleum Exporting Countries (OPEC) had finally managed to stabilize the price of oil at over $50 per barrel. In fact, Brent crude, a classification of low-density, low-sulfur crude that provides one standard benchmark price for oil traders, entered June 2018 at over $75 per barrel. If the price of crude ever holds at that level or higher, it will raise the cost of fuel for cruise lines and other hospitality sectors. Instead, it ended the year at $53.80 per barrel. West Texas Intermediate, as always, was a few dollars cheaper.

As we discussed in Chapter 7, the future course of oil prices has become less clear than it once appeared owing to questions about American oil production and the pace at which people will give up their personal cars in favor of ride-hailing services. Fleet operations like Uber and Lyft are likely to be cheaper than individually owned cars and quicker than individuals to jettison internal-combustion vehicles in favor of more economical electrics.

If these factors drive down the price of oil, it obviously would benefit the cruise lines. Either it would boost cruise-industry profits, or it would allow the lines to cut their prices and build ticket sales more rapidly, particularly among cash-strapped Millennials. This could be especially helpful in growth markets like China and India, where the middle class is expanding fast but still has less real disposable income than counterparts in the industrialized countries.

We continue to believe it more likely that the price of energy, adjusted for inflation, will average less than $65 for the foreseeable future. Then, over the coming decades it will slowly drift downward as electric vehicles increasingly displace the internal combustion engine and more of the world's electricity comes from the sun, wind, and other renewable sources. Renewables already are cheaper than coal or oil in most of the world, and their cost falls almost daily.

In China and India, the industry's quickest future growth markets, the transition to electric vehicles is almost sure to move faster than it will in the West. According to one estimate from the Indian government, by 2030 the country will see its last new internal-combustion car. They are not planning to ban oil-burning cars. Instead, by then only cheap-to-run electrics will still be viable in the Indian market. High demand in countries as populous as China and India could push down the cost of electrics throughout the world, quickly bringing the price of oil down as well.

Fortunately, this is not the make-or-break issue for the cruise industry that it could be for airlines. With fuel costs amounting to only 12 percent of expenses, the cruise lines will remain comfortably profitable even if the cost of crude rises over $65 per barrel and remains there. It could go even higher without significantly harming cruise-company profits. The price of oil is just one of many factors that cruise executives will need to monitor. It is not one they will need to fear.

Cruise lines face growing environmental demands.

If the industry has been conspicuously weak in one area, it is in shrinking its environmental footprint. A typical cruise ship generates about 1 million gallons of gray water in a single week. It also produces 210,000 gallons of sewage, 25,000 gallons of oily bilge water, and over 7 tons of solid waste—and that was in 2008, before the largest ships now operating had set sail.

In the decade beginning with 2008, 228 pollution violations and fines worldwide were reported. As recently as 2016, Princess Cruise Lines paid a $40 million penalty for dumping oily waste into the ocean off Great Britain. It had been doing so since 2005. At least five of the company's cruise ships used clean ocean water to fool onboard sensors that otherwise would have registered the illegal dumping.

This is a long way from being the only such incident. A report in late 2017 claimed that cruise ships have done almost nothing to reduce their pollution. Nabu, a German environmental group, pointed out that cruise companies a year earlier had promised to equip at least 23 ships with soot filters to reduce particulate emissions. A study of 63 cruise ships found that not one carried a working filter. As a result, a mid-size, diesel-powered cruise ship was still pouring out as much particulates as 1 million cars. Only Hapag-Lloyd and TUI had made any progress, installing catalysts to break down nitrogen oxide, a lesser, but still significant, pollutant. In Australia, the New South Wales Environmental Protection Agency warned that docked cruise ships poured out enough fine particles and sulfur dioxide to harm the health of those living near them.

In fact, despite Nabu's grim assessment, cruise lines are beginning a transition that should leave their ships a lot friendlier to the environment. As early as 2015, Royal Caribbean pointed out that it had cut its production of solid waste in half over the previous two years, from 0.91 pounds per passenger per day to only 0.46 pounds. Many lines are being retrofitted to plug into shoreside power, rather than running their engines in port to generate electricity. Cruise lines in 2017 had committed to install exhaust-gas cleaning systems in 29 cruise ships then under construction. Nearly 50 more ships were scheduled to have the equipment retrofitted in the years ahead. By 2018, an estimated 60 percent of the global cruise fleet had upgraded its sewage treatment devices. CLIA requires members to treat sewage and wastewater before releasing it. It's a start.

Many cruise lines have taken to touting their commitment to the environment:

Costa Cruises says its ships compost food waste and process 100 percent of all onboard solid waste for disposal on land, including plastics and lead batteries.

Crystal says it enforces a "nothing overboard" policy. All waste is recycled, incinerated on board, or was sent to landfills on shore. Even the company's dry-cleaning is eco-friendly.

Holland America purifies its wastewater on board, recycles, and donates such items as unused toiletries and surplus furniture to shelters, rather than throwing them away.

Hurtigruten's two new 530-passenger expedition cruise ships for the Arctic and Antarctic, launched in 2018 and '19, were designed with hybrid power systems that should reduce fuel consumption by about one-fifth.

MSC's ships are equipped with water treatment plants and garbage pulpers, grinders, compactors, and incinerators.

Norwegian is equipping its vessels with oily-water separators to make sure that only clean water goes into the sea. The company also recycles more than 30 percent of materials; however, it still jettisons food waste, which the company considers safe because it's biodegradable.

However, the greatest environmental improvement in tomorrow's cruise ships is likely to be their fuel. Seven of Carnival's ships currently on order will be powered by liquid natural gas (LNG). This fuel is not only cleaner-burning and produces lower in emissions than oil, it drastically reduces ship maintenance. Oil-fueled marine engines require major work every 12,500 hours of operation. GE's marine gas turbine division reports that LNG power plants delay extensive maintenance to 25,000 hours and many operate as long as 35,000 hours when not run constantly at full load. It seems that Carnival and other cruise lines will be doing well while doing good.

Such efforts are only the beginning. In the years ahead, cruise lines will place greater emphasis on environmental matters, because tomorrow's cruisers do. In a 2017 poll, fewer than half of Boomers said their choice of a cruise line was strongly influenced by the line's record of "eco-responsibility." Among Millennials, the number is 69 percent. If environmental measures until recently have been an afterthought at best, in the years ahead they will become both a regulatory necessity and a highly effective competitive method.

Technology increasingly dominates both the economy and society.

Recycling equipment and environmentally friendly power trains are only two of many technological innovations coming to the cruise industry. The robot mixing drinks at the Bionic Bar on Carnival's Quantum-class ships is probably the least of them, more novelty than serious addition to the vessel's efficiency or passenger appeal.

One of the most obvious technologies now expanding through the industry is virtual reality. It may be one of the most beneficial. Ignore onboard VR videogames and other entertainments; anyone who's experienced virtual reality at home knows what to expect. Consider instead something passengers will never see, Royal Caribbean's Innovation Center. Nicknamed "The Cave," it is a virtual-reality theater where designers and architects in 3D goggles can take a virtual walk through a new cruise ship and work out the details before the first steel is cut.

Celebrity's new 2,900-passenger *Celebrity Edge*, due in autumn 2018, was designed there. Working first in VR allowed the naval architects to build much of the ship's framework inside, rather than out. This allowed them, in effect, to move the balcony inside the state room, giving passengers more space and providing a so-called "infinity view" unobstructed by structural members. It also helped designers avoid a common guest complaint, the clumsy, crowded process of boarding a launch to go ashore. They created a platform the size of a tennis court that can serve as a disembarkation point at sea level and be lifted higher in the ship to serve as a restaurant or cocktail bar.

We do not know whether other ships will copy that platform, but we do know that virtual reality is likely to be a major asset for ship designers from now on.

Augmented reality (AR), VR's close cousin, appears on Celebrity Cruises' *Celebrity Edge* as "x-ray technology." It's a smartphone app that allows passengers to look straight through bulkheads and decks into the bridge, engine room, and other areas they can't visit in person.

Not quite VR or AR but impressive nonetheless, are the "virtual balconies" on board Royal Caribbean's *Quantum of the Seas*. Each one consists of an 80-inch high-definition LED screen that stretches from floor to ceiling and wall to wall. Digital cameras mounted around the ship relay real-time views of the ocean to the screen, providing a view of the outside that reviewers have pronounced surprisingly realistic. The idea is not original. Disney introduced virtual portholes a few years earlier, inserting animated characters into the live ocean scenery, and Royal Caribbean tested its virtual-balcony concept on *Navigator of the Seas* in 2013. We can expect to see it on other high-end cruise vessels.

Some of the most interesting shipboard tech is the sort of thing guests will seldom really notice—and that is the point. Built into a watchband or pendant, it records guest's personal details and tracks their location and activities to remove the friction from highly personalized cruising experiences. Typical functions include automatically opening stateroom doors, paying for onboard purchases without so much as a wave at a sensor, suggesting nearby activities that might fit the cruiser's interests, and making sure only one activity gets scheduled for a given time. Facial recognition makes it possible to check in within a couple of minutes instead of enduring a long, drawn-out process. And geolocation means guests can order a drink and get it delivered to them almost anywhere in the ship, rather than having to walk to a bar. That also makes it possible to locate missing children instantly so long as they are wearing their interface. The devices also alert crew members when guests are approaching, providing details such as preferences, activities, and dietary restrictions. Carnival's "Ocean Medallion," and MSC's "MSC for Me" are variations on this technology.

This is been only a brief overview of what new technology is bringing to the cruise industry. A comprehensive run-down would require at least another text, very likely an encyclopedia. In the years ahead cruise lines will be using technology not only to improve ship operations and fend off environmentalist criticism, but to give their guests an easier, more personalized, and more satisfying vacation experience. And that is the most basic, effective competitive method of all.

Bottom Line

We conclude with a few statistics from the European Ships and Maritime Equipment Association (SEA), which represents many of the companies that build and maintain vessels for the cruise industry. In 2015, the organization published a forecast of cruise tourism to 2035. It was the most distant projection we have seen to date and, at twenty years, about as far ahead as we can expect a forecast to be even approximately accurate. By then, today's hospitality students will be growing into key positions in the planning and operation of their companies, so SEA's projection amounts to a forecast of their potential careers in the cruise industry.

SEA believes the cruise industry and its executives can look forward to a bright future. The organization expects cruising to grow at its habitual rate of nearly 7.5 percent annually. By 2035, worldwide passenger loads will total more than 54 million per year.

The industry's regional markets will remain in their current order. North America still will be the world's largest cruise market, contributing more than 26 million cruisers that year, some 49 percent of the total. Europe will still be in second position, with over 17.8 million passengers, or slightly more than 33 percent. Asia, they believed, will contribute about 5.7 million passengers, or 10.5 percent. This leaves about 4.5 million coming from rest of the world, about 8 percent. (We know these percentages add up to more than 100. Limiting figures to only one decimal place introduces rounding errors that become noticeable, but not significant.)

Several years after the SEA made its forecast, it has become clear that they probably underestimated growth in the Asian cruise market. The passenger census from China alone should rise to more than 10 million by then. India will add to this, though under today's circumstances we do not believe it possible to estimate how many cruisers that country will contribute so far into the future.

However much larger the Asian market will be in 2035, we must add the extra cruisers to the world's total. This brings passenger loads to nearly 60 million that year. No other segment of the travel and hospitality industry can look forward to that kind of expansion. It adds up to more ships, more crew members, growing need for executives to manage them all, and a warm welcome for hospitality graduates at the beginning of their careers.

We see only one factor that might change this prediction for the worse. This, of course, is the growing power of artificial intelligence and the high-level automation it makes possible. If brainy machines replace millions of human jobs, widespread unemployment could erode elective spending of all forms until the world has adapted to the change. After the Industrial Revolution, creating new jobs for all who needed them required two generations. This is not what we expect, and in this we agree with most credible forecasters. Very tentatively, we believe the world will muddle through the coming change with less disruption than many fear. Yet, this is one factor that potential cruise executives will have to monitor in the coming decade.

Web Assignment

Log into the student website and complete the end of chapter assignment. Try to utilize some of the works you read about from this chapter and apply the key concepts, terms, and theory in your responses.

Tasty Trends for the Restaurant Industry

It's not true, you know. The idea that 90 to 95 percent of restaurants fail in their first year, it's only a myth. Studies of real-world business data find that roughly 30 percent of restaurants fold or change ownership that soon, while 60 percent go under or are sold in three years. This is roughly equal to the failure/sale rate of small businesses in any other industry. (Note that about 30 percent of small businesses are profitable when sold. Their owners cash out for personal reasons.) Building a career in this corner of the hospitality industry is not as risky as it sounds.

Nonetheless, hospitality graduates entering this field will find plenty of challenges to keep them busy. Competition is fierce, profit margins modest—3 to 5 percent for most, though a few outliers make up to 15 percent. Seasonal variations are strong in some regions. And for individual locations, employee turnover is, by the standards of other industries, ridiculous. One study found that 53 percent of restaurant employees quit in 2016. A decade earlier—before the recession reminded many that jobs can be good to have and hard to replace—researchers put it at nearly 75 percent. At the corporate level in large chains, the restaurant industry is much like any other hospitality operation, with the usual concerns about competitive strategies, financing, siting and operation of facilities, and so on. At the retail level, it can be a constant struggle.

We saw one of the reasons in 2008, when the world's major economies entered the worst downturn the world had seen in almost ninety years. As a discretionary expense for most guests, restaurants are more sensitive than many sectors to economic conditions. They felt the recession first and worst.

As GDPs sank, most of the restaurant industry declined with them. Sales at McDonald's were up 7.2 percent worldwide in the fourth quarter of the year, but that prosperity came at the cost of nearly all higher-priced outlets. That December, the National Restaurant Association (NRA) comprehensive index of restaurant activity set its second consecutive record low after fourteen months below its break-even level. Same-store sales were the weakest in the index's history, with nearly two-thirds of operators reporting a decline for the month. The Association's Current Situation Index, which combines same-store sales, traffic, labor, and capital expenditures, also reached a record low. Business at some high-end restaurants was rumored to be off as much as 40 percent from the previous year.

Things have changed since then.

Status Report

A decade since the Great Recession began, it seems in many ways a good time for the industry. The number of restaurants and drinking establishments has grown faster than, for example, the financial industry in every year since 2007. Even in 2009, when the population of financial firms declined by more than 3 percent, growth among the recovering purveyors of food and drink was weakly positive. By the end of 2016, the NRA counted more than 1 million restaurant locations in the United States.

Industry employment has been going up as well. Between March 2010 and February 2017, the number of restaurant jobs in the United States grew by 25 percent—more than double the 12 percent seen in the economy at large. In 2017, about 14.7 million people worked in U.S. restaurants, some 10 percent of the national workforce.

Wage-growth numbers are even more impressive. In the year ending September 2017, median base pay in the United States grew by 1.8 percent year-over-year. In the restaurant industry, it was 2.5 percent. This looks even better compared with recent performance in other employment sectors. In manufacturing, wage growth began to slow in 2016. In retail, it had been slowing since mid-2015; in October 2016, it touched zero for the first time in this century. Restaurant wages have been accelerating almost steadily since mid-2013. In March 2017, their year-over-year growth was closing in on 5 percent.

Better, many new restaurant jobs have been solidly middle-class. Between 2010 and 2015, the national economy gained only 11 percent more jobs paying between $45,000 and $74,999 per year. Among restaurants, the number was 42 percent. This is even more impressive than it seems when we consider that 56 percent of restaurant employees work part-time or for only part of the year.

In fact, the restaurant industry supplied two of the nation's top five jobs with the fastest-rising wages. Baristas earned 5.6 percent more at the end of the period than a year earlier, giving them the fastest growth in the country. Restaurant cooks earned 4.3 percent more, putting them in fifth position. Not even healthcare approached that record.

Industry sales have justified both expansion and rising wages. In 2017, they came to $799 billion, up 4.3 percent from billion the year before. This too continues a long-running trend. Spending at restaurants and bars has grown twice as fast as all other retail spending. In 2015, for the first time in history, Americans spent more in restaurants and taverns than they did in grocery stores.

All this has inspired optimism in the county's restaurant operators. A late-2016 survey by Toast Restaurant POS found 92 percent looking forward to a good year in 2017. Seven of eight said they believe the success of their restaurants was in their control—not the sort of response we would have expected to see in 2008. Even in the fine-dining segment, which usually suffers the first and deepest wounds in a downturn, only 12 percent of operators were at all pessimistic about the coming year.

So why have industry analysts spent much of the last two years (as of mid-2018) talking of a restaurant recession? They have been fretting since an industry downturn began early in 2015.

Bad News

For the NRA's Restaurant Performance Indicex, readings over 100 indicate a period of growth; anything under 100 signals a contraction. In 2004, it reached about 103.7. In late 2008, at the bottom of the recession, it was roughly 96.4.

Since the end of the recession, the Index has remained generally positive, sometimes dipping briefly to contraction levels, but with much longer periods of accelerating growth. However, between late 2014 and much of 2016, the industry slowed sharply. The index can be up or down a point or more from one quarter to the next, but this was a steady decline from 103 to under 100, a brief recovery, and renewed decline. It seemed ominous at best.

Despite rapid growth in the fast-casual segment, the proliferation of restaurants in the United States came to an abrupt end. Their number dropped by about 2 percent in the twelve months through September 2016 and 2 percent more by fall 2017. The decline was even worse among independent restaurants, which were off by 4 percent in 2016 and 3 percent in the following nine months. The stock-market publication *Seeking Alpha* summarized it as the industry's worst recession since 2009. *QSR Magazine* called 2016 "the worst restaurant year since the recession."

At the end of 2017, walk-in traffic at American restaurants had gone six straight years without a good quarter. Restaurant traffic was flat in 2017. It would have declined if not for a 1-percent rise in quickservice visits. Even at chain restaurants, foot traffic slipped nearly 5 percent year-on-year, with same-store sales off by 2.8 percent. By February 2018, the decline in traffic had gone 24 months without a respite. Same-store sales turned weekly positive only in October 2017.

The one bright spot was the size of the average diner's bill. Despite a wave of promotions, the average restaurant check grew by 2 percent in the the first nine months of the 2917. If not for that, sales numbers would have been even worse.

In all, the restaurant industry grew by about 1.4 percent in 2017, with a similar improvement expected in 2018. Fast casual, which suffered during the recession, was up 7.5 percent on the year. Full-service restaurants barely grew at all. In mid-2018, the index is holding between 101 and 102. Many fingers are crossed.

Prosperity Abroad

Unexpectedly hard times in America contrast sharply with restaurant performance elsewhere. Industry statistics are harder to find outside the United States, and often are relatively dated by the time they become available. Yet, it is clear that eateries in most regions are prospering.

American quickservice chains provide some firm data for their end of the market. Domino's Pizza reported same-store sales overseas up 2.6 percent in the second quarter of 2017. McDonald's reported better-than-expected sales throughout the world, with China, Japan, and the U.K. particularly strong.

Probably the broadest picture of international foodservice markets comes from a quarterly survey by NPD Group. In the second quarter of 2017, restaurant traffic was up in all but one of the markets it tracks, including Australia, Brazil, Canada, China, France, Germany, Great Britain, Italy, Japan, Korea, Russia, and Spain. The exception, of course, was the U.S.

Restaurant sales generally show the same pattern. In Japan, sales totaled $38.48 billion in 2015; they were expected to come in at $41.61 billion in 2017, rising to $44.59 billion in 2020.

Throughout the world, nearly all the growth came from the quickservice segment. Higher in the service and price ranges, performance was stable or only slightly off. This pattern seems likely to remain with us for some time.

American Malaise

As we have seen, the decline of restaurant business is not a global issue. That American restaurants are having problems is particularly troubling because their decline is taking place during what the usual statistics say is a time of general prosperity.

What's the problem? No one is really sure. It may be that the market has simply become too crowded, with too many restaurants chasing too few customer dollars. The decline in same-store sales appears to support that reasoning. Yet, we suspect there is more to it than that. There are many partial explanations, and they may add up to a convincing whole. Yet, the situation is complicated, and possible causes are tied closely to some of the country's most powerful trends. Examining them will require a long discussion, so we will save it for the end of this chapter.

For now, let us look at some of the trends that will help to shape the restaurant industry in the years ahead. These issues will occupy foodservice executives throughout their careers.

Major Trends for the Restaurant Industry

In Chapter 7, we examined the most important trends for the travel and hospitality industries. Everything presented there applies to restaurants in very straightforward ways. We will look at the details here. Then we will return to the forces that have eroded profits for America's restaurants since the Great Recession. In varying degrees, they are likely to help shape the industry's environment in the United States and other developed countries in the years ahead.

Economic growth continues throughout the world, yet is slowing in many countries.

As we have seen, the state of the nation's economy does more than most other factors to set profits in the restaurant industry. Fast-growing prosperity means boom times for foodservice. But in bad times, dining out is an elective expense that can be sacrificed with relative ease. Restaurant guests can eat at home or move down the price spectrum from full-service restaurants to fast-casual or from fast-casual to quickservice restaurants. Most of our discussion here will focus on the near-term, where forecasts can be relatively trustworthy. Yet, we will try to derive longer-term lessons as the data permit.

GDP in the United States is expanding steadily and reasonably fast. Annualized, it came in at 2.3 percent in 2017, and many economists with good track records in forecasting believe 2018 will come in around 3 percent. This is close enough to its 3.22-percent average over the last seventy years.

The stock market, for what it's worth, is down from its January high but in August 2018 remains above 25,000 on the Dow Jones industrial average, a level it never saw before 2018. Inflation is finally starting to heat up, though it has yet to become a problem.

The Federal Reserve Board long aimed for an inflation rate of 2 percent yearly since the Great Recession ended. It maintained that rate for most of 2011 and the first few months of 2012. Before and since then, inflation has never held that high for more than a few months at a time. In May 2018, it came in at 2.8 percent, annualized, higher than it had been since 2012. That was high enough for the Federal Reserve Board to raise interest rates a quarter point, to 2 percent, and announce that it expects rates to reach 3.4 percent by 2020.

At the same time, the jobless rate has come down to a scant 3.8 percent, a level generally considered to represent full employment. Even U6, which includes so-called "marginally attached workers"—those who want a full-time job but cannot find one—was down to 7.6 percent. It has not been that low since 2001. In all, this is the best economy the United States has seen since before the Great Recession. It promises to remain so. The Conference Board's Leading Economic Index for the U.S. has been rising almost without interruption since the second quarter of 2009. Its April 2018 reading of 109.4 was the highest it had been in this century. Three months later, it was at 110.7. The index looks only a quarter or two ahead, but the strength and duration of its upward trend invite optimism for the longer term.

Economies in other countries are, if anything, even healthier. For the first time in memory, GDP is growing in all forty-five of the countries tracked by the Organization for Economic Cooperation and Development.

In a rare show of strength, the European Union expanded faster than the U.S. in 2016 and '17. Unemployment is still too high in some member countries, but for the Union as a whole it has declined continuously since mid-2012 and in April 2018 was lower than it had been in this century, save for the overheated period just before the 2007/'08 crash. Despite the growing power of populist and nationalist right wing, Angela Merkel's reelection to an unprecedented fourth term as Germany's chancellor suggests that economic policy on the Continent, and the economy itself, will remain relatively stable into the coming decade. In April 2018, the Conference Board's Leading Economic Index for the Euro Area has been rising steadily since mid-2013 and shows no sign of slowing down. Central bankers there, like their peers in the U.S., can continue scaling back the monetary and fiscal policies they adopted when their economies were in trouble.

China has left behind the double-digit expansion it achieved during the early 1990s and most of the decade before the Great Recession. Yet, even when the global recession savaged its trade markets, China's economic growth never sank below 9 percent. Although a number of weaknesses in the country's economic data make it difficult to be certain, it seems GDP there is now growing at about half that rate–the target Beijing has set for itself. The Chinese economy may accelerate again temporarily, but in the 2020s GDP is expected to slow steadily to 3.5 percent.

All this good news comes with a caveat, however. Productivity is not improving, so economic progress has been much slower than in the recovery from most previous recessions. Political uncertainties in the United States and too many other countries could derail growth throughout much of the world. (We believe this is relatively unlikely, but it cannot be ruled out.) Rather than investing their profits, companies are banking them or using them for unproductive purposes such as buying back outstanding stock. This is likely to remain a drag on wage growth in the years ahead.

Remember, too, that the United States is already several years behind schedule for its next economic downturn. We assume there will be one by, say, 2022. Our best estimate is that it should be relatively shallow and brief, with little lasting effect on hospitality and travel. However, we are carefully watching the growing pile of corporate debt now accumulating in the country. A panic like the mortgage collapse at the end of 2007 and into 2008 is equally possible in the corporate market and likely to appear with as little warning. The result could be as devastating as it was in 2008, leaving hospitality graduates looking for a first job in an inhospitable economy. Again, this is not our default expectation, but a lesser possibility that bears close observation.

In the longer run, economic growth in the developed world is expected to slow. In the United States, for example, most forecasts anticipate average GDP growth in the neighborhood of 2 to 2.5 percent well into the next decade. However, a very gradual downtrend will bring it down to roughly 1.5 percent by 2050. Over the same period, China's economy will slow to about 2.3 percent per year. Japan's will find it difficult to reach even 2 percent. In the Euro area, it will hover around 2 percent through the mid-2020s, then slip gradually, stabilizing at 1.4 percent. Among the major economies, only India will remain relatively buoyant, holding at nearly 6 percent through the middle of the coming decade then beginning to slide to roughly 4 percent by 2050. Overall, the global economy will grow at an average of about 2.6 percent annually between 2016 and 2050, with net growth for the period of 130 percent.

Most of this expansion will take place in the emerging-market and developing countries. The so-called E7 economies–Brazil, China, India, Indonesia, Mexico, Russia, and Turkey–will average almost 3.5 percent growth each year through 2050, compared with 1.6 percent for the advanced G7 nations. As these economies expand, we expect them to be fertile markets for the restaurant industry. There will be more restaurants, with a growing proportion of high-end restaurants. It will take time, but by the 2030s we expect to see the beginning of industry consolidation in many of these countries, with native restaurant chains expanding to drive out independent operators, as is occurring in the United States and other developed lands.

As economies in the developed world slow their growth, many service industries may seem on their way to becoming zero-sum games, with each improvement in one company's business coming at the cost of its competitors. However, this is a concern for the far future. Throughout the careers of today's students, cost efficiencies will be of even greater concern as markets become increasingly competitive. Yet, economic conditions should support steady growth in the restaurant industry for many years to come.

Populations are growing older and more diverse.

Throughout the developed world, where birth rates are declining and life expectancies are stretching, people on average are growing older. They are growing more diverse as well, thanks to a wave of migration that is bringing millions of people from the eastern hemisphere to the western and from south of the equator to the northern lands. Both these trends will change the restaurant market.

We saw many of the details in Chapter 7:

- In the United States, those over 65 made up 15 percent of the population in 2000; by 2050, 27 percent of Americans will be in their traditional retirement years.

- Japan's over-65 population has grown from 17 percent of the total in 2000 to 22 percent in 2010; it is expected to reach more than 36 percent in 2050.
- In China, some 134 million belonged to the over-65 cohort in 2015; by 2050, their numbers will more than double to nearly 300 million.
- Germany, France, Britain, Italy, and many other countries also are growing older.

In many of these countries the transition will be seen well before 2050. As soon as 2030, seniors will make up more than one-fourth of the population in North America and Europe.

In most of these countries, populations also are shrinking. Japan's peaked at 128 million in 2008 and eventually will decline to less than 87 million. China's will peak at over 1.4 billion in 2025, then shrink to 1.34 billion in 2050 and 1.0 billion in 2100. In the EU at large, the population will not reach its maximum until about 2050. However, Germany's is expected to begin shrinking around 2020; the decline would have begun already if not for the arrival of large numbers of refugees. Spain's population, 46.5 million in 2014, already has begun a slow decline; it will be about 45.4 million in 2030, only 43.8 million in 2050. Italy's population reached its maximum in 2011, at 59.8 million, and will lose nearly 2 million by 2030.

Countries are growing more diverse as well, thanks to a wave of migration that is bringing millions of people from the eastern hemisphere to the western, and from south of the equator to the northern lands. In the United States, the Hispanic, Asian, and Middle Eastern populations all are expanding rapidly, and attempts to stem the flow, however determined, are likely to fail in the long run. In 2000, Latinos accounted for about one-eighth of the U.S. population. By 2050, they will be nearly one-fourth. And the number of Asians is almost doubling from 11.2 million in 2000 to 19.6 million in 2020. Similar changes have been seen in Europe for decades. Even before the mass migration of refugees from Syria and Iraq in 2016, hundreds of thousands of immigrants arrived each year from Eastern Europe, North Africa, the Middle East, and the Indian subcontinent.

All these trends will help to shape the restaurant market in the decades ahead.

The aging, and in some cases shrinking, of national populations has obvious implications. Dependency ratios—the number of children and retirees who need support from those of working age—are rising fast in the developed world. As a result, taxes will rise also, to fund social security programs throughout the industrialized countries.

In the United States, where retirement programs are ungenerous and subject to political whim, more retirees struggling with fixed incomes will compete with young people for restaurant jobs. This may provide a more stable, reliable pool of workers in a traditionally volatile industry. Farther ahead, many restaurants are likely to find that a major part of their business consists of delivering take-out meals to local retirement communities.

Although Baby Boomers once dominated restaurant clientele and still provide roughly 40 percent of restaurant spending, restaurateurs are now focused on the Millennials, currently the second-largest generation in the U.S. This is a matter of long-term planning. In 2017, the Millennials spent less than one dollar in four that restaurants brought in. Before 2030, this will grow to $40 for every $100 spent in restaurants, about what the Baby Boomers now provide. At the same time, the Boomers' share of restaurant spending will shrink to roughly one-third and will continue declining thereafter.

Growing diversity will continue restaurant trends that have been in effect for decades. Catering to migrants, and to natives willing to experiment with their cuisines, has been a fast growth market for decades, especially for independent entrepreneurs and small chains. New immigrants and their first-generation children prefer the foods they grew up with. They remain a steady market for native cuisines long after they have otherwise assimilated into their new culture.

In Europe, a generation of immigrants from North Africa, the Middle East, Pakistan, India, and Bangladesh have been opening restaurants that offer their native cuisines for nearly twenty years. This new fare has proved popular with indigenous Europeans. In Britain especially, demand for *halal* food acceptable to strict Muslims has grown rapidly. We can expect a similar trend, but much stronger, in Germany, which accepted more than 1 million refugees from Syria and Iraq in 2015 and '16 and expects around 300,000 more to join their relatives in the next couple of years. Other countries, much less generous in their treatment of those displaced by war, will see much smaller increases in demand for Middle Eastern cuisine.

We see a similar evolution in the United States, where Peruvian ceviche, Vietnamese pho, Thai sriracha, Korean kimchi and bibimbap, and a host of other fads reflect a much deeper trend. Migration has helped to drive the American boom in Asian, Latin, and Caribbean restaurants for upward of two decades. Latin American cuisines remain among the fastest growing segments with the addition of cuisines from Guatemala, Ecuador, Peru, and other countries south of Mexico. This trend is particularly strong in California, Florida, and wherever there are large Hispanic communities. In Florida, too, Jamaican and other Caribbean cuisines have been an established trend, while Vietnamese restaurants have spread from their big-city footholds to many smaller communities.

In the years ahead, we can expect to see more American restaurants featuring foods from out-of-the-way parts of Asia, the Caribbean, Latin America, and North Africa, with a modest boom in Indian fare. More European restaurants are offering cuisine from many of these same regions. And still more restaurants in China and Japan are specializing in American regional fare. Starting a high-quality, reasonably priced restaurant specializing in one of these cuisines may be the best opportunity for success this industry offers small entrepreneurs in the years ahead.

All this fits well with buying habits in the U.S., where Baby Boomers and their descendants have long sought out novelty and variety. The National Restaurant Association reports that 88 percent of American consumers eat at least one "ethnic" item per month, while 17 percent eat seven or more. A third have deliberately sought out a new foreign cuisine in the past year.

In the United States, three-fourths of adults, and especially young adults, say they are open to trying new foods, according to one study. And although two-thirds of Americans say they prefer American food when they go out to eat and Italian and Mexican restaurants remain firmly in second and third place, some 35 percent of consumers polled by Technomics said they would like to see more Middle Eastern and North African dishes in restaurants. About one in four actively seek out cuisines from those regions. One-fifth are curious about cuisines from Albania, Bulgaria, and other countries in the Balkans, and about 16 percent seek them out.

This trend is likely to last, as Millennials and Centennials are even more commonly interested in these cuisines than their elders.

Even more intense flavors lie ahead as well. Aging Baby Boomers will need them to maintain their sense of novelty and excitement as their taste buds lose their sensitivity. Milennials and Centennials will continue this trend, in part because Centennials are a much more diverse generation than their predecessors were. Some 24 percent are Hispanic, guaranteeing the continued proliferation of Latin American restaurants.

In addition to their preference for daring flavors, Centennials display two characteristics that will help to shape tomorrow's restaurants. One is a demand for authenticity inherited from their forebears and elevated to still greater importance. This is helping to drive the growth of ethnic restaurants with a broader range of fare and flavors than previous generations have demanded. The trend is clearest in Asian restaurants, where menus are pushing deeper into Indian, Thai, and Korean food traditions than in the past. Americanized fare like chop suey is passé, and the nation's restaurants will be better for it.

The other Centennial priority is health consciousness. Their demand for organic foods, fresh ingredients, and freshly prepared meals is helping to drive the growth of fast-casual outlets, which many of them prefer to traditional fast-food chains. Panera's long list of ingredients and additives not found in its food is a response to this preference, pioneered by the Millennials and now intensified among the Centennials.

Even the Boomers, whose health-consciousness is often overcome by their preference for economy and convenience, can be expected to join this trend as they reach their senior years and need to watch their weight, blood pressure, and cholesterol levels. Farther ahead, many restaurants are likely to find that a major part of their business consists of delivering take-out meals to local retirement communities.

This is been only a brief introduction to the trends in cuisine, consumer values, and changing tastes resulting from population trends. Hospitality students who enter the foodservice sector will spend much of their time throughout their careers on crafting new competitive methods to attract all these demographic segments.

Travel (especially international) and tourism are growing fast.

As we saw in Chapter 7, international tourism has expanded by roughly 5 percent per year for nearly as long as anyone can remember. In 2016, international tourist arrivals totaled about 1.235 billion. Until 2008, they were expected to reach 1.6 billion annually by 2020. The global recession appeared to set this expansion back by about three years. Yet, at the current rate of growth, international tourist arrivals still could meet this target.

The largest component of this growth, of course, is the expansion of tourism from China and India. This requires some obvious adaptation from all segments of the hospitality industry, and restaurants are no exception.

We can see what is needed in a glance at the world's largest tourist destination, Las Vegas. In 2016, nearly 43 4million people visited the gamblers' Mecca. About 2.9 million tourists from China visited the U.S. that year, and around 200,000 of them made their way to Las Vegas. Yet, a survey of gaming establishments on the Strip found only two staffers who could speak Mandarin.

© Kobby Dagan/Shutterstock.com

Catering to Chinese tourists is quickly becoming an important part of any hospitality business. By 2020, the number of Chinese tourists in the U.S. is expected to reach 5.1 million, which should put the number visiting Las Vegas at nearly 400,000.

Fortunately for the future of Las Vegas, executives both there and in China have been working to improve the city's appeal:

The MGM Grand, Wynn, and Venetian now offer high-quality Chinese food, Chinese-language menus, and Chinese-speaking staff.

In December 2016, Hainan Airlines began offering three flights per week nonstop from Beijing to Las Vegas. Korean Air operates five more, and half of its passengers who connect in Seoul for Las Vegas are from China.

In November 2016, a new attraction opened: the Lucky Dragon Hotel and Casino, a modest 200-room property funded by Chinese investors and located just off the Strip. It is intended to attract Chinese immigrants to the U.S., but it seems a sure bet that visitors from China itself will flock there as well.

A second casino, the 3,100-room Resorts World, should open at the north end of the Strip in March 2019. Originally set to open in 2016, the project is owned by Malaysia-based Genting Group, and its brand is familiar to Asian tourists. Although it is intended primarily for American visitors, the Asian-themed property will be designed and operated to bring in all the Chinese tourists it can. A planned panda habitat should go over well with both groups.

Obviously, the average restaurant in Topeka or Hamburg will not build itself into a casino for tourists from China, or anywhere else. Yet, those in cities where tourists from China or, soon, India are common will need to work for their business. Bilingual menus should be available, and chefs should learn to prepare one or two specialty meals to assure tourists their business is appreciated. However, this kind of business-development effort is likely to work best at the community level, where local hospitality managers will have the greatest chance to make their mark on it.

The opening of European borders caused a boom in Continental tourism, especially among the younger generations, who routinely speak several languages. Young people from Italy, France, England, and Germany have been nearly as likely to spend vacations, and even long weekends, in each other's countries as in their own. The recession throttled back that flow temporarily, and routed many travelers to lower-priced destinations in Eastern Europe.

The greatest immediate change we are likely to see on the Continent is a decline in tourism from Britain as a result of Brexit, and perhaps an increase in the opposite direction. In 2016, according to one report, the fraction of international vacations taken by British travelers slipped to 64 percent of the total, down from 71 percent the previous year. This likely reflects the precipitous and lasting decline in the value of the British pound following the Brexit vote in June 2016. Potential travelers from the EU, on the other hand, reported significantly more interest in visiting England than in previous surveys.

Surprisingly, early bookings for overseas travel from Britain in the summer of 2017 were up 11 percent over their number at the same time in 2016. In some of the top 50 destinations, demand was up over 50 percent. This probably reflects a wish to visit the Continent while British tourists are still considered EU natives. It probably helped that the pound was worth about 10 percent more late in 2017 than it had been in March. How long this will last depends heavily on the terms of the exit agreement negotiated by British and European representatives. While statements from both sides remain largely posturing, the pound's future value remains anyone's guess.

For restaurants in the traditional tourist destinations, this is bad news, though not critical owing to Britain's relatively small contribution to the tourist market. However, it may be more significant for higher-end full-service restaurants, which report that in an average year up to 30 percent of their sales—and more than half in some major European tourist destinations—are to vacationers and business travelers.

Yet, in the long run, restaurants in the traditional destinations of Europe, Asia, and the United States all can look forward to good times. By 2020, we expect to see a modest wave of new establishments in Europe and the United States catering to the needs of travelers from China and India.

Technology increasingly dominates both the economy and society.

Again, we have dealt with this subject extensively in Chapter 7, including several of its applications in restaurants: largely or fully automated restaurants such as Eatsa in the U.S., Muten Kurazushi Sushi Restaurant in Japan, and the image recognition software Baidu and KFC China are developing to make food suggestions likely to be appropriate for the customer's age and sex. We will keep our discussion here relatively short.

A survey by the National Restaurant Association in 2016 concluded, "there is no doubt technology is becoming the new normal in some restaurants…." It found that one in four restaurant operators planned to lay in more tech in 2017. Four out of five agreed that technology helps increase sales, makes their restaurants more productive, and provides a competitive advantage. Those without customer-facing technology cited a few obvious barriers to its adoption: installation and operating costs, lack of infrastructure, the need for service and repair, customer acceptance, and the need for staff training. One title published by the NRA summarized the situation today. It read, "Restaurants hungry for tech without the headache." They will have it just as fast as the restaurant-tech industry can develop it.

Quickservice restaurants are the obvious first target for automation and the only one where it is likely to displace as many workers as today's pessimists fear. McDonald's already has begun to replace human cashiers with technology. In some of its stores, customers can place their orders through a telephone app and either pick up their food at the drive-through or have it delivered to their table. By 2020, the company plans to install kiosks where customers can place and pay for their orders in most of its 14,000 restaurants in the U.S. Much of the $2.4 billion in capital investments it announced in January 2018 will go to buy them. Taco Bell, Subway, and Wendy's all plan to install them, and Panera has had kiosks in some locations for several years. Wendy's executives say that savings on personnel should repay the investment within two years.

State-of-the-art kiosks even use voice recognition, so customers do not need to waste time searching for food on the menu. They place the order automatically when patrons ask for the items they want.

A few stores in the U.S. and one KFC in Beijing are experimenting with facial recognition to offer arriving customers their previous order. If they accept it, the transaction is over in about four seconds. All that remains is to deliver the food.

McDonald's says it will transfer employees to roles like table service rather than firing them. However, those who leave on their own are unlikely ever to be replaced.

© Sorbis/Shutterstock.com

New as kiosks are, they already are starting to evolve, shrinking and moving to the table. Self-service tablets allow patrons to place their own orders (any mistakes in ordering are their own), split the check easily, and pay at their convenience. They are likely to spread rapidly. Among younger Millennials and older Centennials, ages 18 to 34, more than 70 percent polled said they preferred to order for themselves from a tablet than have a server take care of them.

Those who choose to deal with humans are likely to find the experience more efficient, with less waiting, thanks to another new technology. Restaurants are beginning to equip their personnel with wearable devices that notify them when guests have arrived and tell the servers where they're sitting and when their orders are ready. Servers with devices linked to the tablets at the tables can field patrons' requests even when they are not in sight of a wave or nod. And when managers need to notify the staff that a menu item is no longer available, many of these units act as staff intercoms, so the information goes out immediately. Operations are more efficient even as guests receive a better experience.

Mobile apps are already changing the industry. More than 40 percent of consumers say they have downloaded at least one to their smart phone or tablet. Among those ages 18 to 54, about 45 percent actually use their apps. Seven out of ten view menus on their apps, and nearly half use them to read reviews and find restaurant locations.

Again, among restaurants this technology appears to be spreading most rapidly through quickservice chains. In addition to McDonald's, users include Whataburger, Shake Shack, Chick-fil-A, Domino's, and Dunkin' Donuts. They gain a benefit that patrons undoubtedly overlook. Taco Bell reports that people using the app often select extra ingredients, so the average cost of an order goes up by 20 percent.

However, online restaurant-review services have been even quicker to adopt mobile apps. Yelp, Foursquare, Urbanspoon, Zagat, and OpenTable all offer mobile apps customers can use to find their next meal. So do all their competitors.

Some of the most important restaurant technology will operate behind the scenes. This is data-mining software that gathers information from disparate sources and distills it into a single package for easy analysis. Information from restaurants themselves and a variety of other sources can provide information about customers' dining history, their food choices, whether or not they like to linger over a meal, and dozens of other bits of data that can make it easier and more cost-effective to give guests exactly the dining experience they are looking for. Data mining can track server performance to see who is most effective at promoting coffee, dessert, or an extra glass of wine and who may need some remedial training; and analyze food sales to decide which menu items are worth keeping, which are favorites with regular customers, and which should be replaced—and who would be best to handle a large party with children. It can even help companies decide where to expand their chains. And linked to point-of-sale systems, they make it easy to order supplies exactly when they are needed.

In India, KFC is using some of the highest of high-tech in a clever sales ploy. To promote their new five-in-one meal box, customers who buy an I-Box at some stores can get a small figurine 3D-printed in their own image. Although scanning the customer and printing the plastic selfie requires only ten minutes or so, waiting in line to get scanned reportedly can take a lot longer.

New technologies that bid to change the restaurant industry could easily fill more than one book. However, we will end this discussion with just one more: biotechnology companies are beginning to grow meat not on livestock but in laboratories, culturing cells and assembling them into realistic substitutes for animal-derived products. The first hamburger from man-made meat was grilled in 2013. It did not get rave reviews, but so-called "cellular agriculture" has come a long way in a short time. San Francisco-area Memphis Meats has cultured chicken and duck meat and plans to market animal-free hot dogs, meatballs, and sausages around 2022. Three small companies in Israel already have received a $300,000 order for cultured meat from the Chinese government. And a company called Perfect Day plans to begin marketing animal-free dairy products by around 2020. Finally, the makings of a pepperoni pizza even a vegan can love. For restaurants, cultured animal products will eventually provide uniform, high-quality protein with a healthier mix of fats for patrons and much less risk of contamination at prices that could even be lower than those of natural meat.

New competitors are taking business from restaurants.

This is not one of the global trends you will find in Appendix A. Yet, for the restaurant industry it is one of the most important. New products and services are making it easier for potential guests to enjoy the convenience of prepared foods at home or, with a minimum of work, to enjoy restaurant-quality meals without taking the time or braving bad weather to visit a local eatery. Grocery-store prepared-meal departments—"grocerants"—have been stealing business from restaurants for more than twenty years. Lately, meal kits have been doing so as well. There is more to come.

In the last few years, supermarkets have been refining their game. As a result, they are taking more of the sales that once would've gone to restaurants.

Prepared-foods counters are growing into freestanding restaurants inside the grocery store. Food-court seating, full-service areas, and even menus are turning supermarket prepared-foods departments into something closely resembling fast-casual dining. Whole Foods has installed full-service restaurants complete with servers in at least thirty of its locations and opened a variety of quickservice operations in 250 more. The Wegman's chain, with more than ninety locations, offers burgers, crabcakes, and Tuscan fries at some of its locations in Maryland and New York. Mariano's Fresh Market, in Chicago, offers grills, gelato shops, wine tastings, and even live pianists in some of its stores. Many grocerants offer wine and beer, high-profit items that keep customers in the store.

Many industry analysts view this as a response to Millennial attitudes toward food, which are often more demanding than those of their Boomer forebears. A survey by Technomics in late 2016 found that more than half of those polled saw prepared foods at supermarkets as a healthier alternative to quickservice fare. Growing numbers are finding their meals at the local grocery store instead of restaurants. As a result, sales of prepared food at supermarkets grew by 10 percent per year in the decade ending in 2015. In 2016, some 2.4 billion customer visits drove their sales to $10 billion. That was money that once would have gone to traditional restaurants.

In fact, some of it may yet. Before its takover by Amazon, Whole Foods reportedly was dickering with several brands and nationally recognized chefs to set up restaurants within groceries, and Wolfgang Puck is said to be interested in entering the grocerant market. This seems a natural progression for both restaurants and grocery chains, which already sell restaurant-branded products such as California Pizza Kitchen pizzas, Dunkin' Donuts coffee, and P.F. Chang's Asian cuisine.

© Philip Arno Photography/Shutterstock.com

It is likely to be a natural fit as well for Centennials, who find in grocerants a combination of convenience, reasonable prices, and food that seems better for you than a quickservice burger. With the new generation just reaching the age at which they regularly do their own grocery shopping, supermarket meals can only provide more competition for restaurants in the years ahead.

In the last five years, another new industry has begun to compete for restaurant dollars: meal-kit delivery services. Brands like Blue Apron, Green Chef, Purple Carrot, and even Martha Stewart are packaging step-by-step recipes and high-quality ingredients and delivering them to customers fast enough for the meats and greens to arrive still fresh and appetizing. In fact, a quick count finds more than one hundred companies that deliver meal kits, and online Colossus Amazon is said to be getting into the business, competing with many companies that already market kits through the store.

No wonder. Meal-kit services target the same high-income twenty-five-to-forty-four-year-olds that sit-down restaurants do but deliver appetizing meals for an average of about $10 per serving, compared with restaurant prices that often are double that or more. In one mid-2017 survey, nearly one in five consumers said they had already tried a meal-kit service. In another, 27 percent said they wanted to.

Meal kits do have some downsides. Selections are limited, and meals can take a long time to prepare. They also require planning; kits unavoidably must be ordered a few days or a week before they are used. Spontaneity just isn't possible. Waste-conscious consumers can be put off by all the packaging that arrives at their door along with the food. And few people appreciate being locked into a subscription, even when they can put it on hold for months at a time.

Recently, however, yet another competitor has gotten around some of these problems. Grocery chains like Kroger are getting into the business of selling meal kits, enabling customers to decide at the last minute what they feel like eating. And Plated, a well-regarded subscription service, has begun marketing kits through Albertsons stores. This is a small market so far. Nielsen estimates that grocery stores in the U.S. sold just $80.6 million worth of kits in the year ending March 4, 2017, 6.7 percent over the previous year. Yet, this is one market that seems destined to grow rapidly. If TV dinners can survive since the 1950s, meal kits should be an easy sale.

In all, kits are estimated to be a $5 billion business only five years after Blue Apron pioneered the industry. Technomic predicts that by 2020 subscription revenues will double to $10 billion. We will not be surprised if major restaurants begin to package their own kits in an effort to capture some of this market.

Causes for Concern

All this leaves us with one unanswered question. Why did America's restaurant industry look so weak for so long when all the usual environmental factors suggest that the market has not been this good in years? We have some thoughts.

One factor clearly is an excess of competition. In many markets, too many restaurants are chasing too few customers. As a result, store sales are going down even as the overall market grows. Patrons can go to outlets that cater precisely to their preferences in cuisine, cost, convenience, and perceived quality. This helps to explain why many formerly prosperous restaurant chains offering common-denominator fare are shutting stores and struggling to remain afloat.

Yet, we believe there is more to it than that. A few inconspicuous weaknesses in the American economy also may help to explain what has gone wrong. They are issues that foodservice and society at large will be dealing with for many years.

The most obvious is wage stagnation, a problem largely hidden by the statistics we most often see. Average wages in the U.S. have been rising steadily for years. In the 1960s, '70s, and early '80s, they often grew by more than 10 percent per year and seldom dipped below 5 percent annualized for more than a few months. By the 1990s, the rate of growth was coming down, but it never dipped below zero until 2002. Since 2011, when they finished their climb back from the recession, wages have grown at an average of 2.5 percent each year.

But all that is before inflation. The actual buying power of an average wage declined by about 1 percent from 1979 to 2003. It has been essentially flat ever since. Gains made recently, and often cited as proof of the country's economic health in 2017, have done little to make up this loss.

Contrast that with the changing cost of restaurant meals over the same period. According to the Consumer Price Index for "urban consumers: food away from home," the average meal at the end of 2003 was about 1.5 times more expensive in real, post-inflation terms than in January 1979. By July 2017 it had more than doubled again, reaching 3.7 times the price at the beginning of 1979.

Flat wages divided by the rising cost of restaurant meals equals fewer meals bought per capita and a preference for quickservice chains, where food is comparatively cheap. The only surprise may be that this equation did not make itself felt sooner.

There seems little chance that wage growth will accelerate soon or in any lasting way. As we discussed in Chapter 7, wages depend heavily on labor productivity, and productivity is growing only a fifth as fast as it did for more than 25 years. It does not help that federal policies since the 1980s have directed ever more of the GDP into the bank accounts of the wealthy at the cost of the middle class and poor, a direction we do not expect to change in the near future. American workers will not soon have significantly more to spend on anything but essentials.

Demographic Challenges

Several other issues also seem likely to depress restaurant spending. One is the aging of the country. Food budgets decline as we grow older. Between age 55 and 64, mean spending on food is $6,066 per year. From 65 through 74, this declines to $6,303, and to only $4,349 from age 75 onward. As the average age of American consumers continues to rise, the amount per person spent on food can be expected to fall, with restaurant spending slipping at least as fast. This trend is likely to accelerate after 2020, when the enormous Baby Boom generation begins to arrive in its mid-70s.

In this respect, prospects for the American foodservice industry are actually better than those in some other developed countries. In the United States, the large families of new immigrants have helped to slow the rise of the country's average age. In 2010, only 13 percent of U.S. residents were age 65 and older. By 2030, one in five Americans will be in their traditional retirement years. Contrast this with countries like

Germany, where 28 percent of the population already is age 65 or older. By 2060—admittedly a long way off—the number will be one in three. The details vary, but China, Japan, and much of Western Europe show similar trends.

Unlike the United States, these countries also will see their populations shrinking. The German population, currently just over 80 million, is expected to be only 79.2 million in 2030 and just 67.6 million three decades later. Japan's population, now about 128 million, is on its way to 117 million in 2030, and eventually to only 88 million. Much of Europe is in the same position, and China's population is on track to peak around 2025. However much the average resident spends on discretionary items like restaurant meals, the national market will contract unless many more immigrants than any of these countries are inclined to accept arrives to stem the loss. Tourist spending should help to offset this trend in major destinations, but it is difficult to see how consumer-oriented industries like foodservice can avoid declining in the years ahead.

The United States also faces several issues uniquely its own. Three generations of American adults already are struggling to cope with financial problems that did not afflict the so-called "Silent Generation," now in their seventies and beyond. A fourth soon will do so. Because of them, many consumers lack money to spend on much but essentials. Still more will be short of funds in the years ahead.

We will dive deeper into this subject than many readers are likely to enjoy. It is complicated, and even this extended discussion will touch only the highest points. Yet, it has important implications for the restaurant industry. It will be significant as well for many other segments of hospitality and travel.

Baby Boomers are one problem generation. They make up about one-fourth of the adult population, and they have upward of $2.1 trillion in purchasing power. On average, they spend about 42 percent of their food budgets eating out. Their restaurant tabs added up to an average of about $3,100 each in 2016. This is roughly equal to the national average for all consumers.

The question is how long that can last. In 2018, the eldest Boomers are 72 years old, and even the youngest are 54. Financial planners advise that in order to retire comfortably workers need to save about eight times their yearly salary by age 60. For an average married couple filing their income tax jointly, that comes out to about $942,000. Single wage-earners need much less according to this rule, around $272,000 on average.

For previous generations, saving was, if not easy, at least a reliable process for many workers. Those employed by large and medium-sized companies almost universally were covered by defined-benefit pension plans. They could know years in advance how much they would have to spend during retirement. According to a study by the Bureau of Labor Statistics, those who retired on January 1, 1984, at age 65 after thirty years on the job received monthly pensions averaging $385 a month if they earned $15,000 during their last year at work and $866 a month for those who earned $40,000 a year. This does not sound like much today, but after inflation it comes out to $902 in 2016 for the lower-wage earners and nearly $2,030 for the better-off. It has made a big difference in their late-life standard of living.

Fast-forward to 2017. Only about 2 percent of workers in private industry are still covered by defined-benefit pensions. The rest make do with a variety of tax-deferred investment plans and have no guarantee how much money will be available when their working years are over. The Great Recession cost American workers about 25 percent of their retirement savings, on average, in the second half of 2008 alone. By 2016, only 20 percent of workers reported having made up their losses.

In a time of declining real wages, Boomers have not saved nearly enough. Among families age 50 to 55—the youngest Boomers and the oldest of Generation X—median savings are a scant $8,000. Between 56 and 61, median family savings come to only $17,000. The average is not nearly so bad, about $163,600. Yet, that number is driven up by the relatively few highly successful savers. According to the Government Accountability Office, as many as half of all households with members each 55 and older have no savings at all. Those in the bottom fifth—around 15.4 million people—average $10,500 in debt, not counting the value of their homes.

Nearly 20 percent of people who receive Social Security have no other income; for another third it makes up 90 percent of their income. And Social Security counts for less than it used to. Between 2000 and 2017, cost-of-living adjustments have increased Social Security benefits by 43 percent. Unfortunately, the expenses that seniors generally face cost 86 percent more. The price of Medicare Part B has nearly tripled, from $45.50 per month to $134. A year's worth of prescription drugs cost about $1,100 in 2000. By 2017, it reached $3,132, an increase of 184 percent. Average real estate taxes are up from $692 annually to $1,701.50, or 147 percent. And heating oil has risen 130 percent, from $1.15 per gallon to $2.63. The half of retirees who depend primarily or exclusively on Social Security for survival have a lot less to spend on dining out than they used to.

Generation X is better off, largely because they are younger and still have time for course correction. More than three-fourths interviewed in 2016 said they were saving for retirement. However, they are not saving nearly enough. Financial advisers recommend investing 20 percent of income for retirement. For Gen X, the average is only 8.2 percent. (Boomers still on the job are not doing much better; their average is 9.7 percent.) And even that looks better than it really is. Thirty percent say they have had to take a loan, early withdrawal, or hardship withdrawal from their retirement savings. Many of the rest are likely to. Nearly one in four have less than $5,000 in the bank to cover unexpected expenses like medical bills or home repairs.

With the Baby Boomers as undesirable role models, members of Generation X tend to be much more realistic about the likely result of their retirement planning. More than half intend to remain on the job after age 65, and 51 percent say they expect to work during their retirement years, whether they want to or not.

For restaurants, and any other industry that depends on elective spending, the message is clear: Retired Boomers today are less able to dine out than they were while still in the workforce, and less able than they would have been at pre-Recession prices. Those who retire over the next fifteen years or so, and many in Generation X, will be cash-strapped as well. And even if they are not, whatever money they set aside today will not be spent in restaurants for years to come. How much less they spend now and in the years ahead is an issue hospitality executives in all segments will be dealing with long into the future.

Now consider the Millennials. There are nearly as many of them today than there are of Boomers. Compared with the Boomers, they are relatively poor, with less than

$200 billion in buying power among them. Nonetheless, early adulthood is prime time for socializing, and the average Millennial spends about 44 percent of his food and drink budget at restaurants and bars.

The most recent numbers now available come from early 2015. In the previous year, Millennials had made about 14.5 billion visits to American restaurants and spent $96 billion in them. Millennials, on average, eat at a restaurant or get take-out five times a week. In their twenties, more than half of younger Millennials go to a bar at least weekly. Almost 30 percent buy coffee out three times or more each week. (Among the general population, only 40 percent of adults buy brewed coffee or tea even once a week.) In all, Millennials provide about 23 percent of American restaurant revenues. By the late 2020s, when Millennials are no longer stuck with entry-level salaries and Boomers contribute less to restaurant income, they are expected to account for 40 percent of restaurant spending.

The nation's watering holes will see less benefit, as bar patronage falls quickly with age. Where half of Millennials in their early to mid-20s visit a bar weekly, older Millennials do so significantly less often. Only one in four members of Generation X visit a bar weekly, and among Baby Boomers the number declines to one in five.

© thanosquest/Shutterstock.com

Clearly, the Millennials are a crucial market for the food-and-drink sector and will be more so as the Boomers pass from the scene. Anything that discourages their buying is bad news for restaurants and taverns. The Millennials bring a lot of bad news with them.

Many of the Millennials who should be the most prosperous are deep in debt. Centennials—with about $290 billion in buying power, expected to reach $1.4 trillion in the near future—face the same problem, as most people reading this text probably know too well. More than 70 percent of American college students today borrow to finance their education. No doubt it seems like a good idea at the time, and eventually it may prove to have been. Yet, in 2018 these debts are pure burden.

They are likely to remain so well into the future. Some 44 million Millennials and older Centennials are struggling to pay down student loans whether they graduated or not. At the end of 2016, former students owed more than $1.3 trillion. That comes out to over $37,000 each, and the amount is growing by about 6 percent per year. About 15 million young adults owe $50,000 or more in college loans. Two million owe over $100,000. More than 5 million are behind on their payments or cannot pay at all. These numbers can only grow as the Centennial generation leaves college with balances due.

Not even declaring bankruptcy shields former students from school loans (as many readers again probably know all too well), so barring a change in federal law this problem will be with us through the 2020s and into the following decade. Although we cannot quantify how much this factor depresses restaurant spending, it seems likely that restaurants would be noticeably more prosperous without it.

All this, we believe, goes a long way toward explaining why the restaurant industry has appeared so beleaguered when it should have been prosperous. Here in the United States, though not in other lands, many factors are dragging profits down. Each would be easily survivable on its own. In the aggregate, they are a source of friction that even the best performers struggle with.

In the long run, inheritances from baby-boom parents and grandparents will help to rescue the younger generations' finances. This process has already begun. However, the boomers can expect to be the longest-lived generation to date. Improvements in medical care, and in the costly and inefficient system that delivers it in the United States, could keep them with us even longer than demographers now predict.

Barring changes we cannot anticipate, these issues seem likely to be part of the environment for at least the next two decades. Restaurants, as recipients of almost purely discretionary spending, have felt them first, but in the years ahead they will affect all segments of American hospitality and travel. Tomorrow's hospitality executives will spend much of their effort trying to develop competitive methods that attract business from guests facing increasingly tight budgets.

Web Assignment

Log into the student website and complete the end of chapter assignment. Try to utilize some of the works you read about from this chapter and apply the key concepts, terms, and theory in your responses.

CHAPTER 12

Global Trends in the Casino and Gaming Industry

When you think of casinos and gaming, what do you picture? A weekend in Vegas? James Bond besting the baddies at the Casino de Monte Carlo? A room full of high-rollers at The Venetian Macau?

What we think of is a unique, world-spanning segment of the hospitality industry—one that offers unusual opportunities for graduates in this field. Specialized casino jobs like card dealer, pit boss, and about two-dozen other positions have little to do with hospitality in general. Yet, many gaming companies operate so-called "integrated casino resorts" with full hotel and restaurant operations. As anyone who has visited Las Vegas can attest, they include all the standard opportunities found in hotels, restaurants, and sometimes even small amusement parks. Gaming operators also are branching into the MICE market, so meeting and convention specialists also could find a home in this sector.

Gaming once was viewed as immoral, and in parts of the world it still is. Yet, in many places this industry is now praised for its job creation and contribution to local prosperity. This transition began in the United States around 1980 and is still in progress. By 2018, a poll found that 68 percent of Americans considered gambling "morally acceptable." Only 28 percent still considered it "morally wrong." This evolution is getting started today in Asia, where prosperous countries have begun to view gaming as a source of jobs and tax revenue. Opportunities in the gaming segment are growing rapidly in many parts of the world.

They bring with them a variety of challenges for tomorrow's managers. Changing technologies and economic conditions move this sector as any other, but gambling is uniquely shaped by legislation, regulation, and social values. In Macau and some other gaming centers, personnel shortages also guarantee a welcome for qualified expatriates. (In 2016, Macau employed 177,638 foreign workers, over 45 percent of the local workforce!) Hospitality majors may wish to consider building a career in this segment of the industry.

Present Status

According to the most recent count available, there are more than 5,000 casinos in the world, distributed among 150 countries. (We include Hong Kong and Macau as separate nations for our current purpose, as their gaming laws and regulations differ fundamentally from those of mainland China.)

The United States has the largest population of casinos by far. One estimate puts it at 1,954; we suspect this includes horse and greyhound racing tracks, off-track betting offices, poker rooms, and other miscellaneous sites. The most recent and authoritative figure we have found, cleansed of other betting facilities, was 934 at the end of 2017.

By comparison, other countries have relatively few casinos. Canada and Mexico come in second and third with 219 and 205, respectively. Five more countries have over 100 each: France, with 182; the Netherlands, with 166; the United Kingdom, with 154; Latvia, with 123; and Argentina, with 106. Twenty-two countries are home to two casinos, while 18 more have only one.

Gambling qualifies as big business. Casinos brought in an estimated $433 billion in worldwide revenues in 2018. For comparison, analysts estimated that hotels would gross about $130.8 billion that year, cruise lines "only" $45.6 billion.

Gambling also is a growing business. Including casino gaming, lotteries, poker, sports betting, and online gambling, Research and Markets estimates that the industry is on track to expand by 4 percent annually between 2017 and 2023, to an aggregate of $525 billion.

Note that this is the "gross gaming yield," the amount gamblers bet minus the amount paid out to winners. Casinos that provide more than gaming rooms—the ones that primarily concern us here—earn still more from hotels, restaurants, and convention operations that help to support the bottom line when gambling revenues are weak.

We have not found data to show how much these operations add to the global casino industry's revenue, nor how much expenses subtract from the gross profit. However, a look at the mid-2018 financial report from Las Vegas Sands (LVS) makes it clear that gambling is the company's largest profit producer. It also tells us where the world's hot-test gaming market is found.

Most American gamblers probably know the company as an operator of casinos—The Venetian and The Palazzo—on the Las Vegas Strip, but there is considerably more to its business. It owns a third property in the United States, the Sands Casino Resort in Bethlehem Pennsylvania. The company also is the largest provider of convention space in Las Vegas. Despite this, Las Vegas and Bethlehem each rate only a single page in the company's 60-page earnings deck for the second quarter of 2018. The real action is in the Far East. LVS brought in $1.225 billion in revenue before taxes and other deductions that April, May, and June. The United States contributed only 9 percent of it. The company's four casinos in Macau yielded no less than 61 percent, while Singapore produced the remaining 30 percent. In addition to its gaming floors, LVS has roughly 13,000 hotel rooms and suites in Macau plus some 2 million square feet of conference and meeting space and 1.9 million square feet of retail areas.

The company's earnings report offers a detailed look at revenues from the Marina Bay Sands, in Singapore. That location brought in $368 million in 2Q18. Of this, 2,561 hotel rooms contributed 16 percent, mall space a scant 8 percent. "Other" operations brought in 4 percent. This leaves 72 percent of the casino's profits coming straight from the tables and slot machines. The VIP gaming for which Asian casinos are known accounted for 17 percent of the casino's quarterly profits, with another 22 percent derived from slot machines. Fully one-third came from mass table games like craps and baccarat.

We believe this outcome is roughly in line with results at other integrated casino resorts. Whatever else casino operators do for income, gambling remains their cash cow.

Let's take a closer look at some of the world's most significant gaming markets, the places where hospitality graduates are most likely to find a professional home.

Gaming in the United States

Roughly 460 American casinos in 24 states were built and are run by typical profit-seeking corporations at locations approved either by state legislatures or directly by voters as ballot items. There also are 474 Native American casinos in 29 states, located on tribal land and run for the benefit of the tribe's members.

Gaming law in the United States is enormously complex, involving federal and state statutes, and sometimes local zoning regulations as well. Statutes vary widely from one state to another and often differ for commercial and tribal casinos.

The United States, if not the world's biggest gambling market, still provides the industry with substantial profits. According to the American Gaming Association (AGA), commercial casinos brought in a record $41.2 billion in gross revenues for 2017, while the National Indian Gaming Commission reports that tribal casinos garnered $32.4 billion. Add legal gambling that does not appear in these figures—tribal poker rooms, for example, often are exempt from reporting requirements—and the total comes out at roughly $76.6 billion for the year.

This is likely to grow soon. In May 2018, the Supreme Court struck down a federal ban on sports betting. By that August, four states already had legalized the practice, and at year's end sports-betting laws were working their way through legislatures in eleven states and the District of Columbia. One forecast predicts that 32 states eventually will allow sports betting.

The AGA has estimated that income from this source will quickly reach $200 billion a year. However, that organization also estimates illegal sports betting in the U.S. as "at least $150 billion a year." The American Sports Betting Coalition estimates that Americans illegally bet some $58 billion on professional and college football in 2017, including $15 billion on the Super Bowl and March Madness. This seems in line with the AGA's total.

However, we believe sports betting is likely to deliver a much lower total yield. In Britain, the National Gambling Commission reported in January 2018 that bettors there had wagered about £10 billion on sports in the latest fiscal year. Adjusting for population and the value of the pound, that would make the American market worth about $67 billion a year.

H2 Gambling Capital, a century-old data service specializing in this industry, is even more conservative. The firm estimates that illegal sports betting at offshore gaming sites took in a gross gambling revenue from Americans of $10.4 billion in 2017. H2 predicts that the legal sports-betting market in the U.S. will reach only $5.5 billion by 2023.

Much sports betting is expected to take place via mobile phones and online sites, as it does in Europe and Africa. H2 puts the figure at only $2.3 billion in 2023, with interactive market growing much faster than land-based betting. Nonetheless, casinos will receive enough new income to make a useful difference in their bottom lines.

According to the AGA, gambling directly employed some 766,500 employees in 2017 and supported nearly 1 million more indirectly. Las Vegas alone employed 295,500 in leisure and hospitality as of August 2018. Ten of the twenty largest employers there are casino hotels and resorts, according to the Nevada Resort Association. In all, over one-fourth of jobs in Nevada are in leisure and hospitality, 2.5 times as many as in the country at large. All this speaks of a healthy, profitable industry.

© Yevgen Belich/Shutterstock.com

So does the proliferation of new gaming opportunities. No fewer than ten new casinos opened in the United States in 2018. At least 21 more are scheduled to open in 2019 or '20.

However, the spread of casinos throughout the country has raised concerns about how long the gaming market will remain generous to all comers. Until 2016, same-site revenue in commercial casinos grew even as the competition did. Yet, as still more casinos are built, the gambling market could easily grow saturated, so that new venues survive only by poaching gamblers from established casinos. We see this already in several markets.

In once-prosperous Atlantic City, casinos in New York, Pennsylvania, Delaware, and Maryland have siphoned away substantial parts of the market. Nine Atlantic City casinos have closed over the years, and ten proposed casinos were cancelled without opening. In 2018, the city is home to nine casinos, two of them reopened in 2017 by new owners. A proposal to allow casino development in other parts of New Jersey has been on hold since 2016. According to one analysis, four of Atlantic City's casinos would go bankrupt if competition opened elsewhere in the state.

Similar problems have been seen in Maryland and in Tunica, Mississippi.

In Maryland, casinos prospered when there were only five of them. The 2016 opening of a sixth cut revenues at several of its older competitors even as it drove the state's gaming revenues to new highs.

And in Tunica County, gaming employment has shrunk from 13,000 in 2001 to just 5,000 in 2018 as casinos opened in Arkansas and other nearby states. Caesars Entertainment shuttered its giant Harrah's Tunica Hotel & Casino in 2014 and the Tunica Roadhouse Casino in late 2018.

These will not be the last times casinos find that a new competitor erodes their business. If American casinos generally have not yet reached the point of saturation, they are sure to do so within the careers of today's hospitality students.

Gaming in the Far East

Two generations ago, Asia had little to offer the world's gaming industry. Almost 60 percent of humanity lived there—over 2.6 million people—but nearly all lacked the one attribute on which hospitality and travel depend: disposable income. The story of how this changed is too well known to repeat here. Anyone who needs a reminder can review our discussion of tourism, where we said as much as is useful. Leave it that the globalization of manufacturing and services lifted some 800 million Chinese out of poverty. India began its rise a decade or so later and has not progressed as quickly, but it too has developed vibrant middle and upper economic classes. China especially has become the core market for Asian gaming, while India is a potential market worth watching in the years ahead.

As we saw in our look at LVS, this evolution has made Asia the most important gaming market in the world. In 2018, gaming revenues in the Asia-Pacific region were estimated at $71.4 billion, up from $43 billion in three years. By comparison, European casinos were expected to bring in $28.7 billion, those in Latin America only $5 billion.

After looking at population and economic trends in China and India, the Brookings Institution estimates that from 2015 through 2022, China's middle class will grow by 350 million, while India's expands by 380 million. This is 730 million potential new gamblers in Asia. We expect the Asia-Pacific gaming market to continue growing rapidly in the years ahead,

China — Asia's great economic and military power dominates gaming as it does so much else in this region. This is true even though gambling other than state-run lotteries is illegal there. Chinese gamblers eager to visit legal, Las Vegas-style casinos have three nearby options: the autonomous zones of Hong Kong and Macau and Singapore, an independent city-state. Two of these are relatively minor markets. The third is the largest gaming center in the world. We will focus on that one.

Macau is technically part of China, but most of its legal system has been held over from its centuries as a Portuguese colony. Gambling has been officially legal there since 1847.

In 2002, the Macau government granted six companies licenses to operate casinos and market subconcessions in the former colony. Between 2002 and 2014, those firms invested $32.5 billion to develop some of the world's most luxurious integrated gambling resorts and a host of smaller casinos. By late 2018, there were 50 in all. Planned expansions, plus construction of two new casinos, are expected to drive investment in Macau casinos upward of $50 billion before 2020.

Macau's largest casino operators are Galaxy Entertainment Group, with an estimated 2018 market share of 22.8 percent, and Sands China, with 21.1 percent. The others, in descending order, are Melco Resorts and Entertainment, Wynn Macau, SJM Holdings, and MGM China Holdings. This lineup could grow in 2020 and 2022, when current gaming licenses expire. Several companies are known to be interested in entering the local industry.

Gambling has been a good bet for Macau. By 2006, the city's casinos were bringing in more money than Las Vegas. Eight years later, they chalked up revenues of some $45 billion, while Las Vegas remained stuck in the neighborhood of $6.5 billion. By 2014, the territory's GDP was nearly $55.4 billion. All this is thanks to casino gambling.

The Venetian Casino in Macau.

Two influences have shaped Macau's gambling industry. One is crowding. The other is a shared business strategy.

The Macau Peninsula is 3.3 square miles of land attached to the Chinese mainland. Two islands lie not far offshore, Taipa and Coloane. They have grown over time and most recently have been connected by Cotai, 2 square miles of new landfill. In all, Macau covers just 12 square miles. Coloane is largely undeveloped parkland, and the government has shown no interest in changing that. With 30 casinos on the peninsula, six more on Taipa Island, and 14 in Cotai, only four building lots remain available in all of Macau.

Discounting Coloane, that leaves only one opportunity for expansion: Hengqin Island. Located just west of Taipa, Hengqin is a mammoth (by local standards) 41 square miles. Beijing has made it a free trade zone and a "New Area," where development is a priority. What it has not done is open Hengqin to gambling. Despite this, Macau's gaming companies have over thirty non-gambling projects in development there. At the end of 2018, Beijing is believed almost ready to issue Hengqin's first gambling licenses. When it does, we expect to see yet another burst of growth in the Macau gaming industry.

Historically, Macau casinos have earned their revenues by catering to high-rolling VIPs from mainland China. This policy served them well for years. In 2013, two-thirds of gaming revenue in Macau came from VIP baccarat. Slot machines, the mass-market mainstay in Las Vegas, brought in less than 5 percent. A study in 2017 found that VIP gamblers averaged around 1 million yuan—$150,936—per bet.

However, relying on "whales" has a disadvantage. In 2014, President Xi Jinping ordered a crackdown on corruption that sent China's wealthy ducking for cover. This meant a sudden change of lifestyle from consumption, the more conspicuous the better, to equally conspicuous displays of modesty. The high-rollers stayed home in droves.

It hit Macau hard. Casino revenues in 2013 totaled $45.1 billion, up 20 percent in a year. They declined for the next three years and by 2016 were down to $28 billion. One report estimated that lost VIP business accounted for 98 percent of the loss.

Casinos found a new business model in Las Vegas, where catering to the mass gaming market and providing family-friendly attractions as well as gambling has been a winning strategy. In 2017, only one-third of revenue at casinos on the Strip came from gambling; the rest came from food and beverages, hotels, nightclubs, and entertainment. As early as 2015, the Venetian Sands offered Bon Jovi concerts and guitar festivals. Studio City had the Batman Dark Flight ride, while the Grand Lisboa boasted four Michelin-starred restaurants. Other casinos quickly offered non-gaming entertainment.

This new strategic method worked fast and well. On the Cotai Strip, casinos took in a record $16.7 billion in 2015. Less than 35 percent of it was gaming revenue.

The VIPs finally returned in May 2017. Mass-market revenue grew by 10.4 percent for the year. VIP revenue rose by 26.7 percent. Analysts expected it to grow by 36 percent in 2018, leaving mass market revenue still nearly 40 percent larger than that from VIPs. As it turned, gross gaming revenue was up 14 percent in 2018, to $37.6 billion. Growth of VIP revenue slowed in the second half of the year due to the effects of Pres. Trump's trade war. Revenue from VIP baccarat, for example, was up only 3.6 percent in the third quarter of the year, compared with more than 20 percent for mass-market baccarat and 9 percent for the slots. Serving both markets should ensure Macau casinos better profits and greater stability in the years ahead.

A new challenge could erode those profits, however: ambitious local competition. A proposal to allow gambling on Hainan, about 300 miles to the south, could seriously eat into Macau's trade. New rail links, a ferry terminal, and a bridge tying Macau via Hengqin to Hong Kong also raise the possibility that casinos there will be able to attract business that otherwise would go to Macau. Singapore, South Korea, Vietnam, and the Philippines also are angling for Macau's customers. Manila casinos already have found some success in luring Chinese VIPs despite Pres. Rodrigo Duterte's professed hatred of gambling.

Nonetheless, Macau's future seems assured. Economists estimate that the enclave has captured only half of 1 percent of the potential market available to it. As the Chinese middle class continues to grow, raising this to even 1 percent could bring Macau as much gambling revenue as the entire U.S. gaming industry earns today.

Now if only they can figure out where to put all those visitors.

Australia — There are no more devoted gamblers than in the land of Oz. Its residents lost about A$1,380 ($990) per adult per year on gambling in 2016, more than in any other country. Over 80 percent of Australian adults reportedly engage in some form of gambling.

That makes gambling big business for a country of only 24.5 million people. Yet, it seems small when compared with the industry in Macau or the United States. In 2016–'17, casinos brought in just A$24 billion, or $17.3 billion in US currency. Gaming machines outside casinos raked in over A$144 billion. Sports brought only A$1 billion in bets, but that was up 15.3 percent from the previous year, while casino revenues shrank by 7.8 percent.

Casinos had so little revenue because there are so few of them, only 18 in the country, plus nine cruise-ship casinos. Among them, they offered 1,947 table games and 130 poker tables. The country does have 20,250 slots, poker machines—pokies, the most popular—and other gaming machines, but the vast majority are in pubs and other non-casino venues.

Despite some handicaps—problem gambling is a hot topic in Australia, and casinos especially are being targeted by critics—the casino industry is growing. Crown Resorts, which operates casinos in Melbourne and Sydney, is building a 350-room integrated resort in Sydney. Star Entertainment Group is set to open the A$2.9 billion Queen's Wharf development in Brisbane, with hotel space and apartments in addition to the casino itself. Two Chinese-backed casinos are planned for Queensland. They could worry Macau's gaming operators if they work to attract mainland gamblers who otherwise would stay closer to home.

Some years ago, Australian casino operators and regulators set a goal of winning 10 percent of the Asia-Pacific's gambling business. We doubt it will happen soon. New casinos will continue to appear in Australia, but not nearly as fast as they do in other international gaming markets.

Still, for hospitality professionals from English-speaking lands, they could provide some interesting opportunities.

Taiwan — Gambling, aside from lotteries, is banned in Taiwan, as it is in the part of China under Beijing's control. Despite this, an estimated 200,000 Taiwanese work in the gaming industry, nearly all of them employed by foreign-owned online gaming sites that ban participants from Taiwan. Casino gaming does not exist. Taiwanese with an itch to test their luck at roulette or the slots must travel to Macau or the Philippines, both only a short flight away.

However, casino gaming is not likely to remain off-limits in Taiwan. A bill before the legislature in late 2018 would allow the country's offshore islands to accept offers for casino resort projects. Speculation is that the first casino could open its doors as early as 2019. Claremont Partners, a gaming company based in the Isle of Man, already owns a 66-acre site on Penghu Island, where it has long wished to build a casino.

All this comes with a substantial caveat. The Casino Management Act, though not officially stalled, has been before the legislature for a long time. Industry observers once speculated that Taiwan's first casino would open in 2014. It does seem that the day at last is almost at hand, but no one should be surprised if the issue is on hold for a while longer.

Cambodia also bans gambling, at least in theory, but it has an online-gaming services industry that operates much like Taiwan's, employing a reported 100,000 foreign workers. It also has 65 licensed casinos, including ten in Popiet, just over the border from Thailand, where all gambling is banned, save betting on horse races. Thai and Chinese gamblers make this a profitable industry for Cambodia, legal or not. Naga-World in Phnom Penh, the country's largest casino, brought in net profits of $255.2 million in 2017, up 39 percent on the year.

Vietnam is home to no fewer than 38 casinos, with at least two more integrated casino resorts under construction. The casinos are off-limits to local players, but two still under construction will be allowed to entertain high-income Vietnamese citizens. Those admitting local players are likely to be the most profitable in the country. However, if Hainan eventually allows gambling, Vietnamese casinos could lose at least as much business as Macau does.

Japan — Lotteries here are common. So is gambling at pachinko, a kind of upright pinball machine, which brings in an estimated $200 billion a year in revenue. But there isn't a casino in the country.

That is likely to change soon. After a promotional campaign that lasted nearly twenty years, Japan's legislature in July 2018 legalized the operation of "integrated resorts," casinos attached to hotels, entertainment, and conference facilities. Only three casino licenses will be issued at first, and the casinos will operate under some tight restrictions. Japanese residents will have to pay

Pachinko Parlor in Japan.

¥6,000, about $55, to enter and will be limited to no more than three visits each week and ten per month. And no less than 30 percent of revenue will go to local taxes.

There is a long way to go before anyone sees casino revenue in Japan. Bidding for licenses is not expected to begin until 2020, with the first casinos likely to open no sooner than 2025. It will be worth the wait. Goldman Sachs estimates that revenues when all three casinos open will be ¥1.75 trillion a year, or $15.8 billion. That is likely to make Japan Macau's single largest competitor, even for guests from the mainland.

India — Gambling revenue in 2018 was expected to exceed $130 billion. However, nearly all of this will come from online gaming. Internet poker in particular is "insanely popular," among the young, as one industry analyst put it. Illegal, land-based gambling is believed to add another $30 billion a year to the total.

Horse racing and lotteries are generally legal in India. Gambling also is allowed, and common, during festivals in Haranya, Uttar Pradesh, and other largely rural areas.

Casino gambling is governed by India's 29 states and seven union territories. Only three have legalized it, and only within strict limits. Sikkim, bordering Tibet in the northeast, permits two casinos for a population of roughly 650,000 people. In Goa and Daman, casinos may be set up at five-star hotels or on offshore vessels. Daman, a city of about 250,000 on the Arabian Sea in the northwest, has one, with a second reportedly under consideration. The city-state of Goa, with a population of roughly 1.5 million residents and growing rapidly, has ten, four of them aboard boats on the Mondovi River.

This accounts for about 2.4 million people with ready access to a casino out of a population 1.34 billion. Call it 0.18 percent. Those wealthy enough to travel form a ready market for gaming centers elsewhere in the region.

Nonetheless, India's enormous population, growing middle class, and constant need for tax revenue make this a country to watch. It seems likely that more casinos will open there, say from the late 2020s on.

South Korea — For the gaming industry, this is one strange country. It is home to 23 casinos. Koreans are allowed to gamble in exactly one of them, the Kangwon Land Casino & Hotel. It is located in the far northeast of the country, about as far from major population centers as possible without leaving the country.

The Seoul government so much doesn't want its citizens gambling that what happens in Vegas may not stay in Vegas. For South Koreans, even casino gambling in other countries is illegal.

Most casinos in South Korea are just that, casinos and nothing more. Seoul has granted only three licenses for integrated casino resorts, and as of late 2018 only one has opened, the Paradise City in April 2017.

It was a weak opening, just when Beijing retaliated to the arrival of American antimissile systems by banning visits to South Korea by Chinese tour groups. Without Chinese tourists, Paradise City lost a lot of money that quarter. Now that the Chinese are allowed to visit South Korea again, about 25 percent of revenue from the resort's tables originates with high-rollers from the mainland. Yet, the casino is still losing money.

Caesar's and Mohegan Sun are licensed to build integrated resorts in South Korea. Neither has begun construction. Neither is likely to until it sees better results from Paradise City.

Europe

Here we come to the home, not only of Western civilization, but of casinos and most of the games played in them. First in the world was Il Rodotto, in Venice, established in 1638. The next did not appear until 1810, 172 years later, in Wiesbaden, Germany. By 1882, there were six, two in Germany and one each in Italy, the United Kingdom, Monaco, and France. With the exception of Crockford's in London (b. 1823, d. 1970), they remain open today, Il Rodotto under the name Casinò di Venezia. Outside, they speak of European elegance rather than Las Vegas glitz, all classical architecture, marble columns, and the occasional reflecting pool. Inside … neon-lit slot machines look a bit odd under crystal chandeliers.

Despite stylistic and cultural differences, casinos in Europe resemble those elsewhere in basic features, and they perform the same function: Most are integrated casino resorts or are attached to four- and five-star hotels. They attract both local gamblers and tourists, show them an exciting time at the tables or machines, and keep a share of the gross gaming revenue for their investors. They do it very well. Six of the ten countries whose people spend the most on gambling are in Europe. So are nine of the top fifteen. Among the top six, their average per-capita gambling spend ranges from $319 to $519 a year in 2016. This compares with $476 in the United States that year and $541.18 reported for Las Vegas in 2017.

There are an estimated 1,700 casinos in the 54 European countries and semi-independent states (Monaco, San Marino, and others) that allow gambling. Casinos in 28 countries belong to the European Casino Association (ECA), which keeps close track of industry data. ECA reports 1,024 casinos on its roster. Some 97.8 million people visited them in 2017, giving casinos a revenue of €8.546 billion (about $9.73 billion at late-2018 exchange rates).

Note that the revenue figures reported in Europe are not quite comparable to those elsewhere. Most, though not all, countries on the Continent include employee tips as part of casino revenue, somewhat inflating many reports of gross gaming revenue. However, as tips are relatively small in Europe—in the range of 5 to 10 percent—and are generally considered optional at casinos, we believe the excess is small.

Czech Republic has the most casinos in Europe, with 299. However, they average far smaller than those elsewhere, bringing in a national total revenue of only €235 million ($267 million) in 2017. By this measure, Czech Republic has Europe's 11th largest casino industry. The number of gambler visits was unreported.

France comes in second in a census of facilities, with 200 casinos. Some 33 million visits gave its casinos by far the most revenue in Europe, €2.314 billion, ($2.6 billion).

The U.K. offers 145 casinos, putting it in third place. In revenue, however, it came second only to France, with 19.7 million guest visits and revenue of €1.3 billion during the year, about $1.48 billion.

Legal casinos in Europe face competition on two sides. One is illegal gambling. The other, predictably, is the Internet.

One estimate says there are 120,000 gaming machines in Europe and 9,000 table games. This is far more than licensed casinos can account for. The rest are in unlicensed gambling halls. In Finland, Ireland, and Italy, there are illegal gambling outlets on almost every street in major cities. In Italy alone, organized crime is reported to operate hundreds of slot parlors. They are believed to net more profit than licensed gambling establishments and the government combined.

Online gambling captures significant revenue that might otherwise go to Europe's land-based casinos. Exactly how much is unclear, partially because hard income reports are rare in this industry. Also, there is no way to be sure how many of these wagers would have been made if not for the convenience of betting by smartphone.

Predictably, estimates of online gambling revenues in Europe vary widely. According to one, online bets from the five largest national markets there came to no less than €70 billion ($79.5 billion) in 2017. This is not impossible, but we are more inclined to accept another source, which estimated that online gambling revenue worldwide totaled roughly €40 billion ($45.4 billion) that year. It put Europe's share at a bit more than half that, or twice what Europe's land-based casinos took in.

That global online gambling market is believed to be growing by about 10 percent annually, compared with 4 percent at Europe's land-based casinos. At that rate, online gambling revenue worldwide will be upward of $70 billion by 2023. Call Europe's share $39.75 billion, or €35 billion.

At this point in discussing other regions, we will profile the most interesting casino markets, as we did in Asia. For Europe, where there are so many, that would be unproductive.

Details of the gambling environment vary from one country to the next. For example, the minimum gambling age in some countries is 21. In others, it is 18. A few split the difference: The age is 21 for natives, but 18 for tourists. Similarly, most of Europe sets national regulations for online gambling, but several countries in Eastern Europe ban it entirely, and the Netherlands does not specifically regulate it at all. None of this seems significant here.

Similarly, there is occasional news that in some contexts might be worth reporting:

Six new European casinos opened in 2018, in Bath, England; Amsterdam; Limassol, Cyprus; Gibraltar; Belarus; and Ireland. At least four more are scheduled to open in 2019. The pace varies with the state of the economy, but it shows no sign of slowing permanently.

Gross gaming revenues dipped in the Great Recession, and the ill-considered "austerity" that followed depressed them even more. Yet, the damage was not as great as it might have been, and revenues are again growing.

Malta, which earns 12 percent of its $12.54-billion GDP from gambling, recently replaced its entire regulatory system, giving it more power to act against money laundering and other financial crimes. For the rest of us, and even for casinos there, the change was essentially meaningless.

This is true of nearly every development in Europe's gambling scene. The drama we saw in Macau and will see in Latin America do not exist in Europe. The Continent's major gambling markets are as stable as any growing industry can be, and most of the newer markets in Eastern Europe have made good beginnings. Hospitality students interested in this region's integrated casino resorts can focus on investigating the culture and general environment of any country that interests them and then devote themselves to learning the language.

Latin America

For gambling, this populous region barely exists. Gambling is banned in some countries. Other nations are well supplied with casinos, but their gross gambling revenue would barely register on the scale of Macau. According to the latest count, three countries in Central America and eleven on the South American continent officially permit gambling. (Ecuador, the lone holdout in South America, allowed it until nearly half its citizens voted it down in a 2011 referendum.) At last count, there were 291 casinos in South America. Yet, their gross gambling revenue in 2015, the most recent year for which a regional total is available, was only $5.61 billion, little more than half what Las Vegas saw that year.

The reasons are political and economic. Instability in both is endemic to Latin America.

For an extreme case, see Venezuela, where President Hugo Chavez restricted gambling and tourism in the late 1990s and incompetent policy-making and management have all but destroyed the national economy. In theory, Venezuela now has fourteen casinos. In practice, only two appear to be in business, catering primarily to the local elite and occasional foreign visitors.

Elsewhere in Latin America, gambling companies find that profits justify coping with the continent's challenges. There even are signs that international casino operators are beginning to consider expanding into the continent.

Here are some details about the most significant gambling markets:

Argentina is home to 45 million people and 79 casinos. Some 55 percent of its residents belonged to the middle class as of 2015, nearly double the percentage in 1999. This should make the country an attractive market for the gaming industry.

For the most part, it does. When the slot-machine concessions at seven state-owned casinos were up for renewal, Buenos Aires charged companies $500,000 for the right to bid on them. Eight companies paid it.

This is especially impressive because the province's first-term governor, Maria Eugenia Vidal, despises gambling. In 2017, she closed three casinos when their licenses ran out, leaving nine. She also has sued and shut down online casinos in other provinces when they accepted gamblers from her turf without a Buenos Aires license.

Local casino operators take on this kind of challenge for a reason. Gross gaming revenues in Argentina were expected to reach $17.4 billion in 2018, twice what casinos there saw in 2009. And Vidal won't remain in office forever.

And yet...

Argentina's economy is a mess: Of all the 46 national and regional economies tracked by the Organization for Economic Cooperation and Development, it is the only one in recession in 2018 and one of only two expected to shrink in 2019. (The other is Turkey, with a much smaller one-year decline.) In three years, the middle class has shrunk to 44 percent of the population. Public spending has grown to 40 percent of GDP, turning a balanced budget into a deficit equal to 6 percent of GDP. Inequality is severe. In September 2018, inflation was running at 40.5 percent annually, though it was expected to come in at "only" 9.5 percent for the year. None of this promises good times ahead.

Argentina's casino industry, both real-world and Internet, is strong enough to survive its challenges. At the moment, it does not appear strong enough to attract new participants. No new casinos are under construction, planned, or even proposed.

Brazil is Latin America's Japan in the eyes of many gambling-industry analysts—an (almost) untapped market that promises big profits whenever casino gambling becomes legal.

The country's constitution, passed in 1946, bans most forms of gambling. Specific exceptions include betting on horse races, sports betting, and games of pure chance. Gambling in a public place, including hotels, is forbidden. Online gambling is permitted so long as the website is based in another country. Brazilians also have access to an estimated 200,000 illegal gaming machines.

Despite all this, casinos do exist in Brazil. There are six for 210 million people, the fifth-largest population in the world. Most specialize in off-track betting on horse races. Table games are almost an afterthought.

A law proposed in 2017 would license up to 35 casinos with at least one in each of the country's 27 states. We believe it will eventually pass, and there will be many developers eager to build casinos. Las Vegas Sands (LVS), MBM Resorts International, and Caesars Entertainment all reportedly see Brazil as a potentially lucrative new market. LVS head Sheldon Adelson even met with President Michel Temer in 2017 to discuss investing up to $8 billion in Rio de Janeiro.

Legal casinos seem all but certain to appear in Brazil, even if the timing remains unknown. When they do, this country could become the hottest new market since Macau.

There is one caveat. As *The Economist* put it in 2013, "Failing to meet low expectations is becoming a habit for Brazil's economy." Between 2010 and 2016, economic growth in Brazil collapsed from +7.5 percent to −3.6 percent. The current president, conservative Jair Bolsonaro, seems to be turning it around. In 2017, GDP growth was weakly positive, and inflation fell to 3.4 percent. If he can keep this going for a few years, investing in Brazilian casinos will be one of the best bets available.

Colombia is one of the most inviting countries in Latin America, with consistent economic growth to support a well developed gambling industry and upward of 30 million adults, many of them inclined to visit the local casino.

There were 87 of them at last count, most attached to large hotels. Bogotá, the capital, has 24 gambling facilities all on its own. Studies show that 61 percent of the country's adults are regular bettors.

Casinos in Colombia face less competition than in other countries. A clean-up campaign in 2012 eliminated most of the black-market betting operations that provided a tax-free alternative to legal gambling. And the government blocks most unlicensed online gambling sites; in late 2018 only three online casino operators had been licensed.

Inevitably, doing business in Colombia has a downside. There is a 12-percent tax on casino profits in addition to the 16-percent value-added tax that all businesses pay. Despite this, operating casinos in Colombia is an attractive proposition. Gross gaming revenue in 2016 came to $13 billion, up some 25 percent in a year.

Despite this, new casinos are rare in Colombia. The most recent opening was the Millionaires Casino Bogata, in October 2015. However, we will not be surprised to see the kind of consolidation here that has occurred in other countries: International gaming companies will race the largest local operators to buy up the most profitable casinos in Colombia. It is unlikely to take place until the Brazilian casino industry has been developed, but it will happen.

Mexico has a long and extremely odd relationship with gambling. The country's president banned it in 1935. Updates to the law in 1947 and 2004 permit lotteries; betting at horse and greyhound tracks, jai alai frontons, and fairs; even cock fighting. Slot machines, video gaming machines, and bingo all are legal. Sports books are legal. Online gambling sites are permitted as long as the server is located in Mexico. Even phoning a bet to the nearest bookie is legal. Real-world casinos are not.

This does not mean that casinos don't exist. They do. Many are licensed despite being technically banned, and both federal and state governments tax them. All Mexican businesses pay a "profit tax" of about 29 percent. Casinos pay an additional "tax on production and services." Some Mexican states also tax the bettor's winnings.

Mexico offers 205 casinos, by the latest count. This includes eleven in Tijuana, nineteen in Mexico City, and twenty in Monterrey, within driving distance of Brownsville, Texas. There is at least one casino comfortably near almost any major city or tourist area. The exceptions are in states that specifically ban casino gambling; only three of the country's 31 states do.

Since 2014, a law that would officially legalize and regulate casinos has seemed likely to pass "probably next year." Unwelcome as regulations always are, in this case, they are needed. The gray areas that allow casinos to exist also make it hard for them to prosper to the degree regularly seen elsewhere. They are not allowed to advertise, for example. Because of this and other limits, Mexican casinos had gaming revenues totaling $743 million in 2015. Estimates in 2018 say they are closing in on $800 million.

When the law passes and casinos gain official standing, industry observers expect a wave of building to wash over the country. Probable developments include construction of 35 new gambling facilities on the border with Texas; more casinos in Tijuana, Ciudad Juarez, and Mexico City; construction of the first casinos located in, rather

Canacun resort.

than near, the beachfront resort cities of Acapulco, Cancun, and Puerto Vallarta, including $500 million integrated resorts in Acapulco and Mazatlan. Televisia, licensed to operate in up to 55 locations, already has announced plans to expand its chain of 17 PlayCity casinos. And Caesar's has contracted to manage a $200-million, 500-room, non-gambling resort planned for Puerto Los Cabos by Grupo Questro, one of the country's larger developers. It is easy to suspect that gambling will be added to the site the moment casinos are formally legal.

Even with legal protections, doing business in Mexico will involve risks not generally encountered in other markets. Drug cartels there are strong, and other types of crime are rife. More than 29,000 people were murdered there in 2017, and 2018's toll is shaping up to be higher. The country suffers from a chronic police shortage, with 116,000 positions open in mid-2018, so the Mexican army patrols the cities. All this is abetted or ignored by corrupt politicians, and there is no evidence that this will change in the foreseeable future. For attacks on casinos, there is precedent: In 2011, about 50 people died when masked gunmen set fire to a casino in Monterrey.

The bottom line, for hospitality graduates willing to take a risk, is that new opportunities should soon appear in Latin America's largest gambling market, many of them within commuting distance of the U.S. border. Probably next year, whichever "next" it turns out to be.

Northern Africa and the Middle East

Despite the gaming industry's broad reach, some areas remain casino deserts. They include most Muslim-majority nations; Islam forbids gambling. Nonetheless:

Egypt is home to more than 25 casinos, including 20-plus in Cairo and five in the Red-Sea resort town of Sharm El Sheik.

Lebanon offers the Casino du Liban, probably the most famous in the Middle East.

In **Israel**, Prime Minister Benjamin Netanyahu has pushed to legalize gambling since at least 2012. The most likely site for a future casino is a 12-acre lot in Eilat, which has been set aside for the purpose. However, the move is opposed by Orthodox religious groups and the political parties that represent them. So far, it seems that casino gambling in the country will remain limited to four cruise ships operating out of Eilat and one from Haifa.

There is very little more to be said about this region. North Africa and the Middle East are infertile territory for the world's gaming companies. There is no prospect that this will change during the careers of today's hospitality students.

Sub-Saharan Africa

Until recently, there has been little to say about this region of 850 million people. Its residents were too poor, its governments too unstable, to support profitable, predictable gaming industries.

This began to change early in this century. By 2018, the business analysts at McKinsey were reporting that "Hopes are high for Africa's long-term growth, driven by technology and basic services rather than resources." This inspired them to call Africa "one of the 21st century's great growth opportunities." If they are correct, and their track record is good, Africa could become a region where gaming companies can prosper.

Today, Africa has 251 casinos distributed among 34 countries. South Africa and Kenya, have the most vibrant casino industries, with 59 and 30 facilities, respectively. Zambia, with eleven legal casinos, and Botswana, with nine, are the closest runners-up. Online betting is a bigger segment in much of this region, thanks to the continent's ubiquitous smartphones.

It is hard to say anything that applies to all of sub-Saharan Africa. Economies there are too varied, governments too widely distributed along the spectra of competence, corruption, and concern for their citizens. Here is a brief look at the African casino markets that seem closest to significant:

South Africa qualifies as a high-income country, by the World Bank's classification system. Its GDP amounting to $13,600 per capita in 2017, this in a region where per capita GDPs under $5,000 are common and at least two are under $1,000. Only Equatorial Guinea and Gabon are significantly richer, and neither is hospitable to gambling.

A relatively diverse economy makes South Africa somewhat less vulnerable to fluctuating commodities prices than many African lands. Unfortunately, the country suffers widespread poverty, severe economic inequality, 27 percent unemployment and twice that among young black men. Strikes are frequent, and power outages inhibit business growth. Basic services are unreliable low-income areas. On balance, many international companies would pass South Africa by.

Despite all that, South Africa has a reasonably prosperous gambling industry. Gross revenue for all forms of gambling in the twelve months ending with March 2018 were expected to come in at about R30.6 billion ($2.23 billion), up 8.7 percent on the year.

The National Gambling Act authorizes licensing of forty casinos in the country; two remain available. Six mostly local companies operate casinos around the country, with three companies accounting for all but three. Caesars Entertainment, the only participant not based in Africa, owns an integrated casino resort outside Johannesburg.

Casinos delivered 70 percent of South Africa's gambling revenue, 17.9 billion rand in 2016 ($1.3 billion). They were expected to reach R19 billion in 2018 ($1.39 billion) and R21.22 billion ($1.55 billion) in 2021.

The fastest growing gambling segments are bingo and online sports betting via the continent's ubiquitous cell phones. Revenues from bingo grew nearly 37 percent in 2016 and are expected to reach R2.2 billion ($153.6 million) by 2021. Revenues from sports betting grew by 40 percent between 2016 and 2018, with another 7 percent projected for 2023.

Before Las Vegas peaked and Macau became so crowded, a market with as many negatives as South Africa would not have been on anyone's list of potential expansion sites. Today, we suspect that major gambling companies will look at it closely once Mexico and Brazil have been developed. In time, they will decide that absorbing South African casino firms is one of their better opportunities.

Kenya is Africa's third most populous gambling market, following Nigeria and South Africa. Per-capita GDP works out to only $3,500, but on this continent that is enough to support a gaming industry. Gross gambling revenue for the country is estimated at roughly 100 billion Kenyan shillings per year, about $976 million.

Only seven of Kenya's 47 counties now allow gambling.

As in South Africa, sports betting is by far the fastest growing segment. It is expected to deliver 57 percent of all gross gaming revenue in 2019, up from 18 percent in 2010. Some 85 percent of Kenyan adults own a cell phone, and one study found that 35 percent use them for sports betting. Most of the revenue from this market goes to illegal operators in other countries.

"Gambling addiction" is a major concern here. A week rarely passes without a prominent expose of the problem. In one poll, 78 percent of Kenyan college students identified themselves as compulsive gamblers.

In a symbolic attempt to reduce the problem, the legislature early in 2017 raised the tax on gross gaming revenue to 35 percent. One legal sports betting firm and a large operator of lotteries immediately went out of business. In September 2018, the legislature cut the rate to 15 percent, added a new witholding tax of 20 percent on gamblers' winnings, and doubled the excise tax on mobile-phone transactions to 20 percent. Results are yet to be seen.

Early in 2018, the government began its first serious crackdown on illegal gambling, seizing and destroying some 2,700 slots and video gaming machines in the first six months of the year. However, the authorities went after licensed betting shops as well as illegal ones. The country's High Court halted the campaign at the end of June 2018.

Kenya clearly has issues to resolve before outside companies consider investing there. However, the structure of Kenya's gambling industry invites consolidation under stronger management. Some time in the 2030s, gambling companies elsewhere could well see Kenya as an inviting target.

Nigeria is not among the leaders in African gaming. In fact, although we referred to it above as a gambling market, there are only three legal casinos in the entire country.

However, there are people, about 204 million of them in late 2018, with a high birth rate. By 2060, Nigeria is expected to become the third most populous country in the world, with over 473 million. And where there are people, there is gambling.

Nigeria already is the largest economy in Africa. Its GDP was $376.4 billion in 2017, equivalent to $1.121 trillion in local purchasing power. Per capita GDP is $5,900, again calculated as purchasing power parity. That is enough for the World Bank to consider Nigeria an upper middle-income country.

There are issues to be resolved before Nigeria becomes a candidate for casino development. Just over half its people are Muslim and consider gambling immoral; it is not clear that they will ever accept casinos, even for those whose faiths are less restrictive. The economy has been diversifying, but when oil is cheap, Nigeria's growth rate sinks. Terrorism and military conflict destabilize the north. And per capita GDP is only an average; 62 percent of Nigerians live in extreme poverty. Other problems include lack of infrastructure, power shortages, restrictive trade policies, slow and inconsistent regulatory and judicial systems, pervasive corruption, and a life expectancy of only 59 years. If something handicaps emerging economies, it is found in Nigeria.

None of this suggests that Nigeria can ever become an appealing market for gambling. And yet: 190 million people and the largest economy in Africa. If Nigeria manages to eliminate corruption and insurgency and continues diversifying its economy, it might still grow into the kind of country that interests foreign investors. In that case, the gaming industry is likely to be among the beneficiaries.

Five Important Trends for the Casino Industry

1. The global economy is changing.

For convenience, this section combines four trends: 1. Economic growth continues throughout the world, but not as fast as it used to. 2. In the developed world, economic growth is slowing. 3. Developing economies are outpacing the industrialized lands. And 10. The global economy is growing more integrated. As a group, they are changing the business environment in ways that may benefit the global casino industry but are likely to inconvenience some specific markets.

Like other entertainment-oriented hospitality segments, casinos are most prosperous when their potential guests feel economically secure. Going into 2018, the world had enjoyed an almost ideal economy for several years. When we compiled Appendix A, all 46 regional and national economies tracked by the Organization for Economic Cooperation and Development (OECD) were growing for the first time in memory. At the end of 2018, this may have changed. OECD, though not the World Bank, believes Argentina has now fallen into recession and will not recover until 2020. Yet the rest of the world, where the vast majority of casinos are found, remains economically healthy.

In this context, the long-term slowing of global economic growth seems a small concern, and for casino operators in many lands it will be. Yet this trend will help form the strategic plans of multinational companies in every industry. Those seeking the highest possible stability will favor the developed nations for business expansion, despite their slower economic growth. Those willing to accept more risk for greater rewards will look to the developing world.

Casino operators are likely to fall into the second group, in part because managing risk is their business and in part because many of the developed lands appear to be nearing saturation. In these companies, skill in strategic planning will be mandatory in selecting new locations in high-growth, possibly unstable markets. It also will be a key asset for building a career in this industry. Mastery of one or two foreign languages also couldn't hurt.

As this is written, the single greatest source of instability in the global economy is American trade and economic policy. We do not expect to see a severe recession soon in the U.S. Yet, policy changes since 2016 make a recession both more likely and more likely to be deep and prolonged. These include the end of banking regulations designed to prevent another Great Recession and the unsustainable combination of revenue cuts and spending increases requested by the Trump administration and passed by Congress.

The political instability that has made U.S. trade and economic policy erratic in recent years can be expected to continue through the early careers of today's hospitality students. Difficult as it is to imagine a leading economic and military power remaining effectively rudderless for much longer, it is at least as hard to see how the current political impasse in Washington might end.

To whatever extent tariffs and other penalties make it harder to do business with China and other partners, the United States makes itself less influential in the global trade regime. The only comparable example in recent history is Britain's decision to leave the European Union, giving London much less influence in matters of trade and international policy.

In the years ahead, executives at multinationals in all industries will have to keep a closer eye on trade and economic policies in China and other lands that gain the influence the U.S. has ceded. This applies especially to those at expansion-minded casino companies.

11. Militant extremism is spreading and gaining power.

This is a relatively narrow trend, not the kind of umbrella topic we dealt with above. It also is one that has had little impact on the world's casinos. We nonetheless believe it deserves consideration here. Although militant extremists have not yet attacked casinos—the fire bombing in Monterrey appears to have been gang-related—they have a long history of assaulting hotels. An integrated casino resort might well appear to them much like any other such lightly defended guest accommodation, but with an added attraction. And, like other events we classify as "wildcards," their effects could be so devastating that the possibility cannot be ignored.

The world's terrorists have been relatively quiet of late. Relatively. In 2014, nearly 17,000 terrorist attacks around the world killed more than 45,000 people. These numbers have declined in each year since. In 2017, there were "only" 10,000 attacks and 26,000 deaths as a result. It looks like 2018's figures will come in lower still.

The reason is clear. In 2014, 60 percent of deaths from terrorism occurred in just three countries—Afghanistan, Iraq, and Nigeria. The attacks that caused them were committed by members of Islamic State, Boko Haram, and other terrorist organizations. These groups were at their strongest in 2014 and have been declining ever since. The world's terrorist toll has declined with them.

It also has moved. According to the U.S. State Department Country Report on Terrorism for 2017, almost 59 percent of terrorist attacks that year took place in five countries: Afghanistan, Iraq, Nigeria, Somalia, and Syria—countries where casinos are notably absent.

This is particularly good news for the world's hospitality segments. International casino operators, hotel chains, and franchises are exposed to all the local hazards wherever they do business. Varying economic policies, different workplace regulations, fluctuating currency exchange rates, and political instability all figure in. So does terrorist violence.

Not everyone has been spared outside the high-probability nations. Europe has suffered an uptick in attacks, particularly in France, where 23 terrorist incidents have killed 267 people since 2015. The Continent seems likely to see many more such events in the years ahead. More than 4,000 European Muslims journeyed to Afghanistan and the Middle East, where they received training and practice in terrorist warfare. The will bring those skills home with them, and not all will have lost the taste for infidel blood.

It seems likely that some of these home-grown terrorists eventually will target a segment of the hospitality industry that has been spared so far:

Casinos seem the ideal terrorist target. Each distills into a single location almost everything that might offend a young, disaffected Muslim who needs a cause to give meaning to an otherwise hopeless life. Gambling, alcohol, mixed-sex entertainment—a casino gathers these offenses against Islamic modesty into one location, then imports crowds of tourists with their guard down. Almost by definition, an attack on a casino is a blow for radical Islam, and there is no risk of killing devout Muslims as collateral damage.

Yet, in all the world we know of only one casino that has attracted serious attention from terrorists. On September 14, 2017, the U.S. Embassy in Lebanon warned its staff not to visit Casino du Liban, a few miles north of Beirut. No attack took place, but when a terrorist cell tied to Islamic State was broken up the following month its leader claimed that he had been ready to attack Lebanon's only licensed casino. It was the third such plot in as many years.

Casino du Liban's location in a Muslim land draws extremist attention inevitably. Our only surprise here is that its counterparts in other Islamic countries have not been reported as terrorist targets. For example, at last word there were more than two-dozen casinos in Cyprus, many of them in the Turkish-controlled third of the island where they are relatively accessible. The new City of Dreams Mediterranean, the island's first integrated casino resort, seems especially likely to invite terrorist attention despite its location in the majority-Greek Republic.

The threat of terrorism clearly is a concern for authorities in Macau and regions nearby. In November 2018, 800 Macau police officers joined with 49 soldiers from the People's Liberation Army for an antiterrorism drill involving simulated dirty bombs and chemical weapons. And the new Hong Kong-Zuhai-Macau bridge is equipped with 48 high-def surveillance cameras specifically to guard against terrorist attack.

Although an attack on Macau or some other gambling center is a constant low-level concern, we suspect that casinos themselves make relatively poor targets for attack. Their security, although mostly inconspicuous, is generally the best a commercial institution can buy. Being designed primarily to thwart cheats and thieves does not make it any less likely to intercept would-be terrorists before they can do significant damage.

Security will continue to be a major responsibility for casino executives in the decades ahead. It will be particularly important in Europe and other regions too well supplied with potential jihadis.

15. **Tourism, vacationing, and travel (especially international) are growing fast, as they have done for many years.**

Native American and many regional casinos in the United States depend for their business primarily on guests who live within driving distance. So do many in Europe, where open borders encourage Continental travel but natives remain the primary revenue source. The extreme case is the United Kingdom, where casinos once were limited to members and a few still are.

In the developed lands, particularly Europe and Japan (whenever it accepts that casinos can be a valuable source of tax revenue), this will be a difficult model to expand because record low birth rates have begun to shrink national populations and the pool of potential gamblers. This will not be an immediate issue for casinos and hotels, as the decline is slow. However, it will be felt within the careers of today's hospitality students.

In contrast, gambling centers such as the Las Vegas Strip, Macau, and in a smaller way Cyprus depend almost entirely on tourists for their livelihood.

Visitors to Las Vegas and points nearby spent an estimated $34.8 billion on lodging, food, local transportation, and shopping. Gaming revenue in Clark County, where Las Vegas is located, came to $9.6 billion in the fiscal year ending June 30, 2017. The net income of casinos on the Strip that year was $824 million. Essentially all of this came from tourists.

In Macau, casinos earn essentially none of their revenue from local residents. As we have seen, they draw business almost exclusively from visitors, whether VIP or mass-market. Most live on the mainland. The remainder come from farther off—the United States, Hong Kong, Britain, Japan, Australia, and other more distant lands. In gambling revenue alone, tourists contributed $34 billion to Macau's economy in 2017.

In theory, Macau also could find the growth of its business slowing because its primary market, the Chinese mainland, is losing population, and more rapidly than most other lands. In practice, Macau so far has captured so little of its potential market that attracting even a few more tourists from the mainland each year will more than compensate for the shrinking pool of potential gamblers.

In this context, the continuing expansion of international travel and tourism is good news. Hospitality businesses in popular European destinations, especially, will find that the growing flood of tourists from China, and later India, will more than make up for whatever local business the declining population costs them. Punters who usually visit Macau but are far from home will find European casinos a welcome novelty.

30. **Technology increasingly dominates both the economy and society.**

Under this heading, we subsume all the trends related to technology: the growing role of R&D, the rise of artificial intelligence and robotics, the spread of the Internet, medical advances, and so on. This discussion will not be definitive; a comprehensive account of how technology is changing the casino business could easily fill a book of its own. Instead, we offer a few examples to give you the general idea. Readers are encouraged to look into this subject more deeply on their own. This trend will shape careers in casino resort management, as it will those in other hospitality segments.

Look first at the rise of electronic table games and "e-tables." They augment classic games with loud music, flickering lights, new bonuses, and a faster pace of play. Analytical software tracks player performance, giving management new opportunities to adjust gaming on the fly. There are new games as well, designed for impatient, stimulus-hungry players. One variant of roulette lets players win up to 500 times their bet on a single spin. Another e-table product lets them hop from one game to another, flicking from blackjack to roulette to craps with each bet. Gamblers can even play multiple games at the same time.

Virtual reality has become popular in online gaming. Next step: integrate VR and augmented reality technologies into live gaming.

Slots and other gaming machines are becoming more sophisticated, allowing casino operators to analyze play and adjust games without interrupting the bettor playing them. These systems soon will make it possible for machines, or the networks linking them, to figure out individual strategies to keep each player entertained and betting as long as possible.

That brings us to artificial intelligence. AI is fast infiltrating all businesses in every way possible. In casinos, they will function both at the strategic level, helping executives figure out new strategies to optimize profits, and at the tactical level, optimizing games for individual players in real time, as we saw with gaming machines.

Other behind-the-scenes technologies will be equally important. Casino security departments are already using license plate readers and facial recognition to identify card cheats, problem gamblers, and other undesirables long before they reach the tables.

Casinos also are starting to use the same GPS-based systems now beginning to penetrate retail operations outside. Walk near a casino restaurant, and your smartphone will receive a message suggesting that you stop in for a meal. Casinos are adopting the same technology to let managers know when a "whale" walks in.

Of course, the ultimate in high-tech gaming is the online casino that enables hard-core gamblers to play at home or with a smartphone wherever they are. Sign-up bonuses, incentives for hours of play or sums bet, and other online features will be finding their way into brick-and-mortar casinos in the immediate future.

We could go on forever without exhausting the new technologies now making casinos more efficient, more secure, and "stickier" for gamblers. By the time we finished today's list, innovation would have passed us by. But you get the idea. Comfort with new technology and a firm grasp of how it can be applied to both gaming and back-office functions will be critical for tomorrow's casino executives. Fortunately, this is one area in which today's students excel.

45. The Millennial and Centennial generations already are beginning to change society's priorities.

Many of the casino-floor technologies we saw above can be seen as attempts at catering to the Millennial market and to the oldest Centennials. This is a slightly desperate venture, as the younger generations don't seem to be all that interested in gambling.

For evidence, see Las Vegas. In 1985, when the Baby Boomers were the generation du jour, nearly 58 percent of the money visitors spent was spent on gambling. Thirty years later, Millennials spent just 35 percent of their money on slots and games. Only 28 percent of revenue from the Strip comes from gambling these days. The rest is from restaurant and hotel operations, non-gaming entertainment, and the MICE market.

A study at New Jersey casinos was even more revealing. Older visitors spent 23.5 percent of their vacation budget at the slots and tables. Among Millennials, the amount was only 8.5 percent.

One reason for this may be that Millennials have so many more opportunities for gambling these days. Betting on fantasy sports is always an option. Online poker is still appealing, even with federal regulations making it harder to ship money to poker sites and to receive winnings from them.

Millennials also are a lot smarter about the odds than their predecessors were. Boomers largely hadn't a clue. Millennials can find the details in a few moments with their smartphones.

Millennials also seem less interested in random wins and losses. Games of skill are much more appealing. Hence the rise of poker, both online and in the casino. Its element of chance is tempered by the skills to be learned in dealing with hand strength, bet sizing, and figuring out from an opponent's play which hands he might reasonably have. Casinos already are trying to offer games that incorporate this element.

Even gaming machines are being adapted to give younger gamers learning experiences that optimize their chances of winning without entirely sacrificing the house edge. It is not yet clear how much casinos will benefit from this effort. The number of slot machines on the Strip has been declining for several years because new-generation players think of slots as something for their grandparents and about as interesting as staring at a wall. We suspect the number of slot machines will continue to fall for quite some time.

Of course, there is one more obvious factor for generational disinterest in gambling: Millennials just don't have much money to waste. Many earn less in post-inflation income than the Boomers did at the same age. This is not just an American problem. Young-generation incomes have declined in the United Kingdom and Australia as well.

At the same time, Millennials pay more for just about everything than the Boomers did. They carry student debt that would have given previous generations nightmares, cumulatively well over $1 trillion. On average, they pay nearly half their income for rent, compared with 38.4 percent as recently as 1990. They also are saving a lot more for retirement than their predecessors did; unlike the Boomers, who began their careers expecting someday to receive a pension, Millennials know that DIY retirement is the only kind available to them. None of this encourages a flutter at the tables.

This is a primary cause for the growing importance of fine restaurants, A-list performers, and other non-gambling entertainment in Las Vegas and other gaming centers. To attract Millennials, casinos need a lot more than gambling.

We suspect the same will be true of Centennials. This text's readers can check their own interests and attitudes for a hint at what the future holds for casinos and for the hospitality industry in general.

CHAPTER 13

Sports and Entertainment

Written by Dr. William Sutton, the University of South Florida

What Lies Ahead…

One of my favorite essays about the future was written by William O. Johnson, a senior writer for *Sports Illustrated*. In a seminal 1974 piece entitled "Sport in the Year 2000," Johnson made a series of bold predictions, many of which have come to fruition (although not by the year 2000). Some of those predictions (both hits and misses) were as follows:

- The dominant worker in the United States will be a *brainworker*; someone not involved in agriculture or manufacturing but in services, which Johnson defined as trade, finance, transportation, health, education, government, and sport/recreation.
- Sensors will be utilized to help officiating (interpreting this to include the use of instant replay as well).
- Drugs will be sold openly at sporting events. (Edible marijuana products are available at Colorado Rockies games.)
- There will be a move away from the monolithic spectator sports to sports like cycling, volleyball, and orienteering
- Demand for blood sport will disappear. (This is probably a complete miss given the popularity of UFC for both men and women.)
- The most likely source of income for sport in the future will be from gambling. There will be legalized gambling on all sports. (This prediction came from Baseball Hall of Famer Bill Veeck long before fantasy sports and daily fantasy leagues emerged.)
- Pete Rozelle, then NFL Commissioner, speaking on the decline of NFL popularity: "We are a form of entertainment. In the future I hope we can keep our off-field problems removed from the game. The public doesn't want strikes and lawsuits, they want enjoyment. I hope we can make pro football an escape valve for the fan again, an oasis from a troubled world." (This probably is wishful thinking given the concussion- and health-related issues plaguing the NFL in the current decade.)[1]

Johnson also predicted that two forms of sport/recreation would emerge, *ecosports* and *technosports*. Ecosport was defined as sport that springs from the natural relationship between man and his environment, a return of sports to their primitive vigor.[2] Climbing Mt. Everest, running marathons, white water rafting, and ballooning all are evidence of the historical existence of the interest in ecosports. Triathlons and the emergence of endurance sports such as the Iron Man series, and most recently events such as Tough Mudder, have gained popularity as a way to compete against oneself, other participants, and natural obstacles. According to a report from IEG, a consulting group that focuses on sponsorship, spending on endurance sports topped $100 million for the first time in 2012 and is growing at almost 5 percent annually.[3]

Interestingly, this category of endurance sport includes events that, while they are endurance in terms of having to complete a distance, might be deemed as more of a social experience that includes running. Typical examples include the Color Run 5K and the Race for Your Lives, a property that bills itself as the "world's first zombie-infested obstacle race experience."[4] Contrast that with the definition of Tough Mudder's pitch: "We are 10–12 miles of mud and obstacles built to test your mental grit, camaraderie and all-around physical fitness."[5] Tough Mudder may better represent Johnson's image of the primitive vigor that defines ecosport.

Technosport, according to Johnson, is the product of science, machines, and technicians to impact sport performers (athletes), sport venues, and even the sports themselves.[6] The film *Rollerball*, which debuted in 1975, is an excellent example of what Johnson envisioned for the year 2018. In *Rollerball*, technology shapes the game and is present in all levels—the sport, the athletes, and the venue. While *Rollerball* has not come to pass, many of the ideas and applications of technology and science play a huge part of sport in today's sport scene. Their role seems likely to grow in the years ahead. Genetic engineering, growth- and performance-enhancing drugs, computers and analytics as decision-making tools, and technologically enhanced stadiums and arenas for spectator enjoyment are all ideas that Johnson advanced.

One concept that has not emerged is "Feel-a-vision." Feel-a-vision was the ability to be watching a sporting event and be able to feel what the athlete is feeling—from euphoria to pain.[7] Perhaps this opportunity awaits us in the future as an outgrowth of virtual and augmented reality technologies.

Clearly, both the concepts of technosport and ecosport as imagined by Johnson have materialized. They are an integral parts of our sport and recreation practices now and will certainly be part of the evolution of sport going forward. So what can we expect our future to look like?

Continued growth of e-gaming as a hobby and a competitive sport.

E-gaming led by Riot Games, League of Legends, and competitors DOTA 2 and World of Warcraft will continue to grow as a professional sport. We can expect them to become an intercollegiate sport by 2020. ULOL (University League of Legends) already exists as a club sport in the United States and Canada and, as with most of the sports currently in existence, the club is the incubator for varsity competition.

The universe of e-gaming is much larger than most non-participants probably recognize. League of Legends has 27 million daily players and 67 million monthly players. According to Referral Candy, these are the best statistics of any game in the world. Impressed? Consider that in the 2015 World Championships of League of Legends, fans viewed a total of 360 million hours of live e-sports with the average fan watching for at least one hour per session.[8] If you were wondering about compensation, pro players earn average salaries of about $75,000 and compete for a championship that pays as much as $2 million.[9]

If you need even more evidence of the emerging mass popularity of e-gaming or, as it is beginning to be called, e-sports, TBS has created Friday night programming called *Counter Strike: Global Offensive*, the product of a partnership between Turner Broadcasting System and William Morris Endeavor's IMG sports and media division.

While TV ratings averaged 249,000 during the inaugural season, the 18–34 demographic, which has been eroding in terms of TV viewership, represented a whopping 70 percent of the audience.[10] This is a sign of real growth potential.

According to Joost van Dreunen, CEO of game-industry consulting firm SuperData Research, "E-sports appeals to many more people and households as it is a $612-million global market with 134 million fans and growing fast. I would be very bullish in terms of investment."[11]

Augmented reality promises to bring a whole new variety of e-gaming. The recent Pokémon Go phenomenon got everyone's attention, but why and what does it mean for the future? Less than a year after its release on July 6, 2016, Pokémon Go had attracted 65 million users, making it one of the most successful apps ever, while being praised for promoting exercise, facilitating social interactions, and sparking new interest in local landmarks. While electronic games have traditionally caused kids to retreat to couches, Pokémon Go did exactly the opposite.[12]

Although it is much too soon to draw any firm conclusions, many feel that augmented-reality games will make imaginative play, a critical building block in child development, a mainstream form of play again. Research shows that when children have the opportunity to create the experience themselves, they learn all sorts of skills that come in handy later in life, such as problem-solving, inventiveness,[13] and improvisation.

The live viewing experience, home theaters, and virtual reality – what does it mean?

As my coauthors and I stated in the fourth edition of our textbook, *Sport Marketing*, "Getting people to attend live sporting events and leave their home theaters and connectivity will continue be a crucial challenge for sport teams and leagues."[14] Given the political strife and the increasing impact of terrorism throughout the world, it can reasonably be expected that concern for personal safety will at some point have a direct impact upon live attendance. Combine that fear with the cost of going to a game and technological advances in the home viewing experience, and it becomes possible that virtual reality (VR) will evolve into a satisfying surrogate for "being there." It is easy to accept the possibility that the home viewing experience could become even more of a competitive force in markets hosting professional sports teams.

In my monthly *Sports Business Journal* column, Sutton Impact, I opined that virtual reality could be the ultimate viewing experience, offering views from the best seats in the house of the most interesting camera angles and vantage points. "Through [VR] everyone could be a courtside season ticketholder if they chose, or they could elect to have the view of a player or a coach or perhaps a fan. I am sure there are a number of Americans who would relish the opportunity to view an EPL game sitting with the supporters of that particular team or watching from the goalkeepers' viewpoint. Conversely global fans could follow the exploits of their countrymen playing in the MLS to see how they are faring. There are purported to be 659 million Manchester United Fans globally. How many of them will actually ever get to see the game live? VR solves that issue and probably quite lucratively."[15]

Millennials and Centennials—what does their future hold for sport and recreational activities and products?

If the youth of tomorrow are our future, what does that future look like? Here are some startling statistics from TRU Youth Monitor Perceptions and Priorities 2014.[16]

- 52 percent of Centennials (ages 12–19) don't play sports—and the numbers increase as they age out of high school and into adulthood.
- 46 percent of Centennials don't have a favorite team or athlete.
- More Centennials run (31 percent), lift weights (24 percent), or play e-sports (23 percent) than play ANY team sport. (Basketball has the highest participation rate at 20 percent.)
- Centennials are more likely to have watched HBO or Netflix in the past six months than any of the three major sports networks or any of the four major sport leagues. In fact, barely half of all Centennials regularly watch live sporting events on television with their friends.

TRU Youth Monitor explains that participation in sport is often impacted by the increasing expectations of specialization—playing one sport almost exclusively—and the costs related to that participation: club memberships, travel, equipment, and coaching.[17] Combine that with the time required for such exclusive participation, and it all paints a clear picture of why participation may continue to decline.

A variety of other factors help to explain the drop in participation:

© mTaira/Shutterstock.com

- In the United States, the birth rate has been declining since reaching a peak of 4.3 million births in 2007.
- Parental pressure to compete and succeed in sports is waning as many parents recognize that winning a college athletic scholarship is, for most, only a fantasy.
- The shift to elite competition over the past 20 years has resulted in children playing fewer sports, and the less talented are left behind in recreational leagues, carrying the stigma that they aren't good enough. As a result, 70 percent of children quit sports (and find other outlets) by age 13.[18]

According to Mark Hyman, a professor of sport management at George Washington University, "The system is now designed to meet the needs of the most talented kids. We no longer value participation. We value excellence."[19]

So what might the future look like? Following William O. Johnson's approach to looking at the future, my view of the competitive (participatory and spectatorship) and recreational sports world will be built around the letter E. I see six types of sport and recreational activities:

- E-Sports
- Enhanced Sports and Recreation
- Entertainment Sports
- Enjoyment Sports
- Ecosports
- Experiential Sports and Recreation

We will define and examine each of these categories and then provide an overview of what we might see in the year 2100.

E-Sports

As we defined them earlier in this chapter, e-sports are essentially synonymous with e-gaming. Thus far, professional competition is dominated by League of Legends, DOTA 2, and World of Warcraft. It would be logical to assume that more competition will arise and other games will emerge. Because interest and participation already are so high, it also is safe to assume that e-sports will become even more widely accepted and more mainstream. There already are club-level competitions on college campuses, but we can expect intercollegiate gaming competition, complete with scholarships, conference championships, and ultimately NCAA championships.

Interest + popularity + Mass + investment = opportunity. This UCI model will be the first of many spurred by interest and popularity and also by investment by game developers and hardware manufacturers.[20]

E-games have been more popular globally than they have in the U.S., so it should come as little surprise that an initiative called eGames – the Pinnacle of Competitive Gaming debuted in August 2016 at the Rio De Janeiro Showcase, which was held during the Olympics. Launched and supported by the UK government, eGames is a not-for-profit initiative that has been established to positively shape the future of competitive e-sports. eGames is being launched as a medal-only competition; no money prizes are to be awarded. Participants will compete for national pride and gold, silver, and bronze medals. The organization also hopes to promote competitive video gaming to the non-gamer population.[21] You can probably read that as a trial balloon offered in hope of gaining support for the future inclusion of e-games in the Olympics.

We can argue whether an e-sport is a sport or a game and whether or not e-gamers are athletes. Then again, we have had these same arguments with regard to racing: Is a driver an athlete? And who is the athlete, the jockey or his horse? The debate will continue, but it is very clear that e-sports will be a growing force in our future.

Enhanced Sports and Recreation

By "enhanced," I am referring to the use of virtual and augmented realities to make sports and recreational activities more enjoyable and more meaningful. If you think about it, the earliest attempts to augment reality or alter it would include the video monitors on exercise bikes that help users imagine they are riding through the French countryside or along the Pacific Coast Highway. Similarly, golf simulators enable you to imagine you are playing the British Open, and batting cages make it (virtually) possible to face down a legendary HOF pitcher. These rudimentary enhancements have made these repetitive activities much more fun and interesting. What awaits us in the future could be even more enthralling.

At present, factors such as cost, comfort, and appearance are inhibiting the adoption of VR and AR. As technological improvements overcome these limitations the opportunities and applications will continue to grow.[22]

Entertainment Sports

Entertainment sports are those with mass appeal, competitive for the participants but using a delivery system that emphasizes the spectatorship opportunities associated with the sport. Thus, the category includes all televised sport and, most importantly, those sports receiving the highest proportion of their revenue from broadcast and paid admissions. Why refer to them as entertainment sports and not professional or spectator sports? Because as the sports have evolved over time, the entertainment element has actually become the dominant consideration in establishing rules, competition, schedules, and so forth.

Let's take the case of the National Football League (NFL) as an example. The TV format and schedule calls for an NFL game to be played over a three-hour televised period (although some games are longer). The game consists of four 15-minute quarters. That might imply that it could be played in sixty to ninety minutes with a halftime break, but on closer examination there are reasons it fills the three-hour broadcast. The game clock starts and stops depending upon the action, and there are television time outs for commercial messages. According to the *Wall Street Journal*,[23] the time in which there is action—when the ball is in play—averages only eleven minutes per game. The 185 minutes involved in a typical NFL broadcast break down like this:

- 11 minutes of game action;
- 60 minutes of commercials;
- 75 minutes spent on shots of players in the huddle, on the sidelines; or milling around;
- 39 minutes of replays and replay challenges accompanied by commentary.

In entertainment sports, particularly in the United States, the sport itself often is the smallest part of the home spectator's experience—though NFL games are an extreme case.

© Mark Herreid/Shutterstock.com

Sport continues to be the one televised activity that is most likely to be consumed in real-time (when it is actually being played). However, some of the statistics discussed earlier with regard to Centennials and Millennials might necessitate some changes if its popularity and success are to be maintained.

Sports in the United States, because of the importance of the entertainment and broadcast elements, lacks the "flow" of sports in Europe and the rest of the world. For example, attending an NFL game in the United States could be a 12 hour experience because pre- and post-game tailgating are added to the length of the game itself. A game in the EPL featuring Manchester United might involve a commitment of three to four hours at the maximum from door to door, or only one-third of the usual time on the other side of the Atlantic. But giving U.S. sports more flow might allow less time for commercials and less revenue for the teams, leagues, and broadcasters. That will be a difficult change to undergo.

Another potential change might mean fewer games—162 baseball games is widely considered to be too many—82 basketball and hockey games can be seen in a similar fashion. But again, fewer games would be less money for the owners and the players. Or would it? If fewer games were played, each game would have more meaning. If the games had more meaning and there were fewer of them, couldn't it be argued that each game would be worth more? It probably will not be easy to convince executives whose vast income depends on the status quo. Yet declining viewership requires difficult adjustments in the years ahead.

Note that fantasy sports and wagering in general provide significant entertainment value. NBC Sports reported that total annual spending on fantasy sports in the United States and Canada is $26 billion, with the average participant devoting $465 to his hobby each year.[24] That's a lot of entertainment spending, and it seems unlikely to decline in the future.

In any case, entertainment sport, if it wishes to remain so, will need to adapt its games and approaches to fit the lifestyles, expectations, and interests of the emerging generations.

Enjoyment Sports

While one can argue that all sports should be enjoyed, and I agree, these sports are consumed primarily as participatory activities with little regard to perception or skill level, and results may or may not be important. Enjoyment sports also contain a high degree of social interaction, and that is often the more important driver in the decision as to whether or not to participate. Sport and social clubs are a very popular source of enjoyment sports. Activities range from adult intramural sports (usually co-ed) like softball, flag football, soccer, and volleyball to poker, footgolf, corn hole, and kickball. While champions are identified, the true motivation is social networking—meeting new people, having fun, and staying active.[25]

Enjoyment sports fill a variety of needs—intramurals after college, staying fit, meeting new people, adjusting to a new job or a new place to live, and having fun. Activities continually evolve and adapt to new trends and opportunities.

Ecosports

Much as Johnson defined them, ecosports take place outdoors and involve some type of interaction with nature or the environment. The activity can be competitive in a personal sense, providing the satisfaction of accomplishment, or a formalized activity involving other competitors. Ecosport sometimes combines with tourism to provide sporting opportunities in challenging environments. The pinnacle of ecosport in the competitive space might be the World Marathon Challenge: seven marathons on seven continents in seven days. But the physicality combined with the expense of such an undertaking is very limiting, and the field consists on only twelve runners per year.[26]

The lure of travel combined with sport and the societal developments of delayed marriage and declining home ownership promise the steady growth of ecosport tourism in the future. RunFun Travel organizes running events throughout the world in such locations as French vineyards, Loch Ness, the Maui coast, and even a jungle marathon run in the Amazon.[27] Other ecosport tourism options include cycling, white-water rafting, kayaking, and walking. Ecosport tourism will continue to grow and thrive and be part of vacation planning for the next generations.

Experiential Sports and Recreation

Experiential sports and recreation often have a thrill-seeking element and are unique in how they are perceived. They can be a one-time experience, as skydiving is for some, or they can become part of a recreational sport routine like downhill skiing. Some experiential sports—like scuba diving, deep-sea fishing, skiing, and so forth—also have an element of ecosport tourism to them, as they can become destination-focused. These types of activity are often found on many bucket lists, with goals such as traveling and seeing a baseball game in every major-league park, playing golf on courses where the PGA has staged tournaments, and attending and participating in fantasy baseball camps. The activity is intertwined with the feeling of being somewhere special or the thrill of doing something with an element of risk. Parasailing, tandem sky-diving, bungee-jumping, and similar activities minimize the risk without detracting from their appeal.

Brands today such as NASCAR, Tour de France, and others are attempting to connect with their fans and at the same time bring their brands to life by thrilling them with immersive recreational experiences. At the same time, giving participants stories to tell through social media enhances their brand even further. The Richard Petty Experience offers the opportunity to drive a race car for eight, eighteen, or even thirty laps on the Daytona International Speedway or, for the less adventuresome, the opportunity to ride in a race car with a driver for three laps.[28]

Other experiential sports include swimming with dolphins, diving in a shark cage, and even playing baseball with the "ghosts" at the Field of Dreams in Iowa. The rule of thumb in experiential sport and recreation seems to be if you can imagine it, there is a provider out there offering it.

Summary/Conclusion

In short, the age of opportunity and customization that is so much a part of our daily lives will continue long into the future. As they always have, time and money will dictate the actual sport and recreational activities we can participate in, the experiences we can have, and their frequency in our lives.

Sport and recreational activities will be impacted significantly by technological innovation, but will continue to be shaped by our environment, as they have been for thousands of years. Technology will monitor our performance and our health while at the same time contributing to our enjoyment. The social interaction of enjoying each other and competing against each other will continue to be an important part of sport and play. So will the escape to be alone while involved in some type of ecosport or enjoyment sport.

Entertainment sport could involve true world championships in basketball and baseball, but politics, labor unions, and the ongoing threat of terrorism will probably inhibit that development.

I'm not sure whether sport and recreational pursuits will take on a galactic nature on the next 25 years or so, but the Captain Kirk in me, and the one in most of us, hopes that day comes to pass.

References

1. William O. Johnson, "Sport in the year 2000," *Sports Illustrated*, Dec 23, 1974. www.si.com/vault/1974/12/23/628162/from-here-to-2000

2. *ibid.*

3. "Spending on Endurance sports to total $102 million in 2012," *International Events Group Sponsorship Report*, accessed August 6, 2016, www.sponsorship.com/2012/11/05/spending

4. *ibid.*

5. "We are Tough Mudder," accessed August 6, 2016, www.toughmudder.com

6. William O. Johnson, "From Here to 2000," Sports Illustrated, December 23, 1974, accessed August 6, 2016, www.si.com/vault/1974/12/23/628162/from-here-to-2000

7. *ibid.*

8. "How League of Legends became the most popular game in the world," Referral Candy, accessed August 6, 2016, http://www.referralcandy.com/blog/league-of-legends-word-of-mouth-marketing/

9. *ibid.*

10. John Ourand, "Turner looks beyond ELeague's low viewership numbers," *Street and Smiths Sports Business Journal* 19:16 (August 1, 2016) 1–70.

11. Competitive video gaming is set to return to TV in 2016. Los Angeles Times, www.latimes.com/business/la-fi-turner-img-espc

12. Georgia Perry, " Imagination in the Augmented-Reality Age," Atlantic, August 4, 2016, accessed August 12, 2016, http:/www.theatlantic.com/education/archive/2016/08/play-in-the-augmented-reality-age/494597/

13. *ibid.*

14. Bernard Mullin, Stephen Hardy, and William Sutton, Sport Marketing, 4th Edition (Champaign, IL: Human Kinetics, 2014), 456.

15. Bill Sutton, "How sports will evolve and direct consumers in a virtual world," *Street and Smith's Sports Business Journal* 18:32 (November 23–29, 2015) 15, accessed November 8, 2016, http://www.sportsbusinessdaily.com/Journal/Issues/2015/11/23/Opinion/Sutton-Impact.aspx

16. "Youth & Sports: What Centennials and Millennials Play, Watch and Follow," (Chicago, The Futures Group, 2014–15).

17. *ibid.*

18. Bob Cook, "Why Youth Sports Participation Will Fall, Even If Kids Are Having Fun," Forbes, October 24, 2015, accessed November 8, 2016, www.forbes.com/sites/bobcook/2015/10/24/why-youth-sports-participation-will-fall-even-if-kids-are-having-fun/.

19. Michael S. Rosenwald, "Are parents ruining youth sports? Fewer kids play mid pressure." Washington Post, October 4, 2015, www.washingtonpost.com/local/are-parents-running-youth-sports-fewer-kids-platy-amid-pressure/2015/10/04/eb1460dc-686e-11e5-9ef3-fde182507eac_story.html

20. "UCI to launch first-of-its-kind official e-sports initiative in the fall," University of California Irvine, March 30, 2016, https://news.uci.edu/press-releases/uci-to-launch-first-of-its-kind-official-e-sports-initiative-in-the-fall/

21. "The International eGames Committee launches a brand new event: The eGames," egames, April 6, 2016, accessed November 8, 2016, http://www.egames.org/news/the-international-egames-committee-launches-a-brand-new-event-the-egames.html

22. "SXSW Sports: The Future of Virtual and Augmented Reality in Sports, Sportstechie, March 18, 2016, www.sportstechie.com/2015/03/18sxsw-sports-the-future-of-virtual-and-augmented-reality-in-sports/

23. David Biderman, "11 minutes of action," Wall Street Journal, January 15, 2010, www.wsj.com/articles/SB10000142405274870428120457500285205561406

24. Kristen Wong, "The Fantasy Sports Industry, by the Numbers," NBC News, October 6, 2016, www.nbcnews.com/business/business-news/fantasy-sports-industry-mumbers-n439536

25. "About Chicago Sport & Social Club," Chicago Sport and Social Club, accessed August 28, 2016, www.chicagosocial.com/about

26. World Marathon Challenge, accessed August 28, 2016, www.worldmarathon-challenge.com

27. "Your Marathon and Lifestyle Travel Specialists," RunFun Travel, accessed August 28, 2016, www.runfuntravel.com.

28. Richard Petty Driving Experience, accessed August 28, 2016, www.drivepetty.com/race-tracks/daytona-international-speedway.

Web Assignment

Log into the student website and complete the end of chapter assignment. Try to utilize some of the works you read about from this chapter and apply the key concepts, terms, and theory in your responses.

CHAPTER 14

Global Lodging Trends

Written By Dr. Brian Miller, The University of Delaware

As we focus on the international lodging industry there are both winners and losers. However, in most regions the demand for rooms has seen a steady growth since the world financial crisis of 2008. Key performance indicators (KPI) in the U.S. are collectively very strong and many of these are at their highest levels ever. And this is a common thread throughout the world. Therefore, as we begin to look toward 2020, the projections are that the current levels of growth will not be sustained. At best the growth will be modest and negative growth at the worst. This creates a degree of uncertainty as we move toward 2020.

Financial Health of the Hotel Industry

Traditional key performance indicators (KPIs) for the financial health of the hotel industry are occupancy percentages, average daily rates (ADRs), room revenues, and revenue per available room (RevPar). Across the globe these KPIs are generally strong when looking at the data on a macro level.

U.S. Market

In the U.S. hotel market, the trends for all KPIs have remained consistently strong since 2010. As the market heads into February 2018 we have industry-wide metrics nearly all better than 2017. Occupancies are up 0.9 percent, year over year, ADR is up 2.0 percent, hotel room revenue is up 4.8 percent, RevPar is up 2.9 percent. Moreover, overall demand is up by 1.7 percent with supply growing 1.8 percent over the previous year.

The hotel sector has shown to be resilient in response to global economic uncertainty. The U.S. hotel industry has continued to be a leader in the growth of new jobs with over 188,000 new jobs that have attracted smart, dedicated, and hardworking individuals since 2010. However, a study by Kosova and Enz published in the *Cornell Hospitality Quarterly* in September 2012 found that the industry is adept in the ability to successfully address the effects on demand of both the terrorist attacks (9/11/2001) and the financial crisis (2008). Their study determined that the hotel industry didn't implode but rather the sector bounced back to a significant recovery. At the end of 2015, the industry has reached all-time peak levels in several significant metrics.

However, as seen over the past 30 years of data collected in the U.S. hotel industry, it is clear that demand for hotel rooms is cyclical. As such, the industry will have to adjust to ever-changing conditions moving forward over the next five years.

Below are the projections for three key U.S. markets: New York, NY (East Coast), Chicago, IL (Midwest), and San Francisco, CA (West Coast). Each of these major markets has shown to be a solid indicator for the region in which they reside.

New York, NY

The New York market continues to show consistent growth in all hotel indices, and it is projected that these trends will continue. Occupancies are projected to grow at about 0.2 percent per year through 2020. Average daily rate is projected to grow 2 to 3 percent per year. Revenue per available room is projected to grow approximately 4 percent per year. Finally, demand is projected to out-pace new supply by 3 percent over the next 5 years.

Chicago, IL

The Chicago market, similar to New York, has been strong over the last five years; however, moving forward the market is seeing a significant amount of growth in new supply which is projected to out-pace demand by 3 percent through 2020, which will leave the market's occupancies flat. Average daily rate is projected to grow 1.5 to 2 percent per year. Finally, revenue per available room is projected to grow at the same 1.5 to 2 percent per year through 2020.

San Francisco, CA

The San Francisco lodging market, also similar to both New York and Chicago, has shown consistent growth in all of the hotel indices over the last five years. Occupancies are projected to remain flat through 2020. Average daily rate is projected to remain strong with growth projected between 3 to 4 percent per year. Revenue per available room is also projected to show strong growth at 3 to 4 percent per year. Finally, demand and supply growth is projected to be balanced over the next five years.

Factors Affecting the Lodging Industry in the U.S.

As we project the future of the U.S. hotel industry into the future there are several key elements that the segment will need to keep an eye on as we race to 2020 and beyond.

RevPar Growth

Projections of positive growth in RevPar will require that occupancies continue to grow year over year. There is solid evidence that most markets are still below pre-2008 levels in ADR when factoring in inflation, so these should continue to grow and remain strong. If new supply grows faster than demand, then RevPar growth projections will be in jeopardy.

The U.S. market is projected to continue to break demand records into the foreseeable future as it has over the last three years but the growth has been slowing. That there is still growth in demand this will be good news for hoteliers. As for the growth in new supply, currently the projections are for supply to grow by 2.0 percent per year over the next 3 to 5 years. However, growth of new room supply is not equally dispersed in all markets, so for some markets there will be negative impacts with the introduction of new supply. STR (a data benchmarking, analytics, and marketplace forecaster for the global hotel industry) has reported that this new growth in supply may have a more significant impact on the top 25 U.S. markets as almost half of the U.S. pipeline for new supply is found in these markets.

President Trump

As this chapter is being written, U.S. Pres. Donald Trump is eight months into his second year in office. It has been a tumultuous period for the country, and especially for its relationships with other lands. There are, of course, two primary ways in which he can influence travel and hospitality. The first is through economic policy. The economy is healthy—little changed, in fact, from his predecessor's time in office. This is to be expected, as presidents have less immediate influence over the economy than they often claim and too often receive credit for. However, job growth is slowing, and the recent decline in unemployment to only 3.9 percent owes nearly as much to declining workforce participation as it does to growing demand for labor. The promised burst of hiring as a result of recent tax cuts has yet to appear. Experience requires us to expect growing budget deficits ahead—though perhaps not until they can be blamed on some future administration.

The second way presidents can affect the hospitality industry is through the welcome his policies lead international visitors to expect. Here the picture is clearer. In 2015, the U.S. welcomed 77 million international visitors. The projection for 2020 is that the U.S. will welcome over 100 million visitors. The U.S. hotel industry will need to have these projections come to fruition if it is to achieve the positive forecast projected through 2020. Unfortunately, the number of international tourists arriving in the U.S. declined some 4 percent in the first three quarters of 2017—this in a time when international tourist arrivals worldwide grew by 7 percent, the strongest growth seen since 2010. At year's end, international tourist arrivals in the United States still appeared to be off from 2017, though in August the final tally had not yet been released.

Moreover, along with the populist message of President Trump that resonated so profoundly with the U.S. populace, similar populist messages are being accepted in the UK, France, Germany, and Austria. The common thread to these are the politicians' promise to create policies that protect and restrict entrance through their borders. It is still too soon to appreciate fully how these policies will affect the U.S. lodging markets, but the evidence so far is not encouraging.

Airbnb and the Sharing Economy

Airbnb and other sharing-economy platforms in the lodging space are resonating with travelers. Predictably, this is creating tensions between these alternative supply options and hotel operators. The current collection of lawsuits by the lodging industry provides evidence that legitimate hotel operators are worried about these developments as Airbnb has become a mainstream option for travelers. The good news for the lodging industry is that Airbnb and other sharing economy platforms have gotten on the radar of local governments that are worried the growth of these firms' could displace taxable revenues. These challenges and the growth of alternative authentic lodging options for travelers will continue to play out well into the future.

South American Region

For decades, the major brands have been eager to further develop the South American lodging market. As of 2017, Argentina has a new administration and positive political reform the Brazilian currency is being revalued downward, and Ecuador is placing an increased emphasis on tourism development. Additionally, countries such as Peru, Colombia, and Paraguay are showing positive economic growth rates, along with a maturing of regional hotel companies with a workforce to manage new properties.

However, due to the political and economic situation in this part of the world, significant lodging investment is unlikely to materialize over the next five years. As of 2016, the lodging market of South America saw an increase in supply of 3.0 percent but a decrease in demand (-1.5 percent), revenue (-25.0 percent), occupancy (-4.9 percent), ADR (-24.3 percent), and RevPar. (28.6 percent).

Factors Affecting the Lodging Industry in the South American Region

Currency Devaluation

The currencies of Brazil, Uruguay, and Colombia lost over 20 percent in year-on-year value. This fall in the value of local currencies has made investing in high-quality lodging assets affordable.

Increased Tourism in Region

Travel and tourism in South America is projected to grow faster than other developed regions, such as Europe. According to the World Travel & Tourism Council, travel and tourism recorded $371 billion (2015) and is projected to grow to over $530 billion by 2026. Additionally, international tourist arrivals are forecast to grow at 5.3 percent or 73 million arrivals by 2026, contributing significantly to the South American economy. Compared with international standards, there is room for this growth as more international business tourism travels to the South American markets and uses the existing and new hotel supply as opposed to the more common leisure tourism using hotel rooms. At present, international visitors account for 17 percent of the demand for hotel rooms, whereas the global average is 27 percent. Moreover, business demand accounts for 19 percent of total demand compared to a global average of 23 percent. Therefore, there is plenty of optimism for the South American lodging markets.

Asia Pacific Region

China continues to lead the growth for much of the Asian Pacific Region. However, as a region the lodging industry has seen mixed performance results over the last five years. As a region occupancy is growing at about 1.6 percent; however, ADR has remained relatively flat or decreasing, and RevPar has grown modestly at less than 1.0 percent.

Beijing

The Chinese economy continues to outpace every other market in the world. Although its economy is slowing, the GDP growth through 2020 is projected to be in the 6.0 percent range. As pressure for natural resources eases, this should provide opportunities

Regent Beijing Hotel

in new hotel development investment. The government continues to provide for low interest rates, and this fiscal policy is expected to continue for the foreseeable future.

The Beijing lodging market continues to show consistent growth in the hotel indices, and it is projected that these trends will continue. Occupancies are projected to grow at about 1.0 percent per year through 2020. Average daily rate is projected to grow at 3 percent per year. Revenue per available room is projected to grow approximately 4 percent per year. Finally, demand and new supply is expected to be balanced, with a growth of 9 percent each over the next five years.

Australia

International arrivals to Australia are growing at a strong rate, with double-digit increases over the last five years. December 2016 saw the country's highest monthly ADR on record, which was an increase of 3.2 percent over the previous year. The lodging sector is projected for continued growth in demand, along with a modest growth in supply through 2020. Australia has recently been found to be resilient to international crises as Chinese outbound tourists are increasingly seeking to explore the country's vast tourism resources.

Japan

In 2016, Japan had 24 million international visitors, which was an increase of 21.8 percent over 2015. Japan's main markets for international visitors has consistently been from other Asian countries, with China, South Korea, and Taiwan leading the way.

Europe

In light of Brexit and the uncertainties that remain for the countries still belonging to the European Union, the outlook for the European lodging market remains bullish. The weaker Euro compared to the U.S. dollar will benefit the U.S. traveler and should continue to increase demand for lodging in key European markets. Additionally, current oil prices are at 10-year lows and appear to have stabilized as the new normal. More discretionary income that is available due to the lower cost of fuel will benefit both tourists from within the European Union and those who are outside the European Union.

The significant drawback and uncertainty to an otherwise rosy forecast for the European lodging market continues to be the geopolitical uncertainty of the Middle East and the influence of terrorist groups such ISIS and Al Qaeda to motivate home-grown terrorism within their borders

London

Given the Brexit result, projections for business projections will slow due to the heightened uncertainty as to the time table and the terms of the split with the European Union (EU). This impact of this will largely depend on the negations between Theresa May and her fight with Parliament on how to move forward with removing Britain from the EU. The upside to the broader lodging market is the continued projection of a weak British pound to both the U.S. dollar and Euro to at least 2020. The projections of the British pound to the U.S. dollar and Euro are to remain around $1.40 and €1.20, respectively. Finally, British fiscal policy will continue to have a drag on growth generally through 2020.

In the London lodging market occupancies are projected to grow at about 1.5 percent per year through 2020. Average daily rate is projected to grow 2 to 3 percent per year. Revenue per available room is projected to grow 3 to 4 percent per year. And demand is projected to outpace new supply by 3 percent over the next five years. Current pipeline data of new hotel projects stands at 90 properties with 15,000 rooms. However, many of these projects are in the early planning stages.

Berlin

Going beyond the uncertainty of how the UK will dismantle its relationships with their current European Union partners, the Berlin lodging market is projected to remain strong through 2020—notwithstanding expectations of lower annual GDPs, inflation pressures, and immigration unrest. The Berlin market continues to show consistent growth in all hotel economic measures and it is projected that these trends will continue. Occupancies are projected to grow at about 0.5 percent per year through 2020. Average daily rate is projected to grow 2 percent per year. Revenue per available room is projected to grow approximately 2 to 2.5 percent per year. Finally, demand is projected to out-pace new supply by 4% over the next five years. Currently 3,700 new rooms are in the pipeline for Berlin.

Rome

In Italy, the economic forecast is challenged with a limited economic recovery throughout the country as well as continued scrutiny of the banking industry. The good news is that the labor market continues to recover. In the Rome lodging market, occupancies are projected to grow at about 1.0 percent per year through 2020. Average daily rate is projected to grow 2 percent per year. Revenue per available room is projected to grow approximately 3 percent per year. And demand is projected to out-pace new supply by 10 percent over the next five years as few if any new supply is currently in the pipeline.

Budapest

The Hungarian economy appears to be recovering nicely and should continue to be an attractive beacon for Eastern European economies. It is projected that the Budapest lodging market will see occupancies remain flat through 2020 as new supply is added to the market. Average daily rate is projected to grow at 2.5 percent per year. Revenue per available room is projected to grow an average of 3.0 percent per year. And demand is projected to balance out the increase in supply over the next five years.

The Middle East and Africa

In this region of the world the lodging markets are at best mixed. Significant differences of winners and losers are found in this region. In strong markets, potential positive indicators are typically outstripped by major growth in new supply. Without a doubt the Middle East and Africa provide a mixed bag of success for hotel companies.

Dubai

The Dubai lodging market has seen a tremendous growth in both new supply and demand. The destination continues to be desirable to both the business and the leisure traveler. However, over the next five years lodging market KPIs are not positive due to a number of key issues. Low oil prices, currency pressures, and weak property values will continue to make the cost of visiting the destination out of reach of a vast majority of travelers. Additionally, those visitors who have the capacity to travel to Dubai will find 153 new properties with over 44,500 rooms to be developed in the next five years. Occupancies are projected to be negative year over year through 2020. So is average daily rate, which revenue per available room also will decline during this period.

Final Word

Globally, the hotel pipeline is forecasted to remain modest over the next five years, averaging to about 1 percent per year or about 1 million new rooms per year. These levels may change, as individual market conditions will dictate that new supply does not significantly exceed demand conditions.

Branding

Mergers and Acquisitions

The trend of mergers and acquisitions in the lodging market has picked up speed over the last few years; it's projected to continue into the foreseeable future. This is a new development that is driven by the need to continue organizational growth for stockholders.

As companies come under intense pressure to show growth, the easiest way for hotel companies to gain access to new customers and markets is to acquire established assets. This pressure to find opportunities to grow through mergers and acquisitions stems from the proliferation of new hotel brands and a shifting of traveler preferences.

Marriott's CEO Arne Sorensen states that "Today, size matters, and to be successful in today's lodging space, a wide distribution of brands and hotels across price points is critical." Benefits from increased size include economies of scale, elimination of duplication, centralized procurement, and effective distribution networks, to name a few. Many lodging companies now believe that consolidation is key to survival, but it is not clear that a smaller population of competitors that offer more branded stay options (brands) will serve travelers well.

As much as the international hotel companies are trying to support multiple brands, travelers will see fewer options when planning their trips, as consolidation of hotel companies and specifically their brands continues. Consolidation of competitors is a sign of maturity of an industry. Over the next five years, hotel companies, through their brands, will struggle to support greater consumer segmentation and personalization.

In an effort to meet ever-changing demands, lodging brands will view market shifts as either an opportunity or a threat. Eventually, the brands will need to recognize that the growing demand for personalization can't be met by brands known for their "standard" experiences. Being an iconic brand with a consistent product delivery may turn into a limitation when it comes to satisfying a wide variety of experiences and expectations that travelers demand.

Proliferation of Brands

Growth of franchising from new and legacy brands is expected to continue. This will cause a push of new development projects throughout the globe. The rationale for this comes from a continual switch to an asset lite strategy that will provide the brands' parent company with consistent earnings growth.

As the top five brands race to build new rooms into the market this is expected to lead to an advantage for smaller, high-quality brands that are looking for quality locations over uncontained growth. We will see more cautious growth from brands such as Joie de Vivre, Red Lion, and Commune, to name a few.

Brands v. Independents

Since the emergence of the Internet and the growth of online travel websites, competitive advantages between operating hotels as part of a chain versus independent has dwindled. However, over the foreseeable future, branded hotels' development will significantly outpace independent hotels in all hotel markets around the globe. The business franchise model deployed by hotel companies is the number one reason for this. As these hotel companies get bigger over the next five years, mostly through mergers and acquisitions, they will rule the hotel development pipeline and the divide between branded and non-branded hotels will expand.

In North America and Asia/Pacific branded hotels outnumber non-branded hotels 67 percent to 33 percent and 51 percent to 49 percent respectively. In South America, Europe, and Middle East/Africa independent hotels outnumber branded hotels 41 percent to 59 percent, 41 percent to 59 percent, and 44 percent to 56 percent, respectively but the mix will significantly change in the direction of branded hotels.

The Name of the Game is Room Share

As 2015 was coming to a close the hotel companies were racing to be the first company with 1 million rooms. Marriott won the race through the acquisition of Starwood Hotels and Resorts in the first quarter of 2016. The top five hotel companies by the number of rooms are Marriott (1,017,096), Hilton Worldwide Holdings (737,922), Intercontinental Hotel Group (727,876), Wyndham Hotel Group (671,900) and Jia Jiang International Hotels Group (640,000). The number of rooms that each of these hotel companies have in the pipeline is in descending number from first to fifth if these projects are 100 percent completed and opened. Marriott has the most with 373,000 rooms in the pipeline, representing an increase of 34.8 percent of hotel rooms of their various brands. However, Hilton Worldwide Holdings, with its current pipeline projects is projected to have the largest percentage of change at 35.2 percent,

Global Branded Hotels by Class

STR, the leading hotel data company along with information provided by the world's leading hotel brands, developed a typography of hotel segments for the lodging industry in 2014. These segments denote the class of the hotel based on the average daily rates earned by the entire collection of hotels in a brand's portfolio. Currently hotels are divided into six classes, Economy, Midscale, Upper Midscale, Upscale, Upper Upscale, and Luxury.

The Economy class of hotels is the largest percentage of rooms globally with a market share of 29 percent. In this class the mix between branded versus non-branded is 54 percent to 46 percent. The Midscale class represents 14 percent of the market with 69 percent of these hotels branded compared to 31 percent non-branded. The Upper Midscale class of hotels has 21 percent of the market with 85 percent branded and 15 percent non-branded. Upscale hotels make up 16 percent of the global market and are 79 percent to 21 percent branded to non-branded hotels. The Upscale class is projected to be the fastest growing class of hotels globally over the next five years. Upper Upscale hotels have 13 percent of the global market with a mix of branded to non-branded hotels of 79 percent to 21 percent. Finally, the Luxury class represents 5 percent of the global hotel market and is the only hotel class with fewer branded hotels than non-branded hotels at 44 percent to 56 percent. The projection for new hotel development in regions which currently have more non-branded hotels is that the growth will be significantly toward the development of branded hotels in these regions.

Channels of Distribution

Changing Landscape of Options

Over the last 10 years there has been a lot of changes in the distribution of hotel rooms. As the growth of online travel booking increased so did the number of new startups looking to capitalize on the democratization of information required to search and book hotel rooms.

Changing Landscape of Consumers and Consumer Preferences

The belief that consumers must stay in luxury hotels to receive exclusive experiences and individual recognition will shift to other classes of hotels. No longer will this be the expectation only from guests who are willing to spend whatever money to receive these privileges. Guests searching at all price points for hotel rooms will walk in the door expecting this or they will go elsewhere. The local community in which the hotel operates will need to be the backdrop that drives guests to the hotels, which will in turn provide the options to customize an experience that takes into consideration the personal wishes of their guests.

Consumers will continue to be more knowledgeable of their travel options and will seek advice and guidance from friends, family, and strangers from online review sites to make their travel plans. Consumers will drive hotel operators to provide more than a comfortable bed; they will be looking for experiences that provide stimulation. These consumers will also prefer to allocate their travel dollars by spending less on the room and more on the community-based experience. They will be looking for personal immersion through engagement with the local community. It will all be about the activation of the hotel's programming.

© Francesco83/Shutterstock.com

Consumers will continue to grow their expectations of what they want from a hotel experience. These changes will run through the entire guest cycle. They value their time, health, relationships, communications, and experiences. They will want what they want, when they want it, and want it to be seamless within their normal daily activities.

Increased Use of Technology

Data-Focused Systems

Increased use of artificial learning applications that allow better use of operational inputs is an important trend in the hotel industry. Increased use of predictive analytics tools will utilize the tremendous amount of data collected by hotels all around the world. These tools will allow data to develop more accurate forecasting of demand and operational resources. Currently most of these data go unused.

Increased use of management dashboards will provide internal data to key personnel who have the skills and power to act and adjust operational strategies. At the same time, increased development of middleware will allow data and legacy systems to connect for improved operational efficiencies and customer-facing services. (Peter O'Connor, 2016)

Guest-Focused Systems

Amalgamated messaging platforms can assimilate guest data that is collected by brands and use it to connect hotels to guests and to create personalized services for guests. These will identify and collect data regarding guest behavior across distribution channels. These are an important development that is needed for predictive analytics to reach its potential. The biggest challenge for hotel operators will not come from the process of collecting guest data but rather getting the customer-facing operational team to act on the data.

Guest profiler systems will provide individual, customized profiles of guests so that hotel properties can better meet the needs of their guests. These systems will compile data to customize customer profiles so that the guests are provided a unique set of experience options. This will require new forms of communication beyond those currently used by hotels.

Direct, real-time, and two-way communication modes will collect and push data from/to guests. When used appropriately by operational teams, the hotel becomes a platform to develop individualized programming and experiences that will be appreciated by hotel guests.

Key Trends of a Changing Hotel Consumer

Instant Gratification

Instant news, social media, multi-tasking, and general technology overload has created a traveler who simply wants to touch, click, and go. Searching, booking, and experiencing the holiday as easily and quickly as possible will be demanded by an ever-increasing number of travelers. Those hotel companies that can make the booking process as seamless as possible will be rewarded with an increased demand for their hotels.

"Bleisure"

Over the last few years, there has been a growing trend to combine business travel with leisure travel: "Bleisure." This trend has been growing consistently and should continue to pick up steam through 2020. This will put pressure on hotels to identify and deliver products and services that satisfy the needs of guests who are on both business and leisure during a single stay.

Interest to Discover (spending less of their budget on room accommodations)

It is no longer about the hotel experience alone. In fact, the sleeping room and the other amenities that are commonly available at many hotels will continue to play a much smaller role in the travel experience. A growing number of travelers will be more interested in getting a truly authentic experience than in paying for a host of amenities that they have no interest or time to enjoy. Winning hotels will be those that can match their services to the authentic environments and communities in which they operate.

Travel for the Purpose of Creating a Balance in Life

Due to the stresses of their everyday lives, more travelers will see their holiday as a means to balance their hectic work and personal lives. To meet this growing trend, hoteliers will need to redefine and expand their purpose for accommodating their guests. Instead of the traveler being a guest in the hotel, successful hotels will provide an environment in which it is the hotel and its staff who are the guests in the lives of their visitors.

Force Choice – Go Green or Stay Home

There are many things that today's travelers demand when they choose the location and the hotel while traveling. A growing number of travelers will no longer accept a forced choice of either staying home or traveling in an unsustainable manner. Successful hotels will understand how to operate their businesses in the more sustainable way that is transparent and real to both the visitor and to the local communities in which they operate. This trend will continue to be demanded by more visitors over the next five years.

Setting Travel Priorities

A growing number of travelers will eschew amenities that are viewed as lavish trappings with little or no added benefit. More travelers are willing to participate in the experience as active participants (self-service) and are looking for the simple moments and pleasures that make up a meaningful voyage. Concierges, individual bath products, and candies on the pillow will not be the amenities sought by this new breed of visitor.

The Human Touch

This trend identifies that hotel guests spend a growing portion of their daily routines dealing and communicating with technology. As much as hotel operators want to provide the consumer with more and more technology, successful brands will focus on providing authentic and customized human-to-human experiences. More hotel guests will seek and expect a friendly and caring team to meet their traveling demands. These guests say no to robots!

Unparalleled Travel Experience

This trend will continue to gain traction over the next five years as travelers seek and plan travel for prestige. In the daily lives of the traveling public examples of adventurous and unique experiences are constantly on display through social media platforms. A growing number of travelers will search for unique experiences that provide them with social status among their friends and families. Successful hotels will harness this desire and connect their properties with authentic cultural and unique elements of the communities in which they operate.

Web Assignment

Log into the student website and complete the end of chapter assignment. Try to utilize some of the works you read about from this chapter and apply the key concepts, terms, and theory in your responses.

CHAPTER 15

International Strategic Management: Growing the Brand Globally

Growing the Brand Globally: The International Strategy

Why do United States hospitality and travel companies expand internationally? Why are McDonald's and Marriott opening more businesses in China? What are the opportunities and the threats when they perform their corporate SWOT analyses? There are several reasons firms go global. One is that the domestic market may be saturated (complex), and the U.S. economy may be slowing down, while economies abroad may be expanding and opening up opportunities. Another reason may be that firms need to show the continuous growth that stockholders demand. Ways to grow include acquiring new businesses (such as through mergers and acquisitions), developing new concepts and brands, and also expanding their businesses around the globe.

Strategic Global Entry for Companies

Going global and expanding internationally can provide a firm with a competitive advantage in the marketplace. There are clearly rewards to a firm that chooses this strategy, and also risks involved. Applying the strategic planning tools discussed so far (e.g., the STK Tools) will be extremely prudent. Firms can enter the international market first by exporting products and services. They can license their products and services. Strategic alliances and joint ventures with other international firms are popular and afford firms the opportunity to share the country risks and the resources needed to grow a business globally. Resources will have to be shared; yet this minimizes risk and allows the U.S. firm to move up the new country learning curve.

Aramark often formed joint ventures with like-minded companies when they were hired to run the Olympics around the world. In 2000, Aramark formed a joint venture with Spotless, and they did a similar venture in China for the 2008 Olympic Games. This is a good strategy for a company like Aramark, a global services management giant. It has provided them an opportunity to gain market share in that country where they served in the Olympics. Following the Olympic Games, Aramark has the opportunity to stay in the country and expand.

A great case study from the Harvard Business School is the Warsaw Marriott. Marriott was the first U.S. company to move into Eastern Europe, in Poland, and provide a "beachhead" for other U.S. firms to conduct business in finance, engineering, and energy. This allowed Marriott, a pioneer globally, to expand internationally and also to make long-standing relationships with other U.S. firms venturing into new a part of the world. U.S. hotel companies and leading firms like Aramark are pioneers and deserve a lot of credit for often being the first into a country to establish a safe oasis for businesses to grow and expand in foreign lands.

Finally, firms can expand globally through acquisition and startup ventures where firms will build their own presence through owning facilities in strategic international markets. This method may be faster, but starting anew may be the way to go if strategic global partners (for alliances) are not apparent. This of course can carry the highest level of risk. Earlier in the book we discussed transparency of countries, safety and security risks, economic risk, inadequate labor and resources risk, and the Opacity Index (which, regrettably, has not been updated in a decade.) But there is no doubt that major U.S. companies have to expand globally to survive as a significant global player, and this practice will only continue into the future.

One STK Tool for expanding globally is similar to the Boston Consulting Matrix. On the X-axis is "Competitive Strength of Business in a Country," and on the Y-axis is the "Growth Potential of Doing Business in the Country." In the top right quadrant are the star countries that are high/high on both the X and Y-axes. In the lower quadrant are the "dogs" with little strategic opportunity. Star countries should be maintained and enhanced for continued growth. Dogs should be avoided. Companies in the top left hand quadrant where they have "low competitive strength" but the country is "high" in strategic importance are in peril and need attention and investment. On the other hand, in the bottom right quadrant the country has a high competitive strength for the company but is low on importance and should be defended. China is a country many hospitality and travel firms feel they must operate in due to the expanding economy and market potential \\. Therefore, companies will work hard to find a partner, a joint venture in China, to help them bring their competitive strengths to this new market.

In summary, companies seeking to go multinational face three requirements: First, they must develop a sustainable core strategy in their home country in order to develop a worldwide global strategy for future success. Second, they need to internationalize and master the basics of their core and focused business before they can achieve a global strategy. This can be done as discussed earlier via joint ventures, franchising/licensing their brand. Third, companies can realize a global internationalizing strategy by integrating a focused and honed strategy across multiple countries.

Successful multinational companies know these three steps to global expansion and success. They understand the opportunities, threats, and risks for expansion, but they have a plan or map to become a global player over time. The following case looks at restaurant companies such as Chipotle going into China. You should be able to use the STK Tools to provide sound strategic advice, suggestions, and recommendations to these firms as they look beyond U.S. borders. You should be able to scan the environment and to predict their future internationally, or at least make some predictions and forecasts based on your assessments of the strengths and weaknesses of the firm and the opportunity to expand and do business globally. The world is flat, and without question the future of U.S. companies is to be global competitors and players on a complex international stage.

End of Chapter Case Study

The "Chipotle in China" Case Study serves as an "Integrative Case Study" for the entire book

Chipotle Mexican Grill: A Sustainability Champion Going Global with China

Fred DeMicco Dept. of Hotel & Restaurant Management, University of Delaware. Raub Hall, 14 West Main Street, Newark, DE 19716; Tel. (302) 831-6077; Email: hrim-dept@udel.edu

H.G. Parsa 344 Joy Burns Center, Daniels College of Business, University of Denver2044 E. Evans Ave, Denver, CO 80208, (303) 871-3693 hparsa@du.edu

Jing Gao Dept. of Hotel & Restaurant Management, University of Delaware. Raub Hall, 14 West Main Street, Newark, DE 19716; Tel. (302) 831-6077

Vijaya "Vi" Narapareddy Dept. of Management, Daniels College of Business, University of Denver, 2101 S. University Blvd., Denver, CO 80208 vnarpar@du.edu

Abstract

Several U.S. restaurant chains have expanded their business into China, including KFC, Pizza Hut, McDonald's, Starbucks, and Subway. This case focuses on Chipotle Mexican Grill's potential to develop its business in China and the opportunities and challenges it may face in the Chinese market. Students are expected to learn pros and cons of international expansion of U.S. restaurant firms. Additionally, students will learn the impact of unexpected operational challenges, such as foodborne illness outbreaks, on potential growth strategies and how to address the short term and urgent need to do damage control from foodborne illnesses or to modify and pursue the international expansion strategies.

Key Words: China, Restaurants, International Expansion, Chipotle, Strategy, Cultural Differences.

Introduction

A Motley Fool's article sparked rumors that Chipotle Mexican Grill (Chipotle, hereafter) was contemplating expansion into China. Chipotle was no stranger to overseas expansion. Under the leadership of founder-CEO-Chairman Steve Ells and his co-CEO, Montgomery Moran, the Chipotle brand grew into a highly desired brand in the quick service food service industry. Its enviable position in the home market was the result of its unique strategy known as *Food with Integrity*, which reflected Ells' passion for sustainable sourcing of quality food supplies locally. At a time when the term sustainability was little known in the industry, positioning the restaurant using this distinctive strategy gave Chipotle significant first-mover advantages. Sales reached the $5 billion mark in 2015, from $820 million since its Initial Public Offering (IPO) in 2006. The overwhelming demand for the company's shares on the first day of its 2006 IPO resulted in the doubling of the stock's value that day, making it the most lucrative IPO since 2000.

Brief History and Development of Chipotle

Steven Ells, a graduate of the University of Colorado, Boulder, and the Culinary Institute of America in Hyde Park, NY, founded Chipotle in 1993 after working at a San Francisco restaurant. As a line cook earning $12 an hour, Ells found himself regularly "dining on giant burritos at taquerias in the Mission District." During his lunch hours, the long line of customers waiting for Mexican food day-in day-out sparked the idea of starting his own Mexican-themed restaurant.

It was not until July 13, 1993 that Ells could open his first restaurant. Armed with a loan of $75,000 from his father, Ells leased a space previously occupied by the Dolly Madison ice cream shop near the University of Denver campus in Denver, Colorado, made the renovations himself to the property, and opened his first restaurant. The restaurant was an instant success generating $450 on opening day, $800 the next day, and $1000 a day shortly thereafter. Within six months, sales per day grew to $3,000. This high growth fueled by Ells' novel concept attracted the attention of McDonald's which took a minority stake in Chipotle in 1998, followed by a majority stake in 2001. This capital infusion allowed Ells to expand from sixteen restaurants in 1998 to over 500 by October 2006, when McDonald's liquidated its equity in the company. McDonald's was rumored to have reaped over 416-percent return on its $360 million investment in Chipotle.

Business Strategy

Ells entered the highly competitive and fragmented quick service dining industry with a socially responsible strategy that he called *Food with Integrity*. He was the first in the industry to commit to serving only meats from animals that were not raised using non-therapeutic antibiotics and growth hormones. Dairy products like cheese and sour cream were obtained from milk produced by pasture-raised cows. Obtaining ingredients from responsibly raised farms reflected Ells' love for promoting animal welfare and environmental sustainability. Similar high standards were enforced when Chipotle purchased mostly organically grown produce from farmers using sustainable farming practices within a radius of 350 miles from the restaurant where the produce was served. This combination of serving traditionally cooked food with high quality locally grown ingredients in a quick service environment while providing an interactive dining experience blazed the path to Chipotle's success. The restaurant chain, which expanded through the strategy of company-owned stores, attracted celebrities and dignitaries, including President Obama. Using the same quick service

© jejim/Shutterstock.com

concept, Chipotle opened thirteen *Chop House Southeast Asian Kitch*en restaurants serving Asian cuisine, as well as three *Pizzeria Locale* restaurants specializing in pizza and Italian foods.

Products

A key competitive advantage that Chipotle had over its rivals was its fresh ingredients, local sourcing, healthy cooking practices, and ease of ordering. Chipotle offered menu choices that customers could pick and choose from. When ordering food, patrons could create their own burrito with their choice of meats, vegetables, beans, rice, salsa, guacamole, cheese, or sour cream wrapped inside a Mexican-style whole wheat tortilla (a flat bread), rich in fiber. Alternatively, customers who preferred a gluten-free diet could order a bowl without the tortilla and still receive ingredients of their choice. Other menu choices included crispy corn tacos, soft corn tacos, soft flour tacos, or salads. All ingredients were openly displayed. Several staff members standing on the other (opposite) side of the display counter filled the orders in real time as customers chose the main and side items while moving down the line towards the cash register. This ordering process not only shortened the wait time, but also gave customers the chance to feast on the attractive display of the fresh ingredients while their taste buds received stimulation from the exciting flavors that drifted from the freshly made menu items. Compared to other American quick service chains, such as KFC and McDonald's, the food Chipotle offered was freshly prepared in the restaurant, nutritious, wholesome, and obtained from sustainable sources. This fixed menu concept became Chipotle's source of competitive advantage as busy young professionals, Millennials, and students were drawn to the convenience of home-style, high quality food, which offered a range of choices at competitive prices without long wait times.

Employees

By the end of 2015, Chipotle had a total 59,330 non-unionized employees, 5,100 of which were salaried employees. The remaining 54,230 were hourly workers. The company hired only high-performance employees and promoted general managers from within the organization to ensure that they embraced the corporate culture, passion, and vision while working in a high-performance work environment. Consistent with Ells' passion for sustainability and social responsibility, Chipotle entered into partnership with Loomsdale, a sustainable clothing company that also engaged in socially responsible production methods. Chipotle's employees wore organic cotton tee-shirts and hats made by Loomsdale, which also made Chipotle merchandise (graphic tees, polos, and woven shirts) sold online and in the store.

Performance

In 2014, Chipotle ranked fifth in worldwide sales, behind McDonald's, Subway, and Yum Brands. With sales of $27.44 billion, McDonald's was the largest player among all quick service restaurant chains. Subway ranked a distinct second with $20 billion whereas

Yum Brands and Chick-fil-A ranked third and fourth, respectively. Chipotle, which came in fifth in this competitive segment, had sales of $4.11 billion—approximately 15 percent of McDonald's revenues. Chipotle was also ranked in fifth place among the top ten most valuable quick service brands in 2015. This brand recognition was noteworthy as there were key differences between Chipotle and its key competitors. While Chipotle expanded through company-owned stores, its rivals became global brands through franchising.

Chipotle stood out from its competitors with its strong commitment to environmental sustainability and social responsibility. Founder Ells' culinary background influenced the way food was prepared at the Chipotle restaurants. Despite the high costs of obtaining from local and sustainable farmers as well as using organic ingredients wherever possible, Chipotle achieved strong profit performance. The company's indexed performance shown indicates that it outperformed the S&P 500 Index and the S&P 500 Restaurants Index from 2010 through 2015. This high value created by Chipotle for its shareholders was also evident from the Balance Sheet data presented in Figure 15.1, which shows that Chipotle's shareholders' equity grew 203.7 percent, from approximately $1.04 billion in 2011 to $2.13 billion in 2015. The company's Profit & Loss statement (see Figure 15.2) indicates that labor costs constituted one of the major expenditures in operations. Yet, Chipotle's profits (i.e., net income) more than doubled between 2011 and 2015.

In spite of the highly competitive nature of the industry, a large number of restaurants were opened in the U.S. between 2004 and 2015. The continued and steady growth of revenues in the U.S. quick service sector may have helped Chipotle become a household name, but the company's strategic site selection also contributed to its success. Chipotle restaurants were located in colleges, universities, strip malls, local and regional malls, downtown business centers, free-standing buildings, food courts, train stations, military bases, and airports. The site selection process was managed by an internal team, which sought the help of local real estate brokers. On-site visits were supplemented by a rigorous analysis of trade, business, and demographic data as well as the locations of direct and indirect competitors in the area.

The Chinese Market

As China was home to the largest population in the world, the Chinese government sought to legally control the growth of its population through its one-child policy. However, the population grew from 1.34 billion in 2010 to about 1.37 billion in 2014. With the relaxation of the one-child policy, China's population was expected to exceed 1.4 billion by the year 2020. Even though it was home to the largest population, China enjoyed a rising prosperous economy, as measured by the country's growing GDP (Gross Domestic Product) per capita. China lagged behind the U.S. in GDP. In 2015, while the U.S. had the highest GDP of $17,968 billion, China had the second highest with $11,384.76 billion. However, during the same year (2015), China's share of global GDP based on purchasing power parity (PPP) was the largest at 17.24 percent, as opposed to the U.S. (15.88 percent of the global GDP), suggesting that Chinese consumers had greater buying power than consumers in the U.S. or any other country.

	December 31,				
Balance Sheet Data:	2015	2014[1]	2013[1]	2012[1]	2011[1]
Total current assets	$ 814,647	$ 859,511	$ 653,095	$ 537,745	$ 494,954
Total assets	$ 2,725,066	$ 2,527,317	$ 1,996,068	$ 1,659,805	$ 1,419,070
Total current liabilities	$ 279,942	$ 245,710	$ 199,228	$ 186,852	$ 157,453
Total liabilities	$ 597,092	$ 514,948	$ 457,780	$ 413,879	$ 374,844
Total shareholders' equity	$ 2,127,794	$ 2,012,369	$ 1,538,288	$ 1,245,926	$ 1,044,226

(1) Data adjusted to conform to the Financial Accounting Standards Board Accounting (FASBA) standards that required deferred tax liabilities and assets to be classified as non-current. (Source: Statista)

Figure 15.1 Chipotle's Mexican Grill Consolidated Balance Sheet, 2011–2015 (All numbers in thousands; source: MCG's SEC 10K filings)

	Year ended December 31,				
Statement of Income:	2015	2014	2013	2012	2011
Revenue	$ 4,501,223	$ 4,108,269	$ 3,214,591	$ 2,731,224	$ 2,269,548
Food, beverage and packaging costs	1,503,835	1,420,994	1,073,514	891,003	738,720
Labor costs	1,045,726	904,407	739,800	641,836	543,119
Occupancy costs	262,412	230,868	199,107	171,435	147,274
Other operating costs	514,963	434,244	347,401	286,610	251,208
General and administrative expenses	250,214	273,897	203,733	183,409	149,426
Depreciation and amortization	130,368	110,474	96,054	84,130	74,938
Pre-operating costs	16,922	15,609	15,511	11,909	8,495
Loss on disposal of assets	13,194	6,976	6,751	5,027	5,806
Total operating expenses	3,737,634	3,397,469	2,681,871	2,275,359	1,918,896
Income from operations	763,589	710,800	532,720	455,865	350,562
Interest and other income (expense), net	6,278	3,503	1,751	1,820	(857)
Income before income taxes	769,867	714,303	534,471	457,685	349,705
Provision for income taxes	(294,265)	(268,929)	(207,033)	(179,685)	(134,760)
Net income	$ 475,602	$ 445,374	$ 327,438	$ 278,000	$ 214,945
Earnings per share					
Basic	$ 15.30	$ 14.35	$ 10.98	$ 8.82	$ 6.89
Dilited	$ 15.10	$ 14.13	$ 10.47	$ 8.75	$ 6.76
Weighted average common shares outstanding					
Basic	31,092	31,038	30,957	31,513	31,217
Diluted	31,494	31,512	31,281	31,783	31,775

Figure 15.2 Chipotle Mexican Grill Consolidated Profit & Loss Statement, 2011–2015 (All numbers in thousands, except per share data; source: Chipotle's SEC 10K filings)

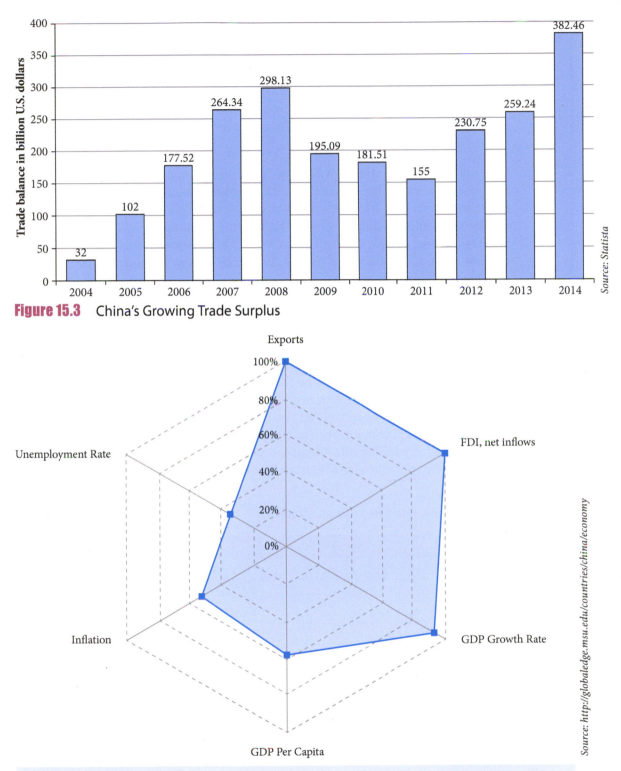

Figure 15.3   China's Growing Trade Surplus

How to interpret the graph: The purpose of this graph is to take a snapshot of a country's economy in comparison to other economies. For example, China's Exports rank is higher than 100% of the countries in the dataset. For Exports, FDI and GDP measures, a higher rank (closer to 100%) indicates a stronger economy. Conversely, for Unemployment and inflation, a lower rank (closer to 0%) indicates a stronger economy.

Figure 15.4   China's Economic Snapshot

Society & Culture

China shares geographical boundaries with fourteen Asian countries, including Mongolia, Russia, North Korea, Taiwan, Vietnam, Laos, Burma, Bhutan, Pakistan, Afghanistan, Tajikistan, India, Kazakhstan, and Nepal. So, it was no surprise that ethnic minorities comprised about 8 percent of the population and the Han Chinese made up the rest, or 92 percent. In addition to Mandarin and Cantonese, the Chinese people speak a multitude of dialects.

China is well known for its high-context culture, where communication rests not only on the spoken words but also the context. Confucianism, which dominates the Chinese philosophy and lifestyle, promotes duty, sincerity, loyalty, honor, and respect for age and seniority, among others. Maintaining harmonious relationships is at the heart of creating a stable society. This collectivistic focus means that individuals act in the best of interest of the group (family, work, etc.) rather than their own self-interest.

Blue Ocean in China's Market

In 2015, there were no Mexican quick service restaurant chains in China. The concept of quick service restaurants was not yet popular in China. As a result, if Chipotle were to enter China's market, it would be the first U.S. chain restaurant offering a unique Mexican quick service food experience. Chipotle could explore a large "blue ocean" in China with greater opportunities than its competition. In this blue ocean, several strategies, such as developing distinct competencies, identifying high traffic restaurant locations, and expanding into the urban markets first could be adopted. Table 15.1 below describes the differences between blue ocean and red ocean.

Table 15.1   Blue and Red Ocean Strategies

Blue Ocean Strategy	Red Ocean Strategy
Create uncontested market space	Compete in existing market space
Make the competition irrelevant	Beat in competition
Create and capture new demand	Exploit existing demand
Break the value-cost trade off	Make the value-cost trade off
Align the whole system of a firm's activities in pursuit of differentiation and low cost	Align the whole system of a firm's activities with its strategic choice of differentiation or low cost

Source: Blue Ocean vs. Red Ocean (W. Chan, 2005)

Place

Location selection was the most critical issue for business expansion, especially in international operations. Traditionally most U.S.-based restaurant chains entered the Chinese market by exploring major urban centers such as Beijing and Shanghai.

Some of the attractive characteristics of these major urban centers included high per capita income, considerable purchasing power, fast-paced urban life demanding conveniences of quick service restaurants, access to technology, modern cultural food habits, exposure to and acceptance of international foods, and a large population of international and domestic tourists seeking American food. Typically, urban customers had pervious exposure to international cuisines, making it easier for Chipotle to enter the Chinese market. In Beijing, highly desired locations were the first floor of upscale office buildings in the Zhongguancun area, SOHO, and food courts in large shopping malls. These locations were often characterized by high foot traffic, thus offering maximum exposure.

Menu Prices

Setting appropriate menu prices in China's market could be a tough decision to make for most U.S. restaurants for the following reasons. Even with the dramatic increase in the size of the middle class in China, the per capita income still lags behind the U.S. Furthermore, news that China experienced high inflation would result in dramatic increases in the cost of raw materials, gas, transportation, labor, real estate etc. In addition, Chipotle must be cognizant of the Chinese culture where numbers are associated with distinct meanings. For example, number "4" is associated with death. Therefore, it is imperative that Chipotle avoid "4" in all menu price-ending choices. In contrast, the number "8" is considered the most lucky, so it is highly advisable to end all prices in the digit 8 or other even digits, such as 6, 2, or 0. At the same time, odd digits have been considered less desirable in Chinese culture since the time of Confucius (Hu, Parsa, & Zhao, 2006). Despite this rule of thumb, one may find some McDonald's using 9 as a price-ending digit in certain locations of China following the policies of the U.S. counterparts. But it is more an exception than a rule.

In Beijing, the average price of a meal at McDonald's and KFC is ¥30, which is the equivalent of U.S. $5. In other words, this price ¥30 can buy a meal at McDonald's and KFC in China. Chipotle must consider these facts in choosing its pricing strategies in order to be competitive. Subway tried to buck the trend by charging ¥70 for their 12" subs. It was no surprise that consumers rejected it even though it was a good value for the size of a 12" sub. Culturally Chinese preferred a 6" sub for ¥30 over the 12" sub for more than twice the price. Eating large amounts of bread, as is the case with a 12" sub at a Subway, is also counter to the Chinese culture, as they prefer eating rice and noodles more than bread.

Promotion

Carefully developed marketing strategies can considerably increase overall brand image and subsequent revenues. The most commonly practiced restaurant marketing strategies in China include: product bundling (meal specials, multi-course deals, lunch discount bundles), special edition gifts (equivalent to holiday specials in U.S., weekend specials, slow Monday deals), and coupon strategies (all types of coupons, from product discounting to free food/drinks). Bundling can provide customers with a feeling of good value for money since things become cheaper when selling together. Chipotle China may want to consider offering bundled meals or platters to offer high value perception. Unlike some of the other cultures, lunch is the main meal of the day for most Chinese; thus, they prefer to have multiple items for lunch—making it a whole meal. Chipotle may want to offer bundled meal deals and include a small dessert cookie, etc.

Similarly, free refills on drinks are often perceived as a good deal in China. In China, it is not uncommon to see a loyalty program where loyal customers accumulate points towards a meal. It plays on the saving psychology of China. A typical Chinese customer is most likely to participate in loyalty programs if there is a reward attached. To attract the younger generations, Chipotle may consider an app where loyalty points are tracked, similar to the Starbucks app used in the U.S.

Physical Evidence

The physical evidence of a company is an impressive logo that can make more customers remember its image and maintain positive word-of-mouth advertising. Almost all popular food service chains in China rely on physical appearance, such as logos, to communicate their value propositions. For example, McDonald's visual image is a yellow capital M, so customers associate the big yellow M with McDonald's taste. KFC's physical evidence is an elderly man with glasses (Col. Sanders), which displays KFC as a worldwide popular brand. Chipotle China, in consultation with local experts, could consider developing a catchy logo/figure for promotional purposes similar to Ronald McDonald of McDonald's. To differentiate from the crowded quick service segment from the U.S., Chipotle may consider a Tex-Mex spokesperson as a champion of Chipotle brand. The hot pepper symbol can also be a good choice, as the colors in the logo are appropriate for the Chinese culture. The color red represents prosperity, so a bright red logo and interior décor may be well received by Chinese customers.

Distribution Strategy

Chipotle China has three options (and may be a hybrid of these three options) with its entry into China: 1) Direct entry as Chipotle corporate-operated restaurants; 2) Joint partnership with a Chinese restaurant company or an investment company; or 3) Franchise solely with local Chinese restaurant investors. All three modes were found to be successful by various companies in China. For example, Starbucks prefers to enter international markets as a direct entry. KFC and others prefer joint partnerships or franchising. Some companies prefer exclusive franchising arrangements. The mode of entry depends on the internal resources of the entering firm, socio-political and economic situation of the host country, the competitive nature of the market, and other macro-environmental markets. It is noteworthy that the Chinese Government banned the use of joint ventures between foreign and domestic Chinese companies in 2004, and that over 90% of Yum Brands' restaurants in China were company-owned resulting in profit margins as high as 15% of its sales in China.

Sustainability

Chipotle's mission includes sustainability and local sourcing. Continuing those practices may be a challenge for Chipotle as they seek local supply chains that are similarly committed to sustainability. Obtaining ingredients such as free-range pork and free-range chicken locally can pose a major challenge in China. Securing a supplier that can reliably supply safe, local produce can be another challenge. Crisis events like the Asian bird flu virus in 2013 serve to remind companies of the importance of establishing and developing good supply chains. If Chipotle could achieve sound local supply chains, it would be a major economic boost to the rural Chinese economy as well. Chipotle can be a good neighbor that supports local economies. It can set new precedents for other companies to follow the mantra of "doing good while doing well." At the same time, Chipotle China may learn from its local suppliers about Chinese taste preferences, regional differences, and cultural taboos.

Advertising Strategies

As a new brand entering a new market, Chipotle can be expected to invest extensively to build brand awareness. In addition, Chipotle may have to educate local consumers about burritos, a product which is not well known in China. Almost all Chinese office workers and college students heavily depend on the Internet both for work and for entertainment. Thus, online advertisement is one of the preferred means to reach these customers. Alternatively, Chinese youth use the Internet exclusively for entertainment. Thus, it would be best to use local social media to reach them.

Long-term Plan

The urban strategy is highly attractive for Chipotle but should be deployed with caution. Slow growth with highly established supply chain systems would be the best method of operation when entering China. A long-term plan may include about fifty Chipotle restaurants in China within the first five years. Most of these fifty outlets could be located in major cities like Beijing or Shanghai, or other major urban markets. To develop new methods and standardize the operational procedures, Chipotle may want to enter the market as a wholly owned subsidiary of Chipotle USA for the first five years. It can be followed by selected franchising for other markets.

Financial Projections

The following section provides financial projections for Chipotle operating units in Beijing in the first operational year, and is based on the research for this paper. This situation analysis is based on previous experiences of other U.S. restaurant chains and the knowledge of the foodservice industry in China. The following estimations are presented.

Table 15.2 Income Statement Projections per Restaurant.

Item	Year 1: Quarters Ended (dollars in thousands)				
	31-Mar	30-Jun	30-Sep	31-Dec	Total
Revenue	1003.8	1003.8	1003.8	1003.8	4015.2
Food, beverage and packaging	281	281	281	281	1124
Labor	302	302	302	302	1208
Occupancy cost	70	70	70	70	280
Other operating costs	50	50	50	50	200
General and admin. expenses	100	100	100	100	400
Depreciation and amortization	50	50	50	50	200
Pre-opening costs	100	20	0	0	120
Marketing	90	30	30	30	180
Total operating costs	1043	903	883	883	3712
Income from operation	**−39.2**	**100.8**	**120.8**	**120.8**	**303.2**
Interest and other expenses	30	30	30	30	120
Income before taxes	**−69.2**	**70.8**	**90.8**	**90.8**	**183.2**
Provision for income taxes	5	5	5	5	20
Net income	**−74.2**	**65.8**	**85.8**	**85.8**	**163.2**

Quick service retail sales in China depict the Asian quick service segment as a dominant component in the country. As shown in Figure 15.5, market shares of the top-five quick service chains in China remained relatively stable. However, quick service sales in China were expected to grow from approximately $85.4 billion in 2013 to about

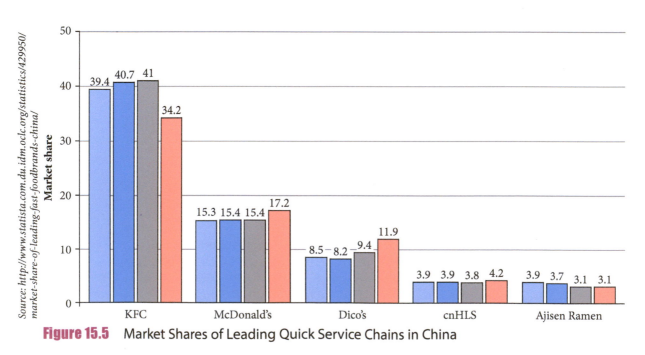

Source: http://www.statista.com.du.idm.oclc.org/statistics/429950/market-share-of-leading-fast-foodbrands-china/

Figure 15.5 Market Shares of Leading Quick Service Chains in China

$107.1 billion in the year 2016. Yum Brands announced that its subsidiary, Taco Bell, would reenter China in 2016–eight years after the latter closed for business in the Chinese market.

The main question facing Chipotle was whether China was the right market for Chipotle to expand. *"Do the right things in a right time at a right place,"* a Chinese adage, properly describes Chipotle's future path in China, which can be explained as exploring a brand-new market with huge potential. Chipotle's entry into the profitable Chinese market potentially could return very high returns on investment and could give Chipotle a worldwide reputation. Additionally, it could provide a platform for further expansion into Asian countries and boost them up the learning "curve." Specifically, if Chipotle China performed well in China, its profit from China's market could become another source of financing for further expansions. These profits could be used for further improvement, such as developing new products, setting more outlets up, and optimizing the internal management. Exploring China's market could also bring Chipotle into a regeneration stage within a huge "red ocean" of competition, and similar to McDonald's and KFC in China, Chipotle has the opportunity to become a household name in their new huge "blue ocean."

If Chipotle were to enter the Chinese market, it could create an integrated supply chain with many logistics centers in China, which could, in turn, simplify further restaurant expansion into other Asian countries, such as India, Japan, and the South Korea, some of the largest economies in Asia. From a financial aspect, a successful expansion in China can enhance the company's overall value, such as increasing the value of their stock and attracting more qualified human talent. In light of the 2015 foodborne illness reports from multiple states in the U.S., the key question was whether it made sense for Chipotle to pursue expansion plans into China at a time when it was mired with food contamination issues in the U.S. Alternatively, should Chipotle hold off on its international expansion plans to China or even consider expanding into China slowly? If Chipotle decides to enter China, what should be the correct mode of entry: totally company owned units, franchising, joint ventures, or some form of hybrid of the three modes of expansion?

As co-CEOs Ells and Moran sought to build their overseas business into a global presence, they faced many questions. Was China the answer to their quest for accelerated growth? Was it the right market for Chipotle? Could Chipotle embrace more sustainable development if it explored this new market properly? Could it gain high customer satisfaction and loyalty in the huge "blue ocean" market of China? Finally, was Chipotle in China a viable strategy for the company?

References

http://www.fool.com/investing/general/2014/04/26/1-thing-that-worries-me-about-chipotle.aspx

https://web.archive.org/web/20080403013733/http://rockymountainnews.com/news/2006/dec/23/chipotlefounder-had-big-dreams/; retrieved on March 17, 2016.

Ibid.

Based on the data presented in the Statista report on China.

Aune, M (2012). Making energy visible in domestic property markets: The influence of Advertisements, *Building Research & Information, 40* (6), 713–723.

Anand S (2011). Yum! Brands seek to add Little Sheep to its stable. *FinanceAsia,* 24–25.

Brady D. (2012). Yum's big game of chicken. *Bloomberg BusinessWeek*, 4273, 64–69.

Bell, D & Shelman, M (2011). KFC's radical approach to China. *Harvard Business Review, 89*(11), 137–142.

Brooks, S (2006). Tomorrow, the world, *Restaurant Business,* 1–8. From: resiauiantbiz.com

Cetron, M; DeMicco, F.J., Davies, O. (2014). *Hospitality 2015: The Future of Hospitality and Travel.* Educational Institute of the American Hotel and Motel Association. Orlando, FL.

Chipotle Mexican Grill, Inc. SWOT Analysis (2012), *Chipotle Mexican Grill, Inc.* 1–8.

Company profile: Chipotle Mexican Grill, Inc. (2012), *Chipotle Mexican Grill, Inc.* 1–8

Chen M & Flannery R (2013). China KFC supplier summer post 1st-Qrt low, business hurt by H7N9, safety concern. From: *Forbes.com*

Collins, M. and H.G. Parsa (2006). Pricing Strategies to Maximize Revenues in the Lodging Industry. *International Journal of Hospitality Management, 25,* 91–107.

Czinkota, M; Grossman, A; Javalgi, R & Nugent, N (2008). Foreign market entry mode of service firms: The case of U.S. MBA programs. *Journal of World Business*, 274–286.

Daley J (2012). Pie in the sky. *Entrepreneur. 40*(1), 96–96.

Fung M, Lain H, Remais J, Xu L & Sun S (2013). Food supply and food safety issues in China. *Lancet, 381* (9882), 2044–2053.

Grewal, D; Javalgi, R; Iyer, G & Randulovich, L (2011). Franchise partnership and international expansion: A conceptual framework and research propositions, *Entrepreneurship, 35*(3), 533–557.

Global Consumer Foodservice –Fast Casual Dining Set for Global Expansion (2009), *Euromonitor International.*

Hu, H.H., H.G. Parsa and J.L Zhao (2006). Magic of Price-ending Choices in European Restaurants: A Comparative Study of USA and Taiwan. *International Journal of Contemporary Hospitality Management, 18*(2), 110–122.

Hu, H.H., H.G. Parsa and M. Khan (2006). Effects of Price Discount Levels and Formats in Service Industries. *Journal of Services Research* 6 (special issue), 67–87 Jerzyk T (2011). Yum! Brands, Inc. *Wall Street Transcript, 187*(6), 2–5.

Jones, S; Peters, M; Otterman, J & Steele, E (2009). Chipotle's Market Potential Analysis, *International Marketing.* 1–17

Karabell, S (2013). What's ahead for 2013, *INSEAD Knowledge Publication*, 1–4.

Klohs, B (2012). Going global, *Economic Development Journal*, *11*(3), 27–34.

Levine-Weinberg, A. (2016). Chipotle Mexican Grill, Inc. Will Forge Ahead With Growth. *The Motley Fool Report*. Feb 6, 2016 at 3:15PM

Miller, P (2004). Quick service hits China, *China Business Review*, *31*(4), 18–28.

Naipaul, S. and Parsa, H.G. and (2001). Menu Price Endings that Communicate Value and Quality. *Cornell HRA Quarterly*, *42*(1), 26–37.

Orr, H (2013). CMG-Chipotle Mexican Grill Inc.—Company analysis and ASR rank report. *Alpha Street Research Reports*. 1–9.

Parsa, H.G. and S. Naipaul (2007). Price-ending Strategies and Managerial Perspective in the Hospitality Industry: A Reciprocal Phenomenon, Part I. *Journal of Services Research 7*(2), 7–26.

Parsa, H.G. and D. Njite (2004). Psychobiology of Price Presentations: An Experimental Analysis of Restaurant Menu Prices. *Journal of Hospitality and Tourism Research*, *28*(3) 263–280.

Parsa, H.G. and H.H Hu (2004). Price-Ending Practices and Cultural Differences in the Food Service Industry: A Study of Taiwanese Restaurants. *Food Service Technology*, *4*(1), 21–30.

Parsa, H.G. and F.A. Kwansa (2001). A Typology for Hospitality Franchise Systems: Strategic Choices for Hospitality Franchisees. *Journal of Restaurant and Foodservice Marketing*, *4*(2), 5–34.

Qi M (2012). The analysis of Chinese food safety issues: Legislations and government supervision, *Chinese Law & Government*, *45*(1), 3–9

Sacks, D (2012). Chipotle: For exploring all the rules of fast food. *Fast Company*. *163*, 124–126.

Terry A, Wang Z & Zhu M (2008). The development of franchising in China. *Journal of Marketing Channel*. *15*(2/3), 167–184.

The China Puzzle (2011). *Journal of Advertising Research*. *51*(4), 634–642.

Tobin, M (2006). Five myths of global expansion. *Financial Executive*, *22*(2), 57–59.

Vignali, C (2001). McDonald's: "think global, act local"- the marketing mix. *British Food Journal*. *103*, 97111.

Wary T (2007). Make you go Yum. *National Provisioner*. *221*(12), 16–19.

Yum Brands Inc. (2011). Case Study: Success fueled by developing markets, Yum Brands. *Inc.,* 1–16.

50 Trends Now Shaping the Future

For more than five decades, Forecasting International has conducted an ongoing study of the forces changing our world. In the 1980s, we condensed what we had learned into a list of trends we had seen at work in the world. We have updated that list frequently in the years since. For each study we undertake, we compare the specific circumstances of the industry, organization, or country with our trends and see how the two interact. The results have been gratifyingly accurate. In all, according to one of our clients, no fewer than 95% of our specific predictions proved correct.

This new edition updates our previous report on the implications for the hospitality industry of 52 major trends now shaping the future. Whatever your concern, some of these trends will have a very direct impact upon it. Others will help to form the general environment in which we live and work. They all merit attention from anyone who must prepare for what lies ahead.

General Long-Term Economic and Societal Trends

1. **Economic growth continues throughout the world, but not as fast as it used to.**

   - In 2017, all 45 national economies tracked by the Organization for Economic Cooperation and Development (OECD) were growing for the first time in memory. By the end of 2018, only Argentina had fallen into recession.

   - At the end of 2018, the yield curve of American interest rates had become inverted, signaling that a recession was likely, with an average lead time of 13 months. In addition, the stock market was in decline, having erased all the gains it had made during the year.

   - As recently as 2011, the global economy grew by about 4.1% per year. By 2015, it had slowed to about 3.1%. A year later, it was down to 2.9%, where it was expected to remain in 2018. Forecasts for the near term vary widely among authorities such as the World Bank, OECD, and the International Monetary Fund. Yet by the 2020s, analysts agree that worldwide economic growth will continue to slow.

     ✓ Reasons include population aging and declining workforce participation in the industrialized countries, the shrinking of China's working-age population, the likely failure of needed financial reforms in many developing lands, and much slower productivity improvement in the industrialized countries.

   Implications: Despite the apparent fragility of the American economy going into 2019 and the stresses visible elsewhere, we believe the recession of 2008 is likely to prove unique, at least through the 2020s. The current round of growth should continue with only brief and relatively minor interruptions for the remainder of this period.

   Under these conditions, global visitor flow is expected to grow more than 15% between 2016 and 2020. This would ensure the steady expansion of hospitality and travel at rates no slower than their accustomed 3+% annually.

Rapid economic growth in the less developed countries should provide investment capital that will encourage foundation of many new travel and hospitality services and destinations. However, slower growth in the wealthy economies could leave them competing for guests whose numbers are not expanding as fast as expected.

China's economy, though not buoyant as it once was, will continue to expand the middle class, making it the world's fastest growing source of international travel.

Although India so far has a much smaller middle class, its faster growth and vast population ensure that this country will be the second major new source of travelers throughout the world.

For the hospitality and travel industry, any future economic downturn is likely to cause, at worst, temporary inconvenience. After the Great Recession, it took less than two years for the industry to grow larger and more prosperous than it had ever been. We see no reason to expect worse from any future recession.

Monitor: Many factors could invalidate this trend. The following list covers the greatest concerns. We do not expect any of them to cause a global recession. Yet their consequences could be too severe to ignore.

International trade agreements have long helped power global economic growth. In 2017 and '18, changing American policy made it necessary to wonder how long this regime could survive. President Donald Trump backed out of the Trans Pacific Partnership, renegotiated the terms of the North American Free Trade Agreement with Canada and Mexico, threatened to back out of the country's trade agreements with the European Union, and pursued a damaging trade war with China. Some economists fear these last two measures could destabilize global trade and send the U.S., China, and the world into recession.

In the United States, too, the issues that triggered financial collapse in 2008 remain troubling. The International Monetary Fund warns that "too big to fail" financial institutions are even bigger today and little better regulated than in 2007, while stock and bond markets are accumulating risky bets that could send panicked investors stampeding for the exits. Welcome to Great Recession II.

This risk grew when the Trump administration set about dismantling the Dodd-Frank Act and other financial regulations that were, in our analysis, too weak to begin with. American finance, like American trade policy, must be watched closely.

In China, vast uncollectible debt, a real estate bubble, and other issues could throw the country into recession, taking the world with it. Beijing has always managed such threats successfully, and we do not expect it to fail this time. Unfortunately, the Chinese financial industry is hard to monitor effectively because data is scarce and widely suspected to be unreliable. Much of the debt is held by so-called "shadow banks," which are unregulated and do not provide financial reports. The trade war with Donald Trump's America could be one more stress than the Chinese economy can sustain.

Europe also faces problems. Brexit alone is expected to halve economic growth in the UK for several years and slow it less severely in the Euro zone. Nationalist movements in France, Spain, and many other parts of the Continent make further withdrawals conceivable. Decline of the European Union would not cause global recession, but it would make the world more vulnerable to other shocks.

See Trend 32 for information about another possible threat to the global economy.

2. In the developed world, economic growth is slowing.

- Performance of the world's largest economies is declining. The "Group of Twenty," or G20, economies—nineteen countries plus the European Union—provide roughly 85% of the world's GDP. OECD predicted G20 growth of 3.5% in 2017, up 0.4% from the previous year, and 3.8% in 2018. Actual growth came in at about 1% in 2017, with wide variation among the countries. and a fraction slower in 2018.
    - ✓ In 2016, only four member states grew faster than average: China, India, Indonesia, and Spain.
    - ✓ The United States, Japan, and much of Europe all trailed well behind.

- U.S. growth estimates from the World Bank, Economist Intelligence Unit (EIU), and United Nations vary between 2.1% and 2.6% growth per year in the near future. EIU calls 2% growth "the new normal" for the United States. OECD predicts that U.S. growth will decline from nearly 3% in 2017 to 2.4% in 2025 and steadily to 1.54% in 2050.

    - ✓ This is even less impressive than it seems. Growth of GDP per capita, which tells more about individual well-being, already has slowed from more than 2% annually to only 0.4%. Median real income has grown in the cities but stagnated in rural areas. In 2017, the American poor have less buying power than they did in 1964. No current or expected economic policies will improve this trend significantly. Many could make it worse.

- Thanks to forced austerity, the Continent was even slower to recover from the recession than the U.S., its growth rate never rising significantly above the 2% seen in 2015. Even without the effect of Brexit, it is not expected ever to break 2% again. In the late 2020s, it will begin a slow decline to 1.35%.

- Japan's long-stagnant economy was expected to grow by about 1.2% in 2017. Japan's GDP ended up 1.7% on the year. After 2018, it is not likely to exceed 0.8% annually through 2020, rising to just over 1.35% in 2030, a level it will not see again for more than twenty years.

Implications: Real incomes will grow more slowly than they used to, if at all. This will continue to erode expectations of personal advancement and the hope that children will have more comfortable lives than their parents did.

Millennials and Centennials will seek personal fulfillment in friendships, leisure activities, and other sources that do not depend on elective spending.

From Generation X on, it will be increasingly difficult for most people to save for retirement. This already has begun to reduce the rate of home ownership, as it is growing more difficult to save for a downpayment. In the longer run, it could reduce college attendance, as fewer families can afford it and the prospect of college debt is increasingly discouraging.

Contingent work will become more important in supplementing incomes, especially in retirement, but growing competition for opportunities means they will pay less well.

The income gap between well-paid and poorly paid workers will continue to grow.

Political instability is likely to grow as positions on the left, and especially the right, become increasingly entrenched.

Most markets, including those for travel and hospitality, will find mid-price, mid-service options squeezed out, as we have seen in family restaurants and the airline industry. Luxury accommodations and services for the rich will prosper, as will those for cash-strapped travelers. The growth segment is likely to be on the lower end of the spectrum, as many consumers are forced to cut back on leisure budgets and opt for "staycations," short-distance travel, and luxury weekends instead of longer, more costly vacations.

3. **Developing economies are outpacing the industrialized lands.**

- The world's emerging markets are growing faster than the wealthy, on average. However, they fall into three distinct groups:

    ✓ Economies based on commodity exports are growing slowly, by only 0.3% in 2016. The International Monetary Fund predicts several years of declining commodities prices, making it unlikely that these economies will accelerate soon. Some are likely to fall into recession.

    ✓ Export-based economies will remain unstable until they find some other way to generate income. This is a task for individual countries, and we do not expect to see much progress in it during the 2020s.

    ✓ Developing economies like China and India, but also Brazil, Egypt, Iran, Kenya, and Thailand are expected to near 6% by 2020. Discounting India and China, it will be around 5.2%.

    ✓ Extreme low-income economies like Angola, Myanmar, and Afghanistan are expected to vary widely, with Afghanistan growing around 3% in 2020, Angola around 2%, and Myanmar upward of 6%.

- China's official, but unreliable, growth rates have remained below 7% since 2015. Some independent observers estimate growth as low as 1% that year. Most estimates put rates at 6.2% to 6.5% through at least 2020. The EIU disagrees, foreseeing a decline to 4.2% in 2018 and '19. Our own best guess is that the Chinese economy will grow at about 6% through 2020, declining to 4% in 2025. Worse performance is entirely possible, especially if the trade war with the United States, under way as this is written, continues.

Implications: China's large economy, fast growth, and infrastructure-focused foreign policy will expand its influence among developing countries. Combined with isolationist policies in the United States, these will give it more global power, politically and economically.

India also will gain a bit of international influence. However, its vast population of the very poor and an entrenched, broadly corrupt bureaucracy will limit its options. The

New Delhi government will find it difficult to participate in foreign development programs, invest in overseas projects, contribute to disaster relief, and otherwise cultivate the kind of sway China is building.

Growing wealth could improve the lot of the poor in some developing lands. However, in many countries, most of the benefits will flow toward the existing oligarchies. Political instability is likely to grow as a result, especially where there are large populations of disaffected young men with little hope of economic or social advancement.

Tourists and business travelers from China, India, the wealthier parts of Latin America, and perhaps Nigeria will form the fastest-growing market for international travel.

4. The world's population will grow to 9 billion by 2050.

- Global population will grow from 7.3 billion in mid-2015 to at least 9.6 billion in 2050.

- The greatest fertility is found in those countries least able to support their existing populations. Countries with the largest population increases between 2000 and 2050 include Uganda (133%), the Democratic Republic of Congo (161%), Angola (162%), Yemen (168%), Niger (205%), and the Palestinian Territory (217%).

- Even these estimates may be too low. According to the Center for Strategic and International Studies (CSIS), most official projections underestimate both fertility and future gains in longevity. This seems entirely possible.

- In contrast to the developing world, many industrialized countries will see fertility rates below the replacement level and hence significant declines in population, excluding the effects of immigration. This means that the developed nations will fall from 23% of the total world population in 1950 and about 14% in 2000 to only 10% in 2050.

- In the mid-2020s, the workforce in Japan and much of Europe will be shrinking by 1% per year. By the 2030s, it will contract by 1.5% annually.

Implications: Growing populations in the better-off developing countries will provide vast new demand for both domestic and international travel and hospitality. In all developing nations and many industrialized countries, we can expect to see new hotels, resorts, and tour operators develop rapidly, both to meet this demand and, in less prosperous lands, to generate income and provide food for many more mouths.

Comparatively rapid population growth—from 319 million in 2014 to 400 million in 2015—will reinforce American domination of the global economy, as the European Union falls to third place behind the United States and China. Unless American policy prolongs the current trade war. In that case, all bets are off.

To meet human nutritional needs over the next 40 years, global agriculture will have to supply as much food as has been produced during all of human history. We believe it will succeed in doing so.

Unless fertility in the developed lands climbs dramatically, China and most of the industrialized nations could face increasingly severe labor shortages. Possible solutions include large-scale automation, the route favored by China and Japan, and encouraging even more immigration from the developing world. As a stopgap, potential retirees could remain on the job a few years longer. This is likely to make retaining experienced workers a priority for the hospitality industry, particularly in the developed countries.

Coping with tight labor markets, particularly in skilled fields, will require new creativity in recruiting, benefits, and perks, especially profit sharing. This hypercompetitive business environment will make it increasingly necessary to reward speed, creativity, and innovation among employees. Hospitality and travel especially will struggle to find greater efficiencies to continue offering the best in personal service with a shrinking workforce.

A fourth alternative is a sharp economic contraction and loss of living standards in countries across the economic spectrum. This is unlikely unless artificial intelligence brings the mass job losses and further concentration of wealth that some observers fear. Nonetheless, we recommend that companies and workers alike examine this scenario and develop a long-term strategy to cope with prolonged economic hardship.

Many developed countries, particularly the United States and much of Europe, are enacting strict immigration controls to slow the arrival of immigrants from lands that are less prosperous, less stable, and especially less white and Christian. We believe these measures will prove temporary, as the need for more workers becomes increasingly urgent. Thus, rapid migration will continue from the Southern Hemisphere to the North, and especially from former colonies to Europe. Hospitality companies, with long practice integrating new arrivals into their staffs, will be uniquely able to benefit from this trend.

5. **The population of the developed world is living longer.**

- Each generation lives longer and remains healthier than the last. Since the beginning of the twentieth century, every generation in the United States has lived three years longer than the previous one. An 80-year-old in 1950 could expect 6.5 more years of life; on average, today's 80-year-olds survive 9.4 more years.

- In 2017, twenty-five countries have average life expectancies at birth over 80 years. These include Japan, Australia, and Monaco, the world's longest-lived nation, where life expectancy is 89-plus. The United States, with a life expectancy of 78.5 and declining for several years, lags in 34th place. China, at 76.4 is 51st on the list.

- A major reason lives are growing longer is the development of new pharmaceuticals and medical technologies, which are making it possible to prevent or cure diseases that would have been fatal to earlier generations.

- In many developed countries, credit also goes to government health programs, which have made these treatments available to many or all residents. The growing restrictions on such programs contributes significantly to the decline of life expectancy in the U.S.

- In the developing lands, a primary cause is the availability of generic drugs, which cut the cost of care and make healthcare affordable even for the poor. Life expectancies should grow faster as China begins to clean its polluted air and water and public sanitation slowly improves in the crowded cities of India and Africa.

- Current forecasts of life expectancy may be much too conservative because they assume that life expectancy will grow more slowly in the future, argues the Center for Strategic and International Studies (CSIS). In fact, it seems more likely to accelerate.

Implications: Global demand for products and services aimed at the elderly can only grow quickly in the coming decades.

Vacation and leisure options for active seniors will be in particularly high demand.

If antibiotic resistance begins to cause outbreaks of untreatable disease, travel and hospitality will face unpredictable contractions wherever they occur. This will increase the need to be well-funded enough to endure severe and prolonged downturns in business.

Developed countries may face social instability as retirement-age boomers begin to compete for resources with their working-age children and grandchildren. CSIS predicts that public spending on retirement benefits in the U.S. and its peers could grow to one-fourth of GDP by 2050, even as the number of workers available to support each retiree declines sharply.

If automation causes widespread unemployment, as some now fear, supporting the elderly, the jobless, and impoverished families will require development of new funding mechanisms.

Barring dramatic advances in geriatric medicine, the cost of healthcare is destined to skyrocket throughout the developed lands. This could create the long-expected crisis in healthcare financing and delivery.

However, dramatic advances in geriatric medicine are all but inevitable. Based on studies in animals, the incidence of late-life disorders such as cancer, heart disease, arthritis, and possibly Alzheimer's disease should decline quickly beginning in the 2020s.

New drugs and technologies, though expensive, could begin to reduce the net cost of caring for patients who would have suffered from the disorders they ameliorate or prevent. Given a practical life-extension technology, the per-person lifetime cost of healthcare may even decline.

Monitor: Several medical developments merit attention:

After decades of research, treatments that slow the fundamental process of aging now seem to be within reach. They could well help today's middle-aged baby boomers to live far longer and in much better health, than even CSIS anticipates today. For the younger generations, such therapies appear almost sure to be available. We expect the first to reach clinical use by 2030.

A counter-trend is the growing resistance of bacteria to antibiotics. Untreatable infections already are seen often in Asia and are beginning to appear in Europe and the United States. They could soon return humanity to an age when a minor scratch could be fatal and common diseases often were. Replacement therapies are under development, but it is not yet clear whether they will be available before infections now considered minor begin to reduce life expectancy.

The third possibility is that entirely new diseases will appear or spread unexpectedly, like Ebola virus in the 1970s, HIV in the 1980s, the Zika epidemic in this decade, and new forms of influenza every few years. It is possible, too, that one or more of these novel pathogens will gain antibiotic resistance when they colonize a patient who already suffers from a resistant infection.

6. The elderly population is growing dramatically throughout the world.

- Throughout the developed world, population growth is fastest among the elderly. In Europe, the United States, and Japan, the aged also form the wealthiest segment of society.
    - ✓ In Germany, the retirement-age population will climb from under 16% of the population in 2000 to nearly 19% in 2010 and 31% in 2050.
    - ✓ By 2050, one in three Italians will be over 65, nearly double the proportion today.
    - ✓ Japan's over-65 population made up about 22% of the total in 2010 and is projected to reach nearly 37% in 2050.
- The world's 65-and-older population will grow from 617 million in 2010, 8.5% of the population, to 1.6 billion, 17%, by 2050. Three-fourths will be in developing countries, principally China, India, Brazil, Indonesia, and Pakistan.

Implications: Not counting immigration, the ratio of working-age people to retirees needing their support will decline dramatically in China, Germany, Italy, Russia, the United States and Japan by 2050. This represents a burden on national economies that will be difficult to sustain under many current medical and social security systems.

The growing concentration of wealth among the elderly, who as a group already are comparatively well off, creates an equal deprivation among the young and the poorer old. This implies a loss of purchasing power among much of the population. In time, it could begin to slow economic growth.

Although seniors average wealthier than other age groups, they include significant proportions of the middle-income and poor. This is especially true in the United States, where retirement and health programs are stingy at best and grow more so each year.

The need to counter the risks of a growing senior population and shrinking workforce is one reason China is investing heavily in automation, robotics, and artificial intelligence. Japan is following the same path, trying to replace the workers it will not have with intelligent manufacturing systems rather than importing labor. Germany, Italy, the U.S., and other countries are likely to adopt the same policy in the 2020s and beyond.

However, with its need for workers outpacing the development of AI and robotics, Japan also has been accepting more foreigners to take jobs that natives are not available to fill. Depending on the pace of AI development, China, many European countries, and the U.S. may be forced to follow Japan's lead.

Like many developing countries, the United States will need more doctors specializing in diseases of the elderly—at least double the 9,000 now available. Yet by 2030 the number of certified American geriatric specialists is expected to decline sharply. Caring effectively for the elderly will become more difficult just when it is needed most.

The nursing shortage is severe today and will grow much worse as the senior population expands. In all, the United States will be short 515,000 nurses by 2020, just as senior Baby Boomers begin to flood the healthcare system. Current and planned healthcare policies seem likely to aggravate this problem. Japan especially is working hard to develop personal-care robots to assist the elderly and make up for the expected shortage of health aides.

For hospitality and travel, this trend is a mixed blessing. Products and facilities for older guests will be in demand at all levels of the price spectrum. However, the elderly are likely to require more service from larger staffs better trained to meet their needs. Restrictions on immigration will make it difficult to serve this market until they are changed.

7. **Society is growing increasingly knowledge-dependent.**

- Information is the primary commodity of more and more industries, from accounting to Internet marketing. It is a critical component in many others, including the travel and hospitality sector. For example, computer outages forced Delta Air Lines to cancel more than 2,000 flights in August 2016 and about 280 the following January.

- By sales, the fastest growing industry in the U.S. is computer systems design and related services, according to a study of company financial statements.

- Online retail, an almost pure information industry, is booming. Ninety percent of American adults now shop online, and over 80% research large purchases online even if they buy from brick-and-mortar stores.

- Analyzing "big data" for useful insights is fast changing industries from healthcare to farming. Current estimates say that many so far capture only a fraction of the value their data have to offer: 30% to 40% in retail, 20% to 30% in manufacturing, and only 10% to 20% in healthcare.
  - ✓ The Chinese government is testing a system of "social credit" in which analyzing vast stores of data about people's social and financial behavior will determine whether individuals have access to travel, education, loans, and insurance coverage.

- The Federal Reserve Bank of St. Louis classifies American workers into four groups. Knowledge workers are by far the largest at about 60 million, up more than 9 million in only five years. Routine cognitive workers, who also trade in information, are in second place with only 33.6 million.

- The U.S. Bureau of Labor Statistics predicts that the number of computer and math jobs will grow by 13.1% in the decade through 2024. Only three occupational groups are growing faster. Two are in healthcare, where IT and other tech skills are mandatory.

- Eurostat, the EU's official statistics keeper, reports that the number of positions for IT professionals is growing eight times faster than total employment.

- Telecommuters are knowledge workers almost by definition. About 3.3 million full-time professionals in the U.S. report working primarily at home, not counting volunteers and freelancers. Some 60% of employed Americans now do at least some of their work at home. About half of all jobs in the U.S. are compatible with remote work.

- In the United States, the "digital divide" seems to be closing. According to Pew Research, at least 78% of households in the U.S. use the Internet, even in the lowest income group. Differences based on age and education are much greater. In the 18 to 29 age group, 97% are Internet users, compared with 60% of retirees. Similarly, 91% of people 18 to 29 own a smartphone, compared with 34% of those over 65, and 96% connect to the Net through a mobile device. Among those with at least a college degree, 96% use the Net, compared with 61% of those without a high-school degree. A much larger gap appears in home broadband use: Only 45% of households with incomes less than $30,000 per year have broadband access at home, compared with 90% of those with incomes between $70,000 and $100,000.

Implications: The travel and hospitality industries will face a growing need for tech skills—for collection of guest data, online marketing, and implementation of competitive methods based on IT. Fortunately, nearly all Millennials and their younger siblings will able to provide them.

As these skills propagate to unserved regions of Africa, Asia, and Latin America, resorts and other far-off destinations there will be better able to attract well-to-do guests from the U.S. and Europe.

Business innovation is becoming "almost costless," according to the World Economic Forum. Because of this, companies will face growing pressure to innovate continuously. They also are likely to face new, fast-changing regulations to encourage the online economy and cope with new technologies.

Knowledge workers are generally better paid than less-skilled workers, and their proliferation is raising overall prosperity. It also raises costs in IT-heavy industries, but the added profits more than compensate.

Even entry-level workers and those in formerly unskilled positions require a growing level of education. For a good career in almost any field, computer competence is mandatory. This is one major trend raising the level of education required for a productive role in today's workforce. For many workers, including most Millennials and Centennials, the opportunity for training is becoming one of the most desirable benefits any job can offer.

New technologies create new industries, jobs, and career paths, which can bring new income to developing countries. One example of many is the transfer of functions such as technical support in the computer industry to Asian divisions and service firms.

For some developing countries, computer skills are making it faster and easier to create wealth than a traditional manufacturing economy ever could. India, for example, is rapidly growing a middle class, largely on the strength of its computer and telecom industries. Other pre-industrialized lands are likely to follow its example.

8. Mass migration is redistributing the world's population.

- Immigration and differential birth rates are quickly changing the ethnic composition of the U.S. By 2044, non-Hispanic whites will be less than half of the population. This process has slowed somewhat since 2017. We expect it to accelerate again in the 2020s.

- Between 2015 and 2065, immigrants and their first-generation children will grow from 324 million to 441 million; immigrants will make up 18% of the American population, their children another 18%. The Hispanic population will rise from 18% to 24%, Asians from 6% to 14%.

- Europe is changing as well, and for similar reasons. In 2014, 784,800 people received EU citizenship. Of these, 29% came from Africa, 21% from the Americas, 20% from Asia, and 18% from non-member states within Europe. On Jan 1, 2015, immigrants from outside the EU made up more than 10% of the populations of Ireland, Austria, Belgium, Cyprus, Latvia, and Estonia. In Luxembourg, they were 46%. Again, this process has slowed in response to local populist movements. It seems unlikely to resume until the growing shortage of workers in the least fertile parts of Europe becomes intolerable. In Eastern Europe, it will take even longer.

- The UN estimates that the Continent's population will decline from about 738 million in 2015 to about 707 million by 2050. At the same time, Christians will shrink from 74.5% of the European population to 65.2%, while Muslims will grow from 5.9% to 10.2%.

- In China, 98 million people have moved from rural areas to cities in recent years. For census and employment data, they are still counted as farm workers and are considered employed by definition. This makes it difficult to track the real condition of the Chinese economy.

- There are about 80 million international migrant workers in the world, according to the United Nations. About half settle in Europe; the rest are divided evenly between North America and Asia.

- In addition, an estimated 65.3 million people have been forcibly displaced from their homes, according to the UN High Commissioner for Refugees. One-third are refugees; 53% of them from just three countries: Somalia, Afghanistan, and Syria. Another 5.2 million are Palestinian. In 2015, only 107,000 refugees were resettled. The Middle East and Africa host 68% of the rest. Only 12% of refugees come to the Americas, 6% to Europe.

Implications: Throughout the U.S. and Europe, demand will grow for restaurants featuring the cuisine of today's migrant-donor countries.

Immigrants who fly home to visit relatives are adding to demand for air travel.

Impoverished migrants are straining social welfare systems in the Middle East and Europe.

Similar problems are likely to afflict the urban infrastructures of China and India in the 2020s.

Remittances from migrants to their native countries are helping to relieve poverty in many developing lands. According to the World Bank, remittances to developing countries totaled $431.6 billion in 2015.

Significant backlashes against foreign migrants already are common, including skin-head movements in Europe and anti-immigration politicians such as Donald Trump and Marine Le Pen. Such reactions will be seen more frequently in the years ahead.

Similar responses will be seen even in the most peaceful lands. For example, in Sweden, resentment against foreign workers is growing, in part because undocumented immigrants are beginning to drive down pay scales for all. Some 163,000 asylum seekers and an unknown number of migrant workers from Eastern Europe arrived in Sweden in 2015. Some 15% of the country's population is foreign-born.

9. Growing acceptance of cultural diversity, aided by the unifying effect of mass media, is promoting the growth of a truly integrated global society. However, this is a slow process and very much subject to local interruptions and reversals.

- Migration is mixing disparate peoples and forcing them to find ways to coexist peacefully and productively, often to the dismay of local majority populations.
- Information technologies promote long-distance communication as people hook up with the same commercial databases and computer networks, and above all social media.
- Television is even more homogenizing, as it encourages the spread of standard accents and language patterns, particularly in the United States.
- Within the United States and Europe, regional differences, attitudes, incomes, and lifestyles are blurring as business carries people from one area to another.
- In many places, intermarriage also mixes cultures geographically, ethnically, socially, and economically.
- Minorities are beginning to exert more influence over national agendas as the growing number of African-Americans, Hispanics, and Asians in the United States is mirrored by the expanding population of refugees and former "guest workers" throughout Europe.
- A 2015 poll found that between 78 and 88% of the populations of France, Germany, Luxembourg, Estonia, and Latvia considered themselves citizens of the European Union, at least secondarily. EU-wide, at least half the population felt like citizens of the Union. Brexit notwithstanding, so did 15% of Britons. About 5% identified with the EU more than their native country.
- Even in the United States, a 2016 poll of young adults found that 35% of 18- to 26-year-olds considered themselves to be more citizens of the world than of the U.S. Among 18- to 21-year-olds, it was 42%.

Implications: Over the next half century, growing cultural exchanges at the personal level will help to reduce some of the conflict that plagued the twentieth century.

However, this already inspires a political backlash, and sometimes a violent one, in societies where xenophobia is common. This can be seen in the rise of populist politicians in the U.S., France, and other countries.

Some of the most fervent "culturist" movements will continue to spring from religious fundamentalism. Would-be dictators and strongmen will use these movements to promote their own interests, ensuring that ethnic, sectarian, and regional violence will remain common. Terrorism especially will be a continuing problem.

Companies will hire ever more minority workers and will be expected to adapt to their values and needs. Much of the burden of accommodating foreign-born residents will continue to fall on employers, who must make room for their languages and cultures in the workplace. Travel and hospitality, of course, have long been accustomed to these challenges.

However, the greatest responsibility will continue to fall on two public institutions, schools and libraries. Primary concerns for schools include providing all students with a solid grounding in the local majority language and, in the United States, finding ways to recruit and reward the best teachers and weed out the least effective. Libraries act as sites for after-hours learning, reference facilities, sources of Net access for those who do not have it at home, and sometimes bad-weather shelters for the homeless.

10. The global economy is growing more integrated.

- The single most powerful force in this process is the Internet, which allows companies to find customers and suppliers in distant lands, competing on an even footing despite differences in size and history. Second is the dense network of cargo ships, aircraft, and package delivery services that carry products quickly and reliably even to remote corners of the world.

- Major trade agreements also help unify large parts of the global economy. These include the European Union, with a population of 522 million and GDP of $16.5 trillion in 2015; the North American Free Trade Agreement, which helped quadruple trade among the U.S., Canada, and Mexico in twenty years and appears to have survived the challenges of 2018; the ASEAN-China Free Trade Area, with eleven member states, a combined population over 580 million, and 40% of global GDP; and Mercosur in Latin America, with four full members and six associate members, total population of 383 million, and $3.2 trillion in combined GDP. Although the effect of such agreements on jobs is disputed, the consensus among economists is that they benefit signatories by accelerating economic growth.

  - ✓ Within the European Union, uniform product standards and the free movement of goods, capital, and people adds an estimated €5,700 of extra income per household, or about 31%.
  - ✓ The Trans-Pacific Partnership scuttled by the Trump administration would have provided for free trade among a dozen countries with a combined population of 800 million and 40% of the world's GDP.

- Outsourcing is yet another factor uniting economies. Rather than pay salaries and benefits for activities that do not contribute directly to the bottom line, companies like IBM, Boeing, Hewlett Packard, and General Motors Powertrain are farming out secondary functions to suppliers, service firms, and consultants, many of them located in other countries.

- ✓ By 2022, the global market for business process outsourcing (BPO) is expected to reach $262.2 billion. BPO to the Asia-Pacific region is growing at a CAGR of 8.5% per year.
- ✓ Knowledge process outsourcing—involving professional-level research and analysis skills in advanced business, engineering, law, and science—is expected to grow by 23% yearly through 2019.
- ✓ Even scientific research and engineering are being outsourced. Cyagen, in China, specializes in bioinformatics and claims it can save American customers 82% of the cost and 64% of the time compared with handling such tasks in-house.

- In the European Union, relaxation of border and capital controls and the adoption of a common currency and uniform product standards have long made it easier for companies to distribute products and support functions throughout the Continent.
- NAFTA has had a similar, though much less sweeping, effect in North America.

Implications: President Trump's reconciliation with China and decision not to leave the North American Free Trade Alliance once suggested that an advisor who understood trade relationships might have won out over the far-right bomb-throwers who formerly had his attention. That impression died in mid-2018, when he imposed tariffs on China, Canada, and the EU—several of America's largest trade partners and its oldest allies—at the cost of American jobs that depended on cheap raw materials. We now believe only one firm forecast is possible: Whatever President Trump does about trade, it will be reversed, and order restored, the moment his successor takes office.

In Europe, any Brexit "deal" between Britain and the EU will be burdensome enough for the U.K. to discourage other member states from making the same mistake.

The growth of global commerce on the Internet reduces some hospitality costs by depressing the price of nonperishable supplies. At the same time, it subjects workers in the industrialized lands to competition by their peers in low-cost economies, helping to keep labor costs under control.

It also ensures that hospitality destinations in one part of the world compete for guests who could find similar attractions elsewhere, putting added pressure on prices in the low-cost and mid-range segments of the industry.

The continuing growth of international trade and competition will increase the need for foreign-language training, employee incentives suited to other cultures, aid to executives going overseas, and the many other aspects of doing business in other countries. These are needs the travel and hospitality sector is well equipped to meet.

11. Militant extremism is spreading and gaining power.

- Although terrorists prefer to attack military, police, and government installations when possible, the hospitality and travel industry is a soft, and therefore inviting, target. An incomplete tally of incidents in 2016 found 23 attacks on restaurants and bars, 13 on hotels, three on airports, one attempted airliner bombing, an old-fashioned hijacking, and an assault on a sports facility.

- The Muslim lands are associated with terrorism for a reason. They are, on average, overcrowded and poor. Virtually all have large populations of young men, often unemployed, who are attracted to violence, especially in service to a cause. When religious extremists seek to advance their political, social, and doctrinal views through terrorism, they have a ready market. They also are, on average, much more eager to cause mass casualties than others.

  ✓ See data on sex selection in Trend 34 for an important aggravating factor.

- Yet, militant extremism is much more widespread around the world and springs from a variety of sources. In its 2015 Country Report on Terrorism, the U.S. State Department reported that terrorism is becoming "increasingly decentralized and diffuse."

- The 32 terrorist attacks completed in the United States between 2010 and 2018 support this analysis.

  ✓ Thirteen were clearly related to Muslim extremism. Three more appear to have been prompted by personal animosity, with religious fervor an after-thought. Two of these involved attackers with histories of mental illness whose motives were even less clearly religious or political.

  ✓ One was motivated by black radicalism.

  ✓ Fifteen emerged from movements associated with the extreme right. Three incidents targeted Planned Parenthood clinics. Four were overtly anti-government attacks by right-wing extremists. Ten were carried out by white supremacists. One was an anti-Semitic attack at a Jewish community center. Another targeted a mosque.

- Most terrorist attacks in the United States and many in Europe are carried out by native-born or naturalized citizens, rather than recent immigrants.

  ✓ Among nine Muslim extremists arrested or killed in the terrorist attacks above, four were foreign-born. Four of them were naturalized citizens, one having lived in the U.S. since the age of two. Three were Muslims born in the United States. One was an American-born convert.

  ✓ A study of 104 individuals indicted in the U.S. for crimes related to the Islamic State and eight more who died while committing them found that nearly two-thirds were born in the United States. Another 20% were nationalized citizens. Only three were refugees, and one of them became radicalized only after arriving in the U.S.

  ✓ About 100 Americans and 4,000 Western Europeans have joined ISIS and other militant groups in Iraq and Syria.

- Afghanistan, Iran, Mauritania, Saudi Arabia, Sudan, and Yemen all are ruled by Muslim theocracies. Only Iran is considered an extremist regime.

  ✓ However, in late 2018 the government of Afghanistan controlled barely more than a third of its provinces, and all but Mauritania have active extremist movements that could gain control or force the government to support their positions. So do many other states.

- The British government lists part or all of 32 countries with "a high risk of terrorism" or advises travelers that "attacks are likely." They include most of North Africa, the Middle East, the Philippines, Russia, and much of Europe, with plus France, Germany, and Italy, rated "very likely."

  ✓ Many more countries are cited as having a "general" or "underlying" threat of terrorism.

- Latin America is an exception to this trend. The region once saw frequent small-scale terrorist attacks, more than any other part of the world. It is much more peaceful than a generation ago.

  ✓ A major reason is Colombia's peace with the Revolutionary Armed Forces of Colombia, ending a half-century war.

  ✓ Lesser threats survive in Colombia, Panama, Paraguay, Venezuela, and Peru. Parts of Mexico are rated dangerous, but violence there is drug-related, not political.

Implications: Terrorism will remain a threat to the hospitality and travel industry for many years. Restaurants, bars, hotels, and public gatherings like concerts rarely have the kind of security that could prevent attacks—hotels in Israel are the exception—and the slaughter of happy innocents guarantees the publicity terrorists seek.

The most common international attacks, and the bloodiest, will continue to emerge from Muslim extremism.

Terrorist events in Europe will continue to grow more frequent, especially as native-born Muslims return home after fighting with ISIS and other terrorist organizations. Countries most at risk will be those that contributed the most fighters: France (estimated at 1,200), the UK (500 to 600), Germany (500 to 600), Belgium (440), and the Netherlands (200 to 250).

Virtually all Muslim lands face an uncertain, and possibly bleak, future of political instability and growing violence. Exceptions may be the oil states, where money can still buy relative peace, at least for now.

Simple solutions to terrorism, such as travel bans, will not work when most terrorist attacks in the U.S. and Europe were carried out by native-born citizens, and many of the rest by naturalized citizens.

Western lands will experience acts of terrorism designed to cause mass casualties so long as they remain active in the Muslim world.

Yet, the greatest risk to the U.S. will be native militants on the anti-government end of the political spectrum.

The takeover of another legitimate government by an extremist regime would give terrorists larger operating budgets, safe havens, the opportunity to coordinate operations by diplomatic communications, perhaps military resources, the use of government laboratories for weapons development, and conceivably access to weapons of mass destruction. At least one can be expected in the 2020s.

Trends in Values, Concerns, and Lifestyles

12. Societal values are changing rapidly, but change inspires strong reactionary movements.

- Developed societies increasingly take their cue from the Millennials, rather than the Baby Boomers who dominated its thinking for most of four decades. Acceptance of same-sex marriage, the protection of LGBTQ rights, marijuana legalization, and the growing concern about inequality all reflect core values of inclusion and personal freedom shared by Generation X and, to an even greater degree, the Millennials and Centennials following close behind.

  - ✓ Acceptance of LGBTQ rights especially has provoked strong, often violent traditionalist reactions in socially conservative lands including Azerbaijan, Chechnya, Egypt, Indonesia, Tanzania, and—less violently, so far—the United States.
  - ✓ Strong populist movements in the United States and Europe are largely a rejection of nontraditional values—obvious examples include freedom of gender choice and expression—and the elevation of free trade over the needs of middle and lower economic classes.

- Millennials tend to be, on average, much less nationalistic than their elders. (See Trend 7.) Even in the United States, a 2016 poll of young adults found that 35% of 18- to 26-year-olds considered themselves to be more citizens of the world than of the U.S. Among 18- to 21-year-olds, it was 42%.

- This will tend to homogenize basic attitudes throughout the world, because younger generations around the globe often have more in common with each other than with their parents and grandparents.

- Industrialization raises educational levels, changes attitudes toward authority, reduces fertility, alters gender roles, and encourages broader political participation. This process is just beginning throughout the developing world. Witness the growing literacy, declining fertility, and broadening voter turnout seen in India since the turn of the century.

- In the U.S., both self-reliance and cooperation are increasingly valued— self-reliance because of the fear that Social Security, pensions, and other benefits soon could be unavailable; cooperation because group action often is the best way to optimize the use of scarce resources, such as retirement savings. In this, society already is beginning to follow where the Millennials lead.

- Post-September 11 worry over terrorist attacks has led Americans to accept almost without comment security measures that once would have seemed intolerable. This continues a long-established tendency in the United States to prefer a greater sense of safety at the cost of increased government surveillance and intervention in private lives. (See also Trend 13.)

- Once national security issues lose their immediacy, family issues will again dominate American society: universal healthcare, day care, early childhood education, the switch from fossil fuels to renewable energy, and stronger protections for the environment. This may be delayed until Millennials inherit political dominance from their elders.

Implications: This change will occur despite fierce opposition from conservative voters and their leaders.

Reaction against changing values is one of the prime motives of cultural extremism in the U.S., Europe, and particularly in the Muslim world and in parts of India.

Nonetheless, the increasingly polarized political environment that has plagued the United States since the 1980s will slowly moderate as the results-oriented Millennials begin to dominate the national dialogue.

Populist changes enacted by the Trump administration and its equivalents in Europe are inherently temporary.

The evolution of values toward inclusion and tolerance will prove to be a global trend, as members of Generation X and the Millennials tend to share values throughout the world.

The market for specialty services like gay-themed cruises can only grow and become more diversified. Some new, entrepreneurial destinations are likely to specialize in extremely narrow market niches based on sexuality, social values—think voluntourism and, less laudably, poverty tourism—perhaps heritage, and other such identifiers.

13. Privacy is dying.

- The greatest change has occurred in the United States, where the impact of the 9/11 attacks have prompted Americans to trade privacy for security to a degree that previously would have been unthinkable.
- The National Security Agency in the United States, the Government Communications Headquarters in Britain, and their counterparts in Russia, Australia, Canada, and many other nations routinely monitor telephone calls, Twitter and Facebook posts, financial transactions, international travel, and many other activities that once would have been considered private.

  - ✓ In the U.S., much surveillance has been contracted out to commercial services. Some 70% of the national intelligence budget is reported to fund private contractors, who are not subject to the Freedom of Information Act or oversight by watchdog organizations.
  - ✓ Under rules passed early in 2017, personal information collected by one American intelligence agency can be shared among 16 others before privacy protections take effect.

- To pre-screen airline passengers, the Transportation Security Administration searches tax data, past itineraries, property records, and reportedly social media accounts, many of which once would have been considered private.
- China has set out to build a nationwide facial recognition system that will monitor the locations and activities of its 1.3 billion residents, identifying any individual within three seconds. The initial target of only 90% accuracy can be expected to rise quickly with improvements in AI. (See Trend 32.)
- Automated license-plate readers perform much the same kind of surveillance in many American cities.

- Commercial credit-reporting services, online marketers, and social media companies routinely gather data on income, spending patterns, credit ratings, medical conditions, and many other sensitive personal characteristics.

  - ✓ In one famous example, parents learned their teenage daughter was pregnant when Internet marketers began sending her advertising for baby supplies.

  - ✓ Google's new "Google Attribution" matches online data with credit-card sales in brick-and-mortar stores to help advertisers better target their campaigns. The service covers 70% of all U.S. card transactions.

- All information in private hands is routinely collected by hackers breaking into private databases, as in the 2017 Equifax breach, which exposed names, addresses, birth dates, Social Security numbers, and other information about nearly 150 million American consumers.

- The "Internet of Things" is expected to carry data from an estimated 100 billion cameras, cars, appliances, factory machines, and other devices by 2025. It will provide still more opportunities for collection of personal data.

Implications: Ready availability of consumer data will improve resource management, allowing manufacturers, utility companies, and government to produce and distribute products and services as needed, with less waste.

In theory, this should reduce the environmental impact of production and distribution activities by eliminating trash, wastewater, and greenhouse gases.

However, totalitarian governments will use unlimited surveillance powers to tighten their grasp on power.

The potential for misuse of personal data is unlimited, even in democratic societies.

If anyone knows something about an individual, virtually anyone who cares to can learn it.

14. Young people place less importance on economic success, which many now believe is in doubt.

- Throughout the 1990s and the beginning of the 21st century—effectively, the adult lives of Generation X and the formative years of Millennials—these generations knew only good economic times. The Great Recession seemed to many a life-changing cataclysm, rather than an exaggerated, but essentially normal, phase of the business cycle.

- Some 80% of Millennials in the U.S. say their version of the American Dream is still possible, and between half and two-thirds throughout the world expect to be better off than their parents' generation. However, top values are family, education, and health/wellness. Wealth came in fourth or fifth, depending on ethnic group and social factors.

  - ✓ Worldwide, 95% say work/life balance is important to them. For 70%, it is very important. Millennials in Japan were least likely to find this issue "very important," but 85% still said it was important.

- In a study of 27 countries, almost 40% of people aged 18 to 30 said they will never have enough money to retire. In the U.S., the number is 20%, but only 45% said they currently had enough money to meet their daily needs. The biggest concern of young adults in North America, Europe, and Asia was the economy.

- In the United States especially, most young people have high aspirations, but many lack the means to achieve them. Millennials are, on average, the best educated generation in history. Yet, only one in three high-school graduates goes on to receive a college degree. Many of the rest wish to, but cannot afford the high cost of further schooling. The real income of American high-school graduates has declined steadily for more than 50 years.

  - ✓ Until 2011, median income among Millennial households was up to 20% less after inflation than their Baby Boom parents earned at the same age. Millennials now have caught up: In 2017, a typical three-person Millennial household earned as much as Boomers or Generation X at the same stage of life. This may reflect the greater proportion of college graduates in this new cohort.

- In Europe, the situation is more complex.

  - ✓ Only 83% of the EU population ages 20 to 24 has attained an "upper secondary level" education, roughly equivalent to high school in the U.S. Nationally, the numbers range from 53.8% in Turkey to 96% in Croatia.

  - ✓ On average, 12% left school without completing any secondary education.

  - ✓ Yet, among those aged 30 to 34, nearly 39% have a college degree or the equivalent. In 17 EU member states plus Norway, Iceland, and Switzerland, more than 40% had completed some form of tertiary education. In the UK, Ireland, Cyprus, Luxembourg, and Lithuania, the number is 50% or more.

- Even with a higher education, many will find it hard to achieve financial stability.

  - ✓ The average American who graduate in 2016 carried $28,446 in student loans, with nearly $40,000 expected for the class of 2017. Many owe several times that. Forty percent report that debt makes it impossible to save. Only 39% believe they will be able to pay off their debt in ten years.

  - ✓ Many find that core American aspirations such as marriage and home ownership are far out of reach. In 1968, 56% of people age 18 to 31 were married and living on their own. Today, 69% of people in that age group said they would like to be married and living in their own household. Yet, only 26% are.

  - ✓ Some 40% of minimum-wage workers hold a college degree.

Implications: As relatively well-off Baby Boomers pass from the scene and more guests come from the younger generations, the market for high-end facilities and services is likely to shrink, while less costly options will be in even greater demand.

This does not mean that luxury travel and hospitality will soon be short of guests. Generation X is expected to inherit more wealth than any generation in history. Nearly all of it will go to those who already are well off. The greater change will come with the Millennials.

Gen X and Millennial entrepreneurs are largely responsible for the current economic growth in India and China. In India, the younger generations dress and think much more like their American counterparts than like their parents. In China, the democratic fervor that once spawned the Tiananmen Square protests has been replaced by capitalist entrepreneurialism.

If younger-generation workers find their ambitions thwarted, they will create growing pressure for economic reform. If reforms do not come fast enough in the developing world, disappointed expectations will raise the number of young people seeking to emigrate to the developed lands.

Disappointment also will drive underemployed young men in the developing world into fringe political and religious movements. This will support continued terrorism and instability, with profound effects on the cultures and economies of the United States and many European countries.

15. Travel (especially international) and tourism are growing fast, as they have done for many years.

- Worldwide, international arrivals passed 1 billion for the first time in 2011 and are now rising by upward of 50 million each year. In 2017, they grew by 7%, well above the UN World Tourism Organizations long-term forecast of 3.8%.

- Outbound tourism is growing equally fast. In 2015, 32.8 million Americans traveled abroad. In 2016, outbound tourism grew by 3.3% from the Americas, 3.8% from Europe, 6% from Asia, and 4.2% from the Middle East. All markets are expected to grow by at least that much in 2017.

- The World Travel and Tourism Council predicts that the industry's direct contribution to global GDP will grow by 3.1% through 2020 and 4.2% annually through 2026, while direct employment climbs by 2.5% per year.

  ✓ The 2020 estimate has been reduced slightly owing to slower-than-expected economic growth in the U.S. and U.K., so expect the longer-term average also to come in a bit below expectations.

- In the United States, the number of international visitors is expected to grow from about 77.5 million in 2015 to 90.1 million in 2020, with travel expenditures rising from $971.1 billion to $1.147 trillion. Domestic travel is expected to grow from about 1.718 billion "person-trips" to 1.871 billion, spending from $814 billion to $958 billion.

- Outbound tourism from China alone is expected to grow from around 125 million in 2016 to nearly 200 million in 2020. By 2030, the Chinese Tourism Outbound Research Institute expects to see 400 million Chinese outbound trips, nearly half of all international travel that year.

- China soon will be the world's most popular destination, with 130 million arrivals expected in 2020. The government's five-year tourism plan projects tourism revenue of about $1 trillion in 2020.

- By 2020, 50 million Indians are expected to tour overseas, up from 13.3 million in 2014. However, only one in five will travel for leisure. The rest will be executives traveling for business, students off to school, and others with goals other than a good vacation.

- Tourism will benefit as Internet "virtual" tours on the Internet, being converted fast to virtual reality, replace printed brochures in promoting vacation destinations.
- Multiple, shorter vacations spread throughout the year will continue to replace the traditional two-week vacation.
- More retirees will travel off-season, spreading travel evenly throughout the year and eliminating the cyclical peaks and valleys typical of the industry. According to the American Association of Retired Persons, 99 percent of retirees plan at least one leisure trip per year, with many aiming for five.

Implications: The high priority of work-life balance among Millennials (see Trend 11) ensures that time off for travel and other forms of recreation will remain a priority for at least the next two generations.

The growing fraction of young adults who view themselves as citizens of the world, rather than of their home country (see Trend 10), also augurs well for international travel.

The hospitality industry will grow at a rate of at least 5% per year for the foreseeable future, and perhaps a bit more. Tourism offers growing opportunities for out-of-the-way destinations that have not yet cashed in on the boom. This will make it an important industry for still more developing countries.

Steady growth will make hospitality one of the most inviting fields for workers seeking stable careers. In the U.S., accommodation and food services lost 4.2% of its workers in the Great Recession, compared with 7.75% for the whole economy. Hospitality made up that loss in less than two years. At the end of 2018, it provided over 22% more jobs than before the recession, compared with only 7.4% in the overall economy.

Marketing to Millennials will require a light touch. Centennials are likely to be even more challenging. Distaste for obvious salesmanship is almost universal. Some 34% of those aged 18 to 35 say they like a brand more if it uses social medial, more than twice as many as older shoppers. Forty-four percent use text messaging to communicate with others about a product, service, or brand, compared with 32% in Gen X and only 15% of Boomers.

By 2030, travel and tourism are expected to provide more than 150 million jobs directly, according to the World Travel & Tourism Council. Including indirect employment, the industry will support 322.67 million jobs, 10.1% of the world total.

16. The physical-culture and personal-health movements will remain strong, but far from universal.

- In one study, Millennials valued health and wellness second only to family. Fully 84% reported exercising at least once a week, and nearly half said exercise was their passion.
- Among Boomers, 46% say "healthy" means not falling sick. Only 29% of Millennials settle for that. Eighty-three percent disapprove of adults smoking one or more packs of cigarettes a day, up from 69% in 1998. Drinking daily earns disapproval from 72%. Nearly one-third make a point of using natural or non-toxic products, and almost 30% prefer organic foods.

✓ Despite this, many health practices their elders consider standard are of much less interest to the young. These include getting regular physical and dental exams, vaccinations, and routine cancer screenings.

- A poll in the U.S. found that Baby Boomers were visiting fast-casual restaurants more often and fast-food outlets 18% less. Gen X had cut fast-food dining by 11 percent. Eighty-nine percent of Millennials preferred fast-casual restaurants, where they considered the food healthier, tastier, and "more customized."

  ✓ Nonetheless, more Millennials than their elders had visited all kinds of economical restaurants in previous three months: "Quick service restaurants" (McDonald's and Subway) led at 96%. Eighty percent had been to a "casual dining restaurant" (Olive Garden and Applebee's.) And 69% had visited a "fast casual restaurant" (Chipotle and Panera Bread).

  ✓ They also were more likely to visit fast-food restaurants eleven or more times per month and fast-casual restaurants eight or more times.

  ✓ Another poll found that 41% of under-twenty consumers said sustainably sourced ingredients were very important in their buying decisions, compared with 38% of Millennials and 34% of Gen X. However, Boomers and their elders were much more concerned that products be low in sugar or sugar-free.

  ✓ A Nielsen survey asked 60,000 people around the world which "healthy" food characteristics were most important to them—all-natural ingredients, low or no cholesterol or sugar, richness in fiber or protein, and so on. In nearly all, the highest ratings were found in Latin America, with the Middle East a close second. North America and Europe led in only one category each—absence of high-fructose corn syrup and of GMO ingredients, respectively.

- At latest count, 110 countries have enacted at least partial bans on smoking, with proscriptions in public places, workplaces, and public transportation the most common. They include seventeen EU members, the Scandinavian countries, Russia, nearly all of Central and South America, India and China, Malaysia, the Middle East, and much of Africa.

  ✓ Bhutan bans smoking in most public places; cultivation and harvesting of tobacco; manufacturing, and distribution, advertisement, sale, and purchase of tobacco products. It does allow importation of tobacco products for personal use, but requires the government to provide counseling and treatment to help users give up smoking.

  ✓ In many places, including most of China, bans are poorly enforced.

Implications: Health and fitness are key values for Millennials and Centennials. Opportunities for exercise and food that is healthful as well as tasty thus are increasingly important. Developing a reputation for providing them without stinting on luxuries will be one of the most effective business strategies. Adventure tourism and sports-oriented destinations especially should benefit from this trend.

Restaurants and resorts will need to emphasize healthy cuisine, and especially fresh, all-natural ingredients. Options for those who must avoid sugar, gluten, potassium and phosphorus, and other ingredients will be expected, both by elders with medical issues and by younger guests who wish to avoid them.

Like tobacco companies, producers of snack foods, liquor, and other medically dubious products will increasingly target markets in developing countries where this trend has yet to be felt.

As the nutrition and wellness movements spread, they will further improve the health of the elderly. The market among fit seniors for activities previous generations would have found too demanding will continue to grow for several more decades.

17. One form of consumerism is still growing rapidly. The other may be reaching its peak, at least in the developed lands.

- A networked society facilitates a consumerist society in the first sense, one in which regulations and availability of data help consumers in selecting purchases and offer significant protections from predatory marketers. Shoppers increasingly have access to information about pricing, services, delivery time, and to customer reviews on the Internet.

- Consumer advocacy agencies and organizations will continue to proliferate, promoting better information—unit pricing, improved content labels, warning notices, nutrition data, and the like—on packaging, TV, and the Internet.

- Online shopping is the single biggest factor giving consumers more power in the marketplace.

  ✓ Price aggregators like Expedia and Travelocity now account for one-third of all hotel bookings and 64% of airline bookings. By 2020, nearly half of all travel bookings and sales will occur online.

  ✓ Among the 44% of travelers who book within two weeks of departure, most within one week, 64% book their trips online. Those booking earlier book only 30% of flights and 25% of hotel stays online.

  ✓ Nearly 60% of Millennials report comparing prices online while in brick-and-mortar stores.

  ✓ Marketers, of course, can also check the competition's offerings. This is shifting competition increasingly to improvements in service and salesmanship, rather than price.

- Discount stores such as Home Depot and Walmart are quickly spreading to Europe and Japan. Six of the largest retail chains in Europe are discounters, in addition to Walmart and operators of warehouse stores. So are two of the eight largest retailers in Asia.

- Consumerism in the second sense—the system in which consumers keep the economy growing by buying ever more goods and services—is being challenged by a shift toward minimalist lifestyles, paring down possessions to the essentials, and buying little except to replace the occasional worn-out item with a high-quality equivalent. Think tiny housing, tiny wardrobes, and as little "stuff" as possible.

  ✓ This movement is driven by the increasing concentration of income and wealth at the high end of the financial spectrum, leaving real incomes among the less well-off either stagnant or shrinking.

  ✓ It is biggest among cash-strapped Millennials.

✓ Nearly four out of five Millennials say they would rather pay for an experience than material goods, compared with only 59% of Baby Boomers.

Implications: Over the next 20 years, Europe and Asia will follow the U.S. in replacing neighborhood stores with cost-cutting warehouse operations and "category killers."

This will inspire social unrest in countries where farmers and owners of small shops have strong cultural or political positions. In Japan, where small farmers have cultural significance, they have gained strong political support and extensive protections in the market. France is, if anything, even more solicitous toward its farmers.

However, the greatest competition will continue to come from online price aggregators and price-comparison sites, particularly as tech-savvy Millennials and Centennials make up more of the market.

As prices fall to commodity levels and online stores can list virtually every product and brand in their industry without significant overhead, service is the only field left in which marketers on and off the Net can compete effectively.

Hotels are fighting the price aggregators with their own online marketing and guest loyalty programs that offer lower rates, room upgrades, and extra services. About one-fourth of hotel bookings now come through hotel websites.

Branded items with good reputations are even more important for developing repeat business.

We expect the minimalist-lifestyles movement to wane among the younger generations as they rise to more senior jobs that provide more disposable income. However, it is likely to remain a permanent feature of the marketplace. Any loss of customers among the young will be made up by cash-strapped Boomers and others who have left the workforce.

18. Women are coming closer to equality with men, but only slowly.

- In the U.S., women's salaries have been rising faster than men's since 1975. However, there still is a long way to go. In 2000, women employed full-time and year-round earned only 74% as much as men in comparable jobs. By 2018, the average was still only 80.5%. At the rate of change seen between 1960 and 2015, women's salaries will not achieve parity with men's until 2050. At the rate seen since 2001, it will take until 2159.
  - ✓ Salaries among Black and Hispanic women average only 63% and 54% as much compared to those of white men.
  - ✓ In "middle-skill" occupations like advanced manufacturing, IT, and logistics women's salaries average only 66% of men's.
- There are exceptions:
  - ✓ Women's salaries equal men's in five fields dominated by men: hazardous material removal workers, telecommunications line installers and repairers, meeting and convention planners, dining room or cafeteria workers, and construction-trade helpers.

- ✓ Outside farm products, women working as wholesale and retail buyers earn 11% more than men.
- ✓ A few companies also are ahead of the trend. A 2015 study at Intel found that men and women were paid equally—to the surprise of the firm's "chief diversity officer."

- Gender gaps are found elsewhere, though not always as great. In the U.K., women earn 9.4% less than men for comparable jobs, down from 19% in 2000.
  - ✓ Women also are less likely to occupy well-paid or prestigious positions. Women make up 56% of workers in the twenty lowest-paid jobs, only 29% of those in the twenty highest-paid jobs, according to the White House Council of Economic Advisors.
  - ✓ Women served as CEO for 24 of the *Fortune* 500 companies in mid-2018. Only 10.6% of board seats in these companies are held by women. Among the S&P 500, only 11% of top earners are women.
  - ✓ Even in the female-friendly hospitality industry, women hold less than 40% of managerial positions, 20% of general management roles, and 9% of board seats. Only 5% of hospitality CEOs are women. There are exceptions: at a 2017 meeting of general managers at Hilton's all-suite brands, 43% were women.

- There are several counter-trends.
  - ✓ From Generation X on, people are virtually gender-blind in the workplace. This is increasingly true even in India and Japan, which have long been male-dominated, though not yet in conservative Muslim lands.
  - ✓ In the U.S., 57% of college students are women. Those aged 25 to 34 are 21% more likely than men to be college graduates and 48% more likely to have completed graduate school. In 2016, for the first time, more than half of law students were female.
  - ✓ One indication of growing dependence on the wife where both spouses work: Life insurance companies are selling more policies to women than to men.
  - ✓ More women are entering the professions, politics, and the judiciary. As we have seen in America's many wars, they also are finding roles as combat soldiers. About 14% of active-duty soldiers and 23% of reservists are women.

Implications: Most careers that remain relatively closed to women will open up by the late 2020s and the gender gap in employment and wages will begin to close more quickly.

Demand for child care and other family-oriented services will continue to grow, particularly in the United States, where national services have yet to appear. Over the next twenty years, this may force American companies to compete on a more even footing with their counterparts in Europe, where taxes pay for national daycare programs and other social services the United States lacks.

However, two-thirds of the jobs rated most likely to be taken over by automation are in the office and administrative categories in which women hold a majority of jobs. The fastest-growing positions are in the STEM categories—science, technology, engineering, and mathematics—in which women are disproportionately rare. This will have relatively little effect through 2025, as it takes time for new technologies to permeate society. Five years later, it will be clear that many more human jobs are at risk. Women will feel this trend first and worst.

In the long run, the need to work with female executives from the developed countries will begin to erode the restrictions placed on women's careers in some developing regions.

Despite an unexpectedly slow start, the hospitality and travel industry is likely to lead this change throughout most of the non-Muslim world.

19. Family structures are becoming more diverse.

- Only 69% of American children lived with two parents in 2016, the fewest ever recorded. This includes parents on their first or a later marriage and those who are unmarried.
  - ✓ Some 46% live in homes with two married, heterosexual parents in their first marriage, down from 73% in 1960 and 61% in 1980.
- Worldwide, between one-fourth and one-third of families are headed by single mothers.
  - ✓ In the U.S., 27% live in single-parent households, 23% with single mothers.
- In 2017, for the first time, a majority of Americans ages 18 to 34 lived with their parents—twice as many as in 1976. Most live at home because stagnant real wages and sharply rising rents make independence unaffordable.
  - ✓ About 12% of American parents also serve as care-givers for at least one adult, usually an elderly parent.
  - ✓ In Europe, 48% of young adults ages 18 to 30 lived with their parents in 2014, including 34% of those who had a job. The number was 79% in Italy, where it is expected, but only 26% in Britain.
- One in five American families is multi-generational, with two or more adult generations or with both grandparents and grandchildren. In 2016, a record 64 million Americans lived in multi-generational households.
  - ✓ Such families made up 21% of the total in 1950 but only 12% in 1980.
  - ✓ In the EU, only 5.8% of households are multi-generational.
  - ✓ UNICEF estimates that in sub-Saharan Africa, roughly half of the 132 million orphaned children live with their grandparents.
- In early 2017, 23 countries had legalized same-sex marriage, including the United States and 13 countries in Europe. Thirteen more European countries had legalized civil unions or given same-sex couples some other form of legal recognition.
  - ✓ An estimated 780,000 Americans were living in same-sex marriages in 2015, about 2 million more in domestic partnerships.

- ✓ In 2016, 55% of U.S. adults supported same-sex marriage, including 75% of Millennials and even more Centennials. One in five Millennials identify as LGBTQ.
- ✓ In 2016, the New York Court of Appeals granted joint custody and visitation rights to non-biological, non-adoptive parents in same-sex partnerships. Many states refuse to recognize non-biological same-sex parents as parents at all.

- Movements to reject or rescind these rights remain strong.

  - ✓ In 2016, the European Court for Human Rights ruled that same-sex marriages are not a human right and lack the standing granted to traditional marriages.
  - ✓ In the U.S., a leaked executive order by President Trump would have stripped legal protections from the LGBTQ community, including those in same-sex marriages. When protests got it sidelined, two Republican Congressmen drafted a bill that would have much the same effect.

Implications: Variant family groupings offer a variety of niche markets for hospitality. For example, same-sex parents might welcome a cruise with similar families.

In the U.S., tax, Social Security, and welfare policies need adjustment to cope with families in which heads of households are retired or unable to work or must support an extended family.

Similar protections are needed for same-sex partners and parents. Strong support among Millennials and Centennials makes it likely that they will be enacted by 2030.

Uniformity of values among the younger generations throughout most of the world makes this a global trend.

Energy Trends

20. Despite efforts to develop alternative sources of energy, oil consumption is still rising rapidly.

- The world used only 57 million barrels of oil per day in 1973, when the first major price shock hit. By 2016, it was using 97 million barrels daily, according to the International Energy Agency (IEA.) Oil use, rising by about 1.5% annually, was expected to pass 100 million barrels daily in late 2018, peaking at 103.5 million in 2040.
- Three markets will maintain demand for oil through 2040: feedstock for petrochemicals and fuel for road freight and aviation. In all three, petroleum is hard to replace.
- However, oil's share of world energy consumption is declining from 34% in 2012 to an expected 32.5% in 2020 and 30% in 2040.
- The United States consumed 19.7 million barrels of oil daily in 2000. By 2017, this was up to 19.9 million barrels per day, about 19% of it imported.

  - ✓ By 2040, U.S. oil consumption is expected to decline by 4 million barrels per day to levels not seen since the 1960s.
  - ✓ In five out of seven forecasts, the U.S. becomes a net energy exporter by 2022.

- Outside the U.S., the largest oil consumers are China, at just under 12 million barrels per day in 2015, and India, at 4.16 barrels per day. By 2020, China is expected to become the world's largest oil importer. India will become the second about 2035. By 2040, Asia will use three-fourths of the world's oil and 60% of its natural gas.

Implications: Most of the hospitality and travel industry will find energy costs rise gradually to peak in the mid-2020s, then remain stable or decline slightly through 2040.

Two segments will see costs rising until oil is replaced by some equally portable energy-dense fuel: air travel and cruise lines. Development of electric and hybrid power systems, and even wind power for ships, could change this forecast in the 2020s.

The U.S. economy will grow much less vulnerable to external price shocks as more of its energy needs are met domestically.

21. Contrary to popular belief, the world is not running out of oil.

- The world's proven oil reserves have climbed steadily from about 660 billion barrels in 1980 to 1.696 trillion barrels at the end of 2017.
- The U.S. Energy Information Agency expects the global supply of crude oil, other liquid hydrocarbons, and biofuels to meet global demand through at least 2040.
- OPEC officials claim the 11 member countries can meet the world's energy needs for the next 70 years or so.
  - ✓ OPEC supplies about 40% of the world's oil and holds 60% of reserves. The group says its production will reach 40.6 million barrels per day by 2020, up from 38.9 million in 2016—nearly half of the world's total projected increase in production.
  - ✓ Even 80% of OPEC's estimated supply would still be enough oil to supply the world through 2050 and beyond.
- Oil production outside the OPEC nations has not yet peaked. In 2016, Russia became the world's largest oil producer. The U.S. was in third place, China in fifth, Canada in seventh, and Brazil in tenth. The top five non-OPEC members pump nearly 29.5 million barrels per day, 18 percent more than the five largest OPEC producers.
  - ✓ One laggard is Venezuela, which owns 20% of the world's proven reserves. The government's catastrophically bad management has cut production to roughly 1.36 million barrels per day, down by 1.7 million over 20 years. No improvement can be expected in the near future.
- India also is believed to own substantial reserves of oil in deposits beneath the Indian Ocean. It had proven reserves of just under 5.7 billion barrels at the beginning of 2016.

Implications: If the price of oil rises significantly beyond current levels, new methods of recovering oil from old wells will become cost effective. Technologies already developed could add nearly 50% to the world's recoverable oil supply.

One global risk is that Saudi Arabia and some smaller producers could be taken over by fundamentalist Islamic governments similar to that of Iran. This likely would deprive the U.S. of a critical oil source and could force Europe to become much more accommodating toward Islamist views.

22. Oil prices are holding stable at $65 to $75 per barrel through at least 2020.

- Prices above $140 per barrel seen in 2008 were an aberration that cannot be sustained now that many non-OPEC oil sources have come on line. The actual cost of producing a barrel of oil and gas equivalent in March 2016 ranged from $44.33 in the U.K. all the way down to $8.98 in Saudi Arabia.

- OPEC estimates that average prices will rise by $5 per year, reaching $65 in 2020. The World Bank puts them at $60 to $65 per barrel through 2020 and rising only to $70 by 2030.
  - ✓ Price increases continue to be restrained in the longer term, reaching $92 per barrel (in 2015 dollars) by 2040.

- Most American drillers kept pumping even when the price of West Texas Intermediate fell to $30 per barrel in 2016. Shale oil, which now accounts for more than half of U.S. oil output, begins to be profitable at $30 per barrel, and most wells at least break even when prices rise to $60. High oil prices therefore have become self-limiting, as per-barrel prices much over $55 bring more reserves online.
  - ✓ Now that an administration friendly to oil interests occupies Washington, drilling almost certainly will begin in the Arctic National Wildlife Reserve and other areas once considered ecologically too sensitive for development.

- The Trump administration also is likely to ease EPA regulations mandating production of super-low sulfur fuels, reducing the cost of gasoline in the U.S. Although this is likely to spur demand for oil, the comparatively low cost of production will continue to keep per-barrel costs in check.

- New oil supplies coming on line in the former Soviet Union, China, and other parts of the world also will make it even more difficult to sustain prices at artificially high levels.

- At full capacity, the twenty most industrialized countries all have at least three-month supplies of oil in strategic reserves. China plans to by 2020. India has about ten days worth. In times of extreme oil prices, many customer nations can afford to cut back their buying until the cost comes down.

Monitor: One development that could change this scenario is the establishment of a Muslim extremist government in Saudi Arabia or another major OPEC producer. Although this seems unlikely, political stability in the Middle East is one factor to monitor.

Even more worth following: acceptance of electric cars. Stanford economist Tony Seba predicts that drivers will switch en masse to electrics by 2024 because the "fuel" is nearly free and the cars should last 1 million miles. In this case, expect oil to sell for less than $30 per barrel.

Implications: Destinations supplying their own renewable energy to well-insulated buildings will have a modest cost advantage over competitors that do not, in addition to attracting guests concerned with the environment. By 2030, this advantage will fade as renewables and energy-efficient construction evolve into business as usual.

This will continue to bolster profits for airlines, which coped with fuel costs that made up nearly 30% of operating expenses when oil prices were their highest, but only 19% in 2016.

This will help the cruise lines as well, despite substantial efficiency improvements in recent years. Carnival reported spending $1.77 billion on fuel in 2008. By 2016, this had come down to $920 million.

23. Growing competition from other energy sources also will help to limit the price of oil.

- Renewable energy sources provided 8.3% of global electricity in 2017, according to the International Energy Agency. Lazard puts it at 12%. Installation of renewable power plants that year came to 167GW—85% of the world's new generating capacity per the International Renewable Energy Agency. Solar and wind energy are developing fastest, but biomass and waste-to-energy, geothermal, small hydro, and marine power all are growing.

- Costs of renewables are dropping fast. Between 2009 and 2017, the average cost of solar energy in North America has fallen from about $352 per megawatt-hour to $50. Wind energy is down from about $138 per megawatt-hour to $45. Coal has held steady at roughly $102 per megawatt-hour.

  ✓ In the U.S., utility-scale photovoltaic energy cost $46 to $61 per MWh, discounting subsidies and taxes, compared with $60 to $143 for coal and $97 to $136 for nuclear. Wind energy was only $32 to $46 per MWh. In about a third of the country, wind energy plants are the cheapest to bring on line, while utility-scale solar is cheapest in much of the Southwest.

  ✓ Some projects have been even cheaper, with bids to build solar projects in 2016 as low as 3 cents per kWh in Mexico and the Middle East. In Chile, a developer in 2016 won a contract to sell solar-generated electricity for only 2.91 cents per kWh, about half the cost of coal.

- Technology is eliminating the largest drawback to renewable energy: sun and wind are not always available. Technologies include Elon Musk's Big Battery Project, storing solar heat in molten salt to run generators at night, and pumping water to high-altitude reservoirs where it can be released to generate electricity when more power is needed.

- Many countries have set ambitious goals to replace conventional energy with renewables.

  ✓ Most of Europe plans to get 12 to 15% of its energy from renewable sources by 2020. EU policy targets 27% by 2030, with a raise to 30% expected.

  ✓ France has committed to 32% by 2030.

  ✓ Norway is aiming for 67.5% renewable energy by 2020, Sweden 49%, Finland 38%, and Denmark 30%.

  ✓ China planned to get 15% of its energy from non-fossil sources by 2020, with non-fossil power climbing 48% in five years. Beijing has ordered a halt to construction of many new coal-fired generators already in process.

Nonetheless, power plants still in development will raise the country's coal-fired generating capacity by 25%, to 1,252 GW.

✓ Coal is still dominant in South and Southeast Asia, where India and other countries are planning to build coal-fired power stations well into the future. According to one study, a new coal-fired electric plant large enough to power a city of around 1.3 million people begins operation in China every seven to ten days.

- Natural gas is a fossil fuel, but a lot better for the environment than oil. It burns cleanly, and there is enough of it available to supply the world's total energy demand for the next 200 years. OPEC predicts that natural gas will overtake oil as the world's greatest source of energy around 2040.

Implications: Though oil will remain the world's most important energy resource for years to come, two or three decades forward it should be less of a choke point in the global economy.

New photovoltaic technologies will continue to raise the efficiency and reduce the cost of solar panels, reducing the space destinations need to generate electricity and making small-scale solar installations as cheap as today's utility-scale power plants. This will make it even more practical for many hotels and resorts to compete as environmentally friendly.

It also will be easier for destinations in remote parts of Africa and other developing lands to supply developed-world luxuries like air condition at competitive prices.

Declining reliance on oil eventually could help to reduce air and water pollution, at least in the developed world. By 2060, a costly but pollution-free hydrogen economy may at last become practical.

Environmental Trends

24. People around the world are becoming increasingly sensitive to environmental issues such as air pollution, as the consequences of neglect, indifference, and ignorance become ever more apparent.

- In the United States, 74% of adults in a 2016 survey said "the country should do whatever it takes to protect the environment." This included more than half of those identifying themselves as Republicans or Republican-leaning.

✓ Some 59% of Americans say their community is already being affected by climate change, according to Pew Research. Within 25 miles of a coast, the number is two-thirds, but 50% agree even 300 miles or more inland.

✓ Some 55% of Americans rated the environment as a top policy issue President Donald Trump and Congress should tackle in 2017. Only protecting against terrorism and improving the economy were named more often as *the* top issue.

✓ Nearly two-thirds of American adults say they worry "a great deal/fair amount" about global warming. And 61% said they always try to live in ways that protect the environment.

- ✓ In China, about one-third of the adult population consider air and water pollution "very big" problems, with another 41% rating them "moderately big." Three-fourth consider climate change to be a "very serious" or "somewhat serious" problem.
- ✓ The Chinese government reportedly considers environmental problems to be the issue most capable of undermining its legitimacy.
- More than half of those polled in Latin America believe protecting the environment is more important than economic development. Numbers ranged from around 23% in Belize to about 63% in Brazil and Colombia.
  - ✓ Add those who consider both important, and the number concerned about the environment ranges from 58% in Belize to 82% in Colombia.
- In a poll about climate change, Pew Research found that 54% of people around the world consider climate change "a very serious problem," and 51% believe it "is harming people now." Regional results:

Region	A very serious problem	Harming people now
Latin America	74%	77%
Africa	61%	52%
Europe	54%	60%
Asia/Pacific	45%	48%
Middle East	38%	26%
United States	45%	41%
China	18%	49%

- In 2016 alone, there were major environmental protests in the United States, Germany, China, Vietnam, Russia (where the government has named 2017 the "Year of Ecology"), India, Brazil (where 185 activists were murdered in 2016), and many other countries.

- Governments are taking more active measures to protect the environment.
  - ✓ An Indian court ruled that glaciers and rivers are "living entities" and "persons" under the law, entitled to protections similar to those granted humans.
  - ✓ New Zealand passed a law recognizing the Whanganui River as a living entity, also with a right to legal protection. The Maori people consider the river to be an ancestor.
  - ✓ A Dutch court ruled in 2016 that the government must cut greenhouse gas emissions by 25% in five years. Plans had called for cuts of only 14 to 17% by 2020.
  - ✓ Norway became the first country to ban deforestation.
  - ✓ Brazil has committed to restoring 12 million hectares of forests by 2030.
  - ✓ China's latest five-year plan, released in 2016, lowered targets for particulate emissions by 25% from previous levels and committed to sharp cuts in the amount of water and energy used and of carbon emitted per unit of GDP.

Water use per unit of GDP was scheduled to fall 23% by 2020, energy use—already down by 18%—by a further 15%, and carbon by 18%. However, failure to halt construction of coal-fired generators despite orders from Beijing may bring these targets into question.

Implications: Worldwide, airborne particulates kill 3 million people a year. In London, the average resident dies nine to sixteen months early owing to air pollution.

If air pollution were halted instantly, it would take an estimated 200 years for carbon dioxide and other greenhouse gasses to return to pre-industrial levels. Whatever global temperature increase results from today's emissions is already inevitable.

Environmental policies will provoke a political backlash wherever they conflict with entrenched interests, as they have long done in the American West. However, the cost of not protecting the environment is too obvious to be ignored. Throughout most of the world, polluters and private beneficiaries of public assets will increasingly confront restrictive regulations designed to serve the interests of the community at large.

25. Water shortages will be a continuing problem for much of the world.

- The world's water supply will fall at least 40% short by 2030, according to the United Nations. One-third of the population of Africa and most of the major cities in the developing world will face water shortages.

  ✓ An estimated 1 billion people already lack access to safe drinking water.

- The northern half of China, home to perhaps half a billion people, already is short of water. The water table under Beijing has fallen nearly 200 feet since 1965.

  ✓ Diversion of water from southern China has begun to reverse this decline, raising Beijing's water table by 0.42 meter in 2016 with more expected in 2017. Two-thirds of the city's tap water now comes by canal and tunnel from Danjiangkou, nearly 900 miles to the south.

  ✓ Desert now covers about 668,000 square miles and is spreading at a rate of about 1,300 square miles per year, affecting more than 400 million people.

  ✓ Arid regions include four of China's five biggest farming provinces.

- Water usage is causing other problems as well. For example, irrigation water evaporates, leaving minerals in the soil. In 2014, 20% of the world's crop land was salty. By 2020, it will be 30%; by 2050, 50%. Salinization already is cutting crop yields in India, Pakistan, Egypt, Mexico, Australia, and parts of the United States.

- Pollution further reduces the supply of safe drinking water. In India, an estimated 77 million people lack access to safe drinking water, due to widespread pollution of rivers and groundwater, compared with 63 million in China and 58 million in Nigeria.

  ✓ In ten countries, more than 40% of people lack access to safe drinking water. All but two are in Africa. The exceptions are Afghanistan and Papua New Guinea, which at 60% has the world's worst supply.

- Water quality is a growing problem even in the developed lands.

  ✓ In the U.S., tap water in at least 33 cities contains over 200 parts per billion (ppb) of lead, one with 10,000 ppb and another with 6,000 ppb. Federal regulations allow no more than 15 ppb, and many believe that standard is too lax.

  ✓ In 2013, the U.S. Environmental Protection Administration rated 55% of the country's rivers and streams in "poor" condition, owing to pollution that often finds its way into city water systems. Forty percent of rivers and 46% of lakes were found too polluted for swimming, fishing, or aquatic life. Tap water in 20% of cities contains toxic levels of lead.

  ✓ In 2018, the Trump administration proposed to exclude some 18% of tributaries and 51% of wetlands from regulation even though pollution in them finds its way to protected rivers.

  ✓ Cities such as Atlanta, where the delivery system is a century old and poorly maintained, suffer frequent water-main breaks, which suck dirt, debris, bacteria, and pollutants into the water supply. There are an estimated 850 such breaks each day in North America, more than 310,000 a year.

- Many ecologists believe that global warming will make drought much more frequent—even the norm—in the U.S. west of the Mississippi.
- Contaminated water is implicated in 80% of the world's health problems. Water borne diseases kill an estimated 3.6 million per year, including 800,000 children who succumb to diarrhea.

Implications: By 2040, at least 3.5 billion people will run short of water, almost 10 times as many as in 1995. By 2050, fully two-thirds of the world's population could be living in regions with chronic, widespread shortages of water.

Water wars are an imminent threat in places like the Kashmir: Much of Pakistan's supply comes from areas of Kashmir now controlled by India. Such problems as periodic famine and desertification also can be expected to grow more frequent and severe in coming decades.

Other present and future water conflicts involve Turkey, Syria, and Iraq over the Tigris and Euphrates; Israel, Jordan, Syria, and Palestine over water from the Jordan River and the aquifers under the Golan Heights; India and Bangladesh, over the Ganges and Brahmaputra; China, Indochina, and Thailand, over the Mekong; Kyrgyzstan, Tajikistan, and Uzbekistan over the Oxus and Jaxartes rivers; and Ethiopia, Sudan, and at least six East African countries, including Egypt, which share the Nile.

Impurities in water will become an even greater problem as the global population ages and becomes more susceptible to infectious diseases.

In the United States, repair of decayed water systems is likely to be a major priority for older cities such as New York, Boston, and Atlanta. Cost estimates for necessary replacement and repair of water mains range up to $1 trillion. If proposed rollbacks of the U.S. Clean Water Act take effect, water quality in the country will be significantly degraded. However, they may be blocked in court until an administration more sympathetic to environmental regulation takes office.

26. The effects of climate change, already making themselves felt, are growing quickly.

- The five warmest years in the global record have come in the 2010s. The years 2014, '15, and '16 each set new records for average global temperature, which is up about 1.1 degrees from pre-industrial times. Sea-surface temperatures also are rising.
- Sea level has risen about 3 inches between 1993 and 2016. There could be much more to come.
  - ✓ The minimum rise now considered likely is about 5 feet by 2100. It could be much higher. If all the ice now known to be melting is lost, it could raise sea level by nearly 50 feet.
- Glaciers have been losing mass steadily since at least 1945. By 2015, they averaged 30% smaller than at the start of the period. Dartmouth researchers found that glaciers on Mt. Hunter, in Alaska, are losing water 60 times faster than before 1850. Temperatures there are rising twice as fast as the global average.
  - ✓ Greenland loses nearly 50 cubic miles each year. An increase of 2 or 3°C could melt all that remains—enough to raise sea level by 24 feet. Climate models say that Greenland will be at least 3°C warmer in this century and perhaps as much as 9°C warmer.
  - ✓ The north-flowing Slims River in Canada, previously 15 miles long and nearly 500 feet wide, disappeared over four days in 2016 when the glacier where it originated melted enough to divert its water to the south.
  - ✓ In western Tibet, a glacier in the Aru Mountains collapsed, killing herders and livestock in a nearby village. Average temperatures in the region have risen about 1.2°C in 50 years.
- Average air temperatures in the Arctic have risen about 5°C in the last century, 3°C since 1971, resulting in a steady loss of sea ice since 1995. Before then, ice covered an average of about 3 million square miles in September. Since 2010, the average has been less than 2 million. Given current trends, the Arctic will be free of ice by 2040. Forecasts say enough ice will melt in this century to raise sea level by about 2.5 feet.
- Antarctica is warming twice as fast as the rest of the planet. The glaciers of West Antarctica are melting rapidly. Evidence suggests that they eventually will melt completely, adding 10 more feet to global sea level. One glacier in East Antarctica also is melting. It is large enough to raise sea level by over 12 feet.
- Extreme weather is growing more common and intense.
  - ✓ Extreme one-day precipitation events in the U.S. have been tracked since 1895. Nine of the top ten years for them have occurred since 1990. The number of such events has grown steadily since the 1980s, and the area affected by them has more than doubled.
  - ✓ Worldwide, there are about six fewer hurricanes per year than in the mid-1980s, but in the North Atlantic the number of Category 4 and 5 storms, the most powerful, has doubled in 40 years. Typhoons in the North Pacific and northern Indian Ocean also are growing stronger.

- Plants and animals already show significant impact from climate change.
  - ✓ A study of 976 plant and animal species worldwide found that 47% already have become extinct in part of their natural ranges.
  - ✓ The Intergovernmental Panel on Climate Change estimates that 20 to 30% of plants and animals it studied could be at risk of extinction if global temperatures rise as much as expected by 2100.
  - ✓ In one study of 35 European non-migratory butterfly species, the ranges of 22 had shifted northward by 30 to 240 km over the past century.
  - ✓ The National Wildlife Federation reports that 177 of 305 North American bird species have shifted their ranges an average of 35 miles north in the last 40 years.
  - ✓ Climate change is warming the oceans, slowing current circulation, and reducing populations of marine creatures. The areas most affected include six regions of exceptional biodiversity and many of the world's most important commercial fisheries.
  - ✓ Warming oceans appear to be responsible for the death of coral reefs that support 25% of marine life. The U.S. has lost half of its Caribbean reefs. Forty percent of Australia's Great Barrier Reef died off in 2016. In the ocean around Japan, corals have shifted their range by up to 14 km in the last century.

Implications: Natural tourist attractions like the Great Barrier Reef seem likely to disappear within this century, some of them within the working lives of today's hospitality students. Small, low-lying ski resorts already are going bankrupt because they lack snow. They are only the first victims of what may be a long, difficult trend in the industry.

Grasses appear especially susceptible to rising temperatures, and they include species like wheat, corn, oats, and rice. A further rise of 1°C, now considered unavoidable, is expected to cut wheat yields by 4.1 to 6.4% just when food demand is rising by at least 60%.

In Africa, 60% of the terrain used to grow beans is expected to become nonviable.

At the same time, ocean warming is likely to reduce fish catches, further impairing global food supplies.

Mosquitoes carrying diseases such as malaria, dengue fever, and West Nile virus are spreading farther from the equator as more temperate regions become habitable. The first known case of West Nile virus infection in the U.S. occurred in 1999. By early 2017, it had been seen in 47 states and the District of Columbia with more than 2,000 cases reported to the Centers for Disease Control and Prevention and 94 deaths.

Destinations in areas affected by these diseases could find tourism becoming less predictable and profits less reliable when vacationers shun outbreak sites as they did Brazil in 2015.

27. Industrial development trumps environmental concerns in some parts of the world.

- In 2018, the United States is chief among them. The Trump administration has done its best to gut the Environmental Protection Agency and NASA's Earth science program. President Trump appointed Scott Pruitt, a prominent climate-change denier, to head the EPA and rescinded Obama-era executive orders intended to protect the environment. Pruitt's replacement, Andrew Wheeler, was a coal lobbyist before appointment to the EPA. Scientific data has been taken off line, government scientists forbidden to speak publicly about climate change. However, Congress overruled White House budget cuts for FY 2018, maintaining EPA funding at its existing level.

- China's continuing construction of coal-fired generators despite Beijing's commitment to environmental reform demonstrates that industrial development retains strong and influential supporters.

- After some 25 years of talking about the environment, Indian politicians now speak of "balancing" environmental protections with economic growth. More than 1,600 attempts to block environmentally damaging or questionable industrial activities have been referred to the National Green Tribunal in recent years, with mixed results.

- In the EU, a coalition of eight countries led by Germany and including Poland, Bulgaria, and Czech Republic attempted to block new limits on power-plant emissions even though the standards were weaker than those in Japan, China, and until recently the United States.

- Hydraulic fracturing for oil and gas faces very few restrictions in the U.S., the UK, Poland, and some other countries despite strong evidence that it pollutes aquifers and drinking water, triggers earthquakes, and releases methane, a powerful greenhouse gas. Bulgaria, France, Germany, the Netherlands, Scotland, and Wales all effectively ban fracking. The U.K. and Ukraine actively promote the practice.

- Brazil recently has backed away from regulations—often poorly enforced—to protect the Amazon rain forest and other natural resources. Up to 59,000 square miles of forest could be legally clearcut as a result of the change.

- Though India has announced that it will stop building coal-fired power plants in 2022, some 600 are now under construction or planned and due for completion by 2030. According to environmentalists, more than 90% of the new generating capacity will be unneeded.

Implications: President Trump's anti-environment measures will survive only as long as his administration does. However, the loss of experienced personnel at the EPA and NASA will have lasting effects on environmental programs until a new generation of scientists and administrators masters their roles.

Measures to raise employment in the coal industry have had no statistically significant effect, as human miners have been replaced by machines and electric utilities have already committed to cleaner natural gas and renewable energy.

Significant regions of the planet will be subject to pollution, deforestation, and other environmental ills in the coming decades.

Attempts to limit global temperature increases to 2°C are doomed to fail, ensuring that the impact of climate change will be much greater than optimistic estimates suggest.

28. Species extinction and loss of biodiversity will be a growing worry for decades to come.

- Some 50,000 species disappear each year, according to an estimate from the United Nations Environmental Program. The rate of extinction from human activity is estimated to be at least 100 times faster than the natural rate, and some authorities make it thousands of times faster.

- The Center for Biological Diversity rates the current wave of species loss the worst die-off since the loss of the dinosaurs 65 million years ago. According to estimates, one in five species alive today now faces extinction, and that could rise to 50% by the end of the century, when the human population is expected to reach 11.2 billion.

- Vulnerable species include:
  ✓ One-third of amphibians;
  ✓ 12% of bird species, and 31% in the U.S.;
  ✓ 21% of fish species evaluated by the UN;
  ✓ 20% of reptiles;
  ✓ 30% of insects and other invertebrates;
  ✓ 50% of mammals, with 20% very likely to disappear;
  ✓ 68% of plant species

- Of the major causes, all are human activities:
  ✓ Introduction of invasive species into fragile ecosystems. Since Burmese pythons were introduced into the Everglades, raccoons, opossum, and bobcats are seen 87 to 99% less often, and rabbits appear extinct within the park.
  ✓ Climate change: The Intergovernmental Panel on Climate Change estimates that 20 to 30% of plants and animals it studied could be lost if global temperatures rise to the levels expected by 2100.
  ✓ Deforestation: Some 46,000 to 58,000 square miles of forest are cleared each year. Orangutans already are near extinction because their habitat is being replaced by palm oil plantations.
  ✓ Urbanization and development: In the first 30 years of this century, cities will triple in area, consuming 463,000 square miles of delicate habitats, farmland, and carbon-storing vegetation. An estimated 200 endangered species will go extinct as a result.
  ✓ Agriculture: People have transformed 37% of the planet's land into farms and pasture where little that is wild survives. Some 17% of the Amazon forest has been cleared for farms in the last 50 years.
  ✓ Poaching: In Africa, elephants, rhinoceros, mountain gorillas, and several other species are expected to die out, either because their habitats are being destroyed or because of illegal hunting. Lions are extinct already in seven African countries.

- Though commercial fishing is not known to have exterminated any species—largely because it costs too much to catch the last few members of a species—it is another important cause of species depletion. Stocks of cod, tuna, swordfish, marlin, and sharks are down 90% since modern industrialized fishing began 40 years ago.

Implications: Species loss has a powerful negative impact on human well-being. Half of all drugs used in medicine are derived from natural sources, including 55 of the top 100 drugs prescribed in the United States. About 40% of all pharmaceuticals are derived from the sap of vascular plants. So far, only 2% of the 300,000 known sap-containing plants have been assayed for potential drugs.

In Indonesia, home to one-eighth of the world's coral reefs, more than 70% of the reefs are dead or dying. The Indonesian economy loses an estimated $500,000 to $800,000 annually per square mile of dead or damaged reef.

Researchers from the United Kingdom's National Environmental Research Council Centre for Population Biology report that diverse ecosystems absorb more carbon dioxide than those with fewer species. Loss of biodiversity thus is a potential cause of global warming.

Destinations specializing in wildlife tours and diving are likely to lose much or all of their business as significant species disappear. This will be especially hard on African resorts and tour operations in the coming decade.

29. Continuing urbanization will improve the world's economic efficiency, but at the cost of aggravating most environmental and social problems.

- Cities are economically productive. Just 600 cities produce some 60% of the world's GDP. They are expected to grow 1.6 times as fast as the world at large.
- Between 2000 and 2030, the global population will grow by an estimated 2.2 billion. Of this total, 2.1 billion people will be added to the world's cities.
  - ✓ In 2017, some 4 billion people—54.9% of the world's population—lived in cities. This was up from 2.8 billion, or 47%, in 2000. By 2030, 60% of the global population will live in cities.
  - ✓ Two-thirds of urban growth will occur in China and India alone.
- The big are getting bigger. In 1990, there were just ten megacities, with populations over 10 million, in the world. In 2020, there will be 27, 18 of them in developing countries.
  - ✓ Twenty-one more have populations over 5 million, 14 of them in developing countries.
  - ✓ All ten of the fastest growing from 2010 to 2020 are in developing countries.
- Urbanization will proceed fastest in the developing lands, where more people are available to move into cities. In the more developed countries, 76% of the population already lives in cities; in the developing lands, only 40%.
  - ✓ However, natural increase now accounts for more than half of urban population growth; at most, little more than one-third of urban growth results from migration.

- Up to 1 billion city dwellers lack adequate shelter, clean water, toilets, or electricity. In India alone, 500 million people defecate in the open because no sanitary system is available. The United Nations estimates that these problems cause 10 million needless deaths annually.
- Urbanization has profound environmental effects, none good.

  ✓ Fuels burned in cities produce 70% of global carbon emissions from human activity.

  ✓ At current growth rates, cities will use over three times more energy in 2050 than they did in 2005.

  ✓ NASA scientists point out that urbanization puts buildings and blacktop on the most fertile land, eliminating carbon-absorbing plants.

  ✓ Urbanization also deprives surrounding areas of water: Instead of sinking into the ground, rain is collected, piped to the city, used, treated as gray water, and then discarded into the ocean. In some regions, such as near Atlanta, water levels in local aquifers are declining rapidly because the water that once replenished them now is lost.

Implications: Cities' contribution to global warming can only increase in the years ahead.

As the world's supply of potable water declines, people are concentrating in those areas where it is hardest to obtain and is used least efficiently.

Deaths due to shortages of shelter, water, and sanitation can only grow. Epidemics will become still more common as overcrowding spreads HIV and other communicable diseases more rapidly.

Since the growth is now due more to natural increase than to migration, programs designed to encourage rural populations to remain in the countryside appear misplaced. Education and family planning seem more likely to rein in the growth of cities. So will economic growth and programs designed to encourage two-income families. Women who work have much more control over their lives than those who do not and reliably produce fewer children.

Urbanization benefits the travel and hospitality industry in at least four ways: It increases demand for hotel space in population centers and air transport among them, makes residents even more eager to escape harried daily lives, and on average gives them more income than they would receive in rural or suburban regions, and more to spend on vacations.

Technology Trends

30. Technology increasingly dominates both the economy and society.

- New technologies are pushing the state of the art in all fields, and the pace of change is accelerating.

  ✓ One critical exception: microprocessors, where it seems that designers have nearly wrung the last increment of performance from conventional chip technology.

- Private, relatively inexpensive launch vehicles and other commercial efforts are creating the infrastructure required for practical space tourism, solar power satellites, asteroid mining, and other space-based activities.
- New materials are enabling stronger, lighter structures, some of which can monitor their own wear and even heal damage.
- Nanotechnology is still in its early stages, but in the years ahead we can expect wonders that range from higher-powered, longer-lived batteries to miniature robots that roam the bloodstream to destroy cancers and ream out blocked arteries.
- Technologies for the "Internet of Things" (IoT) are quickly making it practical to monitor and exchange information among artifacts like smart cars, industrial robots and process controllers, and household appliances.
- Robots are taking over mundane commercial and service jobs, environmentally dangerous jobs, and assembly and repair of the inaccessible. For example, undersea fiber-optic cables are now routinely repaired by remote-control robots.
  - ✓ Also for robots: inspecting nuclear reactors for damage in incidents like the Fukushima disaster.
  - ✓ And space exploration: NASA's two robotic Mars explorers have been spectacularly successful; a third Mars probe is set to launch in 2020. So is a two-legged robot explorer Japan plans to send to the moon.
- Virtual and augmented reality are rapidly nearing general use for applications that range from games to retail marketing, automated tour guides, and maintenance manuals for jet engines and other complex machinery.
- Artificial intelligence (AI) is becoming incomparably more powerful than the simple if-then systems developed in the 1980s and '90s. Applications include robotics, machine vision, voice recognition, speech synthesis, electronic data processing, health and human services, administration, and airline pilot assistance. (See Trend 32 for more information.)

Implications: The current slow pace of improvement in microprocessors is temporary. Faster technologies than silicon-based computer chips are available and will be adopted whenever the demand for greater speed makes mass production profitable. For special purposes, quantum computers will be in general use mid-way through the next decade, quickly solving a variety of problems beyond the reach of today's hardware.

One thing quantum computers do particularly well is factoring large numbers—finding two smaller numbers that when multiplied together yield the big one. For conventional computers, this is so hard that the codes used to protect financial transactions and most secure email rely on its near-impossibility. The arrival of quantum computers is likely to make these codes obsolete.

New technologies should continue to improve the efficiency of many industries, helping to keep costs under control. However, this increased productivity retarded U.S. job creation in the first few years of this century. We will see much more of this effect in the future.

New technologies also will bring thousands of new opportunities to create businesses and jobs but using them effectively requires education and training that few who need jobs will possess. Fortunately, AI, virtual and augmented reality, and other technologies are beginning to reduce the training required for some activities and making training itself quicker and easier.

Technology also brings legal hazards. For example, former guests at Marriott's Starwood hotels filed two federal class-action lawsuits in connection with a four-year hacking attack that affected the personal data of more than 380 million patrons. The suits allege that Marriott did too little to protect its guests' data and, in one, that the company was too slow to provide adequate information about the incident.

In the 2020s, growing evidence that man-made climate change will far exceed the 2°C target set by international treaties, causing major economic dislocation, will overcome political obstacles and spur the development and adoption of clean industry, carbon capture, and other environmentally friendly technologies.

By 2025, the Internet of Things will be responsible, directly and indirectly, for about 10% of the economy in the industrialized countries. An estimated 3.8 billion IoT devices were in use at the end of 2016. By 2020, they will number 25 billion. This will make many devices both more reliable and cheaper.

Hacking of IoT devices like cars, home appliances, and industrial equipment will be a large and growing problem. A "botnet" of 100,000 compromised IoT gadgets knocked some of the Net offline as early as October 2016.

Automation will continue to cut the cost of many B2B products and services, making it possible to reduce prices while still improving profits.

Even at this early stage in its mass adoption, artificial intelligence is changing healthcare, investment, manufacturing, transportation, power generation, transportation, urban planning, and the practice of law. AI will spread rapidly throughout business, industry, and daily life, growing ever more powerful and useful.

General AI, with human versatility and vastly greater speed, is unlikely to appear much before 2040. However, this forecast is unusually subject to change. Developing general AI will require breakthroughs in our understanding of the human mind, and breakthroughs are impossible to predict.

We have seen one claim that researchers already have captured the workings of the mind in a simple algorithm. If this report holds up, the development of general AI in the 2020s will become our default forecast. It will trigger revolutions in almost all aspects of business and daily life. The fabled "Singularity," when AI becomes smarter than humans and prediction becomes impossible, would be likely in the 2030s.

As many studies have suggested, AI, robots, and other forms of automation are bringing a time of mass unemployment. The change will not be as fast as is often predicted, as it takes time for companies to invest in new technology and change their processes to take full advantage of it. However, it will be more complete than currently estimated because still more powerful AI will be developed in the years ahead. New creative jobs will eventually appear for those who can perform them, but not before many of the unemployed reach retirement age. This will necessitate adoption of a guaranteed minimum income and other support systems. By 2025, the direction of events will be obvious to all. And by 2025, McKinsey predicts, AI will be a $13 trillion market opportunity.

The hospitality industry lives primarily on personal interactions and will be relatively immune to this change—with one exception. Restaurants will quickly replace servers and cooks with automated equipment, particularly in the fast-food segment. Recent automated hotels seem more a novelty than a sign of things to come.

Travel will feel much more impact from automation. (See also Trend 32.)

31. R&D plays an increasingly critical role in the economy.

- Consider this an extension of Trend 27.

- R&D pays off better than other activities. Economists attribute up to 80% of modern economic growth to technological innovation. One credible study found that the $5.8 billion the Department of Energy was expected invest in clean-energy research in 2017 would add $8.6 billion to the American GDP, a payoff of $1.60 for every dollar spent. Much of this profit would be spun off to other sectors in taxes and spending by industry employees.

- In 2013, the most recent year for which totals are available, the world spent $1.671 trillion on research and development. Over ten years, this represented a CAGR of 7.2% per year.

- The United States devoted 2.72% of GDP on research and development, making it only the world's seventh most generous funder by that measure. Yet, this amounted to $456.1 billion, the largest national R&D budget in the world. However, see below.

  - ✓ Some $80.5 billion went to basic research, the stuff of Nobel Prizes and the foundation of future economic growth. Of this, 51% came from colleges and universities, only 12% from government. Business and nonprofits supplied the rest.

  - ✓ Applied research received $90.6 billion, 56% from the business sector.

  - ✓ Predictably, business also spent by far the most on development, which aims at short-term profit—88% of the $285 billion spent that year. Another 9% was spent within the federal government, much of it defense-related.

- China spent $336.5 billion for R&D in 2013. To this, add spending hidden in the military budget, which itself is nebulous.

- The European Union as a group spent 2.03% of its GDP on research and development, about $414 billion. Among the "big four" EU economies, Germany led at 2.83% of GDP; Italy lagged at 1.31%.

- America's apparent dominance in R&D is much less impressive than it seems. Measured by Purchasing Power Parity, which adjusts raw numbers to reflect local buying power, the U.S., Canada, and Mexico combined spent 29.4% of the world's R&D budget in 2013. East and Southeast Asia accounted for 36.8%.

- Washington's 2017 budget allocated $144.1 billion to R&D. Defense R&D totaled $66.57 billion, up 9.8% since 2007. Nondefense research, which is widely considered more productive, received $77.53 billion, a cut of 12.8% in a decade.

  - ✓ Among non-defense outlays, $33.63 billion went to health research, $10.9 billion to space, $10.10 billion to general science, $3.55 billion to energy, $2.49 billion to the environment and related fields, and $5.92 billion to "other."

- Western corporations are outsourcing R&D to foreign contractors, just as they do other functions. In the U.S., about 16% of corporate research takes place overseas, according to the National Science Foundation. Although the results are theoretically owned by the company sponsoring the research, foreign contractors often use the findings for their own profit.

Implications: R&D spending in China and other countries is growing much faster than in the U.S. In 2000, China was responsible for 3.5% of scientific studies published in the world. By 2015, Chinese scientists produced 18% of published studies. This strongly suggests that America's technical lead, and the economic benefits it brings, will not survive without changes in federal policy and corporate practice.

China graduates 4.7 million students per year with STEM degrees and awards 30,000 Ph.D.s in these fields annually. India turns out 2.6 million new STEM graduates each year. The U.S., in third place, produces only 568,000 STEM graduates annually. Only 4% of bachelor's degrees in the U.S. are awarded in engineering, compared with 31% in China. OECD predicts that by 2020 37% of the world's STEM majors will come from China. This too is bad news for American technical leadership.

Some 45% of foreign students in American colleges and universities major in STEM subjects. About half wish to remain in the U.S., but recent changes in immigration policy may make that impossible. They have already reduced the number applying for American student visas.

By inhibiting stem-cell research early in this century, the United States made itself a less attractive place for cutting-edge biomedical work. As a result, the United Kingdom and other countries soon recruited top American scientists and benefited from their discoveries. Calls to regulate gene-editing research and other controversial disciplines risk making the same mistake.

Washington's neglect of basic science is being felt in the declining fraction of patents, Nobel Prizes, and other awards going to American scientists. As other countries become more skilled in critical high-tech fields, the United States is fast losing its edge. If this trend is not reversed, it will begin to undermine long-term economic performance and shift both economic and political power to other lands.

This also has security implications, as witness the surprise announcements that Russia and China had developed hypersonic missiles. The U.S. had not entirely neglected this strategically crucial technology, but prior to 2018 it made little effort to develop weapons from what amounted to a low-priority science project. Given budget constraints, easier, but less transformative, concepts took precedence.

32. The power and impact of artificial intelligence and robotics are growing rapidly.

- The rise of "big data" and improved data analytics are providing vast new stocks of information for training AI, both enabling better training of AI programs and opening new fields for their application.
- New computers are bringing new power to run AI programs and are better adapted to their needs. Current improvements are in the development of neuromorphic chips, which imitate networks of nerves. Near-future developments

such as quantum and optical computers are likely to speed AI computing by orders of magnitude.

- ✓ IBM has designed a new programming language, Corelet, that mimics the massively parallel, redundant, and distributed "computing" processes of the human brain on a conventional supercomputer. A similar computing system took about 40 minutes to simulate one second of real neuronal activity among 1.73 billion cells with 10.4 trillion connections. IBM hopes eventually to mimic the activity of 100 trillion neuronal connections.

- A technique called reinforcement learning allows computers to figure out how to do things no programmer can teach them.

- Other advances enable AI to recognize and simulate emotions, making them better adapted to deal with human users.

- Artificial-intelligence software is quickly becoming simpler to use, so non-experts can apply it to practical tasks. Google has even made its TensorFlow machine learning software open-source, so others can not only use it but improve it and adapt it to specific tasks.

- Robots equipped with AI will be more capable, cheaper, more versatile, and safer when operating next to human colleagues.

- For the foreseeable future, artificial intelligence will be so-called "weak AI," focused on specific, narrow tasks such as pattern recognition, natural language processing, and machine learning.

  - ✓ "Strong AI," the kind of general intelligence capable of duplicating human versatility and insight, requires fundamental breakthroughs in the understanding of human cognition. Many AI researchers, especially among psychologists, believe it is fundamentally impossible to achieve.

  - ✓ However, at least one research group has reported discovery of an algorithm it suggests captures the fundamental processes of human thought.

Implications: Expect remarkable advances in medicine as AI is applied to newly available data from genomics, wearable tech that gives a real-time view of the human organism during exercise and under stress, and crowd-sourced data on behavior, nutrition, and other aspects of human life.

Robotic process automation, which uses AI to handle repetitive, rule-based business activities, will be one of the fastest growing markets through the mid-2020s. It grew by 64% in 2016 and was expected expand another 70 to 90 percent through 2018. We expect it to spread at that rate through at least 2025, and probably 2030.

Virtual assistants soon will begin to guide human activities, making sure that we get proper nutrition, for example, and arrive at appointments on time despite unexpected weather and traffic conditions. Software and devices currently marketed under that description is much less helpful than AI-enhanced virtual assistants are expected to become.

Research in linking computers directly to the human brain eventually will give humans direct access to AI, and vice versa, giving us access to more memory and special-purpose computing power than biology can provide.

The pace of scientific discovery will accelerate due to the use of AI lab assistants to extract patterns from experimental data.

Autonomous cars and trucks will dramatically reduce deaths from highway accidents, currently 40,000 per year in the U.S., 1.2 million globally, and rising. This also will save an estimated $100 billion per year in medical care and productivity losses. The insurance industry in this sector will contract sharply as a result. So will the number of professional drivers, now about 5 million in the United States alone.

Private ownership of cars is likely to be largely replaced by on-call fleets, many operated by automakers that have lost revenue from consumer sales. By the mid-2030s, this will eliminate auto dealerships and private repair services, save those specializing in exotic or collectible cars.

Loss of jobs to AI-enhanced automation will be generally recognized in the early 2020s. Nonetheless, warnings that AI and robotics could replace nearly half of human occupations by 2025 are unfounded. AI available then will be capable of eliminating many jobs and job categories, but adapting business processes to use it will take time. However, during this period AI will grow still more powerful. Eventually, it will be able to do nearly all that now occupies human workers.

AI will spin off millions of new jobs, many of them creative, mostly in AI, robotics, automation, and the ecosystem around them. However, fewer will appear than are lost, and many who lose today's jobs will be unable to make the transition into new occupations. Many others will lack the basic talents and skills needed to prosper in the new economy.

Retraining programs to help those who have lost jobs fit into the automated economy will be of temporary benefit, but less than many hope. There is little point in training for jobs that will cease to exist almost before they can be mastered.

Jobs are in their last years as the primary means of distributing buying power and providing a sense of accomplishment and personal worth. Studies find that up to half of them could be automated out of existence by 2025. We do not believe the transition will take place that quickly, but by the 2030s widespread unemployment becomes a near-certainty. In response to growing pressure from the formerly middle class, the industrialized lands are likely to establish a universal basic income. A poll in early 2017 found that 68% of Europeans already favor such a program, up from 64% a year earlier.

The impact of this transition may be even worse than it appears, because the profits from automation will go to those who own the robots. Everyone else will earn proportionally less, and the unemployed will struggle to survive as they wait for new jobs created by AI that will come too late or not at all.

As a result, growing numbers will create occupations to support themselves and their families "off the books" and all but immune to taxation. Some may be paid by barter.

As less income is declared, income taxes from the lower and middle classes will no longer help to support government functions. They are likely to be replaced by some form of value-added tax, as taxing the income of the wealthy seems beyond today's political leaders.

Political conflicts over all these changes will be intense, protracted, and destructive, as they delay society's adaptation to a world of universal AI.

Companies with the biggest stockpiles of data useful for training AI software will have an enormous advantage over those that are less well equipped.

None of these implications depends on the development of super-smart AI with the versatility of the human mind. They emerge from technologies now available or clearly under development. The arrival of "general AI," either as a result of breakthroughs in our understanding of the human mind or as an emergent property of combining many smaller advances, will transform them in ways that cannot yet be anticipated.

Until governments adopt a universal basic income or some other means of distributing buying power is found, the poor and formerly middle class may not be able to afford luxuries like travel. In this case, hospitality will cater to the wealthy, and there will not be nearly enough of them to support the industry in its present form. Creating hospitality products for those with little to spend will be one of the industry's greatest challenges in the years ahead.

33. The Internet is spreading to the remotest corners of the world.

- In 2017, 47% of the world's population is on the Internet, and fast broadband is expanding to cover even the remotest parts of the world.
    - ✓ In 2000, the world's Internet population numbered only 360 million. By March 2017, an estimated 3.8 billion people—nearly half the world's population—were online. By 2020, 5 billion people will be online.
    - ✓ In the U.S., 34% of the population lacks access to 25 megabit-per-second broadband service.
    - ✓ By 2020, global fixed broadband speeds are expected to double.
- The Net is increasingly mobile, with less than half of the Internet population connecting via desktop computers. In the U.S. and China, 71% of online minutes are spent with laptops, tablets, or smartphones. In Indonesia, mobile accounts for more than 90% of online minutes.
    - ✓ In 2015, there were 226 million mobile Net users in Africa, double the number only two years before. By 2020, there will be at least 750 million, and data traffic is expected to increase 15-fold.
    - ✓ Small, cheap solar energy installations allow charging for the two-thirds of people in sub-Saharan Africa who lack grid electricity.
- Among the 35 countries of the Organization for Economic Cooperation and Development in 2016, there were about 101 fixed and 95 mobile broadband subscriptions for every 100 inhabitants.
- As SpaceX, Google, and other companies bring their networks online, broadband will quickly grow to cover the entire planet.
    - ✓ SpaceX plans to loft nearly 12,000 satellites to provide Net access beginning in 2019. The company expects to complete its network in 2024.
    - ✓ Samsung has proposed a similar network involving 4,600 satellites.
    - ✓ Google is working on a system that will use balloons to deliver Net service. Sri Lanka has bought 25% of the project.
- The Net's center of gravity is changing quickly. In the Internet's dawn of time, the early 1990s, almost all Net users outside the United States lived in Europe.

In March 2017, there were 320 million of them in North America, 637 million in Europe, and 1.8 *billion* in Asia.

- ✓ This trend is sure to continue. Over 88% of the North American population is online, and 77% of Europe. Asian Net users make up only 45% of the region's population. In Africa, only 28% are online.
- Only 52% of websites use English. Russian, in second place, accounts for only 6.5%. Less than 3% of websites use Chinese.
  - ✓ However, only 26% of Internet users communicate in English online. Nearly 21% use Chinese. Russian speakers make up only 2.9% of Net users.
- In 2017, the world sent and received 225 million emails per day, the number growing by 3% per year.
  - ✓ In 2017, 53% of email is business messages. The average Net user receives 12 spam messages daily.
- Internet-based commerce is growing by 50% per year. Total e-commerce revenue was expected to be about $2.3 trillion in 2017, $4.5 trillion in 2021, accounting for nearly 10% of consumer spending.
- Worldwide, 53% of Internet users bought something online in 2016. In the U.S., 200 million people—two-thirds of the population—made at least one online purchase in 2016. The average online consumer in the U.S. spends $1,800 via the Internet.
- Internet censorship and surveillance are widespread. In most of Europe, Africa, Central and South America, and Canada, there is little or none. According to the Open Internet Initiative, Freedom House, and other authorities, government censorship or surveillance is pervasive in China, Russia, India, much of the Middle East—and the United States, which in 2014 joined North Korea, Russia, Saudi Arabia, and 15 other countries on a global list of "enemies of the Internet."

Implications: Internet censorship and surveillance will grow more common and intrusive through the foreseeable future.

The Internet will continue to take business from brick-and-mortar stores. As a result, many offline retailers will go out of business.

B2B sales on the Internet are continuing to reduce business expenses throughout the net-connected world, while giving suppliers access to customers they could never have reached by traditional means.

Internet-based commerce requires knowledgeable, well-trained workers. People with the right technical training will find a ready market for their services until artificial intelligence displaces them. The transition to AI will begin to be felt by 2025.

For travel and commerce, the spread of broadband is expanding the online presence of destinations in remote parts of the world. Participation in segments such as adventure travel and "poverty tourism" will grow as a result.

The percentage of revenues arriving from or influenced by the Internet will grow as well. However, profit margins are likely to shrink as online competitors grow in number and sophistication. Discount aggregators like Kayak and Priceline will continue to capture a growing fraction of Internet sales until hospitality and travel companies regain control of online marketing.

These trends call for the continuous development of new and effective competitive methods.

34. It is becoming increasingly hard to recognize what is real and what is not.

- Hollywood uses computer animation extensively, and often believably, to fill in for actors who are unavailable.
  - ✓ In "Rogue One: A Star Wars Story," Peter Cushing's character was portrayed by another actor with Cushing's features "grafted" to him by computer graphics, as Cushing had died more than 20 years earlier. Only his eyes seemed less than real, and then only to viewers looking for flaws. The young Carrie Fisher also appeared via computer-generated imagery.
  - ✓ Young actors who have captured public attention already are being scanned routinely for digital simulation in case they become unavailable or are needed for young roles they already have outgrown.
  - ✓ FaceApp, for smartphones, can realistically add a smile to a photographed face, alter the subject's apparent age, smooth wrinkles, and even change the individual's sex.
  - ✓ Artificial intelligence techniques such as machine learning are quickly eliminating the remaining weaknesses that still make it possible to distinguish graphics from reality.
  - ✓ For movies and 4K, a program called Beauty Box plugs into video production software to smooth rough or wrinkly skin and suppress blemishes such as acne or scars. It gives actors the appearance of perfect skin even in live broadcasts.
- Adobe has demonstrated what it calls "Photoshop for audio," which can edit recorded speech to alter what the person said or create entirely new sentences in the speaker's voice. A Canadian firm called Lyrebird has a similar program, AI-enabled, which creates speech all but indistinguishable from the real thing.
  - ✓ Lyrebird produced simulated, but believable, endorsements from Barak Obama, Donald Trump, and Hillary Clinton.
- The limiting factor is technology. Four minutes of animation equates to 7,500 frames. Each consists of 150 to 200 MB of data, adding up to 1.5TB over all.
  - ✓ In 2014, the 102-minute animated film *How to Train Your Dragon* required as many as 10,000 simultaneous computing cores and 75 million hours of computation, resulting in 500 million digital files.
  - ✓ The computing power required for this kind of task will be commonly available on consumer laptops before 2030—if demand for it materializes.
- "Fake news" during the 2016 U.S. presidential election appears to have been realistic enough to sway many voters.
  - ✓ This likely depended at least as much on the voter's wish to believe it as on the quality of the of the stories.

Implications: It soon will be impossible to recognize when images, video, and audio "recordings" are real and when they have been synthesized.

Faster, more powerful computers and improved AI will soon make it practical to create entirely synthetic "realities" of any length.

In the future, successful actors are likely to sign non-compete agreements requiring them never to act again in video in order to protect the value of their digital replicas.

In the U.S. elections of 2024, clandestine animation shops will begin to produce simulated, but entirely realistic, videos undermining the reputations of their clients' opponents. They will be paid for by anonymous donors to political action committees and similarly protected organizations.

By 2025, surveillance evidence used in criminal prosecutions will be routinely challenged by defense attorneys. By 2035, after several cases in which such evidence has proved to be falsified, it will be considered too unreliable for use in court.

The success of "fake news" in the 2016 election suggests that many voters are less interested in the validity of new information than in having their beliefs confirmed.

35. Advances in transportation technology will make travel and shipping faster, cheaper, and safer, by land, sea, and air.

- Elon Musk's famous Hyperloop appears en route to reality. Traveling at 700 mph, the train-in-a-tube would make the trip from San Francisco to Los Angeles—six hours by car—in only 35 minutes by Hyperloop. Cost to build is only a fraction of that for conventional trains.

  ✓ Hyperloop Transportation Technologies announced in May 2017 that the first Hyperloop passenger capsule was already in production and the first line—from Abu Dhabi to Dubai—could enter operation as early as 2020.

  ✓ Rival Hyperloop One, meanwhile, announced eleven possible routes in the U.S., including runs from Chicago to Pittsburgh, Miami to Orlando, and of course San Francisco to LA.

  ✓ Another possibility: Beijing's proposed Silk Road run from China to Europe—more than 8,000 miles. The trip would take a week on a conventional train, only a day by Hyperloop.

- A radical new air traffic control system called NextGen uses GPS to route airliners straight to their destinations, rather than along fixed air routes, cutting flight times and fuel use. It also allows planes to fly closer together, so more can be in the air at once; air traffic threatened to overwhelm the old system. Parts of NextGen are already in operation, with other functions due for completion through the early 2030s. A compatible system is under development in Europe.

- Supersonic aircraft are on their way back to the civilian market. At least four companies are working to develop supersonic business jets (SSBJ), and two—Lockheed Martin and Airbus—are working on supersonic airliners.

  ✓ Boston-based Spike Aerospace plans low-speed flights of a scaled proof-of-concept demonstrator in 2017, high-speed flights in mid-2018, and crewed supersonic flights in 2019. Deliveries of its 22-passenger craft are scheduled for 2023.

- ✓ Aerion Corp, of Reno, NV, plans the first flight of its SSBJ in 2021. The company foresees a worldwide market for 600 such aircraft in the first 20 years.

- ✓ In 2018, Boom Supersonic raised $100 million in funding for development of a 55-seat airliner capable of traveling at Mach 2.2. First flight of a manned technology demonstrator is scheduled for 2019.

- On-demand air taxis also are nearing operation. Half a dozen companies have models under development.

  - ✓ Best bet: Airbus is working up an autonomous VTOL taxi with room for a single passenger. The aerospace giant reportedly has earmarked $150 million for the project. Testing is set to begin in 2017.

  - ✓ Uber's new air taxi division, Uber Elevate, claims it will be testing an air taxi service in Dallas and Dubai by 2020. Airbus says it will be collaborating with Uber to develop the aircraft.

  - ✓ Ehang, a Chinese drone company, and the German Volocopter are expected to have pilot air-taxi projects flying in Dubai, Singapore, Los Angeles, and Dallas by the early 2020s.

  - ✓ Munich start-up Lilium has already flown an unmanned, two-seat taxi prototype powered by electric jet motors. Plans call for a five-seater that could make the trip from JFK to Manhattan in five minutes instead of nearly an hour by car.

- Modern airliners are taking over many of the pilot's functions. The most sophisticated already can fly on their own from takeoff to terminal. They even take over if the pilot's control inputs conflict with design limits. Expect the first pilotless airliners to be ready for use in the late 2020s, but it will be the early '30s before they are certified to carry passengers.

- There are more than 1 billion cars in the world, and the number is growing quickly, thanks largely to record sales in China. Conventional estimates say the world's auto population will double by 2040.

- A study from Stanford University says virtually all these cars will be electric, as drivers switch to electric cars by 2024. The reason: The "fuel" costs almost nothing, and the cars are expected to run for 1 million miles.

- As a human skill, driving is on the way out. Google's autonomous-car tests have pushed many old-line automakers into the race to be first with a driverless vehicle.

  - ✓ Two self-driving buses are carrying passengers in Helsinki.

  - ✓ Audi's 2018 A8 offers Level 3 autonomy, but not over 37 mph, so a human will still do most of the driving.

  - ✓ Nissan and Audi independently plan to have fully autonomous on the road by 2020.

  - ✓ Ford and BMW both say their autonomous cars will be on the market by 2021. Ford's will be for fleet operation at first but ready for private owners by 2025. The company says its cars can already handle rain and snow.

  - ✓ Uber planned to put self-driving trucks on the road in 2017—with a driver on board for safety—but problems in testing have moved their target date back. Autonomous trucks from Google's Waymo division was slated to begin freight deliveries to the company's Atlanta data centers, but only within its campus.

- Other advances in automobile technology are on the horizon, such as convoy systems that soon will allow cars to pack themselves closer on the highway safer and operate more efficiently.

Implications: Most accidents are caused by operator error, so autonomous cars and airliners will be dramatically safer than conventional vehicles. Tesla CEO Elon Musk points out that the company's autonomous mode already cuts fatalities from one per 94 million miles to one in 130 million.

Pilotless airliners also are expected to cut fuel and maintenance costs. Airline companies will invest heavily in them as soon as they believe the public will accept aircraft that lack human pilots to take over in emergencies.

That will be in the early 2030s, when experience with driverless cars will have eased public concern about trusting their lives to a robot.

Pilotless air taxis may be a harder sell, mostly because cities will find it difficult to provide landing space for door-to-door use. Another challenge will be finding urban air space for hundreds of small aircraft.

The NextGen air traffic control system was originally supposed to be complete in 2025. It has already been delayed and its functions cut back owing to budget problems and mismanagement. Expect it to fall further behind schedule as the roll-out continues.

Driverless trucks and taxies are likely to be arrive faster than autonomous private cars. They make money for their owners, and autonomous vehicles will make more of it. Their biggest advantage won't be safety or lower maintenance: Unlike human drivers, they will be able to stay profitably on the road 24/7.

About 3 million truck drivers will need new careers in the United States alone. Taxi drivers, chauffeurs, and other drivers will add as many as 2 million more to jobless roles.

Experience with the first Hyperloop in Dubai will confirm the system's efficiency and safety, but property rights and liability concerns will slow their construction in the U.S. So will lobbying by regional air carriers, whose routes the Hyperloop eventually will replace.

China and Europe, in contrast, will adopt the Hyperloop as quickly as funding and construction times allow.

More-efficient electric and hybrid vehicles will significantly reduce the demand for oil in the early 2020s, easing one of the few remaining sources of inflation.

Cities increasingly will struggle to reduce auto congestion, either by limiting the use of private automobiles—as in Munich, Vienna, and Mexico City—or by encouraging the development and use of mass transit, as in Copenhagen and Curitiba, Brazil.

New transportation technologies will revolutionize travel, but they will have little effect on the hospitality sector.

36. The pace of technological change continues to accelerate.

- The design and marketing cycle—idea, invention, innovation, imitation—has shrunk steadily. As late as the 1940s, the product cycle stretched to 30 or 40 years. Today, it seldom lasts 30 or 40 weeks. In the fastest-moving industries, such as computers and electronics, it can be two or three weeks. In electronics, consultants in China can reverse-engineer a new product and deliver a knock-off prototype in as little as a week.

- Fast 3D printing, or "additive manufacturing," is making it quicker, easier, and cheaper to create prototypes of complex parts, shortening their path to market.

  - ✓ 3D printing is now being adopted for routine production of complex, high-value items. For example, the turbine blades for some jet engines are now made by additive manufacturing and are lighter, stronger, and more durable than similar blades produced by conventional machining.

  - ✓ Improved technology and materials are quickly broadening the range of products that can be made practically by 3D printing. Even artificial internal organs are being made by 3D printing.

- More than 80% of the scientists, engineers, and doctors who ever lived are alive today—and exchanging ideas real-time on the Internet.

- As artificial intelligence gains power and flexibility, it will begin to take over some aspects of research. (See Trend 32.)

  - ✓ AI is already making it easier for scientists to keep up with research reports in their fields, carry out literature searches for future experiments, and prepare reports.

  - ✓ IBM reports that its AI can scan academic literature and generate scientific hypotheses that research is likely to prove correct.

  - ✓ As early as 2009, one AI program was making its own hypotheses about yeast genetics, designing experiments to test them, and then using automated equipment to carry them out. In one case, it identified three genes that code for an enzyme human scientists had not understood.

- All the technical knowledge we work with today will represent little more than 1% of the knowledge that will be available in 2050.

- A possible counter-trend is the waning of the consumers' urge to possess the newest technology. We see this in the latest generation of smartphones, in which cost has outgrown perceived value and shipments in 2017 and '18 declined from the previous year. Whether other consumer products will follow the smartphone's lead remains to be seen.

Implications: Use of AI for research and engineering will make new product development faster and cheaper in the near future.

The limiting factor in technological progress is no longer the pace of research and discovery, nor the engineering of new products, but funding their manufacture and bringing them to market. This gives even greater importance to the automation of manufacturing and logistics, but still more to advertising and marketing.

Industries will face much tighter competition based on new technologies. Those first to adopt state-of-the-art methods will prosper. Slower competitors eventually will fail.

Lifelong learning is a necessity for anyone who works in a technical field, and for growing numbers who do not.

37. Important medical advances continue to appear almost daily.

- Medical knowledge is doubling every four to five years, and faster in some specialties. Clinical knowledge doubles every 18 months.

- Half of what students learn in their freshman year about the cutting edge of medical science and technology is obsolete, revised, or taken for granted before their junior year is over. Scientists are developing a variety of drugs and techniques to combat infections that survive today's antibiotics.

- Gene editing makes it possible to heal many diseases, but it will be some time before most such cures enter human trials. In theory, the technique could eliminate all the 4,000 or so inherited disorders. Genetic therapies for hemophilia and sickle-cell anemia already appear successful in early human testing.

  - ✓ Gene editing is being developed for treatment of lung, bladder, prostate, and kidney cancer. One form of gene-based therapy for leukemia and lymphoma has already received FDA approval.

  - ✓ Scientists have used gene editing to eliminate viral DNA from test mice, pointing the way to a possible cure for HIV/AIDS and other viral diseases.

  - ✓ Another study found that inserting genes found in a family highly resistant to heart disease reduced cholesterol levels in mice by 40%. Human trials are still some years off.

  - ✓ Editing the genes of reproductive cells or embryos early in development can eliminate hereditary disorders not only from the patient but also from all his or her descendents. Ethical concerns have blocked human research in the U.S. and much of the West. However, scientists in China and some other countries are pursuing this work.

- Immunotherapy is proving remarkably effective against some forms of cancer. For example, two small children with leukemia were cured when injected with genetically modified T-cells from a donor's immune system.

  - ✓ In other experiments, treatment with the patient's own genetically modified T-cells has been astonishingly successful against blood cancers. In one study, 90% of patients with acute lymphoblastic leukemia that had resisted other treatment were cured of the disease.

  - ✓ Experimental vaccines are being used to treat human cancers. In one study, they helped about 40% of patients with advanced melanoma, though only one in twenty had complete cures. The vaccines must be tailored to the individual patient.

- Our growing knowledge of biochemistry, aided by advanced computer modeling, has made it possible to design drugs to fit specific receptors in the cell. Drugs created through this technology often are much more effective than natural derivatives or the products of "synthesize, scan, and hope" methods, and less likely to cause adverse side effects.

  ✓ That last point is critical. About one-third of drugs approved by the FDA later prove to have safety problems.

• Using electronic devices, doctors are beginning to restore useful movement to lab animals paralyzed by spinal injury. However, it will take a decade or more to shrink the hardware for practical human use.

  ✓ Also in the works: the use of stem cells to restore damaged spinal nerves, restoring reasonably normal muscle control.

• New medical imaging systems give unprecedented views inside the body.

  ✓ A new ultrasonic imager is said to reveal bodily structures not even an electron microscope can see.

  ✓ Another technique makes it possible to see inside the body with an ordinary camera.

  ✓ And a new twist on magnetic resonance imaging can look inside opaque tissues without a new $3 million machine or positron emission tomography, which requires injecting the patient with a radioactive tracer.

• Alzheimer's disease and other brain disorders may finally be on their way out thanks to a variety of new developments.

  ✓ Scientists in the UK have found two drugs that—in animals—block nerve loss of the kind seen in Alzheimer's, Parkinson's, and Huntington's diseases, and even in so-called prion diseases, which have never been successfully treated before. Both drugs are already in human use. They cannot repair whatever damage has already occurred or provide an outright cure, but they make the diseases something patients can live with. It will be about 2020 before results from human trials are available.

  ✓ Nicotinamide mononucleotide (NMN) appears to reverse many effects of Alzheimer's disease, again blocking progress of the disease. NMN is found naturally in all cells and, though horribly expensive now, eventually could be sold like any vitamin or nutritional supplement. In the body, NMN is converted to nicotinamide riboside, which already is available and is much less expensive. Human testing is yet to come.

• Other transplanted tissues will come from cloning and related technologies used to grow stem cells. Radical new treatments for diabetes, Parkinson's disease, perhaps Alzheimer's, and many other refractory disorders are can be expected to arrive within the next five to ten years. Whether American physicians will be allowed to use them is still being debated. Forecasting International believes that cloning and related methods eventually will be accepted for the treatment of disease.

• Surgeons working via the Internet will routinely operate on patients in remote areas, using robot manipulators.

• By 2025, the first nanotechnology-based medical therapies should reach clinical use. Microscopic machines will monitor our internal processes, remove cholesterol plaques from artery walls, and destroy cancer cells before they have a chance to form a tumor.

- The latest research suggests that it may be possible to cure, or at least delay, aging itself. Two of the more promising lines of research:
  - ✓ As we get older, the body accumulates cells that no longer work properly. It turns out that their presence is one cause of the symptoms we know as aging. Drugs known as senolytics kill these senescent cells and dramatically extend healthy lifespan—in mice, at least. The first human trials are in progress.
  - ✓ Decades of studies in many different test animals show that blood plasma from the young extends lifespan and reverses many aspects of aging. Research is beginning to identify the mechanisms responsible. Some clinics already are providing youthful plasma to prosperous oldsters, but formal human trials have yet to begin.
- Artificial intelligence is being applied to prostheses so that, for example, a "bionic" hand with a built-in camera can grasp objects automatically, requiring less fine control by the wearer.

Implications: Death rates from cancer, heart disease, and many other common ills are likely to plummet through the 2020s and into the 2030s, while the feared resurgence of infectious diseases should be averted. Fortunately, the incidence of Alzheimer's and other diseases of old age will be falling at least as fast, so many more of the elderly will be self-sufficient. This will reduce the cost of healthcare well below most current projections and ease the shortage of healthcare personnel. However, it is likely to raise the cost of Social Security and the few remaining fixed-benefit pension plans.

Until new therapies reduce the frequency of age-related disorders and rates of death from illnesses that are common today, growing personnel shortages can be expected in high-tech medical specialties, in addition to the continuing deficit of nurses and health aides.

These default expectations assume that there will be no radical breakthrough in the prevention of aging. This almost certainly makes them wrong.

Our current analysis indicates that the first practical techniques for extending human life and health will be available before 2030. Although they will not push average life expectancy much beyond the century mark, they will ensure that those receiving therapy will remain in good health much farther into old age than many observers now imagine possible. In this case, the need for most forms of medical care will decline rapidly, and shortages of medical personnel will ease quickly.

Unfortunately, this will exacerbate the issues of how to distribute buying power and give our lives meaning when jobs no longer serve those purposes.

On average, between 102 and 108 males are born for every hundred females. Numbers much outside that range suggest that parents are choosing the sex of their children, probably by selective abortion. Widespread sex selection is producing many more male than female children throughout the Middle East and Asia. The highest ratios are in Qatar (326 males per 100 females) and the United Arab Emirates (234/100).

India and China will face similar problems. Although both countries report sex ratios at birth within the normal range, population statistics tell a different story. By 2050,

India is expected to have 160 men wanting to marry for every 100 women available. In China, there will be upwards of 180.

The resulting populations of unattached, violence-prone young men will destabilize the affected countries, their neighboring states, and the West. (See Trend 49.)

Trends in Labor Force and Work

38. Education and training are expanding throughout society.

- Rapid changes in the job market and work-related technologies necessitate increased training for many workers.

- The U.S. Bureau of Labor Statistics predicts that the economy will add 11.5 million new jobs in the decade ending 2026, a growth rate of 0.7 percent annually. Nine out of ten will be in service industries. Jobs requiring a high-school diploma were expected to grow by 5.1%. Job categories requiring at least some post-secondary education were growing by an average of 10.8%, including eighteen of the thirty fastest-growing occupations. Ph.D. openings were growing by 13.1%, those requiring a master's degree by 16.7%.

  ✓ Even some manual jobs now require extra training. In the forestry industry, the number of tree fellers is declining because complex machinery, which requires training to operate, gets their work done faster.

  ✓ However, there are so many jobs that do not require post-secondary education—retail salespeople and custodians, for example—that they will gain more openings, even at slower growth rates—8.8 million positions over the decade, compared with 6.8 million that call for more training.

- A second factor is the accelerating pace of R&D.

  ✓ As early as 1966, it was estimated that when engineering students graduated, half of what they had learned was already obsolete. Today, the half-life of an engineer's knowledge is two years or less. After 10 years, only 3% is still relevant.

  ✓ The half-life of biomedical knowledge is about five years. Research not only provides new discoveries, it often proves that what scientists and doctors believe is wrong.

- Teacher shortages, which slow this trend, are endemic throughout the world. The UN Educational, Scientific, and Cultural Organization says providing universal primary and secondary education, one of eight UN Millennium Development Goals, will require 69 million more trained teachers.

  ✓ Shortages are worst in sub-Saharan Africa and South Asia.

  ✓ The Organization for Economic Cooperation and Development says 30% of head teachers in member countries say their school is understaffed or that teachers are poorly qualified.

  ✓ American schools ran short of teachers in 2017, about 100,000 short. At the same time, fewer students are entering the career. This deficit was expected to continue every year thereafter until teachers are paid at fair market rates.

Their salaries average about 70% of those for other positions with similar levels of education.

- ✓ An exception is Finland, where teaching also is underpaid, though less so, but is a high-prestige career. In one case, 660 teaching positions attracted more than 6,000 applicants.

Implications: Both management and employees must get used to the idea of lifelong learning. It will become a significant part of work life at all levels.

A substantial portion of the labor force will be in job retraining programs at any moment. Much of this will be carried out by current employers, who have come to view employee training as a good investment. According to one estimate, the market for corporate training is growing by 7.8% yearly through 2019.

Even small businesses must learn to see employee training as an investment, rather than an expense. Motorola estimated that it reaps $30 in profits for each dollar it spends on training.

The rise of Internet-based education makes it possible for people to educate and train themselves for high-tech careers. In 2012, a 15-year-old from Ulan Bator, Mongolia, got a perfect score in the online version of MIT's sophomore-level Circuits and Electronics course. A year later, he was attending the school in person.

The inevitable obsolescence of human knowledge will help drive the adoption of AI.

AI in turn will make training for new careers largely obsolete. (See Trend 32.)

39. Specialization is spreading throughout industry and the professions.

- For doctors, lawyers, engineers, and other professionals, the size of the body of knowledge required to excel in any one area precludes excellence across all areas.
  - ✓ This is clearest in software engineering, where most companies limit hiring for all but entry-level jobs to candidates whose experience exactly matches not only the position's duties but the software used to carry them out.
- The same principle applies to artisans. Witness the rise of post-and-beam homebuilders, old-house restorers, automobile electronics technicians, and mechanics trained to work on only one brand of car.
- The information-based organization depends on ad-hoc teams of task-focused specialists to get its work done.
- For hundreds of tasks, corporations increasingly turn to consultants and contractors who specialize more and more narrowly as worldwide markets become increasingly accessible and technologies differentiate.

Implications: This trend creates endless new opportunities for small businesses and independent contractors. It also brings more career choices, as old specialties quickly become obsolete but new ones appear even more rapidly.

However, it will be heavily impacted by the growing power of artificial intelligence. For example, in medicine radiologists are fast becoming obsolete as software learns to identify cancerous tumors and other anomalies as well as human specialists and sometimes better. Contractors will find themselves displaced from many fields that require high-level skills but deal with tasks that are essentially routine. This trend also is reducing financial security, as independent contractors do not receive health insurance, retirement programs, and other benefits common among job-holders.

40. Services are the fastest-growing sector of the global economy.

- Service industries accounted for 58.6% of global GDP in 1995, according to data from the World Bank and OECD. By 2015, they made up 68.9%, and 74% in the advanced economies.
- Service industries provided 77% of private nonfarm jobs in the United States in 2008. By 2019, they provided 86.3% of total employment.
  - ✓ In the decade ending 2026, services are expected to account for virtually the entire net gain in U.S. employment. In April 2017, a typical month, service industries added 165,000 new jobs, wholesale and retail trade 14,000, and goods-producing industries only 12,000.
  - ✓ Twenty-nine of the top 30 fastest growing occupations are in the service sector.
  - ✓ The strongest growth is expected in educational services, healthcare and social assistance, personal service, and professional and business services.
- In the EU, services provide more than 70% of both GDP and jobs.
- Service jobs have replaced many of the well-paid positions lost in manufacturing, transportation, and other fields. These new jobs, often part-time, pay half the wages of manufacturing jobs.
  - ✓ Not all service jobs are badly paid. Physicians, computer professionals, and financial planners all are service workers with average earnings near or into six figures. Common factors: extensive training, high skills, and scarce opportunities compared with badly paid low-skill jobs.
- Many low-skilled service positions in administration and transport are being automated quickly. Typical at-risk occupations include positions in banking and booking/reservation work in the hospitality and travel industry.
  - ✓ Despite this, service occupations are trending toward bimodal distribution (see Trend 50), with medium-skill, medium-pay jobs growing slowest and most vulnerable to loss. In Europe, 70% of trade unions report their members are affected by this trend.

Implications: Services now compete globally, just as manufacturing industries have done since the 1990s. By creating competitive pressure on wages in the industrialized lands, this trend helps to keep inflation in check.

However, replacement of well-paid industrial jobs by service occupations has slowed income growth dramatically. This is a major reason American workers have been losing constant-dollar disposable income even as nominal wages have continued to grow.

This is yet another mandate for broad-scale education and training to prepare workers for higher-skill, higher-wage service jobs. This is most urgent for the unemployed. However, the single greatest share of job training—about half in Europe—is conducted or paid for by employers.

This need will become more urgent as it grows clear that AI and automation are supplanting human workers. By the mid-2020s, the need for public job training will become an important political issue in the United States and Europe.

41. Workforce participation in the United States is falling, especially among men.

- Among those age 19 and up, labor force participation topped out at 67.3% in *January 2000*. It declined continuously to the neighborhood of 66% and remained in that area until late 2008. Since then, it has fallen to 62.4% in September 2015 and remained at 63% or less through 2018.
  - ✓ Among men of prime working age, 25 to 54, participation topped out at 91.5% in January 2007. It bottomed at 88% in 2014 and at the end of 2018 had not risen higher than 89.3%.
  - ✓ Among prime-age women, it peaked at 77.3% in April 2000, bottomed at 73.4% in post-recession May 2015, and peaked at 75.8% in July 2018.
  - ✓ Participation rates vary widely among states. In nine, total labor force participation was under 60% at the end of 2018. In West Virginia, it was only 53.8%. Minnesota was highest at 69.8%.
  - ✓ In this, the U.S. is an exception. Data from OECD countries shows that labor force participation among men ages 15 to 64 has recovered from 79.5 at the bottom of the Great Recession to 80.2 in 2017. Among women, it has risen from 61.7 to 64.0 over the same period; in 2000, it was only 59.2.
- The difficulty of finding work after prolonged unemployment contributes to this trend. In a 2016 poll, 43% of jobless reported having completely given up looking for work. Among the long-term unemployed, the number was 59%. In 2017, with the official employment rate approaching 4%, one-third of the unemployed still remained on the sidelines.
- Many suspect that widespread addiction to opioid painkillers in the U.S. also suppresses workforce participation. One study suggested that addiction accounts for about 20% of the decline among prime-age men and 25% of the drop among prime-age women.

Implications: During periods of high employment, this trend aggravates worker shortages and helps to constrain business expansion.

It also reduces income-tax revenues and the federal discretionary spending that requires them.

Because many dropouts from the workforce are recognized as disabled—more than 12% aged 55 to 64 as of 2014—this trend also greatly increases the cost of Social Security disability payments and other services for those who can no longer work.

42. Workers are retiring later as life expectancy stretches and the few traditional pensions still extant disappear.

- OECD data show that a trend toward early retirement in the developed world has ended. In 21 rich countries, age at retirement has been rising since 2006.
  - ✓ The Great Recession accelerated this trend in all but the hardest-hit countries, where there were no jobs to be had.

- ✓ Entrepreneurs are particularly reluctant to call it a career. A poll by AARP found that nearly a third of Baby Boom entrepreneurs were not planning to retire *ever*, and another 19% did not know when they would quit. Three-fourths had no succession plan, compared with 37% of Millennial business owners. This foretells yet another conflict between Boomers and their heirs is coming over opportunities for advancement.

- In the United States, the fraction of workers among those over 65 fell dramatically from the early 1960s to a 1985 minimum of 10.8%. Since then, it has risen almost steadily. By 2016, 31% of people ages 65 to 69 were employed. By 2022, 27% of men and 20% of women are expected to remain in the workforce over age 65.

  - ✓ Over 16% of those age 65 and older are self-employed, by far the largest fraction of any age group.

  - ✓ Better health gives today's seniors more options late in life. In the U.S., more than half of early retirees cite a health problem or disability as the reason they stopped work.

- Americans often return to work and delay complete retirement for several years.

  - ✓ A brief delay is legally required, as the qualifying age for full Social Security benefits rises from 65 to 67 for those born in 1960 or later.

  - ✓ In the U.S., 65% of Baby Boomers expect to continue working after age 65. The youngest will reach that age in 2029.

- In Europe, full-time employment remains rare over 65. The average was only 5.6% in 2015. Nonetheless, labor participation rates have been rising among seniors since about 2005, earlier in some countries, and part-time work is increasingly common. This is due in part to the growing number of women who remain on the job.

  - ✓ Post-65 workforce participation varies widely from one country to another. Spain, at just 5.3%; Belgium, at 2.6%; and France, at 6.3%, are offset by countries like Great Britain, where 21% of people continue work at least to age 69.

  - ✓ The EU's official Europe 2020 Strategy aims to raise the average retirement age to compensate for the shrinkage in the prime-age workforce owing to sub-replacement birth rates.

- Senior workers tend to be most numerous in Asia. In Japan, 42.8% are still at work after age 65. In India, the number is 35.8%. South Korea reports that 45% remain in the workforce. In Indonesia, it was 50.6%. (Data are from 2016.)

  - ✓ China reports that 36% of seniors continue working over age 65. Note that Beijing tracks employment only among those whose paperwork identifies them as city-dwellers. In rural areas, everyone is assumed to work in farming, which may well be accurate.

Implications: This trend will spread throughout the industrialized countries and many industrializing lands as the retirement-age population grows and the number of active workers to support them declines.

It will be strongest in China and other countries where retirement programs are weak or absent and prime-age populations are declining. By 2025, we expect retirement in the United States to be delayed into the 70s, on average, because many in the Baby Boom generation have not saved for retirement. One study found that 55% of workers over age 55 had no retirement savings at all. Another 26% had saved less than $50,000. At age 60, 75% still had not saved enough. About half of Boomers will be living on Social Security or working in the traditional retirement years.

People increasingly will work at one career, "retire" for a while (perhaps to travel) when they can afford it, return to school, begin another career, work part-time at home, and so on in endless variations. True retirement, a permanent end to work, will be delayed until very late in life.

This will help to ease worker shortages during periods of peak employment. For example, in March 2017, nearly one-third of U.S. metropolitan areas had unemployment rates under the 4% usually considered to represent full employment. In some cities, it was as low as 2%, and employers were finding their businesses constrained by lack of workers.

Older workers will partially make up for the shortage of entry-level employees. The chance to remain in the workplace will reduce the risk of poverty for many elderly people who otherwise would have had to depend on Social Security to get by.

Travel and hospitality will find courteous, conscientious post-retirement workers well suited to guest-service roles.

Growing numbers of the semi-retired will find positions in education, helping to make up for the chronic shortage of qualified teachers, especially in the sciences.

In the long run, it may be impossible to maintain the tradition of retirement except through personal savings and investment. The growing ability of AI and other forms of automation to replace human workers will soon abort this trend. (See Trend 32.) We expect the number of elders who remain on the job to begin declining again no later than 2025.

43. Employment mobility is growing, with multiple careers becoming common, as more people make mid-life changes in occupation.

- In the U.S., where statistics are easiest to obtain, younger Baby Boomers, born from 1957 through '64, held an average of 11.7 jobs between ages 18 and 48. Twenty-seven percent held 15 jobs or more.
  - ✓ One-third of the workforce now changes jobs each year.
- The fast pace of technological change makes old careers obsolete, even as new ones open up to replace them. The rise of AI and AI-empowered automation is likely to accelerate this process dramatically.
- It is extremely unlikely that many of those who lose obsolete jobs will be equipped to perform, or even to learn, the new ones. People now change careers every 10 years, on average.
  - ✓ The pace slows rapidly after age 45, when 80% of people consider changing their careers, but only 6% do so.
  - ✓ Rates are lowest among blue-collar workers, who may be most in need of a new way to earn a living.

- A Louis Harris poll found that only 39% of workers say they intend to hold the same job five years from now; 31% say they plan to leave their current work; 29% do not know.
- This trend may be waning, as Pew Research reports that Millennials are remaining with jobs longer than their predecessors did. This may reflect the higher proportion of Millennials with college degrees, as grads tend to stick with one employer longer than others. Nonetheless, 67% of Millennials say they would leave a job that lacked opportunities for growth and leadership development.

Implications: This trend will accelerate once more as AI and advanced automation make ever more of today's occupations obsolete.

Moving displaced workers into new careers will be even more difficult than many observers now recognize.

"Earn while you learn" takes on new meaning: Most people who can will have to study for their next occupation, even as they pursue their current career.

In many two-earner couples, one member or the other will often take a sabbatical to prepare for a new career.

Self-employment is becoming an increasingly attractive option, as being your own boss makes it easier to set aside time for career development. This is especially true for generations X and Dot-com.

Retirement plans will be revised, so that workers can transfer medical and pension benefits from one career to the next—a change that has long been needed.

44. Two-income couples are becoming the norm in many countries.

- The percentage of working-age women who are employed outside the home has grown steadily throughout most of the world. Among OECD countries in 2016, 64% of women were in the labor force. The number ranged from 29% in India and 35% in Turkey to 75% in Norway and 80% in Sweden.

  - ✓ Men's preference for traditional gender roles mayo inhibit women's labor force participation. A 2017 study by OECD found that the number of men who would prefer their wives to stay home ranged from 12% in Northern, Southern, and Western Europe to 51% in Northern Africa. In Burkina Faso, it was 93%!
  - ✓ A worldwide Gallup poll for the International Labor Organization found that 70% of women and 66% of men preferred that women work at paid jobs, including a majority of women not currently in the workforce. We have not found an explanation for the apparent conflict with the OECD study cited above.
- In the U.S. that year, 66% of women were part of the labor force, according to OECD, including 60 percent in couples with children under 18. In 2017, the U.S. Bureau of Labor Statistics reported that only 57% of women actually held paid jobs outside the home.

✓ This has declined since 2000, when 68.8% of women were in the labor force.

✓ Women's preference for outside work is a big reason the richest 25% to 50% of the U.S. population has reached zero population growth. They have no time for children and little interest in having large families.

Implications: Demand for on-the-job child care, extended parental leave, and other family-oriented benefits can only grow. In the long run, this could erode the profitability of some American companies unless it is matched by an equal growth in productivity.

Middle- and upper-class two-career couples can afford to eat out often, take frequent short vacations, and buy new cars and other such goods. They feel they deserve whatever time-savers and outright luxuries they can afford. This is quickly expanding the market for consumer goods and services, travel, and leisure activities.

This trend also promotes self-employment and entrepreneurialism, as one family member's salary can tide couples over while the other works to establish a new business. Look for families that usually have two incomes, but have frequent intervals in which one member takes a sabbatical or goes back to school to prepare for another career. As AI and automation render former occupations obsolete, this is likely to become the new norm.

45. The Millennial and Centennial generations already are beginning to change society's priorities.

- There are 74.5 million Millennials—born from 1981 through 1997—in the United States; worldwide, they already make up one-fourth of the workforce. Centennials, born after 1997, number almost 84 million in the U.S. and about 1.3 billion the world. By 2020, their population is expected to reach 2 billion.

  ✓ Generation X, ages 38 to 53 in 2018 and now beginning to reach upper-management positions, numbers only about 68 million in the U.S.

- There are approximately 50 million people in Europe between the ages of 15 and 24; 30 million more are between 25 and 29. The under-30 cohort represents about 22% of the European population.

- The two youngest generations are particularly vast in India, the Muslim lands, and parts of Africa.

  ✓ More than half of India's population is under 25, 65% under 35.

  ✓ More than half of Egypt's labor force is under 30. Half of Nigeria's population—167 million in all—is between 15 and 34. In Afghanistan, Angola, Chad, East Timor, Niger, Somalia, and Uganda, more than two-thirds of the population is under 25.

- China's one-child policy, now abandoned, has skewed its population toward old age. Only 30% are under 25. By 2025, about 20% of the population will be over 65. By 2050, its workforce will shrink by nearly one-fourth.

- Throughout the world, the Millennial and Centennial generations have more in common with each other than with their own elders, thanks largely to the global reach of the Internet and mass media.

- In the U.S. and Europe, the under-20 group is remaining in school longer and taking longer to enter the workforce than before.
- Generation X, the Millennials, and the Centennials are proving to be very business-oriented, each more so than the last, until the youngest care for little but the bottom line.
  - ✓ Their entrepreneurial impulse is strong. Twice as many say they would prefer to own a business rather than be a top executive. Five times more would prefer to own a business than hold a key position in politics or government. However, seen Trend 47.
  - ✓ Issues of race, gender and ethnicity that obsessed earlier generations are for Millennials and Centennials almost beneath notice. All that matters is whether people can do their job well.
- Many in these generations are economically conservative. On average, those who can begin saving much earlier in life than their parents did in order to protect themselves against adversity.
  - ✓ Gen X made money in the stock market boom of the 1990s, then lost it twice, first in the "dot-bomb" contraction of the early 2000s and again in the Great Recession. Yet, most have left their money in the market.
  - ✓ Millennials and Centennials have learned from their example, but time is still on their side.
  - ✓ This also has reinforced a sense that all things are transient, with few people and no institutions to be trusted.
- They are highly independent in their goals and priorities, yet generally work well in groups when they can reach their goals most efficiently by doing so.
- Growing up with laptops and smartphones has made Millennials and Centennials more adept with technology than Boomers, and even Gen X, ever can be.

  - ✓ Growing up with the Internet has also addicted many to social media. Yet, it is Generation X that spends the most time with Facebook, Twitter, Instagram, and their competitors.

Implications: Although generations have common characteristics, individual variation overwhelms them. Nothing said about any group will apply to all its members.

Employers must adjust their policies and practices to fit the values of these new and different generations, including finding new ways to motivate and reward them. The younger generations all thrive on challenge, opportunity, and training—whatever will best prepare them for their next career move. Cash is just the beginning of what they expect.

For these generations, lifelong learning is nothing new; it's just the way life is. Companies that can provide diverse, cutting-edge training will have a strong recruiting advantage over competitors that offer fewer opportunities to improve their skills and knowledge base. However, they will have to adjust their expectations and incentives to suit unique generational needs and preferences.

From Generation X on, they are increasingly well equipped for work in an increasingly high-tech world, but have little interest in their employers' needs. They also have a powerful urge to do things their way.

As both customers and employees, they will demand even more advanced telecommunications, Net-based transactions, and cutting-edge technology.

Growing up with parents eager to nurture their individuality and sense of security has given Millennials and Centennials an intense need for recognition when they accomplish even modest work tasks.

46. Growing stress increasingly erodes quality of life.

- As real buying power shrinks for the middle and lower economic classes, money is the most important stressor.
    - ✓ In the U.S., 65% of workers polled cited it as a "somewhat" or "very significant" source of stress.
    - ✓ Nearly 75% said money issues had caused them extreme stress in the previous month.
    - ✓ Among those with partners, nearly one-third reported money was a major source of conflict in their relationship.
- Time is another factor. Statistically, American men now work for pay 12 hours a week less than they did 40 years ago, just over 35 hours, on average, or 1,789 hours per year. Yet, many are working longer.
    - ✓ Email and smartphones have turned off-duty hours into working time, whether we get paid for them or not. Sixty percent of workers with smartphones are connected to their jobs 13.5 hours or more each day.
    - ✓ College-educated men lost six hours of leisure over the 20 years ending in 2005.
    - ✓ A survey of 1,000 professionals found that 94 percent averaged at least 50 hours of work per week. Nearly half worked 65 hours.
    - ✓ Outside the U.S., workers regularly spend even more time on the job: 1,853 hours in Israel, 1,985 hours in Russia, and 2,505 hours in Hong Kong.
- This trend does not apply to Europe, where strict regulations limit the number of hours asked of workers.
    - ✓ The UK is an exception: 40% of managers there put in more than 60 hours a week.
- In a Harris poll of Centennials ages 15 to 21 for the American Psychological Association, three-fourths said mass shootings are a significant source of stress. Other issues of concern included sexual harassment and assault and current events such as the separation and deportation of immigrant families.
- Nine out of ten in Generation X said they had experienced at least one physical or emotional symptom of stress such as depression or loss of motivation or energy. Nearly two-thirds found money or work stressful. One-third cited

personal debt as a cause. Other significant issues included housing instability (31%) and hunger (28%.)

- Other issues are significant as well:

  ✓ In Europe, more than 14% of workers report being threatened with physical violence at work. More than 8% in public administration, education, and health report actual incidents of violence.

Implications: Stress-related problems affecting employee morale and wellness will continue to grow. Companies must help employees balance their time at work with their family lives and need for leisure. This may reduce short-term profits but will aid profitability in the long run.

This is especially an issue in the hospitality industry, where staff tensions, harassment, and in hotels and restaurants even threats of violence are too common.

Single workers and two-income couples are increasingly desperate for any product that offers to simplify their lives or grant them a taste of luxury—and many can afford to buy it.

Time pressure offers new opportunities for hospitality companies to provide more weekend getaways, three-day cruises, "staycation" attractions, and similar products. Those including travel to the destination will be particularly attractive.

As time for shopping continues to evaporate, Internet and mail-order marketers will have a growing advantage over traditional stores.

Online marketing and reservations, already a major trend in travel and tourism, will be increasingly significant, even for segments that have resisted these practices.

Management Trends

47. More entrepreneurs will start new businesses.

- The most common and powerful incentive to start a business is unemployment. Worldwide, about 35% of the unemployed say they wish to start a business. This is true even among seniors, who when employed are much less likely to consider starting a business than other generations.

- In Europe, where entrepreneurship once was distrusted and unpopular, 85% of people in a recent survey said that starting your own company is now socially acceptable.

  ✓ According to one count, Europe is home to more than 150 tech incubators and Silicon Valley-style tech centers. In the Netherlands, the High Tech Campus at Eindhoven hosts more than 160 new companies and some 11,000 entrepreneurs and researchers. Companies there are said to be responsible for nearly 40% of Dutch patent applications.

  ✓ Stack Overflow, a popular Internet site for software engineers, estimates that there are now 5.5 million professional developers in Europe, compared with only 4.4 million in the United States.

- In China, where state-owned companies once effectively were the economy, private businesses have largely supplanted them.
  - ✓ Revenues and profits at commercial enterprises have been rising three times faster than those of state-owned businesses.
  - ✓ In the 2016 National People's Congress, Premier Li Keqiang made entrepreneurship a leading agenda of national economic strategy, using that word 22 times and "innovation" 59 times. The country has 115 university science parks and over 1,600 technology business incubators for would-be entrepreneurs.
- In India, 9.2% of adults in a 2015 survey said they expected to start a business within the next three years. Most were going it alone; only 3.5% said they expected to create six or more jobs within five years.
- In the U.S., workers under 30 would prefer starting their own company to advancing through the corporate ranks. Nearly two-thirds of 20-something Americans either own a business or want to start one, according to a survey at the University of Phoenix. About 10% are actively trying to start their own businesses, three times as many as in previous generations.
- However, in practice American Millennials are creating businesses slower than any recent generation. Less than 2% even report being self-employed, compared with 5.4% of Gen X and 8.3% among Baby Boomers. Possible reasons include college debt and un/under-employment, which make it hard to save starting capital, and strong risk-aversion.
  - ✓ Over the decade ending in 2017, the number of startups formed per year in the U.S. fell by 36%.
  - ✓ In contrast, adults aged 55 to 64 made up 14.8% of new entrepreneurs in 1996. By 2016, they accounted for 25.5%.
  - ✓ Nearly 80 percent of people who start businesses with under five people fund the company from their own savings. Millennials, whose real buying power is less than that of earlier generations at the same age, have not had savings to spend. (See Trend 14.)
- Majorities from Generation X on distrust large institutions and believe—correctly—that jobs cannot provide economic security in a time of rapid technological change.
  - ✓ Publicity around $1 billion "unicorns" has reinforced the dream of wealth through entrepreneurship.
- Despite all this, self-employment was slow to spread in the U.S. until the last few years. Only 6.5% of American workers were self-employed in 2015. By 2017, the number was about 14 million, around 8.75% of the workforce.
  - ✓ This includes only the full-time self-employed. Other sources get numbers up to 25% by including Uber drivers, part-time freelancers, those with "side gigs," and others we prefer to omit.
  - ✓ Based on job-holders' ambitions, FreshBooks says the number of full-time self-employed professionals could triple to 27 million by 2020. Best guess: the number will be a bit less than 12%, or 19 million.

✓ In the EU countries, the average in 2016 was about 14%, slightly lower than a year or two earlier.

✓ In South Korea, 29.4% of workers were self-employed in 2017, down from 33% in 2009.

- Women are increasingly entrepreneurial. In 2018, women owned 39% of the 28 million small businesses in the U.S. Between 2007 and 2016, their numbers grew by 45%, according to the U.S. Census Bureau. This was 5 times faster than the national average for all businesses.

- Since the 1970s, small businesses started by entrepreneurs have accounted for nearly all of the new jobs created. For much of this period, giant corporations have actually cut employment. Despite this, they also account for a disproportionately high number of job losses.

Implications: Many countries, and especially the United States, have ample populations of would-be entrepreneurs to ensure the continuing flow of business startups in the decade ahead.

Through 2025, when the effects of AI begin to be felt (see Trend 31), entrepreneurs will continue to produce about 65% of new jobs. However, failed startups also will account for a majority of jobs lost.

The expanding global population (see Trend 4) will need food, resources, transportation, and other goods and services for nearly one-third more people by 2050. These will be a continuing source of entrepreneurial opportunity for at least 30 years.

Entrepreneurial growth is a self-perpetuating trend, as new firms need other companies to handle chores outside their core business. This opens market opportunities for still more startups.

Many startups will be founded on rapid developments in technology, which create endless new opportunities for business development. The application of AI and automation/robotics will provide many of these opportunities, both for small service companies and for individual consultants.

Technology, especially the Internet, has dramatically reduced the capital required to start a business. However, expanding a business much beyond self-employment still can require substantial investment.

This trend will help to ease the poverty of many developing countries, as it already is doing in India and China.

48. Government regulations will continue to take up a growing portion of the manager's time and effort, but not for many more years.

- The World Bank tries to track this, with limited success. Data for most major economies, including the United States, is unavailable. However, in the EU, senior managers in 2005 reported spending an average 11.4% of their time dealing with government regulations. Other countries ranged from 0.1% in South Korea in 2005 to 46.5% in Tunisia in 2013.

- According to the National Small Business Association, 25 percent of small-business owners spend one to ten hours a year dealing with new and existing federal regulations; 56% put it at 40 hours or less, and 70% said state and local regulations cost them 40 hours or less annually. However, 14% said they spent more than 20 hours per month on federal regulation.

- A study at Harvard Business School found that 27 CEOs of major international companies spent an average 9% of their time dealing with government, the media, industry groups, and other relatively unproductive demands.

- Other studies say line managers spend 35% of their time in meetings, 26% counseling bad employees, 18% resolving employee disputes, leaving relatively little for regulations.

- Note: the politician's gambit of displaying a pile of paper representing pages from the Federal Register (FR) is meaningless. Less than a third of FR pages are regulatory, some of them repealing previous regulations. The rest is public comments and other material managers never deal with.

- Note also: the number of pages published each year since Vol. 1 in 1936 shows no obvious difference according to the party in power.

Implications: There is little reason to imagine that the flow of new regulations will slow in the years ahead.

Regulations are necessary, unavoidable, and often beneficial. Yet it is difficult not to see them as a kind of friction that slows both current business and future economic growth.

However, the time and money devoted to complying with them will decline sharply in the next decade. This is an obvious field in which AI can eliminate many demands on human execs.

This position has important political consequences. In the United States, the right promotes it to gain support. In the U.K., it was a significant factor in the Brexit campaign.

A 2016 draft report by the U.S. Congressional Office of Management and Budget estimated the annual cost of major federal regulations enacted in the previous decade at between $74 billion and $110 billion per year. However, the estimated benefits of those regulations added up to between $269 billion and $872 billion annually (in 2014 constant dollars).

The largest benefits in 2014, at least 3.7 times their maximum cost and perhaps as much as 7.1 times, came from rules promulgated by the Environmental Protection Administration. Even neglecting the future costs of climate change, efforts to limit EPA's activities appear likely to cost much more than they save.

Regulations that ensure a stable, fair business environment are especially necessary. Lands such as Russia, India, and even China will remain at a competitive disadvantage until they can pass needed business regulations and enforce them fairly.

Institutional Trends

49. Consumers increasingly demand social responsibility from companies and each other.

- Major companies are being forced to change their operations in important ways
  - ✓ Walmart's Project Gigaton promises to eliminate a billon tons of CO_2 from the retailer's supply chain by 2030.
  - ✓ Unilever, one of the world's biggest sellers of palm-oil products, says it will stop causing net deforestation by 2020.
  - ✓ Apple's 58-page "Environmental Responsibility Report" for 2017—the firm's tenth such annual report—claimed the company got 96% of its energy worldwide from renewable sources in 2016, reducing CO_2 emissions by nearly 585,000 metric tons. Next goal: to use only renewable or recycled materials and eliminate mining from its supply chain.
  - ✓ In 2015, more than 300 companies supported President Barack Obama's clean power plan. When the Trump administration reversed course, corporate leaders at Mars, Staples, The Gap, and even ExxonMobil called on the U.S. to continue working against climate change.
- More than 2,100 companies in over 50 countries have sought and won B Corps certification as meeting rigorous standards of social and environmental performance, accountability, and transparency.
- In a 2016 poll, 96% of Democrats and 89% of Republicans endorsed government financial regulations. Seven out of ten approved of the Consumer Financial Protection Bureau, while only 20%—including less than half of generally business-friendly Republican respondents—called it an example of "job-killing big government."
- Nearly all major banks have refused to finance companies that use mountain-top removal to mine coal. They include Bank of America, Citigroup, JPMorgan Chase, Credit Suisse, and PNC.
- Safety testing of children's products also enforces corporate responsibility. Forced recalls in 2018 included 29 million "Step-It" wristbands given away by McDonalds that could cause skin irritation or burns; 17.3 million IKEA chests and dressers after two tipped over, killing children; and 17 products with parts that could come off, resulting in a choking hazard, more than 1.4 million units in all.
- With 5% of the world's population and 66% of the lawyers on the planet, American citizens will not hesitate to litigate if their demands are not met.

Implications: The Consumer Financial Protection Bureau, effectively gutted by the Trump administration, will be restored by whatever president follows him.

Many companies will adopt practices friendly to consumers and the environment, as others already have done. Likely exceptions include many oil companies, which will declare their commitment to clean practices but find them fundamentally contrary to their corporate interests, and the airlines, which will clean up air travel as best they can but lack the technology to make major improvements.

Access to information on the Net is making it easier for activists to monitor corporate practices.

As the Internet spreads Western attitudes throughout the world, environmental activists in other regions will find ways to use local court systems to promote their goals. Litigation is likely to become a global risk for companies that do not make the environment a priority.

Building a "green" reputation is proving to be an effective competitive method for hospitality and travel companies. By 2025, environment-friendly practices will be standard throughout the industry.

Monitor: In the U.S., the Trump administration and its congressional allies are committed to eliminating government regulations that companies find inconvenient. Weakening the Consumer Finance Protection Bureau, eliminating Internet neutrality, and eliminating the Dodd-Frank law intended to control banking risks that triggered the 2008/'09 recession will be followed by many less conspicuous consumer-unfriendly actions.

Watch corporate annual meetings as well. Shareholders are seldom friendly to measures that others consider socially responsible if they might impair corporate profits. In Shell's 2017 annual meeting, 94 percent of shareholders voted against setting emissions targets to bring the company in line with the Paris climate accord.

50. Institutions are undergoing a bimodal distribution: The big get bigger, the small survive, and the midsized are squeezed out.

- The top six car manufacturers in the world (out of fifty tracked by the International Organization of Motor Vehicle Manufacturers)—Toyota, Volkswagen, Hyundai, General Motors, Ford, and Nissan—built more than half of all cars manufactured in 2016. The bottom twenty-five combined produced less than Toyota, Volkswagen, Hyundai, or GM individually.

- In the third quarter of 2018, the top three personal-computers makers shipped 63.8 percent of the world's total output. The top five sold 78.1 percent.

- In 2017, 4.1 billion people flew. The top five airlines carried 797.2 million people in 2017. The next five airlines carried 364.1 million people.

- In 2000, there were ten major airlines in the United States. By 2015, there were four. In 2017, the top four each carried more than three times as many passengers as the fifth largest. Cumulatively, they carried 93 percent of all domestic passengers.

- Where regulations allow, mergers and acquisitions are an international game. Witness the $104.3 billion merger of the world's two largest brewers, Anheuser-Buschm of Belgium and SABMiller, in the U.K., in 2016. Major takeovers completed that year: U.S.-based Baxalta International by Shire, a London-based drug maker; the merger between Johnson Controls, in the U.S., and Tyco International, in Ireland; and the takeover of Columbia Pipeline Group, in Houston, by TransCanada, in Calgary. This phenomenon carried into 2018 when German Bayer Aktiengesellschaft acquired American Monsanto for $66 billion.

- We are now in the third decade of the micro-segmentation trend, as more and more highly specialized businesses and entrepreneurs search for narrower niches. These small firms will continue to prosper, even as mid-sized, "plain vanilla" competitors die out. This trend extends to nearly every endeavor, from retail to agriculture.

Implications: Thus far, industries dominated by small, regional, often family-owned companies have been relatively exempt from the consolidation now transforming many other businesses. Takeovers are likely even in this last frontier in the next decade.

In the 2020s also, this trend will begin to affect countries where all but high-tech industries remain fragmented and most businesses are small and family-owned.

"Boutique" businesses that provide entertainment, financial planning, and preventive medical care for aging Gen Xers and Millennials will be among the fastest-growing segments of the U.S. economy. Another obvious growth area: specialty hospitality firms in an endless variety of niche markets.

No company is too large to be a takeover target if it dominates a profitable market or has other features attractive to profit-hungry investors. In 2017, companies identified as acquisition candidates include Bristol-Myers Squibb, worth an estimated $120 billion, and Allergan, which Pfizer was set to buy for $160 billion in 2016 until Obama-era tax regulations scuttled the deal.

In Strategic Management for Hospitality and Travel: Today and Tomorrow
© Frederick J. DeMicco, Ph.D.; Marvin J. Cetron, Ph.D.; and Owen Davies
End of Book Case Study

The Wellness Tent: A Poverty Alleviation Tourism Project for Women in Developing Countries

By
© Dr. Chekitan S. Dev. All Rights Reserved. Please do not copy or cite without permission. 1

A Poverty Alleviation Project for Women in Developing Countries

Give a woman a fish, feed her for a day. Teach a woman to fish, feed her and her family for a lifetime.

Introduction

This project is aimed at helping poor women in developing countries escape from persistent poverty. The project is grounded in five key themes: 1. limited opportunities for women, due primarily to social and cultural constraints, to become productive members of the economy; 2. the dramatic growth in special interest travel, especially travel as it relates to health, wellness and culinary tourism; 3. the increasing use of natural treatments and diets in developed countries to help people cope with stress and other ailments, 4. the popularity of micro credit as a financing vehicle for incubating small businesses, and 5. the integration of the global supply chain making it easy to move materials across borders. At the confluence of these five themes lies an opportunity for poor women to create value with their traditionally endowed skills and abilities. Below, I will describe my vision for this idea, and then briefly go into each of these themes and suggest how they may be combined in a novel and interesting way to give poor women an opportunity to climb out of poverty by doing well and doing good at the same time.

Project Outline

Imagine a tented wellness retreat in a village in rural Kerala, the Andes, or a small town in the Bophuthatswana homeland of northern South Africa. In each place, local women are treating visiting women with herbs, oils, grains, spices, massage, song, incense, steam, dance or other methods that they have used to keep their families healthy and nourished for generations. These "treatments", local substitutes for "modern" health care which is typically unaffordable or unavailable, not subjected to double blind studies, are honed for their effectiveness over time by trial and error. The treatment and diet secrets are typically passed down to younger generations, almost exclusively women, by word of mouth. The women are working on women because in many areas, especially in developing countries, it is generally not acceptable for women to touch male strangers. In this way, poor women in depressed economic areas are doing good by helping those more fortunate by sharing their ways of feeling and being better and, in the process, helping themselves do well.

Why Now?

Persistent poverty among women is worst in economically depressed areas where women are discouraged or even prohibited from becoming productive members of the economy by working outside the home. By making it possible for these women to realize an economic benefit from their innate knowledge, they can help their families escape poverty, train other women in wellness methods so they can do the same, and codify these treatments for the healthcare community to investigate. This will then increase the health and nutrition awareness in the community, and increase the education level of the women by the training needed for them to run these businesses.

The Market: Well-Being Tourism

Tourists looking for physiological and nutritional nirvana now have new authentic, natural and ethnic cleansing and healing experiences to add to their travel repertoire. In an article in the April 2008 issue of the *Harvard Business Review* titled The Tourism Time Bomb, the author's state:

International travel is no longer the exclusive province of the rich. Over the next several decades, hundreds of millions of new entrants to the middle class will want not only the things – but also the experiences – that money can buy. … As the scarcity of places grows, many companies will find opportunities to profit by meeting new levels of demand for authentic – and inauthentic – experiences …. A billion or two additional international travelers represent both a massive potential headache and an opportunity for business. Local, natural and ethnic treatments and diets are very popular among international tourists, especially women from developing countries increasingly bedeviled by stress and other modern day ailments.

The global well-being/spa travel market is set to cross the $2 trillion mark, according to a new study, "Spas and the Global Wellness Market," conducted by SRI International.

Key SRI Study Findings include: 81% of consumers are "extremely" or "very interested" in improving their personal wellness; exercising, eating better and visiting a spa are the top three things consumers say they are most likely to do to improve their wellness; 82% of spa industry respondents reported changes in their business to respond to the wellness trend, and the vast majority has seen revenue growth as a result; While medical tourism ($50 billion) has generated far more discussion up to now, "wellness tourism" (consumer travel to pursue holistic, preventive, or lifestyle-based services) represents a market more than twice as large ($106 billion). The study, released at the Global Spa Summit in Istanbul in 2010, defines nine core segments of the market and three mega-trends driving growth in wellness travel. The mega- trends, according to SRI include: (1) an aging world population; (2) failing conventional medical systems, with consumers, healthcare providers and governments seeking more cost-effective, prevention-focused alternatives to a Western medical/"sickness" model focused on solving health problems rather than preventing them; (3) increased globalization, with consumers more aware of alternative health approaches via the Internet and the powerful reach of celebrity wellness advocates such as Oprah Winfrey, Deepak Chopra, and Jamie Oliver. The SRI study reported that there are 289 million active wellness consumers in the world's top 30 industrialized nations alone. The SRI report describes wellness as: (1) multidimensional and holistic, integrating physical, mental, spiritual and social approaches; (2) complementary and proactive, not only treating illness, but more importantly, focused on preventing sickness and improving overall quality of life; (3) consumer driven, relying on consumer choice rather than patient necessity.

How Will It Work?

The tents help lower the cost of the facility, reduce setup time, and can be shipped to other locations when not in use. If Four Seasons can do it in northern Thailand and become the best hotel in the world (2010), we can do it too. Plus, the ability for businesses to harness the power of global supply chains to move factors of production across borders has never been easier. For seasonal locations, these tents can be shipped from say one part of Africa, when it may be low season for tourists, to another part where it might be high season.

How Will It Be Financed?

Localities and countries where poor women live will benefit from this economic value creation. There are only so many basket weaving projects that can be supported in any area. This service business idea represents the new generation of sustainable and low impact value creation activities for the 21st century world economy.

The retreat will be financed by micro credit loan. Micro credit experience with women entrepreneurs in places such as Bangladesh and New York City by Nobel Laureate Mohammad Yunus has shown that women default on their loans less than men. Despite this fact, financing for small businesses is typically hard for women in economically depressed areas to obtain without collateral. The loan will be used to source a sufficient and high quality supply of treatment ingredients and treatment tents. By not being a charity, this program helps women help themselves in a fiscally responsible way.

This project will quantify the market for this economic activity, identify target markets where this might work best, and develop a model to bring the necessary stakeholders (tourism, health care, women's groups, micro credit, funding sponsors in cash and kind) together to make this work. This learning by doing will help us find a way to study poverty alleviation by the building of human capital in a new and interesting way.

This project is grounded in a novel and interesting private sector solution for a seemingly intractable problem. It also ties in with the four key sub-themes identified by the core team-health and nutritional status, educational attainment, labor productivity-enhancing technologies and markets, and risk exposure.

The main outcome of the project is a business aimed at empowering a key target group, women in depressed economic areas, escape poverty by capitalizing on a skill set that they possess. In keeping with the UN's Millennium Development Goals, this project addresses several key priorities: empowering women, improving health and reducing the economic gender disparity in a sustainable way. To paraphrase Muhammad Yunus, one day in the not too distant future, millions of people will visit a poverty museum to reflect on how and why this scourge affected over a billion people. This transformational idea has the potential to change the world.

Next Steps

All that is needed to develop a "proof of concept" is to find a location, donors (e.g., ESPA for wellness equipment and training, Abercrombie and Kent for tents and hospitality training, Doctors Without Borders for expert advice on non-traditional cures, etc.), for materials and training, and build a pilot project. In Africa, targeting the poorest but relatively safe countries (e.g., Malawi or Zambia) might be a good place to start.

End of Chapter Questions

1. Do you think the Wellness Tent concept presented will be effective? Why or why not? Please provide specific strategic management responses.

2. What are the key strengths, weaknesses, opportunities, threats for the Wellness Tent concept presented here for the hospitality and tourism industry for a country?

3. What is meant by the "Triple Bottom Line"? (You can Google this). How this Triple Bottom Line is be related to the Wellness Tent concept presented? How does this concept fit in to an overall tourism and hospitality strategy for a firm?

Case developed by Professor Chekitan S. Dev
Cornell University
College of Business
School of Hotel Administration
252 Statler Hall
Ithaca, NY 14853-6902
E-mail: chekitan.dev@cornell.edu

Vital Signs of National Stability

Socio-Political Indicators

- Population of men between age 15 and 30

  Young men are the most prone to violence.

- Unemployment rate among young males

  Young men are most volatile, and most likely to adopt violent causes, if they are unemployed and without hope. A sudden, permanent loss of job opportunities, as when a war is lost or government policies go far wrong, heightens the possibility of terrorism.

- Educational status of young males

  Young men are most susceptible to terrorist causes if they have been educated for a middle-class life that is no longer available to them.

- Percentage of ethnic minorities

  Ethnic divisions reduce national stability, particularly in regions with traditional tribal animosity. However, division among many ethnic groups, rather than only two or three, can produce relative peace, so long as power and prosperity are shared.

- Political power of ethnic minorities

  An effective political voice promotes stability among minority populations and reduces the likelihood of terrorist activity.

  States dominated by an ethnic minority may be even less stable and more prone to terrorism than those in which the minority is persecuted.

- Percentage of religious minorities

  The effects of religious divisions mirror those of ethnic divisions, but may be even more vicious and intractable.

- Prevalence of political corruption

  Widespread political corruption undermines the legitimacy of governments and tends to promote the growth of dissident and terrorist movements.

- Prevalence of police corruption

  Police corruption is equivalent to political corruption at the local level. It can be even more damaging to social stability, and more conducive to terrorism, because the police have both weapons and a coherent management structure to use them.

- Length of visa lines outside embassies

  Eagerness to leave the country reveals instability; any sudden change in this indicator is particularly important.

- Hoarding of food, medical supplies, and gasoline

These all suggest a general expectation of hard times to come and a decline in national stability.

- Number of foreign students in the United States in technical, business, and liberal arts courses

American colleges are a traditional haven for the younger members of wealthy families in unstable lands. In 2019, high-profile anti-immigration policies and a general impression that America no longer welcomes foreigners has reduced the value of this indicator. We expect it to recover in the 2020s.

- Percent of homes with indoor plumbing

A low number indicates widespread poverty and a population with little investment in the existing regime.

- Degree of religious freedom

Great religious freedom indicates a nation with little to fear from social differences.

- Degree of press freedom

The press can be free, monitored, or controlled; the greater the freedom, the more confident the government is likely to be in the acceptance of its power.

- Consolidation of wealth in the hands of political leaders and their families, of military leaders, and of political cronies of the head of government

The more wealth is consolidated within any elite, the less stable any nation will be.

- Subsidies for food, housing, and medicine or medical care

These indicate that the nation's underlying economy is not adequately providing for all its citizens and—when they become a major source of income for a large fraction of its citizens—suggest that social and political stability are low.

- Changes in subsidies to the poor

Sudden increases in subsidies often are an attempt to buy the loyalty of a population that is no longer willing to grant it.

- Percent of the population below the poverty line

Social and political stability is inversely related to poverty rates.

- Number of AIDS patients

In extreme cases, such as in Central Africa and Thailand, high rates of AIDS can undermine entire economies and cause instability.

- Rates of morbidity and mortality

High rates indicate that the society has not been able to deliver basic social services to its population, which will have little loyalty to the existing government. Rising rates, as seen in parts of the United States, are clear warning that something is going wrong in the society.

- Life expectancy

  This extends the previous indicator.

- Sharing data and information on technology, politics, economics, social conditions, criminal activity, military intelligence, and terrorism

  Governments unwilling to share basic information often are uncertain of their hold on power.

Economic Indicators

- Percentage of home ownership

  A high rate of home ownership suggests that wealth is being distributed relatively fairly and indicates that much of the population has a stake in the country's continued stability and prosperity. Again, a significant decline suggests that social cohesion may be declining as well.

- Percentage of imports

  In the absence of some balancing factor, the need to import an unusually high fraction of a nation's goods suggests the absence of a native manufacturing base, and perhaps the existence of widespread poverty. In some countries, trade data may be more available or more reliable than social indicators.

- Percentage of exports

  Strong exports of manufactured goods suggest a prosperous economy, and therefore a stable nation; an export economy based on raw materials suggests the reverse. Oil-based economies will be vulnerable to unrest for so long as petroleum remains relatively cheap, as we expect it to, minus occasional spikes due to political or military uncertainties, until world reserves are clearly being exhausted.

- Difference in income and wealth between the richest and poorest deciles of the population

  A wide gap between the rich and poor is one of the most reliable warnings of social and political instability. Developed by Forecasting International many years ago, this indicator was adopted by the Central Intelligence Agency for the country reports presented in the *CIA World Factbook*, which is available on the Internet. A similar measure called the Gini coefficient is commonly available. It uses the top and bottom 20 percent.

- Transfer of wealth to other countries

  In the absence of other investment incentives, this may suggest strong doubts about political stability among those well positioned to make such a judgment. Specific data to look for include:

  - Movement of cash to the United States

  - Investment in U.S. stocks or bonds

  - Investment in overseas real estate

- Increased sales of diamonds

  This may reveal conversion of wealth to easily portable form, a traditional sign of instability.

- Increased numbers of expensive homes on the market

  Another harbinger of impending flight by the wealthy.

- Growing investment in homes or real estate in the United States or Canada by the wealthy elite, by high-ranking military officers, and by politicians

  This strongly confirms the previous indicator.

- Form in which workers are paid

  Payment in goods or credit—in any form other than a regular salary—indicates a severely unhealthy economy in which unrest is likely.

  For a time, Russian teachers were paid in vodka, which is easily sold and resisted inflation better than rubles. They had refused to accept payment in toilet paper or credit toward funeral costs.

- Access to drug funds

  Drug money represents a convenient and lucrative way both to support terrorist activity and to make it pay.

Technology Indicators

- Number of automobiles

  A high rate of automobile ownership suggests at least moderate general prosperity and the existence of a well developed infrastructure to maintain and supply the cars and roads; both these implications suggest political and economic stability. The infrastructure itself can be seen—highways on satellite photographs, for example—but hard numbers can be tracked over time or compared with those of other countries.

- Availability of modern communications facilities

  General access to information-related technologies suggests the existence of a high-tech infrastructure to manufacture, operate, and maintain the equipment; a population both sufficiently well educated to have use for telephones, computers, and the like and wealthy enough to buy them; and a government that trusts its citizens with information and with access to the world at large. Specific indicators include:

  - Number of cell phones per capita
  - Number of land-line telephones per capita

- Number of computers per capita
- Number of printers per capita
- Number of copiers per capita
- Number of fax machines per capita
- Number of shortwave radio receivers per capita
- Number of satellite receivers per capita
- Number of Internet users per capita.

Military Indicators

- Percentage of military

  In a stable country, the military usually employs a small fraction of the population and forms a minor segment of the economy.

- Military salaries

  Military pay scales substantially above those of the population at large may indicate a nation with little social cohesion.

- Numbers of palace guard or "elite" guard

  The existence of a strong elite guard indicates that leaders cannot trust even their own military.

- Changes in salary of palace guard per year

  A sudden, substantial pay raise for an elite guard is often an attempt to buy loyalty where none is otherwise available and is a clear sign of impending unrest. This was one of the most important symptoms of social and political instability in Iran in the years before the fundamentalist revolution of 1980. More than any other single factor, it allowed Forecasting International to warn its clients of impending trouble fully two years before the event.

- Role of military in politics

  Relatively few governments remain stable for long unless the military is subservient to civilian rule.

- Nuclear, biological, and chemical weapons capabilities

  There is little impetus for nations to develop weapons of mass destruction in the face of international sanctions unless they perceive some imminent threat to their sovereignty or are planning future aggression.

- Use of underground tunnels or laboratories

  The felt need to hide weapons development and other military preparations is a clear warning that war is contemplated.

Global Growth Strategy for Shaner Hotels: A History and Future International Plans for Hotel Development

Courtesy of Plato Ghinos/Shaner Group

*By Frederick DeMicco, Professor, Alessandro Capocchi, Professor
& Plato Ghinos, Conti Professor and President, Shaner Hotels*

ABSTRACT

This case study aims to describe the strategic international growth history of Shaner Hotels. In begins with expansion in Tuscany, Italy and then extends into the Eleuthera Bahamas to the former Club Med Resort. The case study begins with how the Italian hotel industry is improving its competitiveness, in the globalized economy, in terms of innovation and supplementary services delivered to the customers. Innovation (as implementation of new technologies) and supplementary services represent the driver for the Italian hotel industry to increase the creation of value and to become more competitive in the international arena. An industry that is growing, modernizing and expanding with brand-named hotels due to the projected growth in travelers to Italy in the future, many from Asia and other BRIC economies who perceive Italy as an iconic historical and innovative nation.

Key Words: Italian Caribbean Hotel Industry; Competitiveness; Innovation; Hotel Chain; Brand; Creation of Value.

Introduction

In the last two decades, tourism in Italy has changed its shape even while Italy remains globally one of the leading tourist destinations in the world. The Italian leadership in tourism is based not only on its geographical position, climate and natural beauty, but also on the fact that it has at least 40 percent of the world's wealth of monumental, historical and artistic works. All these reasons are making Italy an interesting destination not only for tourist but also for international investors who decides to become players of the Italian hospitality sector.

A recent study (see A. George Assaf, et al., 2015) of the different factors that attract hotel investors in a destination has analyzed seven pillars of locational attractiveness: 1) quality of tourism and related infrastructure; 2) opportunities for tourism; 3) quality of human resources; 4) political stability; 5) cultural and development proximity; 7) price advantage.

The relevance of tourism for Italy is clear when we consider some economic evidence: the tourist sector represents a share above 10 percent of the Italian GDP and above 11 percent of employment (Source Istat, 2014); both variables steadily display larger values than the world and the European average data. In Italy, the domestic segment of tourism is around 66 percent, as measured by total overstays (see Borowiecki & Castiglione, 2014; Massidda & Mattana, 2013; Accardo, 2012; Marrocu & Paci, 2013, and Lorenzini, Pisati, & Pompili, 2014; Cellini R. and Cuccia T., 2015).

Unfortunately, in Italy the incoming sector hospitality is not so developed in term of management. This is a threat but also a great opportunity. Here are a few points to explain why the Italian incoming sector is not internationally so strong: i) There is no Italian hotel chain that is strong abroad, as there are in countries such as Spain, France, UK, US etc.; ii) Alitalia—the Italian airline company—is experiencing a significant financial crisis, and the business model is not sustainable any longer; iii) In Italy there are 33,202 hotels and similar accommodations (Eurostat2015) with a total number of rooms of 1,091,634; iv) The average numbers of rooms in Italy is 124.8 for international hotel chains, 105.7 for domestic hotel chains and 32.9 for independent hotels. Italy in the European ranking for number of hotels and similar accommodation is n. 3 following UK and Germany while is number one for numbers of total rooms and number two in the world after China; v) In Italy the 95.8 percent of hotels are independents, which means the 85.8 percent in term of number of rooms.

Independent Hotel and Hotel Chain in Italy

In Italy the hospitality sector is composed of both independent hotels and hotel chains. Independent hotels are usually managed as family businesses, with generally poor managerial skills and a limited range of management tools. On the other hand, independent hotels are more open to innovation because the owner has direct contact with customers. This contact with customers is a real driver of innovation, as the independent hotels are more oriented to the creation of value by satisfying the individual customer's needs.

In short Table n. 1 shows the situation concerning the relationship between independent hotels and chain hotels, both domestic and international.

Table n. 1 Key evidences from the Horwath HTL2016

Key Evidences in the Last Four Years	2013	Growth %	2014	Growth %	2015	Growth %	2016
Chain Hotels	1,308	1.70	1,330	2.30	1,360	3.00	1,401
Chain Rooms	143,968	0.70	144,956	2.80	148,963	4.40	155,505
Average Size per Chain Hotel in Rooms	**110**	**−1.00**	**109**	**0.50**	**110**	**1.30**	**111**
Italian Hotel Stock (overall Supply)	33,728	−1.20	33,316	−0.10	33,290	−0.30	33,199
Italian Rooms Stock (overall Supply)	1,093,286	−0.30	1,089,770	0.00	1,090,300	0.10	1,091,569
Average Size per Hotel in Rooms	**32**	**0.90**	**33**	**0.10**	**33**	**0.40**	**33**
Chain penetration % in Hotels	0	2.90	0	2.30	0	3.30	0
Total Number of Brands	148	14.90	170	15.30	196	4.10	204
Domestic Brands	87	12.60	98	12.20	110	12.70	124
International Brands	61	18.00	72	19.40	86	−7.00	80
Source: the Horwath HTL 2016 Census of Chains' Hotels in Italy							

In 2016 the Italian hospitality market suffered two important changes: internationally, the entry Marriot and Starwood into the Italian market with a total of 46 properties, and the acquisition of the former of the Royal Demeures properties by Starhotels; domestically, the ATA Group, joined the UNA Hotels Group, forming the largest domestic hotel chain by numbers of hotels, and some domestic players went international for the first time.

Currently the hotel chains in Italy are mainly positioned in the upscale and luxury segment with a penetration rate of 5.4 percent in the midscale, 31 percent in the upscale and 49 percent in the upper upscale and luxury segment.

Courtesy of Plato Ghinos/Shaner Group

The Horwath HTL 2016 shows as the 61 percent of chain's hotels are managed by domestic players, while the remaining 39 percent is under an international brand, within which 5 percent is managed by domestic white label players. In the same report, they show only one case of foreign white label operator in Italy.

Concerning the different segments of the market in Italy, the hotel chains are more concentrated in the four-star properties, 84 brands are positioned in the luxury tier and there is a very limited presence in the budget and economy market. The different distribution between domestic and international hotel chains is not so far in the upper upscale and luxury market while is more significant in the midscale and upscale tiers in term of rooms:

- Midscale: 9,514 domestic and 16,336 international;
- Upscale: 39,369 domestic and 73,749 international:
- Upper upscale and luxury: 6,723 domestic and 9,198.

Concerning the geographical distribution of the hotel chains' rooms the 28 percent are concentrated in Rome, Milan, Florence and Venice. Lombardia, Lazio, Emilia Romagna, Veneto and Toscana are the regions where hotel chains are more concentrated, not only for the importance of the destination for tourism but also the presence of important business activities.

Finally, the top ten international and domestic hotel chain groups by number of rooms in Italy are: 1) Best Western, 164 hotels and 12,458 rooms; 2) Accor, 77 hotels and 10,015 rooms; 3) Marriott International, 46 hotels and 8,890 rooms; 4) NH Hotels, 52 hotels and 7,992; 5) UNA-ATA, 43 hotels and 5,467 rooms; 6) Valtur, 15 hotels and 4,990 rooms; 7) IHG, 31 hotels and 4,911 rooms; 8) Hilton, 19 hotels and 4,399 rooms; 9) ITI Hotels, 31 hotels and 3,824 rooms; 10) Starhotels, 24 hotels and 3,671 rooms.

380   **Strategic Management for Hospitality & Travel: Today and Tomorrow**

The Meaning of Creation of Value in the Tourism Industry

Tourism remains one of the most important sectors in the globalized economy. As reported in the United Nations World Tourism Organization's (UNWTO) Highlights 2012 Edition, tourism's contribution to worldwide gross domestic product (GDP) is estimated as 5 percent (UNWTO, 2012). Tourism's contribution to employment tends to be slightly higher and is estimated to be in the order of 6–7 percent of the overall number of jobs worldwide (direct and indirect). For advanced, diversified economies, the contribution of tourism to GDP ranges from approximately 2 percent for countries where tourism is a comparatively small sector, to over 10 percent for countries where tourism is an important pillar of the economy (UNWTO, 2012). For small islands and developing countries, the weight of tourism can be even larger, accounting for up to 25 percent in some destinations. The overall export income generated by inbound tourism, including passenger transport, exceeded $1.2 trillion in 2011, or $3.4 billion a day on average. Tourism exports account for as much as 30 percent of the world's exports of commercial services and 6 percent of overall exports of goods and services. Globally, as an export category, tourism ranks fourth after fuels, chemicals and food (UNWTO, 2012). The tourism Industry is going to change very fast: in 2030 57 percent of International arrivals will be in emerging economy destinations (versus 30 percent in 1980) and 43 percent in advanced economy destinations (versus 70 percent in 1980). The global market currently shares of Asia and the Pacific (to the 30 percent in 2030, up from 22 percent in 2010), the Middle East (to 8 percent, from 6 percent) and Africa (to 7 percent, from 5 percent) will all increase. As a result, Europe (to 41 percent, from 51 percent) and the Americas (to 14 percent, from 16 percent) will experience a further decline in their share of international tourism, mostly because of the slower growth of comparatively mature destinations, in North America, Northern Europe and Western Europe (UNWTO, 2012).

Courtesy of Plato Ghinos/Shaner Group

In this international framework the Italian tourism industry has to improve its competitiveness preparing the change for the future (Cetron, DeMicco and Davies, 2010). A significant role is played by the Italian lodging industry which has specific characteristics.

The Italian lodging industry is mainly represented by two different typologies of accommodation: The hotel industry and other typologies of accommodation.

The hotel industry in Italy is composed by 362 five- and five luxury-star hotels with 61,484 beds; 5,083 four stars' hotel with 706,383 beds; 15,217 three stars' hotels with 971,273 beds; 6,764 two-star hotel with 220,001 beds; 3,837 one star hotels with 89,287 beds.

Other types of accommodation are represented by 2,610 camps and tourist village; 456 hostels; 21,852 bed and breakfast (TourisMonitor, 2012). In the Italian hotel industry, the number of rooms is on the average of 46 rooms.

An industry that is growing, modernizing and expanding with brand named hotels due to the projected growth in travelers to Italy in the future, many from Asia and other BRIC economies who perceive Italy as an iconic historical and innovative nation.

In this direction, it is very important to understand how the Italian hotel industry could increase the capacity to create value in order to improve its competitiveness. Creation of value is an important issue in the dynamics of globalized competition. Creation of value can be defined as the ability of a company or of a sector to satisfy its customers. (Kozak, 2001)

In the globalized economy, to create value means to be able to satisfy also the potential customers (Alegre and Garau, 2010). And in a worldwide economy the creation of value is an important tool to attract tourists, as modern competition is based on the capacity to understand customer needs (Kotler et al., 2010).

If this is true, the creation of value is strictly related to the satisfaction of the tourist. And the satisfaction of the tourist could be a way to measure the creation of value in an economic perspective, through the guest's willingness to pay (Kozak and Rimmington, 2000; Choi and Mattila, 2003; Xia et al., 2004; Tallury and Van Ryzin, 2005; Mmoplwa G., 2007; Svensson et al., 2008; Noon and Mattila, 2009).

Tourist satisfaction is an important factor for the globalized competition also for the Italian hotel industry. From a managerial point of view, tourist satisfaction can be considered as "the primary source of future revenue" (Kau and Lim, 2005; Wang X., et al., 2009, page 397; Hasegawa, 2010). In the international literature, there are several studies that investigate and try to identify the main driving factors of tourist satisfaction such as tourist expectations (Bosque I. A. R. et al., 2006), the perceived quality, the perceived value and the destination and the brand image (Chen C. F., Tsai D. C., 2007).

It is also widely recognized that a quality service attitude is vital to building long-term, mutually ratifying relationships between hotels and customers (Martin, 1986; Croby et al., 1990). Several empirical studies also confirm the positive correlation between customer satisfaction and profitability (Anderson et al., 1994; Eklof et al., 1999; Zeithaml, 2000; Kuo, 2009).

The satisfaction of a tourist is also strictly related to the level of innovation (Weiermaier, 2006; Lee et al., 2007). This is the reason this study describes the relation between the uniqueness of the Italian hotel industry and the types of supplementary services provided to the customers.

Supplementary services are related to the innovation issue (Naipaul and Parsa, 2000). And innovation may be considered as a driver to create value for the customer and for the potential customer.

Following Schumpeter's analysis, it is possible to identify five different types of innovation, all of which can also be considered in the tourism industry: the creation of new products or services; new production processes; new markets; new suppliers; changed organizational structure or management system (Schumpeter, 1934).

Innovation can be viewed as the result of a value-adding chain of activities making up the complete or tourist's holistic product called "vacation" or "travel." It stretches from the first tourism encounters through advertising and/or the provision of tourism information to after sales services. Summing up, this study aims to understand whether and how Italy can be more attractive for international players in the hospitality sector, considering the experience of Shaner Group Inc.

Shaner Hotels Group

Shaner Hotel Group is one of the foremost award-winning hospitality owner-operators and development and management companies in the hospitality industry. Its current portfolio consists of 55 full-service, select-service, extended-stay and resort properties with more than 5,000 rooms in 17 states and two countries. Shaner successfully works with investors and brands—including hotel development, design and construction,

Courtesy of Plato Ghinos/Shaner Group

e-commerce and revenue management—and have a proven method for success thanks to Their hardworking and dedicated team and 35 years experience. Shaner Hotels works to deliver extraordinary experiences for guests, solid financial results for owners and partners and a great work environment for every associate.

Shaner Hotel Group in Italy: the Case of Renaisance Tuscany Hotel in Barga

Innovation and tradition

The "Il Ciocco" resort hotel was first developed by the Marcucci Family in the 1960s. It was originally developed and built by the family to serve as a training facility for Kedrion, a pharmaceuticals firm, and MTV Studios for Europe. Located near the corporate headquarters, the hotel would serve to house scientists and managers from Kedrion, coming from Europe and the United States.

The hotel was managed for many years by the Marcucci family, with many local employees, and managers. It is worth noting that the hotel had ample event space and rooms, including a 1000-seat ballroom for conferences and was later known as the MTV Studio Hotel. It also has pools, spa, thousands of acres of land to explore through hiking, horseback riding, rally car and motorbike events.

This worked well operationally for many years. However, as the hotel industry evolved rapidly around the world in an age of high-speed internet bookings and transactions, the family owners of the Il Ciocco Hotel realized they needed a strong management partner and affiliation to help in the global marketing, reservation systems, revenue

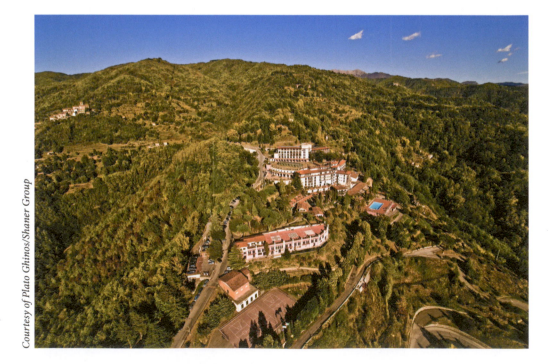

Courtesy of Plato Ghinos/Shaner Group

management and bookings in a more complex and hyper-competitive hotel business environment.

In 2009, the family, through a friend, invited Dr. Frederick DeMicco, a hotel professor from the University of Delaware to visit Il Ciocco. The Marcucci Family dispatched a helicopter to pick Dr. DeMicco up at the Pisa Airport in June. Dr. DeMicco met with Mrs. Marialina Marcucci, the matriarch of the family, on the terrace overlooking the stunning landscape—the Apennine Mountain range, the vineyards and the olive trees. During the meeting, Dr. DeMicco was provided an introduction and tour of the solidly built and venerable hotel. It was explained to that the family was seeking a partner to help modernize the facility and help with marketing in a global context. This was imperative for future financial growth and success of the Il Ciocco Hotel. Dr. DeMicco said he would make an introduction to potential hotel partners. Upon return to the United States the following week, Dr. DeMicco contacted three hotel companies whose presidents he knew. These include Shaner Hotels (Marriott franchisee); Dolce Hotels and Wyndham Hotels. They were all interested. However, Shaner Hotels visited first, and ended up seeing the opportunity and became a partner in the hotel (with the Marcucci family) and the management company for the hotel. The hotel was renovated and now has a Marriott Renaissance Brand. It is a five-star level hotel in Italy and attracts visitors from Europe, U.S. and Asia. It is also used for business conferences and leisure- with its outdoor recreation amenities, spa, and fabulous Tuscan cuisine. It is located near the charming town of Barga, surrounded by olive trees and vineyards and is about 30 minutes from the walled city of Lucca, famed as the birthplace of composer Giacomo Puccini.

Shaner Hotel Group: Expand Strategy in Tuscany

In 2015, Shaner and the Marcucci Family formed a joint venture to purchase an additional property: the historic Hotel Universo in Lucca. It is situated near Piazza Napoleon- where his sister ruled the city. This was the second hotel in Italy for Shaner. Hotel Universo is the only hotel located within the medieval walls of the City of Lucca. It offered the Marcucci/Shaner partnership an opportunity to acquire and reposition the hotel to a Marriott Autograph Collection Hotel under the new name "The Grand Universe" Hotel. This high-end property should open the doors mid 2019.

The Eleuthera, Bahama's Hotel Development Project by Shaner Hotels: Further International Growth

The History of Eleuthera

The island of Eleuthera (adapted from Eleuthera.com) was formed, as many islands are, as a coral reef. It gradually assumed a very unusual shape, long and thin, with much shoreline. It is also unusual in that it is relatively hilly, reaching an elevation of 100 feet, much more than most of the other Bahamian islands and nearby Florida. This fact gives it a scenic advantage, unshared by the other family islands, Generally, Eleuthera is 3 to 4 degrees cooler than Florida, with constant sea breezes; birds abound, and are heard everywhere outside the towns. The history of Eleuthera begins with the Arawaks.

Courtesy of Plato Ghinos/Shaner Group

They came to Eleuthera from the coast of the Yucatan in Mexico, and from Florida. They knew how to weave cotton cloth and made spears with fish hooks from the tortoise shell. They lived primarily on fish and shellfish. (By the way, it is from the Arawaks, that we get the three words, "iguana", "avocado", and "guava"). The Arawaks, a peace-loving people, were not displaced by the warlike Caribs, who did so in all of the other Lesser Antilles.

In the later 1400s, the Spaniards appeared in the area, led by Christopher Columbus. The Spaniards basically decimated the population of the Bahamas by either killing the residents or exporting them for slavery. The Bahamas, including Eleuthera became very desolate, save for small pockets of survivors. Thus, the Bahamas were like this for the next 200 years.

A person who is very prominent in Eleuthera's history, William Sayle, is credited for naming the isle "Eleuthera", which is a variation of the Greek word for freedom. He had been Governor of Bermuda, but had fallen into disfavor with the Crown of England. Therefore, he wanted to leave Bermuda to pursue freedom, and he decided upon Eleuthera, since the Bahamas were the nearest group of islands to Bermuda. He returned to London, and petitioned Parliament to settle Eleuthera in 1654 what he envisioned as a "utopia". He promised each settler 300 acres of land, upon completion of the voyage to Eleuthera.

However, the voyage did not end smoothly; one of the two ship wrecked on the perilous north part of Eleuthera, destroying much of their supplies. He put most of the settlers ashore at Preacher's Cave, and he went to Virginia for more provisions. When he returned with more supplies, he split the group; one group went to the area now known as "The Current", and his group went to Governor's Harbor. The soil was very rocky, and not easily cultivated, and the group continued to endure hardship.

Preacher's Cave today

The next period of history was dominated by pirates and buccaneers. The Bahamas in general, became headquarters for the pirates, especially Nassau. The only real contact Eleuthera had with the pirates was a raid by "Calico" Jack on Harbor Island, where he burned a few fishing vessels.

Next in history, the English took tighter control of the islands, especially after the American War of Independence. After their defeat, many Englishmen did not want to remain in the United States. Therefore, many emigrated with their slaves to the Bahamas, causing the white population of the Bahamas to double and the black population to triple. The British subjects were given land to aid their start in their new country. At this time, "wrecking", or the salvaging of shipwrecked boats, became a mainstay of the economy. In fact, various tricks were used to lure the ships to the reefs in the northern part of the island. At a large reef off Spanish Wells, a reef called "Devil's Backbone", there are many wrecks today, attesting to the success of the following ruse; lanterns were put on donkeys at night and moved to strategic areas to fool the captains into thinking they were the lights of lighthouses and cause the ships to go off course onto the rocks. This was especially popular in Spanish Wells and Harbor Island. The local population even resisted the construction of lighthouses\ in the period from 1845 to 1870; more than 300 vessels had been wrecked over the years, and "wrecking" provided an important boost to the local economy.

Pineapple farms then came into prominence. The pineapple has been introduced earlier, in the mid-18th century. But it was not until the turn of the century that it really became popular. The red soil of Eleuthera was ideal for growing pineapples. A prominent farmer, Jabez Pyfrom was a leading pineapple farmer at that time. Eleuthera's economy thrived and there was much prosperity. At one point, 40 schooners were anchored in Governor's Harbor, awaiting the harvesting of the famous pineapples. But this prosperity was not to last. The US government started to subsidize the pineapple industries of Cuba and Hawaii, undercutting the Eleutheran crop, and this industry, as well as the economy of Eleuthera, collapsed. Quarrying was then started, to try to jumpstart the economy, in the area of Hatchet Bay. George Benson, a retired English officer, was instrumental in this endeavor. He also started construction of the "cut" that is now present in Hatchet Bay, connecting the lake with the ocean. Another man famous in the history of Eleuthera, Austin Levy, arrived in 1927 and formed the "Hatchet Bay Plantations", a combined dairy and poultry farm. He became so successful that he built his own schools and stores. At about this time, Mr. Arthur Vining Davis started the Rock Sound Club as well as establishing a farm, dock, and workshops in the Rock Sound area.

Women notable in this era were Charlotte Blodget and Rosita Forbes. Ms. Blodget arrived in Governor's Harbor in 1937 and found much unemployment. She started a sea shell and weaving business\ and established trade with Boston. Rosita Forbes, an author and journalist of minor repute, wrote copiously and put Eleuthera on the map. She built a house called "Unicorn Cay" on a lagoon called "Half Sound". This house is modelled on the famous "Chateaux on the Loire" in France. She said around this time, Eleuthera had a bit of a scandal involving Count Alfred de Monigny, who had built a house at the site of what was later to become "The French Leave", and then the Club Med. It seems that the father of his bride was murdered in Nassau. He was accused and acquitted, but was required to leave the Bahamas.

Due to its location near Florida, Eleuthera became a relay station between Columbia and Florida, like many other Bahamian islands, for the cocaine trade, in the late '70s and early '80s. Though not heavily involved, the island and its economy and people were definitely affected by this drug trade. However, it has, by and large, disappeared due to police activity.

Today, Eleuthera's economy consists mostly of fishing, boating, and tourism. It is used mainly by Canadian, Italian, German, and American tourists as a vacation spot, and, for some, a winter home. It is not nearly as developed as Grand Bahama (Freeport), or New Providence (Nassau). In Eleuthera, you will find a world of sunshine and brilliant colors, pink sand beaches, and aquamarine and azure water where time stands still, life is leisurely, and peace is a reality and not an illusion. Island visitors are mainly from the U.S. and Europe.

Air travel is available from Fort Lauderdale, Miami and Nassau. Flight time is just over an hour from Florida and approximately 30 minutes from Nassau. North Eleuthera International Airport offers the most flight options from the U.S. Flights from Nassau travel to Governor's Harbour Airport, which is closest to the resort. Medical care is limited to clinics on the island, with limited hours or limited availability of doctors. Emergencies or serious medical conditions would require travel to Nassau or Florida via medical flight service or air ambulance.

Club Med Hotel—the Past Hotels on the Island

Built in 1976 Club Med was a profitable 300-room resort. Yet, when Hurricane Floyd struck in 1999, causing only limited damage, the company's financial position was such that the facility was closed instead of being repaired. Per Plato, Ghinos, president of Shaner, "Visitors are mainly from U.S. and Europe Club Med. It was one of the first ones built. It was destroyed in the early nineties by a hurricane and never rebuilt. The island was left behind in the tourism boom of the 80s and 90s. The lack of development and natural beauty is the biggest thing going for them."

Hotel description from the Shaner Hotel website

For a truly relaxing and unplugged vacation experience, visit French Leave Eleuthera in the Bahamas. The island of Eleuthera is a secluded paradise with no casinos, no cruise ship ports and no constant turnstile of flights carrying thousands of tourists. Instead, you'll find beautiful uncrowded pink sand beaches, azure blue waters, friendly people and great local dining and shopping experiences. Our hotel—which is designed for very low density, the least possible environmental impact, traditional Bahamian architecture and traditional Bahamian values—is one of the Caribbean's best kept secrets, and we invite you to experience this unbelievable paradise. Source: www.shanercorp.com/

The property joined the Marriott International Autograph Collection in 2017 with great success. As Shaner's Plato Ghinos puts it, "the property offers a great gateway with simplistic elegance to our customers."

Summary and Conclusion

This case study aims to describe the history of strategic international growth at Shaner Hotels. In begins with the expansion in Tuscany and then extends into the Bahamas at the former Club Med Resort. The case study analyzes how the Italian hotel industry is improving its competitiveness, in the globalized economy, in terms of innovation and supplementary services delivered to the customers. Innovation (as implementation of new technologies) and supplementary services represent the driver for the Italian hotel industry to create more value and to become more competitive in the international arena. This industry is growing, modernizing and expanding with brand-named hotels due to the projected growth in travelers to Italy in the future, many from Asia and other BRIC economies who perceive Italy as an iconic historical and innovative nation. The representation of the Italian context describes clearly the opportunity for foreign investors such as Shaner Hotel Group. Shaner's development strategy in Italy starts in Tuscany with two different projects based on the same financial partnership with the Marcucci family. The partnership between an Italian family—who are strictly linked to the territory and to the local cultural roots—and an international group, as in the Shaner experience, could become an example and a model for support and development of the Italian hospitality industry in order to make it more competitive in the global economic dynamics. Finally, the case study shows how the development strategy of the Shaner Group in Italy is coherent with other important project that Shaner is realizing in the world.

Acknowledgements

Shaner Hotel Group. is gratefully acknowledged.

References

Accardo, F. M. (2012). Observations on the state of tourism in Italy. *International Business Research*, 5, 67–70.

Ad banjo D. (2003). Classifying and selecting e-CRM applications: an analysis based proposal. *Management Decision*, 41 (6), 570–577.

Akbaba A. (2006). Measuring service quality in the hotel industry: a study in a business hotel in Turkey. *International Journal of Hospitality Management* 25, 170–192.

Alegre J., Garau J. (2010). Tourist satisfaction and dissatisfaction. *Annuals of Tourism Research*, 37 (1), 52–73

Al-Sabbahy H., Ekinci Y., Riley M. (2004). An investigation of perceived value dimension: implications for hospitality research. *Journal of Travel Research*, 42, 226–234.

Anderson E.W., Fornell C., Lehmann D.R. (1994). Customer satisfaction, market share and profitability: finding from Sweden. *Journal of Marketing*, 58(2), 112–122.

Assaf G. A., Josiassen A., Agbola F. A. (2015). Attracting international hotels: Locational factors that matter most. *Tourism Management*, 47, 329–340.

Babin B. J., Griffin M. (2001). International students' s travel behavior: a model of the travel-related consumer /dissatisfaction process. *Journal of Travel and Tourism Marketing*, 10 (10), 93–106.

Baker D. A., Crompton J. L. (2000). Quality, satisfaction and behavioral intentions. *Annals of Tourism Research*, 27(3), 785–804.

Barney J. B. (1991). Firm resources and sustained competitive advantage. *Journal of Management*, 17 (1), 99–120.

Barsky J. D. (1992). Customer satisfaction in the hotel industry: Meaning and Measurement. *Hospitality Research Journal*, 16 (1), 51–73

Barsky J. D., Labagh R. (1992). A strategy for customer satisfaction. *Cornell Hotel and Restaurant Administration Quarterly*, 33 (5), 32–40.

Berry L., (1983). *Relationship marketing.* In Berry L., Shostack G.L. and Upah G. D., (edited by), Perspectives in Services Marketing, American Marketing Association, Chicago (pp. 89–123).

Bigné J., Sánchez M., Sánchez J. (2001). Tourism image, evaluation variables and after purchase behavior: Inter-relationships. *Tourism Management*, 22(6), 607–616.

Bolton R. N. & Kannan P. K. & Bramlett M. D. (2000). Implications of loyalty program membership and service experiences for customer retention and value. *Journal of the Academy of Marketing Science.* 28(1), 95 –108.

Bonnie J. Knutson, Arjun J. Singh, Hung-Hsu Yen & Barbara Everitt Bryant (2004). Guest Satisfaction in the U.S. Lodging Industry Using the ACSI Model as a Service Quality Scoreboard, *Journal of Quality Assurance in Hospitality & Tourism*, 4(3/4), 97–118.

Borowiecki, K. J., and Castiglione, C. (2014). Cultural participation and tourism flows: An empirical investigation of Italian provinces. *Tourism Economics*, 20, 241–262 .

Bosque I. A. R., Martín H. S., Collado J. (2006). The role of expectations in the consumer satisfaction formation process: Empirical evidence in the travel agency sector. *Tourism Management.* 27(4), 410–419.

Boulding W., Staelin R. and Rhret M. (2005). A customer relationship management road-map: what is known, potential pitfalls and where to go. *Journal of Marketing*, 69 (4), 155–166.

Bowie D. (2009). A transactional approach to customer loyalty in the hotel industry, *International Journal of Contemporary Management*, 21 (3), 239–250.

Buttle F. (1996). *Relationship Marketing: theory and Practice*. London: Chapman&Hall.

Buttle F. (2004). *Customer Relationship Management: Concepts and Tools*. Oxford: Elsevier Butterworth-Heinemann.

Cellini R. and Cuccia T. (2015). The economic resilience of tourism industry in Italy: What the "great recession" data show. *Tourism Management Perspective*, 16, 346–356.

Cetron, M., DeMicco., F.J. and Davies, O. (2010). Hospitality and Travel 2015. The Educational Institute of the America Hotel Lodging Association. Orlando, FL. USA.

Chen C. F., Tsai D. C. (2007) How destination image and evaluative factors affect behavioral intentions. *Tourism Management*, 28(4), 1115–1122

Chen I. J. and Popovich K. (2003). Understanding customer relationship management (CRM): people, process and technology, *Business Process Management Journal*, 9 (5), 672–688.

Choi S. and Mattila A. S. (2003). Hotel revenue management and its impact on customers' perceptions of fairness, *Journal of Revenue and Pricing Management*, 2 (4), 303–314.

Christopher M., Payne A., Ballantye D. (1991). Relationship marketing: bringing quality customer services and marketing together. Butterworth-Heinnemann, Oxford.

Christou E. (2003). Guest loyalty likelihood in relation to hotels' corporate image and reputation: a study of three Countries in Europe. *Journal of Hospitality and Leisure Marketing*, 10 (4), 85–99.

Cline R., Warner M. (1999). Hospitality 2000: the technology a global survey of the hospitality industry's leadership. New York, Arthur Andersen Consultancy.

Crick A. P. and Spencer A. (2011). Hospitality quality: new directions and new challenges, *International Journal of Contemporary Hospitality Management*, 23 (4), 463–478.

Croby L.A., Evans K.R., Cowels D. (1990). Relationship quality in service selling: an interpersonal influence perspective. *Journal of Marketing*. 54 (2), 68–81.

Dube L., Renaghan L. M. (1999). How hotel attributes deliver the promised benefits. *Cornell Hotel and Restaurant Administration Quarterly*, 40 (5), 89–95.

Dube L., Renaghan L. M. (2000). Creating visible customer value. *Cornell Hotel and Restaurant Administration Quarterly*, February, 62–72.

Dube L., Renaghan L. M., Miller J. M. (1994). Measuring customer satisfaction for strategic management. *Cornell Hotel and Restaurant Administration Quarterly*, 35 (1), 39–47.

Dwyer L., Forsyth P., Rao P. (2000). The price competitiveness of travel and tourism: a comparison of 19 destinations. *Tourism Management*, 21, 9–22.

Ekinci Y., Dawes P. L., Massey G. R. (2008). An extended model of the antecedents and consequences of consumer satisfaction for hospitality service. *European Journal of Marketing* 42, 35–68.

Eklof J.A., Hackl P., Westlund A. (1999). On measuring interactions between customer satisfaction and financial results. *Total Quality Management*, 10 (4/5), 514–522.

Enz C. A., Siguaw J. A. (2000). Best Practices in Service Quality. *Cornell Hotel and Restaurant Administration Quarterly*, 41 (5), 20–29.

Flint D. J., Woodruff R. B., Gardial S. F. (2002). Exploring the phenomenon of customer's desired value change in a business-to-business context. *Journal of Marketing*, 86, 102–117.

Gallarza M. G. and Saura I. G. (2006). Value dimensions, perceived value, satisfaction loyalty: an investigation on university students' travel behavior, *Tourism Management*, 27, 437–452.

Galloouj F., Winstein O. (1997). Innovation in services. *Research Policy*, 26, 537–556.

Gilmore J. H. and Pine J. (1997). The four faces of mass customization, *Harvard Business Review*, 75 (1), 91–101.

Gundersen M. G., Heide M., Olsson U. H. (1996). Hotel guest satisfaction among business travelers. *Cornell Hotel and Restaurant Administration Quarterly*, 37 (2), 72–83.

Hallberg G. (2004). "Is your loyalty programme really building loyalty? Why increasing emotional attachment, not just repeat buying, is key to maximizing programme success". *Journal of targeting, measurement and analysis of marketing*, 12 (3), 347–360.

Hasegawa H. (2010). Analyzing tourists' satisfaction: a multivariate ordered probit approach, *Tourism Management*, 31, 86–97.

Haywood K. M. (1988). Repeat patronage: cultivating alliances with customers. *International Journal of Hospitality Management*, 7(3), 225–237.

Hjalager A. M. (2002). Repairing innovation defectiveness in tourism. *Tourism Management*, 23 (5), 465–474.

Horwath HTL, Hotel and Chains Report Italy, 2017. The Report Executive Version, 11–68.

Iriana R., Buttle F. (2006). Strategic, operational and analytical customer relationship management: attributes and measures. *Journal of Relationship Marketing*, 5 (4), 23–42.

Jacob M., Tintoré J, Aguilò E., Bravo A., Mulet J. (2003). Innovation in the tourism sector: Results from a pilot study in the Balearic Islands. *Tourism Economics*, 9 (3), 279–295.

Frehse J. (2006). Innovative Product Development in Hotel Operations. *Journal of Quality Assurance in Hospitality & Tourism*, 6(3/4), 129–146.

Kau A. K. and Lim P. S. (2005). Clustering of Chinese Tourists to Singapore: an analysis of their motivations, values and satisfaction. *International Journal of Tourism Research*, 7, 231–248.

Kim W. G, Cha Y. (2002). Antecedents and consequences of relationship quality in hotel industry. *International Journal of Hospitality Management* 21, 321–338.

Kotler P., Bowen J. T., Makens J. C. (2010). Italian Edition edited bt Mauri G. A. Marketing del Turismo, Milan, Pearson Italia.

Kozak M., Rimmington M. (2000) Tourist satisfaction with Mallorca, Spain, as an off-season holiday destination. *Journal of Travel Research*, 38(February), 260–269.

Kozak M. (2001). Comparative assessment of tourist satisfaction with destinations across two nationalities, *Tourism Management*, 22, 391–401.

Kuo C. M., (2009). The managerial implications of an analysis of tourist profiles and international hotel employee service attitude, *International Journal of Hospitality Management*, 28, 302–309.

Lam S. Y, Shankar V., Krishna E. M., Bvsan M. (2004). Customer value, satisfaction, loyalty and switching cost: an illustration forms a business-to-business service context. *Journal of the Academy of Marketing Science*, 32, 293–311.

Lee C. K., Yoon Y. S., Lee S. K. (2007) Investigating the relationships among perceived value, satisfaction, and recommendations: The case of the Korean DMZ. *Tourism Management*, 28(2), 204–214.

Lee S., Jeon S. and Kim D. (2011). The impact of tour quality and tourist satisfaction on tourist loyalty: the case of Chinese tourists in Korea, *Tourism Management*, 32, 1115–1124.

Levitt T. (1974). *Marketing for business growth*. New York, McGraw-Hill.

Levitt T. (1980). Marketing success through differentiation-of anything. *Harvard Business Review*, January-February, 83–91.

Lo A. S. (2010). Customer relationship management for hotels in Hong Kong, *International Journal of Contemporary Hospitality Management*, 22 (2), 139–159

Lovelock C. H. (1996). Adding value to Core Products with Supplementary Services. *Service Services Marketing* (2nd Edition), NJ Prentice Hall, 337–359.

Marrocu, M., and Paci, R. (2013). Different tourists to different destinations. Evidence from spatial interaction models. *Tourism Management*, 39, 71–83.

Martin Ruiz D., Gremler D. D., Wahburm J. H., Cepeda Carrión G. (2008). Service Value Revisited: Specifying a Higher-Order, Formative Measure. *Journal of Business Research*, Special Issue on Formative Measurement, 61 (12), 1278–1291.

Martin W.B. (1986). *Quality Service: The Restaurant Manger's Bible*. School of Hotel Administration, Cornell University, Ithaca, NY.

Martin-Ruiz D. Barroso-Castro I, Rosa-Diaz M. (2012). Creating customer value through service experience: an empirical study in the hotel industry. *Tourism and Hospitality Management* 18 (1), 37–53.

Massidda, C., and Mattana, P. (2013). A SVECM analysis of the relationship between international tourism arrivals, GDP and trade in Italy. *Journal of Travel Research*, 52, 93–105.

Michael C. G. Davidson (2003) An Integrated Approach to Service Quality in Hotels, *Journal of Quality Assurance in Hospitality & Tourism*, 4(1/2), 71–85.

Minghetti V. (2003). Building Customer Value in the Hospitality Industry: towards the definition of a customer-centric information system. *Information Technology and Tourism*, 6, 141–152.

Mmopelwa G., Kgathi D. L. and Molefhe L. (2007) Tourist's perceptions and their willingness to pay for park fees: a case study of self-drive tourist and clients for mobile tour operators in Moremi Game Reserve Botswana, *Tourism Management*, 29, 1044–1056.

Monroe K. (1990) Pricing: making profitable decisions. McGraw-Hill, New York.

Naipaul S., Parsa H. G. (2000). Supplementary Services as a Differentiation Strategy, *Journal of Quality Assurance in Hospitality & Tourism*, 1(1), 67–80

Noon B. M. and Mattila A. S. (2009). Hotel revenue management and the internet: the effect of price presentation strategies on customer's willingness to book, *International Journal of Hospitality Management*, 28, 272–279.

O'Malley L. (1998). Can loyalty schemes really build loyalty? *Marketing Intelligence and Planning*, 16 (1), 47–55.

Oh H., Parks S. C. (1997). Customer satisfaction and service quality: a critical review of the literature and research implication for the hospitality industry. *Hospitality Research Journal*, 20 (3), 35–64.

Olsen S. O. (2002). Comparative evaluation and the relationship quality, satisfaction and repurchase loyalty. *Journal of the Academy of Marketing Science*, 30 (3), 240–249.

Orfila-Sintes F., Crespi-Cladera R., Martinez-Ros E. (2005). Innovation activity in the hotel industry: Evidences from Balearic Islands. *Tourism Management*, 26 (6), 851–886.

Park C., Kim Y. (2003). A framework of dynamic CRM: linking marketing with information strategy. *Business Process Management Journal*, 9 (5), 652–671.

Piccoli G., O'Connor P., Capaccioli C., Alvarez R. (2003). Customer relationship management-a driver for change in the structure of the US lodging industry. *Cornell Hotel and Restaurant Administration Quarterly*, 44 (4), 61–73.

Parvatiyar A. and Sheth J. N. (2002). Customer relationship management: emerging practice, process and discipline, *Journal of Economic and Social Research*, 3 (2), 1–34.

Payne A. and Frow P., (2005). A strategic framework for customer relationship management, *Journal of Marketing*, 69 (4), 167–176.

Porter M. E. (1985). *Competitive Advantage: Creating and Sustaining Superior Performances*, New York, NY, The Free Press.

Reichheld F. (1996). The loyalty effect: the hidden force behind growth, profits and lasting value. Boston, Harvard Business School Press.

Rigby D., Reichheld F., Schefter P. (2002). Avoiding the four perils of CRM. *Harvard Business Review*, 80 (2), 101–109.

Rodrigues- Diaz M. and Espino Rodrigues T. F. (2006). Developing relational capabilities in hotels, *International Journal of Contemporary Hospitality Management*. 18 (1), 25–40.

Schumpeter J. A. (1934). *The theory of economic development*. New York, Oxford University Press.

Shoemaker S. & Lewis R. C. (1999). Customer Loyalty: The future of hospitality marketing. *International Journal of Hospitality Management*. 18, 345–370.

Sigala M. (2005). Integrating customer relationship management in hotel operations: managerial and operational implications, *International Journal of Hospitality Management*. 23 (3), 391–413.

Slater S. F. (1997). Developing a customer value-based theory of the firm. *Academy Journal of Science Marketing*. 25 (2), 162–167.

Svensson P., Rodwell L. D. and Attrill M. J. (2008). Hotel managed marine reserves: a willingness to pay survey. *Ocean and Coastal Management*. 51, 854–861.

Talluri K. T., Van Ryzin G. J. (2005). The theory and practice of revenue management. *International Series in Operations Research & Management Science*, 68, Springer, New York.

Teare R. (1993). Designing a contemporary hotel service culture, *International Journal of Service Industry Management*. 4 (2), 63–73.

TourisMonitor, TCI Edition, 2012.

Tyng-Ruu Lin G. and Lin J. (2006). *Ethical Customer Creation: Drivers and Barriers*, *Journal of Business Ethics*. 67, 93–105.

UNWTO, Tourism Highlights, 2012 Edition.

Volo S. (2004). Foundation for an innovation indicator for tourism: An application for SME. In P. Keller and Th Bieger (Eds.), AIEST 54th Congress: *The Future of Small and Medium Size Enterprises in Tourism* Vol. 46. St. Gallen. Switzerland: AIEST pp. 361–376.

Volo S. (2006). A consumer-based measurement of tourism innovation. *Journal of Quality Assurance in Hospitality and Tourism*. 6 (3/4), 73–87.

Wang X., Zhang J., Gu C. & Zhen F. (2009). Examining antecedents and consequences of tourist satisfaction: a structural modeling approach. *Tsinghua Science and Technology*. 14(3), 397–406.

Wang Y., Lo H. P., Chi R., Yang Y. (2004). An integrated framework for customer value and customer-relationship-management performance: a customer based perspective from China. *Management Service Quality*. 14, (2/3), 169–182.

Weiermair K. (2006). Prospects for Innovation in Tourism, *Journal of Quality Assurance in Hospitality & Tourism*. 6(3/4), 59–72.

Wu S. I., Li P. C. (2011). The relationship between CRM, RQ and CLV based on different hotel preferences. *International Journal of Hospitality Management*. 30, 262–271.

Wilson H., Daniel E. and McDonald M. (2002). Factors for success in customer relationship management (CRM) systems, *Journal of Marketing Management*. 18 (1–2), 193–219.

Xia L., Monroe K. B, and Cox J. L. (2004). The price is unfair. A conceptual framework of price fairness perceptions, *Journal of Marketing*. 68, 1–15.

Yoo M. & Bai B. (2007). Value Creation. *Journal of Quality Assurance in Hospitality & Tourism*. 8(2), 45–65.

Yoon Y. and Uysal M. (2005). An examination of the effects of motivation and satisfaction on destination loyalty: a structural model, *Tourism Management*. 26, 45–56.

Zeithaml, V.A. (2000). Service quality profitability and the economic worth of customers: what we know and what we need to lean. *Journal of the Academy of Marketing Science*. 28(1), 67–85.

The Role of International Hotel Chains in the Growth Process of Italian Hospitality Industry

Fred De Micco (PhD) – The University of Delaware and Alessandro Capocchi (PhD) – University of Milano Bicocca

Introduction

The global relevance of tourism is easily explained by the recent report of the United Nations World Tourism Organization (UNWTO): Tourism is a major category of international trade in services. In addition to receipts earned in destinations, international tourism also generated US$216 billion in exports through international passenger transport services rendered to non-residents in 2016. This brought the total value of tourism exports up to US$1.4 trillion, or US$4 billion a day on average (UNWTO, 2017: 2). International tourism represents 7 percent of the world's exports in goods and services, after increasing one percentage point from 6 percent in 2015. Tourism has grown faster than world trade for the past five years.

"As a worldwide export category, tourism ranks third after chemicals and fuels and ahead of automotive products and food. In many developing countries, tourism is the top export category."

International tourist arrivals worldwide are expected to increase by 3.3 percent a year between 2010 and 2030 to reach 1.8 billion by 2030, according to UNWTO's long-term forecast report *Tourism Towards 2030*. Between 2010 and 2030, arrivals in emerging destinations (+4.4 percent a year) are expected to increase at twice the rate of those in advanced economies (+2.2 percent a year). The market share of emerging economies increased from 30 percent in 1980 to 45 percent in 2016, and is expected to reach 57 percent by 2030, equivalent to over 1 billion international tourist arrivals. years of double-digit growth in spending, and after rising to the top of the ranking in 2012. Expenditure by Chinese travelers grew by 12 percent in 2016 to reach US$261 billion. The number of outbound travelers rose by 6 percent to reach 135 million in 2016. Tourism expenditure from the United States, the world's second largest source market, increased by 8 percent in 2016 to reach US$124 billion. Germany, the United Kingdom and France are Europe's top source markets, and rank third, fourth and fifth respectively in the world. Germany reported an increase of 3 percent in spending last year to reach US$80 billion. Demand from the United Kingdom remained sound last year, despite the significant depreciation of the British pound following the referendum on EU membership (Brexit). UK residents' overnight visits abroad were up by 5 million (+8 percent) to reach 69 million, with expenditure close to US$64 billion (+14 percent). France reported a 3 percent growth in tourism expenditure in 2016 to reach US$40 billion.

Moving from this global context and from the analysis of the international literature, in this chapter we aim to investigate with regard to the Italian situation 1) whether the International chain can support the development of tourism and if yes 2) how their presence on the territories has contributed to change the shape of the Italian tourism industry.

In particular, following first a qualitative approach, the chapter aims to describe the presence of international hotel chains in Italy considering how they changed in the last decades. The empirical research aims to represent an innovative perspective to analyze the new trend in the Italian tourism industry.

It is clear that in the last two decades tourism in Italy changed its shape even if Italy remains globally one of the leading tourist destinations in the World. The Italian leadership in tourism is based not only on its geographical position, climate and natural beauty, but also on the fact that it has at least 40 percent of the world's wealth of monumental, historical and artistic works. The relevance of tourism for Italy is clear, considering some economic evidence: 1) The tourist sector represents a share above 10 percent of the Italian GDP, and a share above 11 percent of employment (Source Istat, 2014); 2) Both variables steadily display larger values than the world and the European average data; 3) The domestic segment of tourism is around 66 percent, as measured by total overstays (see Borowiecki & Castiglione, 2014; Massidda & Mattana, 2013; Accardo, 2012; Marrocu & Paci, 2013); 4) The performances of tourist arrivals and stays in Italy strongly differ across different types of accommodation: the performance of hotels is worse than the performance of extra-hotel structures; 5) Within the hotel structures, the best performance pertains to the high value segment of hotels. Five- and four-star hotels are increasing of both arrivals and overnight stays, and this holds for both the foreign and the domestic tourist flows. In 3 star hotels a contraction of the domestic segment has occurred, which is in a large part counterbalanced by foreign tourists; 6) At the end, the total contraction in arrivals is around 1 percent, and the contraction of overnight stays is about 5 percent. A sharp decrease of both arrivals and stays has occurred for one- and two-star hotels; the decrease is clearly larger for the domestic part of the demand.

These figures can be easily explained considering the development of new kind of accommodation supported also by the new technologies as the case of Airbnb. (see Cellini and Cuccia, 2015). Italy climbed to 8th place with US$25 billion in outbound tourism expenditure, up 2 percent from 2015, while reporting a 3 percent growth in overnight trips to 29 million. Australia moved up to 9th place with a 6 percent growth in spending to US$25 billion, and a 5 percent increase in outbound trips to 10 million. Hong Kong (China) completes the Top 10 with 5 percent growth in expenditure to US$24 billion and 92 million outbound trips (+3 percent). (UNETO, 2017: 13).

Literature Review

The theoretical framework of this investigation is mainly based on two dimensions: the first concerns the analysis of Assaf, Josiassen and Agbola (see Assaf, Josiassen and Agbola, 2015) regarding the locational factors that play a significant role on the attractiveness of international hotel chains; the second dimension concerns the study of Ivanov and Ivanova regarding more generally the globalization issue and the impact of hotel chains' presence in a country on a country's level of globalization (see S. Ivanov and M Ivanova, 2016). In this theroretical framework, this appendix aims to investigate and to describe the state of the art in Italy.

In the international literature, there are several theories to explain firms' internationalization and locational strategies. Economists have largely paid their attention to the theory of foreign direct investment (FDI) and related sub-theories such as market imperfection theory, international production theory, and internationalization theory (see Byckley, 1983, 1988; Hymer, 1970). More recently a new theory has started to be more popular: the network theory (see Burton, Kahler, & Montgomery, 2009). Assaf, Josassen and Agbola provide an overview of the most important theories and methodological approaches.

The international production theory argues that the motivation of a firm to internationalize is depending on the resource advantages available in its home market in comparison to host locations (see Dunning & Kundu, 1995). In particular, Dunning (1993) and Johnson and Vanetti (2005) analyzed in their studies the locational strategies of firms in international markets. These theories, however, are not specifically focused on locational factors that help to attract firms to international markets. For these reasons, Dunning (1993) and Johnson and Vanetti (2005) developed a new paradigm to explain the locational choice of hotel companies in international markets. The new paradigm is based on three main pillars: ownership advantages (O), location advantages (L), and internationalization advantages (I) (see Dunning, 1993; Dunning & McQueen, 1982).

Hence, while internationalization theory does focus on the choice of location, the new paradigm is seen as more holistic as it addresses three broader factors.

Following this new approach the ownership advantages consists of the advantages of a firm seeking to engage in international activities, while the internationalization advantages concerns the advantages that companies "*derive from the modality of foreign involvement selected when going international*" (see Johnson & Vanetti, 2005, p. 1081).

The location advantages are directly connected to the destination-level analysis, including specific host destination advantages such as the presence of infrastructure, restrictions and regulations and political stability, etc. (see Dunning, 1993).

The new approach has been tested in the hotel industry and it comes out as perfectly suitable for the study of location as it has location as one its three main pillars. In this framework Assaf, Josassen and Agbola, following Dunning (1993) and Johnson and Vanetti (2005), they selected the new paradigm as the main theoretical framework for their research.

Their research has been focused on seven pillars: i) quality of tourism and related infrastructure; ii) opportunities for tourism; iii) quality of human resources; iv) restrictions and regulations; v) political stability; and vi) cultural and development proximity; vii) price advantage. Each pillar was divided in few different point.

The output of the research points out how several locational factors influence a destination's attractiveness to international hotels. The most important factors are classified by an elasticity coefficient: i) travel and tourism welcomeness; ii) quality of transport infrastructure; iii) prevalence of foreign ownership; iv) Size of host economy; v) growth rate of host economy; vi) performance of the hotel industry; vii) government expenditure on travel and tourism; viii) growth of the tourism industry; ix) crime rate.

Concerning the second theoretical dimension, the analysis took also into consideration the recent studies concerning the globalizations of an economy and in particular the impact of hotel chains' presence in a country on a country's level of globalization (see S. Ivanov and M Ivanova, 2016). Several factors in the international literature are indicated as able to stimulate globalization: i) the falling economic and political barriers between nations; ii) political liberalization; iii) international trade; iv) integration of world financial markets; v) international travel and tourism; vi) demography and migration; vii) global environmental problems; viii) the new information and communication technologies; ix) and other factors that may increase the interconnectedness of individuals, firms and institutions on global a scale (see (Lechner, 2009; Steger, 2013; Waters, 2001; Bhagwati, 2007; Rodrik, 2011; Stiglitz, 2003; Dwyer, 2014; Cavusgil, Knight, Riesenberger, Rammal, & Rose, 2015; Dwyer, 2015; Hjalager, 2007; Ietto-Gillies, 2011; Waters, 2001; Wild & Wild, 2015).

In this scenario it is easy to argue that TNCs, including TNCs in tourism and hospitality, increase the international interconnectedness of individuals, firms and institutions through their involvement in the international movement of goods, services, capital and people.

Also the economic and political liberalization are significantly important as they can improve transportation networks, promote the development of common currencies, they can support Governments to synchronize legislation at a supranational level, they can support the removal of barriers to international travel and the global market visibility provided by information technologies, and they can support tourism companies' involvement in international operations and their entry into new cross-border markets.

The Hotel Industry in Italy: an economic overview

The Italian economy is recovering after a long and profound recession, though the recovery is not as strong as expected and productivity continues to decline. Structural reforms, monetary and budgetary policies and low raw-material prices have contributed in the last five years to the improvement of the situation.

Since the beginning of the economic recession, Italian GPD has declined by 10 percent and now at the same level of 1997. Absolute poverty has almost doubled, and it concerns mainly the new generations. The situation in Italy in a hush of well-being has mixed results: Italy has a very good performance in term of times of life, work, social relationships, and health; under the average of countries belonging to the Organization for Security and Co-Operation in Europe (OCSE) in terms of employment, income, housing, education and skills. There are considerable disparities at regional level and also a significant disparities among different segment of population divided by incomes, health and employment.

To address the challenges in the economic field, Italy needs to increase the efficiency of public administration, improve the conditions for doing business and increase available skills by reducing poverty.

The Italian hospitality industry in 2016 decreases its performances, as represented in Table n. 1 and Table n. 2 below.

Table n. 1   Italian hospitality industry performance 2016-2015

Country Performance (Data in Euros)

For the Month of: August 2016

	Occ (%)		ADR		RevPAR		Percent Change from YTD 2015		
	2016	2015	2016	2015	2016	2015	Occ	ADR	RevPAR
Total Europe	69,8	69,7	109,75	112,38	76,58	78,31	0,1	−2,3	−2,2
Countries									
Austria	71,0	70,0	99,11	98,91	70,34	69,24	1,4	0,2	1,6
Belgium	61,0	71,9	98,09	97,86	59,88	70,38	−15,1	0,2	−14,9
Bulgaria	58,7	57,9	68,22	63,25	40,05	36,61	1,4	7,9	9,4
Croatia	54,9	52,6	140,74	111,91	77,32	58,91	4,4	25,8	31,3
Czech Repulic	70,3	69,3	74,92	73,90	52,70	51,20	1,5	1,4	2,9
Finland	64,3	62,4	96,97	91,28	62,31	56,99	2,9	6,2	9,3
France	63,3	66,9	131,92	140,69	83,48	94,17	−5,5	−6,2	−11,3
Germany	69,1	68,4	99,61	96,70	68,83	66,15	1,0	3,0	4,0
Greece	68,1	67,6	120,03	115,81	81,69	78,32	0,6	3,7	4,3
Hungary	72,4	72,0	72,31	66,22	52,37	47,67	0,6	9,2	9,9
Ireland	78,8	77,6	121,83	105,46	96,01	81,87	1,5	15,5	17,3
Israel	66,3	66,9	182,05	183,39	120,64	122,77	−1,0	−0,7	−1,7
Italy	**65,3**	**65,1**	**140,79**	**143,04**	**91,88**	**93,11**	**0,3**	**−1,6**	**−1,3**
Latvia	68,7	67,8	65,99	67,99	45,33	46,11	1,3	−2,9	−1,7
Lithuania	67,1	64,0	60,34	57,84	40,48	36,99	4,9	4,3	9,4
Malta	73,3	76,1	123,73	114,28	90,71	87,02	−3,7	8,3	4,2
Netherlands	72,3	70,7	111,36	104,67	80,50	73,99	2,3	6,4	8,8
Poland	71,4	68,0	61,84	60,21	44,13	40,97	4,9	2,7	7,7
Portugal	69,4	67,2	99,82	92,02	69,26	61,85	3,2	8,5	12,0
Romania	67,2	63,7	70,72	68,11	47,50	43,38	5,5	3,8	9,5
Russia	58,3	53,7	70,23	72,73	40,96	39,04	8,7	−3,4	4,9
Slovakia	62,8	59,0	62,75	59,56	39,41	35,13	6,4	5,4	12,2
Spain	74,5	71,1	109,24	100,55	81,34	71,46	4,8	8,6	13,8
Switzerland	65,4	65,5	202,34	209,98	132,39	137,56	−0,1	−3,6	−3,8
Turkey	49,7	63,6	82,08	110,37	40,81	70,22	−21,8	−25,6	−41,9
United Kingdom	76,4	77,1	108,65	119,05	83,06	91,75	−0,8	−8,7	−9,5

(Source STR Global)

Table n. 1 shows how the occupancy rate increased between 2015 and 2016, while the ADR and the RevPar decrease.

Table n. 2 is interesting because Milan—the city that hosted EXPO in 2015—reduces in 2016 its Occupancy Rate around 5.6 percent but not the RevPar.

Regarding the hotel industry, the average size in Europe in 2014 was 32.7 rooms and Italy was one of the five top countries in terms of hotel capacity account. Italy was also number three in Europe, with around 33,300 hotels and similar accommodation, while Italy was at the top in number of rooms (1.1. million), followed by Germany and Spain.

As represented in Table n. 3, in Italy tourism demand in the last decade increased with a weak flexion in the period 2007/2008 and 2011/2013.

Table n. 2 Bottom Five Markets in terms of Occupancy. Rate and RevPar

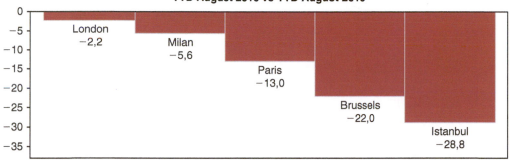

Bottom 5 Markets: Occupancy Percent Change
YTD August 2016 vs YTD August 2015

London −2,2
Milan −5,6
Paris −13,0
Brussels −22,0
Istanbul −28,8

Bottom 5 Markets: RevPAR Percent Change
YTD August 2016 vs YTD August 2015

London −11,8
Paris −16,1
Brussels −21,1
Baku −24,8
Istanbul −44,7

(Source STR Global)

The European market is still the first market for the Italian hotel industry with Germany, France and UK. Outside the European Union, the USA and China are the main markets, with a significant increase of the demand coming from the emerging economies as Brazil, India and Russia. An important point is represented by the changed mix of the demand during the last decade: i) the growth of international

Table n. 3 Tourism demand in Italy from 2004 to 2014

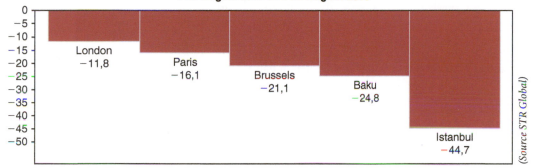

Arrivals, overnight stays and avg. stay in hotels in Italy, 2004–2014 (ISTAT)

Avg. Stay: 3.3 3.3 3.3 3.3 3.3 3.2 3.2 3.1 3.1 3.1 3.0 — CAGR % 2014/2004

Overnight stays in hotel (Min): 234 240 248 254 252 247 251 260 256 255 255 — 0,9

Domestic arrivals in hotels (Min): 41 41 43 43 43 44 44 45 44 43 43 — 0,6

International arrivals in hotels (Min): 30 31 34 35 34 33 35 38 39 40 41 — 3,1

Arrivals in 5* and 5* L hotels (Min): 1.89 1.97 2.36 2.36 2.31 2.40 2.72 2.90 2.91 2.97 3.12 — 5,1%

2004 2005 2006 2007 2008 2009 2010 2011 2012 2013 2014

— International arrivals in hotels (Min)   — Domestic arrivals in hotels (Min)
— Arrivals in 5* and 5* L hotels (Min)   — Overnight stays in hotel (Min)

The Role of International Hotel Chains in the Growth Process of Italian Hospitality Industry   403 demand hotels; ii) the continuous steady growth of demand in the luxury and upscale segments; iii) the loss of appeal of the economy scale.

In this context, the hotel chains increased significantly the number of rooms in the period from 2003 to 2015: from 35,600 rooms to 148,402 rooms, as represented in Table n. 4

Table n. 4 Key evidences in the last four years.

Key Evidences in the Last Four Years	2013	Growth %	2014	Growth %	2015	Growth %	2016
Chain Hotels	1.308	1,70	1.330	2,30	1.360	3,00	1.401
Chain Rooms	143.968	0,70	144.956	2,80	148.963	4,40	155.505
Average Size per Chain Hotel in Rooms	**110**	**−1,00**	**109**	**0,50**	**110**	**1,30**	**111**
Italian Hotel Stock (overall Supply)	33.728	−1,20	33.316	−0,10	33.290	−0,30	33.199
Italian Rooms Stock (overall Supply)	1.093.286	−0,30	1.089.770	0,00	1.090.300	0,10	1.091.569
Average Size per Hotel in Rooms	**32**	**0,90**	**33**	**0,10**	**33**	**0,40**	**33**
Chain penetration % in Hotels	0	2,90	0	2,30	0	3,30	0
Total Number of Brands	148	14,90	170	15,30	196	4,10	204
Domestic Brands	87	12,60	98	12,20	110	12,70	124
International Brands	61	18,00	72	19,40	86	−7,00	80
Source: the Horwath HTL 2016 Census of Chains' Hotels in Italy							

The hotel chains are still the 4,1 percent of the total hotels in Italy: the most important market is based in independent family business hotels. This figure is a distinct competence of Italian hospitality industry as in the rest of Europe the evidence significantly different: Spain 28 percent, France 23 percent, UK 40 percent, Germany 11 percent.

At the end of 2015, Italy accounted for 1,365 chain hotels and 148,400 rooms. The most important point is represented by the growth of brands that have at least one flag in Italy: from 148 in 2013 to 176 at the end of 2015. 2015 has been an important year also for the concentration in the hotel industry, as the top 10 chains group have grown in size with a penetration rate in the market of 4.1 percent on total hotel supply and of 13.6 percent on total rooms supply. At this stage the Italian hospitality industry is ready to receive international capital and strategic alliance both on the side of property and on the side of management. Domestic chains represent the 58 percent of the market in terms of branded room stock, even if domestic affiliated hotels are usually smaller than international affiliated ones: 102 rooms and 121 rooms per hotel on average. These figures are significant compared to the number of rooms of the independent hotels: 33 rooms on average.

The concentration is higher in the luxury segment, where it reaches the 49 percent of overall five-star room supply. Chain presence is significant also in upscale segment (30 percent) which explains the 72 percent of all affiliated rooms. Regarding the distribution of hotel chains, the majority of chains are concentrated on affiliating four-star properties, with 73 brands operating in the luxury segment and a very limited presence in the budget and economy segments: this probably is because in these segments there are many independent hotels, which are stronger on the territory.

Regarding geographical concentration one third of all branded rooms are located in Rome, Milan, Venice and Florence. Lombardi, Lazio, Veneto, Emilia Romagna and Toscana are the regions where chains are mostly concentrated.

Regarding the model of affiliation, the 41 percent of the hotel belonging to chain are under the ownership model, 27 percent is under lease and 24 percent is under franchising. Franchising is the best option for the international chains, and it represent the first option for the international player's growth. Franchising is becoming very popular also in the midscale segment, defending its leadership in the upscale one. Less important in Italy (just 8 percent) is the management model.

Best Western, with three brands, is still the number one in Italy, followed by Accor and NH, as represented in Table n. 5 below.

Table n. 5 Top 20 Chain Groups by Rooms in Italy 2015

Rank	Top 20 Chain Groups by Rooms in Italy 2015	Hotels	Rooms
1	BEST WESTERN	172	12,523
2	ACCOR	77	9,953
3	NH HOTELS	55	8,660
4	ATA HOTELS	21	5,670
5	IHG	33	5,222
6	STARWOOD	24	5,148
7	HILTON	19	4,430
8	OROVACANZE	23	4,353
9	ITI HOTELS	29	3,486
10	STARHOTELS	20	3,403
11	BLU HOTELS	30	3,214
12	BLUSERENA	8	3,130
13	MARRIOTT INTERNATIONAL	18	3,117
14	UNA	31	2,968
15	AEROVIAGGI	12	2,680
16	B&B	24	2,261
17	GETURHOTELS	15	2,115
18	PARC HOTELS	13	2,004
19	JSH	18	1,997
20	ALPITOUR	7	1,755

Table n. 5 shows that the first domestic chain is Ata Hotels, recently merged with Una Hotels. In the luxury segment, the situation is quiet stable, with ITI Hotels Colonna Luxury, GB Thermae Hotels and Boscolo at the top of the ranking in term of rooms: 828, 542 and 464.

The Role of International Hotel Chains for the Development of Tourism in Italy

In this background, the investigation aims to show whether there is a significant correlation between the presence of hotel chains in Italian regional capitals and the size of the flow of foreign tourists in the same regions.

The analysis starts moving from the assumption that the concentration of hotels belonging to international chains varies considerably in Italy. To verify the correctness of this assumption, the analysis calculated the number of hotels affiliated to the most important international chains, present in the twenty Italian regional capitals as represented in Table n. 5.

Moving from Table n. 5, the investigation concentrated its attention not on all the international chains, but just considering the most important in term of number of hotels in Italy, as represented below in Table n. 6.

Table n. 6　International Chain with hotels in Italy

Hotel Chains	Milano	Torino	Venezia	Genova
Accor	35	7	38	5
NH Hotels	12	5	2	2
IHG	9	2	3	1
Starwood	9		6	
Hilton	4		3	
StarHotels	6	1	1	1
MELIA'	2			1
Marriott	4	1	1	1
Total	81	16	54	11

Table n. 6 shows as the International Chains considered are: Accor (FR), NH Hotels (ES), IHG Hotels, Starwood (US), Hilton (US), StarHotels, MELIÝ (ES), and Marriott (US). This point is very important because if the International chain have more hotels it is more significant in the results of the investigation.

Following this method, the information extracted from Table n. 6 were compared with the number of foreign arrivals on the regional basis by associating each regional capital to its Italian region, as represented in Table n. 7 below.

Performing linear regression and considering i) the foreign flows for arrivals (on the Regional basis) expressed in millions as the independent variable ii) and the number of international chain hotels per region capital as the dependent variable it is possible to obtain the analysis represented in Graph n. 1 below.

The linear regression shows the significant correlation between the two variables. Note that the squared linear regression coefficient $R^2 = 0.68$ ca., and it indicates a close positive correlation: in the regions where the number of hotels belonging to the international hotel chains are significant as the number of foreign tourists increases.

Table n.7   Number of Hotels per Regions/Town

Cities	Hotels Number	Foreign flows for arrivals in 2015 (on a regional basis)
Roma	90	7,053
Milano	81	8,129
Venezia	54	11,213
Firenze	36	7,062
Napoli	23	2,318
Torino	16	1,883
Bologna	13	2,619
Genova	11	1,967
Palermo	8	2,007
Cagliari	5	1,208
Perugia	5	0,709
Trieste	5	1,104
Trento	5	5,682
Ancona	3	0,405
Potenza	3	0,095
Bari	2	0,73
Aosta	1	0,409
Campobasso	1	0,013
Catanzaro	1	0,247
L'Aquila	1	0,171

Graph n.1   Linear Correlation between number of hotels and tourist flows

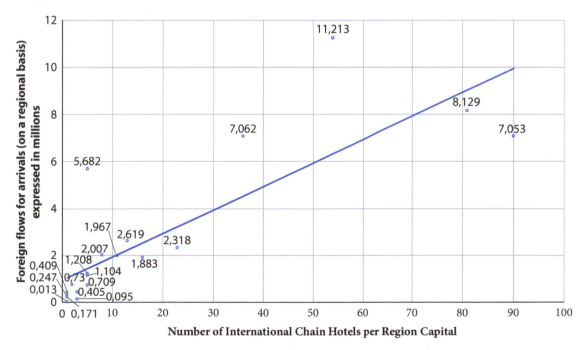

The Role of International Hotel Chains in the Growth Process of Italian Hospitality Industry   407

In short, the evidence of the investigation confirm that the presence of Hotels belonging to International Chains serves as a catalyst for foreign tourists, recording a proportional increase in terms of tourist flows to the increase in the number of hotels.

This should make local governments and municipalities reflect on the actual potential of the International Hotel Chains. In fact, thanks to the satisfaction of quality standards and even quantitatively they represent a showcase for the cities that provide of such hotels. International Hotel Chains are an important development driver for Italian Regions in term of tourism.

As tourism is not considered as an economic sector—tourism is a multiplicator of economic, cultural and social value—it is possible to state that the role played by international chains is very important, not just to develop the tourism industry, but it is strategic to active economic, cultural and social development.

Conclusion

In the last two decades, tourism in Italy has been changing, particularly with respect to branded hotel chains moving into Italy, a country dominated by independent hotel ownership. Italy remains one of the leading tourist destinations in the World. The Italian leadership in tourism is based not only on its geographical position, climate and natural beauty, but also on the fact that it has at least 40 percent of the world's wealth of monumental, historical and artistic works.

This chapter investigated how the presence of international hotel chain is enhancing the delivery of hospitality and tourism services, demonstrating how the presence of international hotel chains—in particular, the focus of the chapter is on the western companies—has contributed to change the shape of Italian tourism and hospitality industry. Following a qualitative approach, this appendix described the presence of international hotel chains in Italy considering how they changed in the last decade. The empirical research aims to represent an innovative perspective to analyze the new trend in the Italian hotel and tourism industry.

References

Alegre, J., & Cladera, M. (2006). Repeat visitation in mature sun and sand holiday destinations. Journal of Travel Research, 44(3), 288–297.

Assaf, A. G., et al. (2012). Internationalization and performance of retail firms: a Bayesian dynamic model. Journal of Retailing, 88(2), 191–205.

Assaf, A., & Josiassen, A. (2012). Identifying and ranking the determinants of tourism performance a global investigation. Journal of Travel Research, 51(4), 388–399.

Balaguer, J., & Cantavella-Jorda, M. (2002). Tourism as a long-run economic growth factor: the Spanish case. Applied Economics, 34(7), 877–884.

Barkema, H. G., Bell, J. H., & Pennings, J. M. E. (1996). Foreign entry, cultural barriers and learning. Strategic Management Journal, 151–166.

Barros, C. P., & Machado, L. P. (2010). The length of stay in tourism. Annals of Tourism Research, 37(3), 692–706.

Barros, C. P., Botti, L., Peypoch, N., Robinot, E., Solonandrasana, B., & Assaf, A. (2011). Performance of French destinations: tourism attraction perspectives. Tourism Management, 32(1), 141–146.

Beerli, A., & Martín, J. D. (2004). Tourists' characteristics and the perceived image of tourist destinations: a quantitative analysis: a case study of Lanzarote, Spain. Tourism Management, 25(5), 623–636.

Bhagwati, J. (2007). In defense of globalization. Oxford: Oxford University Press.

Brouthers, K. D., Brouthers, L. E., & Werner, S. (1996). Dunning's eclectic theory and the smaller firm: the impact of ownership and locational advantages on the choice of entry-modes in the computer software industry. International Business Review, 5(4), 377–394.

Buckley, P. (1983). New theories of international business: some unresolved issues. In M. Casson (Ed.), The growth of international business. London: George Allen & Unwin.

Buckley, P. (1988). The limits of explanation: testing the internationalisation theory of the multinational enterprise. Journal of International Business Studies, (2, Summer), 181–193.

Buckley, P., Clegg, J. L., Cross, A., Liu, X., Voss, H., & Zheng, P. (2007). The de- terminants of Chinese outward foreign direct investment. Journal of Interna- tional Business Studies, 38, 499–518.

Burton, E. H., Kahler, M., & Montgomery, A. H. (2009). New theories of international business: some unresolved issues. In M. Casson (Ed.), The growth of international business. London: George Allen & Unwin.

Capocchi, A. (2014). An overview of the Italian Industry Today, in Journal of Quality Assurance in Hospitality & Tourism, 14(4), 425–446.

Cavusgil, S. F., Knight, G., Riesenberger, J. R., Rammal, H. G., & Rose, E. L. (2015). International business. The new realities (2nd ed.). Melbourne: Pearson Australia.

Cunill, O. M., & Forteza, C. M. (2010). The franchise contract in hotel chains: A study of hotel chain growth and market concentrations. Tourism Economics, 16(3), 493–515.

De Micco, F and L. F. Hume. (2007). Bringing Hotels to Healthcare, in Journal of Quality Assurance in Hospitality & Tourism, 8(1), 75–84.

Dreher, A. (2006). Does globalization affect growth? Evidence from a new index of globalization. Applied Economics, 38(10), 1091–1110.

Dunning, J. H. (2001). The eclectic (OLI) paradigm of international production: past, present and future. International Journal of the Economics of Business, 8(2), 173–190.

Dunning, J. H., & Kundu, S. K. (1995). The internationalization of the hotel industry: some new findings from a field study. MIR: Management International Review, 101–133.

Dunning, J. H., & McQueen, M. (1982). Multinational corporations in the international hotel industry. Annals of Tourism Research, 9(1), 69–90.

Eryiğit, M., Kotil, E., & Eryiğit, R. (2010). Factors affecting international tourism flows to Turkey: A gravity model approach. Tourism Economics, 16(3), 585–595.

Hjalager, A. -M. (2007). Stages in the economic globalization of tourism. Annals of Tourism Research, 34(2), 437–457.

Ivanov, S., & Webster, C. (2013a). Tourism's impact on growth: The role of globalisation. Annals of Tourism Research, 41, 231–236.

Ivanov, S., & Webster, C. (2013b). Globalisation as a driver of destination competitiveness. Annals of Tourism Research, 43, 628–633.

Ivanova, M., & Ivanov, S. (2015). Affiliation to hotel chains: Hotels' perspective. Tourism Management Perspectives, 16, 148–162.

Johanson, J., & Vahlne, J. E. (1990). The mechanism of internationalisation. International Marketing Review, 7(4).

Johnson, C., & Vanetti, M. (2005). Locational strategies of international hotel chains. Annals of Tourism Research, 32(4), 1077–1099.

Kapoulas, A., & Ratković, D. (2015). E-CRM dilemmas in developing markets: The case of a tourism company in Serbia. European Journal of Tourism Research, 9, 24–40.

Lechner, F. J. (2009). Globalization: The making of world society. Chichester: John Wiley & Sons Ltd.

mobile reservation systems: A technology-organization-environment framework. Tourism Management, 53, 163–172.

Ozturk, A. B., & Hancer, M. (2014). Hotel and IT decision-maker characteristics and information technology adoption relationship in the hotel industry. Journal of Hospitality and Tourism Technology, 5(2), 194–206.

Stiglitz, J. (2003). Globalization and its discontents. New York: W.W. Norton & Company.

Su, Y. -W., & Lin, H. -L. (2014). Analysis of international tourist arrivals worldwide: The role of world heritage sites. Tourism Management, 40, 46–58.

Wang, Y. -S., Li, H. -T., Li, C. -R., & Zhang, D. -Z. (2016). Factors affecting hotels' adoption of

Waters, M. (2001). Globalization (2nd ed.). London: Routledge.

Wild, J., & Wild, K. (2015). International business: The challenges of globalization Global edition (8th ed.). Harlow: Pearson Education Ltd.

Index